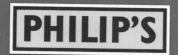

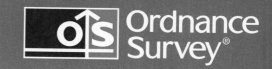

STREET ATLAS Oxfordshire

First published 1992 by

Philip's, a division of
Octopus Publishing Group Ltd
2–4 Heron Quays, London E14 4JP

Second colour edition 2002
First impression 2002

ISBN 0-540-08108-6 (hardback)
ISBN 0-540-08109-4 (spiral)

Printed and bound in Spain
by Cayfosa-Quebecor

Contents

III **Key to map symbols**

IV **Key to map pages**

VI **Route planning**

VIII **Administrative and Postcode boundaries**

1 **Street maps** at 3½ inches to 1 mile

261 **Town maps** of Reading and Swindon

263 **Index** of towns and villages

264 **Index** of streets, hospitals, industrial estates, railway stations, schools, shopping centres, universities and places of interest

Digital Data

The exceptionally high-quality mapping found in this atlas is available as digital data in TIFF format, which is easily convertible to other bit mapped (raster) image formats.

The index is also available in digital form as a standard database table. It contains all the details found in the printed index together with the National Grid reference for the map square in which each entry is named and feature codes for places of interest in eight categories such as education and health.

For further information and to discuss your requirements, please contact Philip's on 020 7531 8440 or george.philip@philips-maps.co.uk

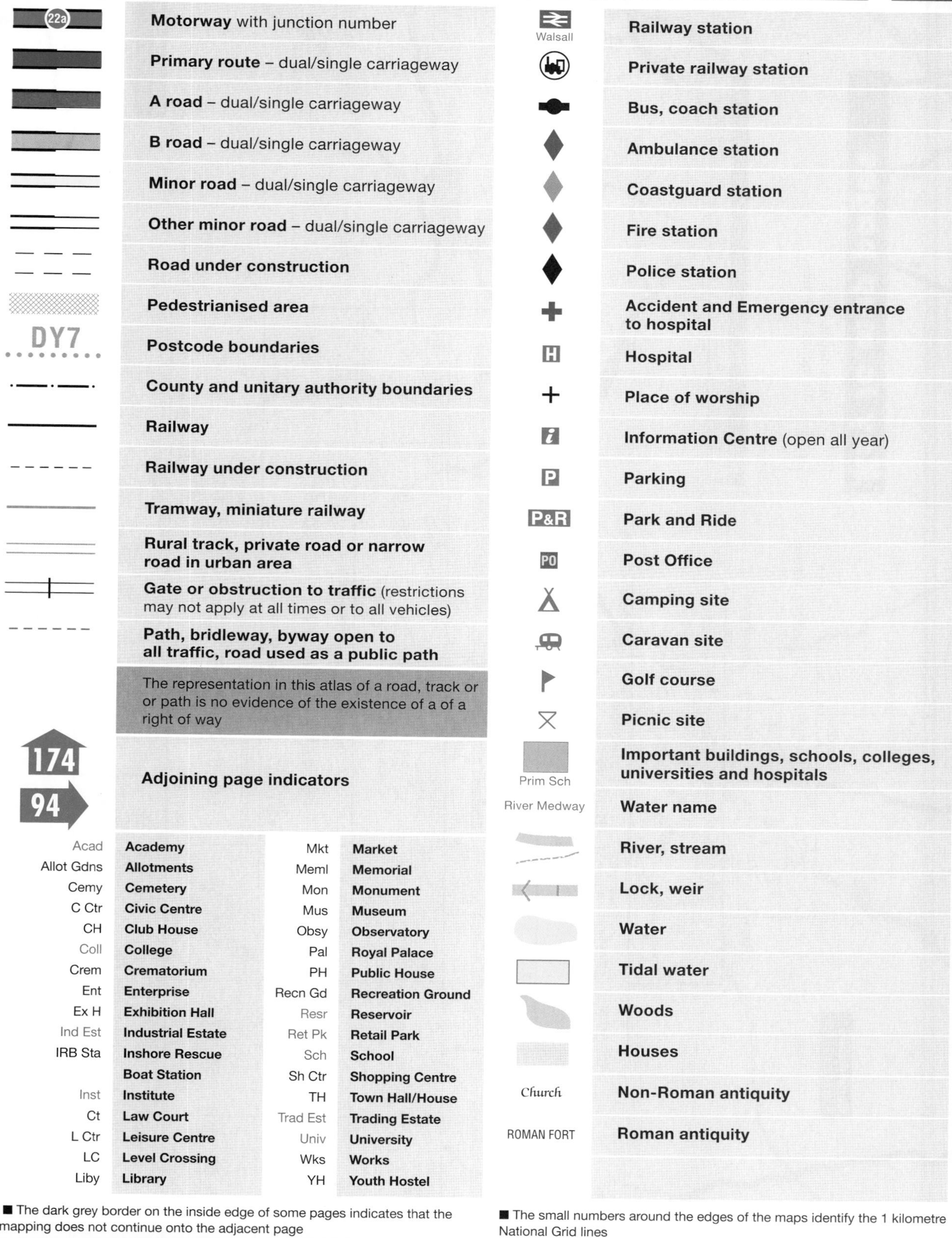

22a	**Motorway** with junction number
	Primary route – dual/single carriageway
	A road – dual/single carriageway
	B road – dual/single carriageway
	Minor road – dual/single carriageway
	Other minor road – dual/single carriageway
	Road under construction
	Pedestrianised area
DY7	**Postcode boundaries**
	County and unitary authority boundaries
	Railway
	Railway under construction
	Tramway, miniature railway
	Rural track, private road or narrow road in urban area
	Gate or obstruction to traffic (restrictions may not apply at all times or to all vehicles)
	Path, bridleway, byway open to all traffic, road used as a public path

The representation in this atlas of a road, track or or path is no evidence of the existence of a of a right of way

174
94 **Adjoining page indicators**

Railway station		Walsall
Private railway station		
Bus, coach station		
Ambulance station		
Coastguard station		
Fire station		
Police station		
Accident and Emergency entrance to hospital		
Hospital		H
Place of worship		
Information Centre (open all year)		i
Parking		P
Park and Ride		P&R
Post Office		PO
Camping site		
Caravan site		
Golf course		
Picnic site		
Important buildings, schools, colleges, universities and hospitals		Prim Sch
Water name		River Medway
River, stream		
Lock, weir		
Water		
Tidal water		
Woods		
Houses		
Non-Roman antiquity		Church
Roman antiquity		ROMAN FORT

Abbr	Full	Abbr	Full
Acad	**Academy**	Mkt	**Market**
Allot Gdns	**Allotments**	Meml	**Memorial**
Cemy	**Cemetery**	Mon	**Monument**
C Ctr	**Civic Centre**	Mus	**Museum**
CH	**Club House**	Obsy	**Observatory**
Coll	**College**	Pal	**Royal Palace**
Crem	**Crematorium**	PH	**Public House**
Ent	**Enterprise**	Recn Gd	**Recreation Ground**
Ex H	**Exhibition Hall**	Resr	**Reservoir**
Ind Est	**Industrial Estate**	Ret Pk	**Retail Park**
IRB Sta	**Inshore Rescue Boat Station**	Sch	**School**
		Sh Ctr	**Shopping Centre**
Inst	**Institute**	TH	**Town Hall/House**
Ct	**Law Court**	Trad Est	**Trading Estate**
L Ctr	**Leisure Centre**	Univ	**University**
LC	**Level Crossing**	Wks	**Works**
Liby	**Library**	YH	**Youth Hostel**

■ The dark grey border on the inside edge of some pages indicates that the mapping does not continue onto the adjacent page

■ The small numbers around the edges of the maps identify the 1 kilometre National Grid lines

The scale of the maps on the pages numbered in blue is 5.52 cm to 1 km • 3¹/₂ inches to 1 mile • 1: 18103

0	¹/₄	¹/₂	³/₄	1 mile
0	250 m	500 m	750 m	1 kilometre

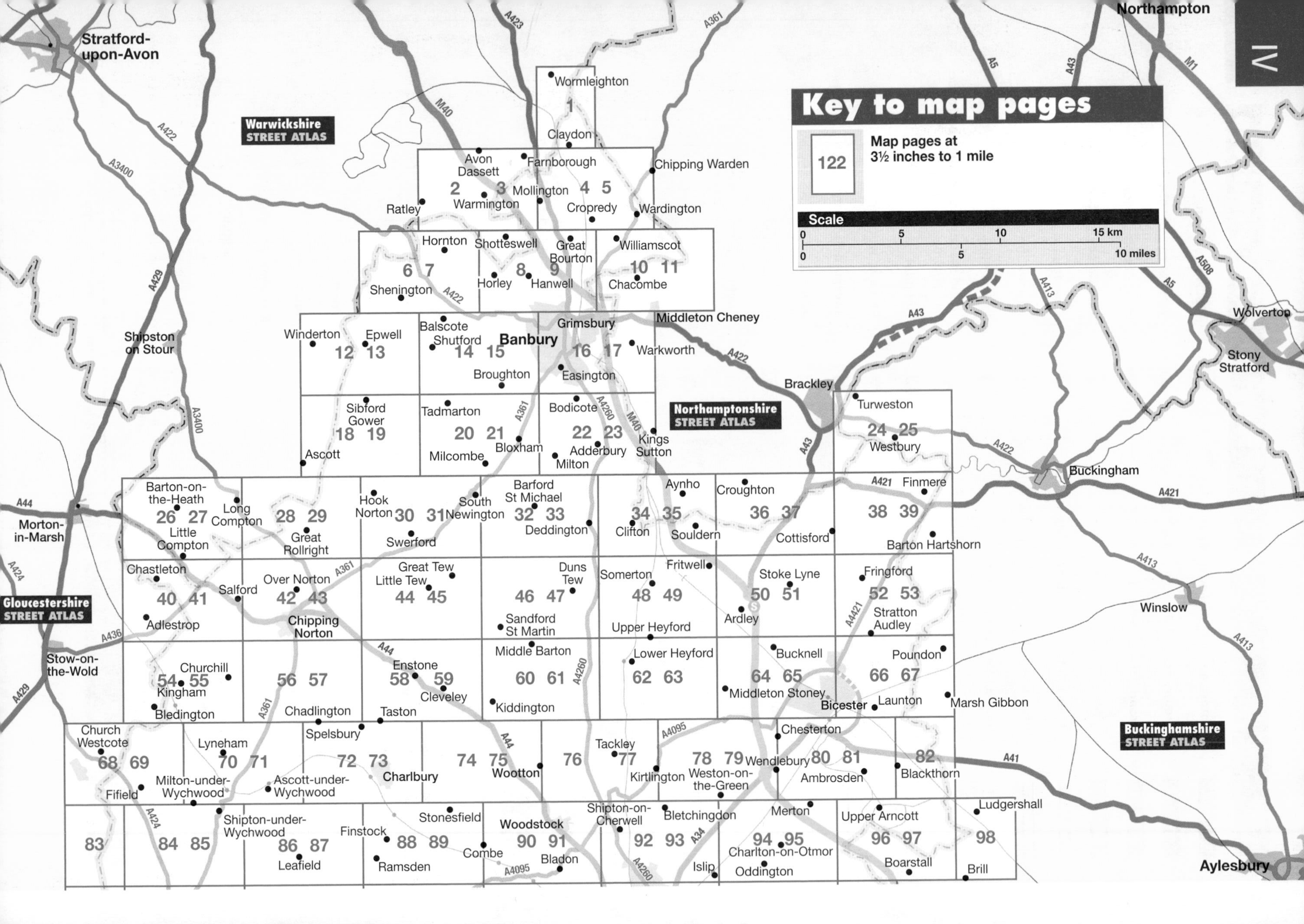

IV

Key to map pages

Map pages at
3½ inches to 1 mile

122

Scale

10 miles

15 km

Northampton

Aylesbury

Stratford-upon-Avon

Buckinghamshire STREET ATLAS

Northamptonshire STREET ATLAS

Warwickshire STREET ATLAS

Gloucestershire STREET ATLAS

Wolverton
Stony Stratford
Buckingham
Winslow
Ludgershall
Brill
Marsh Gibbon
Barton Hartshorn
Finmere
Poundon
Blackthorn
Boarstall
Upper Arncott
Launton
Stratton Audley
Fringford
Chesterton
Ambrosden
Merton
Charlton-on-Otmor
Oddington
Islip
Bletchingdon
Weston-on-the-Green
Wendlebury
Middleton Stoney
Bucknell
Stoke Lyne
Cottisford
Ardley
Kirtlington
Shipton-on-Cherwell
Tackley
Lower Heyford
Upper Heyford
Fritwell
Somerton
Souldern
Croughton
Aynho
Clifton
Kings Sutton
Warkworth
Milton
Adderbury
Bodicote
Easington
Grimsbury
Banbury
Hanwell
Great Bourton
Shotteswell
Horley
Cropredy
Williamscot
Chacombe
Wardington
Chipping Warden
Middleton Cheney
Turweston
Westbury
Brackley
Wormleighton
Claydon
Farnborough
Mollington
Avon Dassett
Warmington
Ratley
Shenington
Hornton
Balscote
Shutford
Epwell
Sibford Gower
Winderton
Ascott
Broughton
Bloxham
Milcombe
Tadmarton
South Newington
Barford St Michael
Deddington
Duns Tew
Sandford St Martin
Middle Barton
Kiddington
Wootton
Woodstock
Bladon
Combe
Stonesfield
Finstock
Ramsden
Leafield
Shipton-under-Wychwood
Milton-under-Wychwood
Lyneham
Ascott-under-Wychwood
Charlbury
Spelsbury
Chadlington
Taston
Cleveley
Enstone
Little Tew
Great Tew
Swerford
Hook Norton
Over Norton
Great Rollright
Chipping Norton
Salford
Chastleton
Adlestrop
Kingham
Bledington
Churchill
Fifield
Church Westcote
Long Compton
Little Compton
Barton-on-the-Heath
Morton-in-Marsh
Stow-on-the-Wold
Shipston on Stour

M1
A43
A5
A508
A5
A421
A413
A422
A43
A422
A361
A423
M40
A422
A4260
A361
A422
A3400
A429
A424
A436
A44
A44
A4260
A4095
A34
A4260
A41
A413
A421

1 2 3 4 5 6 7 8 9 10 11
12 13 14 15 16 17 18 19 20 21 22 23 24 25
26 27 28 29 30 31 32 33 34 35 36 37 38 39
40 41 42 43 44 45 46 47 48 49 50 51 52 53
54 55 56 57 58 59 60 61 62 63 64 65 66 67
68 69 70 71 72 73 74 75 76 77 78 79 80 81 82
83 84 85 86 87 88 89 90 91 92 93 94 95 96 97 98

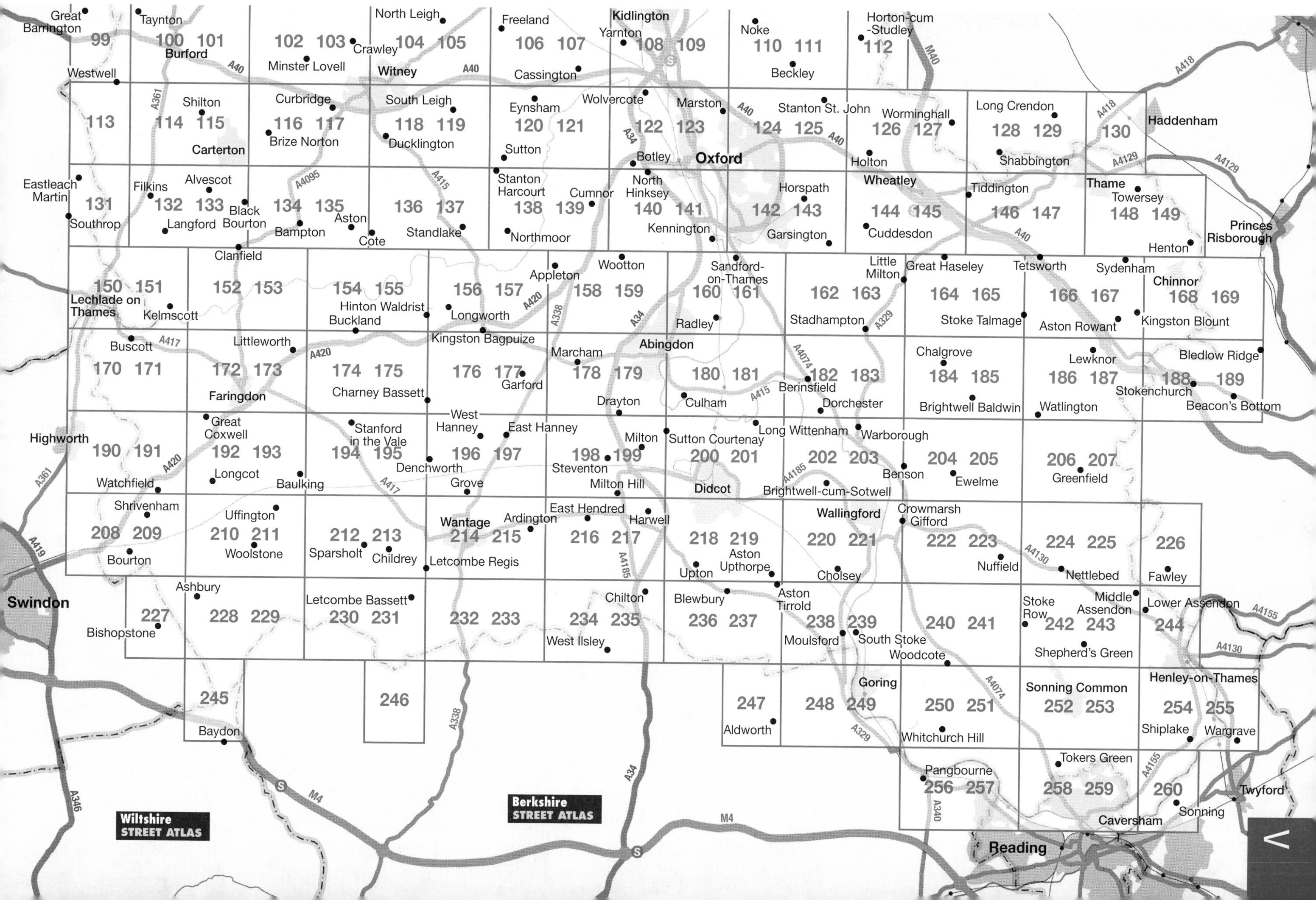

Haddenham 130

Princes Risborough

Thame

Towersey 148 149
Henton
Sydenham
Chinnor 168 169
Kingston Blount
Bledlow Ridge
Beacon's Bottom
Stokenchurch 188 189
Tetsworth 166 167
Aston Rowant
Lewknor
Watlington 186 187
Greenfield
206 207
Fawley
226
Lower Assendon 244
Henley-on-Thames
Shiplake 254 255
Wargrave
Twyford
Sonning
A4155
Caversham 260

Long Crendon 128 129
Shabbington
Tiddington 146 147
Great Haseley 164 165
Stoke Talmage
Chalgrove
Brightwell Baldwin 184 185
Warborough
204 205
Ewelme
Nettlebed 224 225
Middle Assendon 243
Shepherd's Green
Sonning Common 252 253
Tokers Green
258 259
Reading

Horton-cum-Studley 112
Worminghall 126 127
Holton
Wheatley 144 145
Cuddesdon
Little Milton 162 163
Stadhampton
Berinsfield 182 183
Dorchester
Benson 202 203
Brightwell-cum-Sotwell
Crowmarsh Gifford
Wallingford 220 221
Cholsey
Nuffield 222 223
Stoke Row
242
South Stone 238 239
Woodcote 240 241
Whitchurch Hill
250 251
Pangbourne 256 257

Oxford
Kidlington
Yarnton 108 109
Marston 122 123
Noke
Beckley
110 111
Stanton St. John 124 125
Horspath 142 143
Garsington
Sandford-on-Thames 160 161
Radley
Culham 180 181
Long Wittenham
Sutton Courtenay 200 201
Didcot
Aston Upthorpe 218 219
Aston Tirrold 236 237
Blewbury
247
Aldworth

Freeland 106 107
Cassington
Eynsham 120 121
Sutton
Stanton Harcourt 138 139
Northmoor
North Hinksey
Botley
Kennington 140 141
Wootton 158 159
Appleton
Marcham 178 179
Drayton
Milton 198 199
Steventon
Milton Hill
East Hendred 216 217
Harwell
Chilton 234 235
West Ilsley
Goring 248 249

North Leigh 104 105
Crawley
Witney
South Leigh 118 119
Ducklington
136 137
Standlake
Cote
156 157
Longworth
Kingston Bagpuize 176 177
Garford
West Hanney 196 197
Grove
Ardington 214 215
Letcombe Regis
232 233
246

Burford
100 101
Minster Lovell
Curbridge
116 117
Brize Norton
Aston 134 135
Bampton
154 155
Hinton Waldrist
Buckland
Charney Bassett 174 175
Stanford in the Vale 194 195
Denchworth
Wantage
212 213
Childrey
Letcombe Bassett 230 231

Taynton
Burford
100 101
Shilton 114 115
Carterton
Alvescot
Black Bourton 132 133
Langford
Clanfield 152 153
Littleworth 172 173
Faringdon
Great Coxwell 192 193
Longcot
Baulking
Uffington 210 211
Woolstone
Sparsholt 228 229
Ashbury
245
Baydon

Great Barrington 99
Westwell
113
Eastleach Martin
Southrop 131
Filkins
Lechlade on Thames 150 151
Kelmscott
Buscot 170 171
Highworth 190 191
Watchfield
Shrivenham 208 209
Bourton
227
Bishopstone
Swindon

Berkshire STREET ATLAS

Wiltshire STREET ATLAS

Route planning

Scale

0 1 2 3 4 5 6 7 8 km
0   1   2   3   4 5 miles

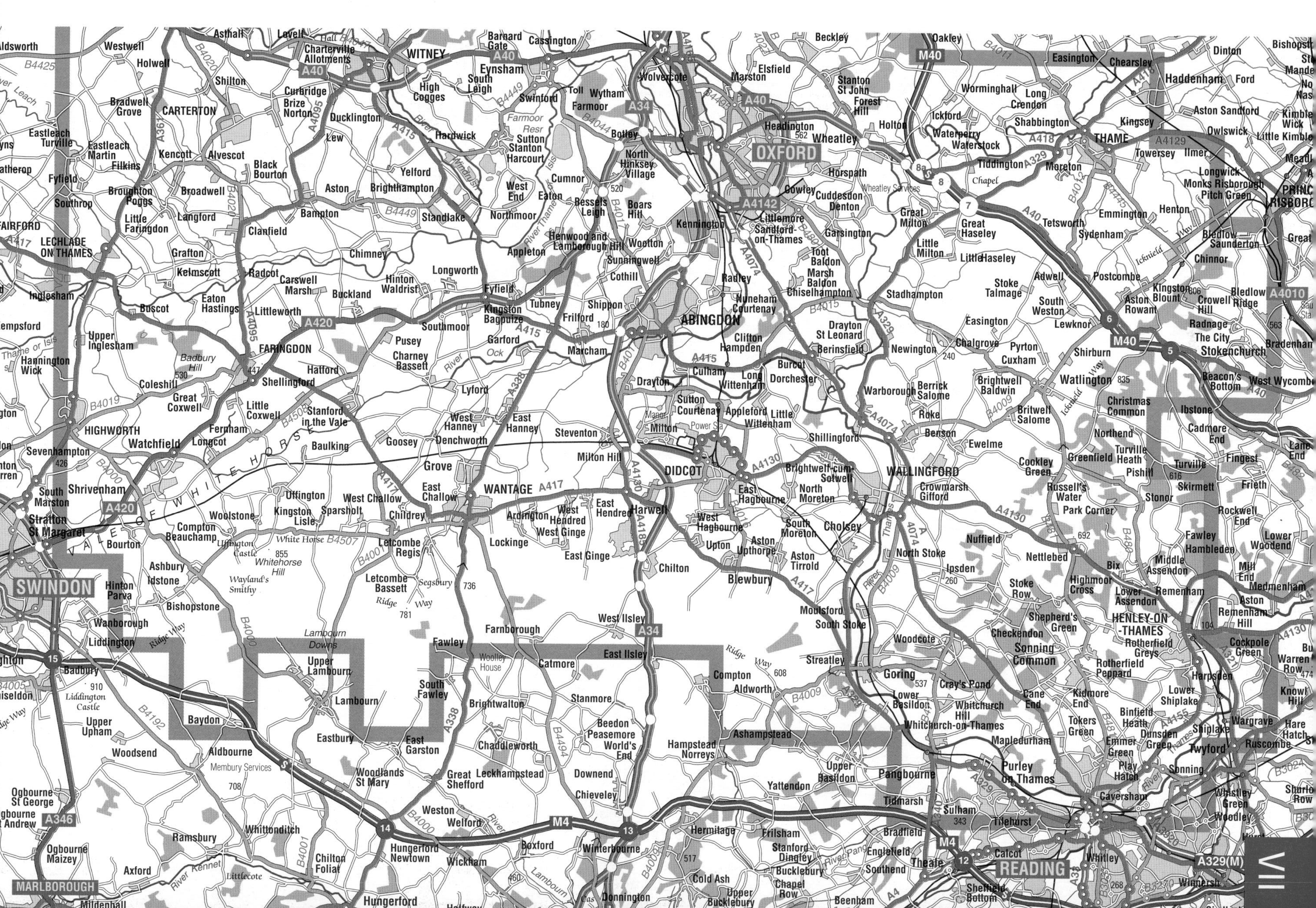

VII
OXFORD
READING
SWINDON
WITNEY
ABINGDON
DIDCOT
WANTAGE
WALLINGFORD
THAME
HENLEY-ON-THAMES
FARINGDON
CARTERTON
HIGHWORTH
MARLBOROUGH
HUNGERFORD
LECHLADE ON THAMES
FAIRFORD
M40
M4
A34
A40
A420
A417
A4074
A4130
A338
A329(M)
A346
Kennington
Botley
Wheatley
Headington
Cowley
Eynsham
Cumnor
Radley
Culham
Dorchester
Benson
Ewelme
Watlington
Goring
Pangbourne
Theale
Tilehurst
Caversham
Woodley
Twyford
Wargrave
Sonning
Purley on Thames
Streatley
Cholsey
Blewbury
Harwell
Chilton
East Ilsley
West Ilsley
Compton
Hermitage
Lambourn
Upper Lambourn
Letcombe Regis
Grove
Stanford in the Vale
Shrivenham
Bampton
Standlake
Ducklington
Stanton Harcourt
Appleton
Fyfield
Kingston Bagpuize
Steventon
Sutton Courtenay
Milton
Chinnor
Stokenchurch
Christmas Common
Nettlebed
Sonning Common
Nuffield
Chalgrove
Great Haseley
Tetsworth
Aldbourne
Ramsbury
Baydon
Ashbury
Uffington
Wanborough
Liddington
Whitehorse Hill
Ridge Way
Lambourn Downs
VALE OF WHITE HORSE

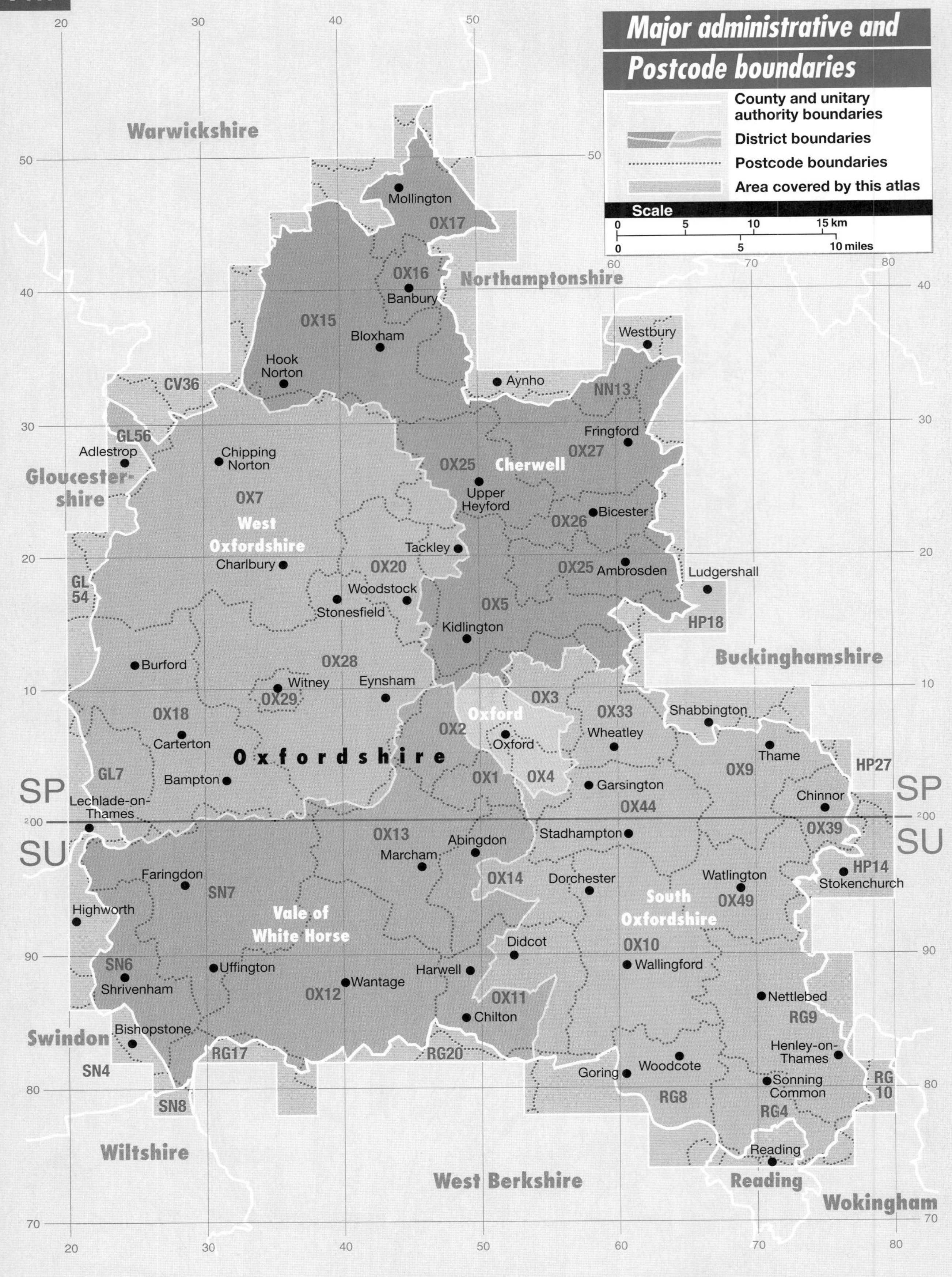

Major administrative and
Postcode boundaries

County and unitary
authority boundaries

District boundaries

Postcode boundaries

Area covered by this atlas

Scale

0   5   10   15 km

0   5   10 miles

Warwickshire

50

40

Mollington

OX17

OX16

Banbury

OX15

Bloxham

Hook
Norton

CV36

Northamptonshire

Aynho

NN13

Westbury

Fringford

OX27

Cherwell

GL56

Adlestrop

Chipping
Norton

OX7

Gloucester-
shire

West
Oxfordshire

Charlbury

OX25

Upper
Heyford

OX26

Bicester

OX25

Ambrosden

Ludgershall

Tackley

OX20

Woodstock

Stonesfield

OX5

Kidlington

HP18

GL
54

OX28

Witney

Eynsham

Buckinghamshire

Burford

OX29

OX3

Oxford

OX33

Shabbington

OX18

Carterton

O x f o r d s h i r e

OX2

Oxford

Wheatley

OX9

Thame

HP27

GL7

Bampton

SP

OX1

OX4

Garsington

OX44

Chinnor

SP

Lechlade-on-
Thames

200

Stadhampton

OX39

200

SU

OX13

Marcham

Abingdon

SU

Faringdon

SN7

OX14

Dorchester

Watlington

OX49

HP14

Stokenchurch

Highworth

Vale of
White Horse

South
Oxfordshire

90

SN6

Uffington

Didcot

OX10

Wallingford

90

Shrivenham

OX12

Wantage

Harwell

OX11

Chilton

Nettlebed

RG9

Bishopstone

Goring

Woodcote

Henley-on-
Thames

RG
10

Swindon

RG17

RG20

RG8

Sonning
Common

RG4

SN4

80

SN8

80

Wiltshire

West Berkshire

Reading

Reading

Wokingham

70

70

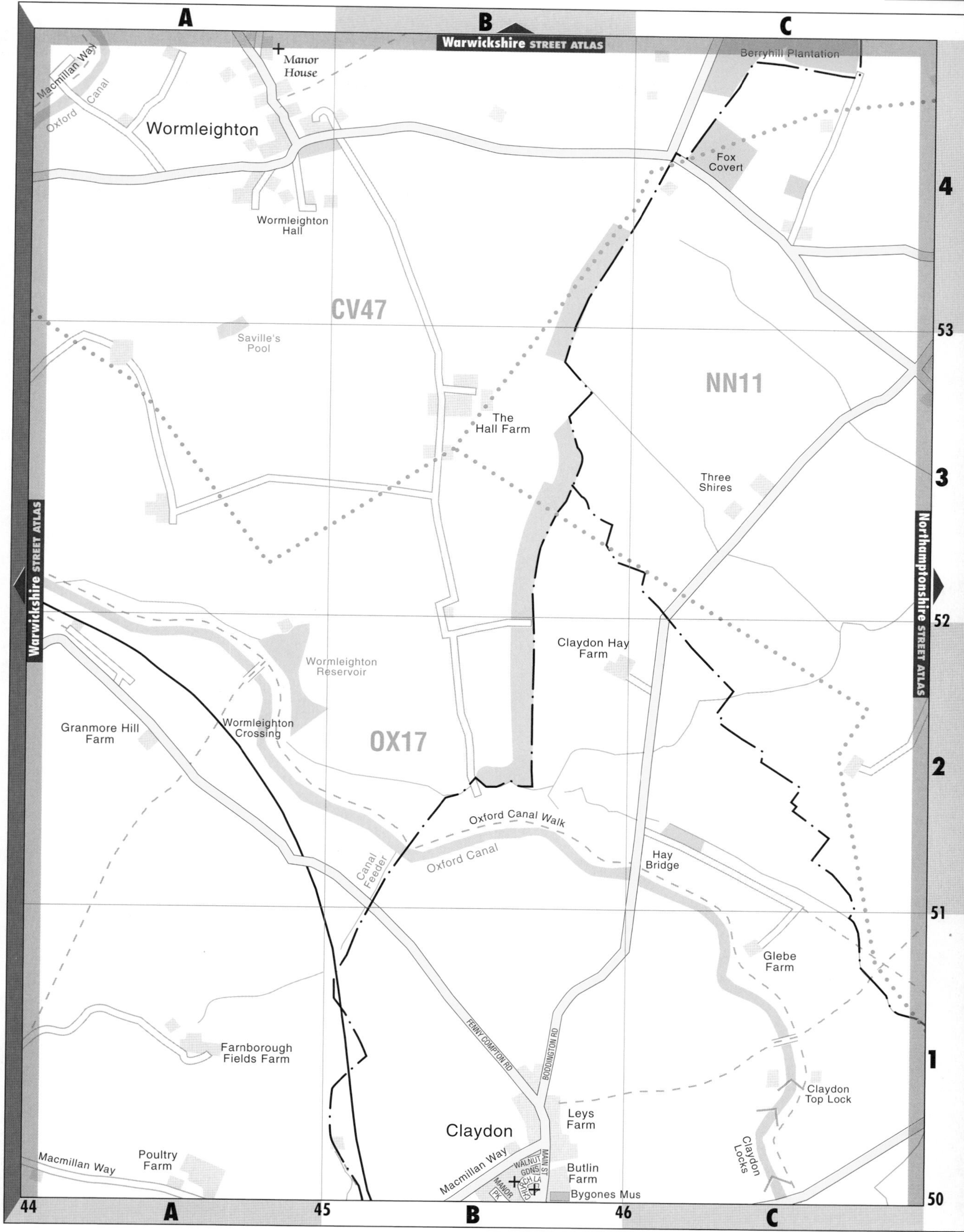

Macmillan Way

Oxford Canal

+ Manor House

Wormleighton

Wormleighton Hall

Berryhill Plantation

Fox Covert

CV47

Saville's Pool

The Hall Farm

NN11

Three Shires

4

53

3

Warwickshire STREET ATLAS

Northamptonshire STREET ATLAS

52

Claydon Hay Farm

Wormleighton Reservoir

Granmore Hill Farm

Wormleighton Crossing

OX17

Oxford Canal Walk

Canal Feeder

Oxford Canal

Hay Bridge

51

Glebe Farm

2

Farnborough Fields Farm

FENNY COMPTON RD

BODDINGTON RD

Claydon Top Lock

1

Claydon Locks

Poultry Farm

Macmillan Way

Claydon

Leys Farm

Butlin Farm

Macmillan Way

WALNUT GDNS

MAIN ST

MANOR PK

CH LA

Bygones Mus

44

A

45

B

46

C

50

2

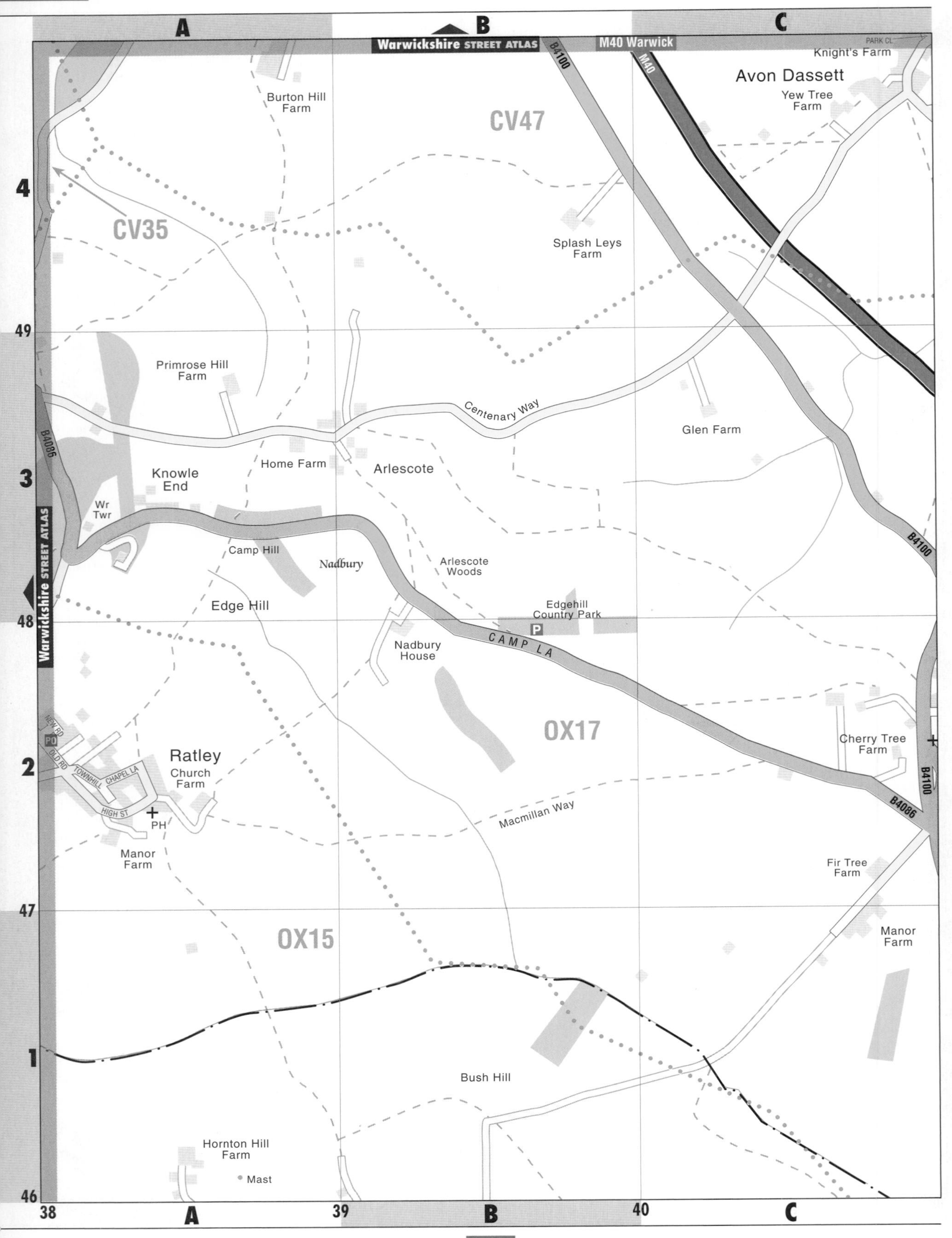

CV47

CV35

Avon Dassett

Knight's Farm

Yew Tree Farm

Burton Hill Farm

Splash Leys Farm

Primrose Hill Farm

Centenary Way

Glen Farm

Knowle End

Home Farm

Arlescote

Wr Twr

Camp Hill

Nadbury

Arlescote Woods

Edge Hill

Edgehill Country Park

CAMP LA

Nadbury House

OX17

Cherry Tree Farm

Ratley

Church Farm

Manor Farm

Macmillan Way

Fir Tree Farm

OX15

Manor Farm

Bush Hill

Hornton Hill Farm

Mast

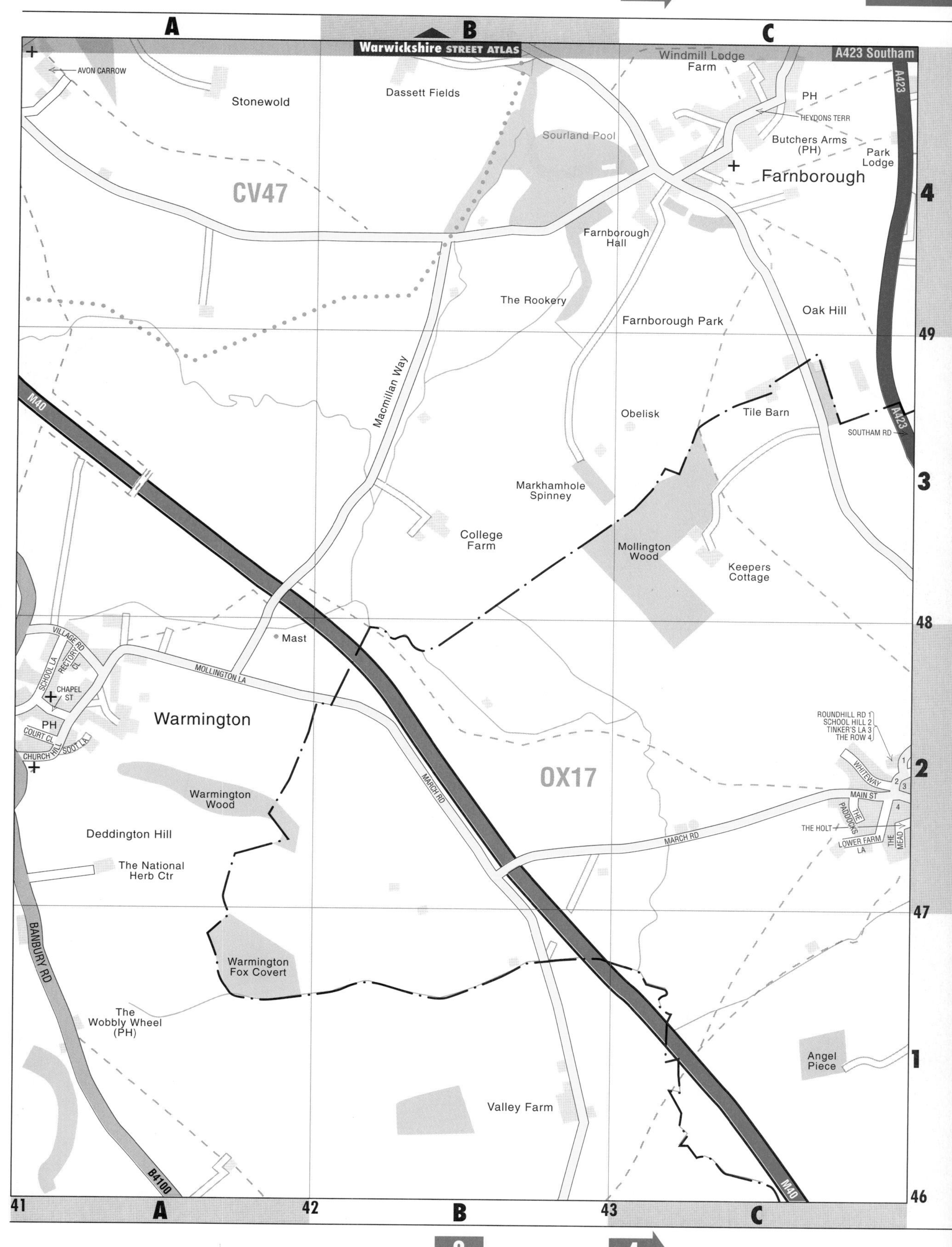

4 →

A **B** **C**

Warwickshire STREET ATLAS

A423 Southam

+ ← AVON CARROW

Stonewold

Dassett Fields

Windmill Lodge Farm

PH
HEYDONS TERR

Sourland Pool

Butchers Arms (PH)

Park Lodge

CV47

+ Farnborough

4

Farnborough Hall

The Rookery

Oak Hill

Farnborough Park

49

M40

Macmillan Way

Obelisk

Tile Barn

SOUTHAM RD

A423

3

Markhamhole Spinney

Mollington Wood

College Farm

Keepers Cottage

• Mast

48

Village RD
SCHOOL LA
RECTORY RD
CL

MOLLINGTON LA

ROUNDHILL RD 1
SCHOOL HILL 2
TINKER'S LA 3
THE ROW 4

CHAPEL ST

Warmington

OX17

WHITEWAY
1
2
3

PH
COURT CL
CHURCH HILL
SCOT LA

MARCH RD

MAIN ST
4
THE PADDOCKS
THE
M40

+

THE HOLT
LOWER FARM LA

2

Warmington Wood

Deddington Hill

MARCH RD

The National Herb Ctr

47

BANBURY RD

Warmington Fox Covert

Angel Piece

The Wobbly Wheel (PH)

1

Valley Farm

M40

B4100

41 **42** **43** **46**

A **B** **C**

8 ↓ **4** →

3
1

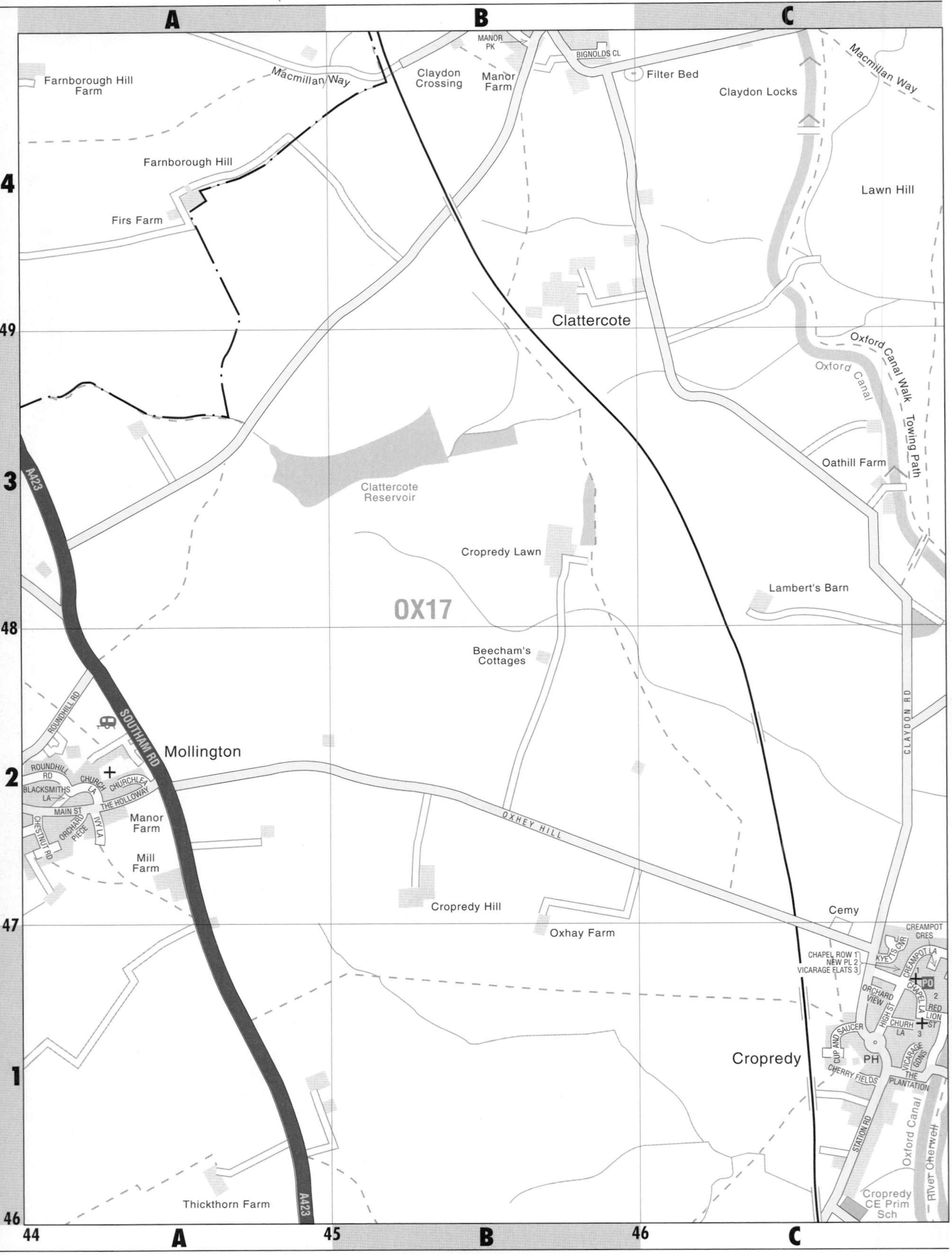

A **B** **C**

Farnborough Hill Farm

Macmillan Way

Claydon Crossing

MANOR PK

BIGNOLDS CL

Manor Farm

Filter Bed

Claydon Locks

Macmillan Way

Farnborough Hill

Lawn Hill

4

Firs Farm

Clattercote

49

Oxford Canal Walk

Oxford Canal

Towing Path

3

A423

Clattercote Reservoir

Oathill Farm

Cropredy Lawn

Lambert's Barn

OX17

48

Beecham's Cottages

ROUNDHILL RD

SOUTHAM RD

Mollington

CLAYDON RD

2

ROUNDHILL RD

CHURCH

CHURCHLA

BLACKSMITHS LA

THE HOLLOWAY

MAIN ST

ORCHARD PIECE

IVY LA

CHESTNUT RD

Manor Farm

Mill Farm

OXHEY HILL

Cropredy Hill

Cemy

CREAMPOT CRES

47

Oxhay Farm

CHAPEL ROW 1
NEW PL 2
VICARAGE FLATS 3

KYE'S CNR

CREAMPOT LA

PO

ORCHARD VIEW

HIGH ST

CHURCH LA

CHERL LA

RED LION ST

2

1

CUP AND SAUCER

CHERRY FIELDS

PH

VICARAGE GDNS

THE PLANTATION

Cropredy

STATION RD

Oxford Canal

River Cherwett

Thickthorn Farm

A423

Cropredy CE Prim Sch

46

44 **A** 45 **B** 46 **C**

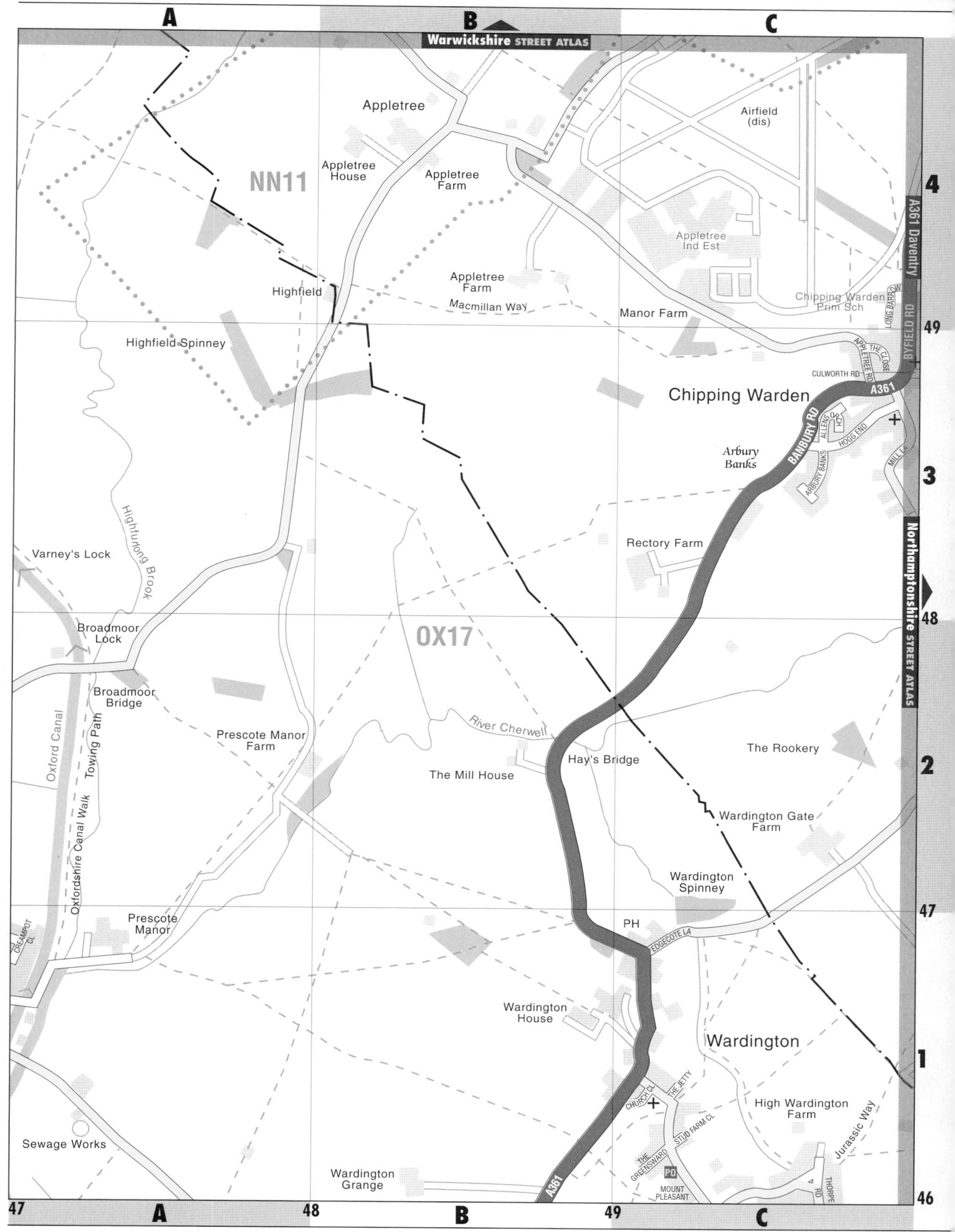

A   B   C

Appletree

NN11

Appletree House

Appletree Farm

Airfield (dis)

Highfield

Appletree Farm

Macmillan Way

Manor Farm

Appletree Ind Est

Chipping Warden Prim Sch

Highfield Spinney

LONG BARROW

THE CLOSE

APPLETREE RD

BYFIELD RD

A361 Daventry

4

49

CULWORTH RD

A361

Chipping Warden

BANBURY RD

ALLENS

HOGG END

MILL LA

Arbury Banks

ARBURY BANKS

3

Varney's Lock

Highfurlong Brook

OX17

Rectory Farm

48

Broadmoor Lock

Broadmoor Bridge

Prescote Manor Farm

River Cherwell

The Mill House

Hay's Bridge

The Rookery

Wardington Gate Farm

2

Oxford Canal

Oxfordshire Canal Walk

Towing Path

Wardington Spinney

47

PH

EDGECOTE LA

Prescote Manor

CREAMPOT CL

Wardington House

Wardington

1

Sewage Works

CHURCH CL

THE JETTY

THE GREENSWARD

STUD FARM CL

PO

MOUNT PLEASANT

High Wardington Farm

Jurassic Way

THORPE RD

Wardington Grange

46

47   A   48   B   49   C

Northamptonshire STREET ATLAS

A361

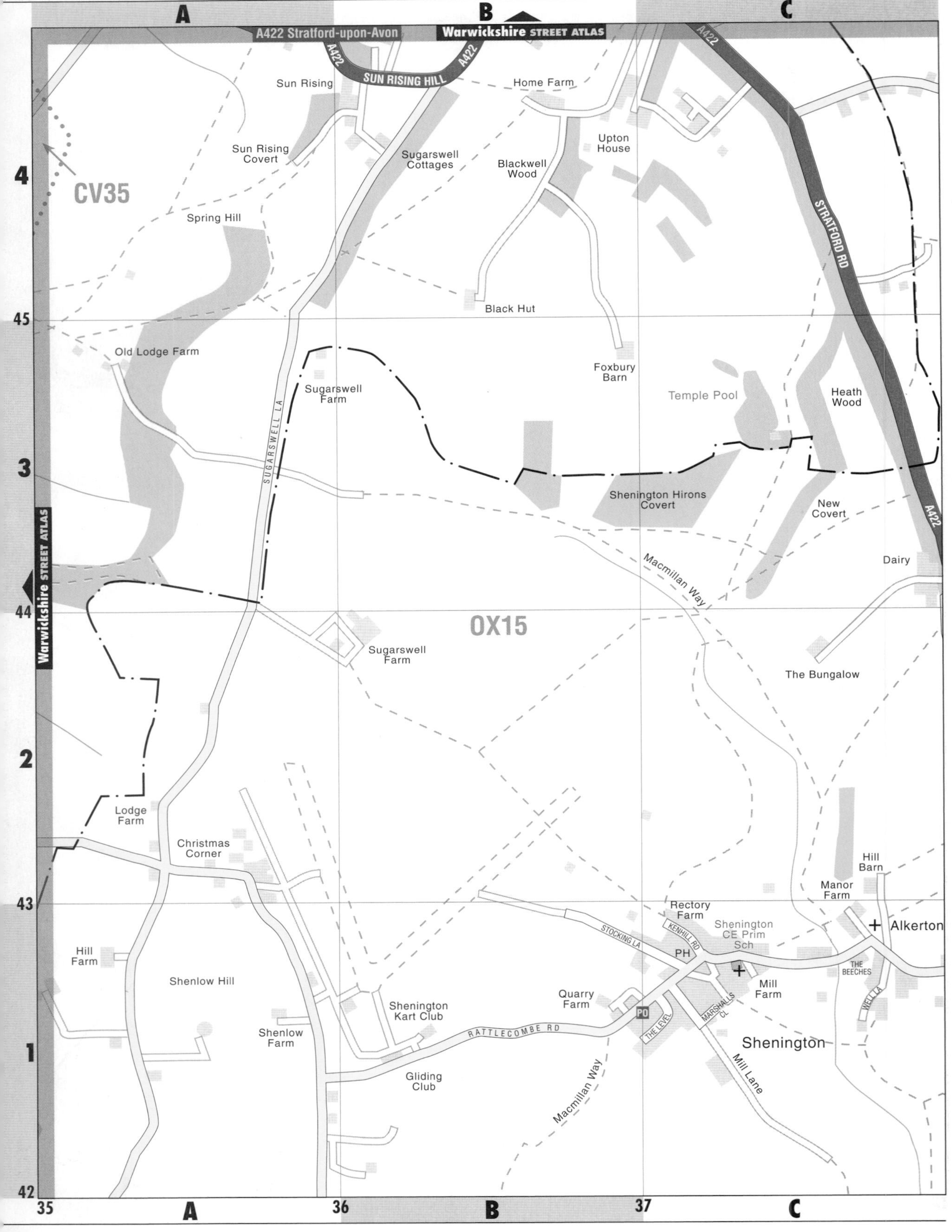

A422 Stratford-upon-Avon

Warwickshire STREET ATLAS

A422

SUN RISING HILL

A422

Sun Rising

Home Farm

A422

Sun Rising
Covert

Sugarswell
Cottages

Blackwell
Wood

Upton
House

4

CV35

Spring Hill

STRATFORD RD

Black Hut

45

Old Lodge Farm

SUGARSWELL LA

Sugarswell
Farm

Foxbury
Barn

Temple Pool

Heath
Wood

3

Shenington Hirons
Covert

New
Covert

A422

Macmillan Way

Dairy

Warwickshire STREET ATLAS

44

Sugarswell
Farm

OX15

The Bungalow

2

Lodge
Farm

Christmas
Corner

Hill
Barn

Manor
Farm

43

Rectory
Farm

KENHILL RD

Shenington
CE Prim
Sch

+ Alkerton

Hill
Farm

PH

THE BEECHES

STOCKING LA

+

Mill
Farm

WELL LA

Shenlow Hill

Shenington
Kart Club

Quarry
Farm

MARSHALLS
CL

Shenington

Shenlow
Farm

PO

RATTLECOMBE RD

THE LEVEL

1

Gliding
Club

Macmillan Way

Mill Lane

42

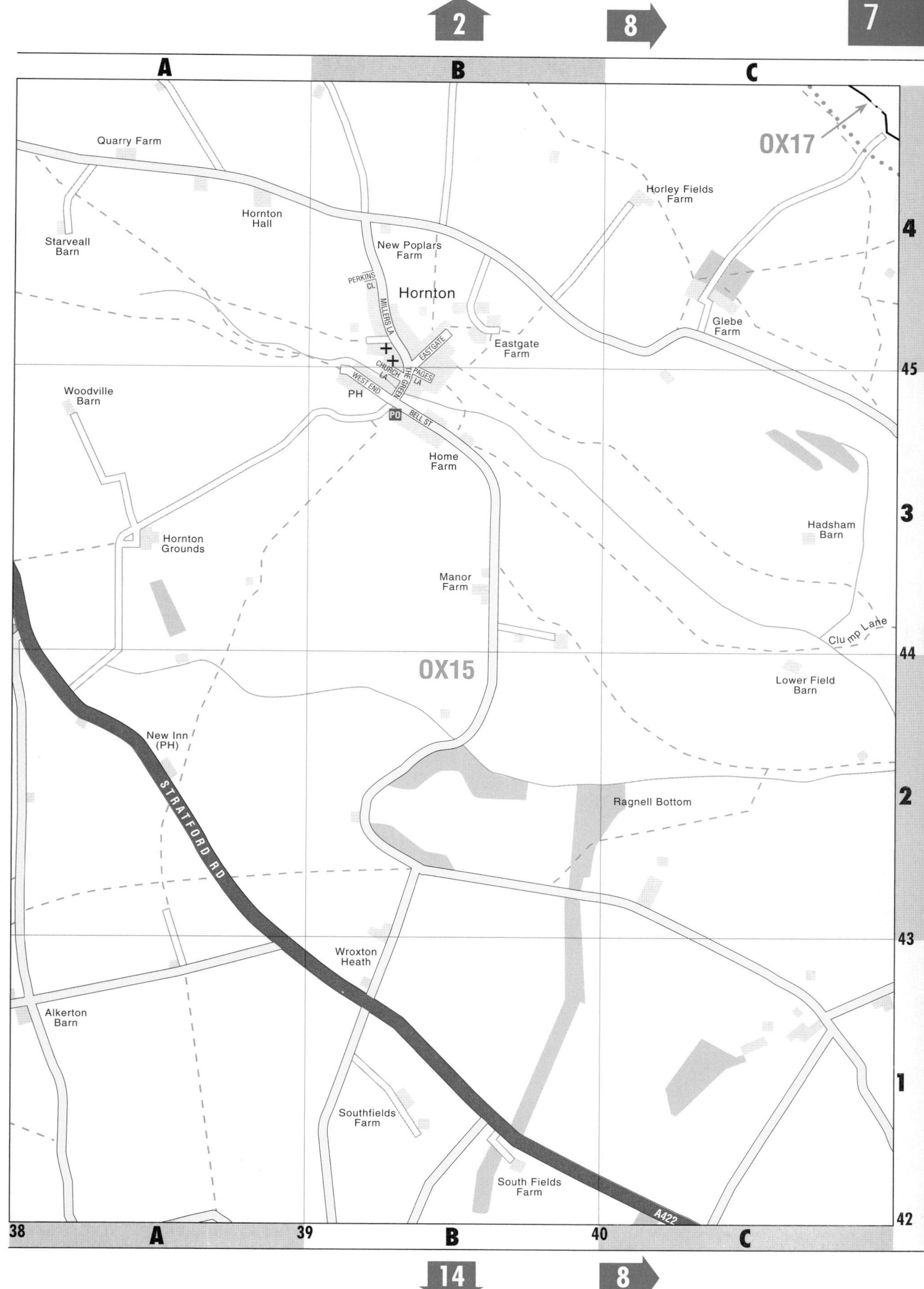

A   B   C

4

45

3

44

2

43

1

42

OX17

Quarry Farm

Hornton Hall

Starveall Barn

New Poplars Farm

Horley Fields Farm

PERKINS CL

Hornton

MILLERS LA

EASTGATE

Eastgate Farm

Glebe Farm

PAGES LA

CHURCH LA

THE GREEN

WEST END

PH

BELL ST

PO

Woodville Barn

Home Farm

Hadsham Barn

Hornton Grounds

Manor Farm

Clump Lane

OX15

44

Lower Field Barn

New Inn (PH)

STRATFORD RD

Ragnell Bottom

Wroxton Heath

Alkerton Barn

Southfields Farm

South Fields Farm

A422

A   B   C

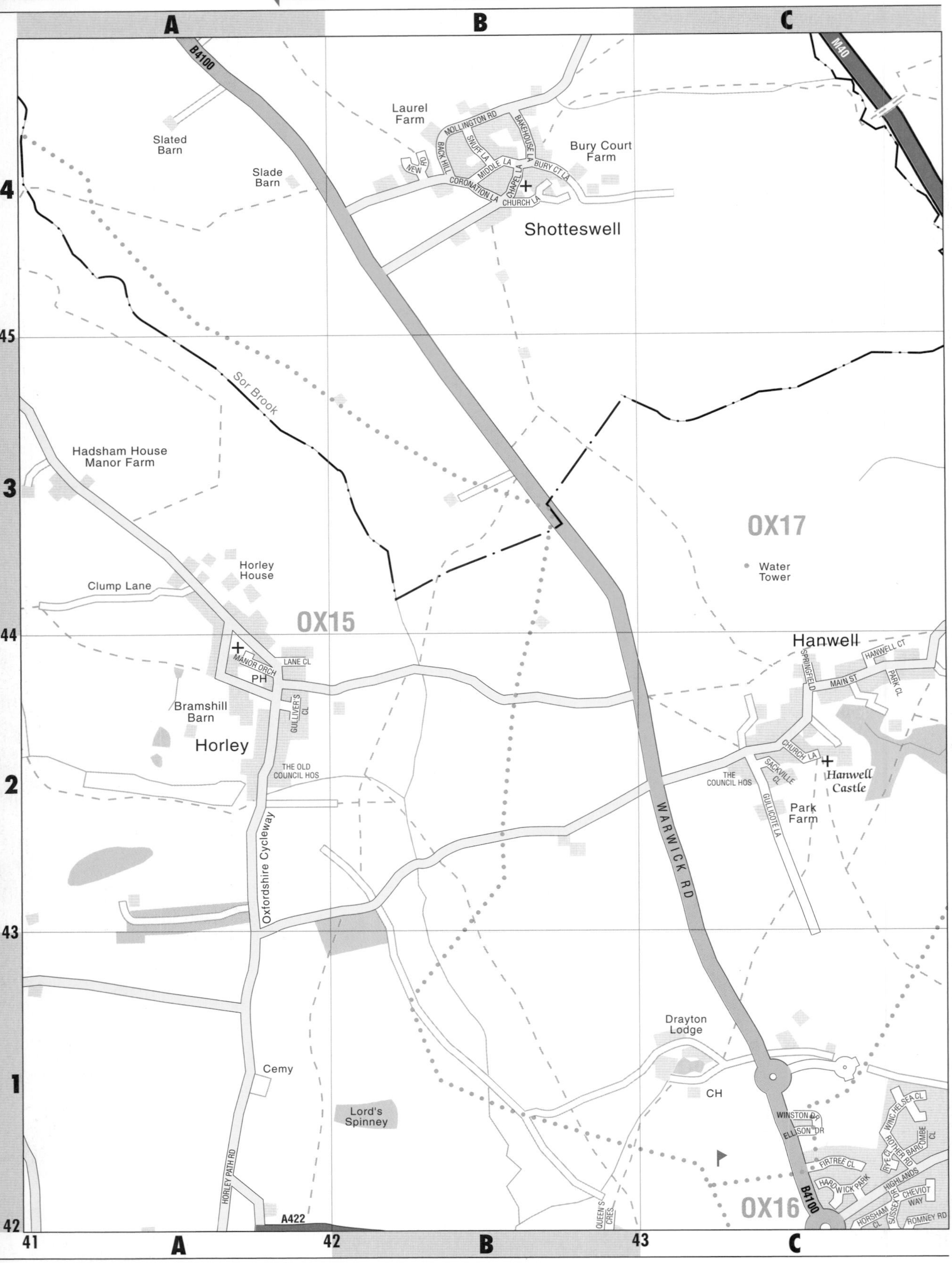

B4100

Slated Barn

Slade Barn

Laurel Farm

NOLLINGTON RD
BACK HILL
NEW RD
SNUFF LA
MIDDLE LA
CORONATION LA
CHURCH LA
CHAPEL LA
BANGHOUSE LA
BURY CT LA

Bury Court Farm

Shotteswell

M40

4

45

Sor Brook

Hadsham House
Manor Farm

OX17

3

Water Tower

Horley House

Clump Lane

OX15

44

Hanwell

MANOR ORCH
PH
LANE CL
GULLIVER'S CL

HANWELL CT
SPRINGFIELD
MAIN ST
PARK CL

Bramshill Barn

Horley

CHURCH LA
SACKVILLE CL
GULLICOTE LA

Hanwell Castle

2

THE OLD COUNCIL HOS

THE COUNCIL HOS

Park Farm

Oxfordshire Cycleway

WARWICK RD

43

Drayton Lodge

CH

1

Cemy

Lord's Spinney

WINSTON DR
ELLISON DR
FIR TREE CL
HARDWICK PARK
RYE CL
CHELSEA CL
WINCH CL
ROTHER CL
BARCOMBE CL
HIGHLANDS
SUSSEX RD
CHEVIOT WAY
HORSHAM CL
ROMNEY RD

HORLEY PATH RD

A422

QUEEN'S CRES

B4100

OX16

42

41   A   42   B   43   C

4
10

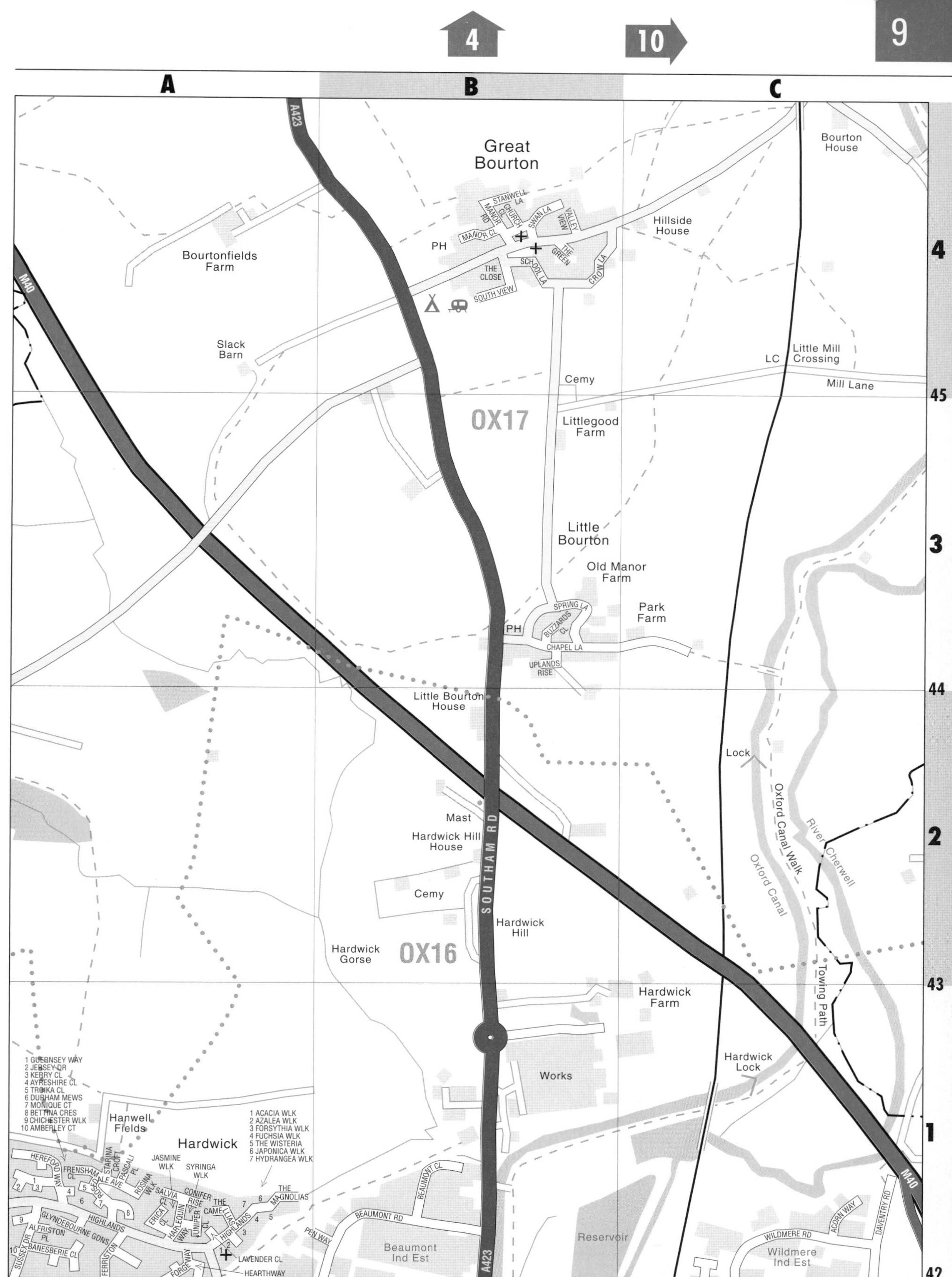
A
B
C
A423
M40
Great Bourton
STANWELL LA
MANOR RD
CHURCH CL
SWAN LA
VALLEY VIEW
MANOR CL
PH
THE GREEN
SCHOOL LA
CROW LA
THE CLOSE
SOUTH VIEW
Bourtonfields Farm
Hillside House
Bourton House
Slack Barn
LC
Little Mill Crossing
Mill Lane
Cemy
OX17
Littlegood Farm
Little Bourton
Old Manor Farm
Park Farm
SPRING LA
BUZZARDS CL
PH
CHAPEL LA
UPLANDS RISE
Little Bourton House
Lock
Oxford Canal Walk
Oxford Canal
River Cherwell
Mast
Hardwick Hill House
SOUTHAM RD
Cemy
Hardwick Hill
Hardwick Gorse
OX16
Towing Path
Hardwick Farm
Works
Hardwick Lock
1 GUERNSEY WAY
2 JERSEY DR
3 KERRY CL
4 AYRESHIRE CL
5 TROIKA CL
6 DURHAM MEWS
7 MONIQUE CT
8 BETTINA CRES
9 CHICHESTER WLK
10 AMBERLEY CT
Hanwell Fields
Hardwick
1 ACACIA WLK
2 AZALEA WLK
3 FORSYTHIA WLK
4 FUCHSIA WLK
5 THE WISTERIA
6 JAPONICA WLK
7 HYDRANGEA WLK
HEREFORD WAY
FRENSHAM CL
STARINA CROFT
PASCALI PL
ROSEDALE AVE
ROSINA WLK
JASMINE WLK
SYRINGA WLK
SALVIA CL
CONIFER RISE
THE CAMELLIAS
THE MAGNOLIAS
GLYNDEBOURNE GDNS
HIGHLANDS
ERICA CL
HARLEQUIN WAY
JUNIPER CL
ALFRISTON PL
SUSSEX DR
BANESBERIE CL
FERRISTON
FORGE WAY
LAVENDER CL
HEARTHWAY
PEN WAY
BEAUMONT CL
BEAUMONT RD
Beaumont Ind Est
A423
Reservoir
WILDMERE RD
ACORN WAY
DAVENTRY RD
Wildmere Ind Est
4
45
3
44
2
43
1
42
44
45
46

16
10

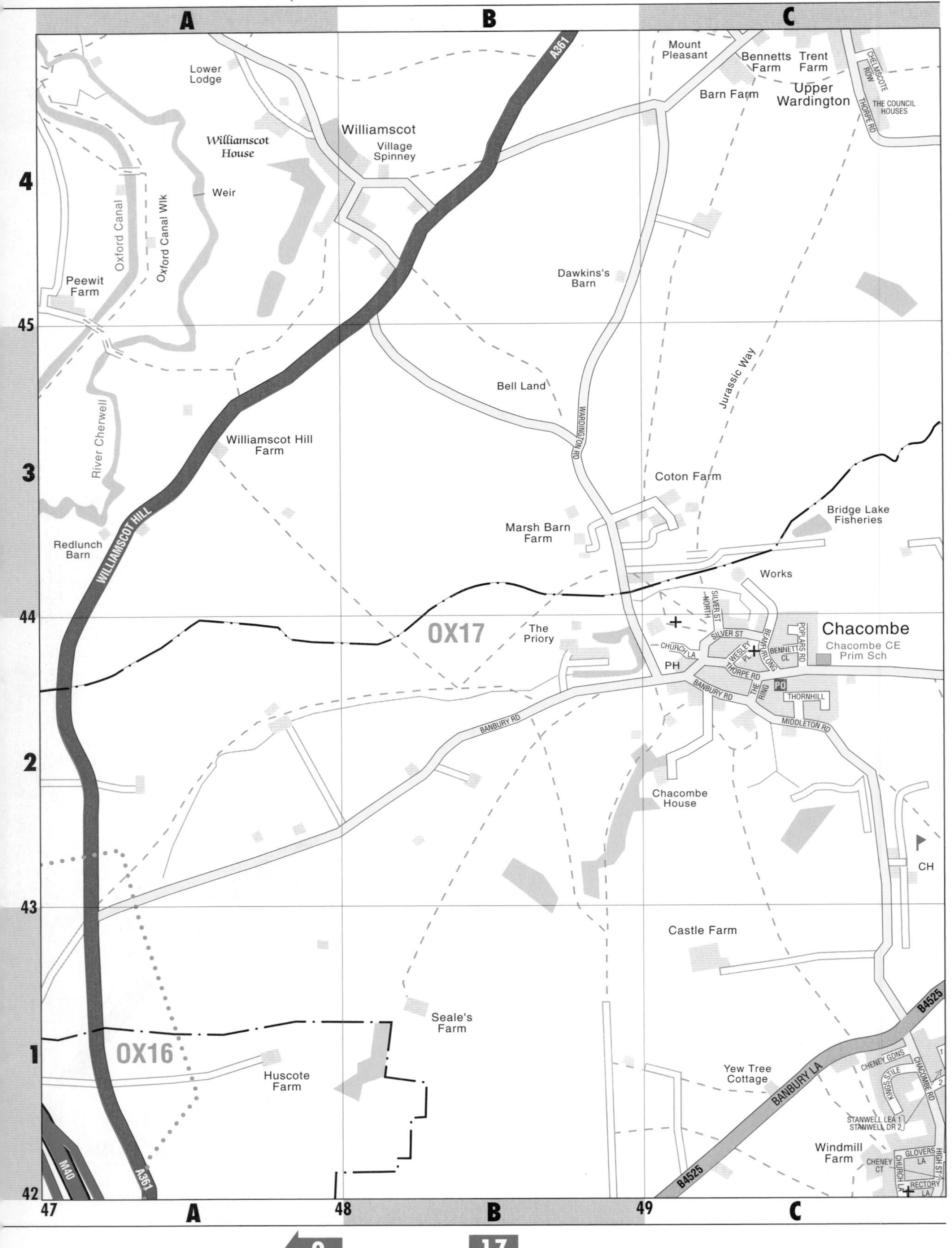

A   B   C

Mount Pleasant
Bennetts Farm   Trent Farm
Lower Lodge
Barn Farm   Upper Wardington
CHELMSCOTE ROW
THE COUNCIL HOUSES
THORPE RD

Williamscot
Williamscot House
Village Spinney

A361

4

Weir

Dawkins's Barn

Oxford Canal
Oxford Canal Wlk

Jurassic Way

45

Peewit Farm

Bell Land

WARDINGTON RD

River Cherwell

Williamscot Hill Farm

Coton Farm

3

Bridge Lake Fisheries

Redlunch Barn

Marsh Barn Farm

WILLIAMSCOT HILL

Works

SILVER ST NORTH

44

OX17

The Priory

SILVER ST
WESLEY PL.
BEAR GdLING
BENNETTS CL
POPLARS RD
Chacombe
Chacombe CE Prim Sch

CHURCH LA
PH
THORPE RD
THE SPINN
BANBURY RD
PO
THORNHILL
MIDDLETON RD

BANBURY RD

2

Chacombe House

CH

43

Castle Farm

B4525

1

OX16

Seale's Farm

Yew Tree Cottage

CHENEY GDNS
STILE SPINX
CHACOMBE RD

Huscote Farm

BANBURY LA
STANWELL LEA 1
STANWELL DR 2

M40
A361

Windmill Farm

CHENEY CT
GLOVERS CT
CHURCH LA
HIGH ST
RECTORY LA

B4525

42

47   A   48   B   49   C

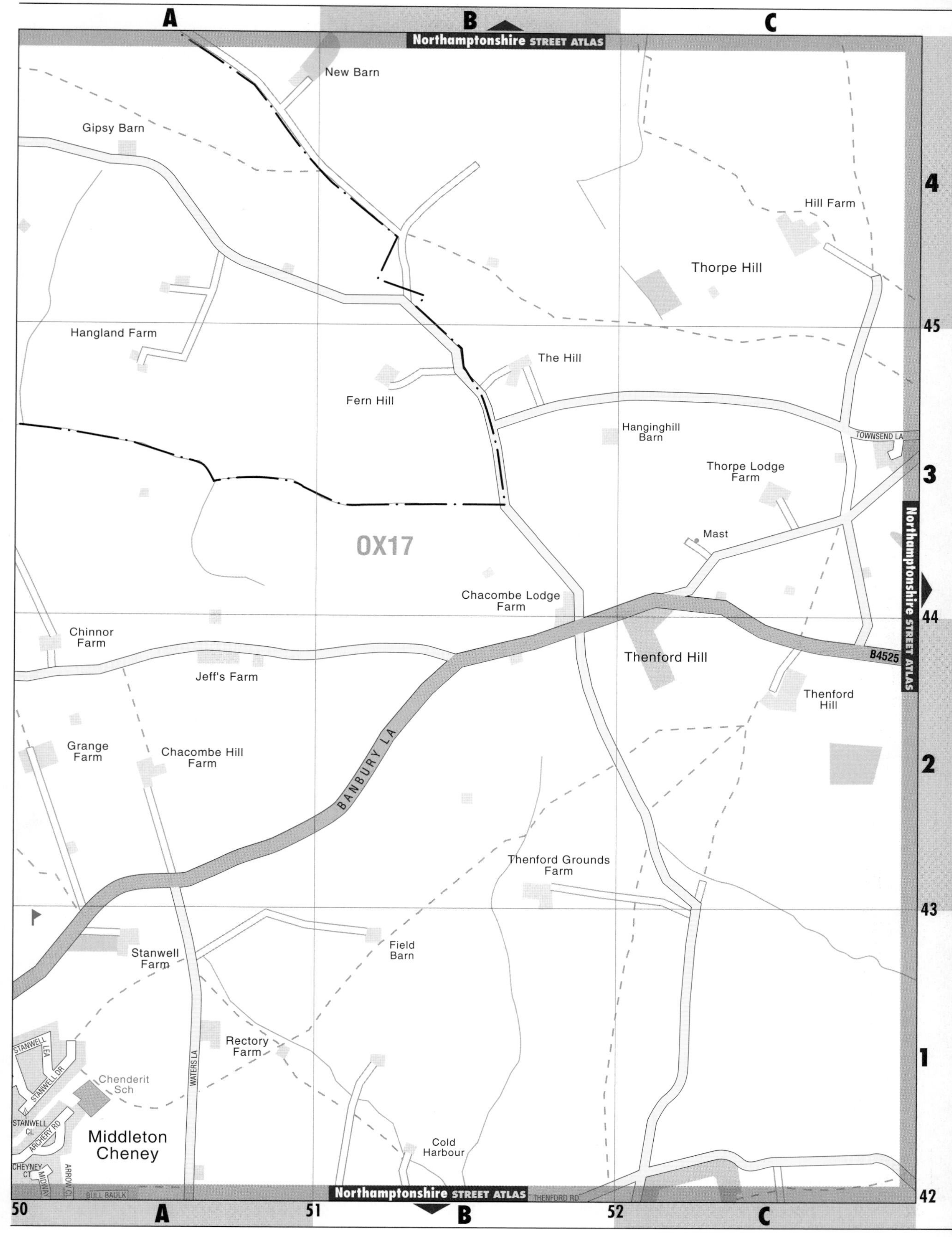

New Barn

Gipsy Barn

Hill Farm

4

Thorpe Hill

Hangland Farm

45

The Hill

Fern Hill

Hanginghill Barn

TOWNSEND LA

Thorpe Lodge Farm

3

OX17

Mast

Chacombe Lodge Farm

44

Thenford Hill

B4525

Chinnor Farm

Jeff's Farm

Thenford Hill

Grange Farm

Chacombe Hill Farm

BANBURY LA

2

Thenford Grounds Farm

43

Stanwell Farm

Field Barn

STANWELL LEA

STANWELL DR

WATERS LA

Rectory Farm

1

STANWELL CL

ARCHERY RD

Chenderit Sch

CHEYNEY CT

MIDWAY

ARROW CL

BULL BAULK

Middleton Cheney

Cold Harbour

THENFORD RD

42

50

A

51

B

52

C

Northamptonshire STREET ATLAS

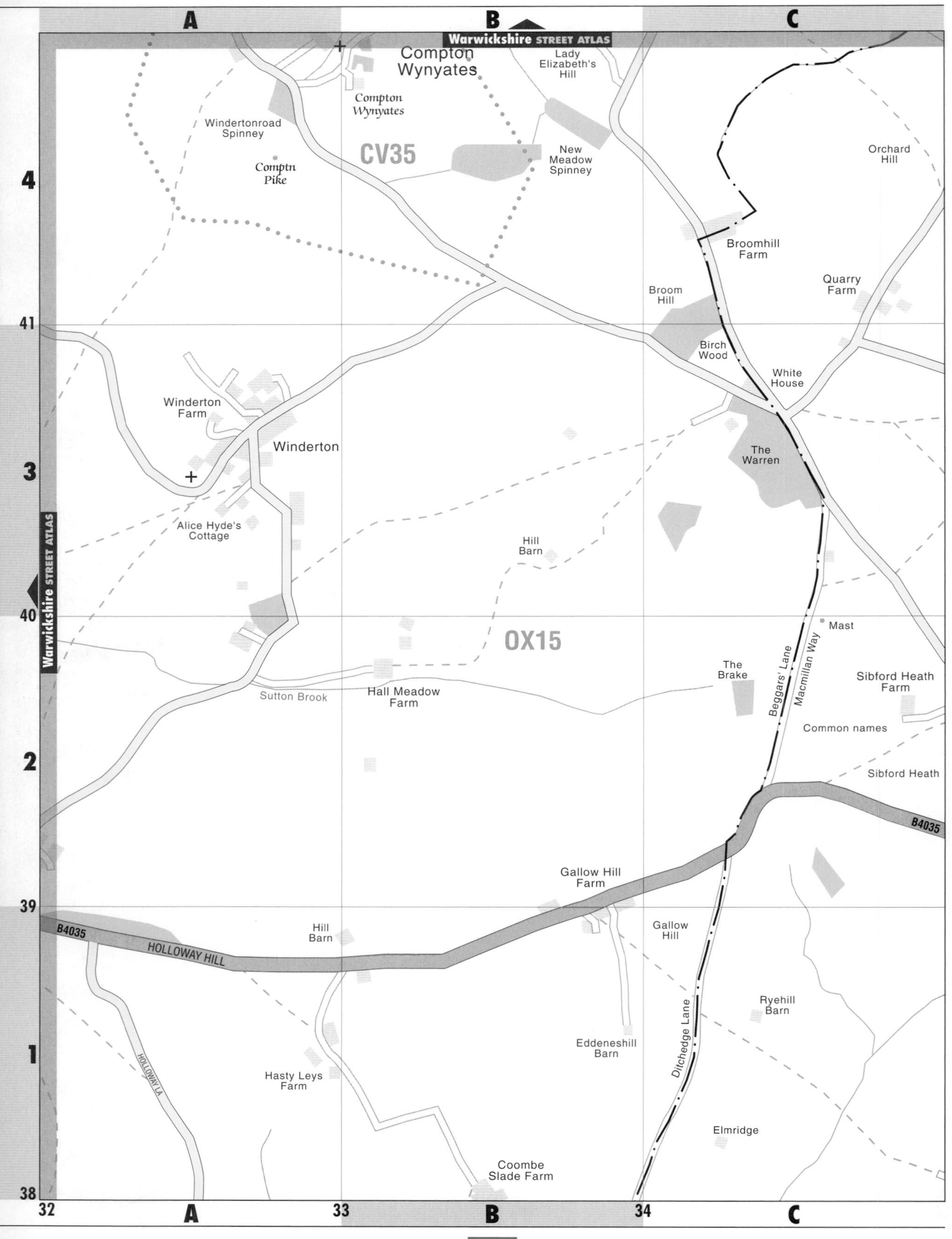

Compton
Wynyates

Lady Elizabeth's
Hill

Orchard
Hill

Windertonroad
Spinney

Compton
Wynyates

CV35

New
Meadow
Spinney

Broomhill
Farm

Quarry
Farm

Comptn
Pike

Broom
Hill

Birch
Wood

White
House

Winderton
Farm

The
Warren

Winderton

Alice Hyde's
Cottage

Hill
Barn

OX15

Mast

The
Brake

Sibford Heath
Farm

Beggars' Lane

Macmillan Way

Common names

Sutton Brook

Hall Meadow
Farm

Sibford Heath

B4035

Gallow Hill
Farm

B4035

HOLLOWAY HILL

Hill
Barn

Gallow
Hill

Ryehill
Barn

Ditchedge Lane

HOLLOWAY LA

Eddeneshill
Barn

Hasty Leys
Farm

Elmridge

Coombe
Slade Farm

32   A   33   B   34   C

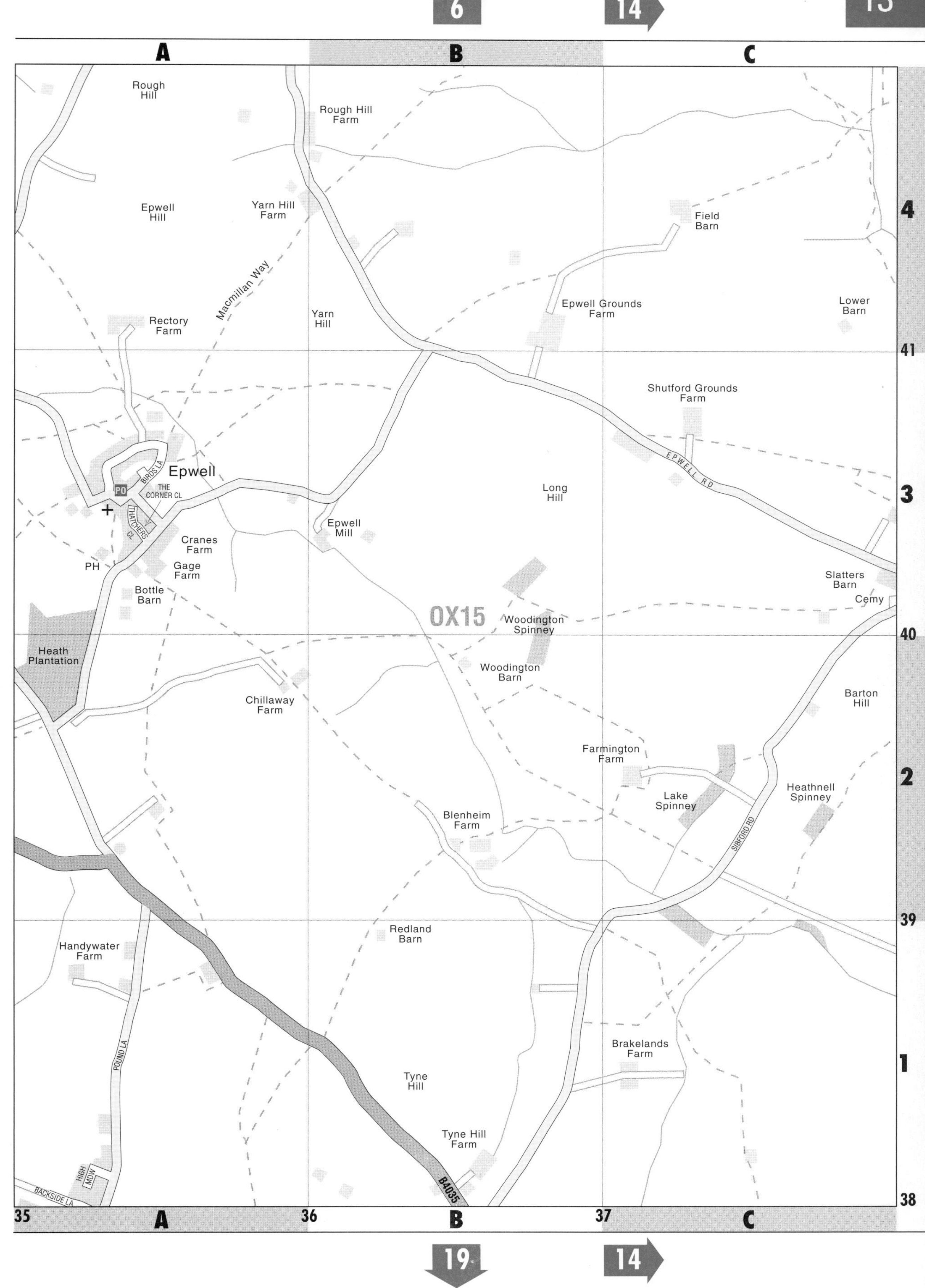
A
B
C
Rough Hill
Rough Hill Farm
Epwell Hill
Yarn Hill Farm
Field Barn
Macmillan Way
Rectory Farm
Yarn Hill
Epwell Grounds Farm
Lower Barn
Shutford Grounds Farm
EPWELL RD
Epwell
BIRDS LA
PO
THE CORNER CL
THATCHERS CL
Long Hill
Epwell Mill
Cranes Farm
PH
Gage Farm
Bottle Barn
Slatters Barn
Cemy
OX15
Woodington Spinney
Heath Plantation
Woodington Barn
Chillaway Farm
Barton Hill
Farmington Farm
Lake Spinney
Heathnell Spinney
Blenheim Farm
SIBFORD RD
Redland Barn
Handywater Farm
POUND LA
Brakelands Farm
Tyne Hill
Tyne Hill Farm
HIGH MDW
BACKSIDE LA
B4035
4
41
3
40
2
39
1
38
35
36
37

13
7

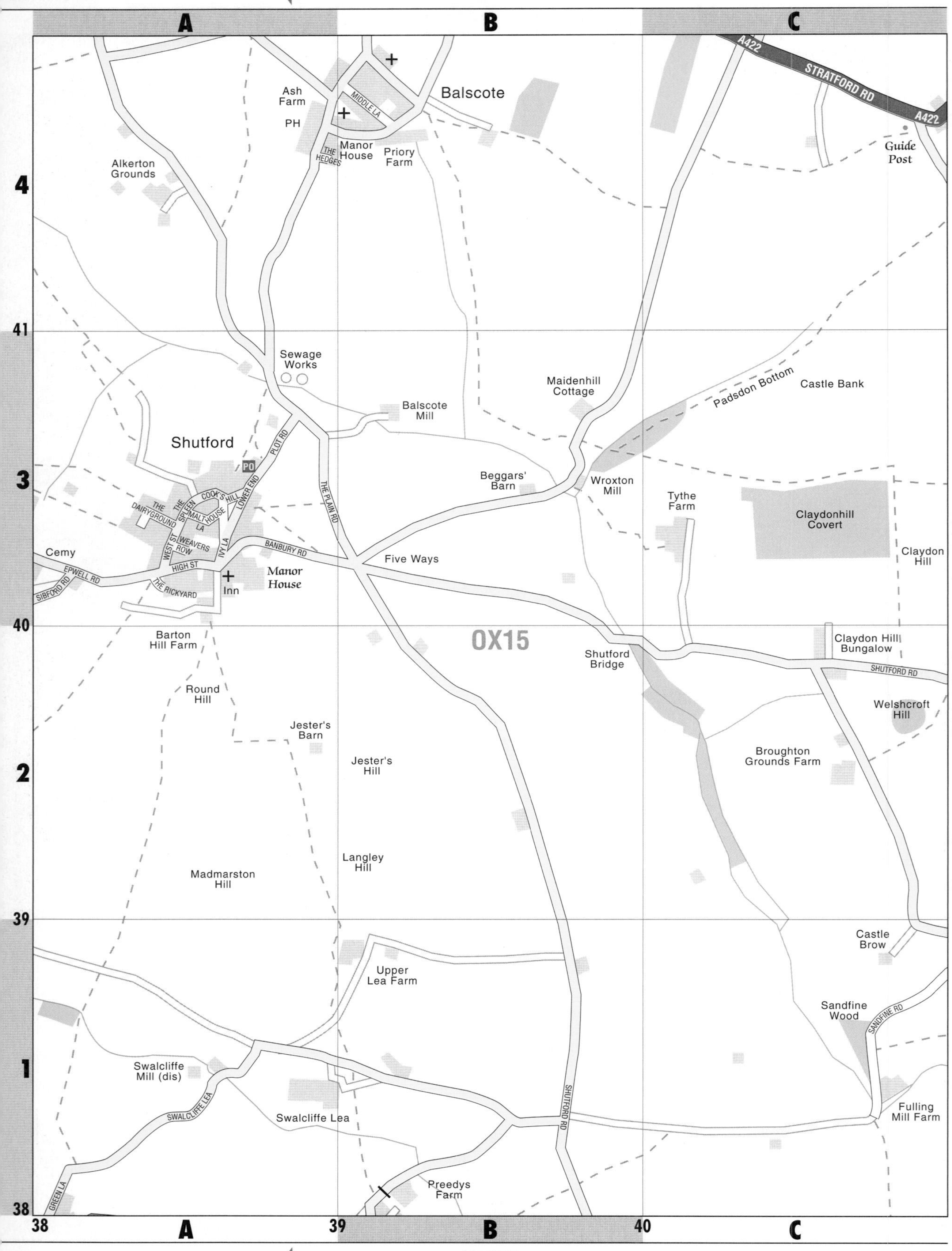
A
B
C
A422
STRATFORD RD
A422
Balscote
Ash Farm
PH
MIDDLE LA
THE HEDGES
Manor House
Priory Farm
Guide Post
Alkerton Grounds
4
41
Sewage Works
Maidenhill Cottage
Padsdon Bottom
Castle Bank
Balscote Mill
Shutford
PLOT RD
PO
3
Beggars' Barn
Wroxton Mill
Tythe Farm
Claydonhill Covert
THE DAIRYGROUND
THE SPLEEN
COOK'S HILL
MALTHOUSE LA
LOWER END
WEST ST
WEAVERS ROW
IVY LA
THE PLAIN RD
BANBURY RD
Cemy
HIGH ST
EPWELL RD
SIBFORD RD
THE RICKYARD
Inn
Manor House
Five Ways
Claydon Hill
40
OX15
Barton Hill Farm
Shutford Bridge
Claydon Hill Bungalow
SHUTFORD RD
Welshcroft Hill
Round Hill
Jester's Barn
2
Jester's Hill
Broughton Grounds Farm
Madmarston Hill
Langley Hill
39
Castle Brow
Upper Lea Farm
Sandfine Wood
SANDFINE RD
1
Swalcliffe Mill (dis)
SWALCLIFFE LEA
Swalcliffe Lea
SHUTFORD RD
Fulling Mill Farm
GREEN LA
Preedys Farm
38
38
39
40

13
20

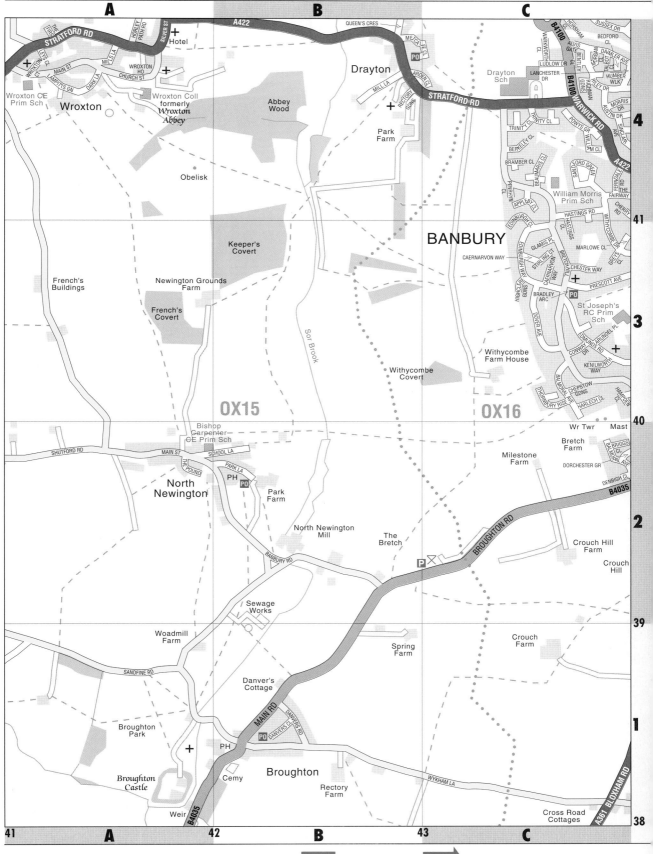

8
16

A B C

STRATFORD RD
A422
THE FIRS
HORLEY PATH RD
SILVER ST
Hotel
QUEEN'S CRES
METCALFE CL
PO
B4100
HORSHAM CL
SUSSEX DR
BEDFORD CL
WARKWORTH CL
ALVIS GATE
BENTLEY CL
MORGAN CL
DAIMLER AVE
TALBOT CL
LEYS CL
WROXTON CT
MILLS LA
MAIN ST
WROXTON HO
CHURCH ST
LAMPITTS GN
DARK LA
Drayton
ARDEN CL
MILL LA
RECTORY GDNS
Drayton Sch
LUDLOW DR
LANCHESTER DR
RICHMAN GDNS
RILEY DR
HUMBER WLK
Wroxton CE Prim Sch
Wroxton
Wroxton Coll formerly *Wroxton Abbey*
Abbey Wood
STRATFORD RD
WARWICK RD
MORRIS DR
AUSTIN DR
TRINITY CL
POWYS GR
SINCLAIR AVE
WILLIAM CL
Park Farm
BERKELEY CL
BRAMBER CL
BEAUMARIS CL
SANDFORD GREEN
FERNDALE RD
THE FAIRWAY
Obelisk
PENRHYN CL
APPLEBY CL
William Morris Prim Sch
CHERRY RD
HASTINGS RD
HASTINGS CL
EDINBURGH CL
WITHYCOMBE DR
Keeper's Covert
BANBURY
GLAMIS PL
MARLOWE CL
GREYS CL
CAERNARVON WAY
STIRLING CT
EDINBURGH WAY
CAERNARVON WAY
BRETCH HILL
CHESTER WAY
French's Buildings
Newington Grounds Farm
PRESCOTT AVE
HIGHCLERE GDNS
BRADLEY ARC
PO
French's Covert
St Joseph's RC Prim Sch
DOVER AVE
Sor Brook
EDMUNDS RD
ARUNDEL PL
CONWAY DR
Withycombe Farm House
KENILWORTH WAY
Withycombe Covert
BALMORAL AVE
CHEPSTOW GDNS
THORNBURY RISE
HARLECH CL
HAMPDEN CL
OX15
OX16
Bishop Carpenter CE Prim Sch
Wr Twr
Mast
SHUTFORD RD
MAIN ST
SCHOOL LA
THE POUND
PARK LA
PH
PO
Bretch Farm
Milestone Farm
BRIGGS CL
BALMORAL AVE
DORCHESTER GR
DENBIGH CL
B4035
North Newington
Park Farm
BROUGHTON RD
North Newington Mill
The Bretch
Crouch Hill Farm
Crouch Hill
BANBURY RD
P
Sewage Works
Woadmill Farm
Spring Farm
Crouch Farm
SANDFINE RD
Danver's Cottage
MAIN RD
DANVERS RD
DANVERS CL
PO
Broughton Park
PH
Broughton
WYKHAM LA
Broughton Castle
Cemy
Rectory Farm
A361 BLOXHAM RD
Weir
B4035
Cross Road Cottages

4 41 3 40 2 39 1 38
41 A 42 B 43 C

21
16

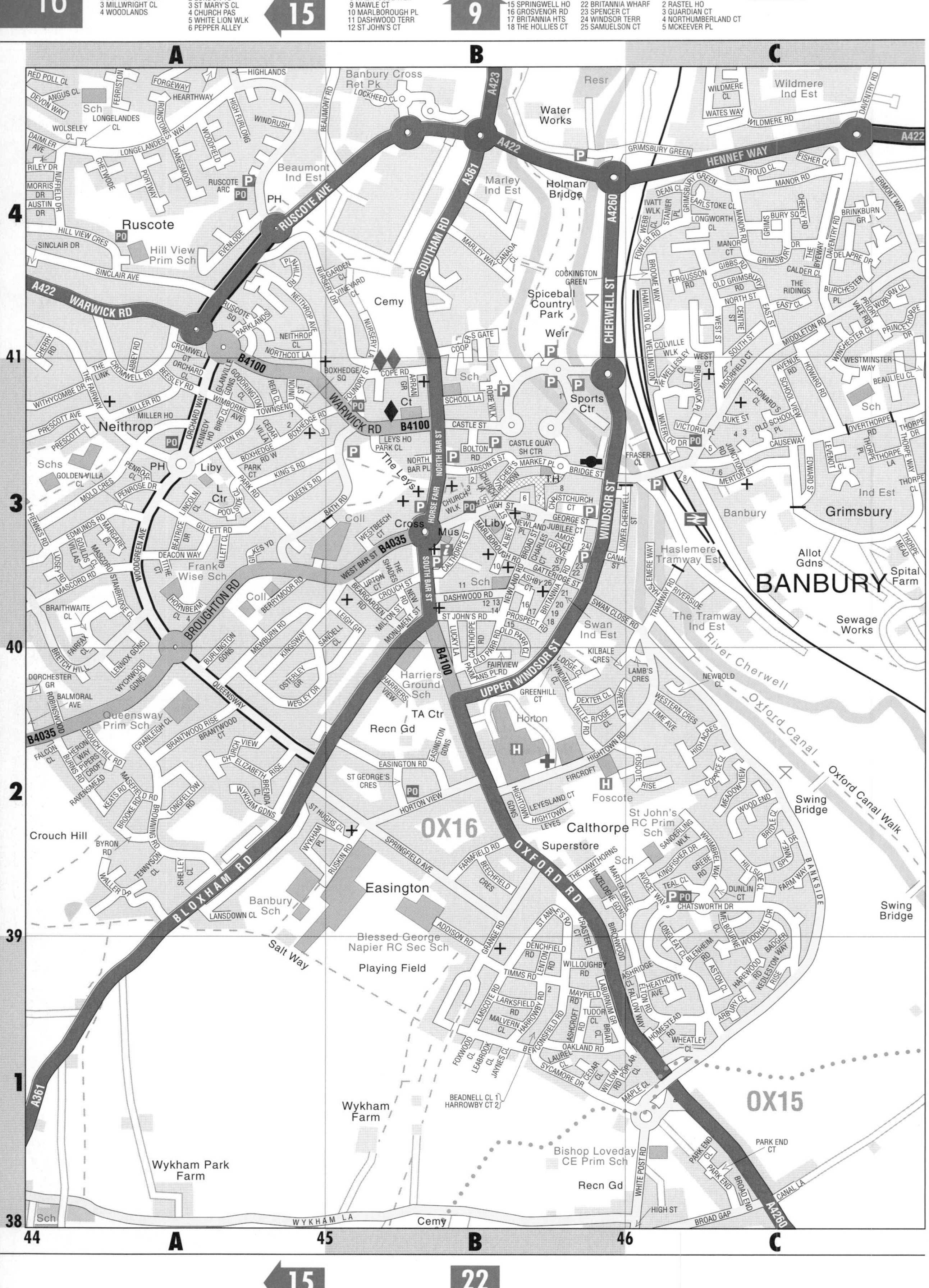

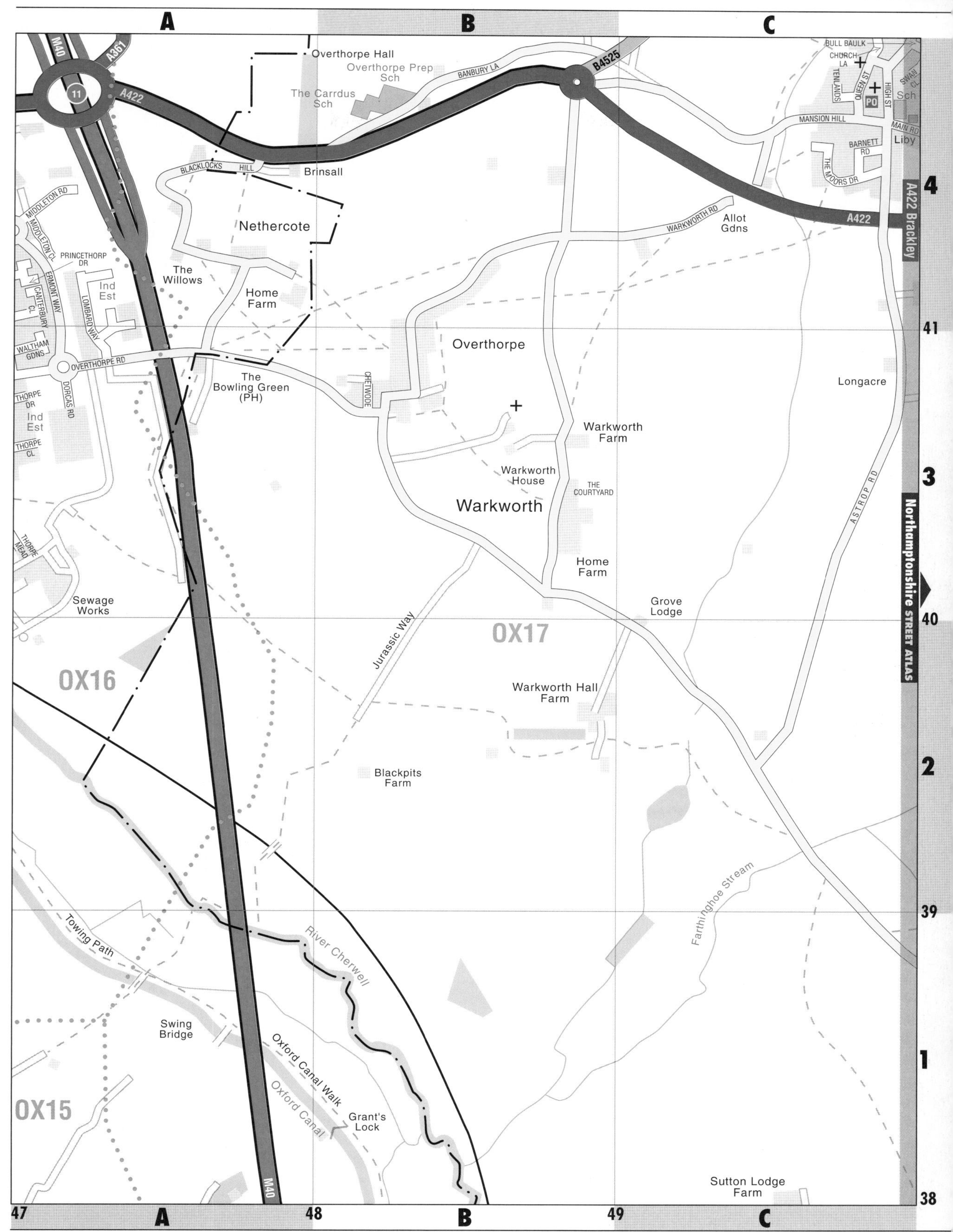

Overthorpe Hall

Overthorpe Prep Sch

BANBURY LA

B4525

The Carrdus Sch

BULL BAULK
CHURCH LA
TENLANDS
QUEEN ST
MAIN RD
HIGH ST
SWAN
Sch
PO
Liby

MANSION HILL

BLACKLOCKS HILL

Brinsall

THE MOORS DR

BARNETT RD

Nethercote

WARKWORTH RD

Allot Gdns

A422

A422 Brackley

4

MIDDLETON RD
MIDDLETON CL
PRINCETHORP DR
ERMONT WAY
CANTERBURY CL
LOMBARD WAY
WALTHAM GDNS
THORPE DR
DORCAS RD
THORPE CL

Ind Est

The Willows

Home Farm

Overthorpe

Longacre

41

11

A422

A361

M40

Overthorpe Rd

The Bowling Green (PH)

CHETWODE

+

Warkworth Farm

Warkworth House

THE COURTYARD

ASTROP RD

Northamptonshire STREET ATLAS

3

Ind Est

THORPE MEAD

Sewage Works

Warkworth

Home Farm

Grove Lodge

40

OX16

Jurassic Way

OX17

Warkworth Hall Farm

Blackpits Farm

2

39

River Cherwell

Farthinghoe Stream

Towing Path

Swing Bridge

Oxford Canal Walk

Oxford Canal

Grant's Lock

1

OX15

Sutton Lodge Farm

38

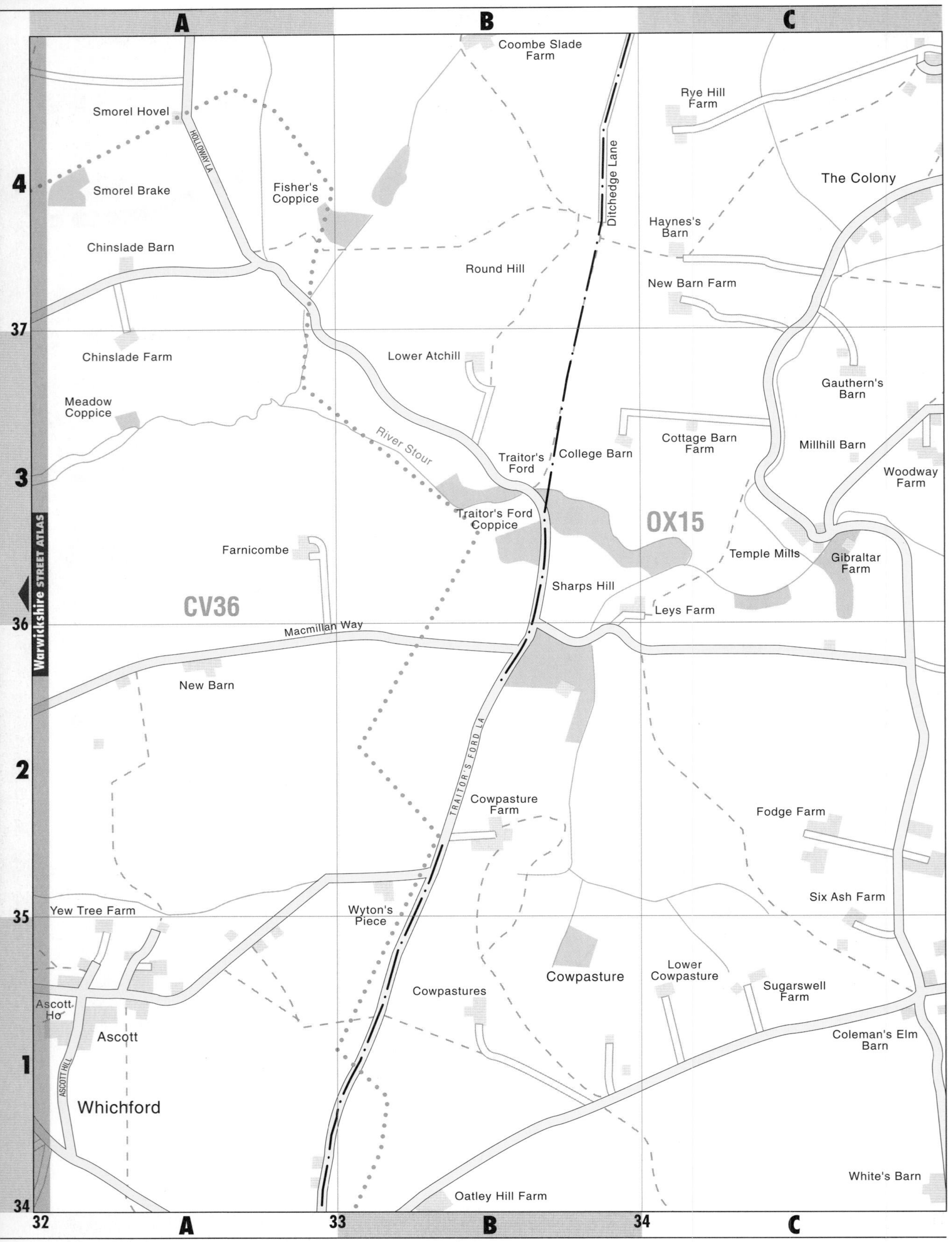

A   **B**   **C**

Coombe Slade Farm

Smorel Hovel

HOLLOWAY LA

Smorel Brake

Fisher's Coppice

Rye Hill Farm

The Colony

Chinslade Barn

Round Hill

Ditchedge Lane

Haynes's Barn

New Barn Farm

4

37

Chinslade Farm

Lower Atchill

Gauthern's Barn

Meadow Coppice

River Stour

Cottage Barn Farm

Millhill Barn

Woodway Farm

3

Warwickshire STREET ATLAS

Traitor's Ford

College Barn

OX15

Farnicombe

Traitor's Ford Coppice

Temple Mills

Gibraltar Farm

Sharps Hill

CV36

Leys Farm

36

Macmillan Way

New Barn

TRAITOR'S FORD LA

2

Cowpasture Farm

Fodge Farm

Six Ash Farm

35

Yew Tree Farm

Wyton's Piece

Ascott Ho

ASCOTT HILL

Ascott

Cowpastures

Cowpasture

Lower Cowpasture

Sugarswell Farm

Coleman's Elm Barn

1

Whichford

White's Barn

34

32   **A**   **33**   **B**   **34**   **C**

Oatley Hill Farm

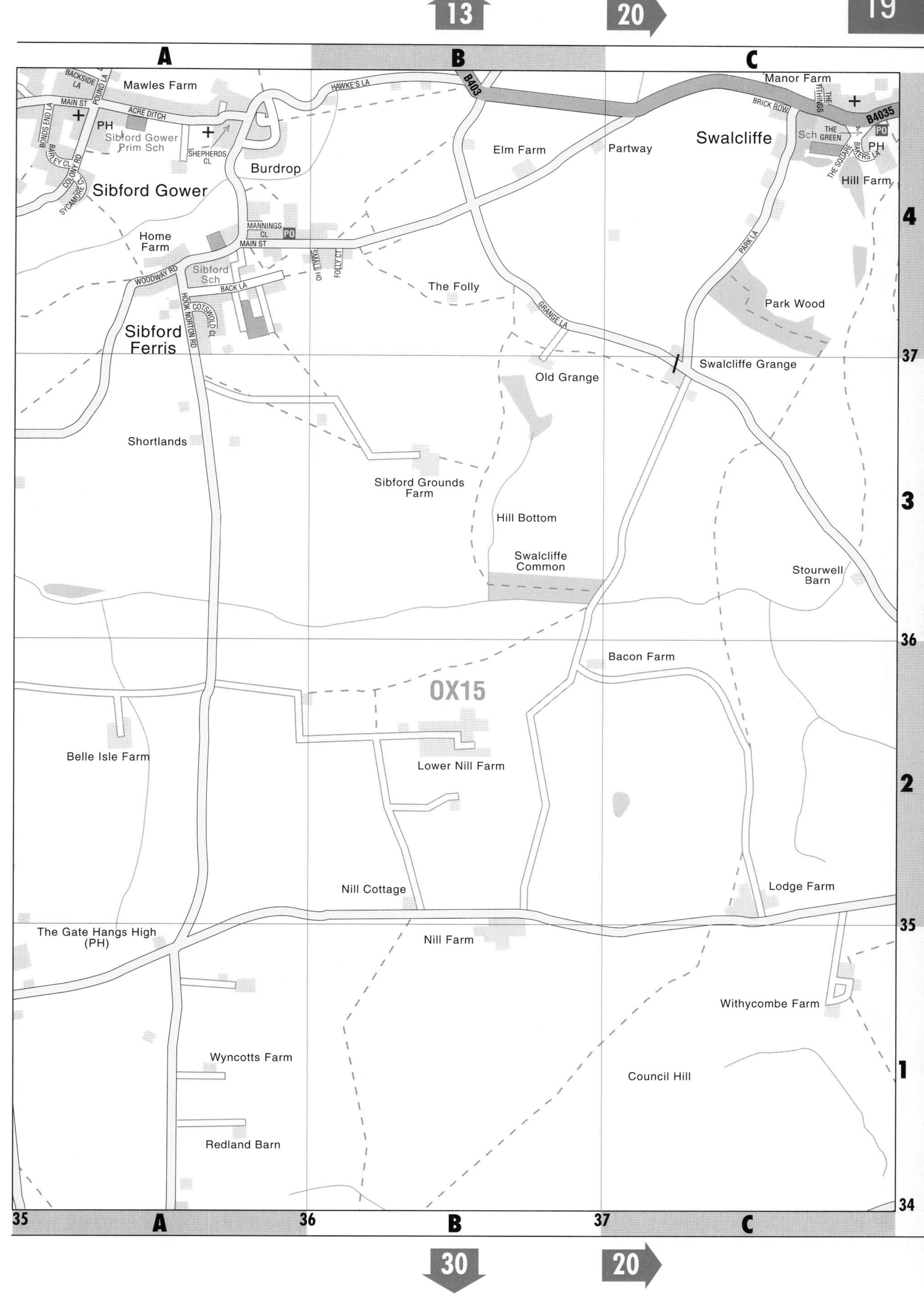
13
20
A
B
C
Mawles Farm
BACKSIDE LA
POUND LA
MAIN ST
ACRE DITCH
HAWKE'S LA
B403
Manor Farm
BRICK ROW
THE YITHINGS
B4035
BONDS END LA
PH
Sibford Gower Prim Sch
SHEPHERDS CL
Burdrop
Elm Farm
Partway
Swalcliffe
Sch
THE GREEN
PO
PH
BARLEY CL
COLONY RD
SYCAMORE CL
Sibford Gower
THE SQUARE
BAKERS LA
Hill Farm
Home Farm
MANNINGS CL
MAIN ST
SMALL HO
FOLLY CT
PARK LA
4
WOODWAY RD
Sibford Sch
BACK LA
The Folly
Park Wood
HOOK NORTON RD
COTSWOLD CL
GRANGE LA
Sibford Ferris
37
Swalcliffe Grange
Old Grange
Shortlands
Sibford Grounds Farm
3
Hill Bottom
Swalcliffe Common
Stourwell Barn
36
Bacon Farm
OX15
Belle Isle Farm
Lower Nill Farm
2
Nill Cottage
Lodge Farm
The Gate Hangs High (PH)
35
Nill Farm
Withycombe Farm
Wyncotts Farm
1
Council Hill
Redland Barn
34
35
A
36
B
37
C
30
20

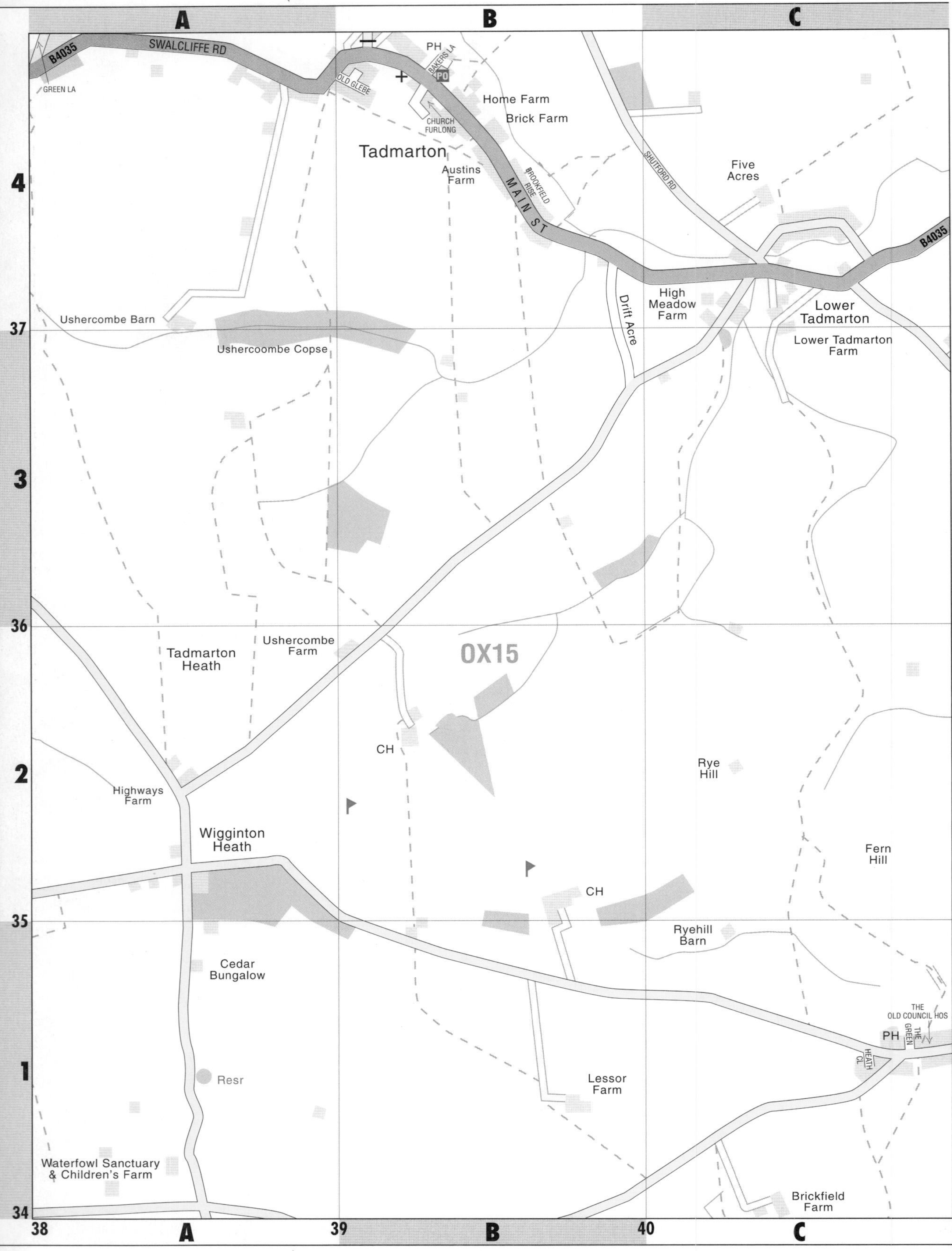

A
B
C

B4035
SWALCLIFFE RD
GREEN LA

OLD GLEBE

PH
BAKERS LA
PO
CHURCH FURLONG

Home Farm
Brick Farm

Tadmarton

Austins Farm

BROOKFIELD RISE

MAIN ST

SHUTFORD RD

Five Acres

B4035

4

Drift Acre

High Meadow Farm

Lower Tadmarton

Ushercombe Barn

37

Ushercoombe Copse

Lower Tadmarton Farm

3

36

OX15

Tadmarton Heath

Ushercombe Farm

CH

Rye Hill

2

Highways Farm

Fern Hill

Wigginton Heath

CH

Ryehill Barn

35

Cedar Bungalow

THE OLD COUNCIL HOS
THE GREEN

PH
HEATH CL

1

Resr

Lessor Farm

Waterfowl Sanctuary & Children's Farm

Brickfield Farm

34

38
A
39
B
40
C

15
22

A B C

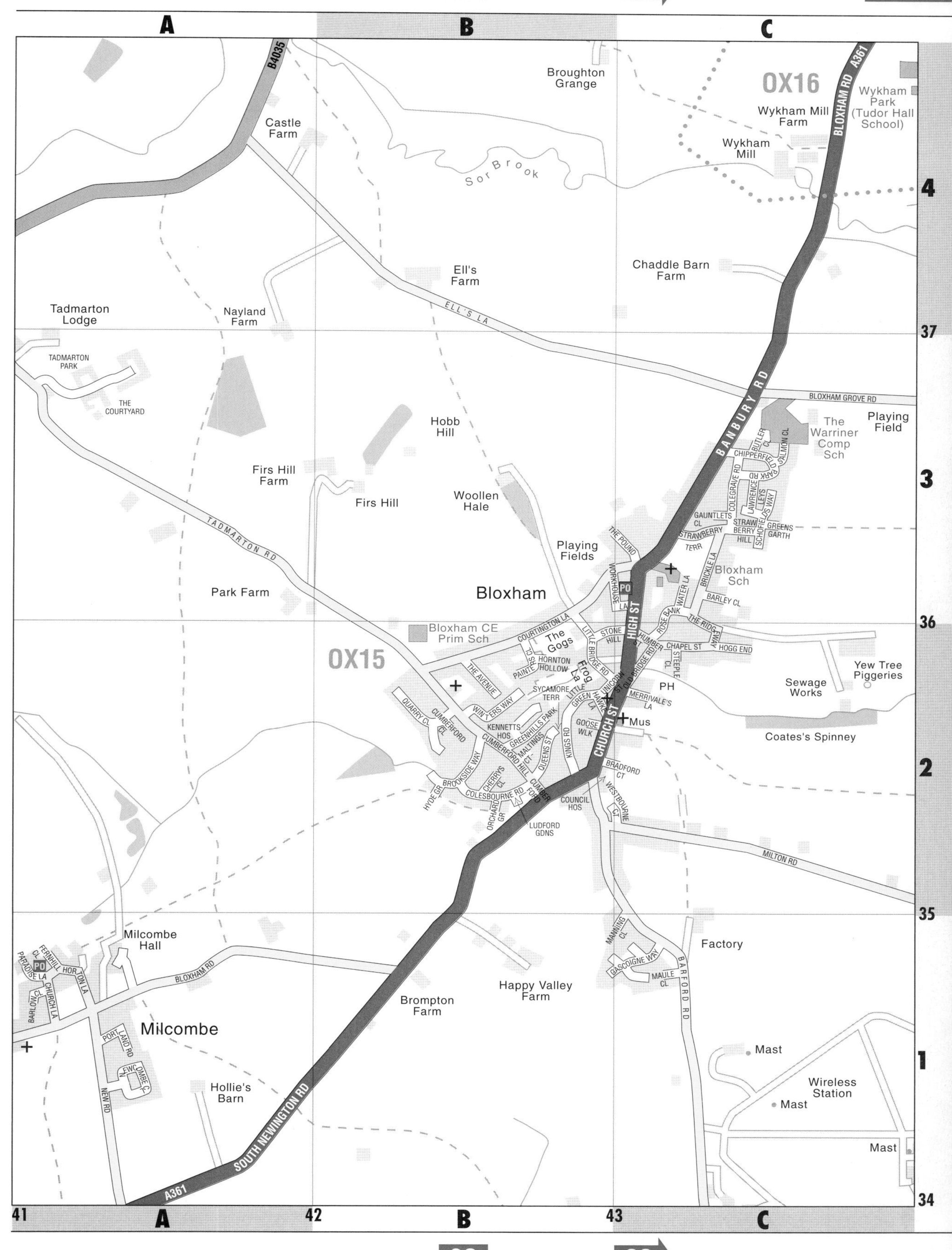
B4035
Castle Farm
Broughton Grange
OX16
Wykham Park (Tudor Hall School)
Wykham Mill Farm
Wykham Mill
BLOXHAM RD A361
Sor Brook
Ell's Farm
Chaddle Barn Farm
Tadmarton Lodge
Nayland Farm
ELL'S LA
TADMARTON PARK
THE COURTYARD
BLOXHAM GROVE RD
BANBURY RD
The Warriner Comp Sch
Playing Field
Hobb Hill
Firs Hill Farm
Firs Hill
Woollen Hale
TADMARTON RD
Playing Fields
Park Farm
Bloxham
Bloxham Sch
Bloxham CE Prim Sch
OX15
The Gogs
HIGH ST
CHURCH ST
Frog La
PH
Mus
Sewage Works
Yew Tree Piggeries
Coates's Spinney
MILTON RD
Factory
Milcombe Hall
BLOXHAM RD
Happy Valley Farm
Brompton Farm
Milcombe
BARFORD RD
Mast
Wireless Station
Mast
Mast
Hollie's Barn
NEW RD
SOUTH NEWINGTON RD
A361

4
37
3
36
2
35
1
34

41 A 42 B 43 C

32
22

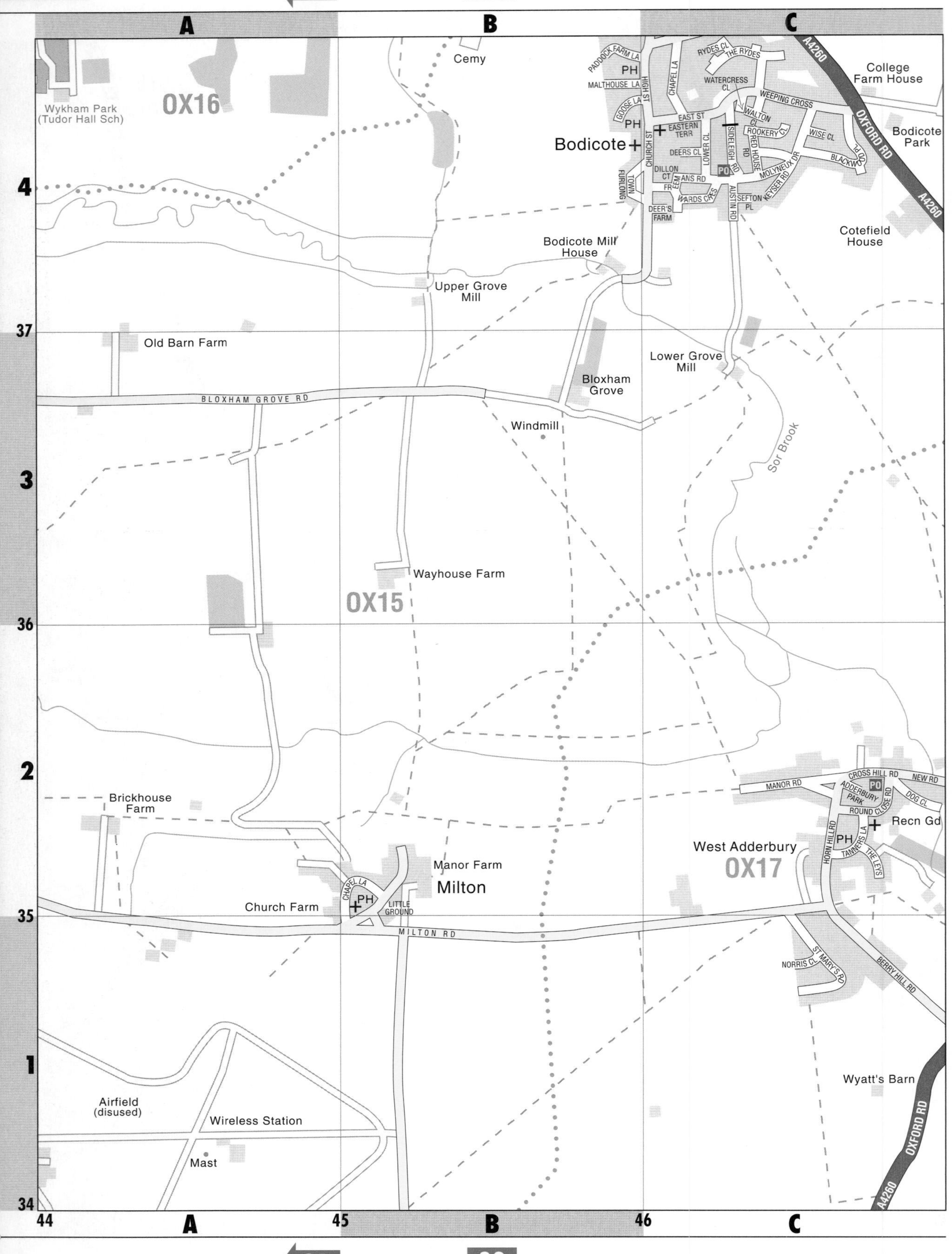

A   B   C

Wykham Park
(Tudor Hall Sch)

OX16

Cemy

PADDOCK FARM LA
RYDES CL
THE RYDES
PH
CHAPEL LA
HIGH ST
MALTHOUSE LA
GOOSE LA
WATERCRESS CL
WEEPING CROSS

College
Farm House

A4260
OXFORD RD

PH
EAST ST
EASTERN TERR
WALTON CL
RED HOUSE
ROOKERY CT
WISE CL
BLACKW

Bodicote
DEERS CL
LOWER CL
SIDELEIGH
PO
MOLYNEUX DR
KEYSER RD
SEFTON PL

Bodicote
Park

DILLON CT
EVANS RD
TOWN FURLONG
CHURCH ST
FR
WARDS CRS
AUSTIN RD

Bodicote Mill
House

DEER'S
FARM

Cotefield
House

4

Upper Grove
Mill

Lower Grove
Mill

37

Old Barn Farm

Bloxham
Grove

BLOXHAM GROVE RD

Sor Brook

Windmill

3

Wayhouse Farm

OX15

36

2

MANOR RD
CROSS HILL RD
NEW RD
ADDERBURY PARK
PO
ROUND CLOSE RD
DOG CL

Brickhouse
Farm

West Adderbury
OX17
HORN HILL RD
PH
TANNER'S LA
THE LEYS
Recn Gd

Manor Farm

Milton

Church Farm
CHAPEL LA
PH
LITTLE GROUND

35

MILTON RD

NORRIS CL
ST MARY'S RD
BERRY HILL RD

1

Wyatt's Barn

Airfield
(disused)

Wireless Station

OXFORD RD
A4260

Mast

34

44   A   45   B   46   C

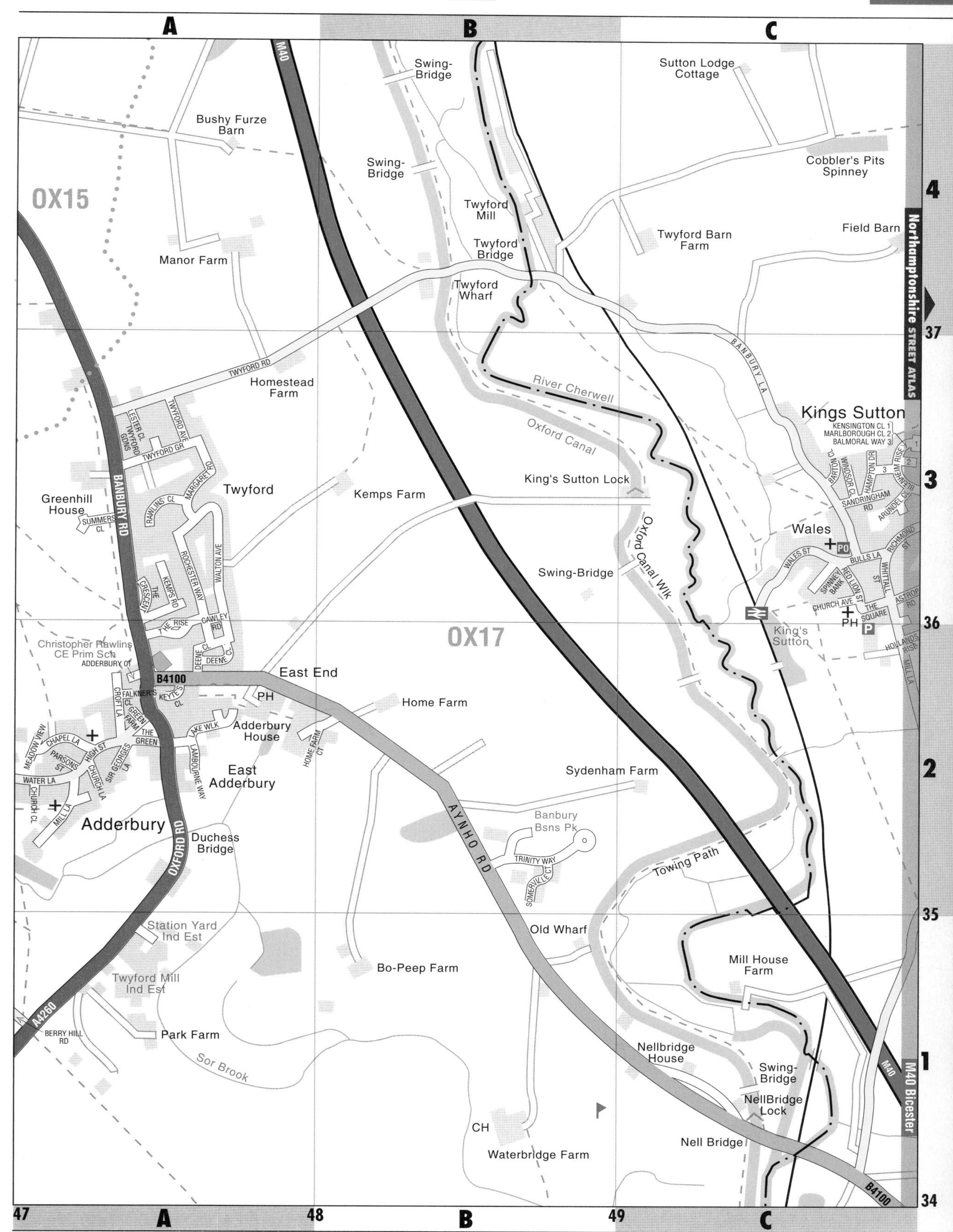
A
B
C
OX15
OX17
Bushy Furze Barn
Manor Farm
Swing-Bridge
Twyford Mill
Twyford Bridge
Twyford Wharf
Sutton Lodge Cottage
Cobbler's Pits Spinney
Twyford Barn Farm
Field Barn
Homestead Farm
TWYFORD RD
River Cherwell
Oxford Canal
BANBURY LA
Kings Sutton
KENSINGTON CL 1
MARLBOROUGH CL 2
BALMORAL WAY 3
Greenhill House
Twyford
Kemps Farm
King's Sutton Lock
Oxford Canal Wlk
Wales
PO
BULLS LA
WALES ST
CHURCH AVE
THE SQUARE
PH
P
King's Sutton
HOLLANDS RISE
MILL LA
Swing-Bridge
BANBURY RD
Christopher Rawlins CE Prim Sch
ADDERBURY CT
B4100
East End
Home Farm
Adderbury House
East Adderbury
Sydenham Farm
AYNHO RD
Banbury Bsns Pk
TRINITY WAY
Adderbury
Duchess Bridge
OXFORD RD
Towing Path
Station Yard Ind Est
Old Wharf
Bo-Peep Farm
Twyford Mill Ind Est
Mill House Farm
A4260
BERRY HILL RD
Park Farm
Sor Brook
Nellbridge House
Swing-Bridge
NellBridge Lock
CH
Waterbridge Farm
Nell Bridge
M40
Northamptonshire STREET ATLAS
M40 Bicester
4
37
3
36
2
35
1
34
47
48
49

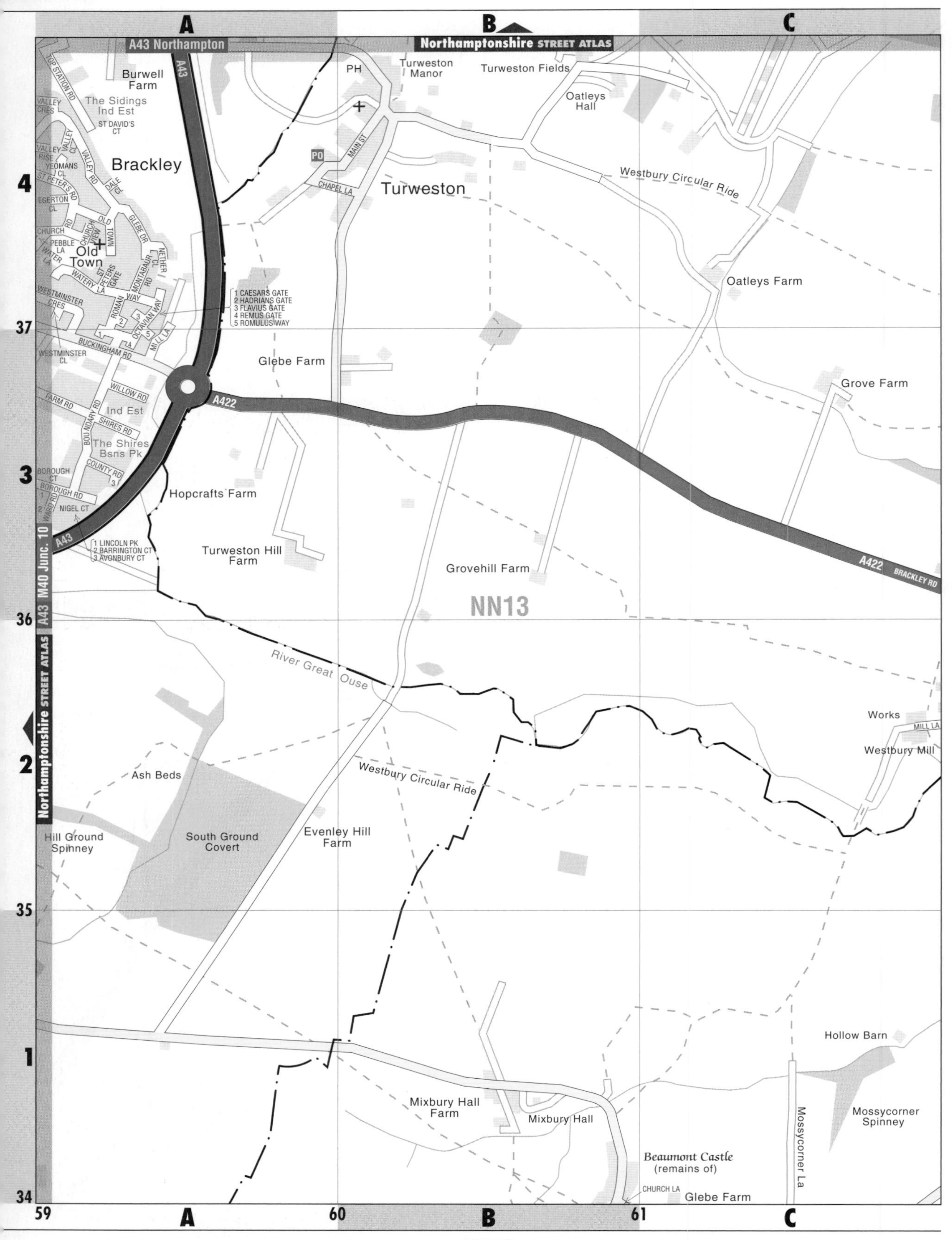

Brackley

Burwell Farm

The Sidings Ind Est

ST DAVID'S CT

Old Town

PH

Turweston Manor

Turweston Fields

Oatleys Hall

Westbury Circular Ride

Turweston

PO

CHAPEL LA

MAIN ST

Glebe Farm

Oatleys Farm

Grove Farm

1 CAESARS GATE
2 HADRIANS GATE
3 FLAVIUS GATE
4 REMUS GATE
5 ROMULUS WAY

A422

Ind Est

The Shires Bsns Pk

BOROUGH CT

Hopcrafts Farm

Turweston Hill Farm

Grovehill Farm

NN13

A422 BRACKLEY RD

1 LINCOLN PK
2 BARRINGTON CT
3 AVONBURY CT

River Great Ouse

Works

MILL LA

Westbury Mill

Ash Beds

Westbury Circular Ride

Hill Ground Spinney

South Ground Covert

Evenley Hill Farm

Hollow Barn

Mixbury Hall Farm

Mixbury Hall

Mossycorner La

Mossycorner Spinney

Beaumont Castle (remains of)

CHURCH LA

Glebe Farm

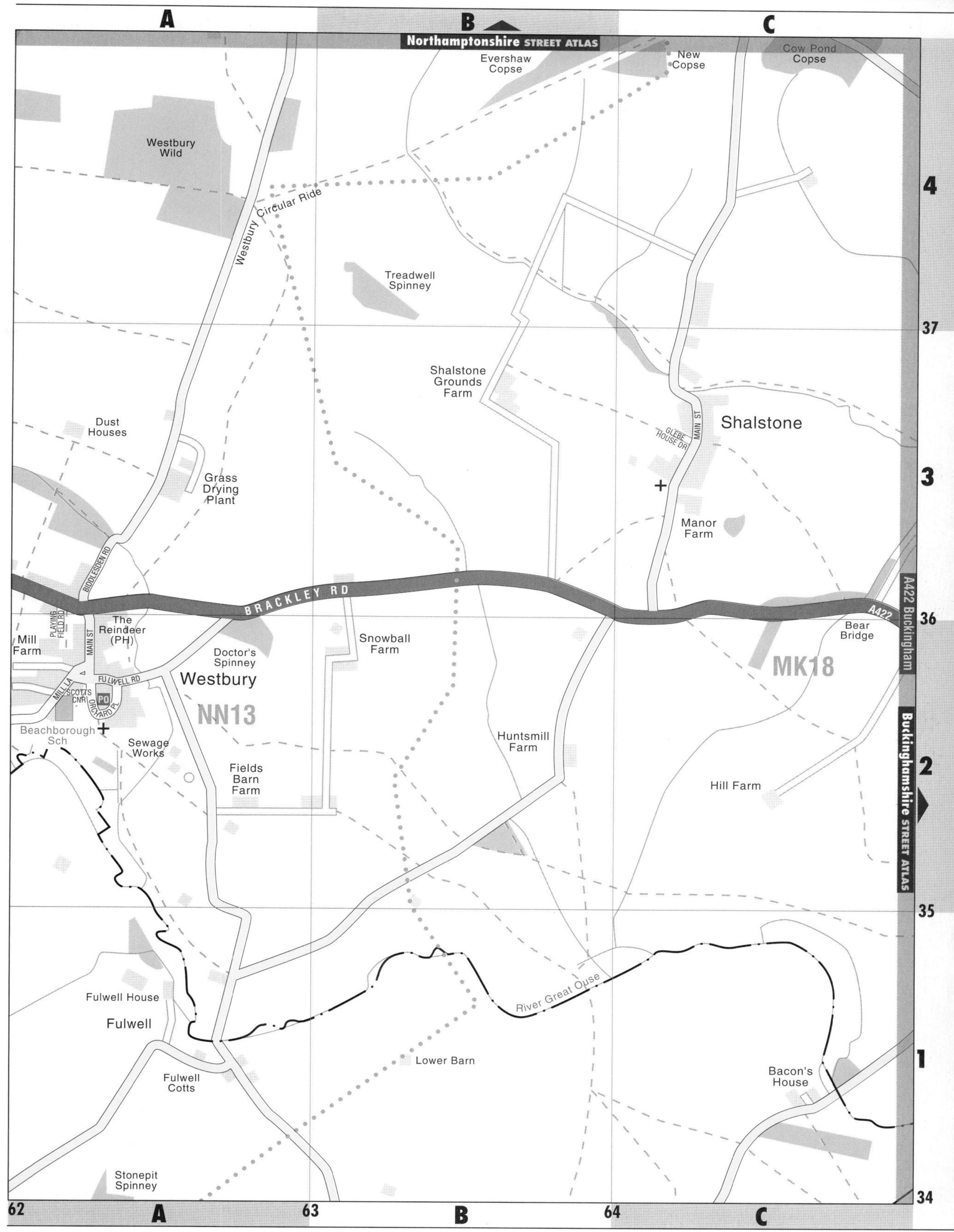

Evershaw Copse

New Copse

Cow Pond Copse

Westbury Wild

Westbury Circular Ride

4

Treadwell Spinney

37

Shalstone Grounds Farm

GLEBE HOUSE DRI

MAIN ST

Shalstone

Dust Houses

Grass Drying Plant

3

+

Manor Farm

BIDDLESDEN RD

BRACKLEY RD

A422

A422 Buckingham

36

Mill Farm

PLAYING FIELD

MAIN ST

The Reindeer (PH)

Doctor's Spinney

Snowball Farm

Bear Bridge

MK18

Beachborough Sch

MILL LA

SCOTT'S CNR

FULWELL RD

PO

ORCHARD PL

Westbury

NN13

+

Sewage Works

Fields Barn Farm

Huntsmill Farm

Hill Farm

Buckinghamshire STREET ATLAS

2

35

River Great Ouse

Fulwell House

Fulwell

Lower Barn

Bacon's House

1

Fulwell Cotts

Stonepit Spinney

34

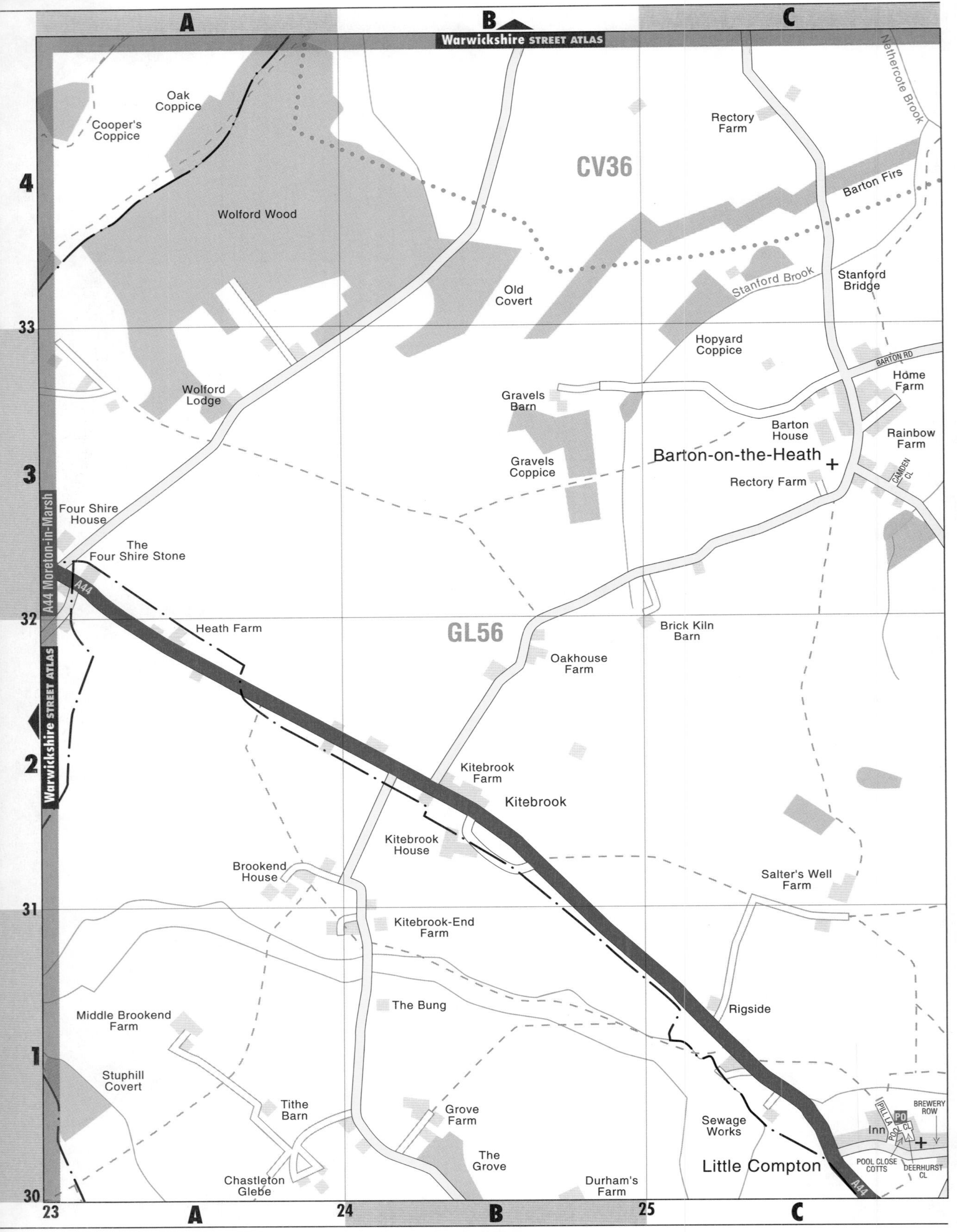

CV36

Oak Coppice

Cooper's Coppice

Wolford Wood

Old Covert

Rectory Farm

Barton Firs

Stanford Brook

Stanford Bridge

Nethercote Brook

33

Wolford Lodge

Gravels Barn

Hopyard Coppice

Home Farm

BARTON RD

Barton House

Rainbow Farm

CAMPEN CL

Gravels Coppice

Barton-on-the-Heath +

Rectory Farm

Four Shire House

3

A44 Moreton-in-Marsh

The Four Shire Stone

A44

Heath Farm

GL56

Oakhouse Farm

Brick Kiln Barn

32

Warwickshire STREET ATLAS

Kitebrook Farm

Kitebrook

Kitebrook House

Brookend House

Salter's Well Farm

Kitebrook-End Farm

2

31

Middle Brookend Farm

The Bung

Rigside

1

Stuphill Covert

Tithe Barn

Grove Farm

Sewage Works

Little Compton

BREWERY ROW

Inn

PILL A PO

POOL CL

POOL CLOSE COTTS

DEERHURST CL

A44

Chastleton Glebe

The Grove

Durham's Farm

30

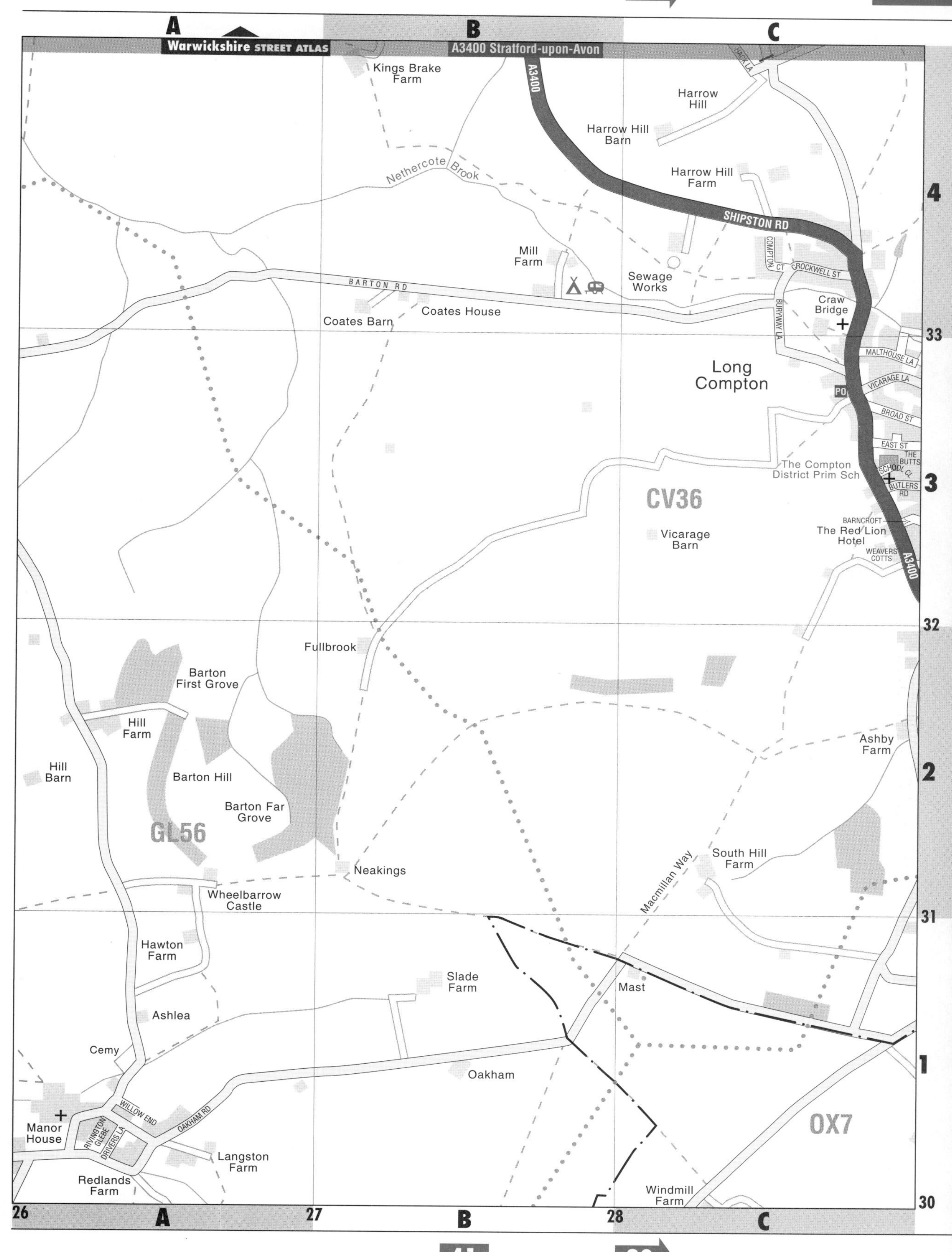

Warwickshire STREET ATLAS

A3400 Stratford-upon-Avon

Kings Brake Farm

A3400

Harrow Hill

Harrow Hill Barn

Harrow Hill Farm

SHIPSTON RD

Nethercote Brook

Mill Farm

Sewage Works

COMPTON CT

CROCKWELL ST

BURWAY LA

Craw Bridge

MALTHOUSE LA

4

33

BARTON RD

Coates House

Coates Barn

Long Compton

PO

VICARAGE LA

BROAD ST

EAST ST

SCHOOL CL

THE BUTTS

The Compton District Prim Sch

BUTLERS RD

3

CV36

Vicarage Barn

BARNCROFT

The Red Lion Hotel

WEAVERS COTTS

A3400

32

Fullbrook

Barton First Grove

Hill Farm

Hill Barn

Barton Hill

Barton Far Grove

GL56

Ashby Farm

2

Neakings

Wheelbarrow Castle

Macmillan Way

South Hill Farm

31

Hawton Farm

Slade Farm

Mast

Ashlea

Cemy

Oakham

1

Manor House

RIVINGTON GLEBE

WILLOW END

OAKHAM RD

DRIVERS LA

Langston Farm

OX7

Redlands Farm

Windmill Farm

30

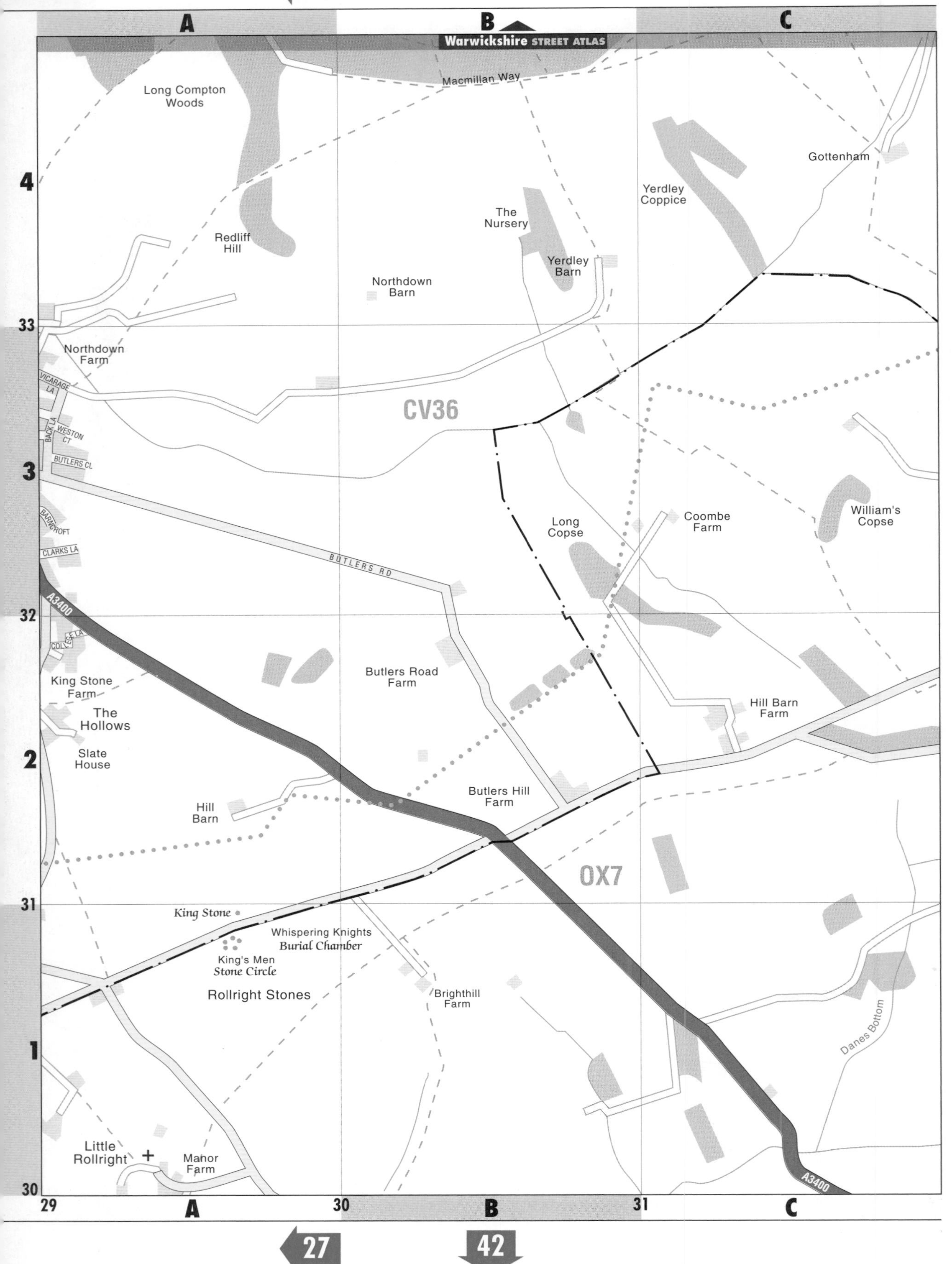

Macmillan Way

Long Compton
Woods

4

Gottenham

Yerdley
Coppice

The
Nursery

Redliff
Hill

Yerdley
Barn

Northdown
Barn

33

CV36

Northdown
Farm

William's
Copse

VICARAGE
LA

WESTON
CT
BACK LA

Long
Copse

Coombe
Farm

BUTLERS CL

3

BARKCROFT

BUTLERS RD

CLARKS LA

32

A3400

COLLEGE LA

Butlers Road
Farm

Hill Barn
Farm

King Stone
Farm

The
Hollows

2

Slate
House

Hill
Barn

Butlers Hill
Farm

OX7

31

King Stone

Whispering Knights
Burial Chamber

King's Men
Stone Circle

Brighthill
Farm

Rollright Stones

Danes Bottom

1

Little
Rollright

Manor
Farm

A3400

30

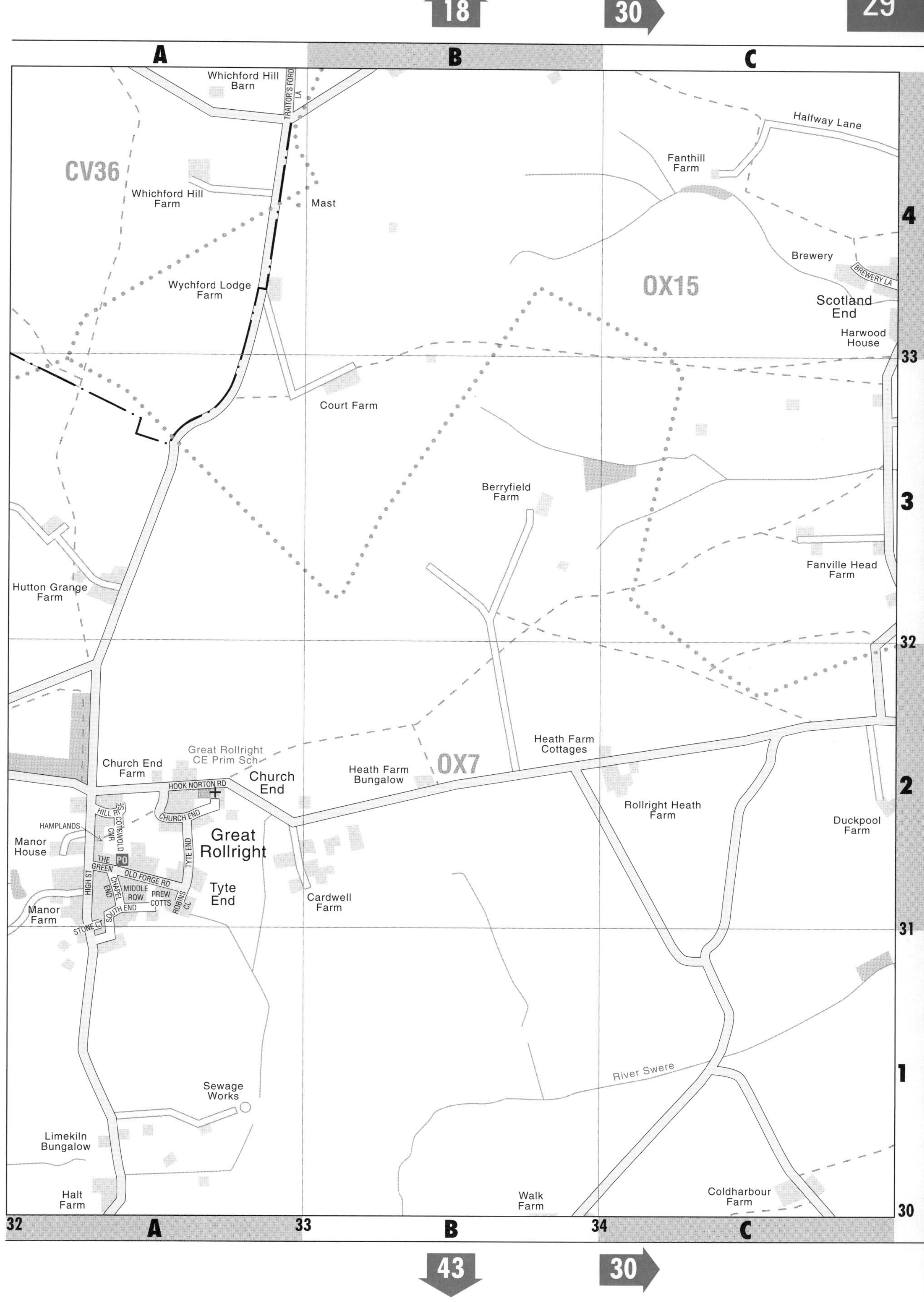
18
30
A
B
C
Whichford Hill Barn
TRAITOR'S FORD LA
CV36
Whichford Hill Farm
Mast
Halfway Lane
Fanthill Farm
4
Brewery
BREWERY LA
Wychford Lodge Farm
OX15
Scotland End
Harwood House
33
Court Farm
Berryfield Farm
3
Hutton Grange Farm
Fanville Head Farm
32
Great Rollright CE Prim Sch
Church End Farm
Church End
HOOK NORTON RD
Heath Farm Bungalow
OX7
Heath Farm Cottages
2
CHURCH END
HILL RE
COTSWOLD CNR
HAMPLANDS
Great Rollright
Rollright Heath Farm
Duckpool Farm
Manor House
TYTE END
PO
THE GREEN
OLD FORGE RD
HIGH ST
CHAPEL END
MIDDLE ROW
PREW COTTS
ROBINS CL
Tyte End
Cardwell Farm
Manor Farm
SOUTH END
STONE CT
31
River Swere
1
Sewage Works
Limekiln Bungalow
Halt Farm
Walk Farm
Coldharbour Farm
30
32
33
34
43
30

29
19

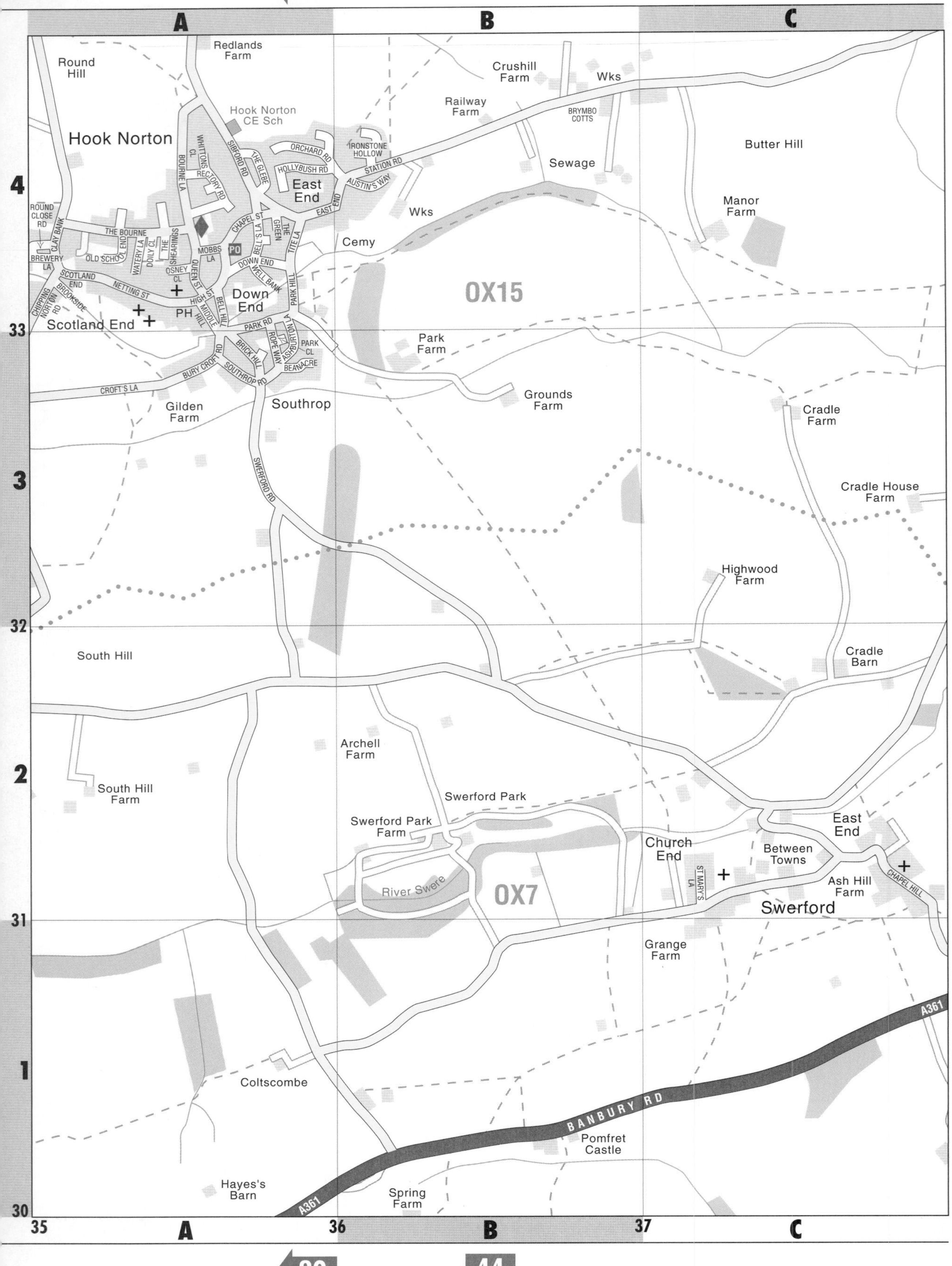
A
B
C
Round Hill
Redlands Farm
Crushill Farm
Wks
Railway Farm
Hook Norton
Hook Norton CE Sch
BRYMBO COTTS
Butter Hill
Sewage
ORCHARD RD
IRONSTONE HOLLOW
HOLLYBUSH RD
STATION RD
East End
AUSTIN'S WAY
EAST END
THE GLEBE
SIBFORD RD
WHITTONS CL
RECTORY RD
BOURNE LA
ROUND CLOSE RD
CLAY BANK
THE BOURNE
Wks
Manor Farm
CHAPEL ST
THE GREEN
TITE LA
BELL'S LA
Cemy
PO
MOBBS LA
THE SHEARINGS
WATERY LA
DOILY CL
OLD SCHOOL END
BREWERY LA
OSNEY CL
QUEEN ST
DOWN END
WELL BANK
PARK HILL
SCOTLAND END
NETTING ST
OX15
BROOKSIDE
CHIPPING NORTON RD
Down End
HIGH ST
MIDDLE HILL
BELL HILL
PH
Scotland End
PARK RD
ROPE WAY
ASHBURTON LA
PARK CL
Park Farm
BRICK HILL
BEANACRE
BURY CROFT RD
SOUTHROP RD
CROFT'S LA
Grounds Farm
Cradle Farm
Gilden Farm
Southrop
SWERFORD RD
Cradle House Farm
Highwood Farm
South Hill
Cradle Barn
Archell Farm
South Hill Farm
Swerford Park
Swerford Park Farm
East End
Church End
Between Towns
ST MARY'S LA
Ash Hill Farm
CHAPEL HILL
River Swere
OX7
Swerford
Grange Farm
A361
BANBURY RD
Coltscombe
Pomfret Castle
Hayes's Barn
Spring Farm
A361
4
33
3
32
2
31
1
30
35
36
37
A
B
C

29
44

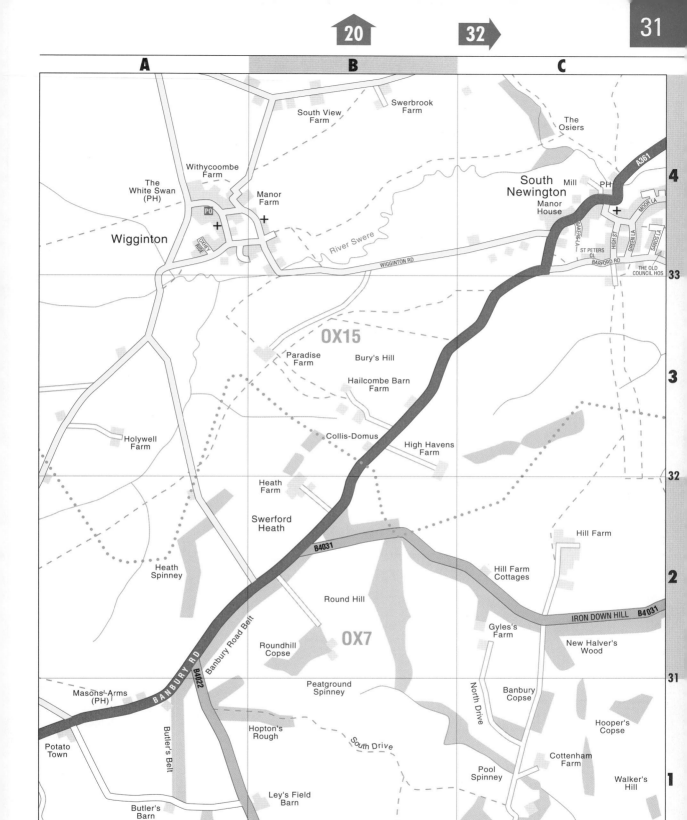

A B C

Swerbrook Farm
South View Farm
The Osiers
Withycoombe Farm
The White Swan (PH)
Manor Farm
PO
Wigginton
OXHEY RISE
River Swere
WIGGINTON RD
South Newington
Mill
PH
A361
Manor House
MOOR LA
BAKERS LA
ST PETERS CL
HIGH ST
GREEN LA
SANDS LA
BARFORD RD
THE OLD COUNCIL HOS
4
33
OX15
Paradise Farm
Bury's Hill
Hailcombe Barn Farm
3
Holywell Farm
Collis-Domus
High Havens Farm
32
Heath Farm
Swerford Heath
Hill Farm
B4031
Heath Spinney
Hill Farm Cottages
2
Round Hill
IRON DOWN HILL B4031
Gyles's Farm
Banbury Road Belt
Roundhill Copse
OX7
New Halver's Wood
BANBURY RD
B4022
31
Masons' Arms (PH)
Peatground Spinney
North Drive
Banbury Copse
Butler's Belt
Hopton's Rough
Hooper's Copse
Potato Town
South Drive
Cottenham Farm
Pool Spinney
Walker's Hill
1
Ley's Field Barn
Butler's Barn
Buttercombe Farm
Chescoombe Clump
Horse Hill
Cow Hill
Groveash Lane
B4022
Lodge Ponds
30

38 A 39 B 40 C

45
32

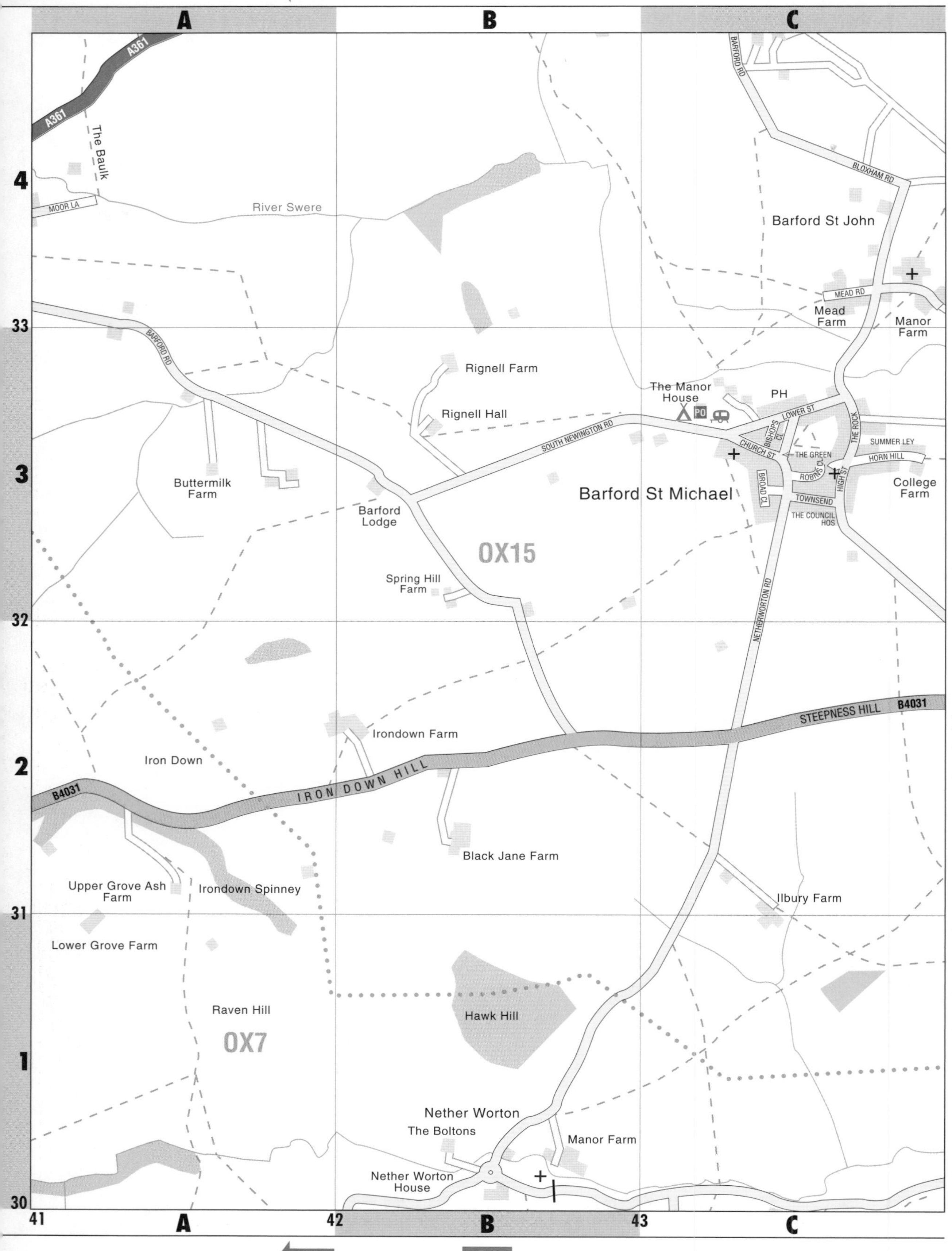

A   B   C

A361

The Baulk

MOOR LA

4

River Swere

Barford St John

BLOXHAM RD

BARFORD RD

MEAD RD

Mead
Farm

Manor
Farm

33

BARFORD RD

Rignell Farm

Rignell Hall

The Manor
House

PH

LOWER ST

SUMMER LEY

THE ROCK

HORN HILL

South Newington Rd

PO

BISHOPS CL

CHURCH ST

THE GREEN

ROBINS CL

HIGH ST

Buttermilk
Farm

Barford St Michael

BROAD CL

College
Farm

TOWNSEND

THE COUNCIL
HOS

3

Barford
Lodge

OX15

NETHERWORTON RD

Spring Hill
Farm

32

STEEPNESS HILL

B4031

Irondown Farm

Iron Down

IRON DOWN HILL

2

B4031

Black Jane Farm

Ilbury Farm

Upper Grove Ash
Farm

Irondown Spinney

31

Lower Grove Farm

Raven Hill

OX7

Hawk Hill

1

Nether Worton

The Boltons

Manor Farm

Nether Worton
House

30

41   A   42   B   43   C

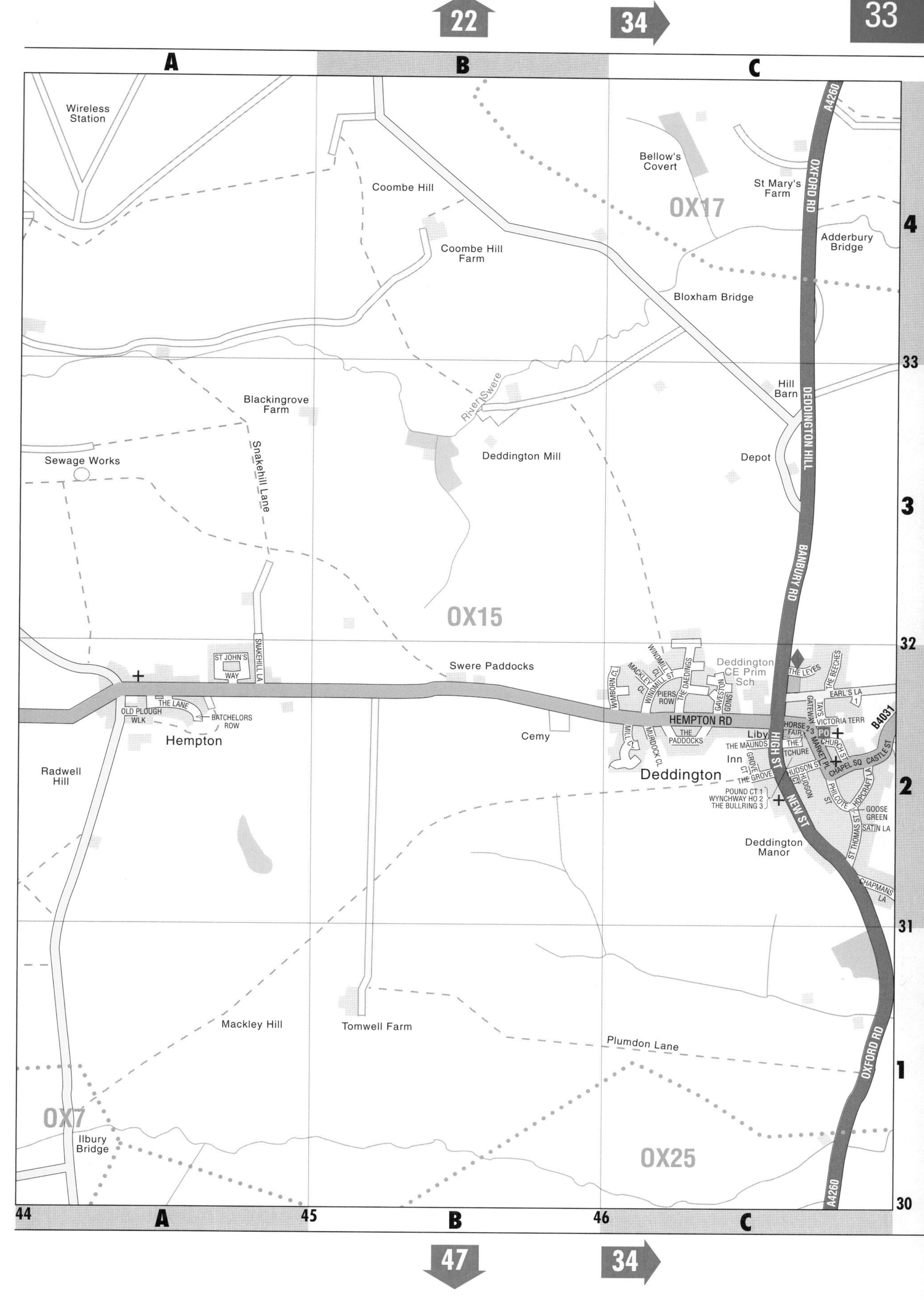

A
B
C

Wireless Station

Bellow's Covert

OX17

St Mary's Farm

A4260

OXFORD RD

Coombe Hill

Adderbury Bridge

4

Coombe Hill Farm

Bloxham Bridge

DEDDINGTON HILL

33

River Swere

Blackingrove Farm

Hill Barn

Sewage Works

Deddington Mill

Depot

Snakehill Lane

BANBURY RD

3

OX15

32

Swere Paddocks

Deddington CE Prim Sch

THE LEYES

THE BEECHES

WINDMILL ST

ST JOHN'S WAY

MACKLEY CL

PIERS ROW

THE DAEDINGS

GAVESTON GDNS

EARL'S LA

B4031

SNAKEHILL LA

WINDMILL CL

HEMPTON RD

THE LANE

WINDMILL CL

MILL CL

MURDOCK CL

THE PADDOCKS

THE MAUNDS

VICTORIA TERR

Cemy

TAYS

GATEWAY

MARKET PL

CHURCH ST

CASTLE ST

CHAPEL SQ

PO

OLD PLOUGH WLK

BATCHELORS ROW

Liby

HORSE FAIR

HIGH ST

THE

Hempton

Inn

HUDSON ST

PHILCOTE ST

2

Deddington

THE GROVE

HUDSON ST

ST THOMAS ST

HOPCRAFT LA

GOOSE GREEN

Radwell Hill

POUND CT
WYNCHWAY HO 2
THE BULLRING 3

NEW ST

SATIN LA

Deddington Manor

CHAPMANS LA

31

Mackley Hill

Tomwell Farm

Plumdon Lane

OXFORD RD

1

OX7

A4260

Ilbury Bridge

OX25

30

44
45
46

A
B
C

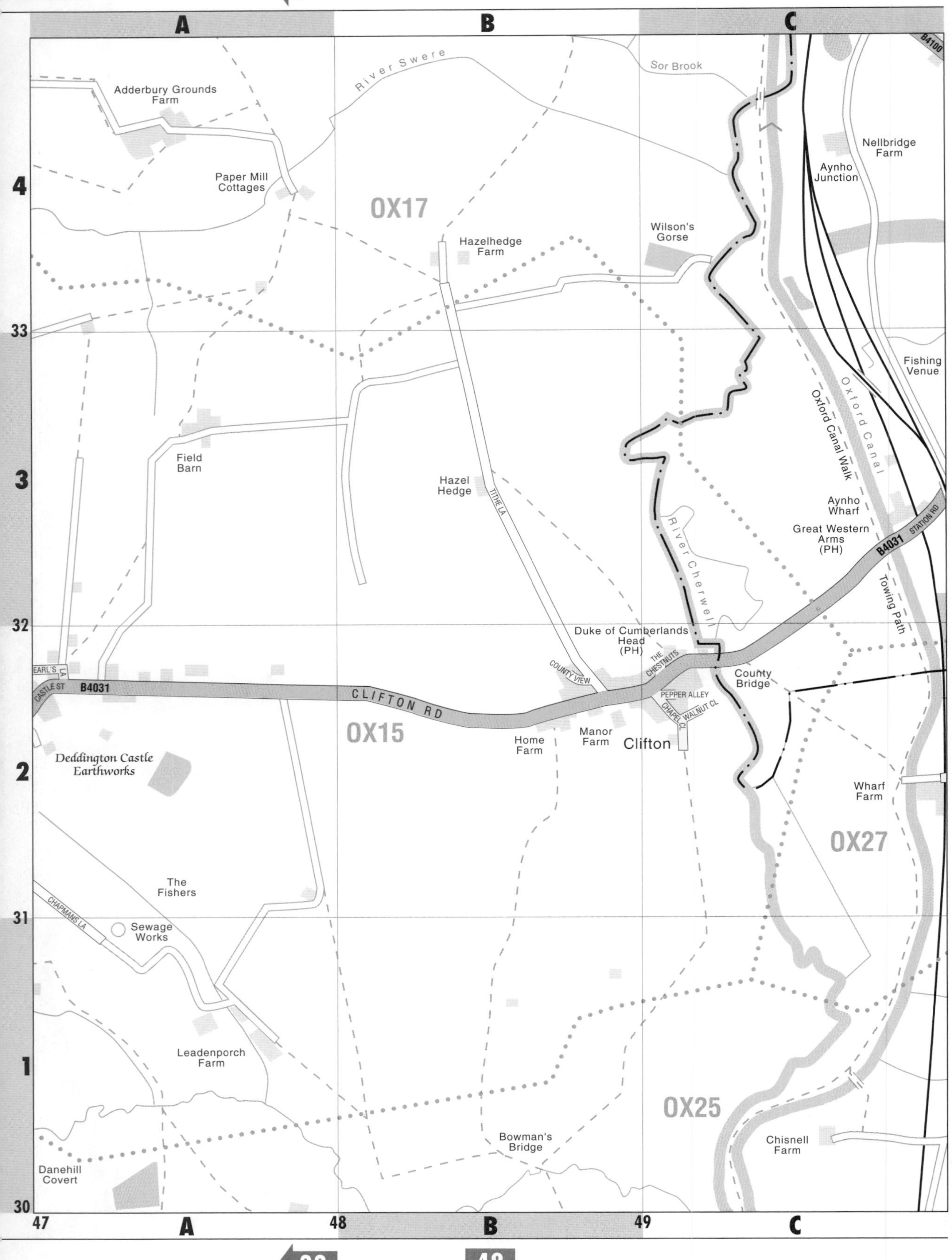

A   B   C

River Swere

Sor Brook

B4100

Adderbury Grounds
Farm

Nellbridge
Farm

Aynho
Junction

Paper Mill
Cottages

4

OX17

Wilson's
Gorse

Fishing
Venue

Hazelhedge
Farm

33

Oxford Canal Walk

Oxford Canal

Field
Barn

3

Hazel
Hedge

TITHE LA

Aynho
Wharf

Great Western
Arms
(PH)

River Cherwell

B4031   STATION RD

Towing Path

32

Duke of Cumberlands
Head
(PH)

COUNTY VIEW

THE CHESTNUTS

County
Bridge

EARL'S LA

CASTLE ST

B4031

CLIFTON RD

CHAPEL CL

PEPPER ALLEY

WALNUT CL

OX15

Home
Farm

Manor
Farm

Clifton

Deddington Castle
Earthworks

2

Wharf
Farm

OX27

The
Fishers

CHAPMANS LA

31

Sewage
Works

Leadenporch
Farm

1

OX25

Bowman's
Bridge

Chisnell
Farm

Danehill
Covert

30

47   48   49

A   B   C

36

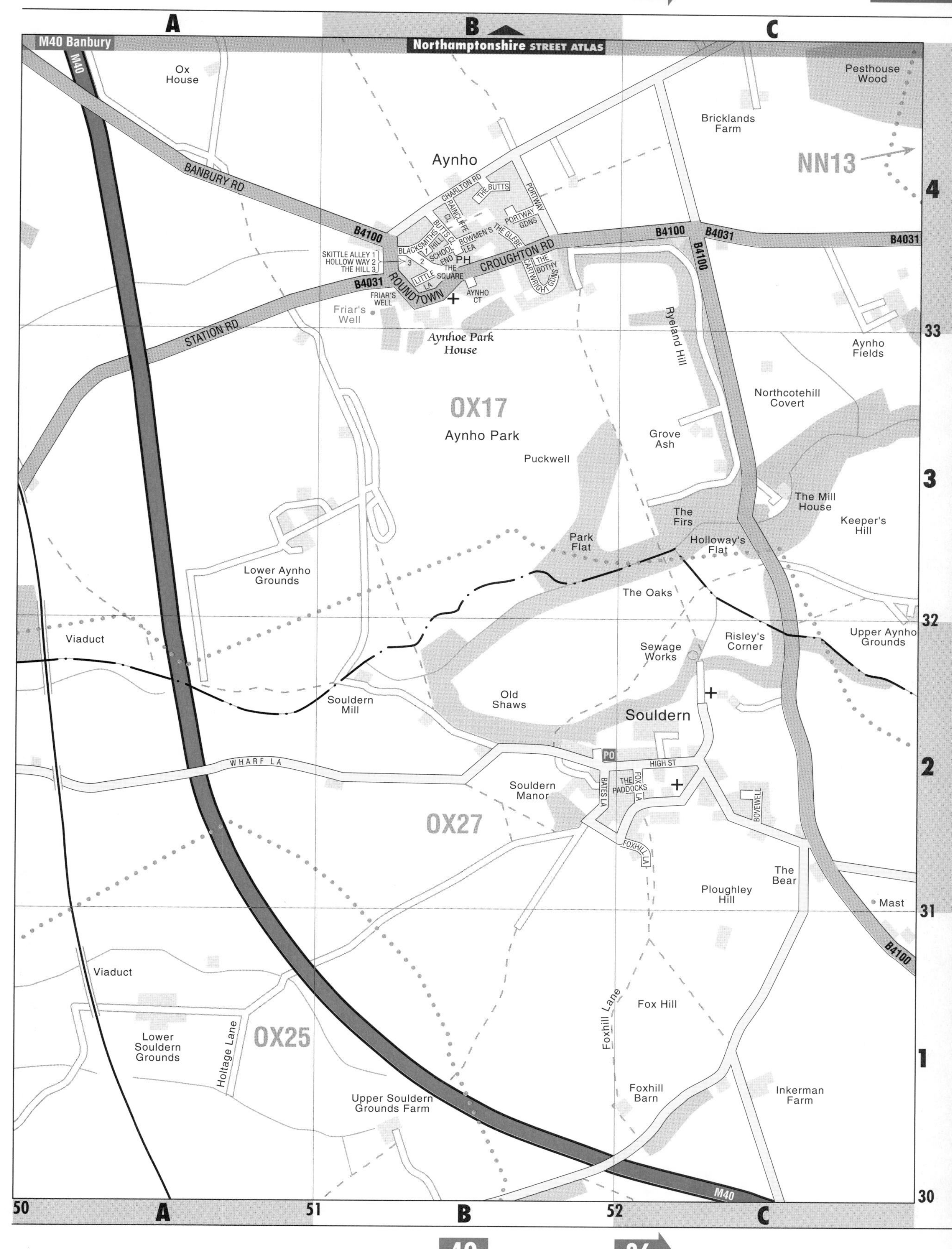

A
B
C
M40 Banbury
Northamptonshire STREET ATLAS
M40
Ox House
Pesthouse Wood
Bricklands Farm
NN13
Aynho
BANBURY RD
CHARLTON RD
THE BUTTS
PORTWAY
RAINCLIFFE CL
PORTWAY GDNS
BUTTS CL
BLACKSMITHS HILL
BOWMEN'S LEA
THE GLEBE
SCHOOL END
B4100
B4031
SKITTLE ALLEY 1
HOLLOW WAY 2
THE HILL 3
CROUGHTON RD
THE SQUARE
PH
THE BOTHY
CARTWRIGHT GDNS
LITTLE LA
ROUNDTOWN
FRIAR'S WELL
AYNHO CT
Friar's Well
Aynhoe Park House
STATION RD
Ryeland Hill
Aynho Fields
Northcotehill Covert
OX17
Aynho Park
Grove Ash
Puckwell
The Mill House
Keeper's Hill
The Firs
Park Flat
Holloway's Flat
Lower Aynho Grounds
The Oaks
Viaduct
Sewage Works
Risley's Corner
Upper Aynho Grounds
Old Shaws
Souldern Mill
Souldern
WHARF LA
PO
HIGH ST
THE PADDOCKS
FOX LA
BATES LA
Souldern Manor
BOVEWELL
OX27
FOXHILL LA
The Bear
Ploughley Hill
Mast
Viaduct
Fox Hill
Foxhill Lane
Lower Souldern Grounds
Holtage Lane
OX25
Foxhill Barn
Inkerman Farm
Upper Souldern Grounds Farm
4
33
3
32
2
31
1
30
50
51
52

49
36

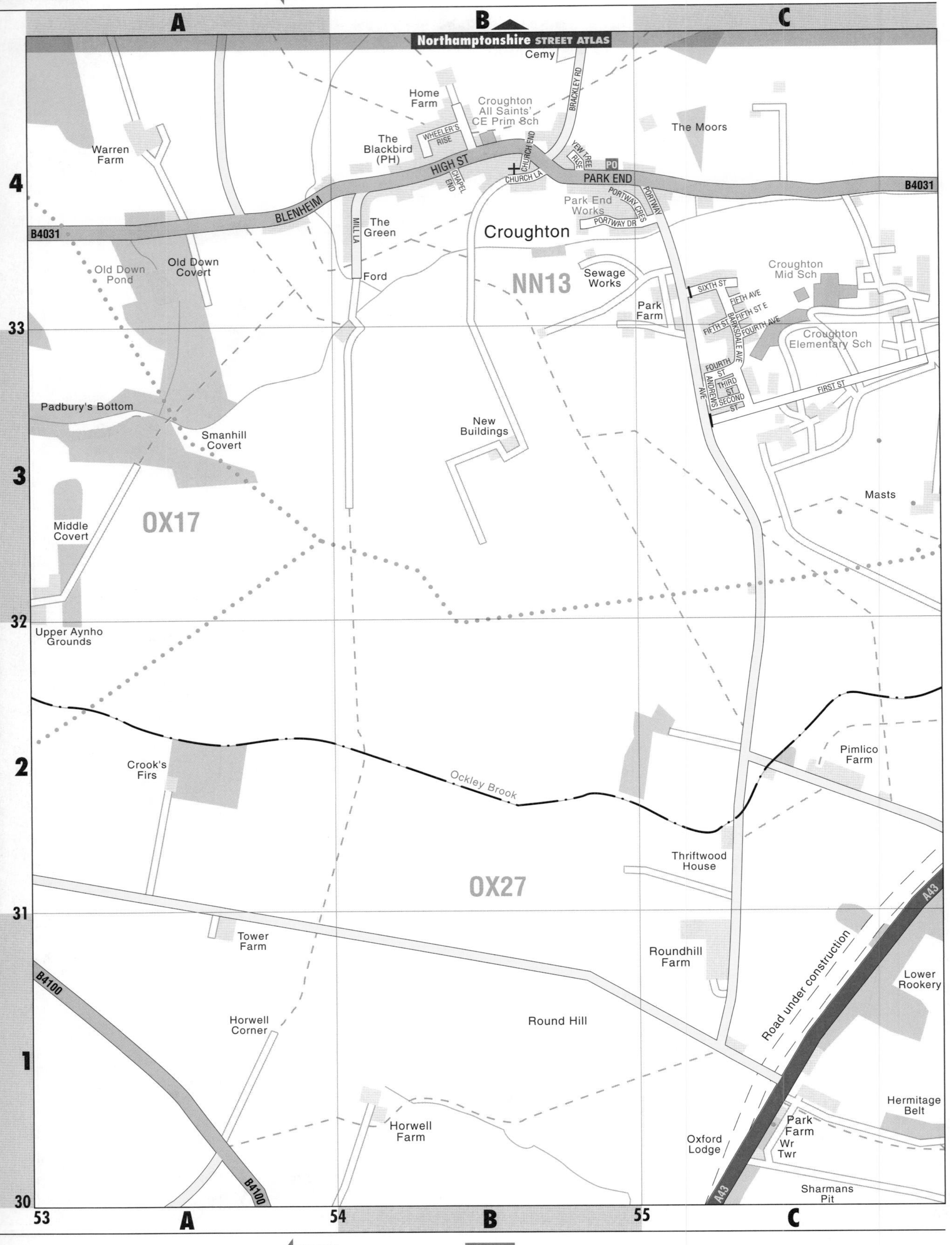

Cemy

Home
Farm

Croughton
All Saints'
CE Prim Sch

BRACKLEY RD

The Moors

The
Blackbird
(PH)

WHEELER'S
RISE

YEW TREE
RISE

PO

CHURCH END

CHURCH LA

PARK END

PORTWAY

B4031

HIGH ST

CHAPEL END

BLENHEIM

PORTWAY CRES

PORTWAY DR

4

Warren
Farm

B4031

MILL LA

The
Green

Ford

Croughton

Park End
Works

Park End

NN13

Sewage
Works

Croughton
Mid Sch

Old Down
Pond

Old Down
Covert

Park
Farm

SIXTH ST

FIFTH AVE

FIFTH ST E

FIFTH ST

BARKSDALE AVE

FOURTH AVE

Croughton
Elementary Sch

33

Padbury's Bottom

Smanhill
Covert

New
Buildings

FOURTH
AVE

ST ANDREWS
AVE

THIRD
ST

SECOND
ST

FIRST ST

Masts

3

OX17

Middle
Covert

32

Upper Aynho
Grounds

Pimlico
Farm

2

Crook's
Firs

Ockley Brook

Thriftwood
House

OX27

Roundhill
Farm

Road under construction

A43

Lower
Rookery

31

Tower
Farm

B4100

Horwell
Corner

Round Hill

Hermitage
Belt

1

Horwell
Farm

Oxford
Lodge

Park
Farm
Wr
Twr

A43

B4100

Sharmans
Pit

30

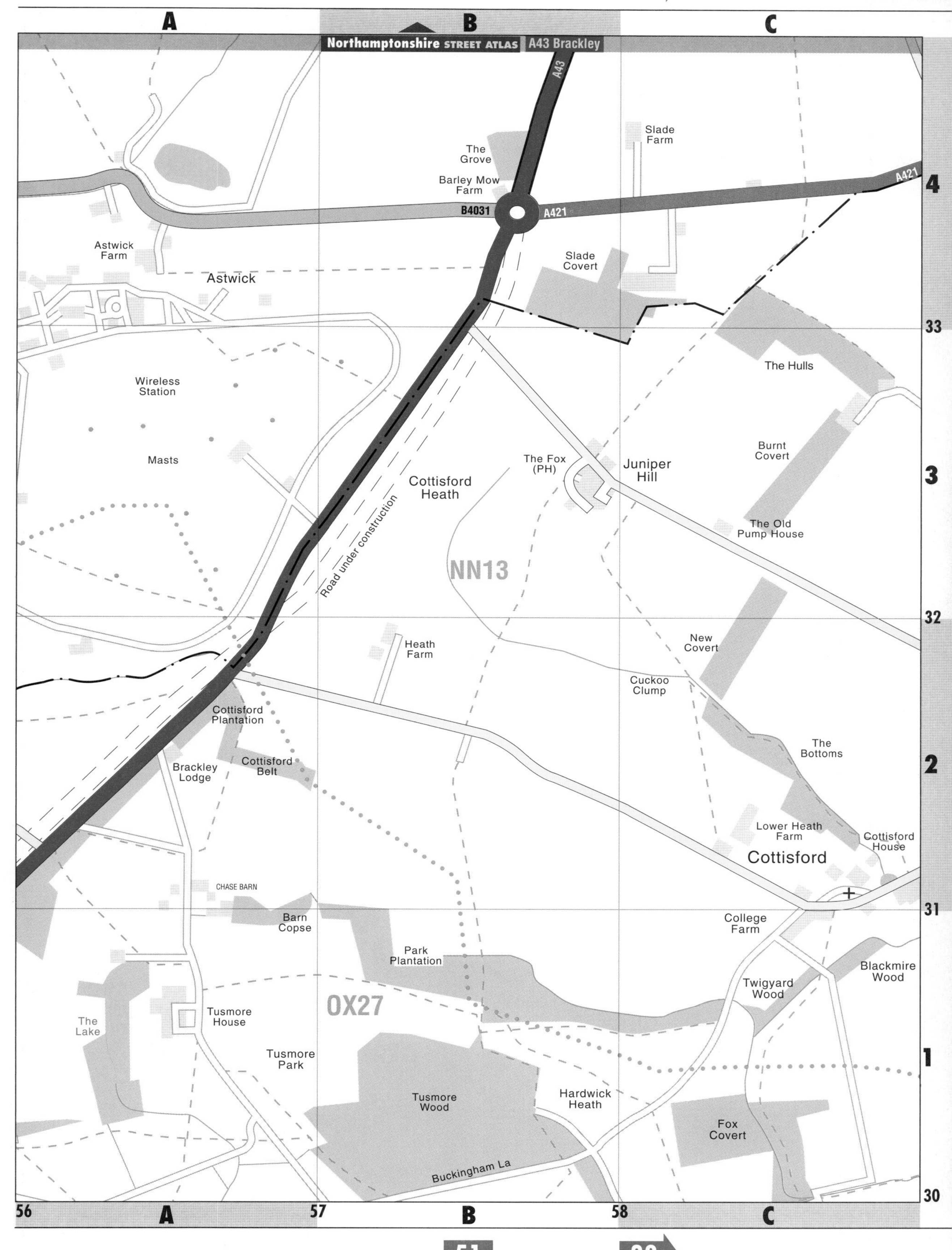

Northamptonshire STREET ATLAS A43 Brackley

A43

The Grove

Barley Mow Farm

Slade Farm

B4031 A421

A421

Astwick Farm

Astwick

Slade Covert

The Hulls

Wireless Station

Burnt Covert

Masts

Cottisford Heath

The Fox (PH)

Juniper Hill

The Old Pump House

NN13

Road under construction

Heath Farm

New Covert

Cuckoo Clump

The Bottoms

Cottisford Plantation

Brackley Lodge

Cottisford Belt

Lower Heath Farm

Cottisford House

Cottisford

CHASE BARN

Barn Copse

College Farm

Blackmire Wood

Park Plantation

Twigyard Wood

The Lake

OX27

Tusmore House

Tusmore Park

Tusmore Wood

Hardwick Heath

Fox Covert

Buckingham La

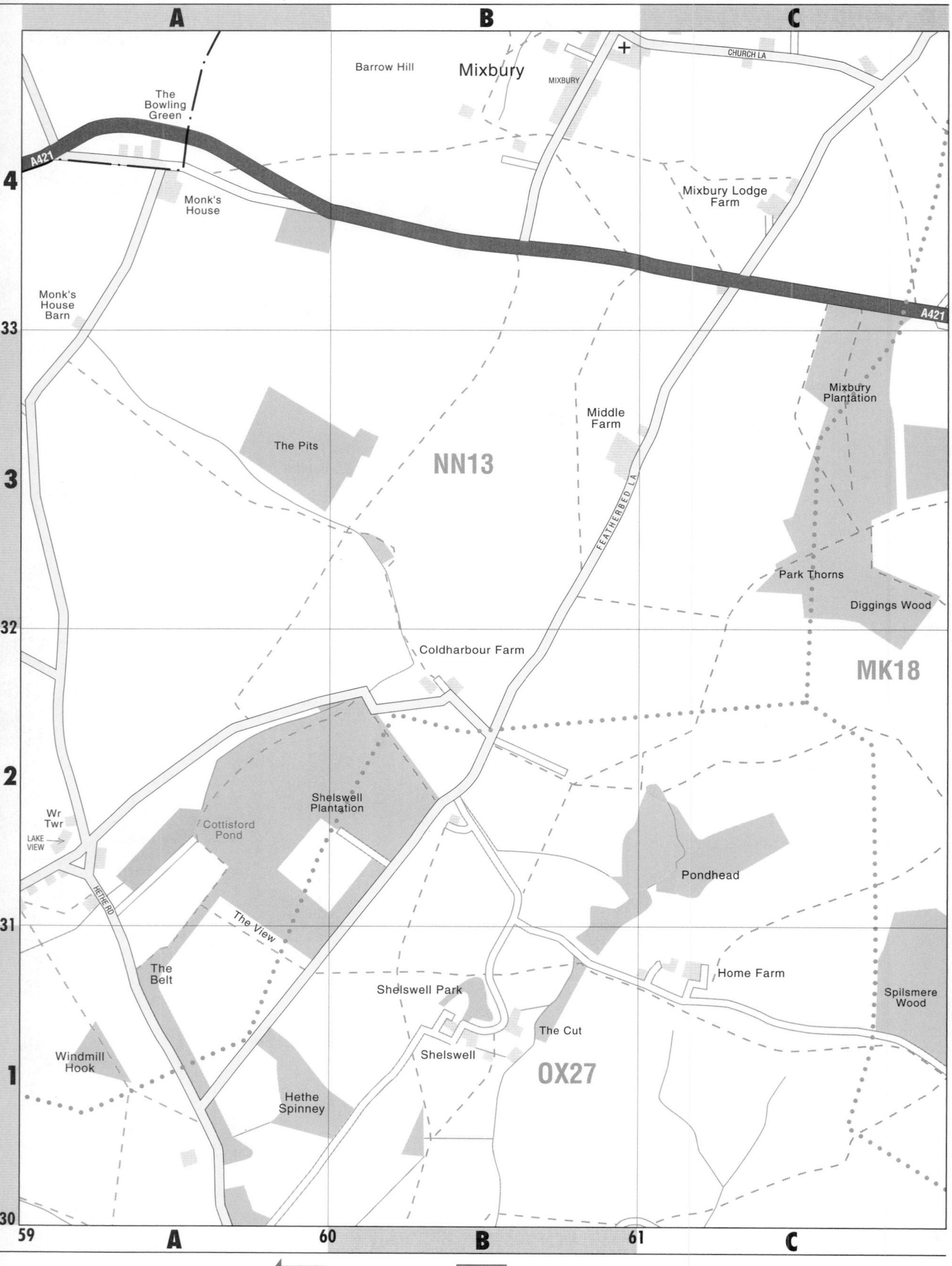

A **B** **C**

Barrow Hill

Mixbury

MIXBURY

CHURCH LA

The Bowling Green

Mixbury Lodge Farm

A421

4

Monk's House

Monk's House Barn

33

Mixbury Plantation

Middle Farm

The Pits

NN13

A421

FEATHERBED LA

3

Park Thorns

Diggings Wood

32

Coldharbour Farm

MK18

2

Shelswell Plantation

Wr Twr

LAKE VIEW

Cottisford Pond

Pondhead

31

The View

HETHE RD

The Belt

Shelswell Park

Home Farm

Spilsmere Wood

Windmill Hook

Shelswell

The Cut

1

OX27

Hethe Spinney

30
59 **A** 60 **B** 61 **C**

25

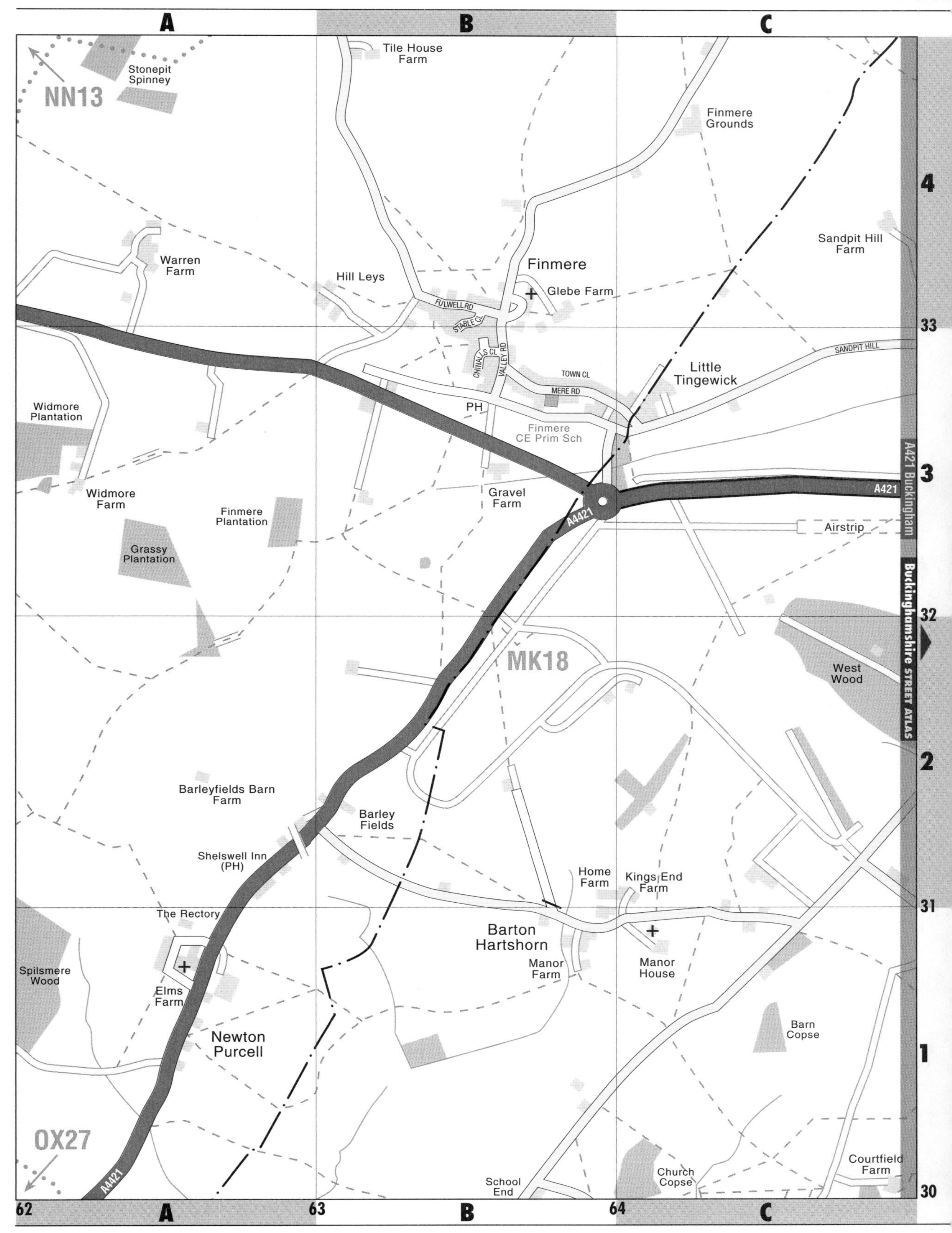

A
B
C
Tile House Farm
Stonepit Spinney
NN13
Finmere Grounds
4
Sandpit Hill Farm
Warren Farm
Finmere
Hill Leys
Glebe Farm
FULWELL RD
STABLE CL
33
CHINALLS CL
VALLEY RD
SANDPIT HILL
Little Tingewick
TOWN CL
MERE RD
Widmore Plantation
PH
Finmere CE Prim Sch
A421 Buckingham
3
A421
Widmore Farm
Gravel Farm
Finmere Plantation
A4421
Airstrip
Grassy Plantation
Buckinghamshire STREET ATLAS
32
MK18
West Wood
2
Barleyfields Barn Farm
Barley Fields
Shelswell Inn (PH)
Home Farm
Kings End Farm
31
The Rectory
Barton Hartshorn
Spilsmere Wood
Manor Farm
Manor House
Elms Farm
Newton Purcell
Barn Copse
1
OX27
A4421
Church Copse
School End
Courtfield Farm
30
62
A
63
B
64
C

53

26

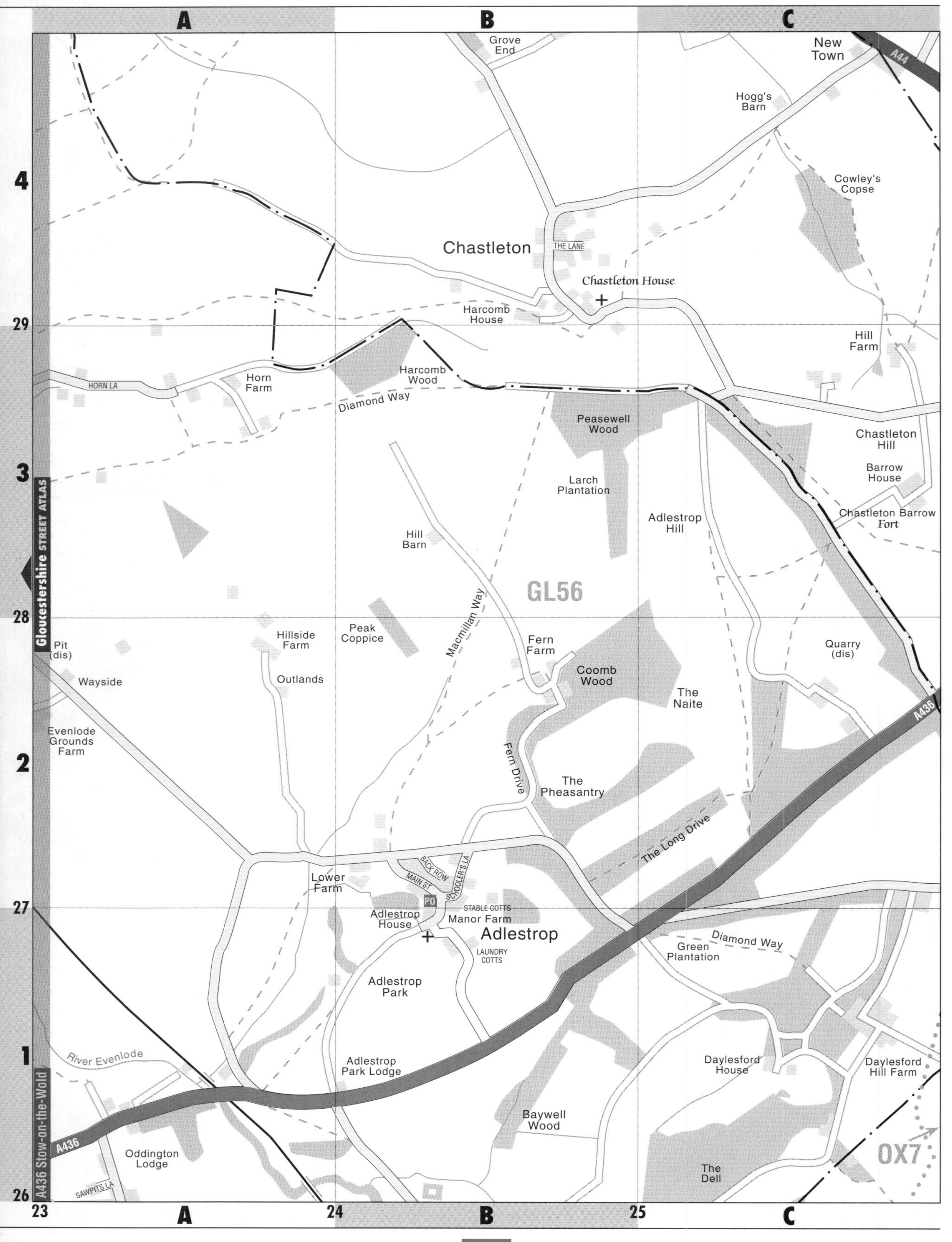
A
B
C
Grove End
New Town
A44
Hogg's Barn
Cowley's Copse
Chastleton
THE LANE
Chastleton House
Harcomb House
Hill Farm
HORN LA
Horn Farm
Harcomb Wood
Diamond Way
Peasewell Wood
Chastleton Hill
Barrow House
Larch Plantation
Adlestrop Hill
Chastleton Barrow Fort
Hill Barn
GL56
Macmillan Way
Hillside Farm
Peak Coppice
Pit (dis)
Fern Farm
Quarry (dis)
Wayside
Outlands
Coomb Wood
The Naite
A436
Evenlode Grounds Farm
Fern Drive
The Pheasantry
The Long Drive
BACK ROW
SCHOOLER'S LA
MAIN ST
Lower Farm
PO
Adlestrop House
STABLE COTTS
Manor Farm
Adlestrop
LAUNDRY COTTS
Diamond Way
Green Plantation
Adlestrop Park
River Evenlode
Adlestrop Park Lodge
Daylesford House
Daylesford Hill Farm
Baywell Wood
A436
Oddington Lodge
OX7
The Dell
SAWPITS LA
A436 Stow-on-the-Wold
Gloucestershire STREET ATLAS
4
29
3
28
2
27
1
26
23
24
25
A
B
C

54

27
42

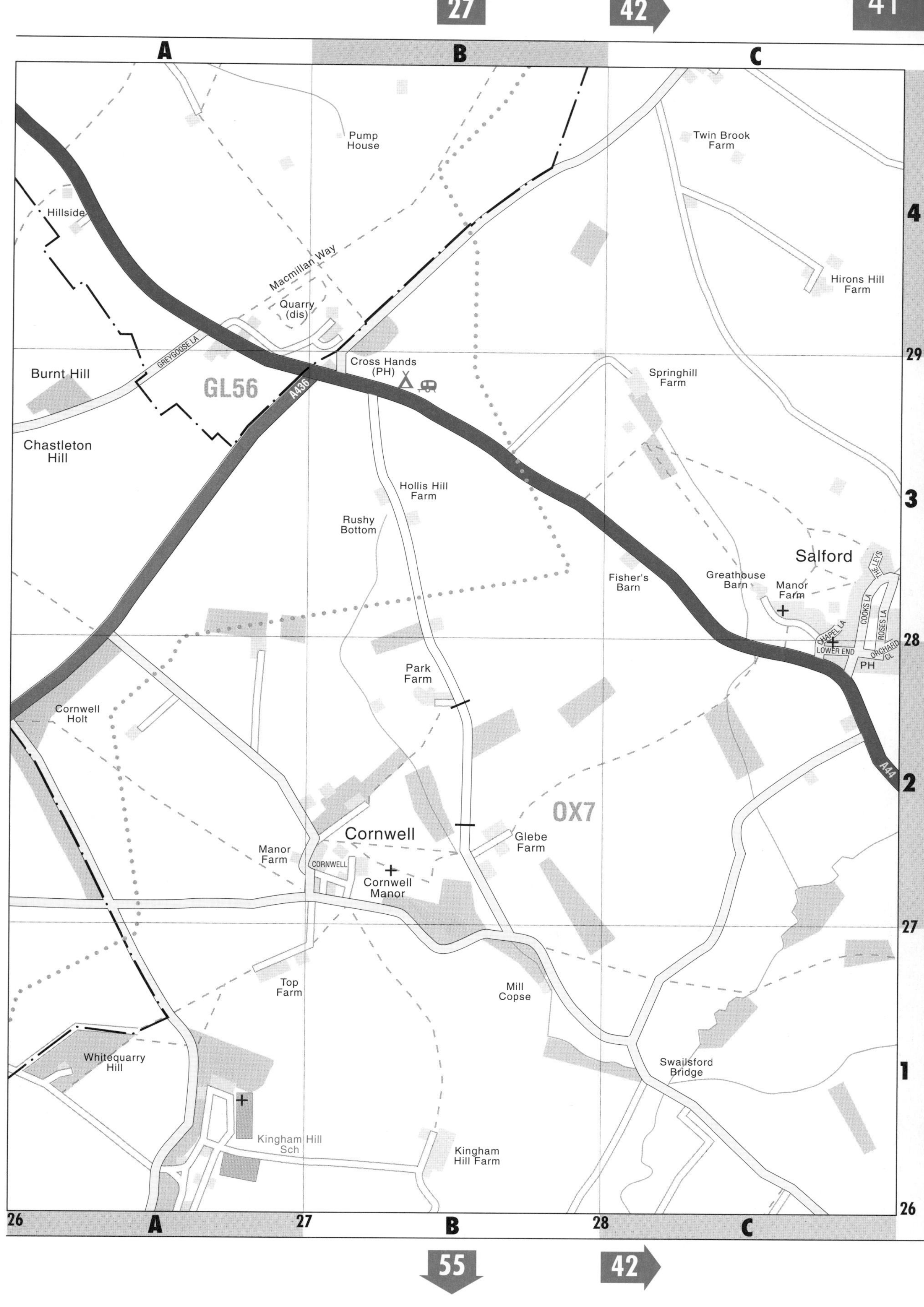
A
B
C
Pump House
Twin Brook Farm
Hillside
Hirons Hill Farm
Macmillan Way
Quarry (dis)
GREYGOOSE LA
Burnt Hill
GL56
A436
Cross Hands (PH)
Springhill Farm
Chastleton Hill
Hollis Hill Farm
Rushy Bottom
Salford
THE LEYS
Fisher's Barn
Greathouse Barn
Manor Farm
COOKS LA
CHAPEL LA
ROSES LA
LOWER END
ORCHARD CL
PH
Park Farm
Cornwell Holt
A44
OX7
Cornwell
Glebe Farm
Manor Farm
CORNWELL
Cornwell Manor
Top Farm
Mill Copse
Swailsford Bridge
Whitequarry Hill
Kingham Hill Sch
Kingham Hill Farm
4
3
2
1
29
28
27
26
26
27
28
A
B
C

55
42

A · B · C

4

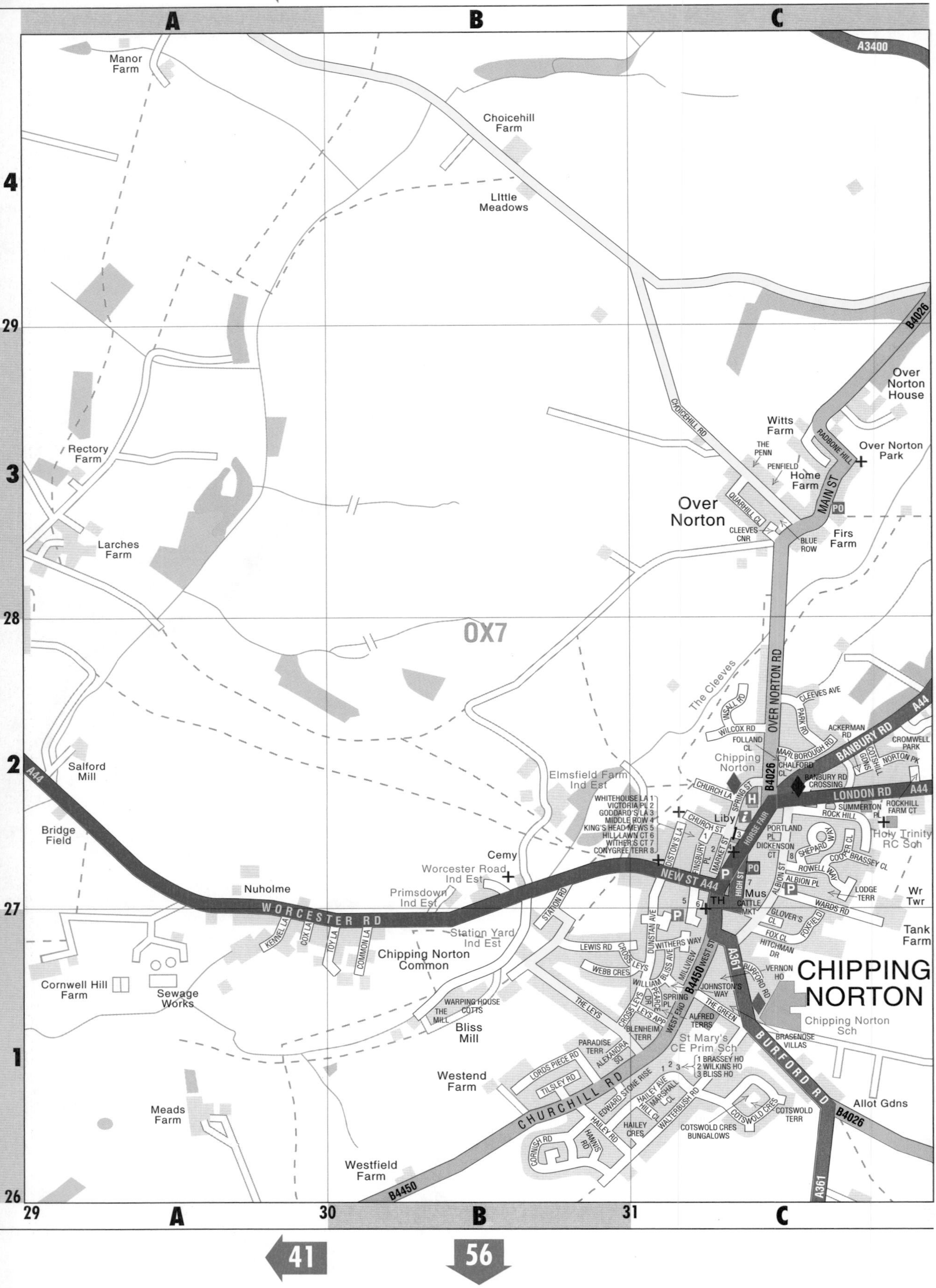

Manor Farm

Choicehill Farm

Little Meadows

A3400

29

Over Norton House

Over Norton Park

Witts Farm

THE PENN

PENFIELD

Home Farm

Rectory Farm

3

Over Norton

QUARHILL CL

CLEEVES CNR

MAIN ST

PO

BLUE ROW

Firs Farm

CHOICEHILL RD

RADBONE HILL

Larches Farm

B4026

28

OX7

The Cleeves

OVER NORTON RD

PARK RD

CLEEVES AVE

ACKERMAN RD

COTSWOLD

CROMWELL PARK

NORTON PK

WKSALL RD

WILCOX RD

FOLLAND CL

Chipping Norton

MARLBOROUGH RD

CHALFORD RD

BANBURY RD

A44

B4026

Banbury Rd Crossing

ROCK HILL

SUMMERTON WAY

ROCKHILL FARM CT

Elmsfield Farm Ind Est

WHITEHOUSE LA 1
VICTORIA PL 2
GODDARD'S LA 3
MIDDLE ROW 4
KING'S HEAD MEWS 5
HILL LAWN CT 6
WITHER'S CT 7
CONYGREE TERR 8.

CHURCH LA

CHURCH ST

Liby

H

i

LONDON RD

A44

PORTLAND PL

DICKENSON CT

SHEPARD WAY

Holy Trinity RC Sch

COOK CL

BRASSEY CL

2

Salford Mill

A44

Bridge Field

Cemy

Worcester Road Ind Est

HORSE FAIR

MARKET ST

HIGH ST

PO

Mus

ALBION PL

ROWELL WAY

FOXTEL CL

LODGE TERR

Wr Twr

NEW ST A44

P

CATTLE MKT

WARDS RD

Nuholme

WORCESTER RD

Primsdown Ind Est

STATION RD

Station Yard Ind Est

TH

GLOVER'S CL

FOX CL

HITCHMAN DR

Tank Farm

27

KERNELLA CT

COX LA

TOY LA

COMMON LA

Chipping Norton Common

LEWIS RD

CROSS LEYS

DUNSTAN AVE

WITHERS WAY

P

BLISS AVE

MILL VIEW

VERNON HO

A361

BURFORD RD

CHIPPING NORTON

Cornwell Hill Farm

Sewage Works

WEBB CRES

THE LEYS

WARPING HOUSE COTTS

THE MILL

Bliss Mill

WILLIAM ST

CROSS LEYS

SPRING

WEST END

JOHNSTON'S WAY

THE GREEN

ALFRED TERR

Chipping Norton Sch

1

PARADISE TERR

ALEXANDRA SQ

BLENHEIM TERR

St Mary's CE Prim Sch

1 BRASSEY HO
2 WILKINS HO
3 BLISS HO

BRASENOSE VILLAS

Westend Farm

LORDS PIECE RD

TILSLEY RD

EDWARD STONE RISE

CHURCHILL RD

HAILEY AVE

MARSHALL CL

WATERBUSH RD

HAILEY CRES

COTSWOLD CRES

COTSWOLD TERR

Allot Gdns

B4026

Meads Farm

CORNISH RD

HARRIS RD

HAILEY CRES

COTSWOLD CRES BUNGALOWS

A361

Westfield Farm

B4450

26

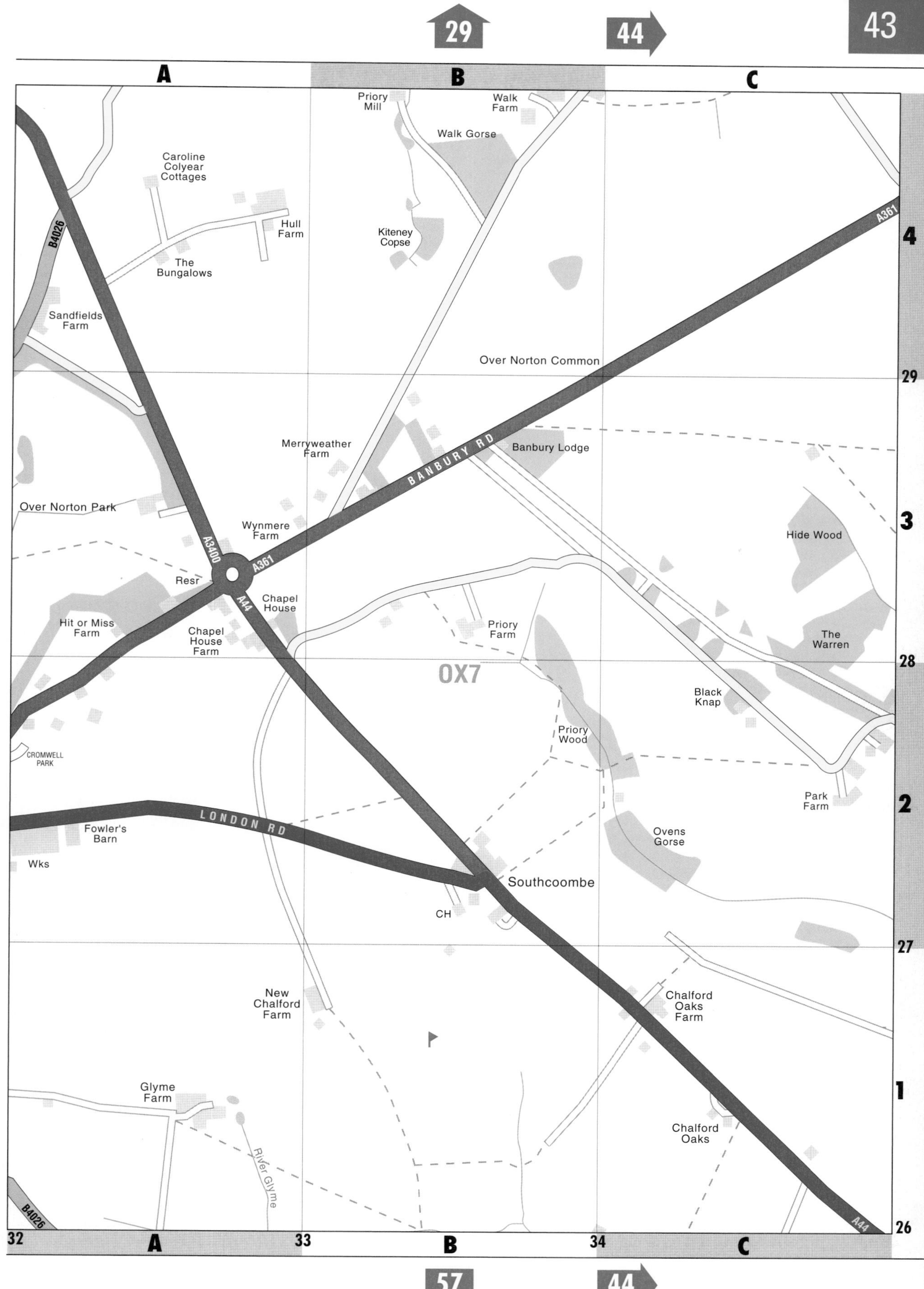

A
B
C

Priory Mill
Walk Farm
Walk Gorse

Caroline Colyear Cottages

B4026

Hull Farm

Kiteney Copse

The Bungalows

A361

Sandfields Farm

Over Norton Common

4

29

Merryweather Farm

Banbury Lodge

BANBURY RD

Over Norton Park

Hide Wood

3

A3400

Wynmere Farm

A361

Resr

Chapel House

Priory Farm

The Warren

Hit or Miss Farm

A44

Chapel House Farm

OX7

28

Black Knap

CROMWELL PARK

Priory Wood

Park Farm

2

LONDON RD

Fowler's Barn

Ovens Gorse

Wks

Southcoombe

27

CH

Chalford Oaks Farm

New Chalford Farm

Glyme Farm

Chalford Oaks

1

River Glyme

B4026

A44

26

32
A
33
B
34
C

A B C

A361

4

A361

Cherwell Barn

The Meetings

Showell Bungalow

Showell Farm

Showell Copse

29

River Dorn

Magpie Farm

3

Dunthrop

Chivelcorner Plantation

Chivel Farm

GREEN LA

28

OX7

Heythrop

Little Tew Grounds Farm

+

Wheatfield Copse

2

Deerpen Wood

Iron's Copse

Foxberry Wood

West Wood

27

Harris's Bottom

Heythrop Park

Fattingfield Copse

1

Broadstone Hill

Heythrop Park Staff Training College

Kite Grove

The Wilderness

26

35 A 36 B 37 C

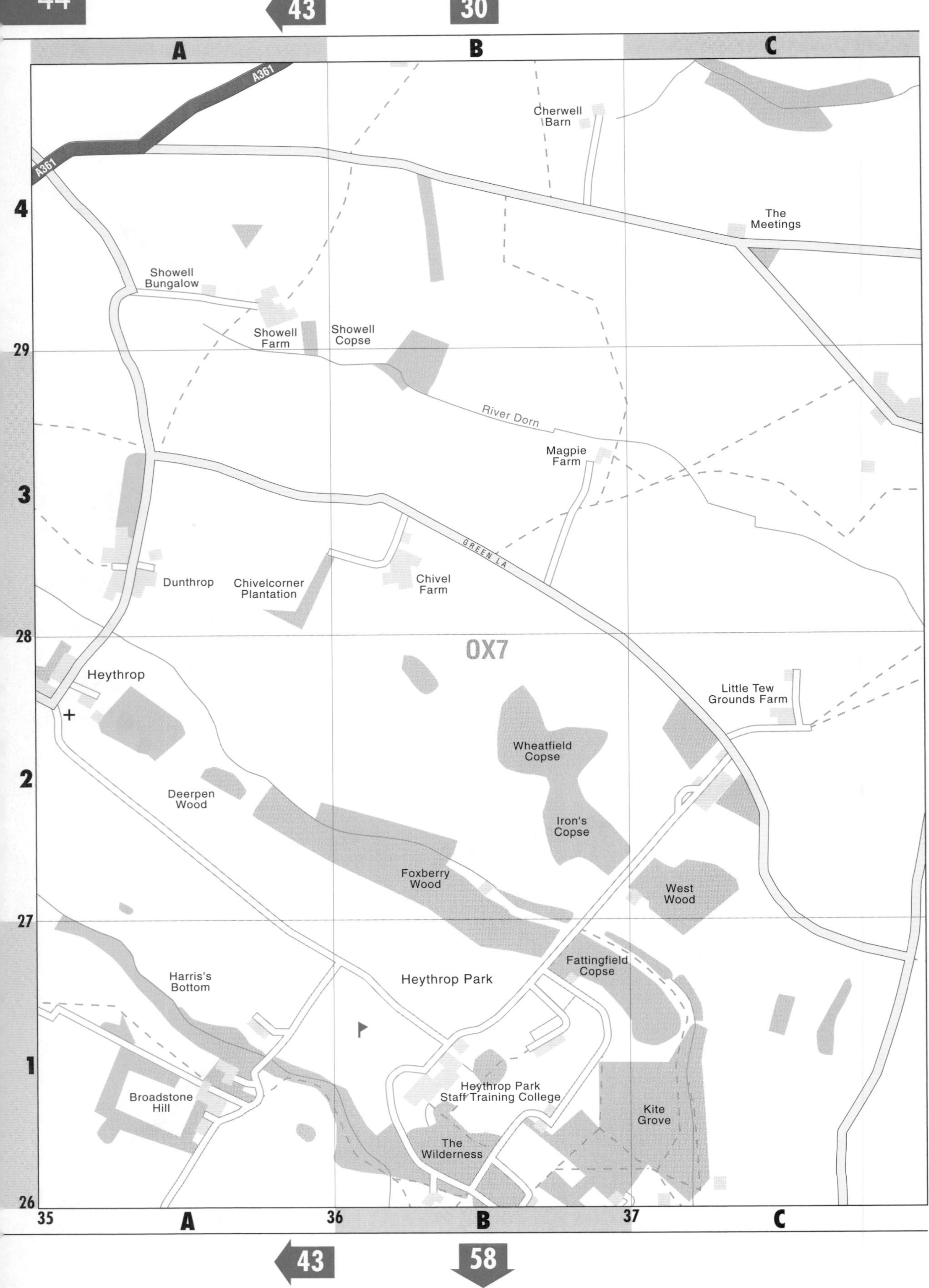

31
46

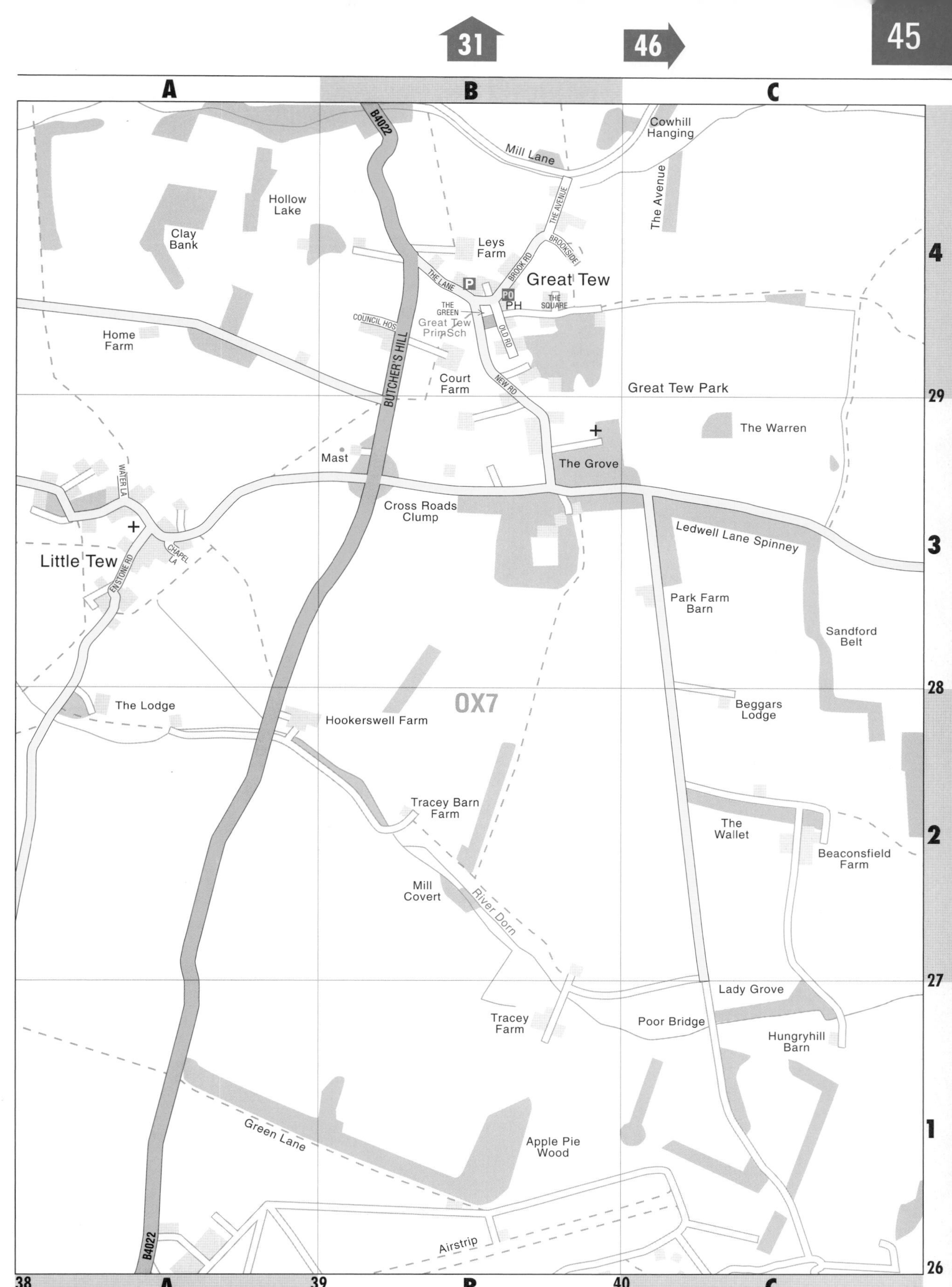
A
B
C
Cowhill Hanging
Mill Lane
The Avenue
Hollow Lake
Clay Bank
Leys Farm
BROOKSIDE
BROOK RD
THE LANE
Great Tew
THE GREEN
THE SQUARE
PH
COUNCIL HOS
Great Tew PrimSch
OLD RD
Home Farm
BUTCHER'S HILL
B4022
Court Farm
NEW RD
Great Tew Park
The Warren
Mast
The Grove
WATER LA
Cross Roads Clump
Ledwell Lane Spinney
CHAPEL LA
Little Tew
ENSTONE RD
Park Farm Barn
Sandford Belt
The Lodge
OX7
Hookerswell Farm
Beggars Lodge
Tracey Barn Farm
The Wallet
Beaconsfield Farm
Mill Covert
River Dorn
Lady Grove
Tracey Farm
Poor Bridge
Hungryhill Barn
Green Lane
Apple Pie Wood
Airstrip
38
39
40
4
29
3
28
2
27
1
26

59
46

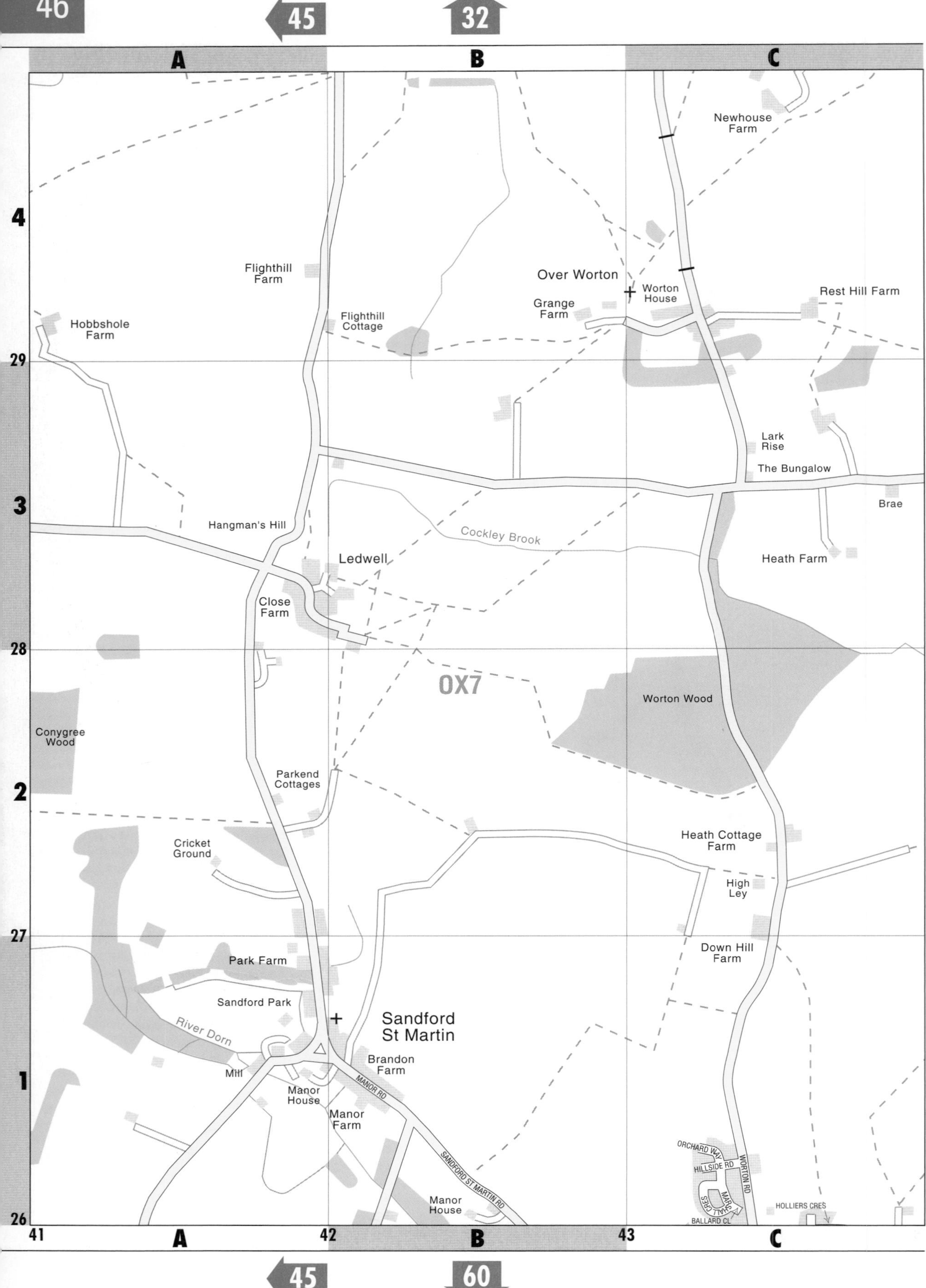

A
B
C

45
60

41
42
43

A
B
C

4

29

3

28

2

27

1

26

Newhouse Farm

Flighthill Farm

Flighthill Cottage

Hobbshole Farm

Over Worton

Grange Farm

Worton House

Rest Hill Farm

Lark Rise

The Bungalow

Brae

Hangman's Hill

Cockley Brook

Ledwell

Heath Farm

Close Farm

OX7

Worton Wood

Conygree Wood

Parkend Cottages

Heath Cottage Farm

Cricket Ground

High Ley

Down Hill Farm

Park Farm

Sandford Park

River Dorn

Sandford St Martin

Mill

Brandon Farm

Manor House

Manor Farm

MANOR RD

ORCHARD WAY

HILLSIDE RD

MARSHALL CRES

WORTON RD

BALLARD CL

HOLLIERS CRES

SANDFORD ST MARTIN RD

Manor House

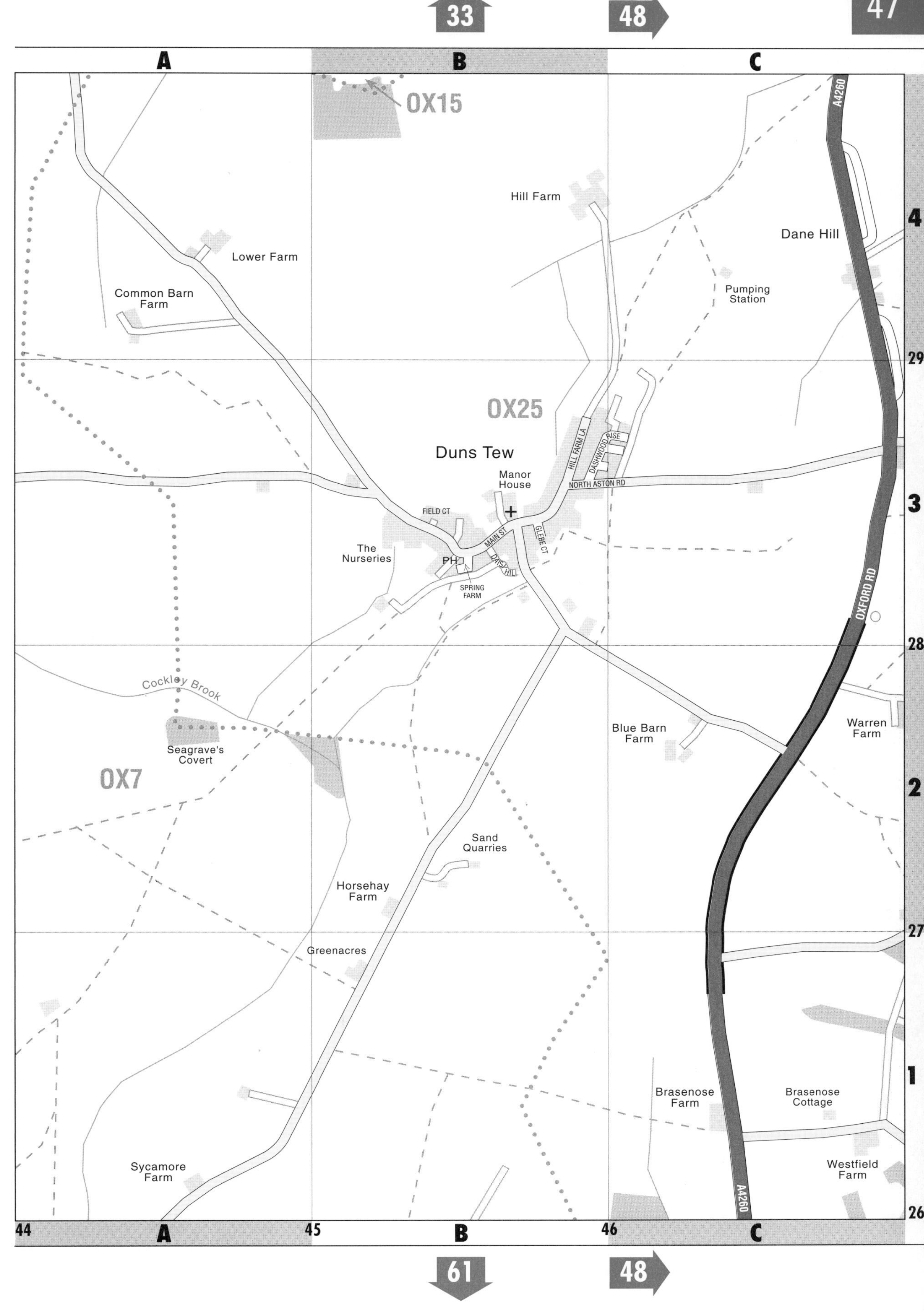

A
B
C

OX15

Hill Farm

Dane Hill

4

Lower Farm

Common Barn
Farm

Pumping
Station

29

OX25

Duns Tew

HILL FARM LA
DASHWOOD RISE
NORTH ASTON RD

3

FIELD CT

Manor
House

The
Nurseries

MAIN ST
GLEBE CT
DAYS HILL

PH

SPRING
FARM

28

Cockley Brook

Blue Barn
Farm

Warren
Farm

Seagrave's
Covert

OX7

2

Sand
Quarries

Horsehay
Farm

27

Greenacres

1

Brasenose
Farm

Brasenose
Cottage

Sycamore
Farm

Westfield
Farm

26

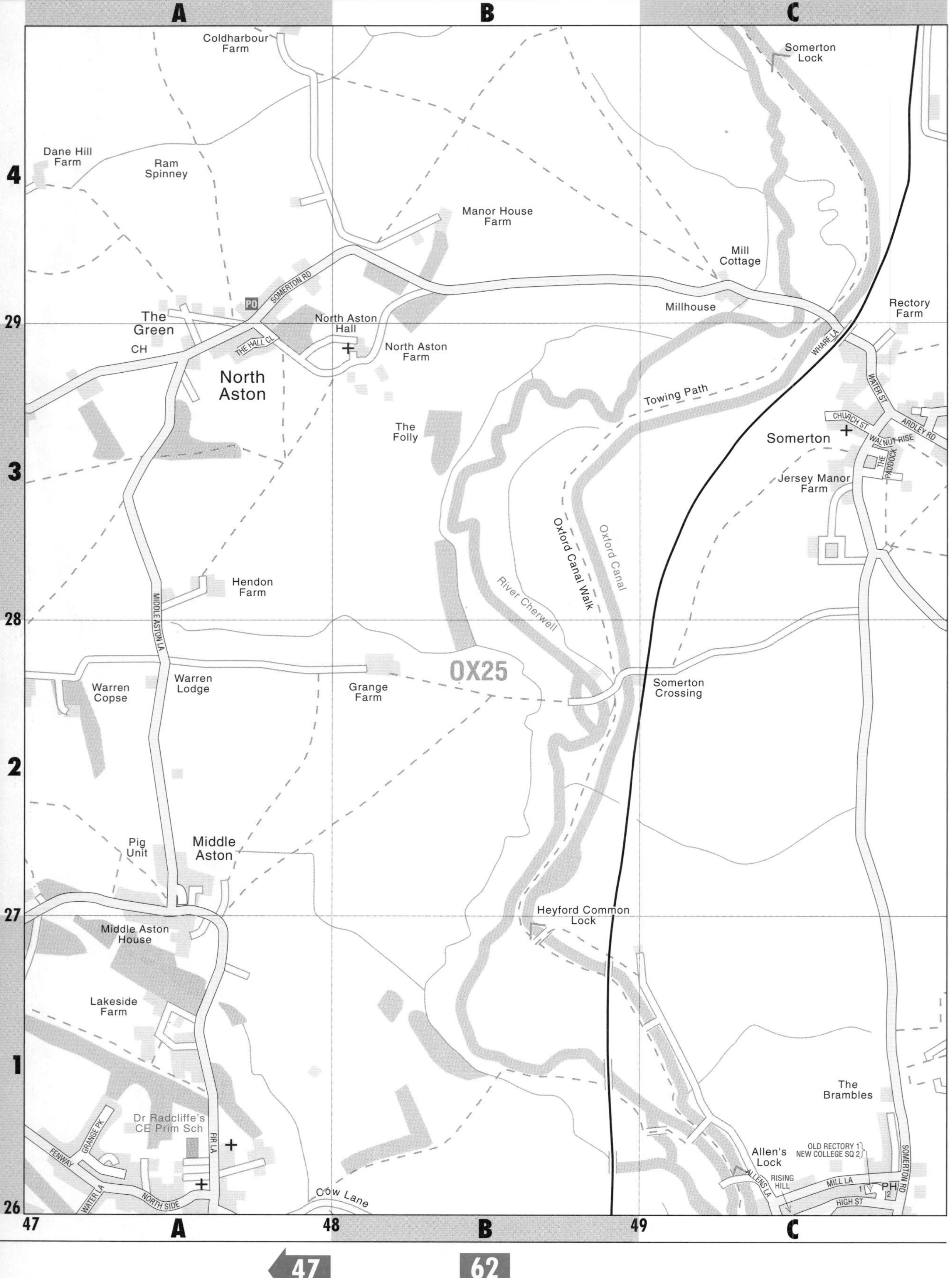

A

B

C

Coldharbour Farm

Dane Hill Farm

Ram Spinney

4

Manor House Farm

Somerton Lock

Mill Cottage

PO

SOMERTON RD

Millhouse

Rectory Farm

29

The Green

CH

North Aston Hall

North Aston Farm

THE HALL CL

Towing Path

WHARF LA

WATER ST

CHURCH ST

ARDLEY RD

Somerton

THE PADDOCK

WALNUT RISE

North Aston

The Folly

Jersey Manor Farm

3

MIDDLE ASTON LA

Hendon Farm

Oxford Canal Walk

Oxford Canal

River Cherwell

28

Warren Copse

Warren Lodge

Grange Farm

OX25

Somerton Crossing

2

Pig Unit

Middle Aston

Heyford Common Lock

27

Middle Aston House

Lakeside Farm

1

The Brambles

FENWAY

GRANGE PK

WATER LA

NORTH SIDE

FIR LA

Dr Radcliffe's CE Prim Sch

Cow Lane

Allen's Lock

ALLEN'S LA

RISING HILL

OLD RECTORY 1
NEW COLLEGE SQ 2

MILL LA

PH

HIGH ST

SOMERTON RD

26

35
50

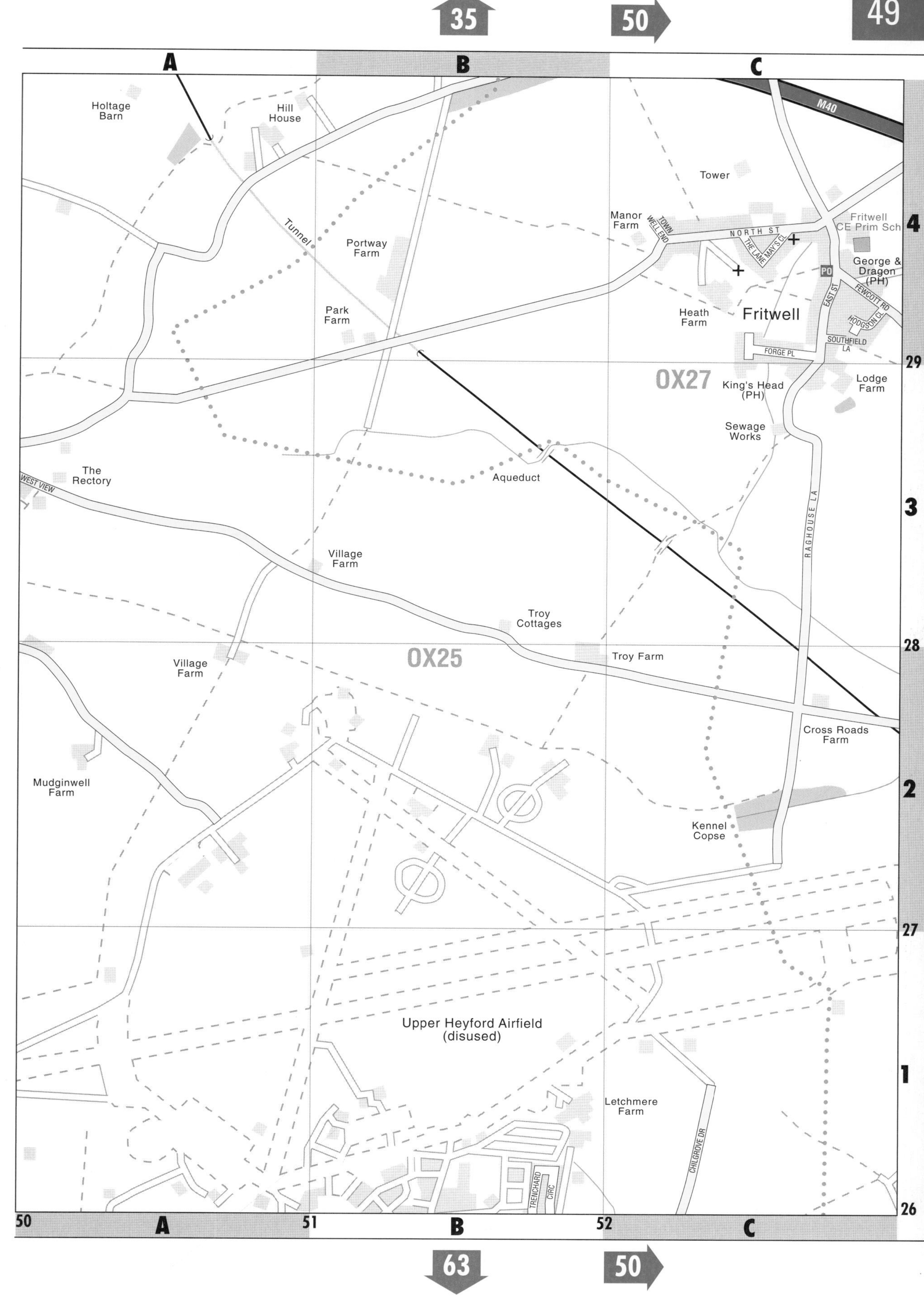
A
B
C
M40
Holtage Barn
Hill House
Tower
Manor Farm
TOWN WELL END
NORTH ST
THE LANE
MAY'S CL
Fritwell CE Prim Sch
George & Dragon (PH)
PO
FEWCOTT RD
EAST ST
HODGSON CL
Tunnel
Portway Farm
Park Farm
Heath Farm
Fritwell
FORGE PL
SOUTHFIELD LA
OX27
King's Head (PH)
Lodge Farm
Sewage Works
The Rectory
WEST VIEW
Aqueduct
RAGHOUSE LA
Village Farm
Troy Cottages
OX25
Troy Farm
Village Farm
Cross Roads Farm
Mudginwell Farm
Kennel Copse
Upper Heyford Airfield (disused)
Letchmere Farm
CHILGROVE DR
TRENCHARD CIRC
4
3
2
1
29
28
27
26
50
51
52

63
50

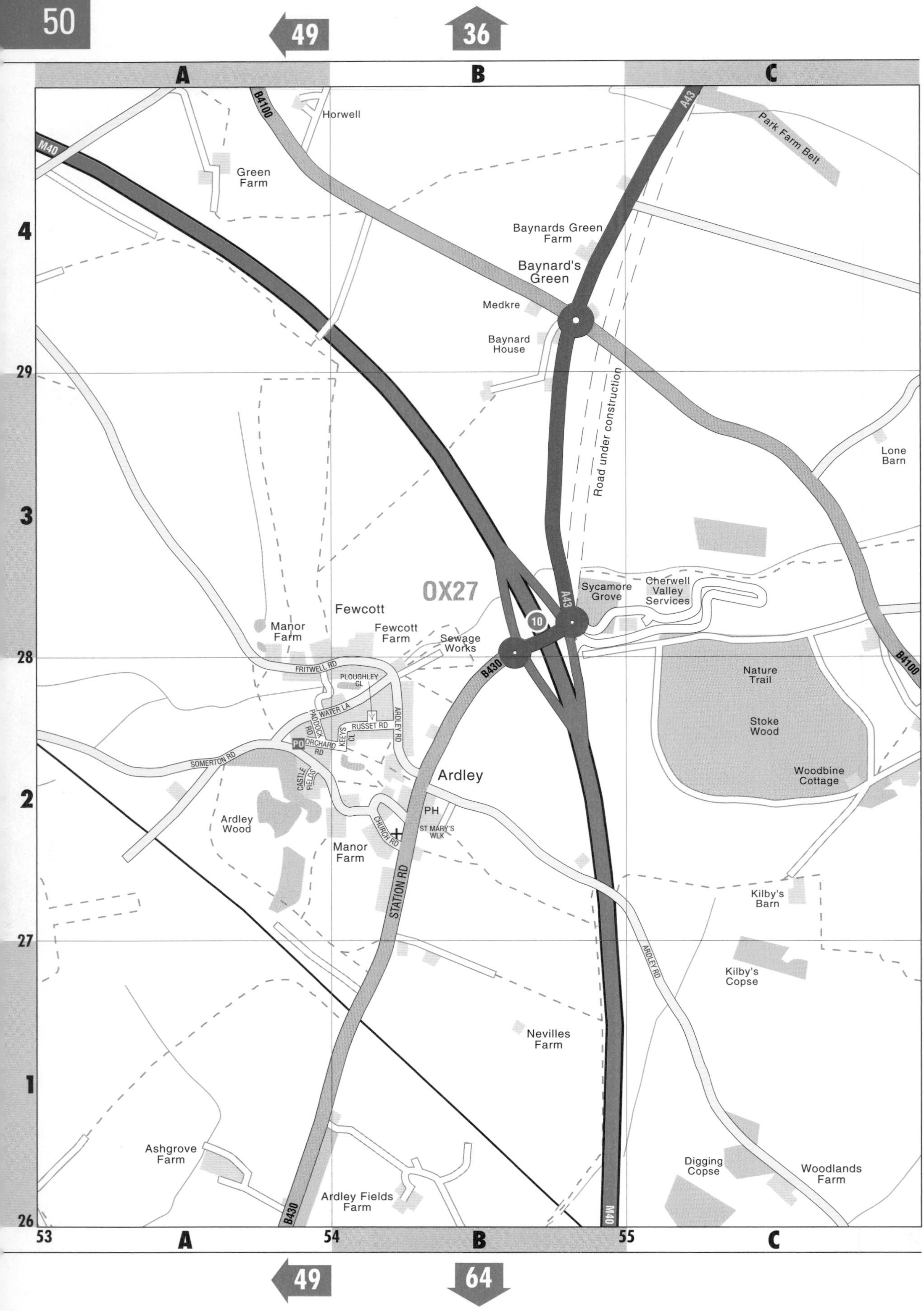

A   B   C

← M40

B4100

Horwell

Green
Farm

A43

Park Farm Belt

Baynards Green
Farm

4

Baynard's
Green

Medkre

Baynard
House

Lone
Barn

29

Road under construction

3

OX27

Sycamore
Grove

Cherwell
Valley
Services

A43

Fewcott

Fewcott
Farm

Sewage
Works

Manor
Farm

FRITWELL RD

PLOUGHLEY
CL

Nature
Trail

28

B430

Stoke
Wood

B4100

WATER LA

PADDOCK

RUSSET RD

KEEY'S
CL

ARDLEY RD

Woodbine
Cottage

PO

ORCHARD
RD

SOMERTON RD

⑩

2

CASTLE
FIELD

Ardley

Ardley
Wood

CHURCH RD

PH

St MARY'S
WLK

Manor
Farm

Kilby's
Barn

STATION RD

Kilby's
Copse

27

ARDLEY RD

Nevilles
Farm

1

Ashgrove
Farm

Digging
Copse

Woodlands
Farm

Ardley Fields
Farm

B430

M40

26

53   A   54   B   55   C

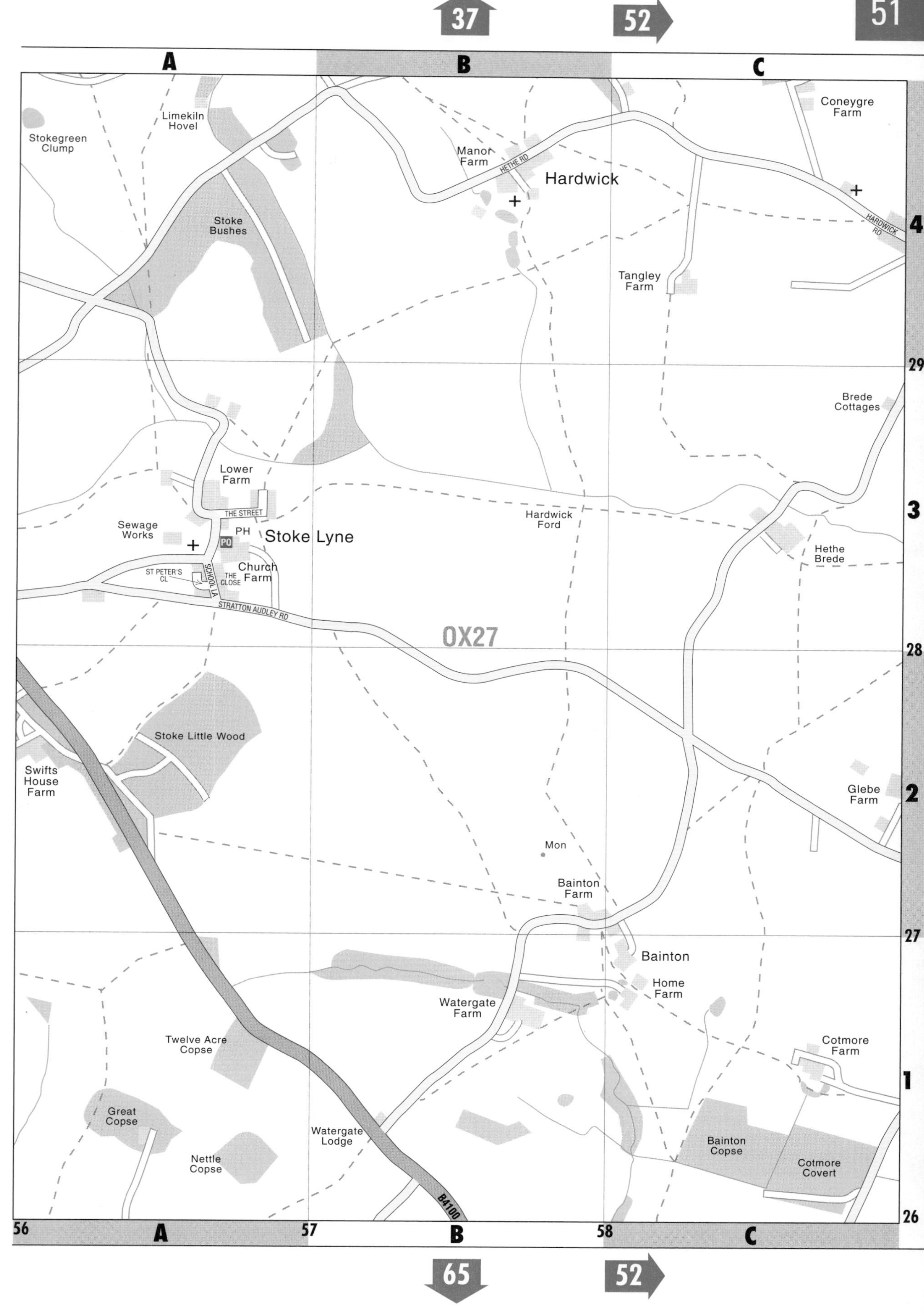

A   B   C

Stokegreen
Clump

Limekiln
Hovel

Stoke
Bushes

Manor
Farm

HETHE RD

Hardwick

Coneygre
Farm

HARDWICK RD

Tangley
Farm

4

29

Brede
Cottages

Lower
Farm

THE STREET

Sewage
Works

PH
PO

Stoke Lyne

Hardwick
Ford

Hethe
Brede

3

ST PETER'S
CL

SCHOOL LA

THE
CLOSE

Church
Farm

STRATTON AUDLEY RD

OX27

28

Stoke Little Wood

Swifts
House
Farm

Glebe
Farm

2

Mon

Bainton
Farm

27

Bainton

Home
Farm

Watergate
Farm

Twelve Acre
Copse

Cotmore
Farm

1

Great
Copse

Watergate
Lodge

Nettle
Copse

B4100

Bainton
Copse

Cotmore
Covert

26

56   A   57   B   58   C

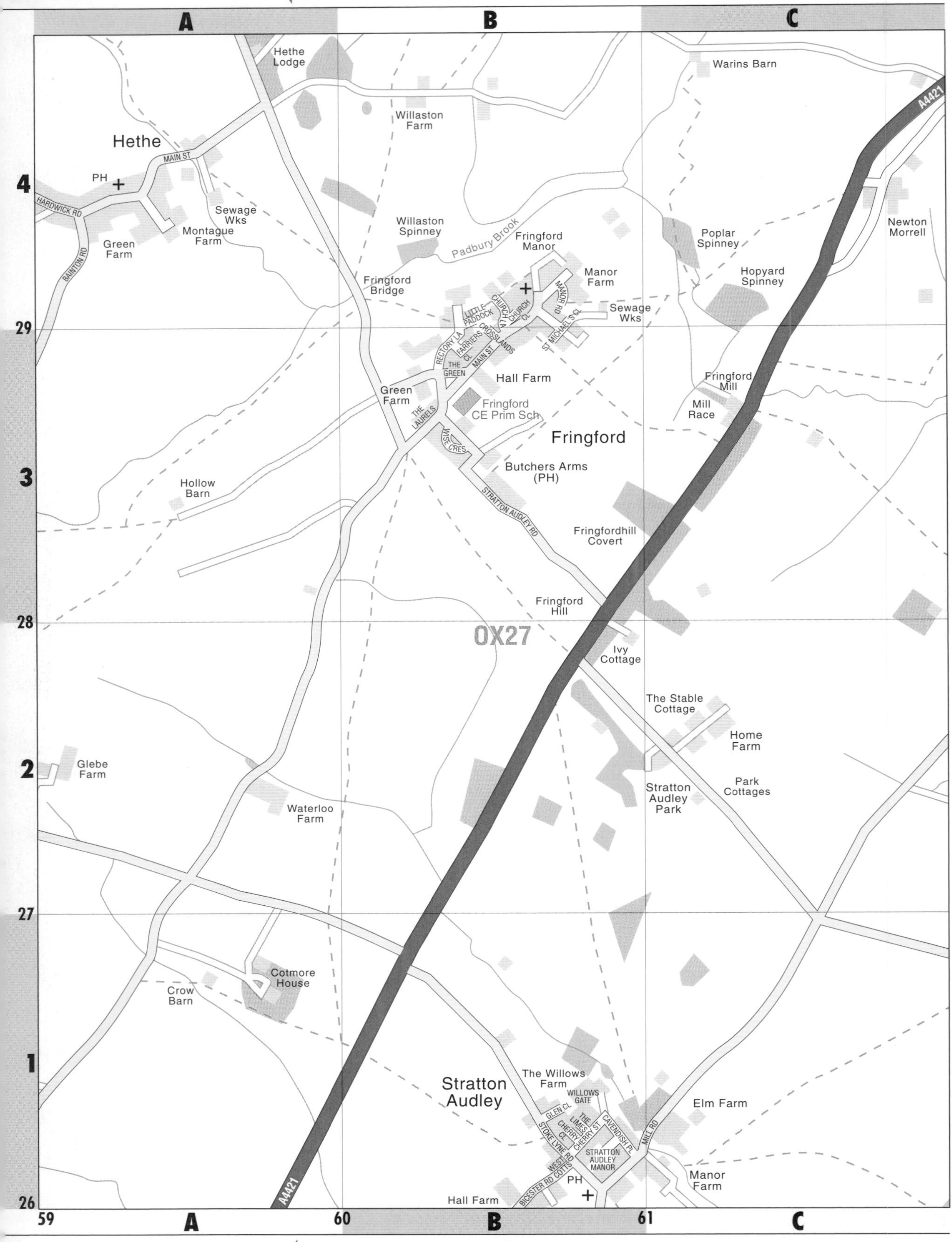

A   B   C

Warins Barn

Hethe Lodge

Willaston Farm

Hethe

Main St

PH +

Willaston Spinney

Fringford Manor

Poplar Spinney

Newton Morrell

A4421

4

HARDWICK RD

BAINTON RD

Sewage Wks

Montague Farm

Green Farm

Padbury Brook

Manor Farm

Hopyard Spinney

Fringford Bridge

MANOR RD

+

Manor RD

St Michael's Cl

Sewage Wks

29

RECTORY LA

LITTLE PADDOCK

CHURCH LA

FARRIERS CL

CROSS LANDS

CHURCH CL

MAIN ST

THE GREEN

Fringford Mill

Mill Race

Green Farm

THE LAURELS

Hall Farm

Fringford

3

Hollow Barn

Fringford CE Prim Sch

WISE CRES.

Butchers Arms (PH)

STRATTON AUDLEY RD

Fringfordhill Covert

Fringford Hill

28

OX27

Fringford Hill

Ivy Cottage

The Stable Cottage

Home Farm

2

Glebe Farm

Waterloo Farm

Stratton Audley Park

Park Cottages

27

Crow Barn

Cotmore House

1

The Willows Farm

Stratton Audley

WILLOWS GATE

GLEN CL

THE LIMES

CHERRY ST

CAVENDISH CT

Elm Farm

STONE LYNE RD

CHERRY CT

MILL RD

WISE CL

Stratton Audley Manor

BICSTER RD COTTS

PH +

Manor Farm

26

Hall Farm

59   A   60   B   61   C

A4421

39

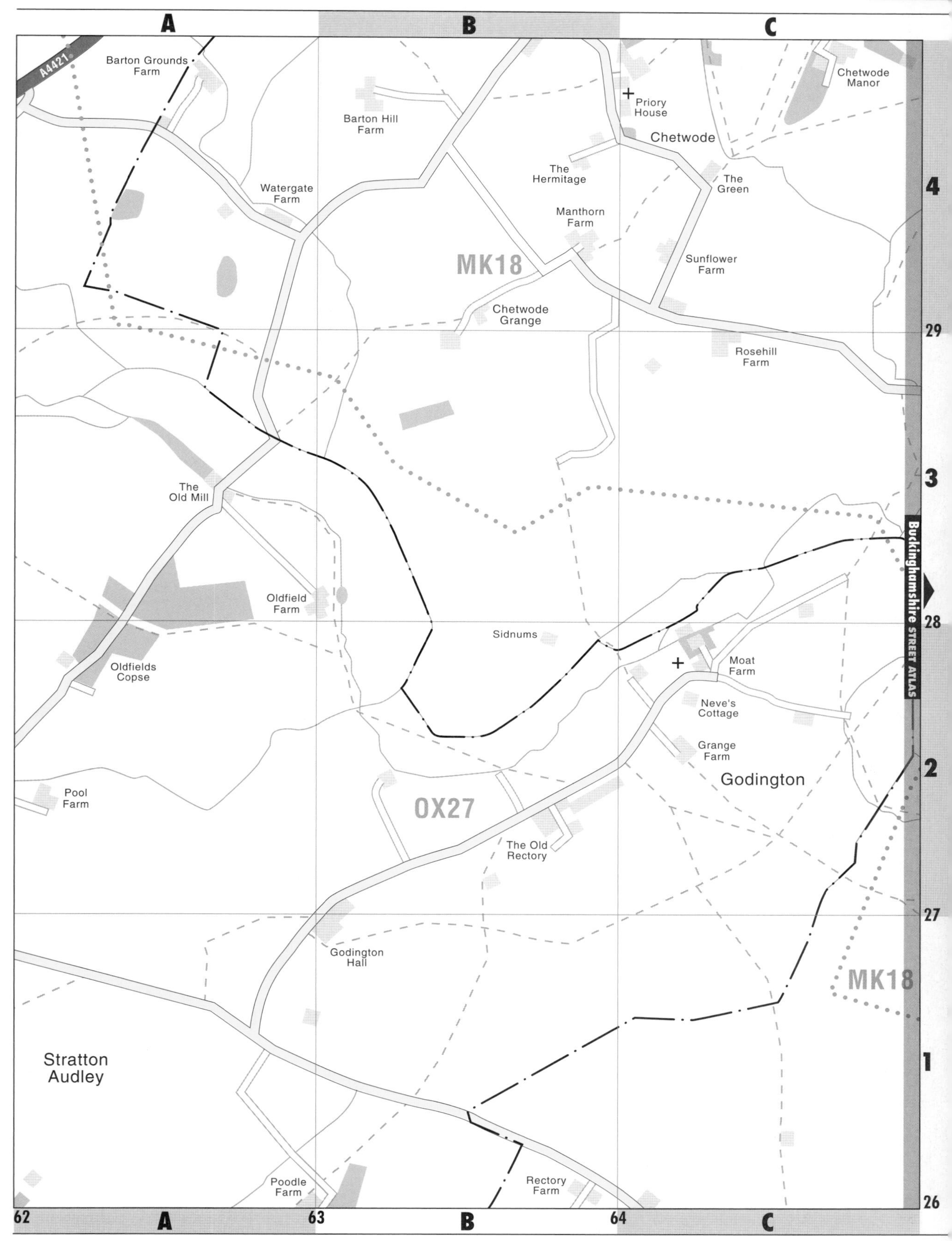
A
B
C
A4421
Barton Grounds Farm
Barton Hill Farm
Priory House
Chetwode Manor
Chetwode
The Hermitage
The Green
Watergate Farm
Manthorn Farm
4
MK18
Sunflower Farm
Chetwode Grange
29
Rosehill Farm
3
The Old Mill
Buckinghamshire STREET ATLAS
Oldfield Farm
28
Sidnums
Oldfields Copse
Moat Farm
Neve's Cottage
Grange Farm
2
Godington
Pool Farm
OX27
The Old Rectory
27
Godington Hall
MK18
1
Stratton Audley
Poodle Farm
Rectory Farm
26
62
63
64

67

40
A B C

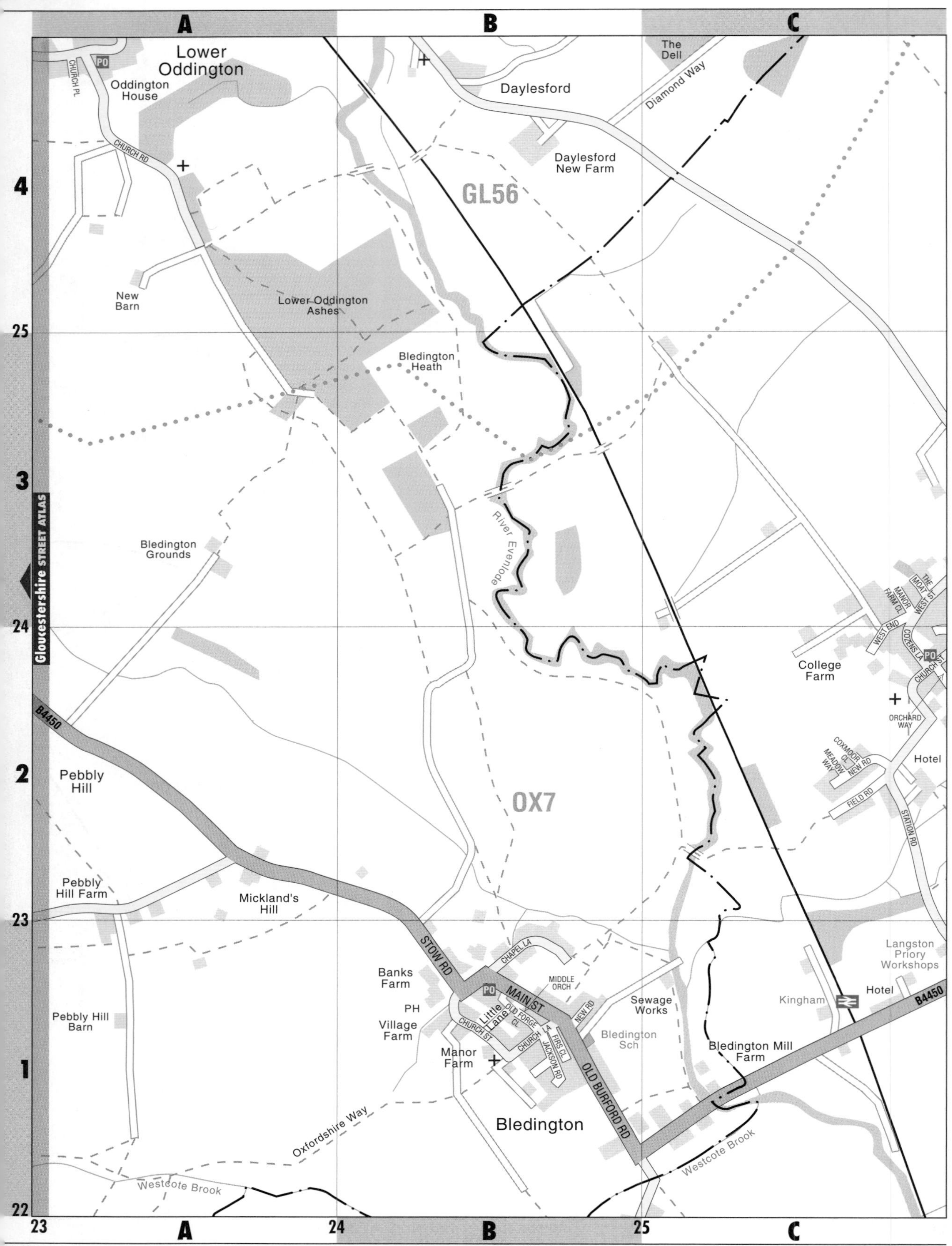
Lower Oddington
Oddington House
CHURCH PL
PO
CHURCH RD
Daylesford
The Dell
Diamond Way
Daylesford New Farm
GL56
New Barn
Lower Oddington Ashes
Bledington Heath
River Evenlode
Bledington Grounds
College Farm
THE MOAT
WEST ST
MANOR FARM CL
WEST END
COZENS LA
CHURCH ST
ORCHARD WAY
COXMOOR CL
MEADOW WAY
NEW RD
FIELD RD
STATION RD
Hotel
B4450
Pebbly Hill
OX7
Pebbly Hill Farm
Mickland's Hill
Langston Priory Workshops
STOW RD
CHAPEL LA
Banks Farm
MIDDLE ORCH
MAIN ST
PH
Village Farm
Little Lane
OLD FORGE CL
CHURCH LA
FIRS CL
JACKSON RD
NEW RD
Sewage Works
Kingham
Hotel
Pebbly Hill Barn
Bledington Sch
Manor Farm
OLD BURFORD RD
Bledington Mill Farm
Oxfordshire Way
Bledington
Westcote Brook
Westcote Brook
Gloucestershire STREET ATLAS

4
25
3
24
2
23
1
22
23 A 24 B 25 C

69

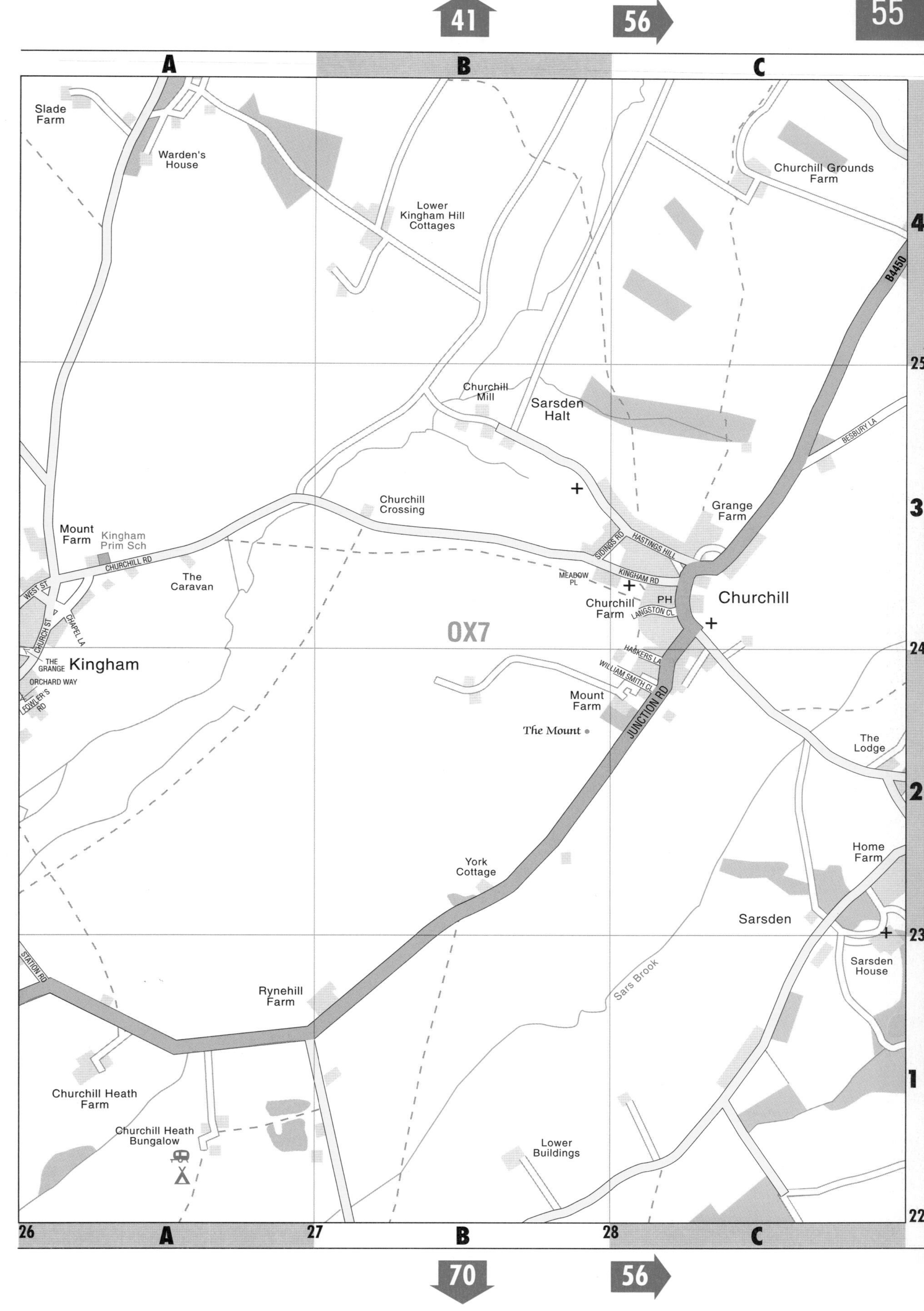

A B C

Slade Farm

Warden's House

Lower Kingham Hill Cottages

Churchill Grounds Farm

B4450

4

25

Churchill Mill

Sarsden Halt

BESBURY LA

Churchill Crossing

+

Grange Farm

3

Mount Farm

Kingham Prim Sch

CHURCHILL RD

The Caravan

SIDINGS RD

HASTINGS HILL

MEADOW PL

KINGHAM RD

Churchill Farm

LANGSTON CL

PH

Churchill

+

+

WEST ST

CHAPEL LA

OX7

HARKERS LA

CHURCH ST

THE GRANGE

Kingham

ORCHARD WAY

WILLIAM SMITH CL

24

FOWLER'S RD

Mount Farm

JUNCTION RD

The Mount •

The Lodge

2

Home Farm

York Cottage

Sarsden

+

23

STATION RD

Sarsden House

Rynehill Farm

Sars Brook

1

Churchill Heath Farm

Churchill Heath Bungalow

Lower Buildings

22

26 A 27 B 28 C

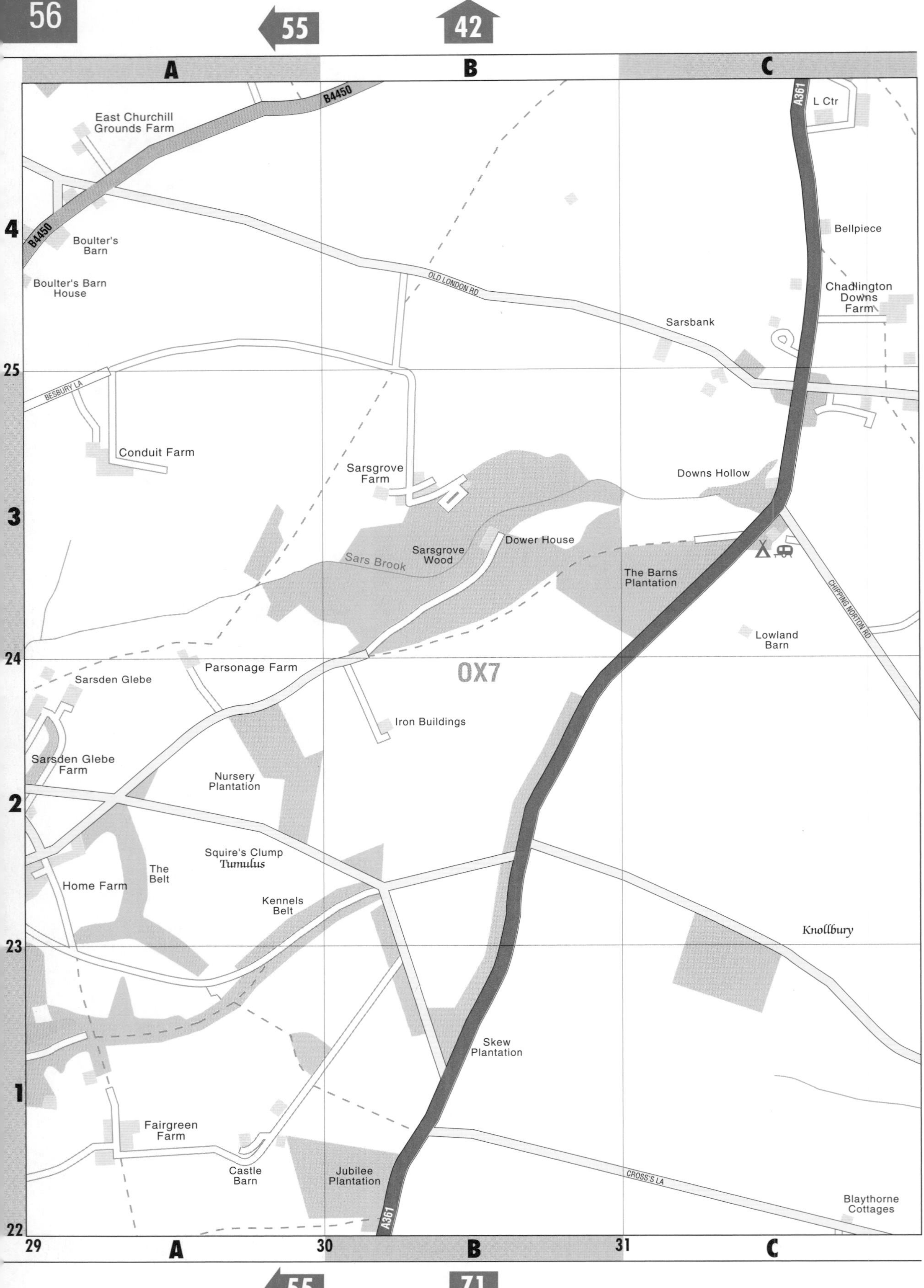

55
42

A　　　　　　B　　　　　　C

B4450

East Churchill
Grounds Farm

4

B4450

Boulter's
Barn

Boulter's Barn
House

OLD LONDON RD

Sarsbank

L Ctr

Bellpiece

Chadlington
Downs
Farm

25

BESBURY LA

Conduit Farm

Sarsgrove
Farm

Downs Hollow

3

Sars Brook

Sarsgrove
Wood

Dower House

The Barns
Plantation

CHIPPING NORTON RD

24

Sarsden Glebe

Parsonage Farm

Iron Buildings

OX7

Lowland
Barn

Sarsden Glebe
Farm

Nursery
Plantation

2

Squire's Clump
Tumulus

The
Belt

Home Farm

Kennels
Belt

Knollbury

23

Skew
Plantation

1

Fairgreen
Farm

Castle
Barn

Jubilee
Plantation

CROSS'S LA

Blaythorne
Cottages

A361

22

29　　　　　A　　　　30　　　　B　　　　31　　　　C

55
71

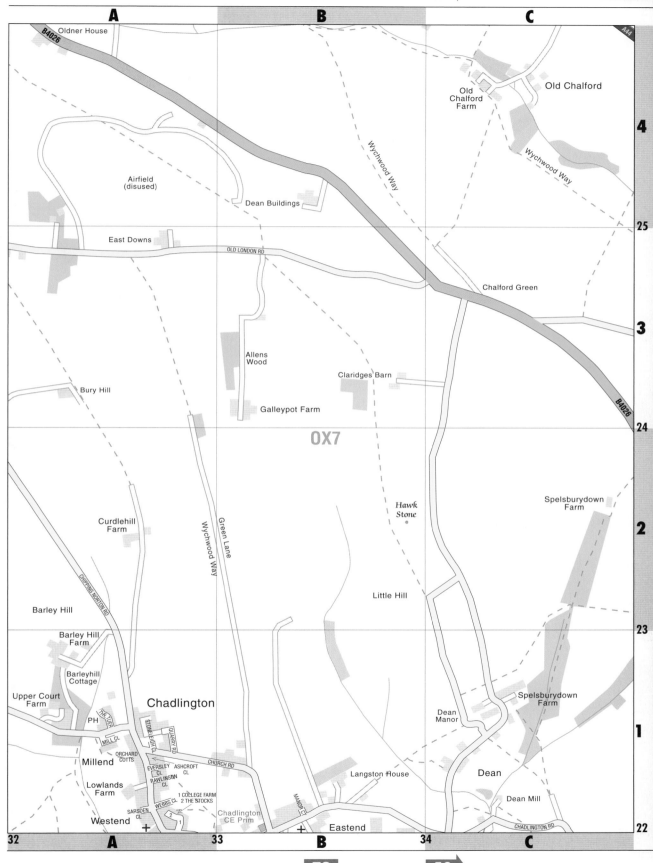

A B C

Oldner House

B4026

Old Chalford Farm

Old Chalford

Wychwood Way

Wychwood Way

A44

4

Airfield (disused)

Dean Buildings

25

East Downs

OLD LONDON RD

Chalford Green

3

Allens Wood

Claridges Barn

Bury Hill

Galleypot Farm

B4026

OX7

24

Curdlehill Farm

Hawk Stone

Spelsburydown Farm

Green Lane

Wychwood Way

2

Barley Hill

Little Hill

23

Barley Hill Farm

Barleyhill Cottage

CHIPPING NORTON RD

Upper Court Farm

Chadlington

Spelsburydown Farm

Dean Manor

THE TUER

PH

STONELEIGH CL

QUARRY RD

MILL CL

ORCHARD COTTS

CHURCH RD

Dean

1

Millend

EVERSLEY CL

ASHCROFT CL

RAWLINSON CL

WEBBS CL

Langston House

Dean Mill

Lowlands Farm

1 COLLEGE FARM
2 THE STOCKS

SARSDEN CL

Westend

MANOR CT

Chadlington CE Prim

Eastend

CHADLINGTON RD

22

32

A

33

B

34

C

57
44

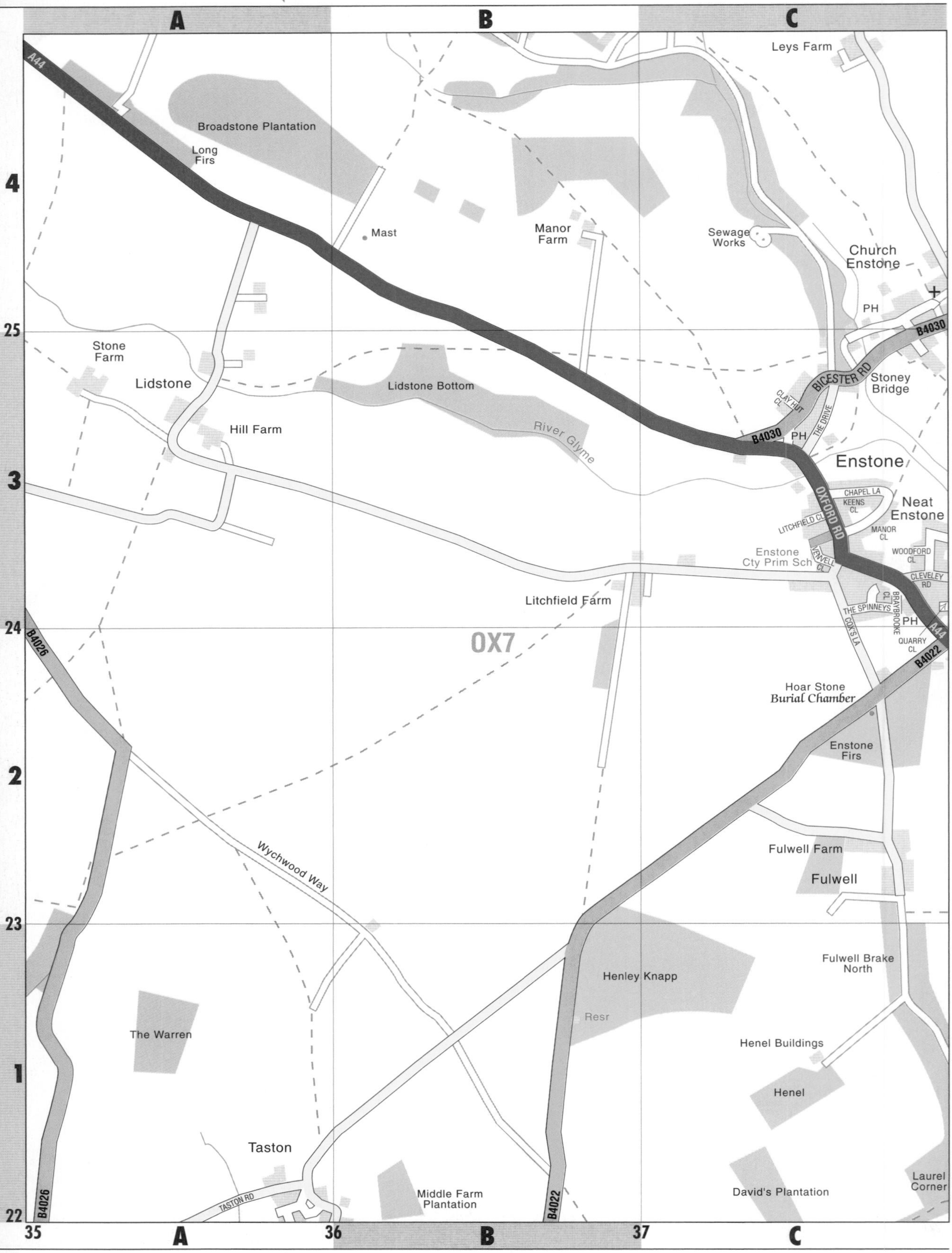

A **B** **C**

A44

Broadstone Plantation

Long Firs

Leys Farm

Mast

Manor Farm

Sewage Works

Church Enstone

PH

B4030

4

Stone Farm

Lidstone

Hill Farm

Lidstone Bottom

River Glyme

BICESTER RD

CLAY TFT

THE DRIVE

CLAY CL

Stoney Bridge

25

B4030

PH

Enstone

CHAPEL LA

KEENS CL

OXFORD RD

Neat Enstone

MANOR CL

WOODFORD CL

3

LITCHFIELD CL

IRWELL

Enstone Cty Prim Sch

CLEVELEY RD

Litchfield Farm

THE SPINNEYS

COX'S LA

BRAYBROOKE CL

PH

QUARRY CL

A44

24

B4026

OX7

B4022

Hoar Stone Burial Chamber

Enstone Firs

2

Wychwood Way

Fulwell Farm

Fulwell

23

Henley Knapp

Resr

Fulwell Brake North

Henel Buildings

1

The Warren

Henel

Taston

TASTON RD

Middle Farm Plantation

B4022

David's Plantation

Laurel Corner

22

B4026

35 **A** **36** **B** **37** **C**

57
73

45
60

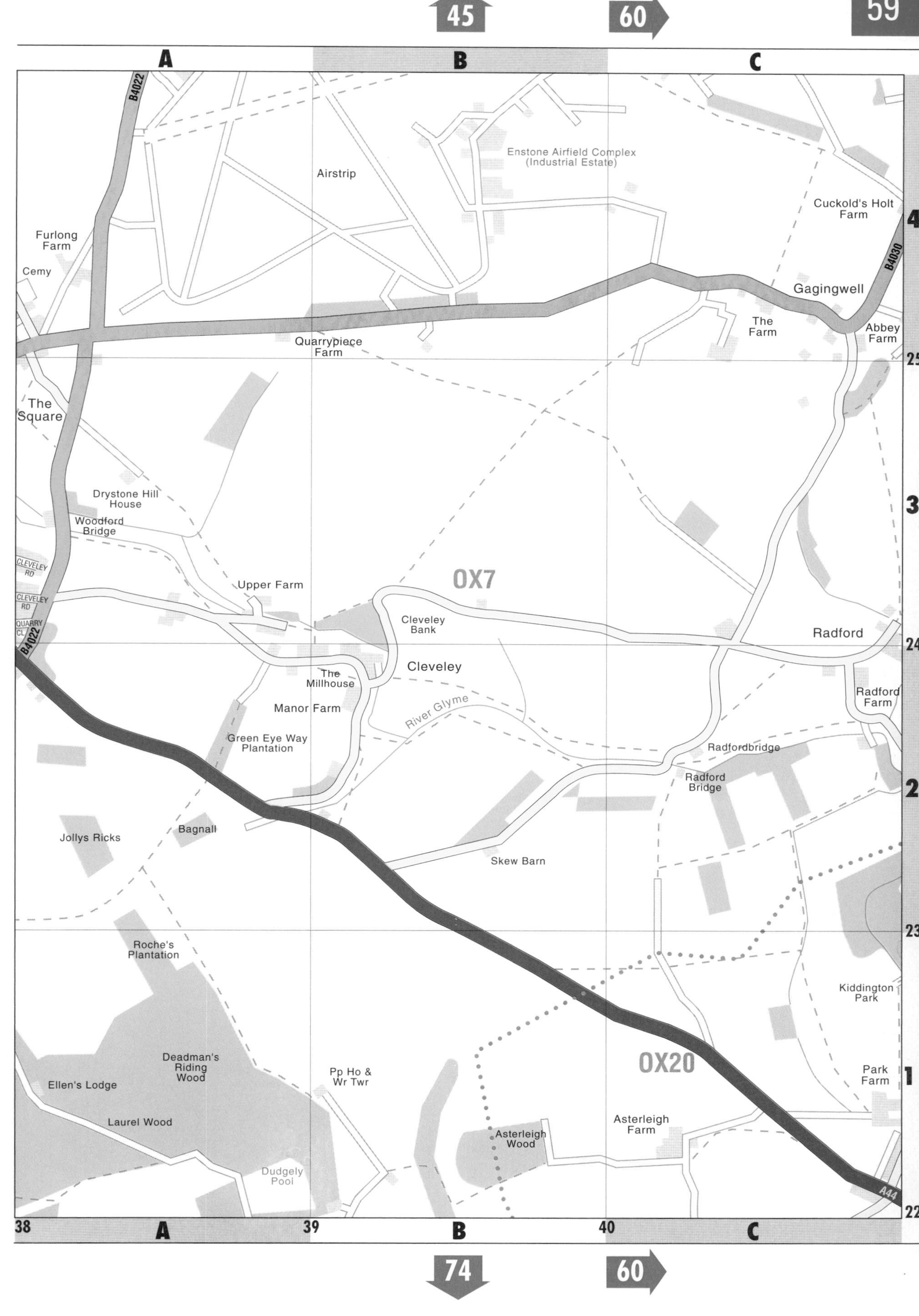
A
B
C
B4022
Airstrip
Enstone Airfield Complex
(Industrial Estate)
Cuckold's Holt
Farm
Furlong
Farm
Cemy
B4030
Gagingwell
The
Farm
Abbey
Farm
Quarrypiece
Farm
The
Square
Drystone Hill
House
Woodford
Bridge
OX7
CLEVELEY
RD
CLEVELEY
RD
QUARRY
CL
Upper Farm
Cleveley
Bank
Radford
B4022
Cleveley
The
Millhouse
Manor Farm
River Glyme
Radford
Farm
Green Eye Way
Plantation
Radfordbridge
Radford
Bridge
Jollys Ricks
Bagnall
Skew Barn
Roche's
Plantation
Kiddington
Park
Deadman's
Riding
Wood
Ellen's Lodge
Pp Ho &
Wr Twr
OX20
Park
Farm
Laurel Wood
Asterleigh
Wood
Asterleigh
Farm
Dudgely
Pool
A44
4
25
3
24
2
23
1
22
38
39
40
A
B
C

74
60

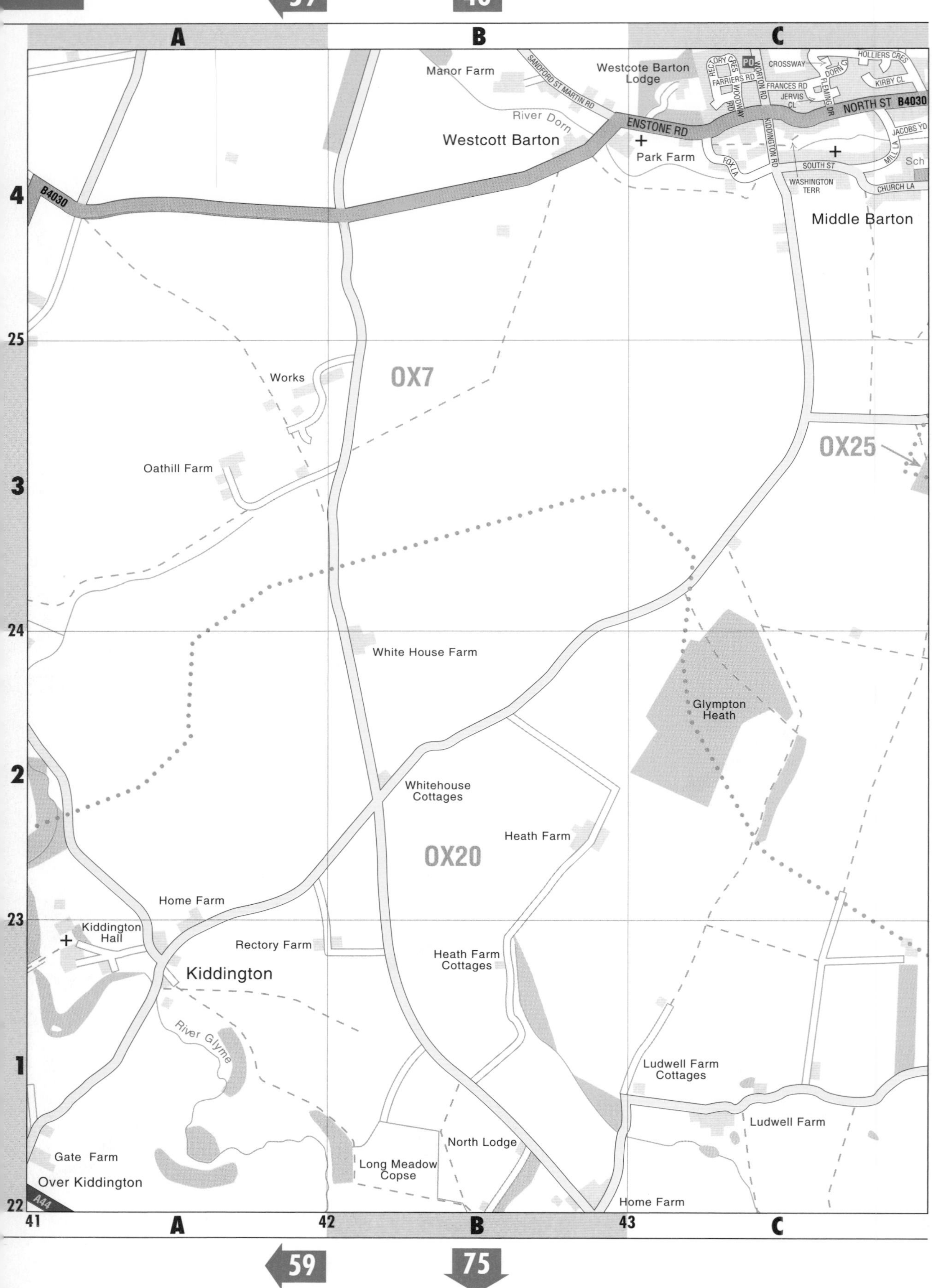

59
46

A   B   C

Manor Farm

Westcote Barton Lodge

RECTORY CRES
FARRIERS RD
WOODWAY
CROSSWAY
NORTON RD
FRANCES RD
JERVIS CL
HOLLIERS CRES
KIRBY CL
DORN CL
FLEMING DR
NORTH ST B4030
JACOBS YD

River Dorn

ENSTONE RD

Westcott Barton

Park Farm

KIDDINGTON RD
FOX LA
SOUTH ST
WASHINGTON TERR
MILL LA
CHURCH LA
Sch

Middle Barton

4   B4030

25

Works

OX7

OX25

Oathill Farm

3

White House Farm

24

Glympton Heath

Whitehouse Cottages

2

Heath Farm

OX20

Home Farm

23

Kiddington Hall

Rectory Farm

Heath Farm Cottages

Kiddington

River Glyme

1

Ludwell Farm Cottages

Ludwell Farm

Gate Farm

Over Kiddington

North Lodge

Long Meadow Copse

Home Farm

22   A44

41   A   42   B   43   C

47
62

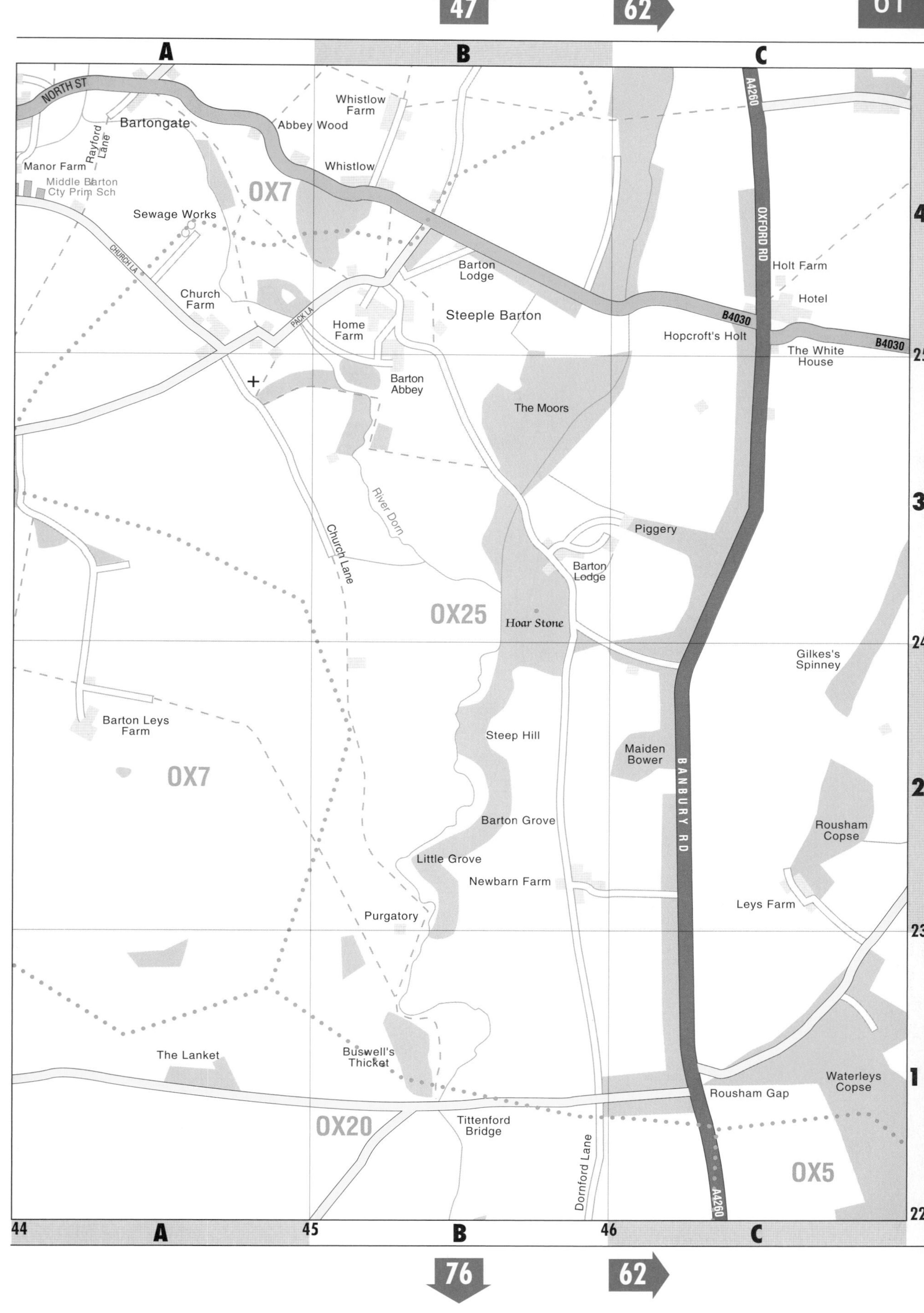
A
B
C
NORTH ST
Bartongate
Rayford Lane
Manor Farm
Middle Barton Cty Prim Sch
Whistlow Farm
Abbey Wood
Whistlow
OX7
Sewage Works
CHURCH LA
Church Farm
PACK LA
Home Farm
Barton Lodge
Steeple Barton
Barton Abbey
A4260
OXFORD RD
Holt Farm
Hotel
B4030
Hopcroft's Holt
The White House
The Moors
River Dorn
Church Lane
Piggery
Barton Lodge
OX25
Hoar Stone
Gilkes's Spinney
Barton Leys Farm
Steep Hill
Maiden Bower
BANBURY RD
OX7
Barton Grove
Rousham Copse
Little Grove
Newbarn Farm
Leys Farm
Purgatory
The Lanket
Buswell's Thicket
Waterleys Copse
Rousham Gap
Tittenford Bridge
OX20
Dornford Lane
OX5
A4260
4
25
3
24
2
23
1
22
44
A
45
B
46
C

76
62

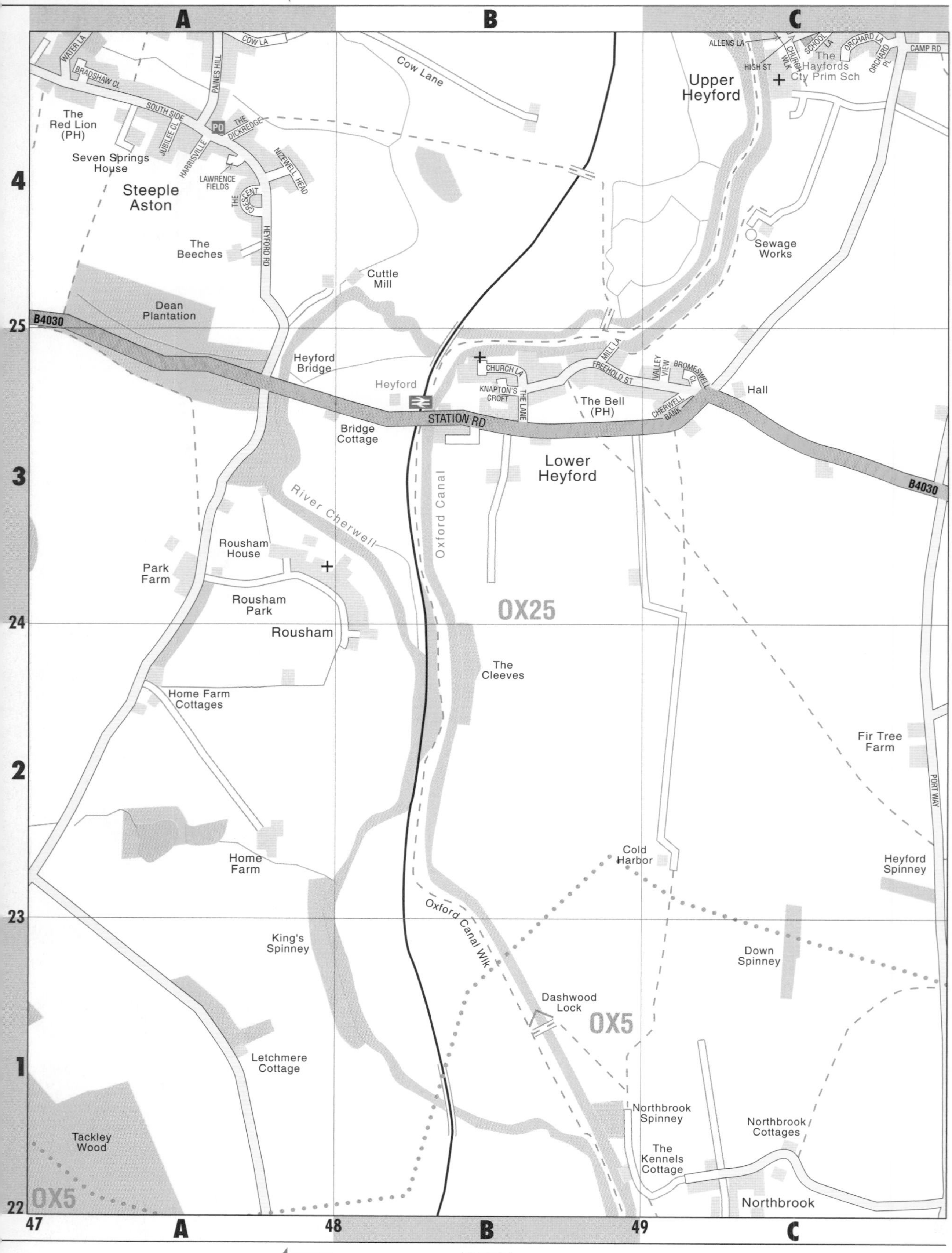

A B C

Upper
Heyford

ALLENS LA
HIGH ST
CHURCH WLK
SCHOOL LA
ORCHARD LE
ORCHARD PL
CAMP RD

The
Hayfords
Cty Prim Sch

Steeple
Aston

The Red Lion
(PH)

Seven Springs
House

4

WATER LA
BRADSHAW CL
SOUTH SIDE
JUBILEE CL
PAINES HILL
COW LA
THE DICKREDGE
PO
HARPISVILLE
LAWRENCE FIELDS
THE CRESCENT
NIZEWELL HEAD
HEYFORD RD

The Beeches

Cuttle
Mill

Sewage
Works

Cow Lane

Dean
Plantation

25 B4030

Heyford
Bridge

Heyford

STATION RD

CHURCH LA
KNAPTON'S CROFT
THE LANE
FREEHOLD ST
MILL LA
VALLEY VIEW
BROMESWELL
CHERWELL BANK

Hall

The Bell
(PH)

B4030

Bridge
Cottage

Lower
Heyford

3

River Cherwell

Rousham
House

Park
Farm

Rousham
Park

Oxford Canal

Rousham

OX25

24

Home Farm
Cottages

The
Cleeves

2

Fir Tree
Farm

PORT WAY

Home
Farm

Cold
Harbor

Heyford
Spinney

23

King's
Spinney

Oxford Canal Wlk

Down
Spinney

Dashwood
Lock

OX5

1

Letchmere
Cottage

Northbrook
Spinney

Northbrook
Cottages

Tackley
Wood

The
Kennels
Cottage

Northbrook

22 OX5

47 A 48 B 49 C

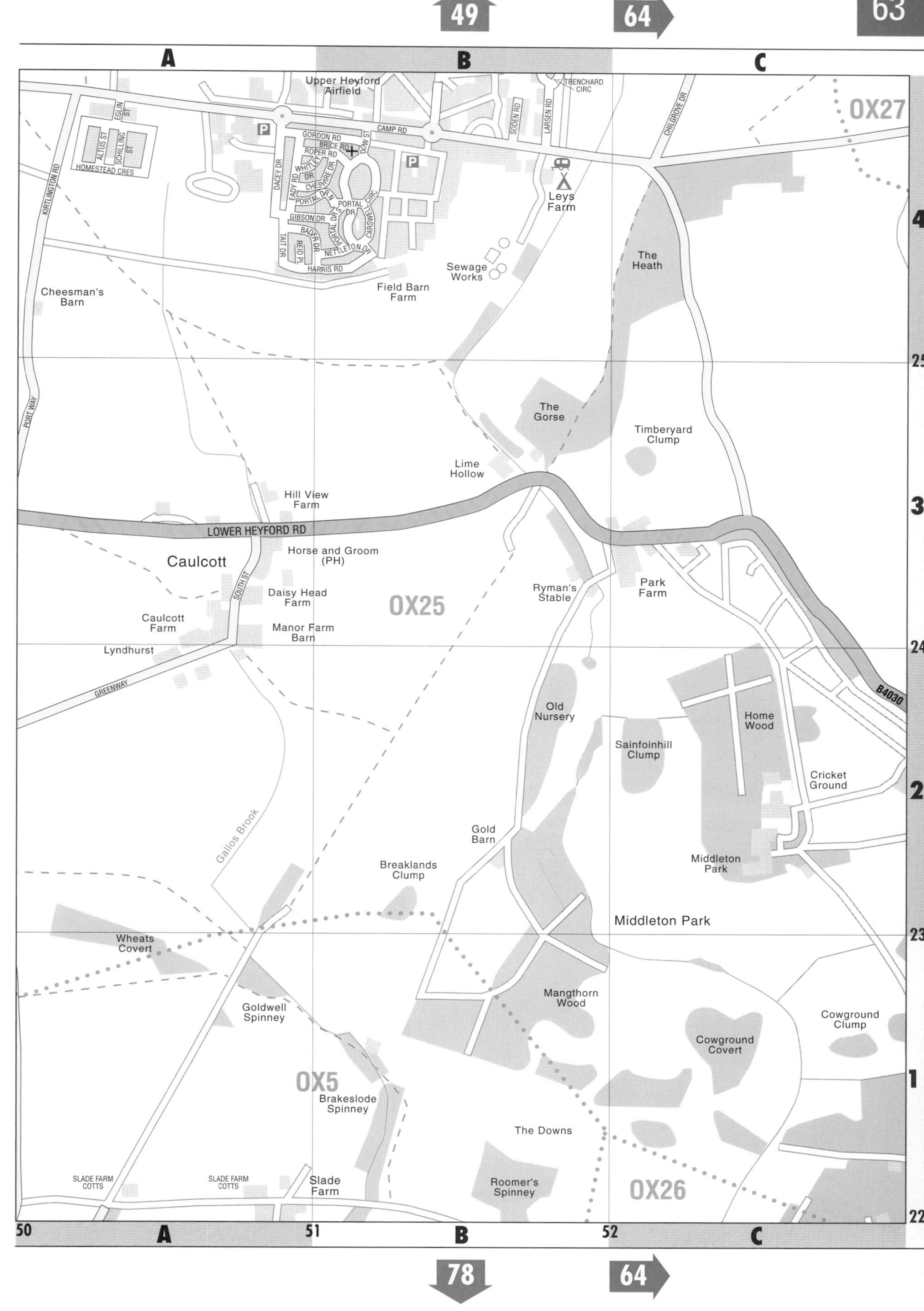

A **B** **C**

OX27

Upper Heyford
Airfield

TRENCHARD
CIRC

CAMP RD

SODEN RD

LARSEN RD

CHILGROVE DR

Cheesman's
Barn

GORDON RD
BRICE RD
ROPER RD
WHITLEY DR
CHESHIRE DR
PORTAL DR
PORTAL DR
GIBSON DR
NETTLETON DR
CARSWELL CIRC
BAZIN DR
REID PL
TAIT DR
HARRIS RD
DACEY DR
EADY RD

KIRTLINGTON RD
EGLIN ST
ALTUS ST
SCHILLING ST
HOMESTEAD CRES

Leys
Farm

The Heath

4

Field Barn
Farm

Sewage
Works

PORT WAY

25

The Gorse

Timberyard
Clump

Lime
Hollow

Hill View
Farm

LOWER HEYFORD RD

3

Horse and Groom
(PH)

Caulcott

OX25

Ryman's
Stable

Park
Farm

Daisy Head
Farm

SOUTH ST

Caulcott
Farm

Manor Farm
Barn

Lyndhurst

GREENWAY

24

B4030

Old
Nursery

Home
Wood

Sainfoinhill
Clump

Cricket
Ground

Gallos Brook

Gold
Barn

Middleton
Park

2

Breaklands
Clump

Middleton Park

23

Wheats
Covert

Mangthorn
Wood

Cowground
Clump

Goldwell
Spinney

Cowground
Covert

OX5

Brakeslode
Spinney

1

The Downs

SLADE FARM
COTTS

SLADE FARM
COTTS

Slade
Farm

Roomer's
Spinney

OX26

22

A **B** **C**

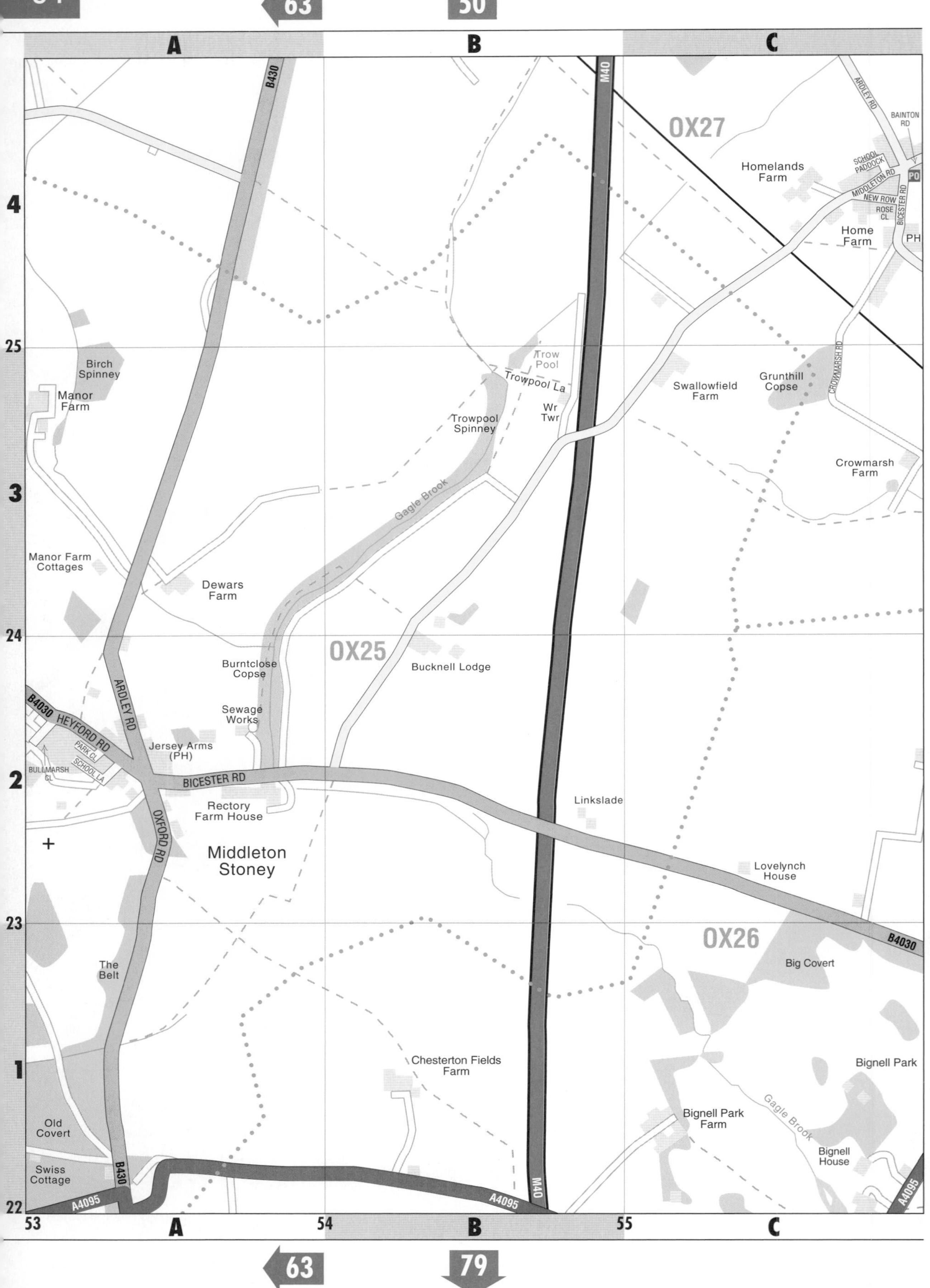

A
B
C

OX27

4

Homelands Farm

BAINTON RD

ARDLEY RD

SCHOOL PADDOCK
MIDDLETON RD
NEW ROW
ROSE CL
BICESTER RD
PO

Home Farm

PH

25

Birch Spinney

Trow Pool

Trowpool La

Swallowfield Farm

Grunthill Copse

CROWMARSH RD

Manor Farm

Trowpool Spinney

Wr Twr

3

Gagle Brook

Crowmarsh Farm

Manor Farm Cottages

Dewars Farm

24

OX25

Burntclose Copse

Bucknell Lodge

B4030
HEYFORD RD

ARDLEY RD

Sewage Works

PARK CL
SCHOOL LA

Jersey Arms (PH)

BULLMARSH CL

2

BICESTER RD

Linkslade

Rectory Farm House

+

OXFORD RD

Middleton Stoney

Lovelynch House

23

OX26

B4030

The Belt

Big Covert

1

Chesterton Fields Farm

Bignell Park

Old Covert

Bignell Park Farm

Gagle Brook

Swiss Cottage

B430

Bignell House

A4095

22

A4095

M40

A4095

53

A

54

B

55

C

Map: Bicester

Grid columns: A B C (top), A B C (bottom)
Grid rows: 4, 25, 3, 24, 2, 23, 1, 22

Place names and labels

Manor Farm
Lower Farm
BAINTON RD
Bucknell Manor Farm
Manor House
Bucknell
BICESTER RD
OX27
Lodge
Caversfield House
Caversfield
Home Farm
SPRINGFIELD RD
WARHAVEN RD
ELDERFIELD RD
TRUEMPER GR
WILSON WAY
OLD SCHOOL CL
THOMPSON DR
BAKER CL
CASTLE CL
DANES GDNS
PAYNES END
SHEEN CL
BLENCOWE
BARNFIELD CL
SKIMMINGDISH LA
Bricknells Farm
CUCKOO CL 1
MANZEL RD 2
Hawkwell Farm
MARIGOLD WLK 1
SPEEDWELL CROFT 2
STONECROP LEYES 3
VERVAIN CL 4
BUTTERBUR GDNS 5
TAMARISK GDNS 6
SALLOW CL 7
THE MAGNOLIAS 8
A4421
A4095
JASMINE PL
Lord's Farm
Aldershot Farm
Gowell Farm
Himley Farm
HOWES LA
OX26
BICESTER
Woodfield
BANBURY RD
Bure Park Prim Sch
Highfield
B4100
Bicester North
Ind Est
B4030
A4095
Bignell Belt
Brookside Prim /St Edburg's CE Sch
Sports Ctr
Bicester Com Coll
St Mary's RC Prim Sch
NORTH ST
MANORSFIELD RD
Longfields Prim Sch
MIDDLETON STONEY RD
B4030
King's End Services
Whitelands Farm
OXFORD RD
Bicester Com Sch
St Edburg's CE Prim Sch
Cemy
Liby
LONDON RD B4100
Garth Park
Bicester Crossing
McKay Trading Est
ALCHESTER TERR

Index

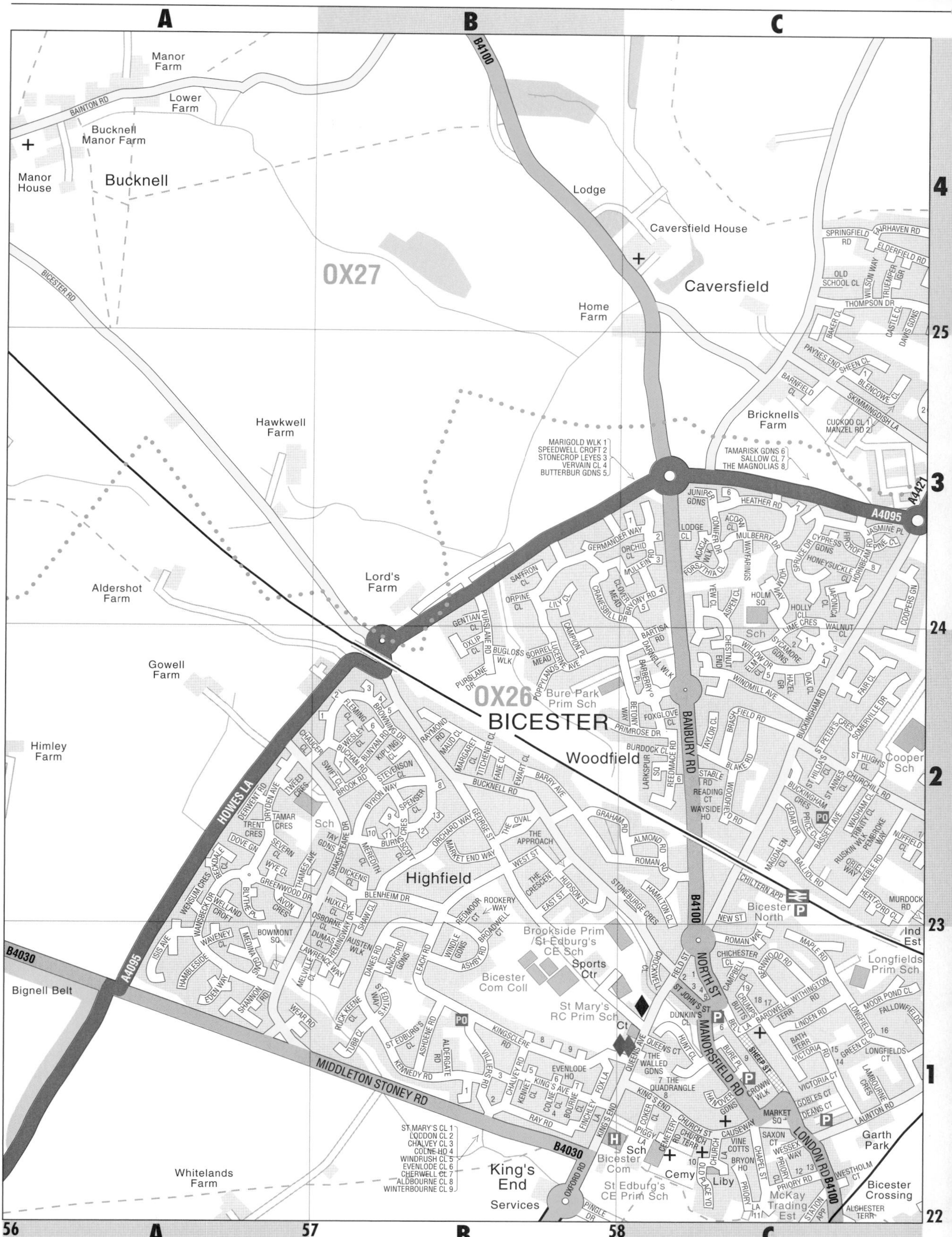

80 66

B2
1 COLERIDGE CL
2 COWPER CL
3 GOLDSMITH CL
4 KEATS CL
5 KINGSLEY RD
6 WORDSWORTH CL
7 WALPOLE CL
8 LONGFELLOW CL
9 SHELLEY CL

B2
10 MASEFIELD CL
11 MILTON CL
12 MACKENZIE CL
13 MACAULAY CL

C1
1 TWITCHERS ALLEY
2 FANE HO
3 REYNARD CT
4 TOLLGATE HO
5 HARCOURT HO
6 WESLEY LA
7 BICESTER HO
8 THE SOUTH LODGE
9 EVANS YD
10 DOVE CT
11 PRIORY CT
12 AMBASSADOR CT
13 REGAL CT
14 NEWPORT TERR
15 MANCHESTER TERR
16 FOLLOWFIELDS CT
17 BELL LODGE
18 HENLEY GDNS
19 DRAYMANS CROFT

C2
1 SPINDLESIDE
2 HAWTHORN WLK
3 SOUTHWOLD
4 MAYCROFT
5 LARCH CL
6 BLUEBELL CL
7 MERTON WLK

St Mary's area index:
ST MARY'S CL 1
LODDON CL 2
CHALVEY CL 3
COLNE HO 4
WINDRUSH CL 5
EVENLODE CL 6
CHERWELL CL 7
ALDBOURNE CL 8
WINTERBOURNE CL 9

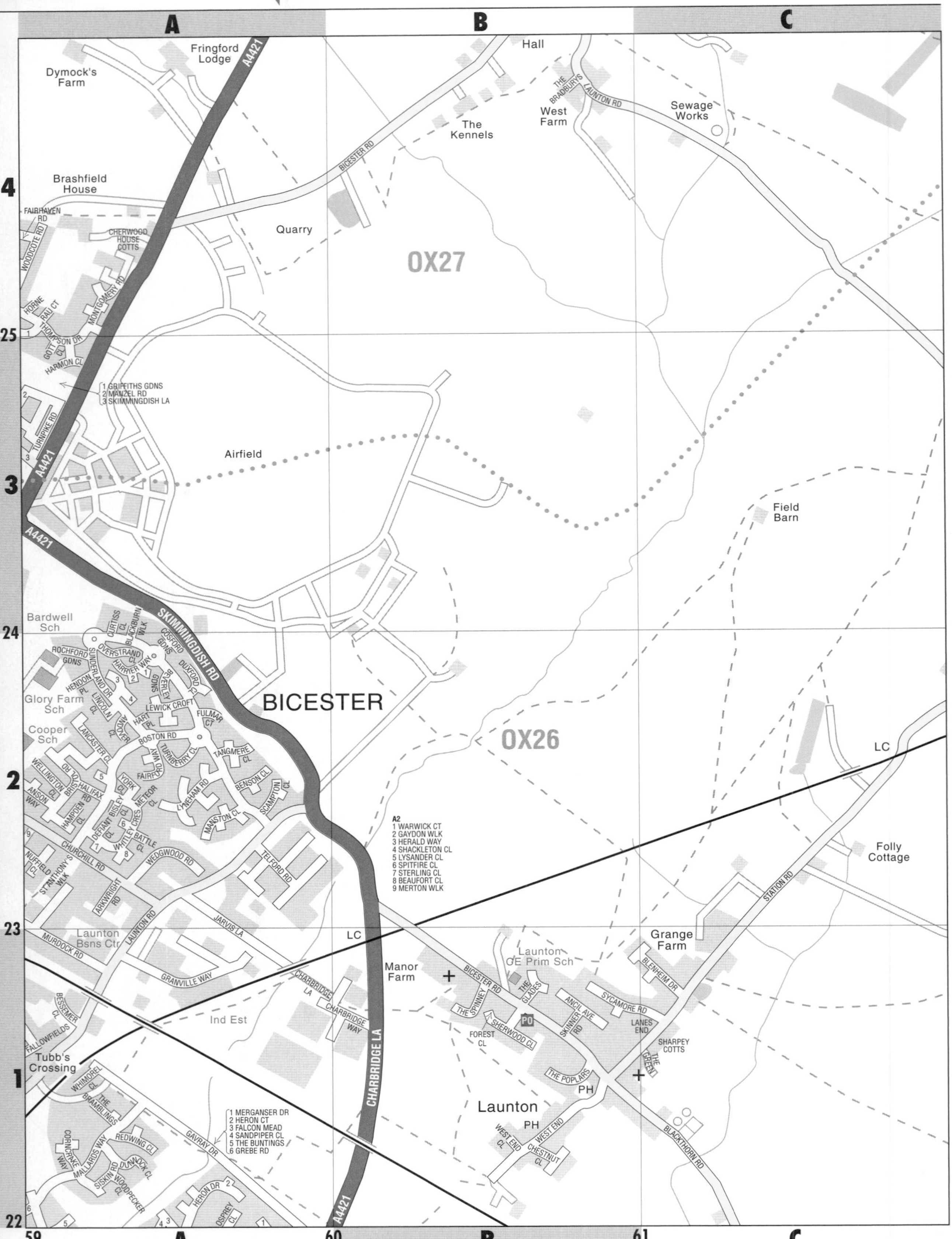

A   B   C

Fringford Lodge

Dymock's Farm

Hall

A4421

The Kennels

West Farm

Sewage Works

THE BRADBURYS

LAUNTON RD

4

Brashfield House

FAIRHAVEN RD

WOODCOTE RD

CHERWOOD HOUSE COTTS

Quarry

BICESTER RD

OX27

HORNE

HALL CT

MONTGOMERY RD

25

THOMPSON DR

GRITT

HARMON CL

1 GRIFFITHS GDNS
2 MANZEL RD
3 SKIMMINGDISH LA

Airfield

TURNPIKE RD

A4421

3

A4421

SKIMMINGDISH RD

Field Barn

Bardwell Sch

CURTISS

BLACKBURN WK

OSSFORD

GOSFORD

OVERSTRAND

DUZFORD

ROCHFORD GDNS

SUNDERLAND PL

HARRIER WAY

BRIERLEY

24

HENDON PL

LINCOLN

Glory Farm Sch

LANCASTER CL

LEWICK CROFT

HART

FULMAR CT

Cooper Sch

WELLINGTON CL

HAMPDEN

DEFIANT

BISLEY

YORK

BOSTON RD

TURNBURY CL

AVRO WAY

TANGMERE CL

BICESTER

HALIFAX

FAIRPLAY

METEOR

BATTLE

LYNEHAM RD

SCAMPTON

BENSON CL

OX26

ANSON WAY

WHITLE CRES

MANSTON CL

LC

CHURCHILL RD

WEDGWOOD RD

TELFORD RD

NUFFIELD CL

STANTON WK

FAIRWRIGHT RD

Folly Cottage

STATION RD

A2
1 WARWICK CT
2 GAYDON WLK
3 HERALD WAY
4 SHACKLETON CL
5 LYSANDER CL
6 SPITFIRE CL
7 STERLING CL
8 BEAUFORT CL
9 MERTON WLK

Grange Farm

23

MURDOCK RD

JARVIS LA

LC

Launton CE Prim Sch

BLENHEIM DR

Launton Bsns Ctr

LAUNTON RD

GRANVILLE WAY

Manor Farm

BICESTER RD

SYCAMORE RD

ANCIL AVE

BESSEMER CL

CHARBRIDGE LA

Ind Est

CHARBRIDGE WAY

THE SPINNEY

THE GLEBES

PO

SKINNER RD

LANES END

SHARPEY COTTS

2

FALLOWFIELDS

FOREST CL

SHERWOOD CL

THE GREEN

1

Tubb's Crossing

WITHMERE CL

THE BRAMBLINGS

GAVRAY DR

CHARBRIDGE LA

THE POPLARS

PH

+

Launton

PH

WEST END

BLACKTHORN RD

WHIMBREL

1 MERGANSER DR
2 HERON CT
3 FALCON MEAD
4 SANDPIPER CL
5 THE BUNTINGS
6 GREBE RD

REDWING CL

CORMORANT WAY

MALLARDS WAY

SISKIN RD

DUNNOCK CL

WOODPECKER

HERON DR

OSPREY CL

WEST END CL

CHESTNUT CL

A4421

22

59   A   60   B   61   C

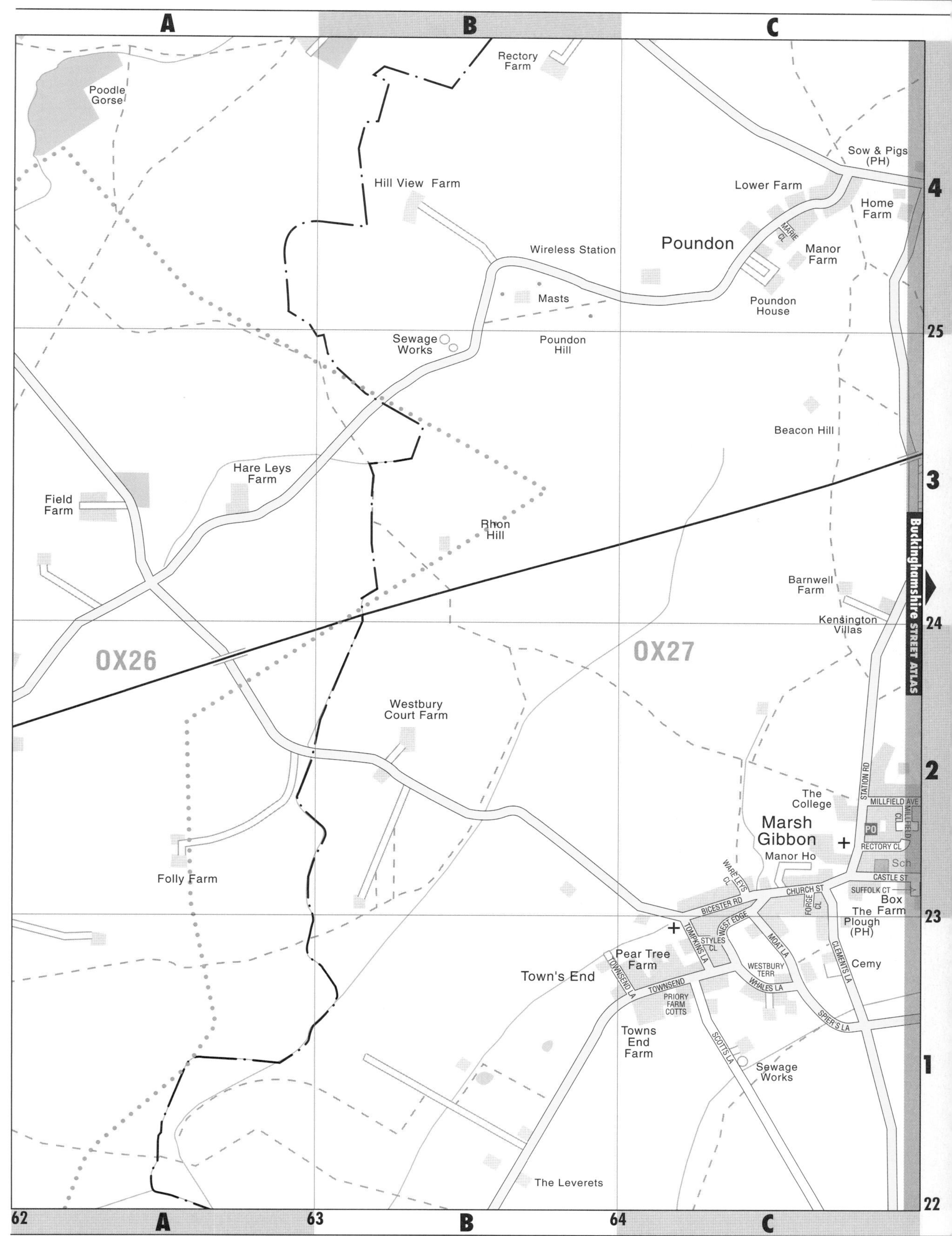

A B C

Poodle Gorse

Rectory Farm

Hill View Farm

Sow & Pigs (PH)

Lower Farm

Home Farm

Poundon

Wireless Station

Manor Farm

Masts

Poundon House

4

Sewage Works

Poundon Hill

25

Beacon Hill

Hare Leys Farm

3

Field Farm

Rhon Hill

Barnwell Farm

Kensington Villas

OX26

OX27

24

Westbury Court Farm

2

The College

MILLFIELD AVE

STATION RD

Marsh Gibbon

PO

RECTORY CL

Folly Farm

Manor Ho

Sch

CASTLE ST

WARE LEYS CL

CHURCH ST

SUFFOLK CT

Box The Farm

BICESTER RD

FORGE CL

Plough (PH)

23

Pear Tree Farm

STYLES CL

TOMPKINS LA

MOAT LA

WESTBURY TERR

Cemy

CLEMENTS LA

Town's End

TOWNSEND LA

TOWNSEND

WHALES LA

SPER'S LA

PRIORY FARM COTTS

Towns End Farm

SCOTTS LA

Sewage Works

1

The Leverets

22

62 A 63 B 64 C

Buckinghamshire STREET ATLAS

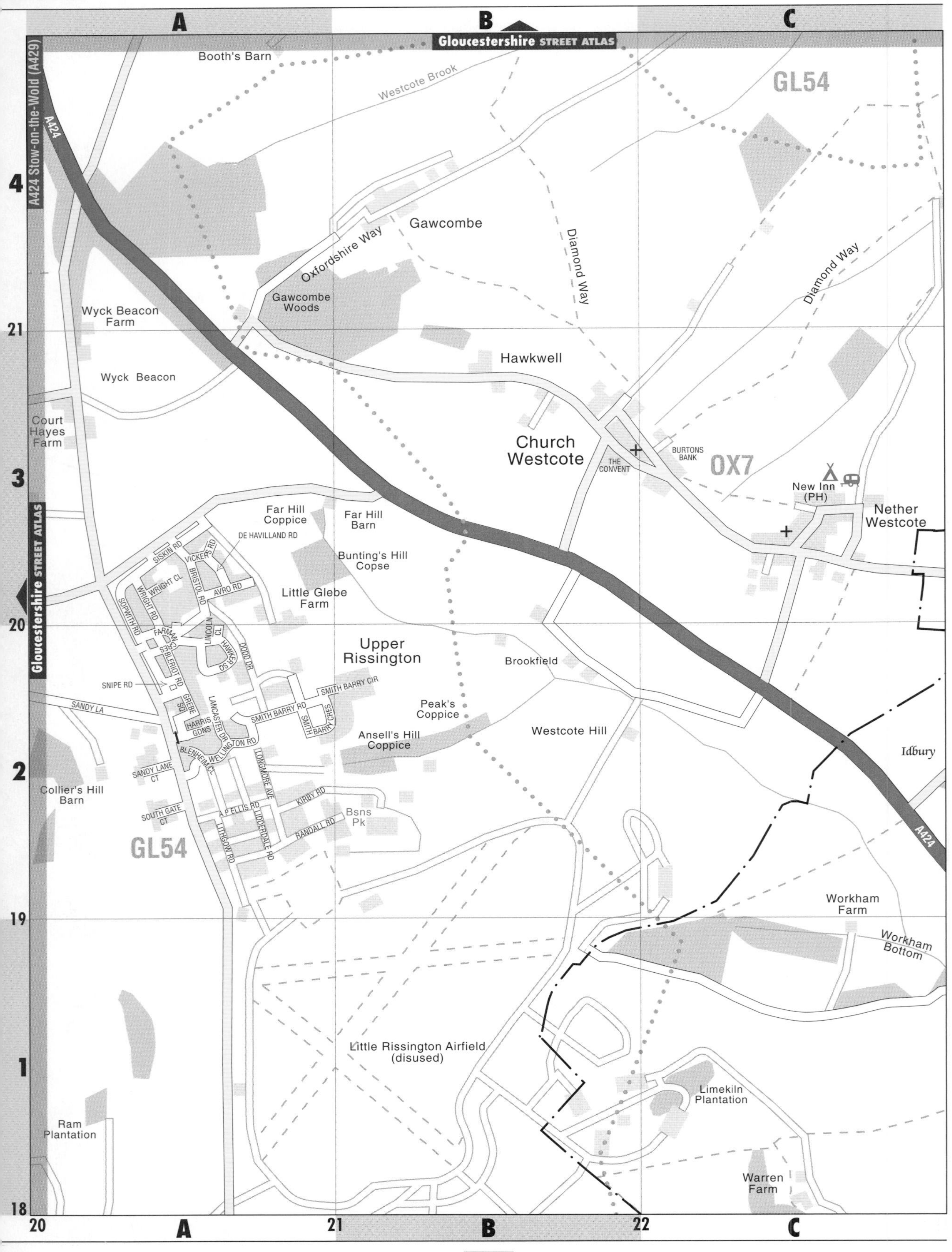

GL54

A424 Stow-on-the-Wold (A429)

A424

Booth's Barn

Westcote Brook

Gawcombe

Oxfordshire Way

Gawcombe Woods

Diamond Way

Diamond Way

Wyck Beacon Farm

Wyck Beacon

Hawkwell

Court Hayes Farm

Church Westcote

THE CONVENT

BURTONS BANK

OX7

New Inn (PH)

Nether Westcote

Gloucestershire STREET ATLAS

Far Hill Coppice

Far Hill Barn

DE HAVILLAND RD

SISKIN RD

VICKER? RD

BRISTOL RD

AVRO RD

WRIGHT CL

Bunting's Hill Copse

Little Glebe Farm

SOPWITH RD

FARMAN

N TOMLIN CL

HAWKS RD

SELFRIDGE RD

DOUG DR

Upper Rissington

Brookfield

SNIPE RD

SANDY LA

GREBE SQ

LANCASTER DR

SMITH BARRY RD

SMITH BARRY CRES

SMITH BARRY CIR

Peak's Coppice

Westcote Hill

Idbury

HARRIS GDNS

BLENHEIM CL

WELLINGTON RD

LONGMORE AVE

Ansell's Hill Coppice

Collier's Hill Barn

SANDY LANE CT

SOUTH GATE CT

A P ELLIS RD

LIDDERDALE RD

KIRBY RD

RANDALL RD

Bsns Pk

LITHGOW RD

GL54

A424

Workham Farm

Workham Bottom

Little Rissington Airfield (disused)

Limekiln Plantation

Ram Plantation

Warren Farm

20 A 21 B 22 C

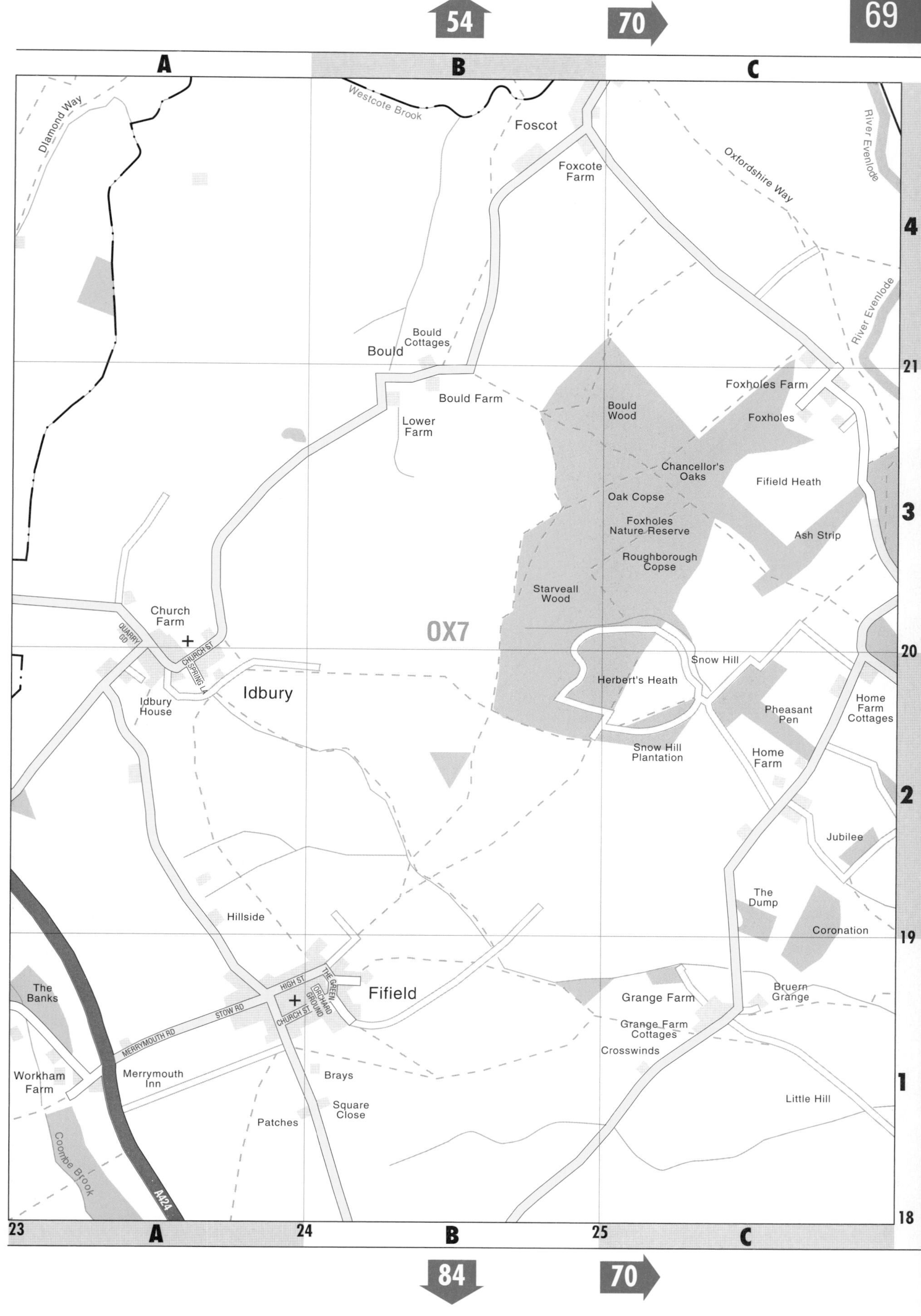

A   B   C

Diamond Way

Westcote Brook

Foscot

Foxcote
Farm

Oxfordshire Way

River Evenlode

4

River Evenlode

Bould
Cottages

Bould

21

Bould Farm

Bould
Wood

Foxholes Farm

Foxholes

Lower
Farm

Chancellor's
Oaks

Fifield Heath

Oak Copse

Foxholes
Nature Reserve

Ash Strip

3

Roughborough
Copse

Starveall
Wood

OX7

Church
Farm

Snow Hill

QUARRY RD

CHURCH ST

Herbert's Heath

Pheasant
Pen

Home Farm
Cottages

20

SPRING LA

Idbury

Snow Hill
Plantation

Home
Farm

Idbury
House

Jubilee

2

The
Dump

Coronation

Hillside

19

High St

The Green

Stow Rd

Fifield

Orchard Ground

Grange Farm

Bruern
Grange

The
Banks

Merrymouth Rd

Church St

Grange Farm
Cottages

Crosswinds

Workham
Farm

Merrymouth
Inn

Brays

Little Hill

1

Patches

Square
Close

Coombe Brook

A424

23   A   24   B   25   C

18

69
55

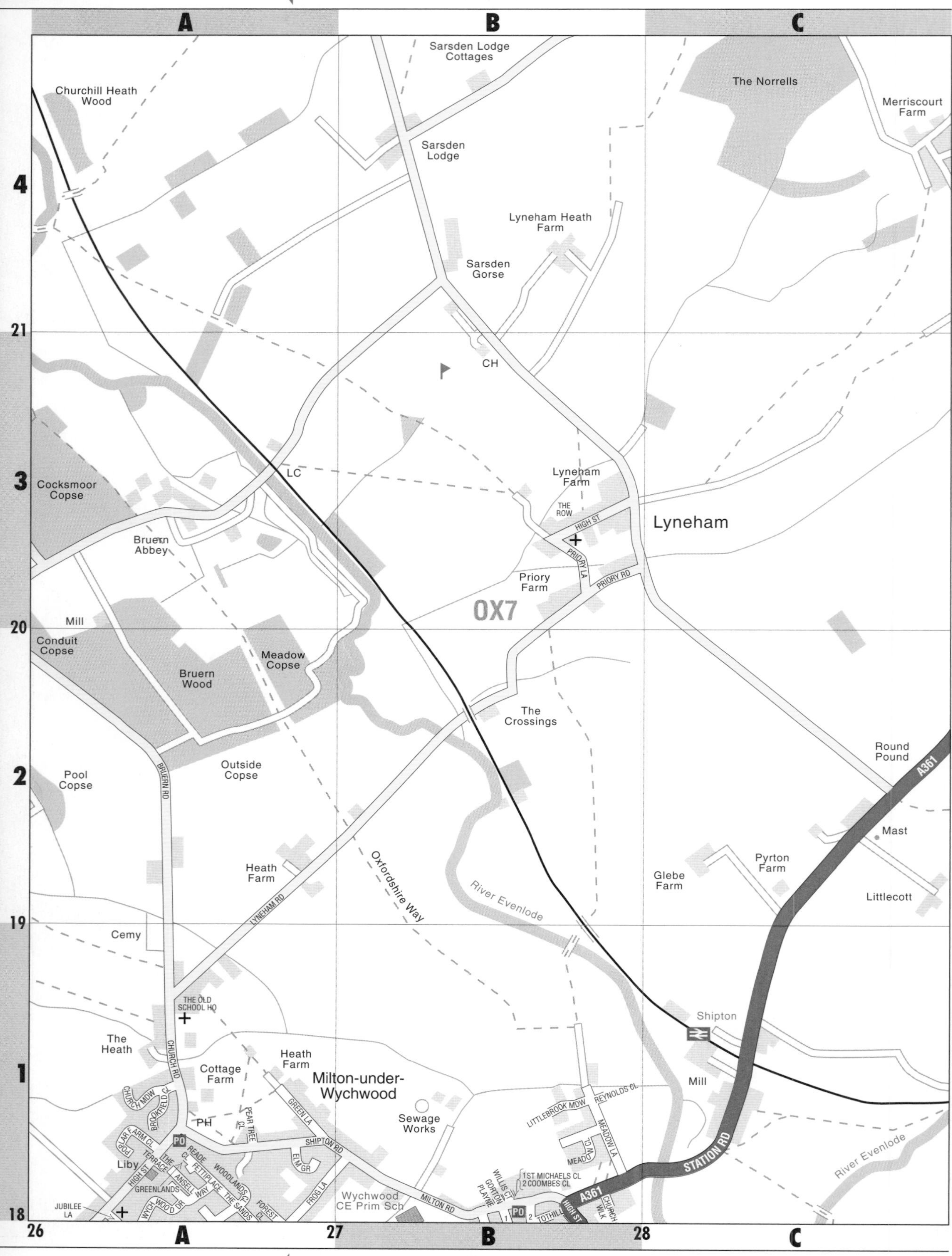
A
B
C
4
3
2
1
21
20
19
18
26
27
28
Churchill Heath Wood
Sarsden Lodge Cottages
The Norrells
Merriscourt Farm
Sarsden Lodge
Lyneham Heath Farm
Sarsden Gorse
CH
LC
Cocksmoor Copse
Lyneham Farm
THE ROW
HIGH ST
Lyneham
Bruern Abbey
PRIORY LA
PRIORY RD
Priory Farm
OX7
Mill
Conduit Copse
Meadow Copse
Bruern Wood
The Crossings
Round Pound
A361
Outside Copse
Pool Copse
BRUERN RD
Mast
Heath Farm
Oxfordshire Way
Pyrton Farm
Glebe Farm
Littlecott
River Evenlode
LYNEHAM RD
Cemy
THE OLD SCHOOL HO
Shipton
The Heath
CHURCH RD
Cottage Farm
Heath Farm
Milton-under-Wychwood
Mill
REYNOLDS CL
CHURCH MDW
BROOKFIELD CL
PH
PEAR TREE CL
GREEN LA
Sewage Works
LITTLEBROOK MDW
MEADOW LA
POPLAR FARM CL
PO
THE CL
READE
SHIPTON RD
ELM GR
MEADOW CL
STATION RD
Liby
HIGH ST
TERRACE
PETTIPLACE
WOODLANDS
ANSELL WAY
GREENLANDS
THE SANDS
FOREST CL
FROG LA
WILLIS CT
GORTON PLAYNE
1 ST MICHAELS CL
2 COOMBES CL
River Evenlode
JUBILEE LA
WYCH WOOD DR
Wychwood CE Prim Sch
MILTON RD
PO
TOTHILL
HIGH ST
A361
CHURCH WLK

69
85

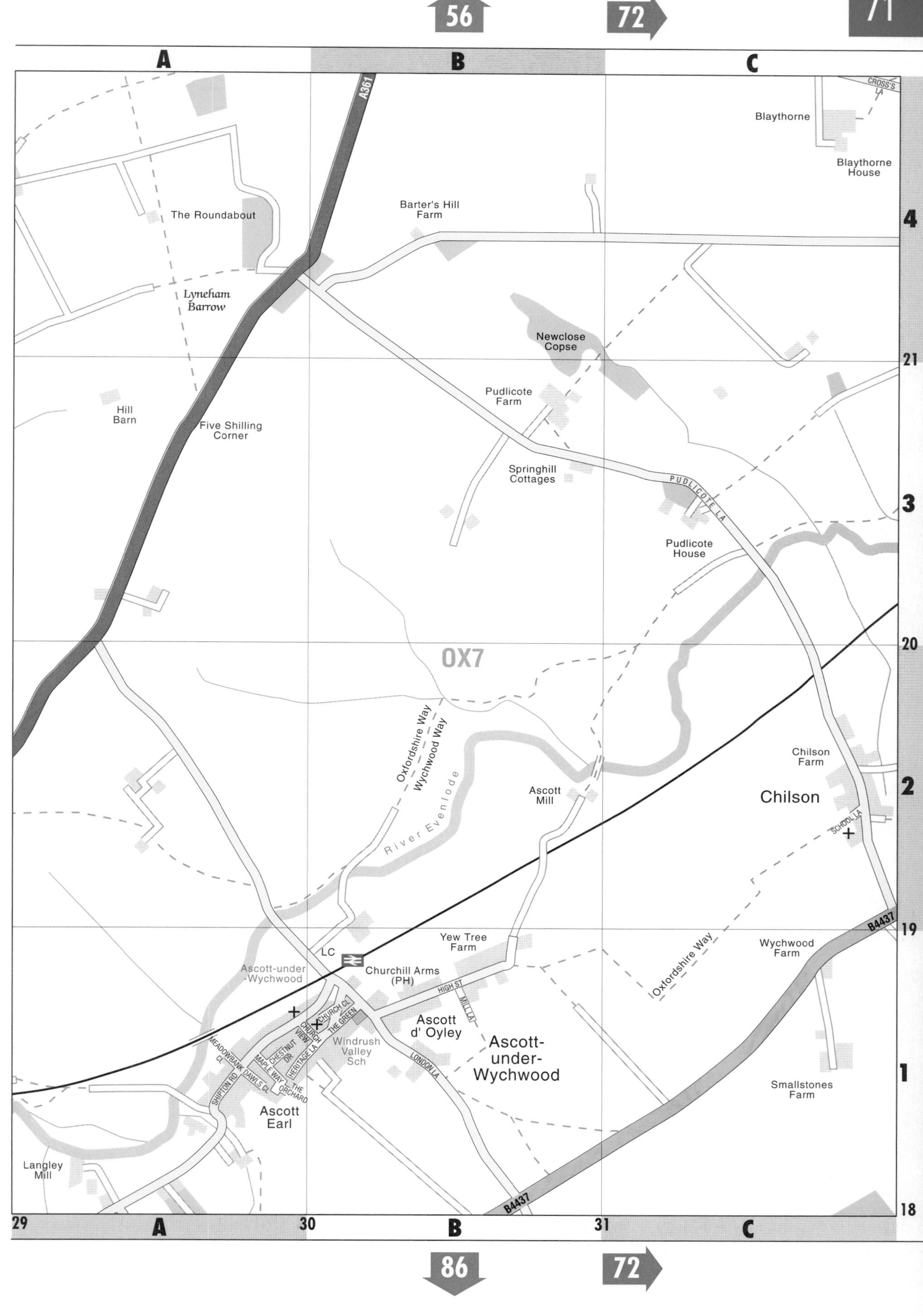
56
72
A
B
C
A361
The Roundabout
Barter's Hill Farm
Blaythorne
Blaythorne House
CROSS'S LA
4
Lyneham Barrow
Newclose Copse
21
Hill Barn
Five Shilling Corner
Pudlicote Farm
Springhill Cottages
PUDLICOTE LA
3
Pudlicote House
20
OX7
Oxfordshire Way
Wychwood Way
River Evenlode
Ascott Mill
Chilson Farm
Chilson
2
SCHOOL LA
19
B4437
Yew Tree Farm
Wychwood Farm
Oxfordshire Way
LC
Ascott-under-Wychwood
Churchill Arms (PH)
HIGH ST
MILL LA
CHURCH CL
THE GREEN
CHURCH VIEW
CHESTNUT DR
MAPLE WAY
HERITAGE LA
MEADOWBANK CL
DAWLS CL
THE ORCHARD
SHIPTON RD
LONDON LA
Windrush Valley Sch
Ascott d' Oyley
Ascott-under-Wychwood
Ascott Earl
1
Smallstones Farm
Langley Mill
B4437
18
29
30
31
A
B
C
86
72

71
57

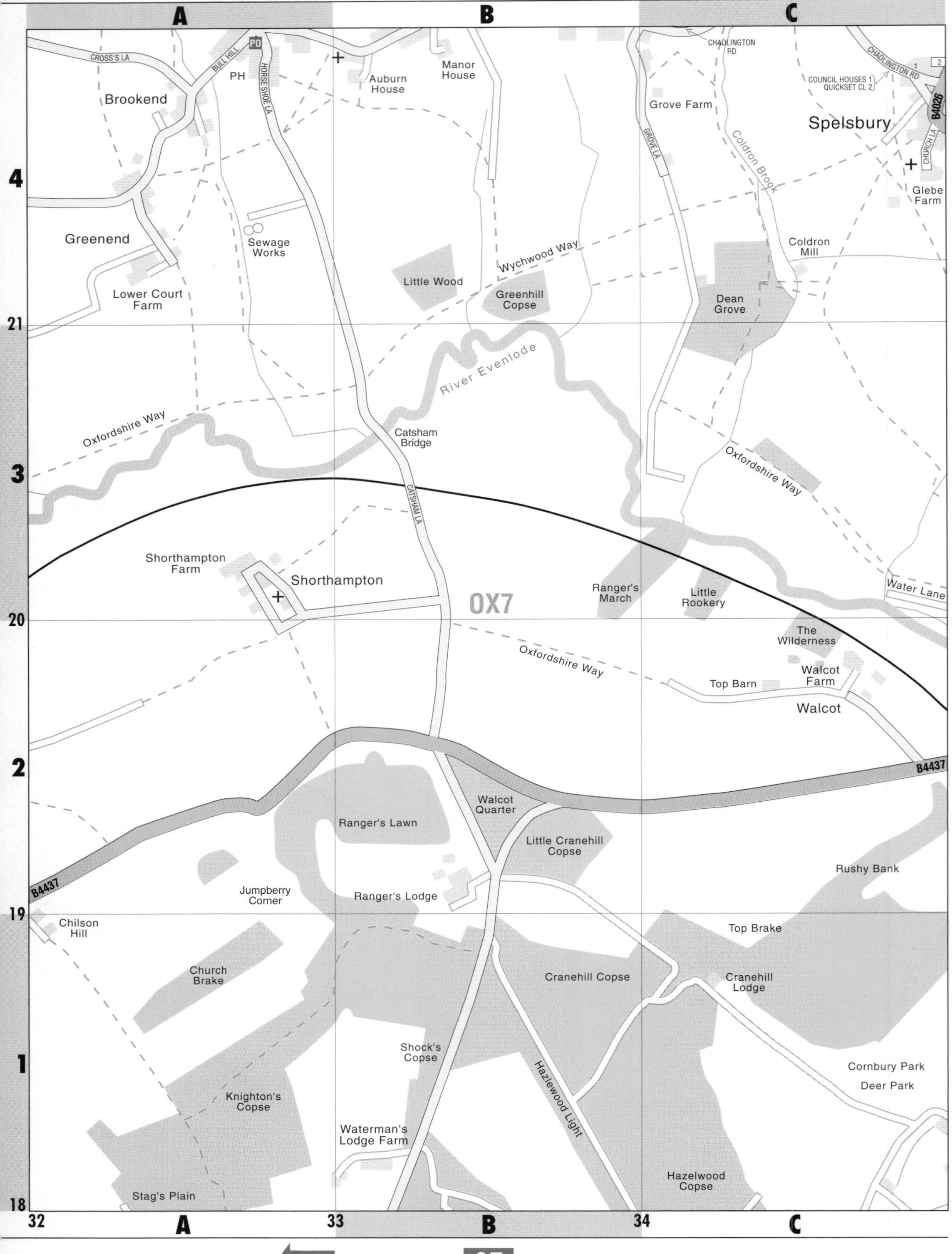
A
B
C
4
21
3
20
2
19
1
18
32
33
34
CROSS'S LA
BULL HILL
PO
PH
HORSE SHOE LA
Brookend
Auburn House
Manor House
CHADLINGTON RD
CHADLINGTON RD
COUNCIL HOUSES 1
QUICKSET CL 2
Grove Farm
Spelsbury
B4026
GROVE LA
Coldron Brook
CHURCH LA
Glebe Farm
Greenend
Sewage Works
Wychwood Way
Coldron Mill
Little Wood
Greenhill Copse
Dean Grove
Lower Court Farm
River Evenlode
Oxfordshire Way
Catsham Bridge
Oxfordshire Way
CATSHAM LA
Shorthampton Farm
Shorthampton
OX7
Ranger's March
Little Rookery
Water Lane
The Wilderness
Oxfordshire Way
Walcot Farm
Top Barn
Walcot
B4437
Walcot Quarter
Ranger's Lawn
Little Cranehill Copse
Rushy Bank
B4437
Jumpberry Corner
Ranger's Lodge
Chilson Hill
Top Brake
Church Brake
Cranehill Copse
Cranehill Lodge
Shock's Copse
Hazlewood Light
Cornbury Park
Deer Park
Knighton's Copse
Waterman's Lodge Farm
Hazelwood Copse
Stag's Plain

71
87

58
74

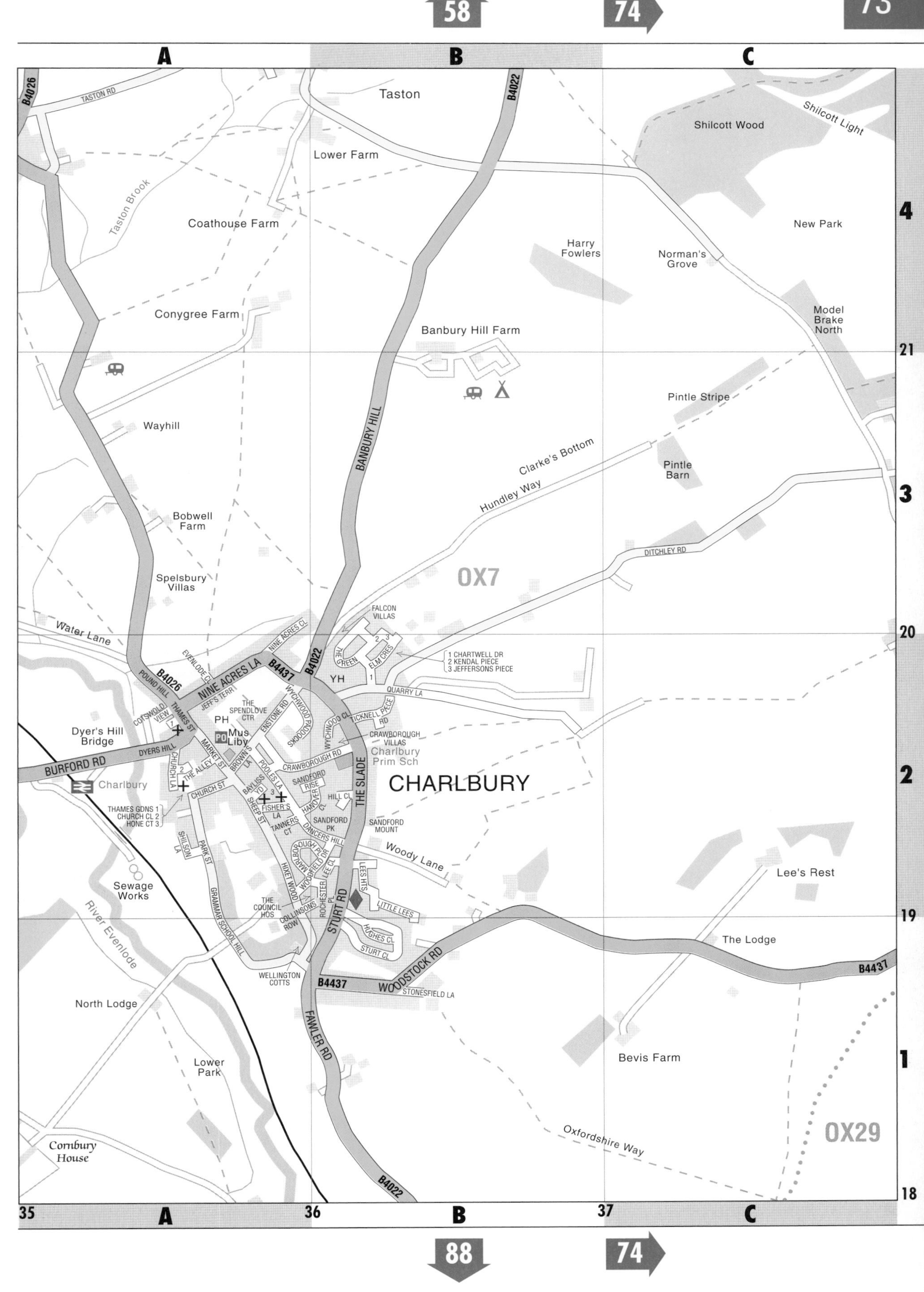
A
B
C
Taston
TASTON RD
B4026
B4022
Shilcott Wood
Shilcott Light
Lower Farm
Taston Brook
Coathouse Farm
New Park
Harry
Fowlers
Norman's
Grove
Conygree Farm
Banbury Hill Farm
Model
Brake
North
Wayhill
Pintle Stripe
BANBURY HILL
Clarke's Bottom
Pintle
Barn
Hundley Way
Bobwell
Farm
DITCHLEY RD
OX7
Spelsbury
Villas
FALCON
VILLAS
Water Lane
NINE ACRES CL
EVENLODE CL
B4026
NINE ACRES LA
B4437
B4022
THE GREEN
ELM CRES
1 CHARTWELL DR
2 KENDAL PIECE
3 JEFFERSONS PIECE
YH
QUARRY LA
POUND HILL
JEFF'S TERR
THE
SPENDLOVE
CTR
COTSWOLD
VIEW
THAMES ST
PH
ENSTONE RD
WYCHWOOD PADDOCKS
WYCHWOOD CL
TICKNELL PIECE
RD
Dyer's Hill
Bridge
Mus
Liby
CRAWBOROUGH
VILLAS
DYERS HILL
MARKET ST
BROWN'S
LA
Charlbury
Prim Sch
BURFORD RD
CHURCH LA
THE ALLEY
POOLES LA
CRAWBOROUGH RD
CHARLBURY
Charlbury
SANDFORD
RISE
THE SLADE
CHURCH ST
BAYLISS
YD
HILL CL
SHEEP ST
HANOVER
CT
THAMES GDNS 1
CHURCH CL 2
HONE CT 3
FISHER'S
LA
SANDFORD
PK
TANNERS
CT
SANDFORD
MOUNT
SHILSON
LA
PARK ST
DANCERS HILL
Woody Lane
MARLBOROUGH PL
Sewage
Works
WOODFIELD DR
LEE CL
LEES HTS
Lee's Rest
HIXET WOOD
River Evenlode
GRAMMAR SCHOOL HILL
THE
COUNCIL
HOS
ROCHESTER PL
STURT RD
LITTLE LEES
COLLINSONS
ROW
HUGHES CL
The Lodge
STURT CL
WOODSTOCK RD
B4437
WELLINGTON
COTTS
B4437
STONESFIELD LA
North Lodge
FAWLER RD
Lower
Park
Bevis Farm
Oxfordshire Way
OX29
Cornbury
House
B4022
4
21
3
20
2
19
1
18
35
36
37

88
74

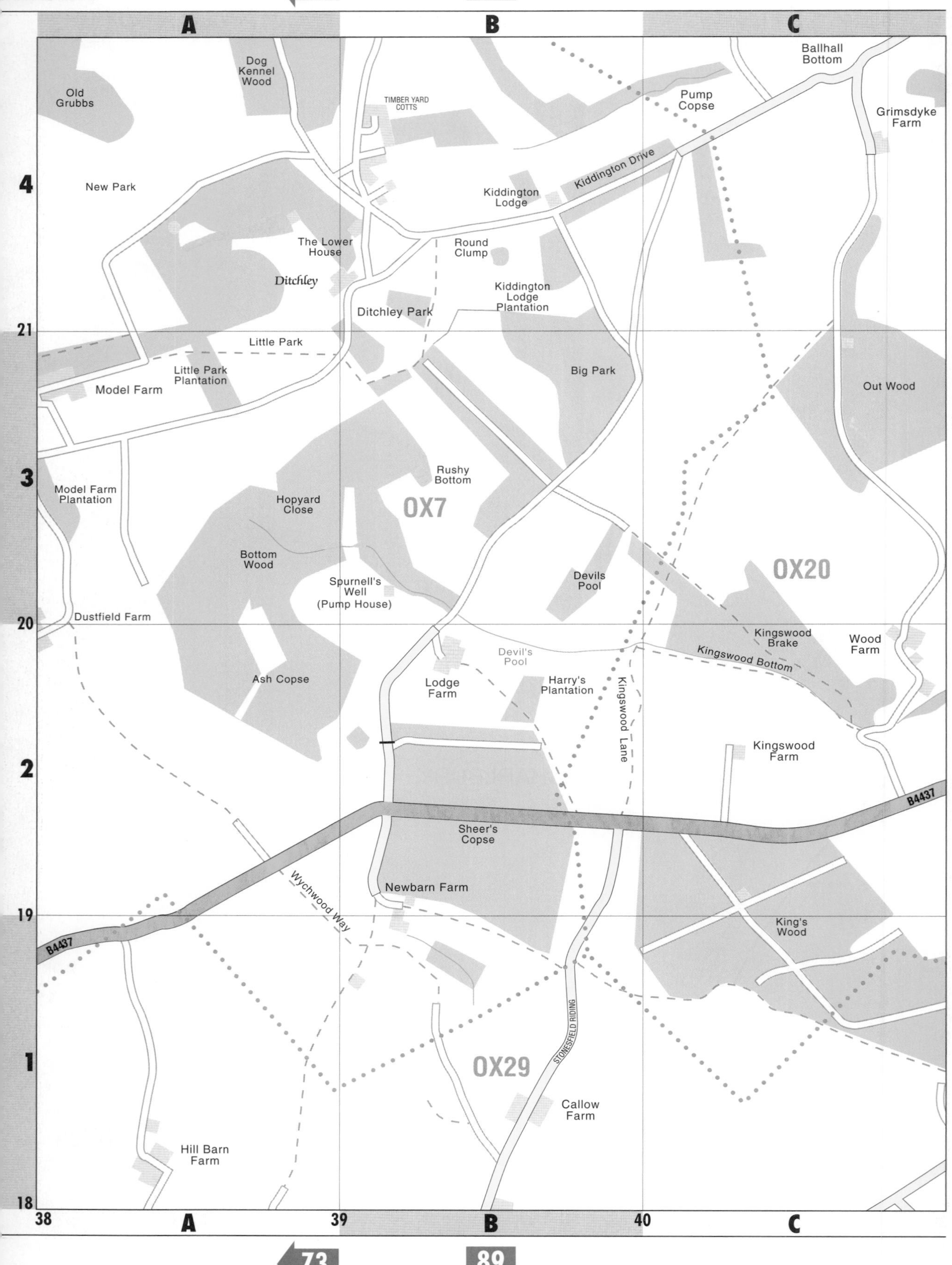

73
59

A   **B**   **C**

Ballhall
Bottom

Old
Grubbs

Dog
Kennel
Wood

TIMBER YARD
COTTS

Pump
Copse

Grimsdyke
Farm

4

New Park

Kiddington
Lodge

Kiddington Drive

The Lower
House

Round
Clump

Ditchley

Ditchley Park

Kiddington
Lodge
Plantation

21

Little Park

Big Park

Out Wood

Little Park
Plantation

Model Farm

3

Model Farm
Plantation

Hopyard
Close

Rushy
Bottom

OX7

OX20

Bottom
Wood

Devils
Pool

Spurnell's
Well
(Pump House)

20

Dustfield Farm

Kingswood
Brake

Wood
Farm

Ash Copse

Lodge
Farm

Devil's
Pool

Harry's
Plantation

Kingswood Bottom

Kingswood Lane

Kingswood
Farm

2

B4437

Sheer's
Copse

Wychwood Way

Newbarn Farm

King's
Wood

19

B4437

STONESFIELD RIDING

1

OX29

Callow
Farm

Hill Barn
Farm

18

38   **A**   39   **B**   40   **C**

73
89

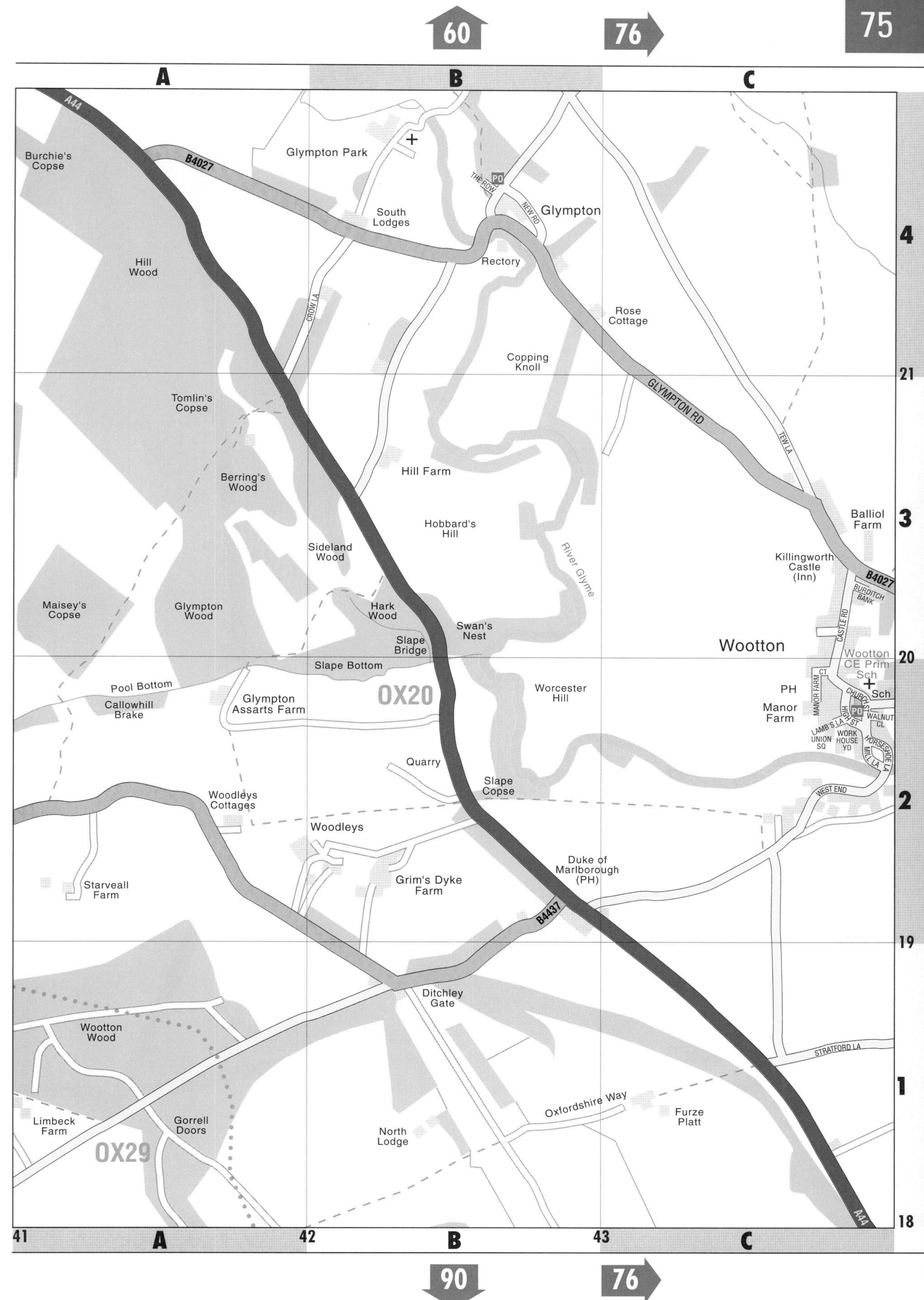
A
B
C
A44
B4027
Burchie's Copse
Glympton Park
South Lodges
THE ROW
PO
NEW RD
Glympton
Rectory
Hill Wood
CROW LA
Rose Cottage
Copping Knoll
GLYMPTON RD
Tomlin's Copse
TEW LA
Hill Farm
Berring's Wood
Hobbard's Hill
Balliol Farm
Sideland Wood
River Glyme
Killingworth Castle (Inn)
B4027
BURDITCH BANK
Maisey's Copse
Glympton Wood
Hark Wood
Swan's Nest
CASTLE RD
Slape Bridge
Wootton
Wootton CE Prim Sch
Slape Bottom
Pool Bottom
OX20
Worcester Hill
PH
MANOR FARM CT
CHURCH ST
Sch
Callowhill Brake
Glympton Assarts Farm
Manor Farm
HIGH ST
WALNUT CL
LAMB'S LA
UNION SQ
WORK HOUSE YD
HORSESHOE LA
MILL LA
Quarry
Slape Copse
WEST END
Woodleys Cottages
Woodleys
Duke of Marlborough (PH)
Starveall Farm
Grim's Dyke Farm
B4437
Ditchley Gate
Wootton Wood
STRATFORD LA
Oxfordshire Way
Furze Platt
Limbeck Farm
Gorrell Doors
North Lodge
OX29
4
21
3
20
2
19
1
18
41
42
43

75
61

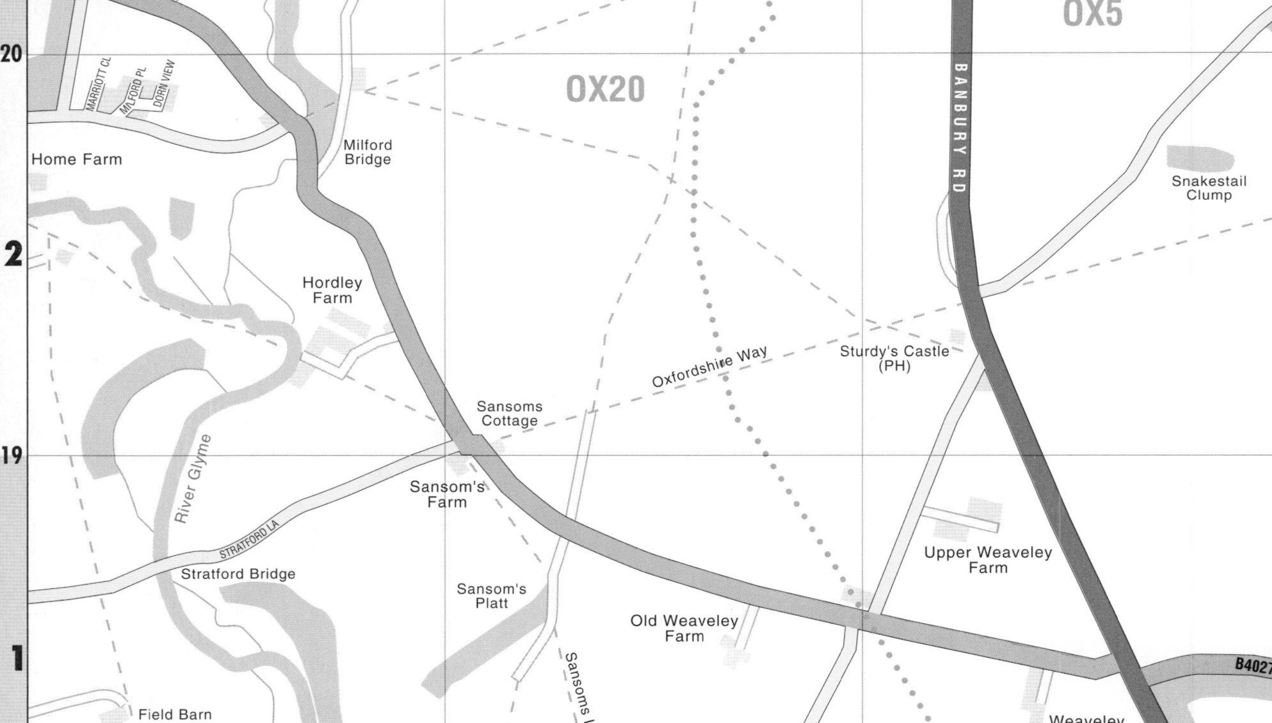

A   B   C

4

Woottondown Farm

Woottondown Cottages

Upper Dornford Farm

Upper Dornford Cottages

A4260

Tackley Heath

21

Old Man Leys Cottage

Old Man Leys

Holly Bank

River Dorn

Lower Dornford Farm

Dornford Lane

OX5

3

Dornford Grove

B4027

20

MARRIOTT CL

MILFORD PL

LODIN VIEW

OX20

BANBURY RD

Home Farm

Milford Bridge

Snakestail Clump

2

Hordley Farm

River Glyme

Oxfordshire Way

Sturdy's Castle (PH)

19

Sansoms Cottage

Sansom's Farm

Upper Weaveley Farm

STRATFORD LA

Stratford Bridge

Sansom's Platt

Sansoms Lane

Old Weaveley Farm

BANBURY RD

1

B4027

Field Barn

Weaveley Farm

Weaveley Furze

A4260

18

44   **A**   45   **B**   46   **C**

75
91

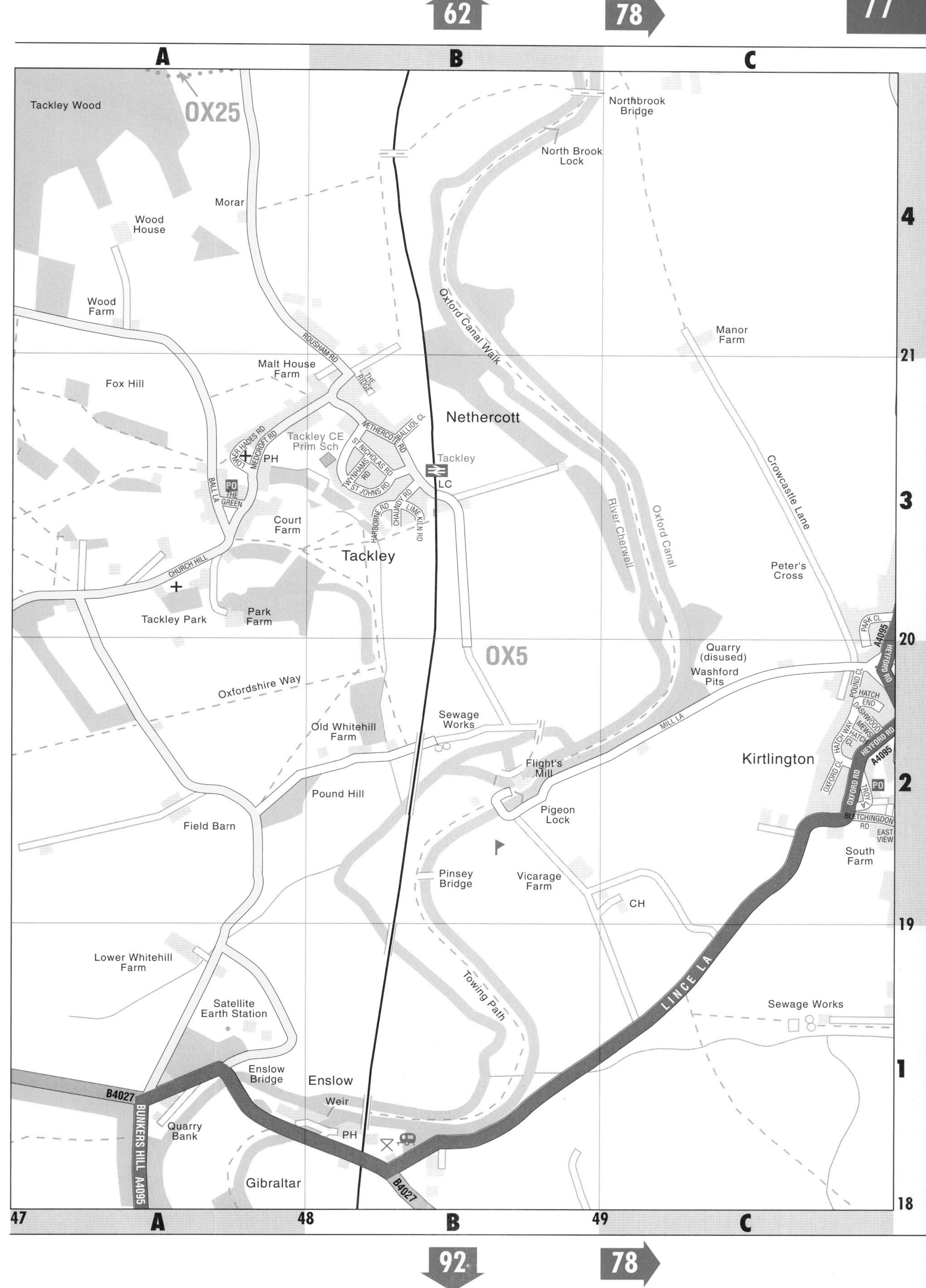

62
78

A B C

Tackley Wood

OX25

Morar

Wood House

North Brook Lock

Northbrook Bridge

Manor Farm

4

Wood Farm

ROUSHAM RD

Oxford Canal Walk

21

Fox Hill

Malt House Farm

THE RIDGE

Nethercott

Crowcastle Lane

LOWER HAYES RD

MEDCROFT RD

Tackley CE Prim Sch

NETHERCOTT RD

BALLIOL CL

Tackley

3

BALL LA

PH

PO

THE GREEN

WYNHAMS RD

ST NICHOLAS RD

ST JOHNS RD

HARBOURNE RD

CHINNEY RD

LIME KILN RD

LC

River Cherwell

Oxford Canal

Peter's Cross

Court Farm

Tackley

CHURCH HILL

Tackley Park

Park Farm

PARK CL

A4095

HEYFORD RD

20

OX5

Quarry (disused)

Washford Pits

Oxfordshire Way

POUND CL

HATCH END

DASHWOOD

Old Whitehill Farm

Sewage Works

MILL LA

Kirtlington

HATCH WAY

HATCH CL

MEWS

HEYFORD RD

2

Pound Hill

Flight's Mill

OXFORD CL

OXFORD RD

TROY CL

PO

Field Barn

Pigeon Lock

Vicarage Farm

BLETCHINGDON RD

EAST VIEW

South Farm

CH

Pinsey Bridge

19

Lower Whitehill Farm

Towing Path

LINCE LA

Sewage Works

Satellite Earth Station

B4027

BUNKERS HILL A4095

Enslow Bridge

Enslow

Weir

1

Quarry Bank

PH

Gibraltar

B4027

18

47 48 A 49 B C

A
B
C

Hoarstone
Spinney

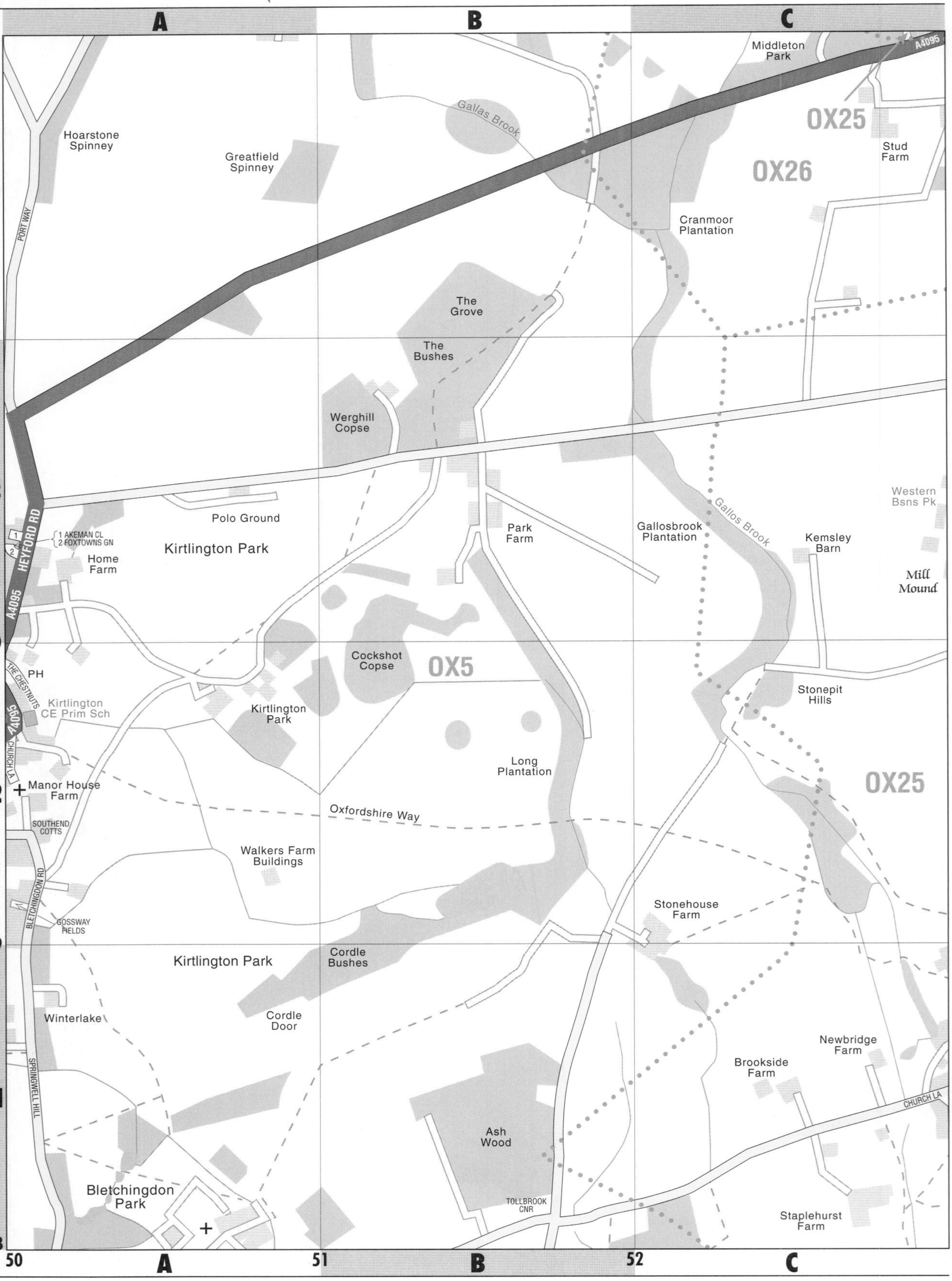

Greatfield
Spinney

Gallas Brook

Middleton
Park

OX25

OX26

Stud
Farm

4

Cranmoor
Plantation

The
Grove

21

The
Bushes

Werghill
Copse

Gallos Brook

3

Polo Ground

Western
Bsns Pk

PORT WAY

HEYFORD RD

1 AKEMAN CL
2 FOXTOWNS GN

Kirtlington Park

Park
Farm

Gallosbrook
Plantation

Kemsley
Barn

Mill
Mound

Home
Farm

A-4095

20

PH

THE CHESTNUTS

A-4095

CHURCH LA

Kirtlington
CE Prim Sch

Kirtlington
Park

Cockshot
Copse

OX5

Stonepit
Hills

Long
Plantation

OX25

2

Manor House
Farm

Oxfordshire Way

SOUTHEND
COTTS

Walkers Farm
Buildings

Stonehouse
Farm

BLETCHINGDON RD

GOSSWAY
FIELDS

19

Kirtlington Park

Cordle
Bushes

Winterlake

Cordle
Door

Brookside
Farm

Newbridge
Farm

SPRINGWELL HILL

CHURCH LA

1

Ash
Wood

Bletchingdon
Park

TOLLBROOK
CNR

Staplehurst
Farm

18
50
A
51
B
52
C

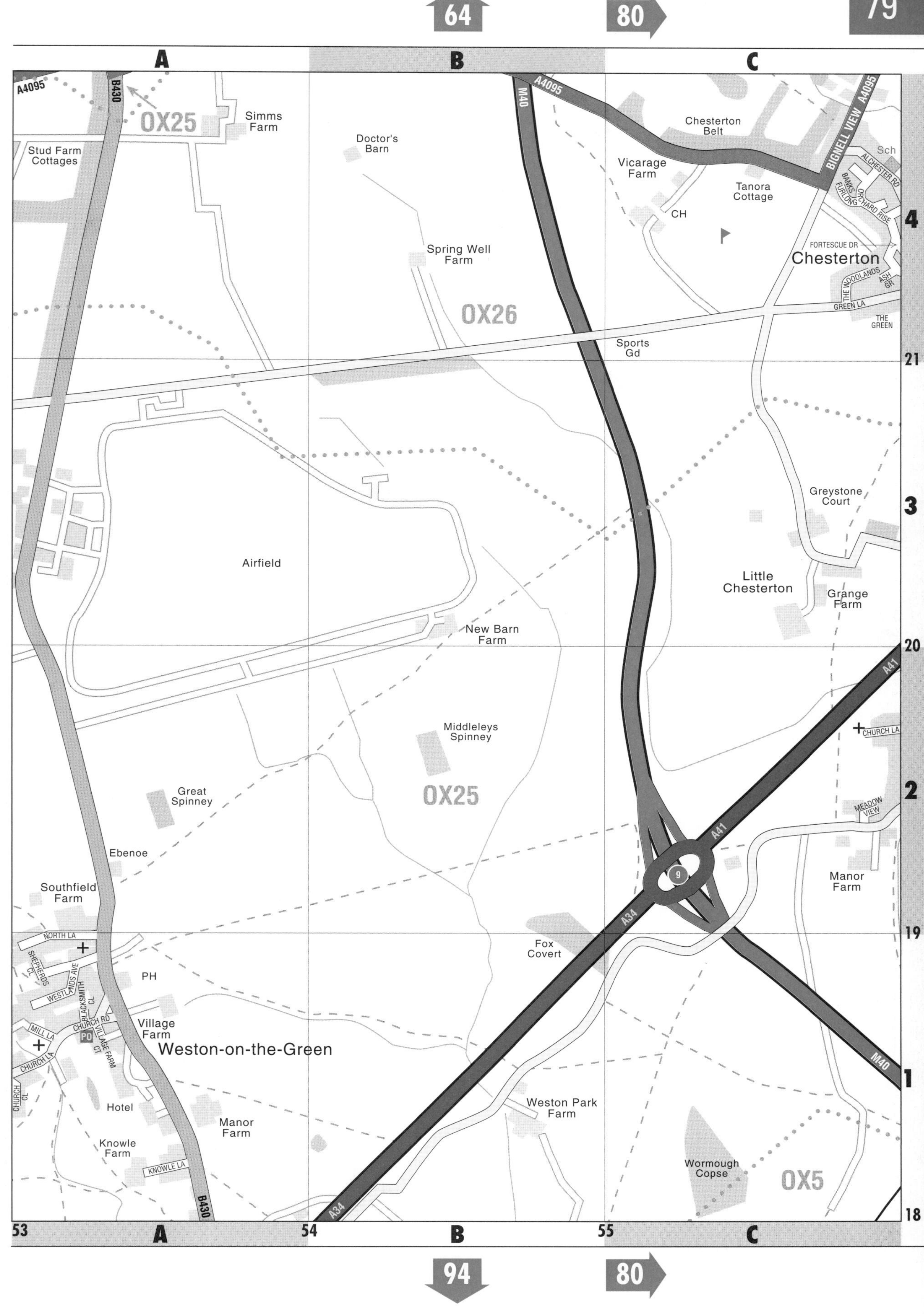
64
80
A
B
C
A4095
B430
OX25
Simms Farm
Stud Farm Cottages
Doctor's Barn
M40
A4095
Chesterton Belt
BIGNELL VIEW A4095
Sch
Vicarage Farm
Tanora Cottage
ALCHESTER RD
BANKS FURLONG
ORCHARD RISE
CH
FORTESCUE DR
Chesterton
THE WOODLANDS
ASH GR
GREEN LA
THE GREEN
Spring Well Farm
OX26
Sports Gd
Airfield
Greystone Court
Little Chesterton
Grange Farm
New Barn Farm
A41
CHURCH LA
Middleleys Spinney
OX25
Great Spinney
MEADOW VIEW
A41
Ebenoe
9
Manor Farm
Southfield Farm
A34
NORTH LA
SHEPHERDS CL
WESTLANDS AVE
BLACKSMITH CL
PH
Fox Covert
MILL LA
CHURCH RD
PO
VILLAGE FARM CT
Village Farm
Weston-on-the-Green
CHURCH LA
CHURCH CL
M40
Hotel
Weston Park Farm
Manor Farm
Knowle Farm
KNOWLE LA
Wormough Copse
OX5
B430
A34
4
21
3
20
2
19
1
18
53
A
54
B
55
C
94
80

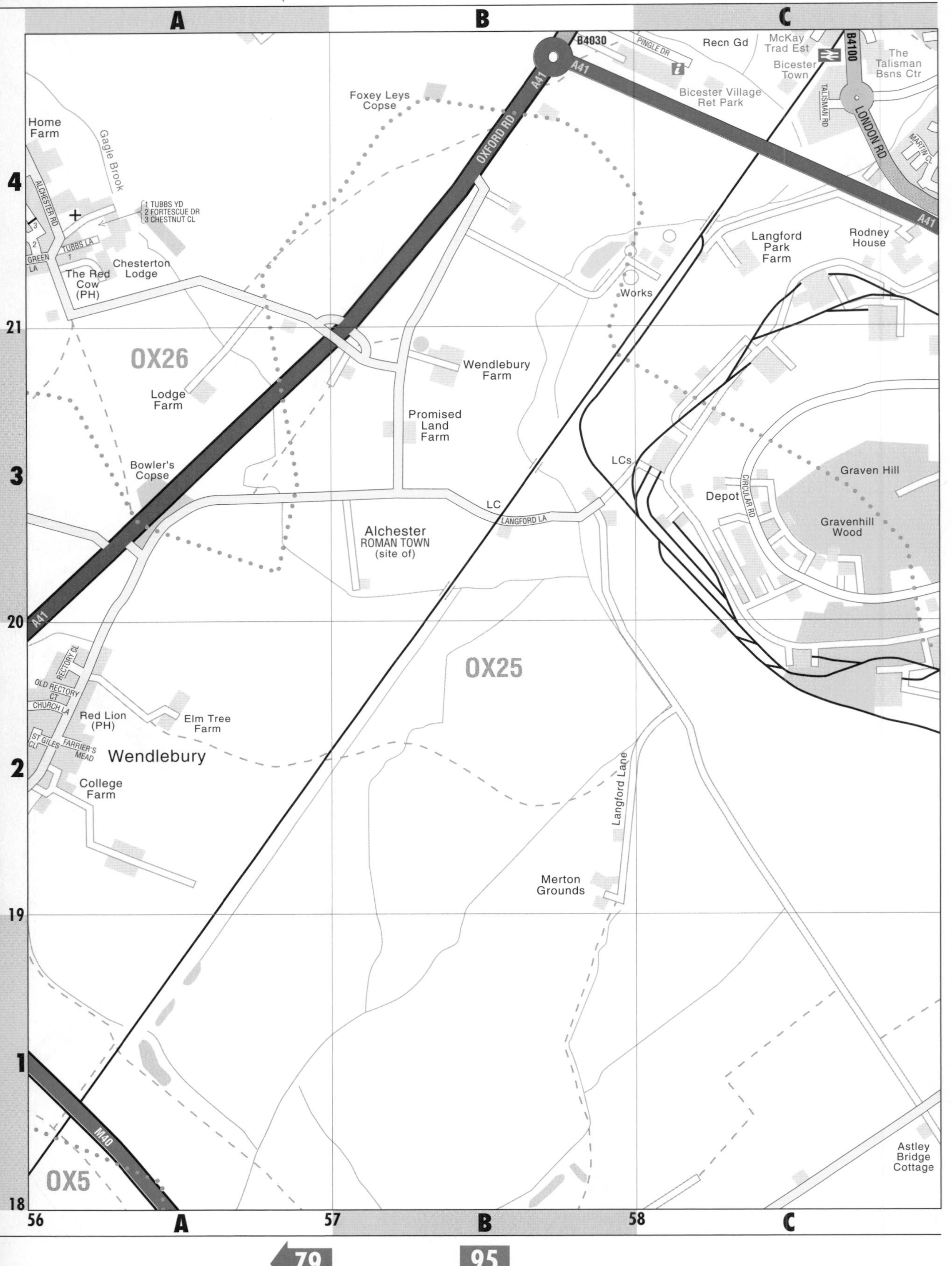

79
65

A
B
C

B4030
PINGLE DR
Recn Gd
McKay
Trad Est
Bicester
Town
The
Talisman
Bsns Ctr
B4100

A41
A41

Foxey Leys
Copse
OXFORD RD
Bicester Village
Ret Park
TALISMAN RD
LONDON RD
MARTIN CT

Home
Farm
Gagle Brook
Works
Langford
Park
Farm
Rodney
House

4

ALCHESTER RD
1 TUBBS YD
2 FORTESCUE DR
3 CHESTNUT CL
GREEN LA
TUBBS LA
The Red
Cow
(PH)
Chesterton
Lodge

21

OX26
Wendlebury
Farm

Lodge
Farm
Promised
Land
Farm
LCs
CIRCULAR RD
Graven Hill

3

Bowler's
Copse
LC
LANGFORD LA
Depot
Gravenhill
Wood

Alchester
ROMAN TOWN
(site of)

20

A41
OX25

RECTORY CL
OLD RECTORY
CT
CHURCH LA
Red Lion
(PH)
Elm Tree
Farm

ST GILES
CL
FARRIER'S
MEAD
Wendlebury

Langford Lane

2

College
Farm

19

Merton
Grounds

1

M40

Astley
Bridge
Cottage

OX5

18

56
A
57
B
58
C

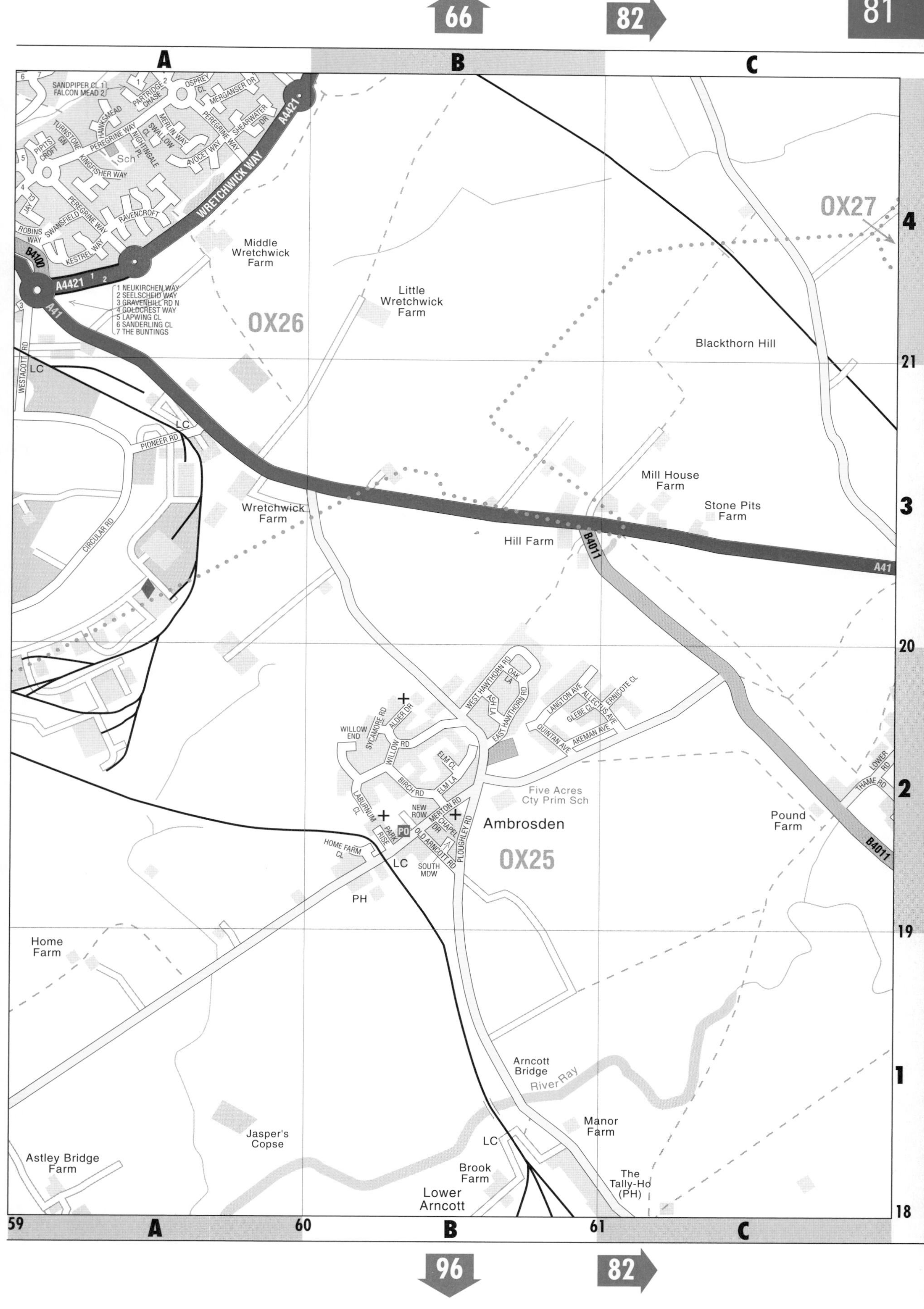

WRETCHWICK WAY

A4421

B100

A4421

A41

WESTACOTT RD

LC

1 NEUKIRCHEN WAY
2 SEELSCHEID WAY
3 GRAVENHILL RD N
4 GOLDCREST WAY
5 LAPWING CL
6 SANDERLING CL
7 THE BUNTINGS

SANDPIPER CL 1
FALCON MEAD 2

PARTRIDGE CHASE

OSPREY CL

MERGANSER DR

MERLIN WAY

SHEARWATER

PEREGRINE WAY

SWALLOW

NIGHTINGALE

AVOCET WAY

PEREGRINE WAY

RAVENCROFT

Sch

TURNSTONE GR

HAWKSMEAD

PIPITS CROFT

KINGFISHER WAY

JAY CL

ROBINS WAY

SWANSFIELD WAY

PEREGRINE WAY

KESTREL WAY

Middle
Wretchwick
Farm

OX26

Little
Wretchwick
Farm

Blackthorn Hill

OX27

21

PIONEER RD

CIRCULAR RD

LC

LC

Wretchwick
Farm

Mill House
Farm

Stone Pits
Farm

Hill Farm

B4011

A41

3

20

WEST HAWTHORN RD

EAST HAWTHORN RD

LANGTON AVE

ALLECTUS AVE

GERNICOTE CL

GLEBE CL

QUINTAN AVE

AKEMAN AVE

SYCAMORE RD

ALDER DR

WILLOW RD

WILLOW END

ELM CL

ELM LA

BIRCH RD

LABURNUM CL

NEW ROW

MERTON RD

CHAPEL RD

OLD ARNCOTT RD

PLOUGHLEY RD

PARK RISE

PO

Five Acres
Cty Prim Sch

Ambrosden

OX25

HOME FARM CL

LC

SOUTH
MDW

PH

Pound
Farm

LOWER THAME RD

B4011

2

Home
Farm

19

Jasper's
Copse

Astley Bridge
Farm

Arncott
Bridge

River Ray

LC

Manor
Farm

Brook
Farm

Lower
Arncott

The
Tally-Ho
(PH)

1

18

A   B   C

← OX26

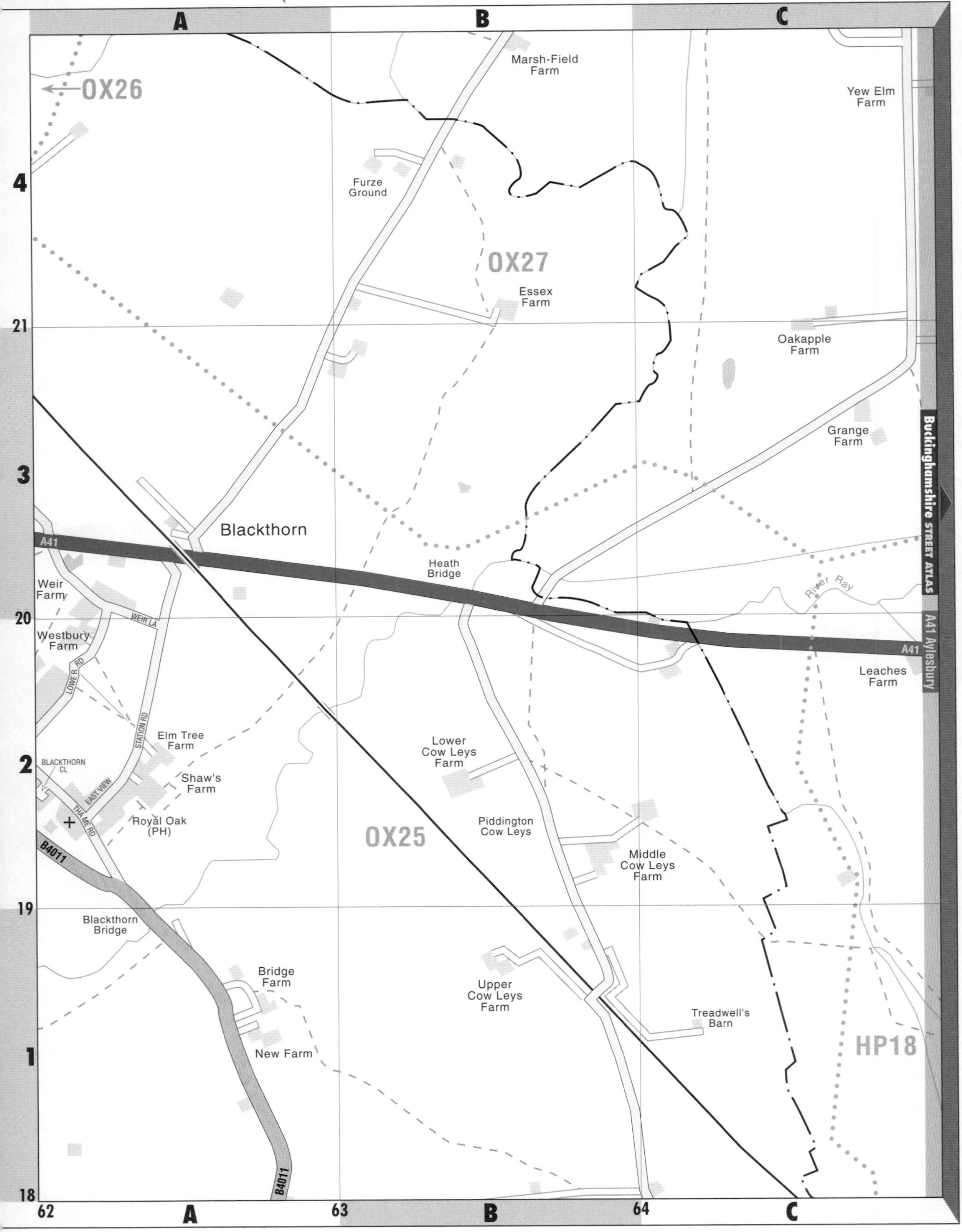

OX27

Marsh-Field
Farm

Yew Elm
Farm

Furze
Ground

Essex
Farm

Oakapple
Farm

Grange
Farm

4

21

3

A41

Blackthorn

Heath
Bridge

Weir
Farm

WEIR LA

Westbury
Farm

River Ray

A41

A41 Aylesbury

20

LOWER RD

STATION RD

Elm Tree
Farm

EAST VIEW

BLACKTHORN
CL

Shaw's
Farm

Lower
Cow Leys
Farm

Leaches
Farm

2

THAME RD

Royal Oak
(PH)

OX25

Piddington
Cow Leys

Middle
Cow Leys
Farm

B4011

19

Blackthorn
Bridge

Bridge
Farm

Upper
Cow Leys
Farm

Treadwell's
Barn

HP18

1

New Farm

B4011

18

62   A   63   B   64   C

Buckinghamshire STREET ATLAS

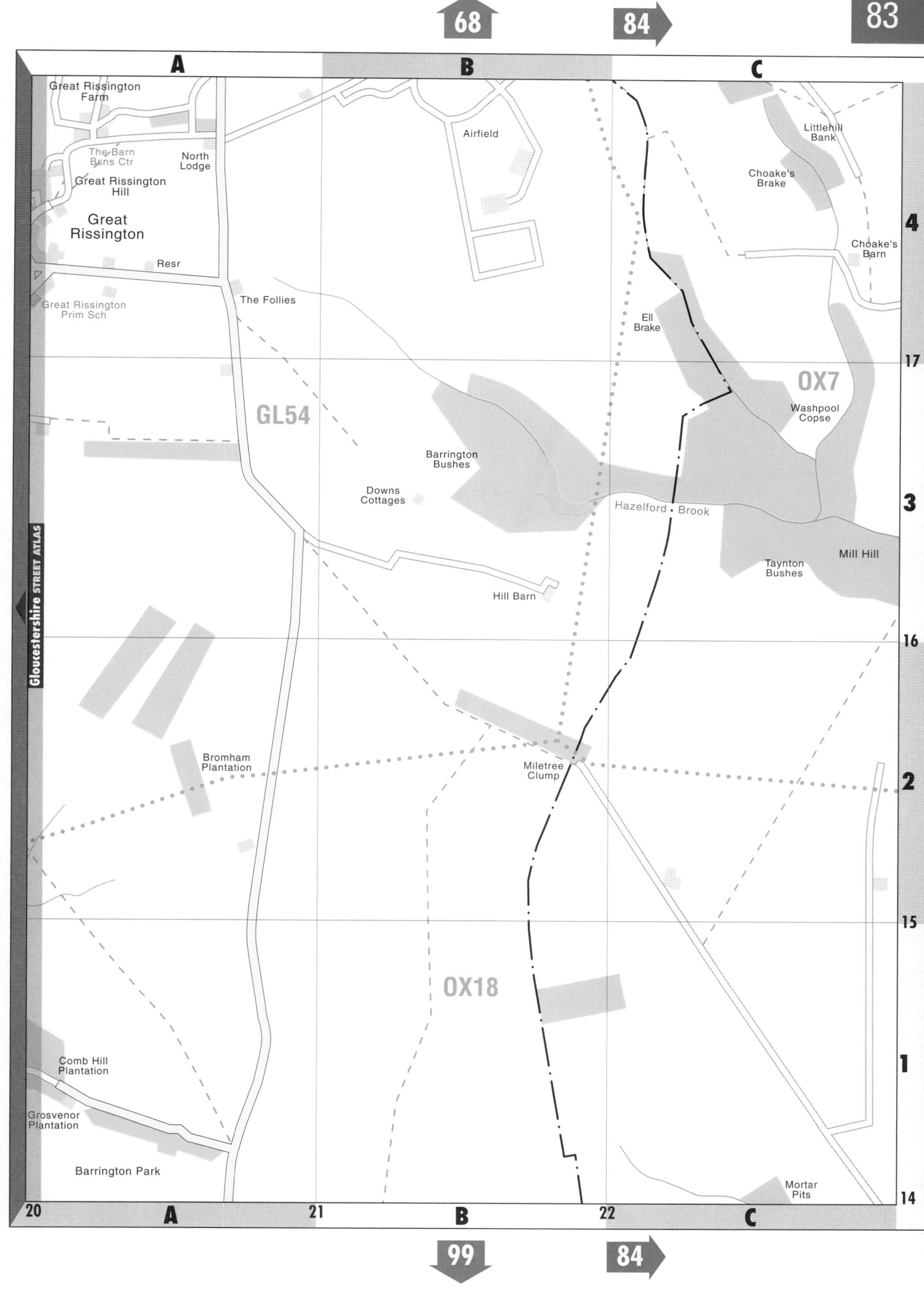

68
84

A

B

C

Great Rissington Farm

The Barn Bsns Ctr

North Lodge

Great Rissington Hill

Great Rissington

Resr

Great Rissington Prim Sch

The Follies

GL54

Airfield

Littlehill Bank

Choake's Brake

Choake's Barn

4

Ell Brake

OX7

Washpool Copse

17

Barrington Bushes

Downs Cottages

Hazelford Brook

Taynton Bushes

Mill Hill

3

Hill Barn

16

Bromham Plantation

Miletree Clump

2

OX18

15

Comb Hill Plantation

Grosvenor Plantation

1

Barrington Park

Mortar Pits

14

20

A

21

B

22

C

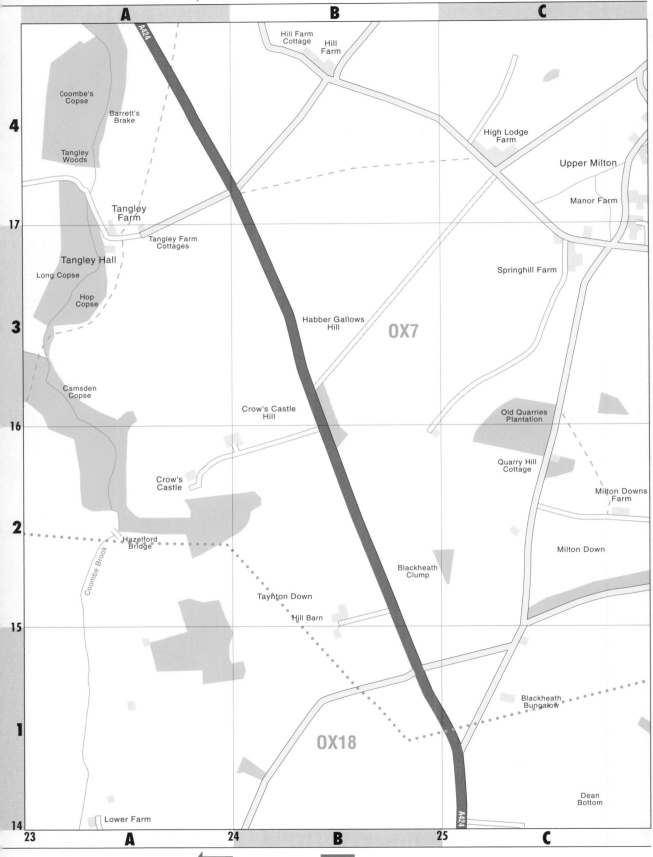

A424

Hill Farm
Cottage

Hill
Farm

Coombe's
Copse

Barrett's
Brake

High Lodge
Farm

Upper Milton

Tangley
Woods

Manor Farm

Tangley
Farm

Tangley Farm
Cottages

Tangley Hall

Springhill Farm

Long Copse

Hop
Copse

Habber Gallows
Hill

OX7

Camsden
Copse

Crow's Castle
Hill

Old Quarries
Plantation

Crow's
Castle

Quarry Hill
Cottage

Milton Downs
Farm

Hazelford
Bridge

Coombe Brook

Milton Down

Blackheath
Clump

Taynton Down

Hill Barn

Blackheath
Bungalow

OX18

Dean
Bottom

Lower Farm

A424

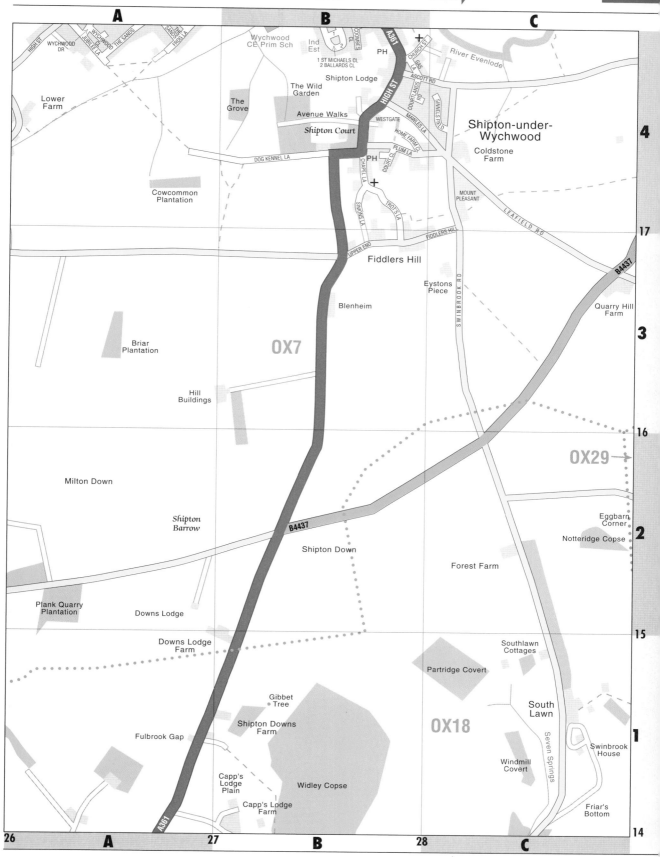

A

B

C

1 ST MICHAELS CL
2 BALLARDS CL

Wychwood CE Prim Sch

Ind Est

Shipton Lodge

The Wild Garden

The Grove

Avenue Walks

Shipton Court

WESTGATE

Home Farm Cl

PLUM LA

CHAPEL LA

SIMONS LA

TROT'S LA

DOG KENNEL LA

UPPER END

Lower Farm

Wychwood Dr

HIGH ST

THE SANDS

JUBILEE LA

FROG LA

COOMBES CL

CHURCH ST

ASCOTT RD

COURT LANDS RD

MAWLES LA

SINNELS FIELD

A361

River Evenlode

Shipton-under-Wychwood

Coldstone Farm

MOUNT PLEASANT

LEAFIELD RD

SWINBROOK RD

FIDDLERS HILL

B4437

Quarry Hill Farm

4

17

3

16

OX29

Eggbarn Corner

Notteridge Copse

2

Eystons Piece

Fiddlers Hill

Blenheim

OX7

Cowcommon Plantation

Briar Plantation

Hill Buildings

Milton Down

Shipton Barrow

B4437

Shipton Down

Plank Quarry Plantation

Downs Lodge

Downs Lodge Farm

Forest Farm

15

Southlawn Cottages

Partridge Covert

South Lawn

Gibbet Tree

Shipton Downs Farm

OX18

Seven Springs

Swinbrook House

Windmill Covert

1

Fulbrook Gap

Capp's Lodge Plain

Capp's Lodge Farm

Widley Copse

A361

Friar's Bottom

14

26

A

27

B

28

C

85
71

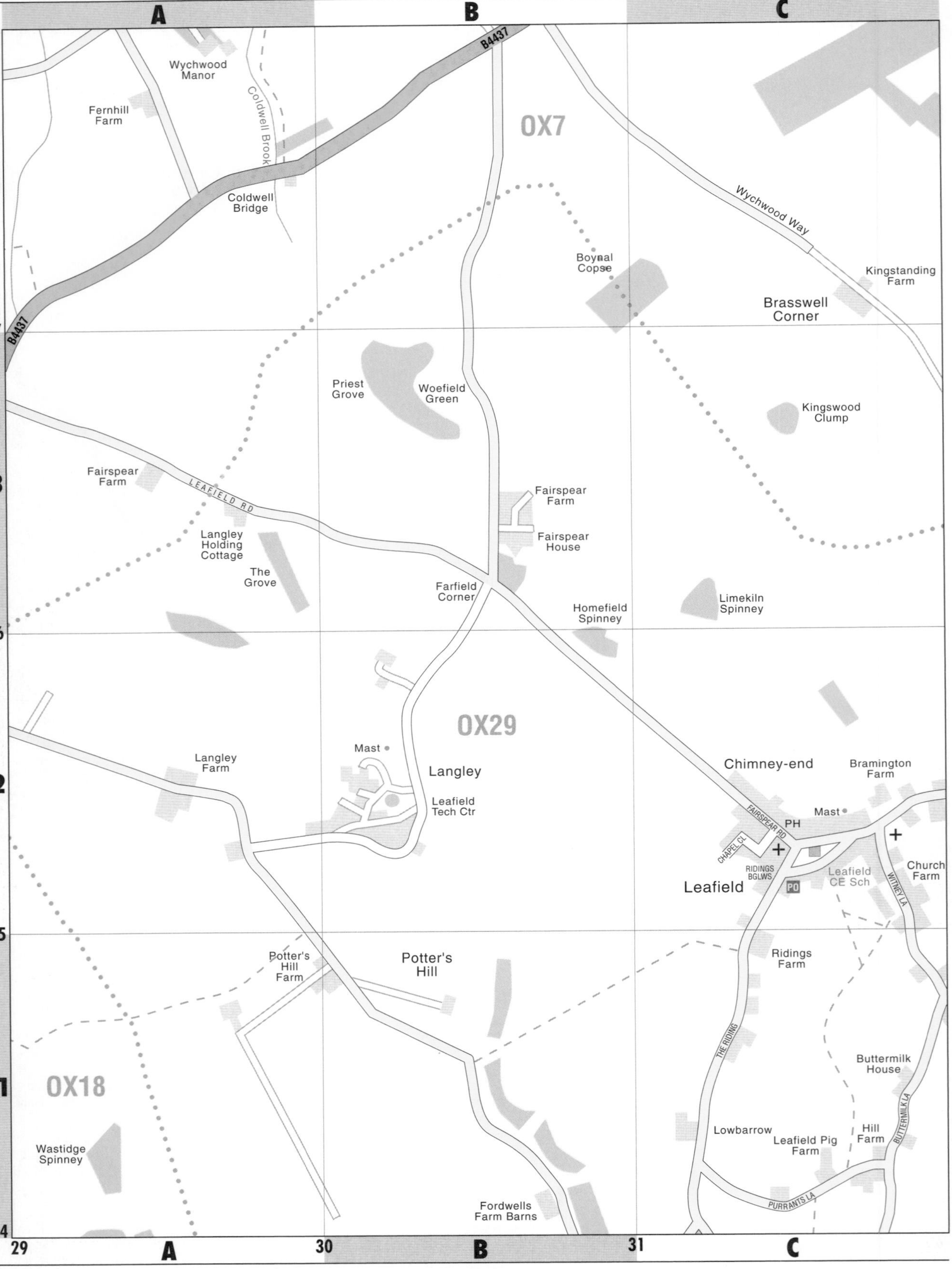

A   B   C

B4437

Wychwood Manor

Fernhill Farm

Coldwell Brook

Coldwell Bridge

OX7

4

B4437

Boynal Copse

Wychwood Way

Kingstanding Farm

Brasswell Corner

17

Priest Grove

Woefield Green

Kingswood Clump

Fairspear Farm

LEAFIELD RD

3

Langley Holding Cottage

The Grove

Fairspear Farm

Fairspear House

Farfield Corner

Homefield Spinney

Limekiln Spinney

16

OX29

Langley Farm

Mast

Langley

Leafield Tech Ctr

Chimney-end

Bramington Farm

FAIRSPEAR RD

Mast

PH

CHAPEL CL

Church Farm

2

RIDINGS BGLWS

Leafield CE Sch

WITNEY LA

PO

Leafield

15

Potter's Hill Farm

Potter's Hill

Ridings Farm

THE RIDING

Buttermilk House

BUTTERMILK LA

1

OX18

Wastidge Spinney

Lowbarrow

Leafield Pig Farm

Hill Farm

Fordwells Farm Barns

PURRANTS LA

14

29   A   30   B   31   C

85
102

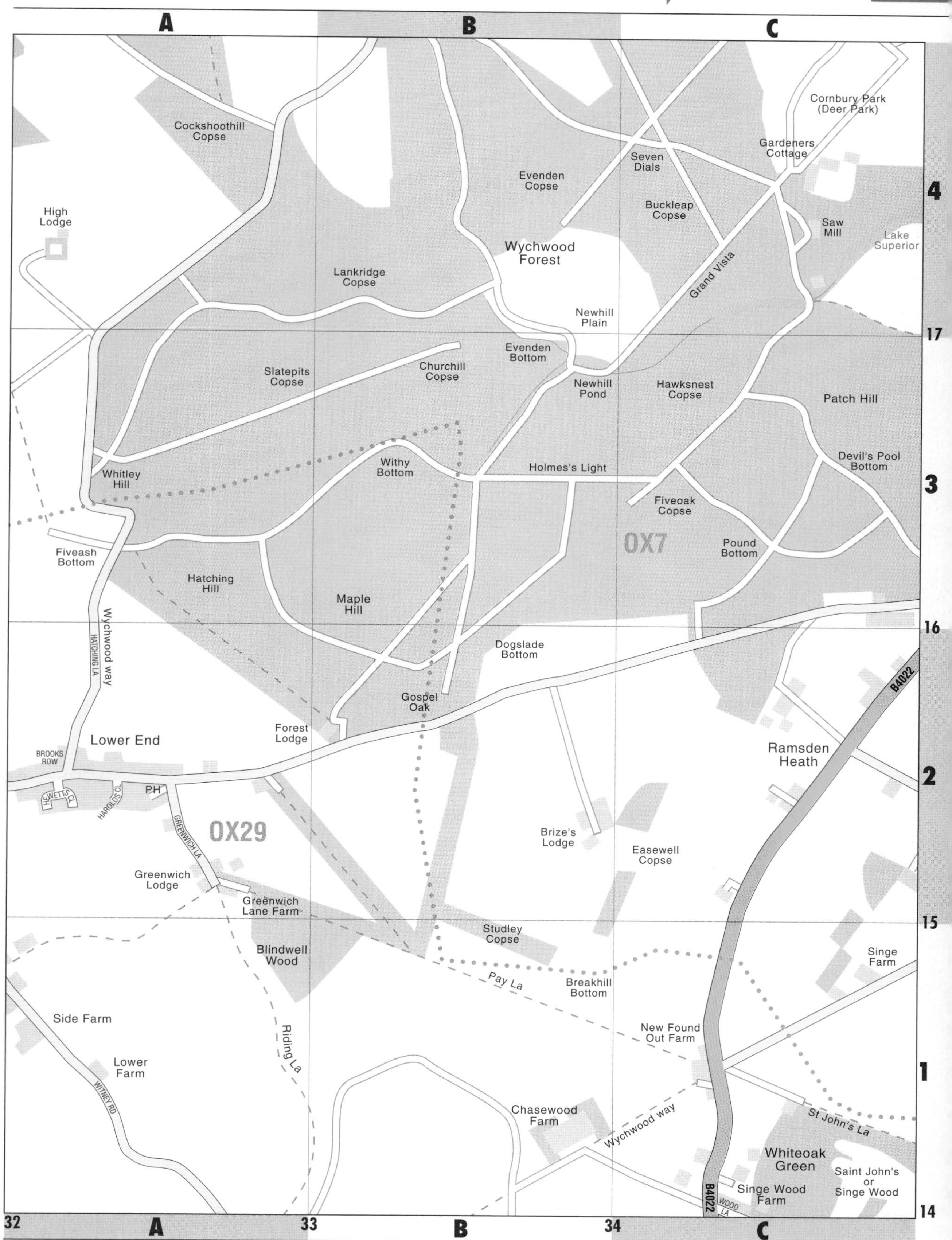

72
88

A

B

C

Cornbury Park
(Deer Park)

High
Lodge

Cockshoothill
Copse

Evenden
Copse

Seven
Dials

Buckleap
Copse

Gardeners
Cottage

Saw
Mill

Lake
Superior

4

Wychwood
Forest

Lankridge
Copse

Grand Vista

Newhill
Plain

17

Slatepits
Copse

Churchill
Copse

Evenden
Bottom

Newhill
Pond

Hawksnest
Copse

Patch Hill

Whitley
Hill

Withy
Bottom

Holmes's Light

Fiveoak
Copse

Devil's Pool
Bottom

OX7

3

Fiveash
Bottom

Hatching
Hill

Maple
Hill

Pound
Bottom

Dogslade
Bottom

16

Wychwood way

HATCHING LA

Gospel
Oak

Forest
Lodge

B4022

Lower End

Ramsden
Heath

2

BROOKS
ROW

HEWETT'S

HAROLD'S CL

PH

OX29

Brize's
Lodge

Easewell
Copse

GREENWICH LA

Greenwich
Lodge

Greenwich
Lane Farm

Singe
Farm

15

Blindwell
Wood

Studley
Copse

Pay La

Breakhill
Bottom

Side Farm

Riding La

New Found
Out Farm

St John's La

1

WITNEY RD

Lower
Farm

Chasewood
Farm

Wychwood way

Whiteoak
Green

Saint John's
or
Singe Wood

Singe Wood
Farm

B4022

WOOD LA

14

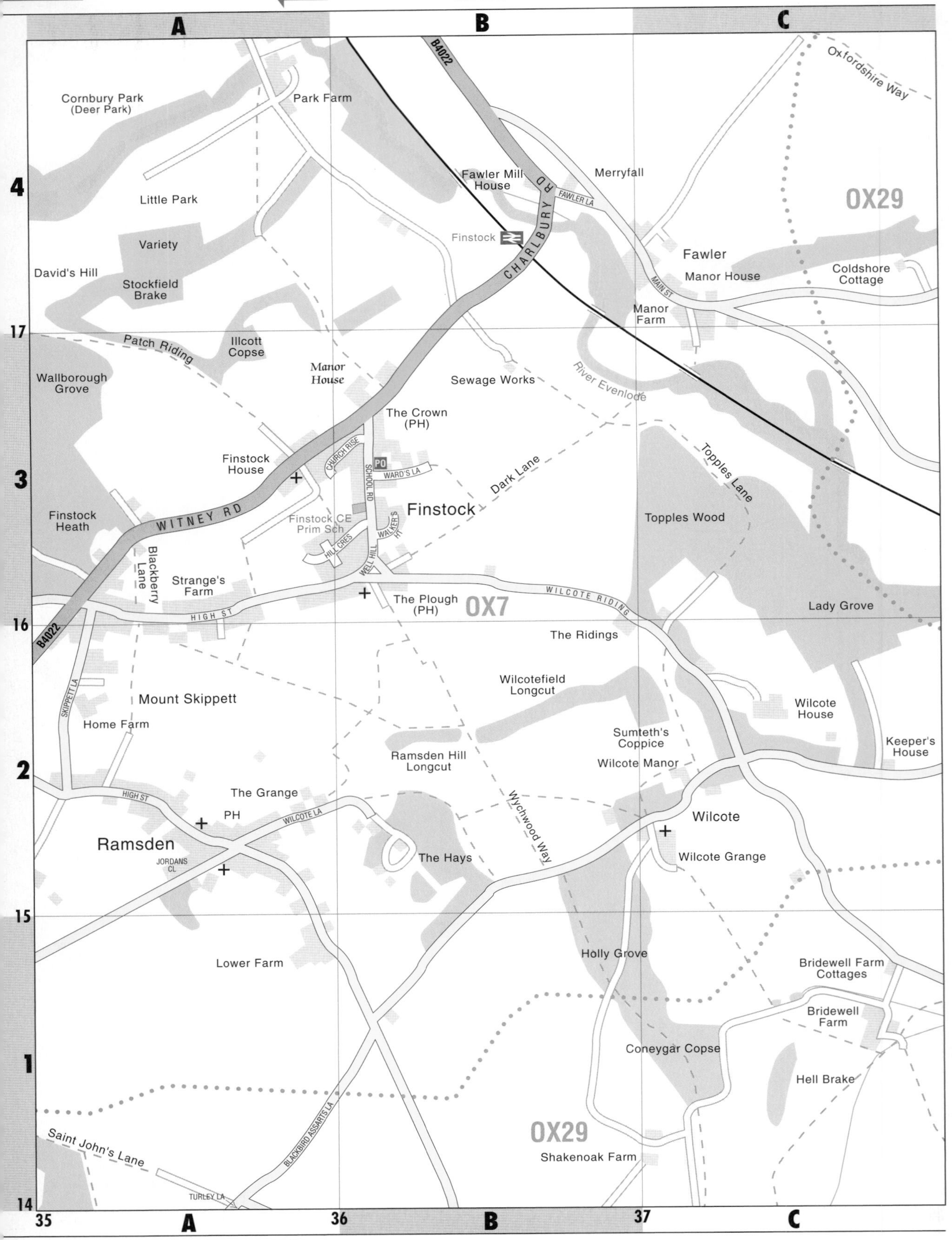

OX29

Oxfordshire Way

Cornbury Park
(Deer Park)

Park Farm

B4022

Fawler Mill
House

Merryfall

CHARLBURY RD

FAWLER LA

Finstock

MAIN ST

Fawler

Little Park

Manor House

Coldshore
Cottage

Variety

Manor
Farm

David's Hill

Stockfield
Brake

Patch Riding

Illcott
Copse

Manor
House

Sewage Works

River Evenlode

Wallborough
Grove

The Crown
(PH)

Topples Lane

CHURCH RISE

Finstock
House

PO

Dark Lane

Topples Wood

SCHOOL RD

WARD'S LA

Finstock

WITNEY RD

Finstock CE
Prim Sch

WALKER'S

Finstock
Heath

Blackberry
Lane

HIL CRES

WELL HILL

Strange's
Farm

The Plough
(PH)

OX7

WILCOTE RIDING

Lady Grove

HIGH ST

B4022

The Ridings

Wilcotefield
Longcut

Wilcote
House

Mount Skippett

SKIPPETT LA

Home Farm

Ramsden Hill
Longcut

Sumteth's
Coppice

Wilcote Manor

Keeper's
House

HIGH ST

The Grange

PH

WILCOTE LA

Wychwood Way

Wilcote

Ramsden

JORDANS
CL

The Hays

Wilcote Grange

Lower Farm

Holly Grove

Bridewell Farm
Cottages

Bridewell
Farm

Coneygar Copse

Hell Brake

OX29

Saint John's Lane

Shakenoak Farm

BLACKBIRD ASSARTS LA

TURLEY LA

74
90

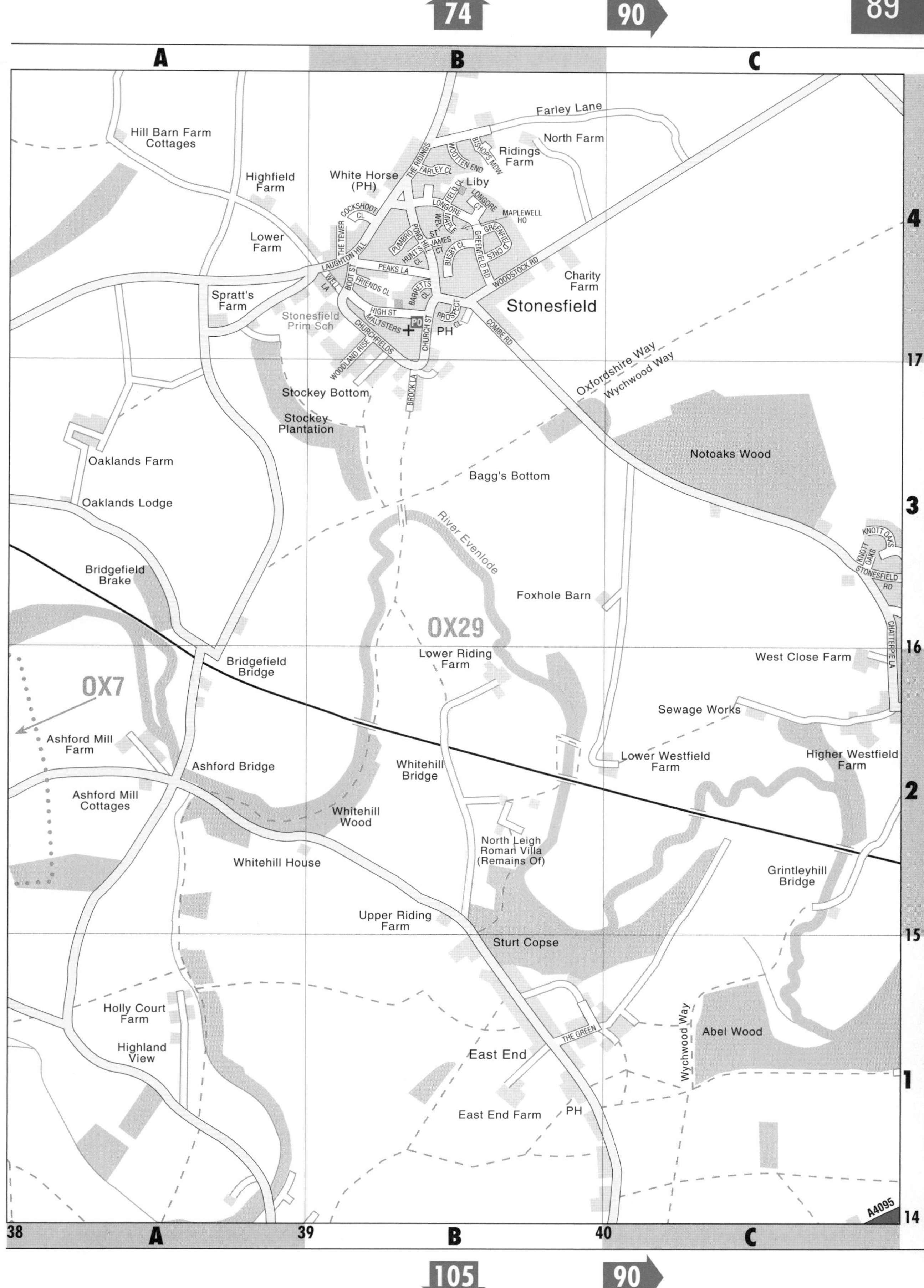
A
B
C
Hill Barn Farm Cottages
Highfield Farm
White Horse (PH)
Lower Farm
Spratt's Farm
Stonesfield Prim Sch
Farley Lane
North Farm
Ridings Farm
Liby
MAPLEWELL HO
Charity Farm
Stonesfield
PH
THE RIDINGS
FARLEY CL
WOOTTEN END
BISHOPS MDW
COCKSHOOT CL
LONGORE
LONGORE CT
FIELD CL
MAPLE
WELL
THE TEWER
LAUGHTON HILL
PLUMBRO
POND HILL
HUNT'S CL
ST JAMES CT
BUSBY CL
GREENFIELD RD
GREENFIELD CRES
WOODSTOCK RD
PEAKS LA
WELL LA
BOOT ST
FRIENDS CL
BARRETTS CL
HIGH ST
MALTSTERS
CHURCHFIELDS
CHURCH ST
PROSPECT CL
COMBE RD
WOODLAND RISE
BROOK LA
PO
Stockey Bottom
Stockey Plantation
Oxfordshire Way
Wychwood Way
Oaklands Farm
Oaklands Lodge
Notoaks Wood
Bagg's Bottom
River Evenlode
KNOTT OAKS
STONESFIELD RD
Bridgefield Brake
Foxhole Barn
OX29
CHATTERPIE LA
Lower Riding Farm
West Close Farm
Bridgefield Bridge
OX7
Sewage Works
Ashford Mill Farm
Ashford Bridge
Whitehill Bridge
Lower Westfield Farm
Higher Westfield Farm
Ashford Mill Cottages
Whitehill Wood
North Leigh Roman Villa (Remains Of)
Whitehill House
Grintleyhill Bridge
Upper Riding Farm
Sturt Copse
Holly Court Farm
THE GREEN
Wychwood Way
Abel Wood
Highland View
East End
East End Farm
PH
A4095
17
4
3
16
2
15
1
14
38
39
40
A
B
C

105
90

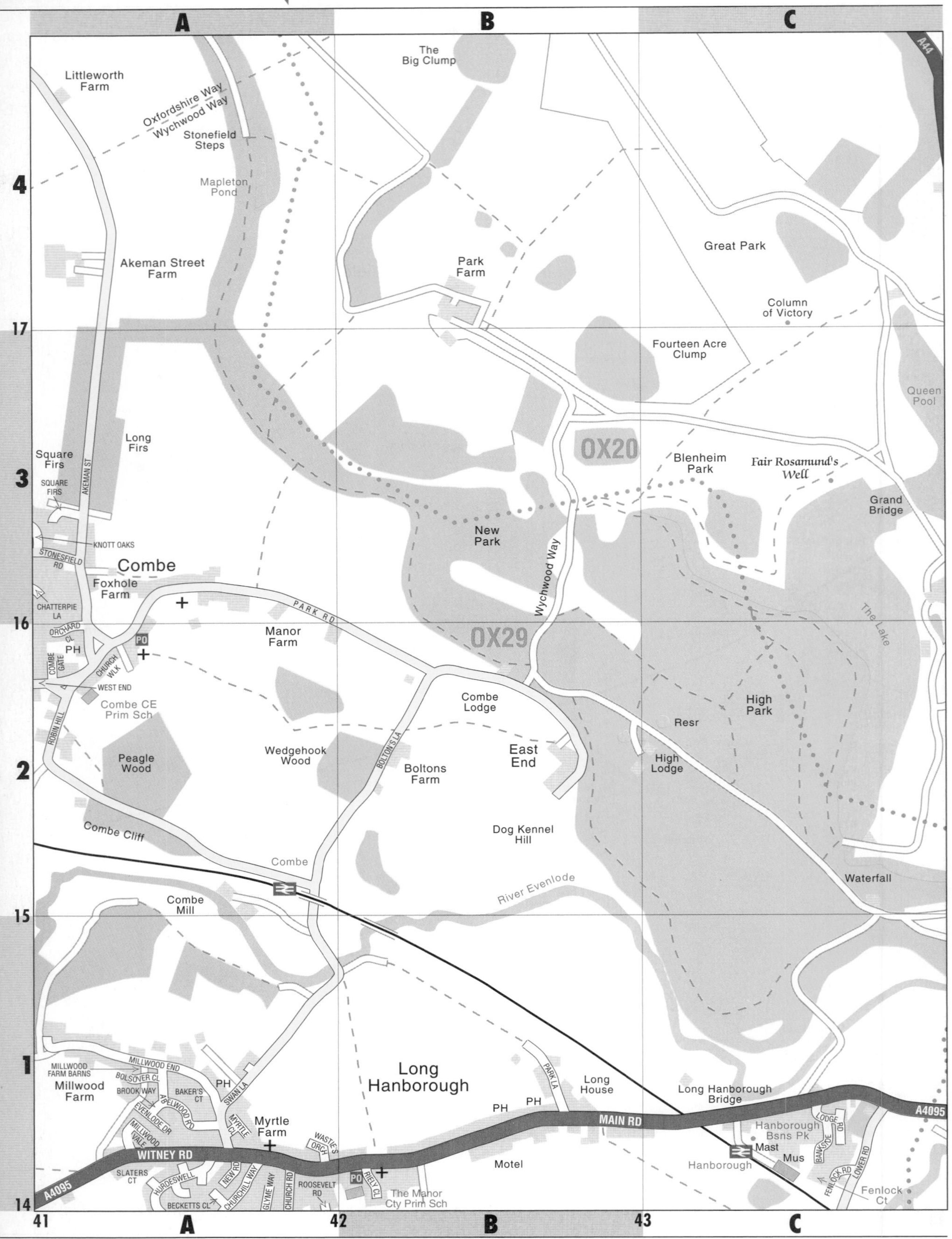

A
B
C

4

17

3

16

2

15

1

14

Littleworth Farm
Oxfordshire Way
Wychwood Way
Stonefield Steps
Mapleton Pond
Akeman Street Farm
The Big Clump
Park Farm
Great Park
Column of Victory
Fourteen Acre Clump
Queen Pool
OX20
Blenheim Park
Fair Rosamund's Well
Grand Bridge
Square Firs
SQUARE FIRS
Long Firs
AKEMAN ST
STONESFIELD RD
KNOTT OAKS
Combe
Foxhole Farm
CHATTERPIE LA
ORCHARD CL
PH
PO
COMBE GATE
CHURCH WLK
WEST END
ROBIN HILL
Combe CE Prim Sch
PARK RD
Manor Farm
New Park
Wychwood Way
The Lake
OX29
Combe Lodge
High Park
Resr
Peagle Wood
Wedgehook Wood
BOLTON'S LA
Boltons Farm
East End
High Lodge
Combe Cliff
Combe
Dog Kennel Hill
Waterfall
Combe Mill
River Evenlode
Millwood Farm Barns
MILLWOOD END
BOLSOVER CL
Millwood Farm
BROOK WAY
FELWOOD DR
BAKER'S CT
PH
SWAN LA
Long Hanborough
PARK LA
Long House
Long Hanborough Bridge
A4095
EVENLODE DR
MILLWOOD DALE
MYRTLE RD
NEW RD
Myrtle Farm
WASTIE'S ORCH
PH
PH
MAIN RD
Hanborough Bsns Pk
LODGE RD
BANKSIDE
WITNEY RD
SLATERS CT
HURDESWELL
BECKETTS CL
GLYME WAY
CHURCH RD
ROOSEVELT RD
CHURCHILL WAY
PO
RILEY CL
The Manor Cty Prim Sch
Motel
Hanborough
Mast
Mus
FENLOCK RD
LOWER RD
Fenlock Ct
A4095

76
92

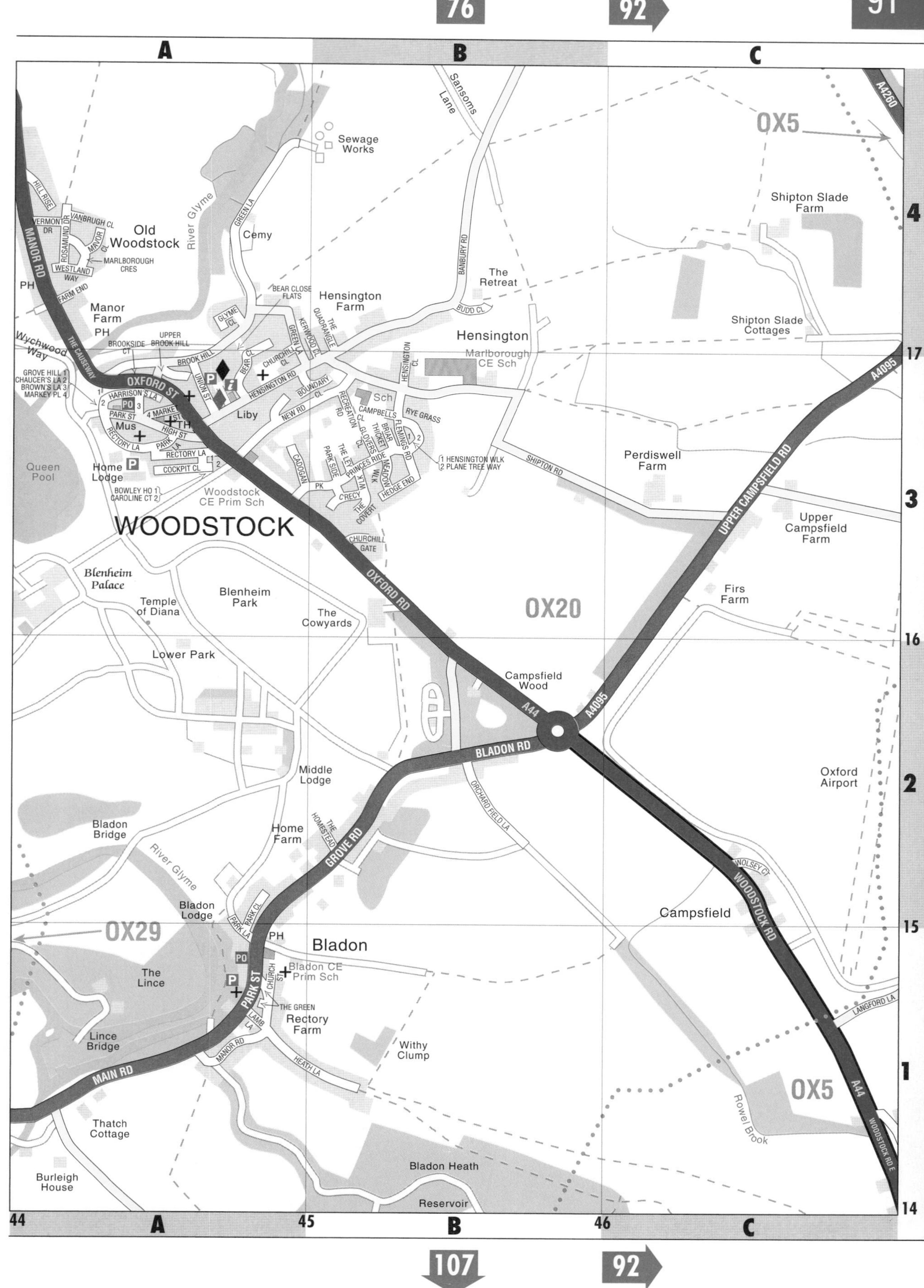
A
B
C
WOODSTOCK
Old Woodstock
Manor Farm
Hensington Farm
Hensington
Marlborough CE Sch
Sewage Works
Cemy
The Retreat
Shipton Slade Farm
Shipton Slade Cottages
OX5
Perdiswell Farm
Upper Campsfield Farm
Firs Farm
OX20
Queen Pool
Home Lodge
Woodstock CE Prim Sch
Blenheim Palace
Temple of Diana
Blenheim Park
The Cowyards
Lower Park
Campsfield Wood
Middle Lodge
Oxford Airport
Bladon Bridge
River Glyme
Home Farm
Bladon Lodge
OX29
Bladon
Bladon CE Prim Sch
The Lince
Lince Bridge
Rectory Farm
Withy Clump
Campsfield
OX5
Rowel Brook
Thatch Cottage
Burleigh House
Bladon Heath
Reservoir
MANOR RD
OXFORD ST
OXFORD RD
A44
A4095
A4260
UPPER CAMPSFIELD RD
BLADON RD
GROVE RD
WOODSTOCK RD
MAIN RD
PARK ST
SHIPTON RD
BANBURY RD
Sansoms Lane
Wychwood Way
Liby
Mus
TH
PO
PH
Sch
1 HENSINGTON WLK
2 PLANE TREE WAY
GROVE HILL 1
CHAUCER'S LA 2
BROWN'S LA 3
MARKEY PL 4
BOWLEY HO 1
CAROLINE CT 2
44
45
46
14
15
16
17
1
2
3
4

107
92

91
77

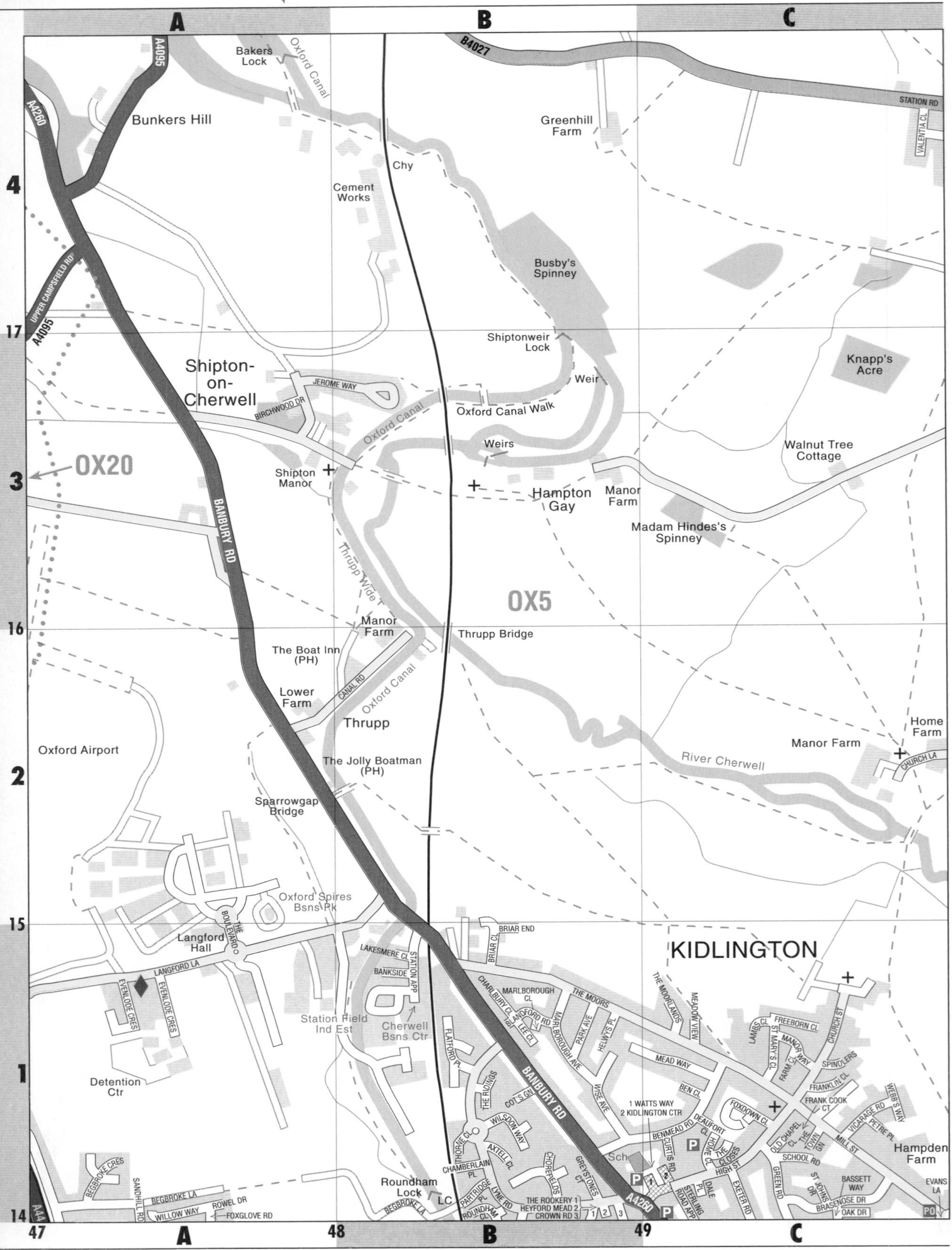
A
B
C
Bakers Lock
Oxford Canal
Bunkers Hill
A4095
A4260
B4027
Greenhill Farm
STATION RD
VALENTIA CL
Chy
Cement Works
Busby's Spinney
UPPER CAMPSFIELD RD
A4095
Shiptonweir Lock
Knapp's Acre
Shipton-on-Cherwell
JEROME WAY
Weir
BIRCHWOOD DR
Oxford Canal Walk
Oxford Canal
Weirs
Walnut Tree Cottage
OX20
Shipton Manor
Hampton Gay
Manor Farm
Madam Hindes's Spinney
BANBURY RD
Thrupp Wide
OX5
Manor Farm
Thrupp Bridge
The Boat Inn (PH)
Lower Farm
CANAL RD
Oxford Canal
Thrupp
Home Farm
Manor Farm
Oxford Airport
The Jolly Boatman (PH)
River Cherwell
CHURCH LA
Sparrowgap Bridge
Oxford Spires Bsns Pk
THE BOULEVARD
Langford Hall
BRIAR END
BRIAR CL
KIDLINGTON
LAKESMERE CL
STATION APP
BANKSIDE
LANGFORD LA
EVENLODE CRES
EVENLODE CRES
CHARLBURY CL
MARLBOROUGH CL
THE MOORS
THE MOORLANDS
MEADOW VIEW
LANGFORD RD
LEE CL
MARLBOROUGH AVE
PARK AVE
HELWYS PL
Station Field Ind Est
Cherwell Bsns Ctr
LAMBS CL
FREEBORN CL
ST MARY'S CL
MANOR WAY
CHURCH ST
FLATFORD PL
MEAD WAY
FARM CL
SPINDLERS
Detention Ctr
THE RIDINGS
COT'S GN
BANBURY RD
WISE AVE
BEN CL
FRANKLIN CL
FRANK COOK CT
WEBB'S WAY
WILSDON WAY
1 WATTS WAY
2 KIDLINGTON CTR
FOXDOWN CL
VICARAGE RD
PETRE PL
MORTON CL
BENMEAD RD
DEAUFORT CL
HOME CL
THE CLOSES
OLD CHAPEL CL
THE TOWN GN
MILL ST
Hampden Farm
AXTELL CL
CHOREFIELDS
GREYSTONES CT
CURTIS RD
SCHOOL RD
CHAMBERLAIN PL
HIGH ST
BEGBROKE CRES
Roundham Lock
PARTRIDGE PL
LYNE RD
DALE PL
EXETER RD
GREEN RD
ST JOHNS DR
BASSETT WAY
EVANS LA
SANDHILL RD
BEGBROKE LA
ROWEL DR
BEGBROKE LA
LC
ROUNDHAM CL
THE ROOKERY 1
HEYFORD MEAD 2
CROWN RD 3
A4260
STERLING ROAD APP
BRASENOSE DR
OAK DR
WILLOW WAY
FOXGLOVE RD
A44
PO
4
17
3
16
2
15
1
14
47
48
49
A
B
C

91
108

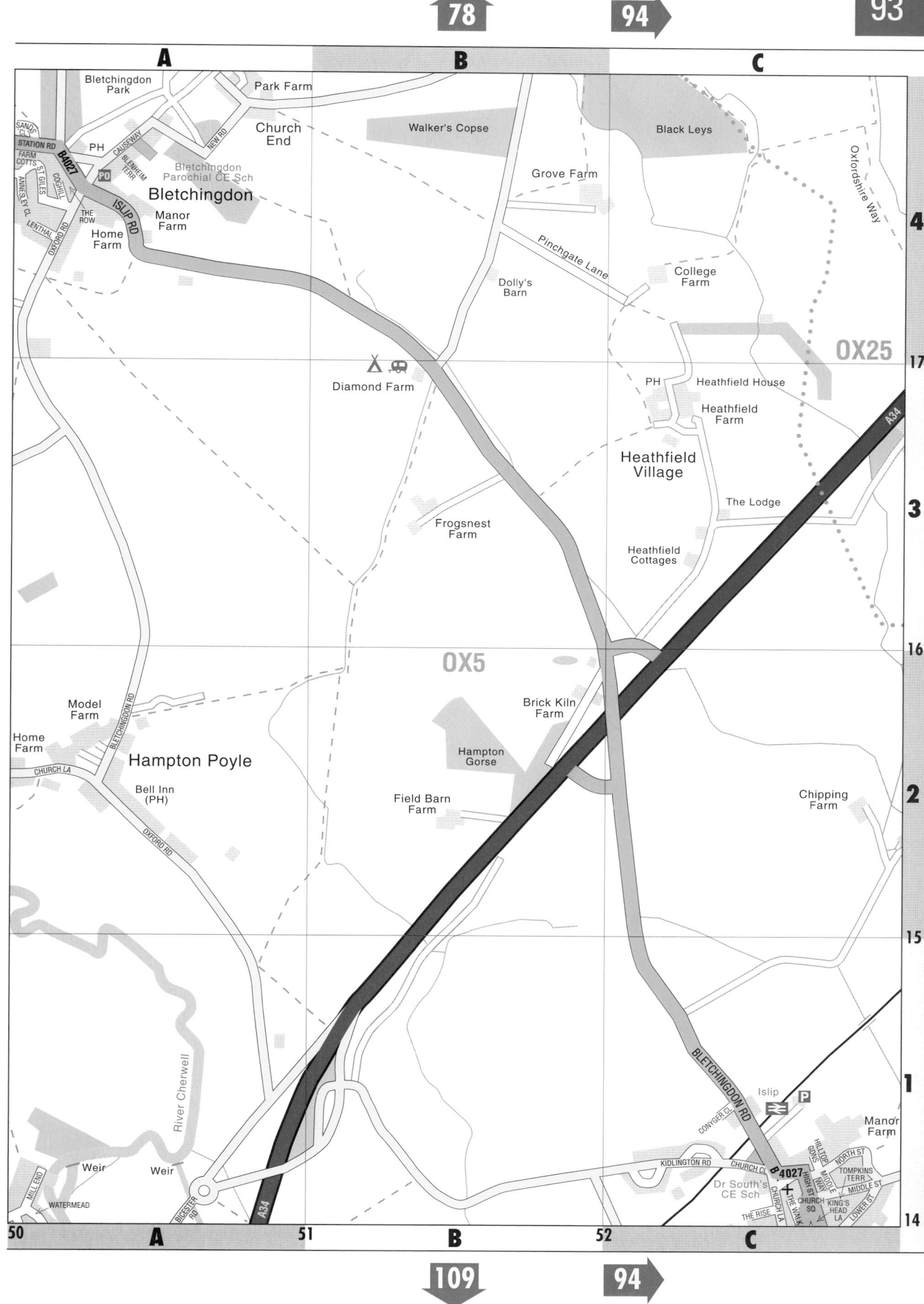

A

B

C

Bletchingdon Park

Park Farm

Walker's Copse

Black Leys

Oxfordshire Way

4

SANDY CL
STATION RD
FARM COTTS
ST GILES
ANNESLEY CL
LENTHAL
OXFORD RD
COGHILL
B4027
PH
CAUSEWAY
BLENHEIM TERR
NEW RD
PO
ISLIP RD
THE ROW

Church End

Bletchingdon Parochial CE Sch

Bletchingdon

Grove Farm

Manor Farm

Home Farm

Pinchgate Lane

Dolly's Barn

College Farm

OX25

17

Diamond Farm

PH
Heathfield House

Heathfield Farm

Heathfield Village

The Lodge

3

Frogsnest Farm

Heathfield Cottages

OX5

16

Model Farm

BLETCHINGDON RD

Home Farm

CHURCH LA

Hampton Poyle

Brick Kiln Farm

Hampton Gorse

A34

Chipping Farm

2

Bell Inn (PH)

OXFORD RD

Field Barn Farm

15

River Cherwell

BLETCHINGDON RD

CONYGER CL

Islip
P

1

Manor Farm

Weir

Weir

BICESTER RD

A34

KIDLINGTON RD

CHURCH CL

B4027

KIDLINGTON RD

HILL TOP
EDINS
MIDDLE
HIGH ST
NORTH ST

TOMPKINS TERR

Dr South's CE Sch

CHURCH LA
THE WALK
CHURCH SQ
KING'S HEAD LA
MIDDLE ST
LOWER ST

MILL END

WATERMEAD

THE RISE

50

A

51

B

52

C

14

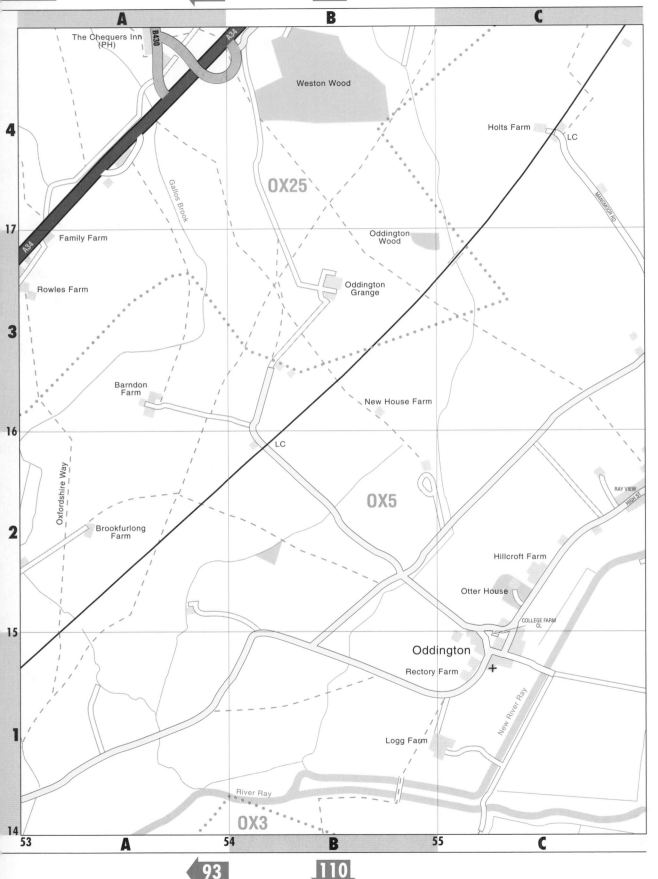

A
B
C

The Chequers Inn (PH)

B430

A34

Weston Wood

Holts Farm
LC

MANSMOOR RD

4

OX25

Oddington Wood

17

A34

Family Farm

Gallos Brook

Rowles Farm

Oddington Grange

3

Barndon Farm

New House Farm

16

LC

Oxfordshire Way

OX5

RAY VIEW

HIGH ST

2

Brookfurlong Farm

Hillcroft Farm

Otter House

COLLEGE FARM CL

15

Oddington

Rectory Farm

+

New River Ray

1

Logg Farm

River Ray

14

OX3

53
A
54
B
55
C

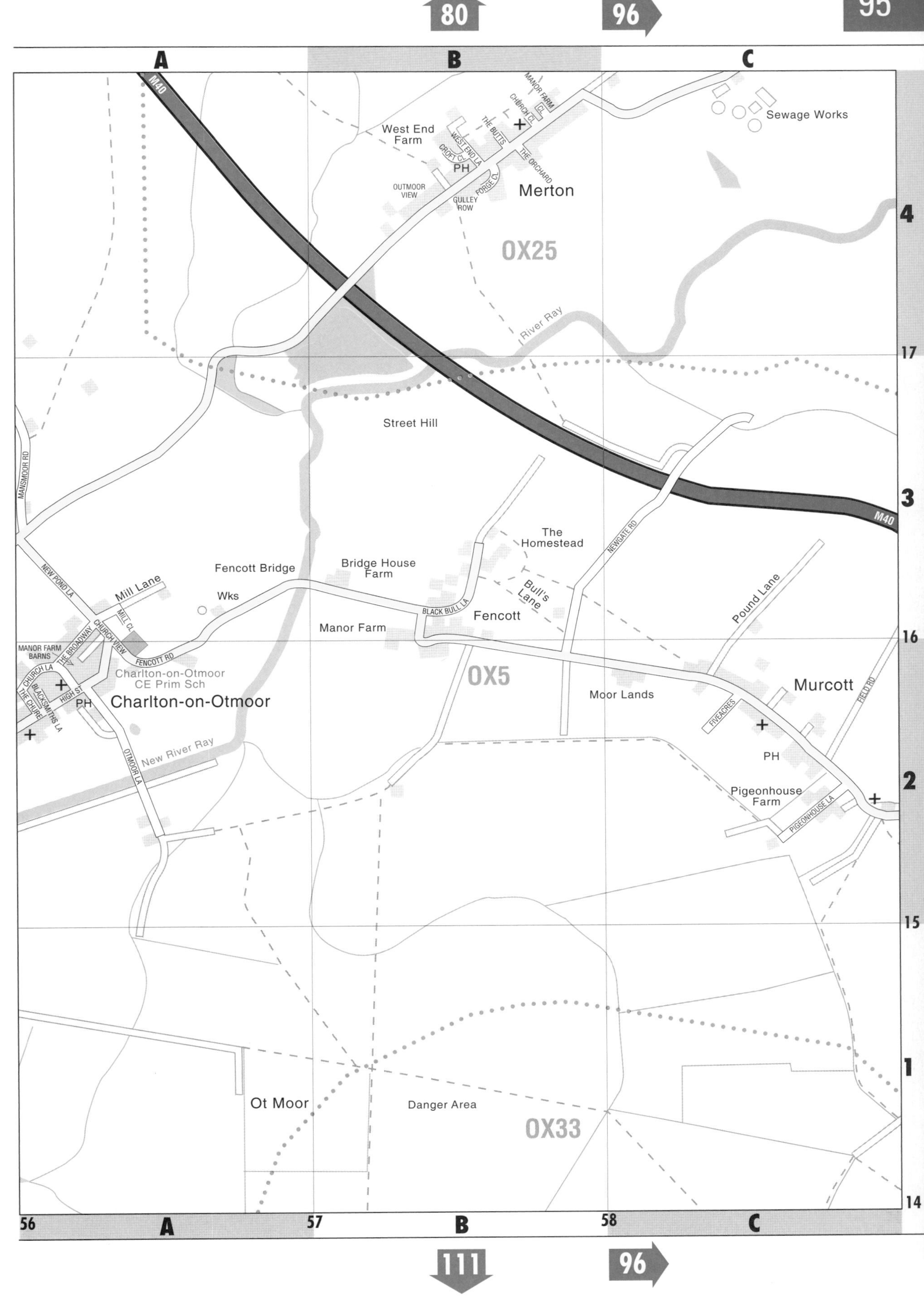

A   B   C

M40

Sewage Works

West End
Farm

Manor Farm

West End La

Church Cl

The Butts

Croft Cl

Forge Cl

The Orchard

PH

Outmoor
View

Gulley
Row

Merton

OX25

River Ray

17

Street Hill

Mansmoor Rd

The
Homestead

Newgate Rd

3

M40

New Pond La

Fencott Bridge

Bridge House
Farm

Bull's
Lane

Pound Lane

Mill Lane

Mill Cl

Wks

Black Bull La

Fencott

Charlton-on-Otmoor
CE Prim Sch

Church View

The Broadway

Fencott Rd

Manor Farm

OX5

Murcott

16

Manor Farm
Barns

Church La

Blacksmiths La

The Church

High St

PH

Charlton-on-Otmoor

Otmoor La

New River Ray

Moor Lands

Fiveacres

PH

Field Rd

Pigeonhouse Farm

Pigeonhouse La

2

15

Ot Moor

Danger Area

OX33

1

56   A   57   B   58   C   14

95 81

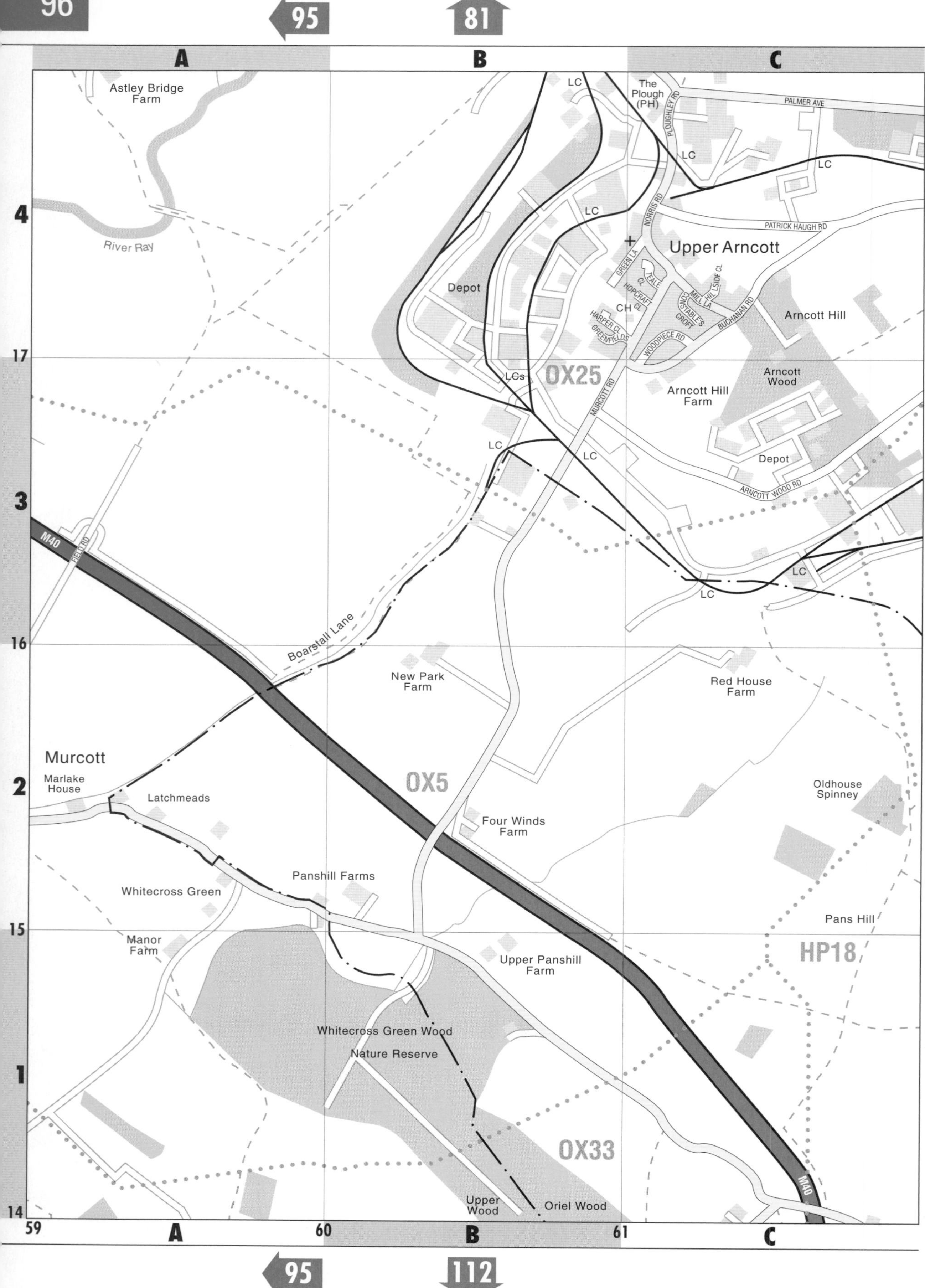

A **B** **C**

4

Astley Bridge Farm

The Plough (PH)
PALMER AVE
LC
LC
LC

River Ray

Upper Arncott

Depot

Arncott Hill

PATRICK HAUGH RD

17

OX25

Arncott Wood

Arncott Hill Farm

LCs

LC

LC

Depot

ARNCOTT WOOD RD

3

M40

FIELD RD

LC

LC
LC

16

Boarstall Lane

New Park Farm

Red House Farm

Oldhouse Spinney

Murcott

Marlake House

2

Latchmeads

OX5

Four Winds Farm

Pans Hill

HP18

Whitecross Green

Panshill Farms

15

Manor Farm

Upper Panshill Farm

1

Whitecross Green Wood
Nature Reserve

OX33

M40

14

Upper Wood

Oriel Wood

59 **A** 60 **B** 61 **C**

95 112

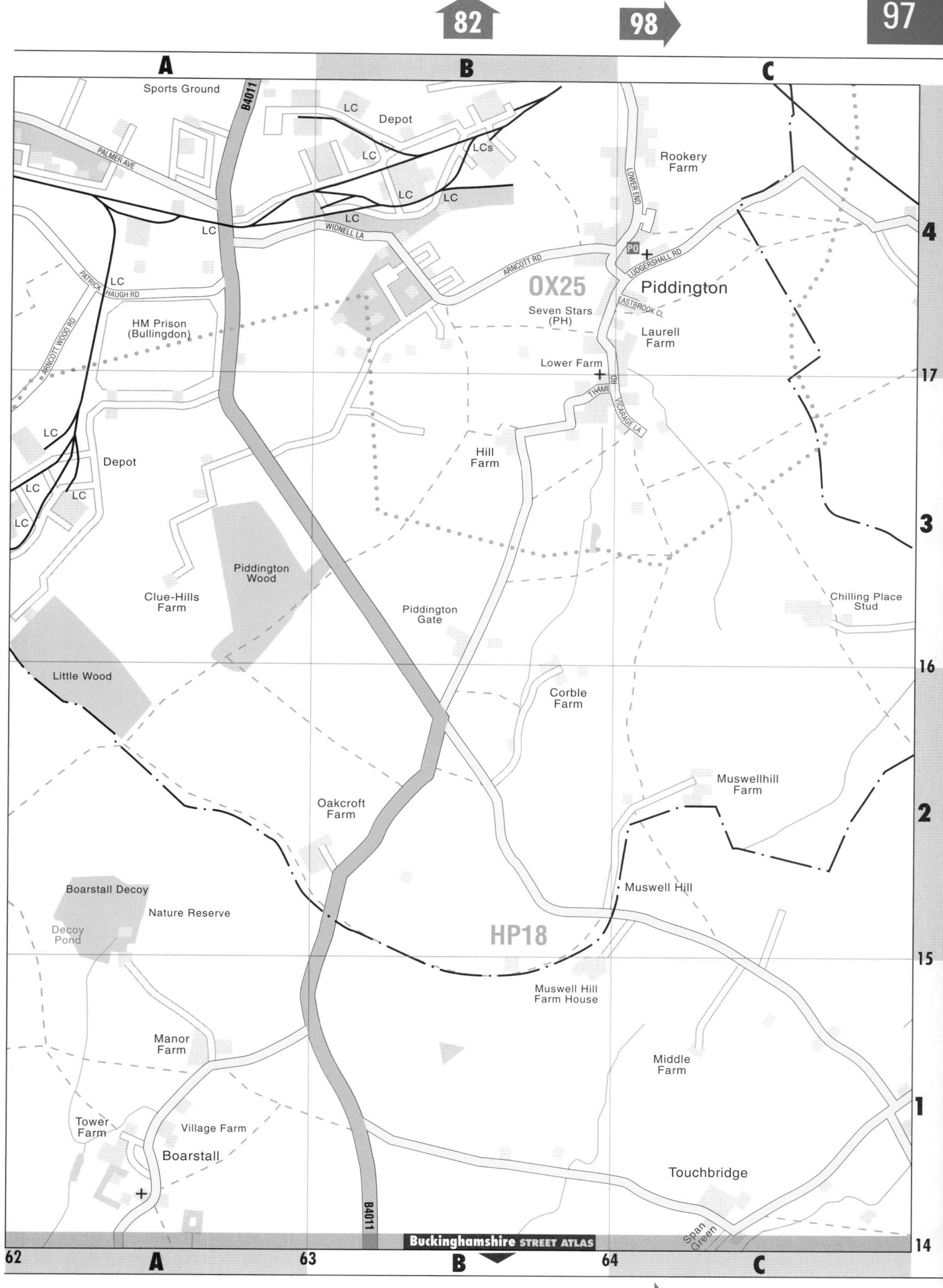

A B C

LC
Depot
LCs
LC
LC
LC
LC
LC
Sports Ground
PALMER AVE
B4011
WIDNELL LA
LC
Rookery Farm
LOWER END
PO
LUDGERSHALL RD
4
ARNCOTT RD
OX25
Piddington
Seven Stars (PH)
EASTBROOK CL
PATRICK HAUGH RD
LC
ARNCOTT WOOD RD
HM Prison (Bullingdon)
Laurell Farm
Lower Farm
17
THAME RD
VICARAGE LA
LC
Depot
LC
LC
LC
Hill Farm
3
Piddington Wood
Clue-Hills Farm
Piddington Gate
Chilling Place Stud
Little Wood
16
Corble Farm
Muswellhill Farm
Oakcroft Farm
2
Muswell Hill
Boarstall Decoy
Nature Reserve
Decoy Pond
HP18
Muswell Hill Farm House
15
Manor Farm
Middle Farm
Tower Farm
Village Farm
1
Boarstall
Touchbridge
B4011
Span Green
14

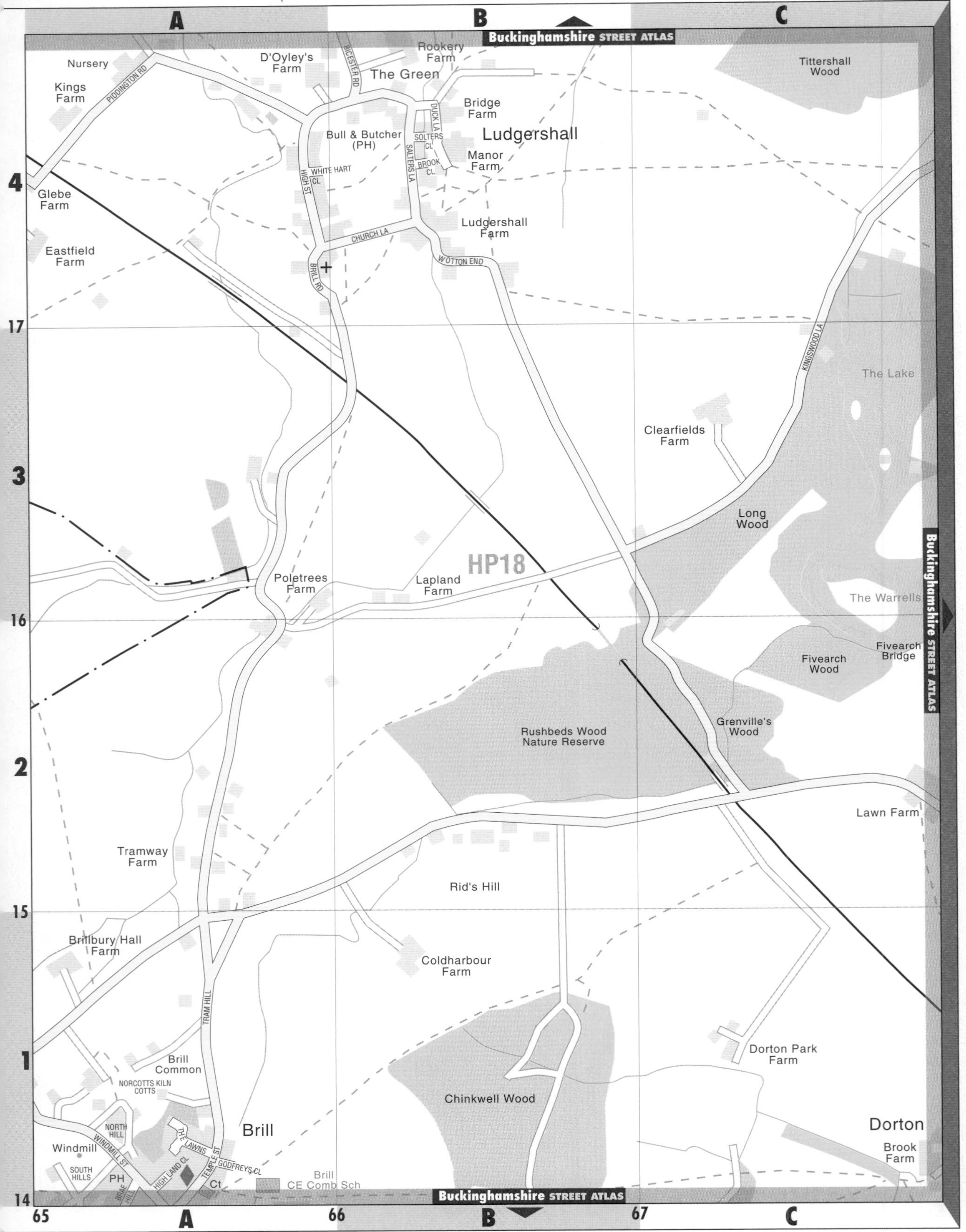

A   B   C

Nursery

Kings
Farm

PODDINGTON RD

D'Oyley's
Farm

BICESTER RD

The Green

Rookery
Farm

DUCK LA

Bridge
Farm

Ludgershall

4

Glebe
Farm

Bull & Butcher
(PH)

SOLTERS CL

SALTERS LA

BROOK CL

Manor
Farm

WHITE HART CL

HIGH ST

Eastfield
Farm

CHURCH LA

Ludgershall
Farm

BRILL RD

WOTTON END

Tittershall
Wood

17

Clearfields
Farm

KINGSWOOD LA

The Lake

3

Long
Wood

Poletrees
Farm

Lapland
Farm

HP18

The Warrells

16

Fivearch
Wood

Fivearch
Bridge

Rushbeds Wood
Nature Reserve

Grenville's
Wood

2

Lawn Farm

Tramway
Farm

Rid's Hill

15

Brillbury Hall
Farm

Coldharbour
Farm

TRAM HILL

Dorton Park
Farm

1

Brill
Common

NORCOTTS KILN
COTTS

NORTH
HILL

WINDMILL ST

THE LAWNS

GODFREYS CL

Chinkwell Wood

Dorton

Windmill

SOUTH
HILLS

PH

BRILL HILL

HIGH LAND CL

TEMPLE ST

Ct

Brill
CE Comb Sch

Brill

Brook
Farm

14

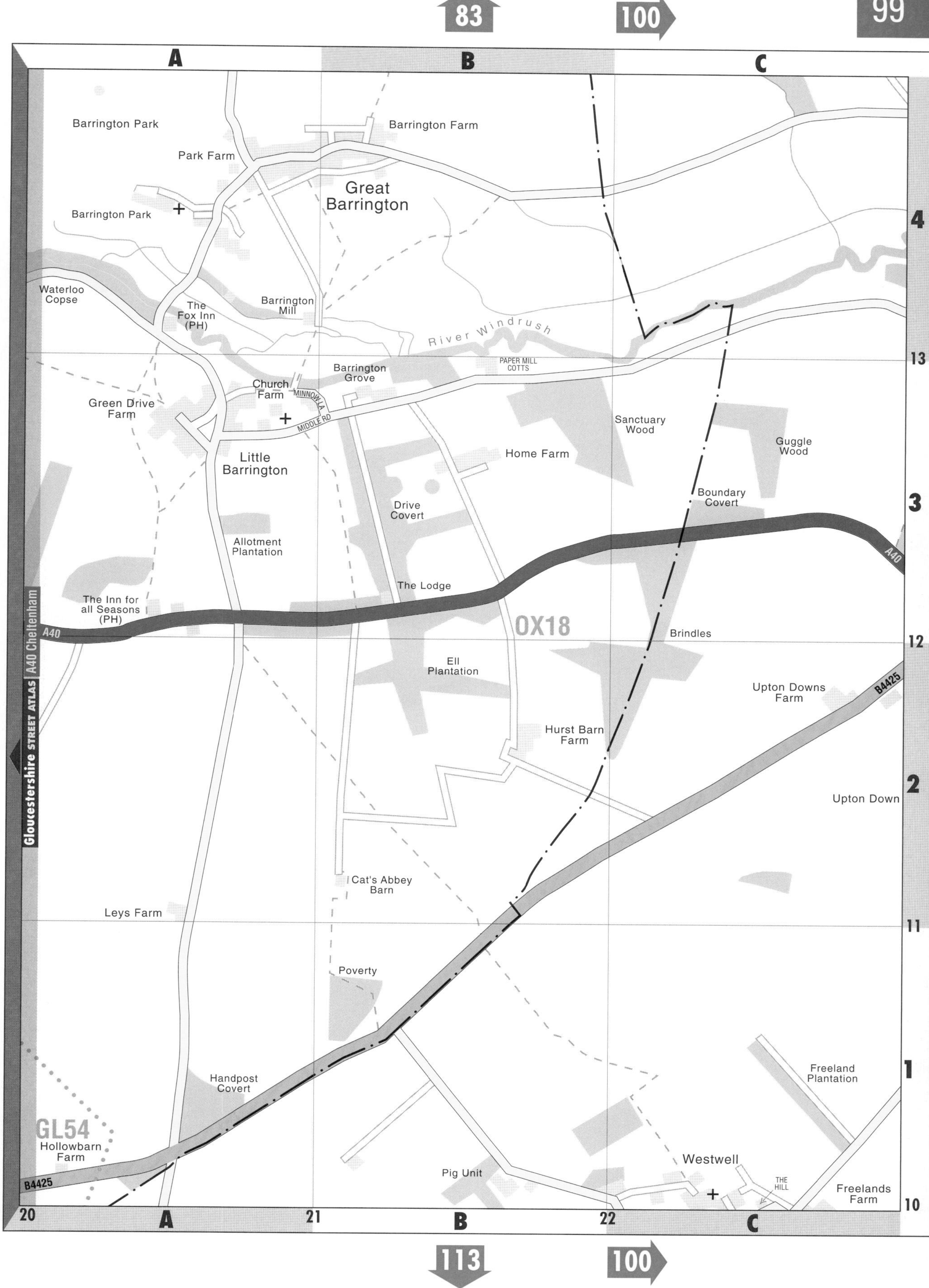

A **B** **C**

Barrington Park

Park Farm

Barrington Farm

Barrington Park

Great
Barrington

4

Waterloo
Copse

The
Fox Inn
(PH)

Barrington
Mill

River Windrush

13

PAPER MILL
COTTS

Church
Farm

MINNOW LA

Barrington
Grove

Sanctuary
Wood

Guggle
Wood

Green Drive
Farm

MIDDLE RD

Home Farm

Little
Barrington

Drive
Covert

Boundary
Covert

3

Allotment
Plantation

The Lodge

A40

The Inn for
all Seasons
(PH)

A40

OX18

Brindles

12

Ell
Plantation

Upton Downs
Farm

B4425

Hurst Barn
Farm

2

Upton Down

Leys Farm

Cat's Abbey
Barn

11

Poverty

Handpost
Covert

Freeland
Plantation

1

GL54

Hollowbarn
Farm

Westwell

B4425

Pig Unit

THE
HILL

Freelands
Farm

10

A 21 **B** 22 **C**

20

Gloucestershire STREET ATLAS | A40 Cheltenham

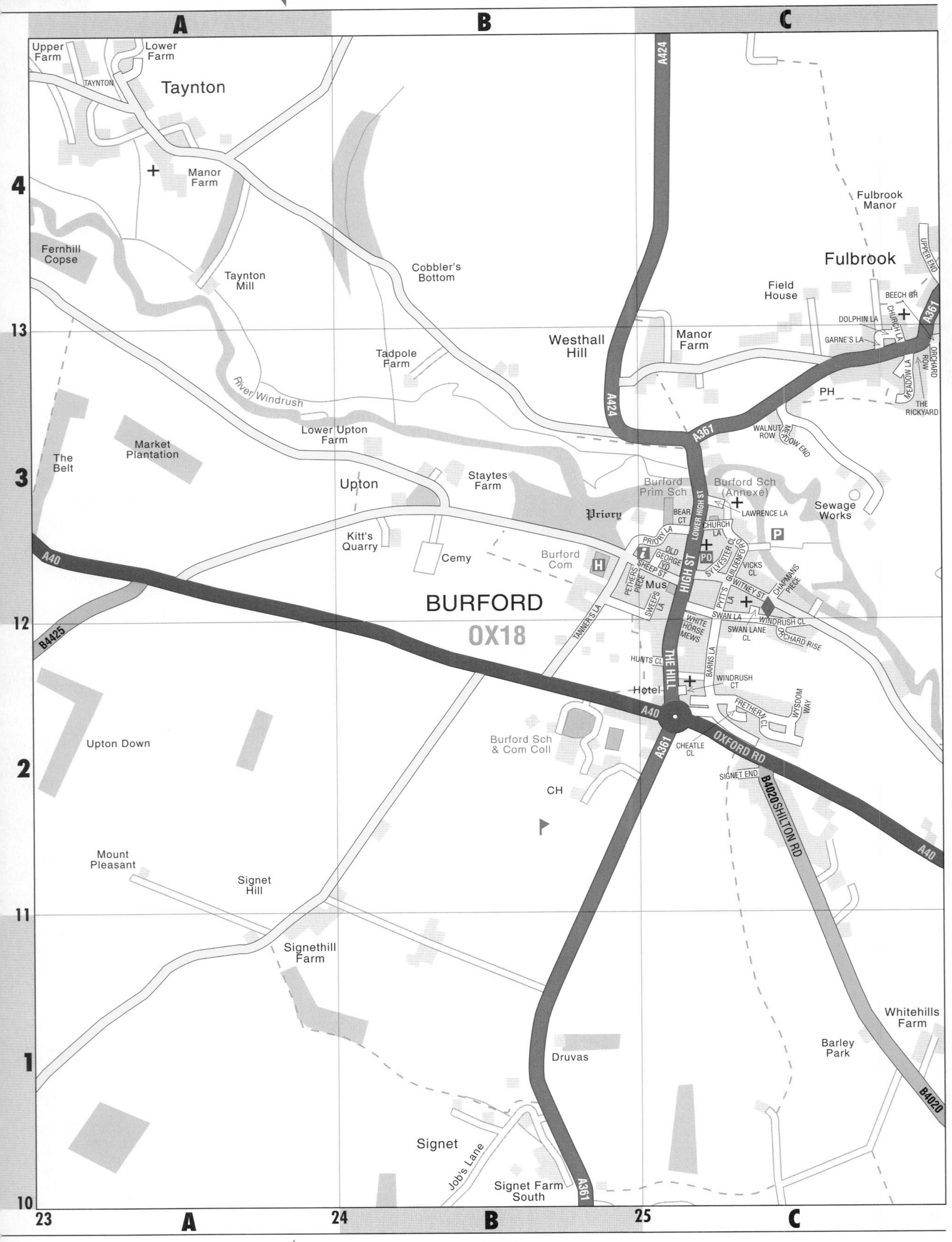

A
B
C

4

13

3

12

2

11

1

10

23
A
24
B
25
C

Upper Farm
Lower Farm
TAYNTON
Taynton
Manor Farm
Fernhill Copse
Taynton Mill
Cobbler's Bottom
River Windrush
Tadpole Farm
Westhall Hill
A424
A424
Fulbrook Manor
Fulbrook
Field House
BEECH GR
DOLPHIN LA
GARNE'S LA
UPPER END
A361
CHURCH LA
MEADOW END
ORCHARD ROW
PH
THE RICKYARD
Manor Farm
A361
WALNUT ROW
MEADOW END

The Belt
Market Plantation
Lower Upton Farm
Upton
Staytes Farm
Priory
Burford Prim Sch
Burford Sch (Annexe)
LAWRENCE LA
Sewage Works
A40
Kitt's Quarry
Cemy
Burford Com
BEAR CT
PRIORY LA
CHURCH LA
LOWER HIGH ST
HIGH ST
i
OLD GEORGE YD
SYLVESTER CT
GUILDENFORD
P
PO
VICKS CL
CHARMANS PIECE

B4425
BURFORD
OX18
TANNER'S LA
H
Mus
PETHER'S PIECE
SHEEP ST
SWEEP'S LA
WITNEY ST
PITT'S
WHITE HORSE MEWS
SWAN LA
SWAN LANE CL
WINDRUSH CL
ORCHARD RISE

Upton Down
Hotel
HUNTS CL
BARNS LA
THE HILL
A40
A361
WINDRUSH CT
FRETHERN CL
WYSDOM WAY

Mount Pleasant
Signet Hill
Burford Sch & Com Coll
CH
CHEATLE CL
OXFORD RD
SIGNET END
B4020 SHILTON RD

Signethill Farm
Whitehills Farm
Barley Park

Druvas
B4020

Signet
Job's Lane
A361
Signet Farm South

85
102

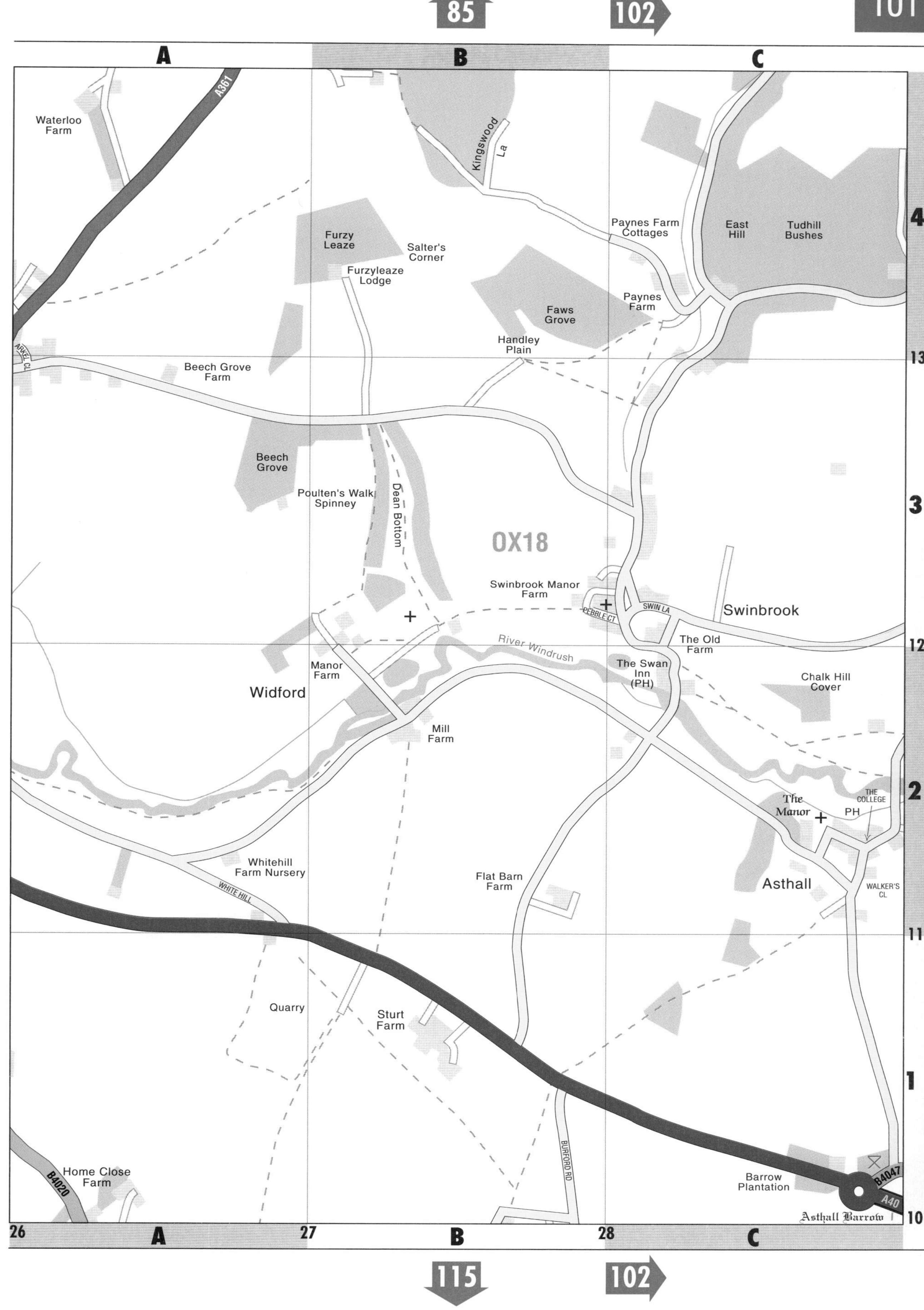
A
B
C
4
13
3
12
2
11
1
10
26
27
28
A361
Waterloo Farm
Kingswood La
Furzy Leaze
Salter's Corner
Furzyleaze Lodge
Paynes Farm Cottages
East Hill
Tudhill Bushes
Paynes Farm
Faws Grove
Handley Plain
ARKELL CL
Beech Grove Farm
Beech Grove
Poulten's Walk Spinney
Dean Bottom
OX18
Swinbrook Manor Farm
PEBBLE CT
SWIN LA
Swinbrook
The Old Farm
River Windrush
Manor Farm
Widford
The Swan Inn (PH)
Chalk Hill Cover
Mill Farm
The Manor
PH
THE COLLEGE
Whitehill Farm Nursery
WHITE HILL
Flat Barn Farm
Asthall
WALKER'S CL
Quarry
Sturt Farm
BURFORD RD
Home Close Farm
B4020
Barrow Plantation
B4047
A40
Asthall Barrow

115
102

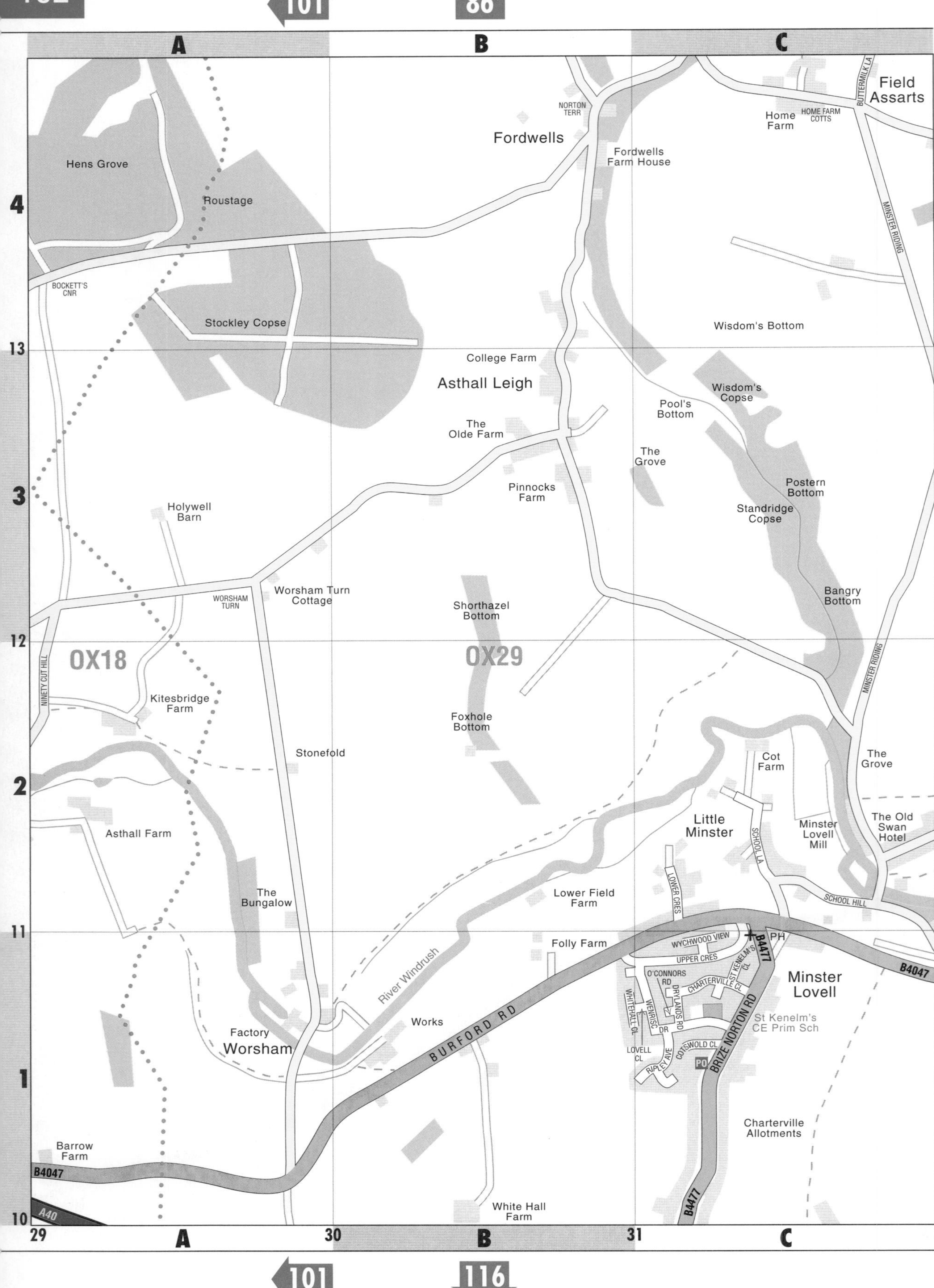

A B C

4

Hens Grove

Roustage

BOCKETT'S CNR

Fordwells

NORTON TERR

Fordwells Farm House

Home Farm

HOME FARM COTTS

BUTTERMILK LA

Field Assarts

MINSTER RIDING

13

Stockley Copse

College Farm

Asthall Leigh

Wisdom's Bottom

Wisdom's Copse

3

Holywell Barn

The Olde Farm

Pinnocks Farm

Pool's Bottom

The Grove

Postern Bottom

Standridge Copse

12

Worsham Turn Cottage

WORSHAM TURN

NINETY CUT HILL

OX18

Shorthazel Bottom

OX29

Bangry Bottom

MINSTER RIDING

Kitesbridge Farm

Stonefold

Foxhole Bottom

Cot Farm

The Grove

2

Asthall Farm

Little Minster

Minster Lovell Mill

The Old Swan Hotel

The Bungalow

Lower Field Farm

SCHOOL LA

SCHOOL HILL

11

River Windrush

Folly Farm

WYCHWOOD VIEW

UPPER CRES

LOWER CRES

PH

B4477

B4047

Minster Lovell

O'CONNORS RD

CHARTERVILLE CL

ST KENELM'S CL

Works

BURFORD RD

WHITEHALL CL

DRYLANDS RD

WEBBS CL

DR

COTSWOLD CL

BRIZE NORTON RD

St Kenelm's CE Prim Sch

Factory

Worsham

LOVELL CL

RIPLEY AVE

PO

1

Barrow Farm

Charterville Allotments

B4047

B4477

A40

White Hall Farm

10

29 A 30 B 31 C

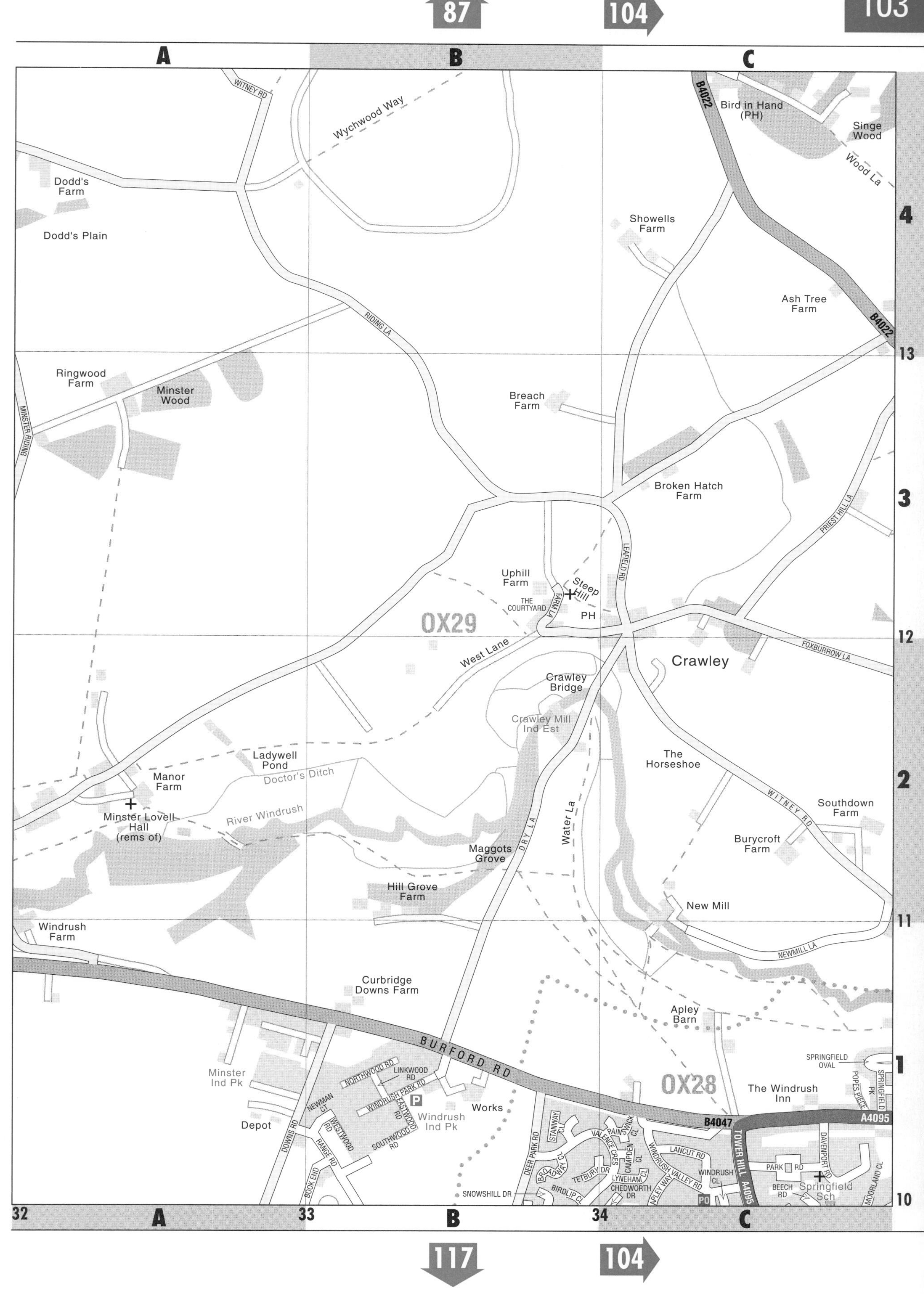

A
B
C

WITNEY RD
Wychwood Way

B4022
Bird in Hand (PH)
Singe Wood
Wood La

Dodd's Farm

Dodd's Plain

Showells Farm

4

Ash Tree Farm

B4022

RIDING LA

Ringwood Farm

Minster Wood

MINSTER RIDING

13

Breach Farm

Broken Hatch Farm

PRIEST HILL LA

3

Uphill Farm

THE COURTYARD

Steep Hill
PH

LEAFIELD RD

FARM LA

OX29

West Lane

Crawley

FOXBURROW LA

12

Crawley Bridge

Crawley Mill Ind Est

The Horseshoe

WITNEY RD

2

Ladywell Pond

Doctor's Ditch

Manor Farm

Minster Lovell Hall (rems of)

River Windrush

DRY LA

Water La

Southdown Farm

Burycroft Farm

Maggots Grove

Hill Grove Farm

New Mill

11

Windrush Farm

NEWMILL LA

Curbridge Downs Farm

Apley Barn

SPRINGFIELD OVAL

POPES PIECE

SPRINGFIELD PK

1

BURFORD RD

Minster Ind Pk

OX28

The Windrush Inn

A4095

NEWMAN CT
NORTHWOOD RD
LINKWOOD RD
WINDRUSH PARK RD
EASTWOOD RD
P

Windrush Ind Pk

Works

B4047

TOWER HILL A4095

Depot

DOWNS RD
WESTWOOD RD
RANGE RD
BROAD END
SOUTHWOOD RD

DEER PARK RD
STANWAY CL
BROADWELL RD
BIRDLIP RD
LYNEHAM RD
TETBURY DR
PAINSWICK
VALENCE CRES
CAMWICK
CHEDWORTH DR
PEDWICK
APLEY WAY
WINDRUSH VALLEY RD
LANCUT RD
WINDRUSH CL
PO

PARK RD
BEECH RD
Springfield Sch
DAVENPORT RD
MOORLAND CL

SNOWSHILL DR

10

103
88

A   B   C

4

Turley Farm
Gigley Farm
The Bungalow
North Leigh La
TURLEY LA
Common Leys Farm
Wynchwood Way
Delly End
Taylor's Copse
WOOD LA
WHITINGS LA
DELLY CL
Hickrall
New Yatt Farm
New Yatt
GREEN LA
KILE LA
Manor House
Breach Lane
The Hydes
HATFIELD PITS LA
NEW YATT LA
Keepers Cottage
Bsns Ctr
Breach Farm
The Saddler's Arms (PH)
Moorland Farm
New Yatt

13

B4022
PRIEST HILL
Middletown
Job's Copse
Home Farm
Heath Holm Farm
GLYFRINALS RD
FISHERS CL
Hailey CE Prim Sch
DELLY HILL
Hailey
PH
POFFLEY END HOS
NEW RD
FLOREY'S CL
TOWNS END
PO
HEMPLANDS
Spicers Lane

3

CHURCH LA
Poffley End
CHAPEL LA
POFFLEY END LA
SWANHALL LA
Swanhall Farm
Witheridge Farm
Witheridge Cross
WATER LA

12

FOXBURROW LA
COX CL
OX29
Downhill Farm
University Farm
Osney Hill Farm
A4095
DOWNHILL LA
The Bungalow

2

MILKING LA
Highcroft Farm
Merryfield Farm
Witney Com Sch
The King's Sch
Cogges Wood
Middlefield Farm
SCHOFIELD GDNS
HOYLE CL
HAILEY RD
EASTFIELD
WITNEY RD
WESTFIELD RD
QUARRY RD
SCHOFIELD AVE
TAPHOUSE AVE
VANNER RD
NEW YATT RD
TARRANT AVE

11

WOODSTOCK RD
CRAWLEY RD
B4022
BAKERS PIECE
FARMERS CL
FARMERS CL
GREEN CNR
CHESTNUT CL
VINER CL
EARLY RD
MADLEY CL
THE CRESCENT
Woodgreen
Northfield Farm
River Windrush
Wks
CAPTAINS MILL
MILLER'S MEWS
WEST END
PO
WOODGREEN
SYCAMORE CL
WOODLANDS CT
WOODLANDS RD
Wood Green Sch
Springfield Oval

1

Springfield Park
Mills
West End Ind Est
BRIDGE ST
GRANGERS PL
RIVERSIDE GDNS
THE OLD WAREHOUSE FLATS
ALMSHOUSES
PENSCLOSE
WITNEY
A4095 BURFORD RD
MILL ST
MOORA AVE
PUCK LA
DARK LA
GLOUCESTER PL
UPP OBS
WITAN WAY
HIGH ST
THE WILLOWS
NEWLAND
Newland
MADLEY BROOK
Tower Hill Com Sch
MOORLAND RD
Witney Com
GLOUCESTER CT MEWS
THE OLD COACHYARD
B4022
KINGSFIELD CRES
COURTS GDNS
JUDD'S CL
H
Bridge Street Mill Bsns Pk

10

35   36   37

A   B   C

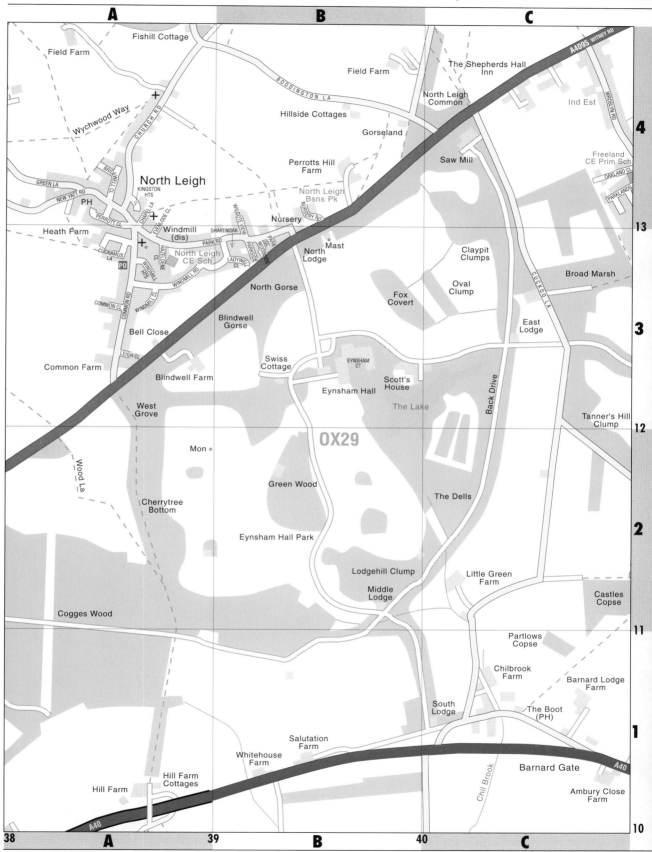
89

106

A B C

Fishill Cottage
Field Farm
Field Farm
BODDINGTON LA
The Shepherds Hall Inn
A4095 WITNEY RD
North Leigh Common
Ind Est
WROSLYN RD
Hillside Cottages
Wychwood Way
CHURCH RD
Gorseland
Saw Mill
Freeland CE Prim Sch
OAKLAND CL
PARKLANDS
Perrotts Hill Farm
North Leigh
BRIDEWELL CL
GREEN LA
KINGSTON HTS
NEW YATT RD
PH
North Leigh Bsns Pk
NURSERY RD
CHAPEL LA
EVENLODE CL
WILCOTE VIEW
PERROTT CL
Nursery
Heath Farm
Windmill (dis)
SHAKENOAK
PARK CL
PARK RD
Mast
WOODSIDE
PARKSIDE
North Lodge
Claypit Clumps
CUCKAMUS LA
HAZELDENE CL
North Leigh CE Sch
LADYWELL CL
PO
WINDMILL HTS
WINDMILL RD
Broad Marsh
North Gorse
Oval Clump
Fox Covert
CUCKOO LA
COMMON CL
COMMON RD
WINDMILL CL
Blindwell Gorse
East Lodge
Bell Close
LEIGH CL
Swiss Cottage
EYNSHAM CT
Common Farm
Blindwell Farm
Scott's House
Eynsham Hall
Back Drive
West Grove
The Lake
Tanner's Hill Clump
OX29
Mon
Wood La
Green Wood
The Dells
Cherrytree Bottom
Eynsham Hall Park
Lodgehill Clump
Little Green Farm
Castles Copse
Middle Lodge
Cogges Wood
Partlows Copse
Chilbrook Farm
Barnard Lodge Farm
South Lodge
The Boot (PH)
Salutation Farm
Whitehouse Farm
Barnard Gate
A40
Chil Brook
Hill Farm Cottages
Hill Farm
Ambury Close Farm
A40

4
13
3
12
2
11
1
10

38 A 39 B 40 C

119

106

105 90

A B C

HURDSWELL

GLYME WY
MARLBOROUGH CRES
CHURCHILL WAY
ROOSEVELT RD
PINSLEY RD
QUEEN ELEANOR CT

Allot Gdns

Pinsley Wood

Mill Farm

LOWER RD

4

Cook's Corner

Cemy

CHURCH RD

OAKLAND CL
Freeland CE Prim Sch
PARKLANDS
PO

Freeland

WADSWYN RD
HURST LA
MASH LA
WOODLANDS
THE BLOWINGS
ASH LA
CHURCH LA
WALKERS

13

Little Blenheim

Sewage Works

MANSELL CL

Church Hanborough

PH

College Farm

BUSBY CL
WEBSTER'S CL
BROAD MARSH LA
BLENHEIM LA

PH

+

+

+

Whitehouse Farm

PIGEON HOUSE LA

Dreydon House

Goose Eye Farm

3

Freeland House

Elm Farm

The Thrift

The Green

12

Lady Grove

OX29

New Barn Farm

River Evenlode

Vincents Wood

CUCKOO LA

2

Bowles Farm

CUCKOO LA

City Farm

11

Eynsham Mill

MILL LA

1

Acre Hill Farm

New Wintles Farm

A40

Evenlode Farm

Acre Hill House

A40

Chil Brook

10

41 A 42 B 43 C

105 120

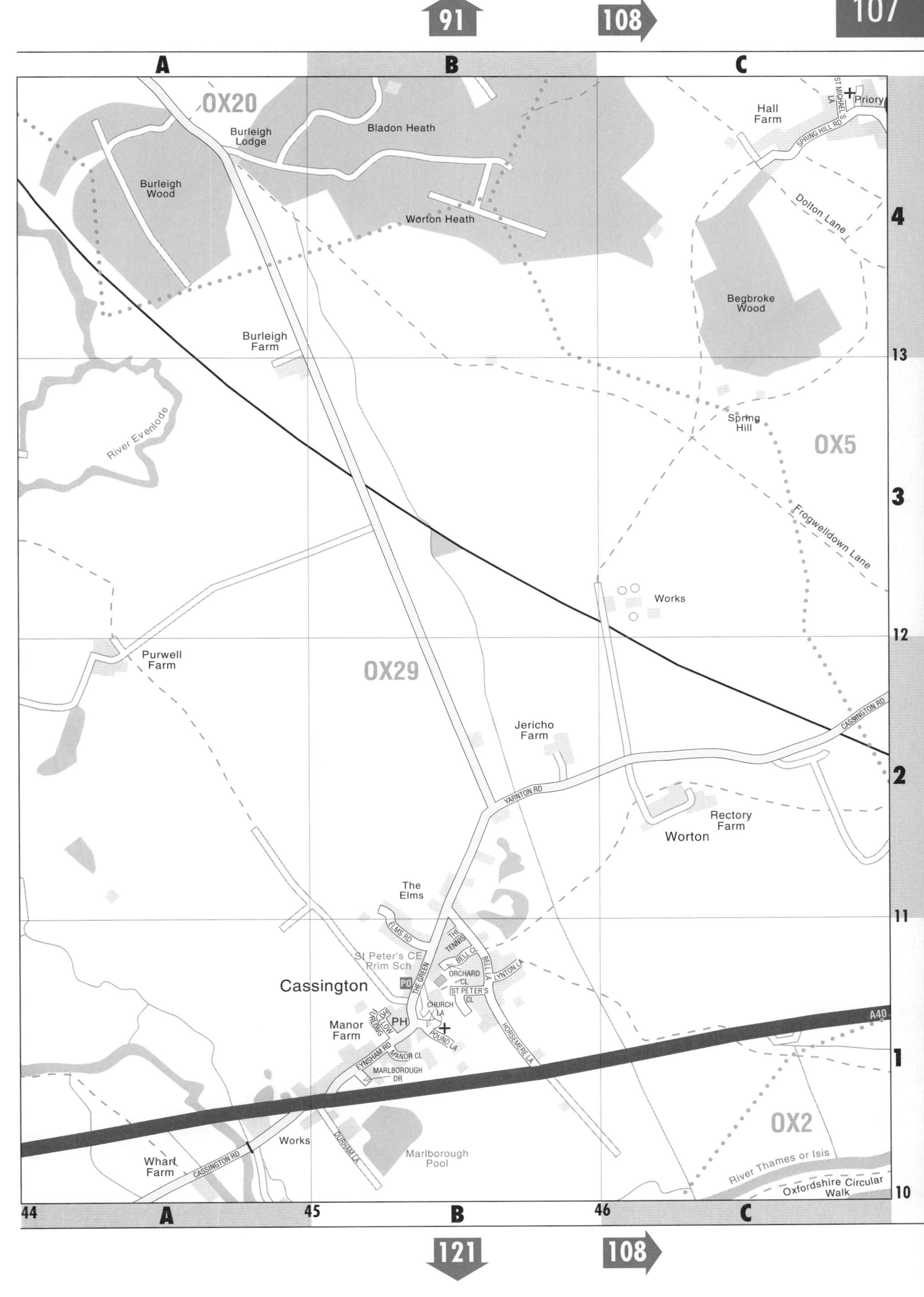

A B C

OX20

Burleigh Lodge
Bladon Heath
Hall Farm
ST MICHAEL'S LA
Priory
SPRING HILL RD

Burleigh Wood

Worton Heath
Dolton Lane

4

Begbroke Wood

Burleigh Farm

13

Spring Hill

River Evenlode
OX5

Frogwelldown Lane

3

Works

12

Purwell Farm

OX29

CASSINGTON RD

Jericho Farm

2

YARNTON RD
Rectory Farm

Worton

The Elms

11

ELMS RD
THE TENNIS
BELL CL
BELL LA
LYNTON LA

St Peter's CE Prim Sch
PO
ORCHARD CL
ST PETER'S CL

Cassington
THE GREEN
CHURCH LA
A40

Manor Farm
PH
FURLONG
MANOR CL
POUND LA
HORSEMERE LA

EYNSHAM RD
MARLBOROUGH DR

1

OX2

Wharf Farm
CASSINGTON RD
Works
DURHAM LA
Marlborough Pool

River Thames or Isis
Oxfordshire Circular Walk

10

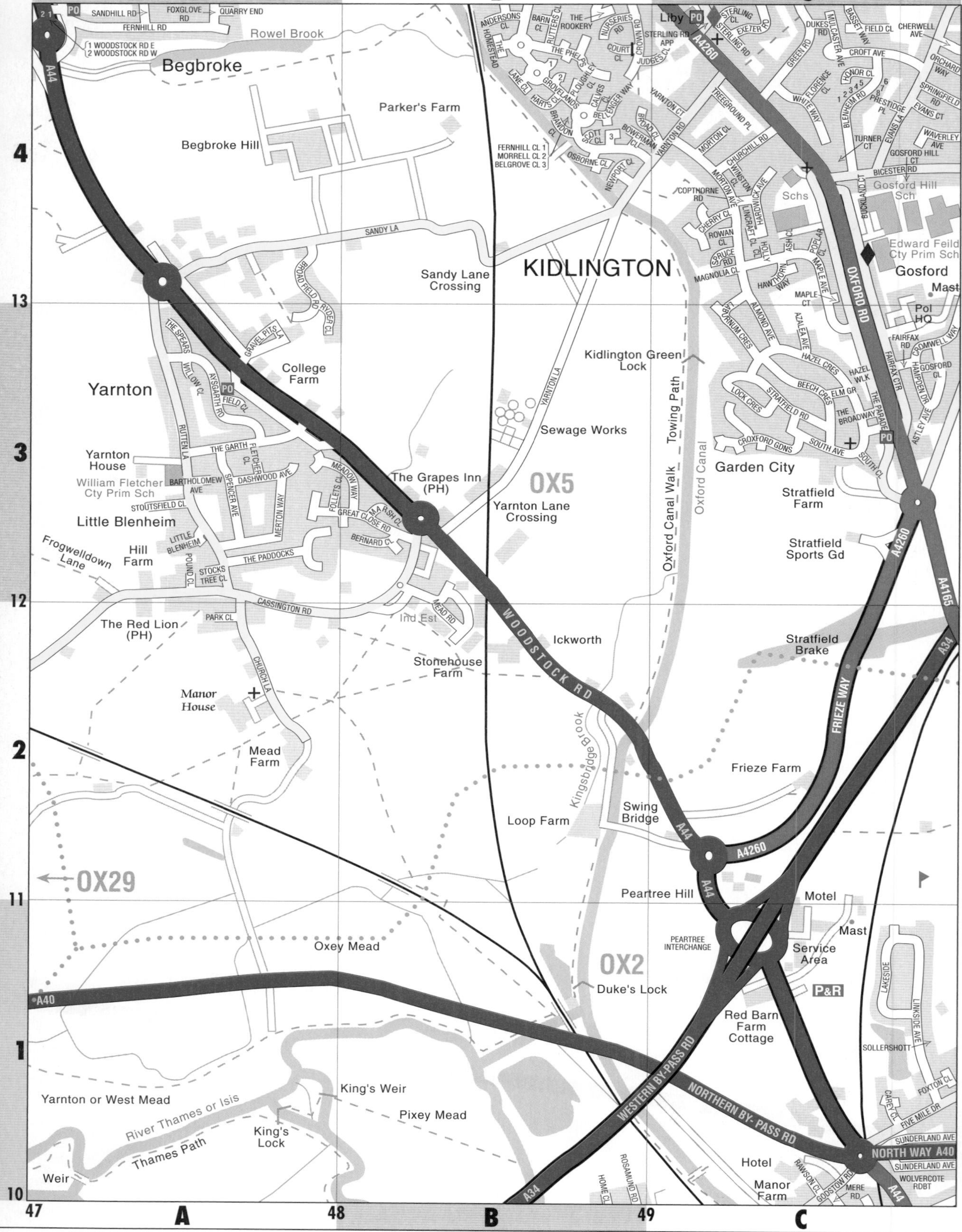

C4
1 ANDOVER CT
2 BLENHEIM CT
3 CLEVEDON CT
4 DORCHESTER CT
5 EXETER CT
6 FARNHAM CT
7 GUILDFORD CT
8 HERTFORD CT

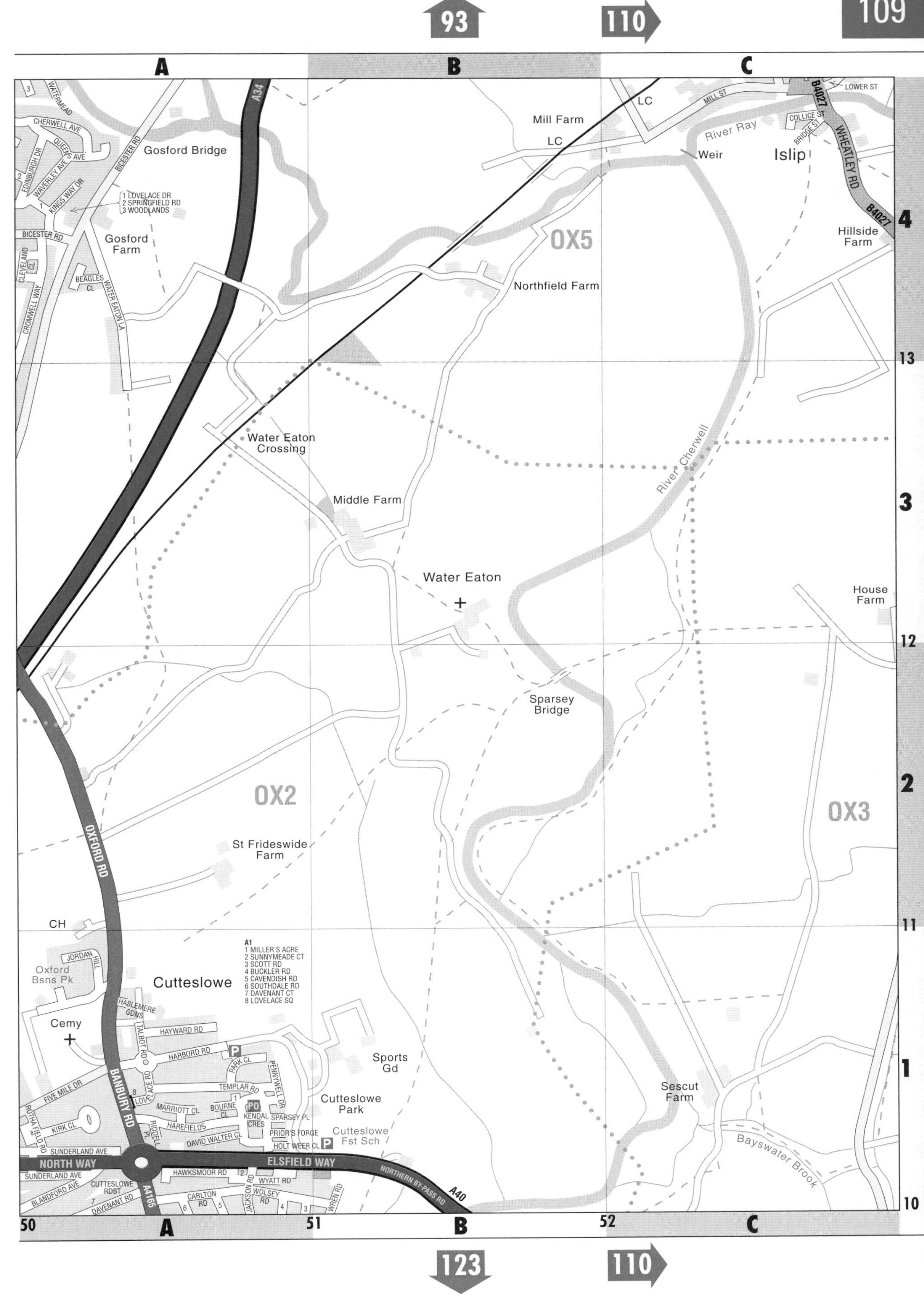
93
110
A
B
C
Gosford Bridge
1 LOVELACE DR
2 SPRINGFIELD RD
3 WOODLANDS
Gosford Farm
Mill Farm
LC
River Ray
Weir
Islip
WHEATLEY RD
B4027
LOWER ST
MILL ST
COLLICE ST
BRIDGE ST
Hillside Farm
OX5
Northfield Farm
A34
CHERWELL AVE
QUEENS AVE
WAVERLEY AVE
EDINBURGH DR
KINGS WAY DR
BICESTER RD
CLEVELAND CL
CROMWELL WAY
BEAGLES CL
WATER EATON LA
WATERMEAD
Water Eaton Crossing
Middle Farm
River Cherwell
Water Eaton
House Farm
Sparsey Bridge
OX2
OX3
St Frideswide Farm
OXFORD RD
CH
JORDAN HILL
Oxford Bsns Pk
Cutteslowe
A1
1 MILLER'S ACRE
2 SUNNYMEADE CT
3 SCOTT RD
4 BUCKLER RD
5 CAVENDISH RD
6 SOUTHDALE RD
7 DAVENANT CT
8 LOVELACE SQ
HASLEMERE GDNS
Cemy
HAYWARD RD
TALBOT RD
HARBORD RD
PARK CL
PENNYWELL DR
Sports Gd
TEMPLAR RD
FIVE MILE DR
LOVELACE RD
MARRIOTT CL
BOURNE CL
KENDAL CRES
SPARSEY PL
Cutteslowe Park
ROTHAFIELD RD
KIRK CL
HAREFIELDS
RIDDELL PL
DAVID WALTER CL
PRIOR'S FORGE
Cutteslowe Fst Sch
HOLT WEER CL
SUNDERLAND AVE
BANBURY RD
NORTH WAY
ELSFIELD WAY
NORTHERN BY-PASS RD
A40
HAWKSMOOR RD
WYATT RD
JACKSON RD
WOLSEY RD
CARLTON RD
WREN RD
CUTTESLOWE RDBT
BLANDFORD AVE
DAVENANT RD
A4165
Sescut Farm
Bayswater Brook
4
13
3
12
2
11
1
10
50
51
52
123

109
94

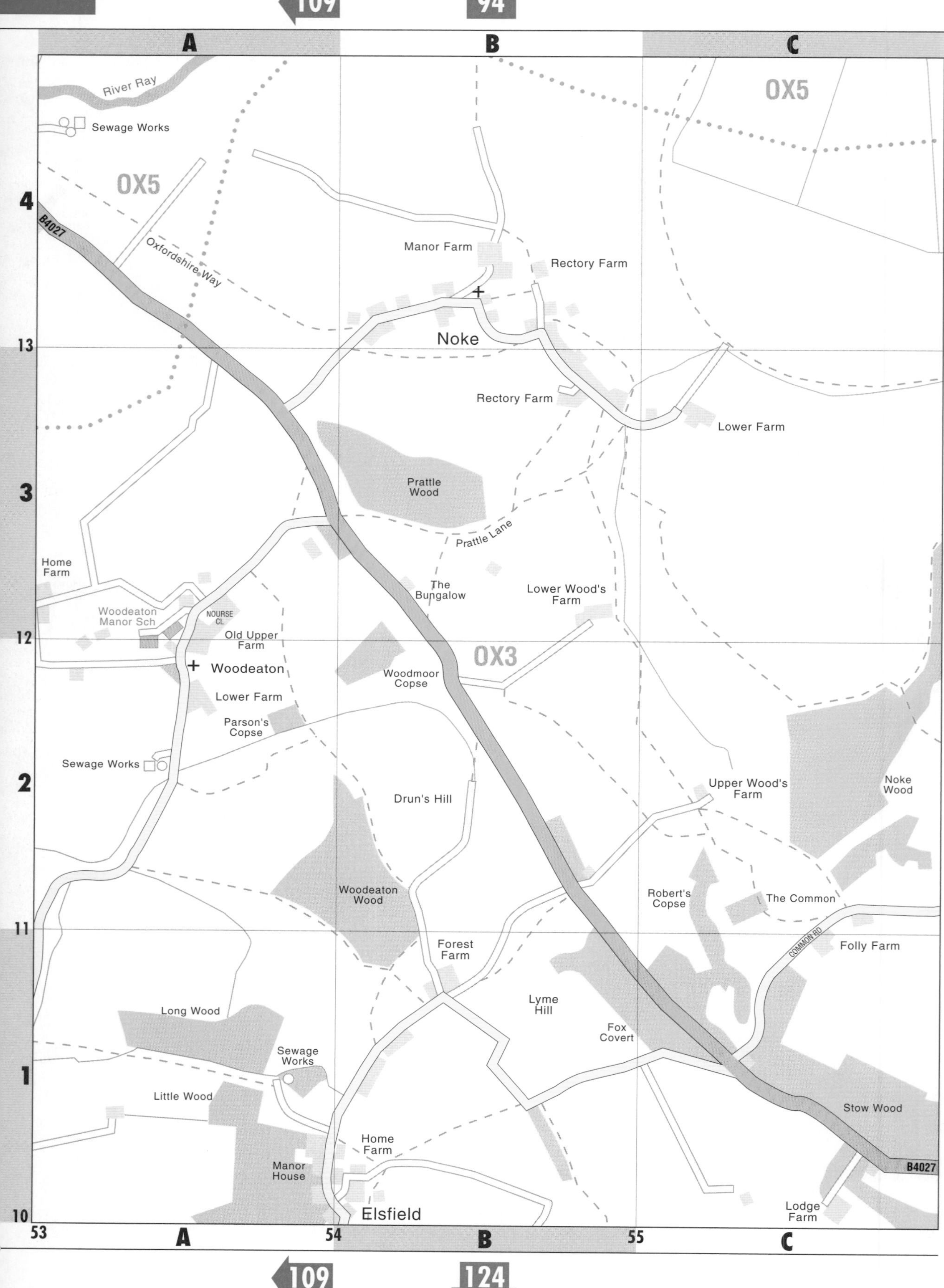
A
B
C
River Ray
Sewage Works
OX5
OX5
B4027
Oxfordshire Way
Manor Farm
Rectory Farm
Noke
Rectory Farm
Lower Farm
Prattle Wood
Prattle Lane
Home Farm
The Bungalow
Lower Wood's Farm
Woodeaton Manor Sch
NOURSE CL
Old Upper Farm
Woodeaton
OX3
Woodmoor Copse
Lower Farm
Parson's Copse
Sewage Works
Drun's Hill
Upper Wood's Farm
Noke Wood
Woodeaton Wood
Robert's Copse
The Common
Forest Farm
COMMON RD
Folly Farm
Long Wood
Lyme Hill
Fox Covert
Sewage Works
Little Wood
Stow Wood
Home Farm
Manor House
B4027
Elsfield
Lodge Farm
4
13
3
12
2
11
1
10
53
54
55

109
124

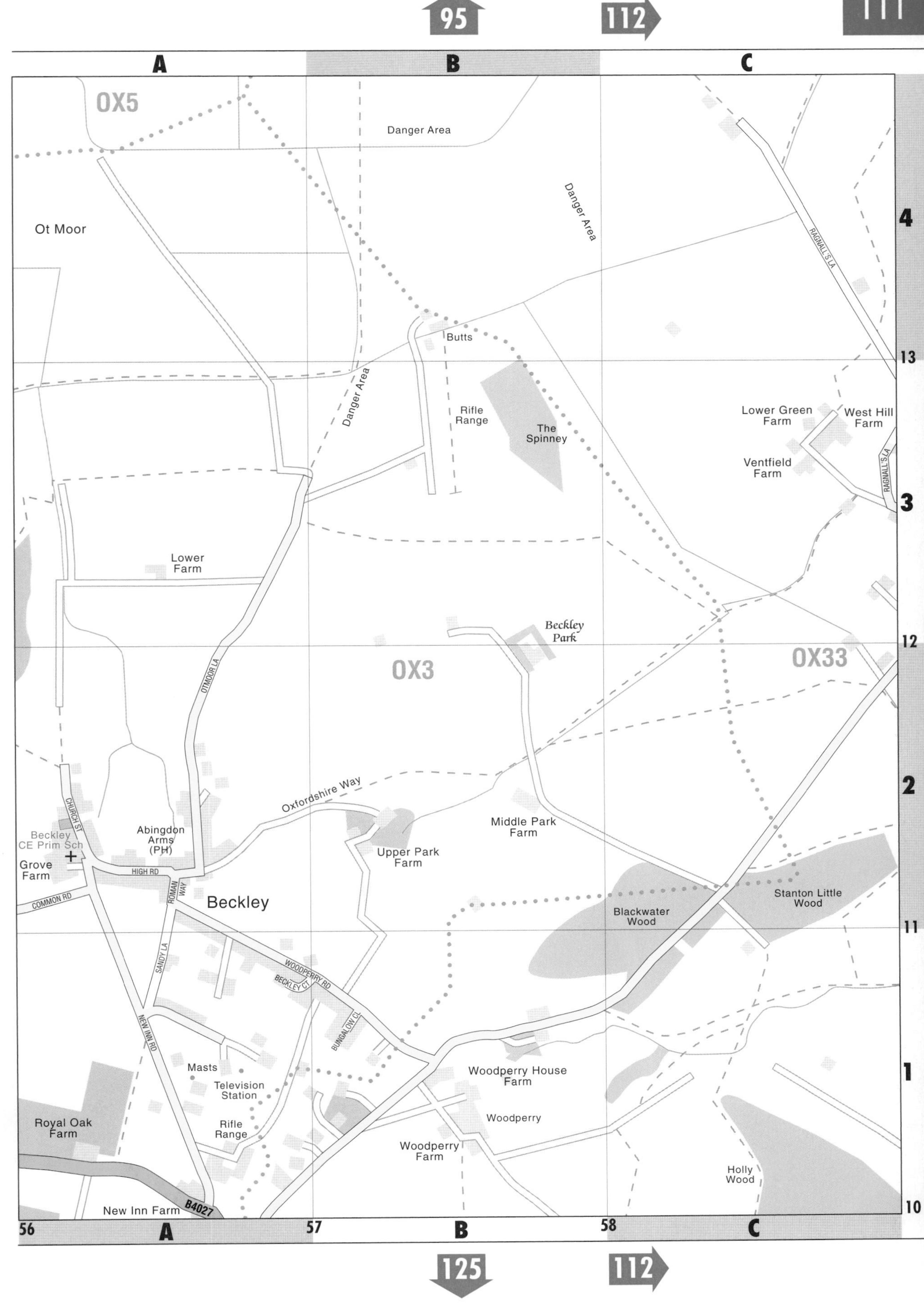

OX5

Ot Moor

Danger Area

Danger Area

Danger Area

RAGNALL'S LA

Butts

Rifle Range

The Spinney

Lower Green Farm

West Hill Farm

Ventfield Farm

RAGNALL'S LA

Lower Farm

OTMOOR LA

Beckley Park

OX3

OX33

Oxfordshire Way

Middle Park Farm

Upper Park Farm

CHURCH ST

Beckley CE Prim Sch

Grove Farm

Abingdon Arms (PH)

HIGH RD

ROMAN WAY

Beckley

COMMON RD

Blackwater Wood

Stanton Little Wood

SANDY LA

WOODPERRY RD

BECKLEY CT

BUNGALOW CL

NEW INN RD

Masts

Television Station

Rifle Range

Royal Oak Farm

Woodperry House Farm

Woodperry

Woodperry Farm

Holly Wood

New Inn Farm

B4027

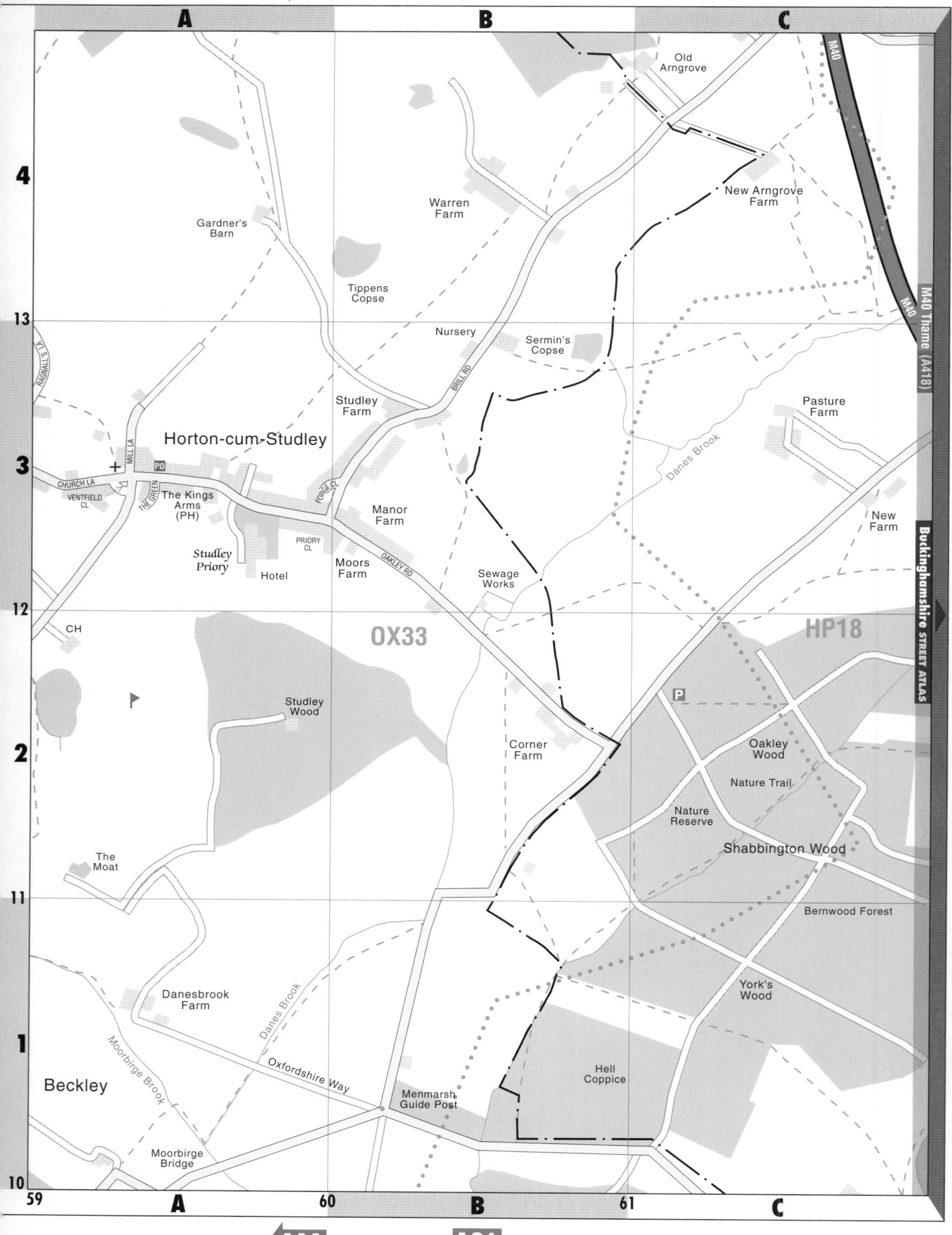

A **B** **C**

4

New Arngrove Farm

Old Arngrove

Warren Farm

Gardner's Barn

Tippens Copse

13

Nursery

Sermin's Copse

Pasture Farm

Danes Brook

Studley Farm

BRILL RD

Horton-cum-Studley

3

CHURCH LA

VENTFIELD CL

MILL LA

PO

The Green

The Kings Arms (PH)

FORGE CL

Manor Farm

New Farm

Studley Priory

PRIORY CL

Hotel

Moors Farm

OAKLEY RD

Sewage Works

CH

12

OX33

HP18

P

Studley Wood

Oakley Wood

Nature Trail

Nature Reserve

Corner Farm

Shabbington Wood

The Moat

11

Bernwood Forest

Danes Brook

Danesbrook Farm

York's Wood

Moorbirge Brook

1

Oxfordshire Way

Beckley

Menmarsh Guide Post

Hell Coppice

Moorbirge Bridge

10

59 **A** 60 **B** 61 **C**

M40

M40 Thame (A418)

Buckinghamshire STREET ATLAS

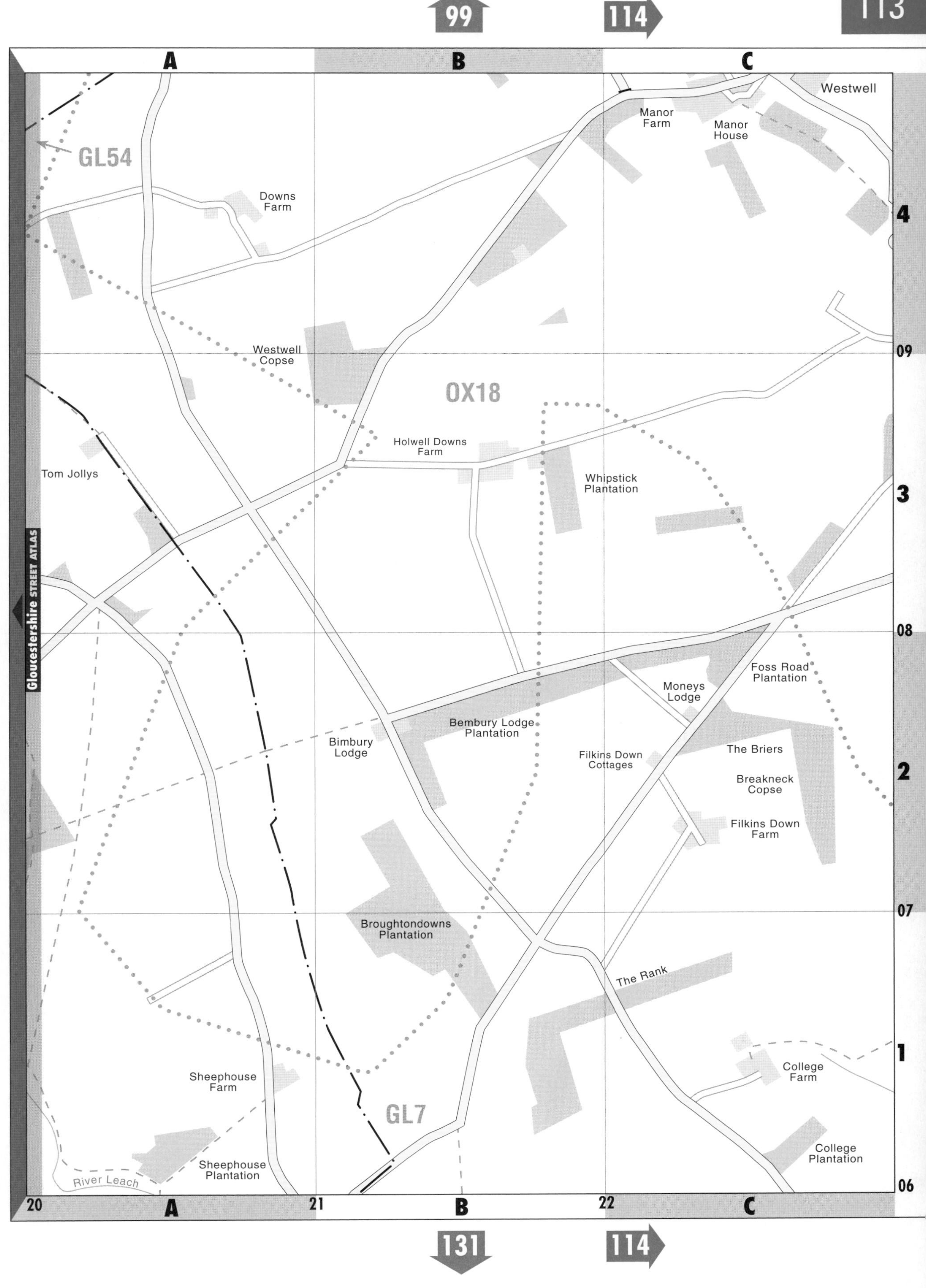
99
114
A
B
C
Westwell
Manor Farm
Manor House
GL54
Downs Farm
4
Westwell Copse
09
OX18
Holwell Downs Farm
Tom Jollys
Whipstick Plantation
3
Gloucestershire STREET ATLAS
08
Foss Road Plantation
Moneys Lodge
Bembury Lodge Plantation
Bimbury Lodge
Filkins Down Cottages
The Briers
Breakneck Copse
2
Filkins Down Farm
07
Broughtondowns Plantation
The Rank
1
College Farm
Sheephouse Farm
GL7
College Plantation
Sheephouse Plantation
River Leach
06
20
A
21
B
22
C
131
114

113
100

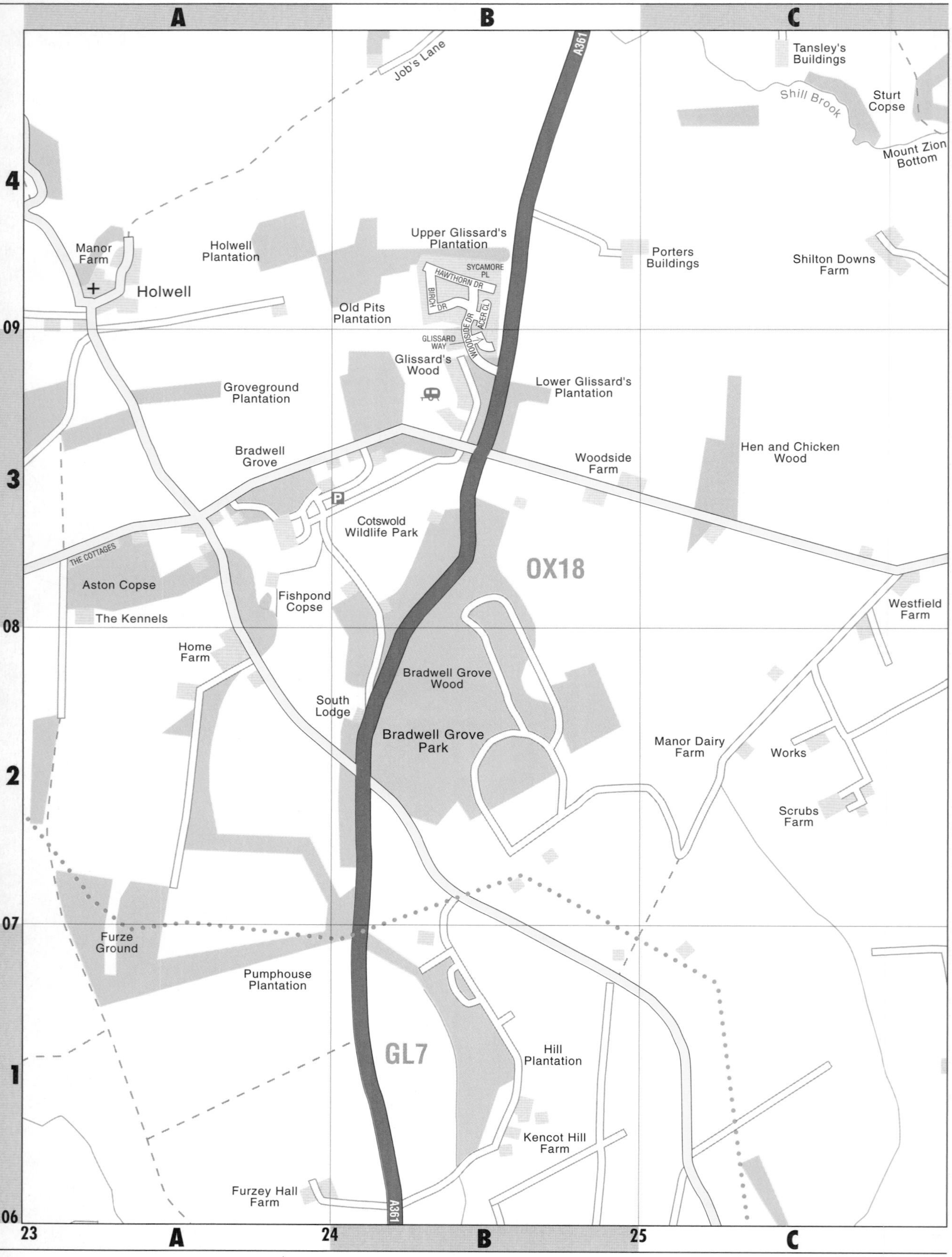

A **B** **C**

Job's Lane

Tansley's
Buildings

Shill Brook

Sturt
Copse

Mount Zion
Bottom

4

Manor
Farm

Holwell
Plantation

Upper Glissard's
Plantation

Porters
Buildings

Shilton Downs
Farm

Holwell

SYCAMORE
PL

HAWTHORN DR

BIRCH DR

ACER CL

Old Pits
Plantation

WOODSIDE DR

GLISSARD
WAY

09

Glissard's
Wood

Lower Glissard's
Plantation

Groveground
Plantation

Bradwell
Grove

Woodside
Farm

Hen and Chicken
Wood

3

P

Cotswold
Wildlife Park

OX18

THE COTTAGES

Aston Copse

Fishpond
Copse

Westfield
Farm

08

The Kennels

Home
Farm

Bradwell Grove
Wood

South
Lodge

Bradwell Grove
Park

Manor Dairy
Farm

Works

2

Scrubs
Farm

07

Furze
Ground

Pumphouse
Plantation

GL7

Hill
Plantation

1

Kencot Hill
Farm

Furzey Hall
Farm

A361

06

23   **A**   **24**   **B**   **25**   **C**

113
132

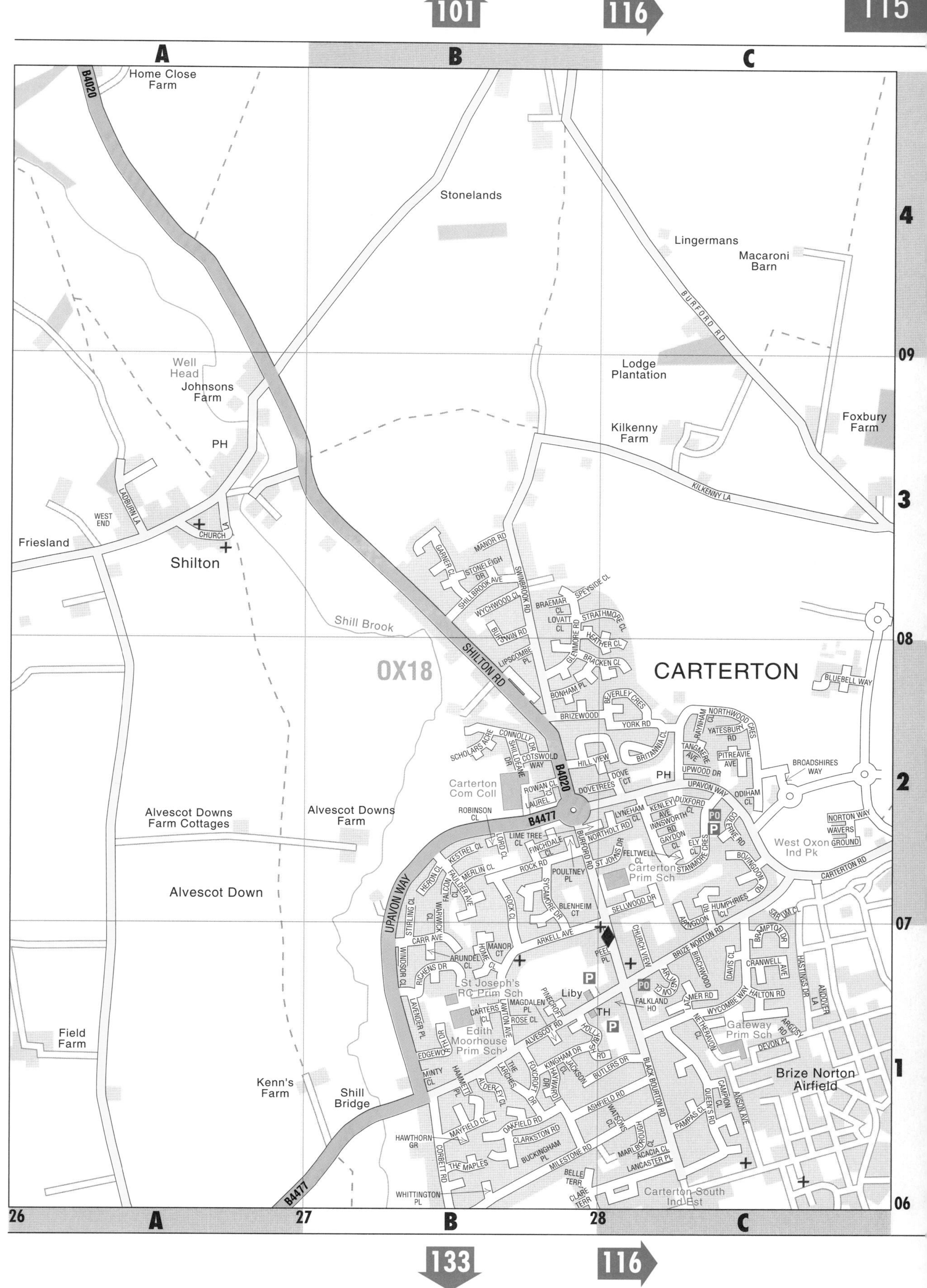

101
116

A
B
C

Home Close Farm

B4020

Stonelands

4

Lingermans

Macaroni Barn

BURFORD RD

Well Head

09

Johnsons Farm

Lodge Plantation

PH

Kilkenny Farm

Foxbury Farm

WEST END

LADBURN LA

KILKENNY LA

Friesland

CHURCH

3

Shilton

MANOR RD

GARNER CL

STONELEIGH DR

SHILLBROOK AVE

SWINBROOK RD

SPEYSIDE CL

Shill Brook

WYCHWOOD CL

BALDWIN RD

BRAEMAR CL

LOVATT CL

GLENMORE RD

STRATHMORE CL

HEATHER CL

SHILTON RD

LIPSCOMBE PL

BRACKEN CL

08

OX18

BONHAM PL

BEVERLEY CRES

CARTERTON

BLUEBELL WAY

BRIZEWOOD

YORK RD

NORTHWOOD CRES

CONNOLLY DR

BRAYTHAM

YATESBURY RD

SCHOLARS ACRE

SHILL DEANE DR

COTSWOLD WAY

HILL VIEW

DOVE CT

TANGMERE AVE

PITREAVIE AVE

BROADSHIRES WAY

2

Carterton Com Coll

ROWAN CL

DOVETREES

PH

UPWOOD DR

ODIHAM

LAUREL

BURFORD RD

B4020

LYNEHAM

KENLEY AVE

DUXFORD

NORTON WAY

ROBINSON CL

B4477

NORTHOLT RD

INNSWORTH RD

WAVERS

West Oxon Ind Pk

Alvescot Downs Farm Cottages

Alvescot Downs Farm

KESTREL CL

LIME TREE CL

FINCHDALE CL

GAYDON

ST JOHNS DR

FELTWELL CL

ELY CL

STANMORE CRES

BOVINGDON RD

CARTERTON RD

HERON CL

FALCON

MERLIN CL

ROCK RD

SYCAMORE RD

POULTNEY PL

Carterton Prim Sch

ABINGDON RD

HUMPHRIES

UPAVON WAY

STIRLING CL

WARWICK CL

FALLOW AVE

ROCK CL

BLENHEIM CT

SELLWOOD DR

BRIZE NORTON RD

07

Alvescot Down

CARR AVE

WINDRUSH

RICHENS DR

ARUNDEL CL

MANOR CT

ARKELL AVE

PEEL PL

CHURCH VIEW

BIRCHWOOD

DAVIS CL

CRANWELL AVE

HASTINGS DR

ANDOVER LA

St Joseph's RC Prim Sch

Liby

BRAMPTON DR

HOME CL

LAVENDER PL

CARTERS

MAGDALEN PL

PINECROFT

Libby

PO

AMER RD

WYCOMBE WAY

HALTON RD

NETHERAVON

Gateway Prim Sch

ARGOSY

Field Farm

EDGEWORTH

ROSE CL

LAWTON RD

ALVESCOT RD

FALKLAND HO

TH

FOLLY RD

BLACK BOURTON RD

DEVON CL

1

Edith Moorhouse Prim Sch

THE LARCHES

KINGHAM DR

BUTLERS DR

CAMPION

AINSLIE AVE

Brize Norton Airfield

Kenn's Farm

MINTY CL

ALDER CL

FOXCROFT DR

HAWTHORN GR

Shill Bridge

MAYFIELD CL

OAKFIELD CL

CLARKSTON RD

ASHFIELD RD

MILESTONE RD

HIGHFIELD

WATSONS CL

MARLBOROUGH

PAMPAS CL

OLEEN'S RD

LANCASTER PL

ACACIA CL

CORBETT RD

THE MAPLES

BUCKINGHAM PL

BELLE TERR

CLARE TERR

Carterton South Ind Est

WHITTINGTON PL

B4477

06

26
A
27
B
28
C

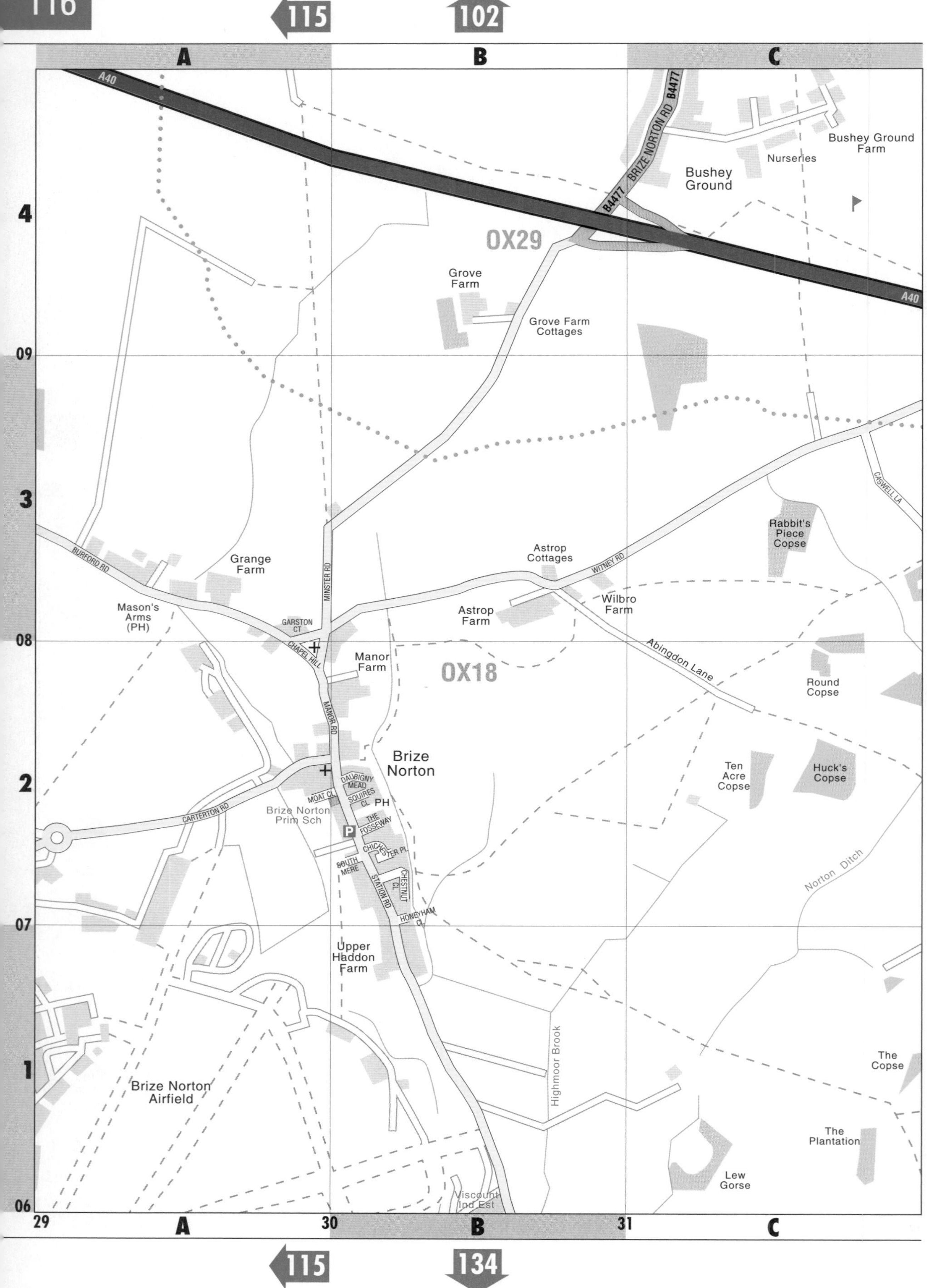

115
102

A
B
C

4

OX29

A40
A40
B4477
BRIZE NORTON RD
B4477

Bushey Ground Farm

Nurseries

Bushey Ground

Grove Farm

Grove Farm Cottages

09

Caswell La

3

Rabbit's Piece Copse

Burford Rd

Grange Farm

Minster Rd

Astrop Cottages

Witney Rd

Mason's Arms (PH)

Garston Ct

Astrop Farm

Wilbro Farm

Abingdon Lane

Round Copse

08

OX18

Manor Farm

Chapel Hill

Manor Rd

Ten Acre Copse

Huck's Copse

2

Brize Norton

Daubigny Mead

Squires Cl

PH

Carterton Rd

Moat Cl

Brize Norton Prim Sch

P

The Fosseway

Chichester Pl

Norton Ditch

South Mere

Chestnut Cl

Station Rd

07

Honeyham Cl

Upper Haddon Farm

Highmoor Brook

The Copse

1

Brize Norton Airfield

The Plantation

Lew Gorse

06

Viscount Ind Est

29
A
30
B
31
C

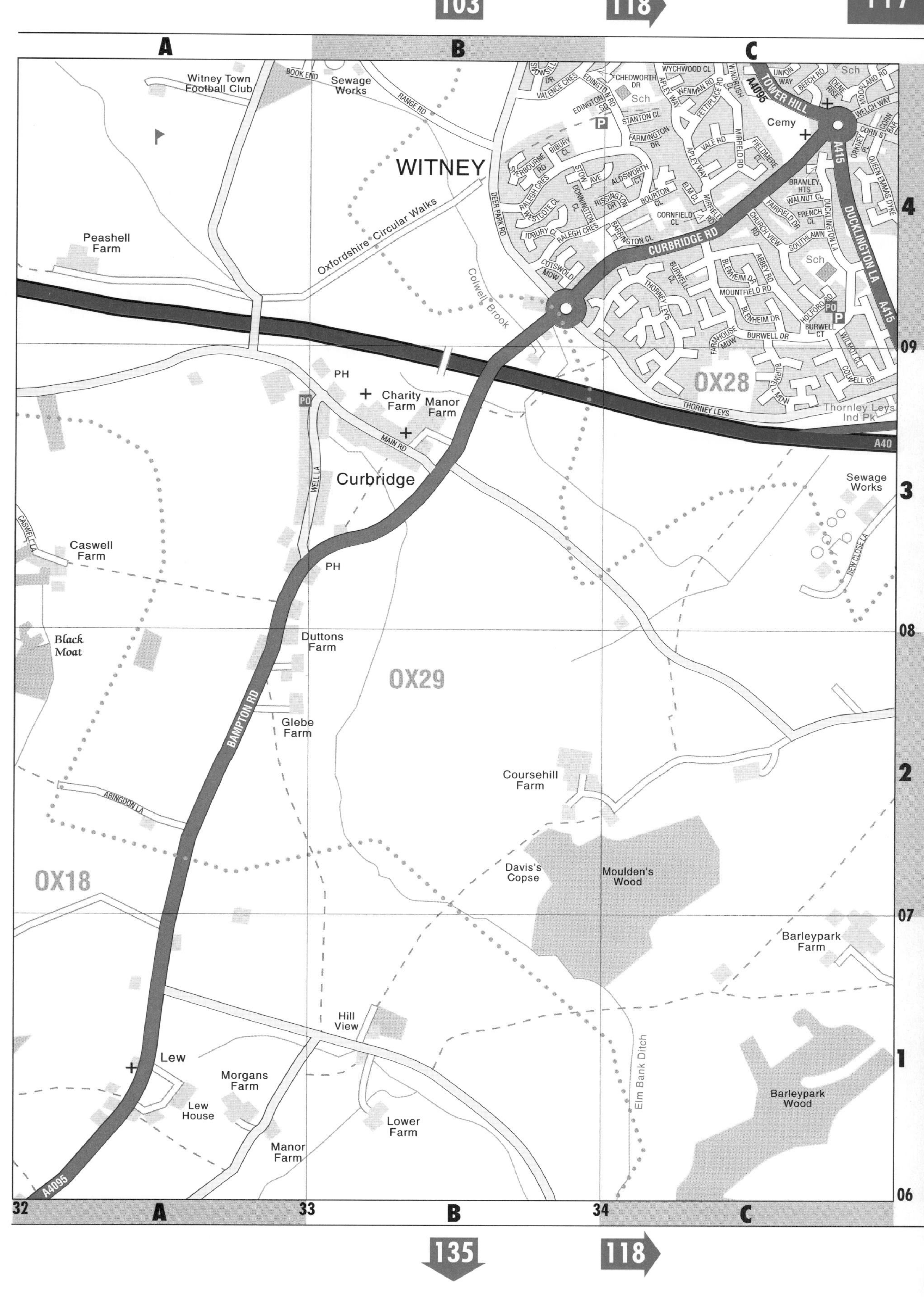

A
B
C

Witney Town Football Club
BOOK END
Sewage Works
RANGE RD
SNOWSHILL
CHEDWORTH DR
WYCHWOOD CL
VALENCE CRES
EDINGTON RD
Sch
BEECH RD
UNION WAY
WELCH WAY
DEER PARK RD
EDINGTON SQ
STANTON CL
WENMAN RD
APLEY WAY
FETTIPLACE RD
A4095
TOWER HILL
CORN ST
ROWLAND CL

WITNEY
CHERBOURNE RD
BIBURY CL
FARMINGTON DR
WINDRUSH
Cemy
P
STOW AVE
RISSINGTON DR
VALE RD
MIRFIELD RD
A415
GRANGE CL
QUEEN EMMAS DYKE
IDBURY CL
PRESCOTE CL
DONNINGTON CL
BOURTON CL
ELM CL
CHURCH VIEW
BRAMLEY HTS
WALNUT CL
FAIRFIELD DR
FRENCH CL
SOUTHLAWN

Peashell Farm
RALEGH CRES
ALDSWORTH CT
CORNFIELD CL
ABBEY RD
CHURCH LA
Sch
4

Oxfordshire Circular Walks
COTSWOLD MDW
MOUNTFIELD RD
BLENHEIM CL
BLENHEIM DR
HOLFORD RD
CURBRIDGE RD
BURWELL
FARMHOUSE MDW
PO
P
WILDMOT CL
BURWELL CT
BURWELL DR

Colwell Brook
THORNEY LEYS
OX28
COLWELL DR
09

PH
PO
+ Charity Farm
Manor Farm
MAIN RD
+
THORNEY LEYS
Thornley Leys Ind Pk
A40

WELL LA
Curbridge
Sewage Works
3

PH
Caswell Farm
CASWELL LA

Black Moat
Duttons Farm
08

BAMPTON RD
OX29

Glebe Farm

Coursehill Farm
2

ABINGDON LA
Davis's Copse
Moulden's Wood
07

OX18
Barleypark Farm

Hill View
1
Lew
+
Morgans Farm
Lower Farm
Elm Bank Ditch
Barleypark Wood

Lew House
Manor Farm
A4095
06

32
A
33
B
34
C

117
104

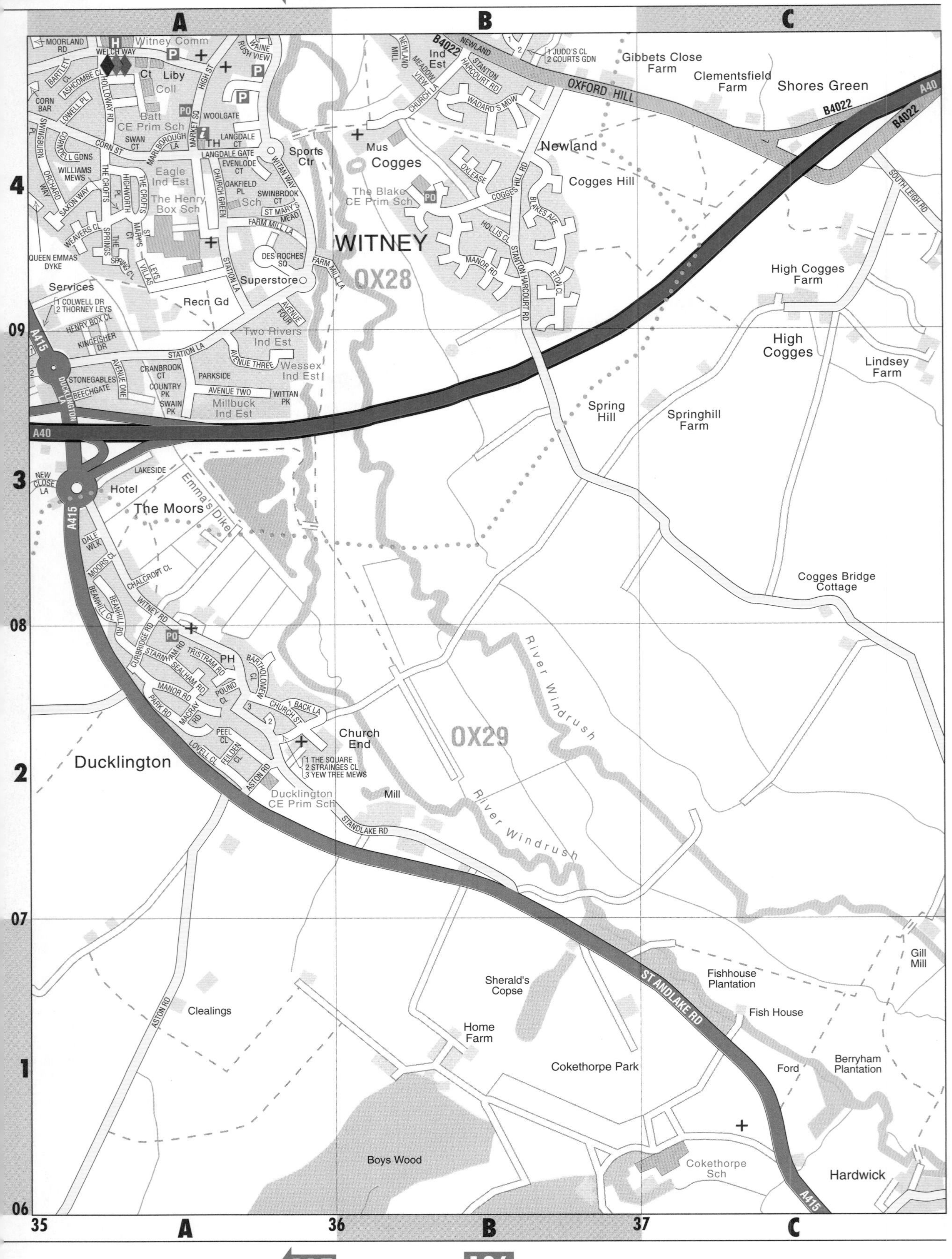
A
B
C
4
09
3
08
2
07
1
06
35
36
37
WITNEY
OX28
OX29
Witney Comm
Ct
Liby
Coll
Batt CE Prim Sch
Eagle Ind Est
The Henry Box Sch
Sch
TH
Sports Ctr
Superstore
Recn Gd
Services
Two Rivers Ind Est
Wessex Ind Est
Millbuck Ind Est
Mus
Cogges
The Blake CE Prim Sch
Ind Est
Newland
Cogges Hill
Gibbets Close Farm
Clementsfield Farm
Shores Green
High Cogges Farm
High Cogges
Lindsey Farm
Spring Hill
Springhill Farm
Cogges Bridge Cottage
OXFORD HILL
B4022
A40
A415
Hotel
The Moors
Emma's Dike
PH
Church End
Ducklington
Ducklington CE Prim Sch
Mill
River Windrush
STANDLAKE RD
ST ANDLAKE RD
Clealings
Sherald's Copse
Home Farm
Cokethorpe Park
Boys Wood
Cokethorpe Sch
Fishhouse Plantation
Fish House
Gill Mill
Ford
Berryham Plantation
Hardwick
ASTON RD
MOORLAND RD
WELCH WAY
HIGH ST
WOOLGATE
MARKET SQ
CORN ST
LANGDALE GATE
WITAN WAY
FARM MILL LA
STATION LA
DES ROCHES SQ
AVENUE FOUR
AVENUE THREE
AVENUE TWO
AVENUE ONE
PARKSIDE
STATION LA
DUCKLINGTON LA
SOUTH LEIGH RD
STANTON HARCOURT RD
COGGES HILL RD
BLAKES AVE
HOLLIS CL
MANOR RD
ETON CL
OXLEASE
WADARD'S MDW
CHURCH LA
NEWLAND
1 JUDD'S CL
2 COURTS GDN
1 COLWELL DR
2 THORNEY LEYS
1 THE SQUARE
2 STRAINGES CL
3 YEW TREE MEWS
LAKESIDE
NEW CLOSE LA
DALE WLK
MOORS CL
CHALCROFT CL
WITNEY RD
BEANHILL CL
CURBRIDGE RD
STARNHAM RD
TRISTRAM RD
SEALHAM RD
MANOR RD
PARK RD
MACRAY RD
POUND CL
BARTHOLOMEW CL
CHURCH ST
BACK LA
PEEL CL
FEILDEN CL
LOVELL CL

A
B
C
35
36
37

117
136

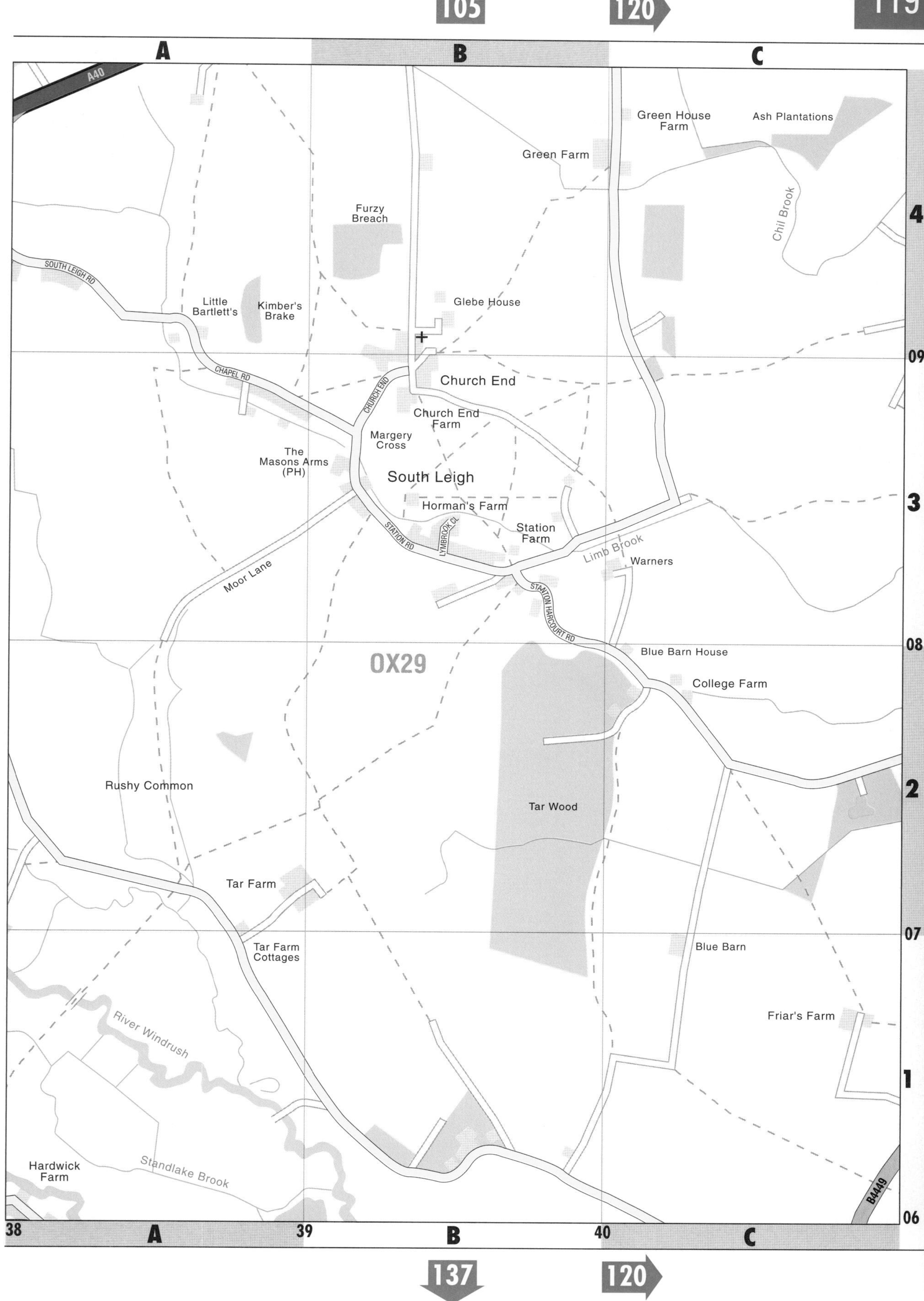

A40

A   B   C

SOUTH LEIGH RD

Green House Farm

Ash Plantations

Green Farm

Furzy Breach

Chil Brook

4

CHAPEL RD

Little Bartlett's

Kimber's Brake

Glebe House

09

CHURCH END

Church End

Church End Farm

Margery Cross

The Masons Arms (PH)

South Leigh

3

Horman's Farm

STATION RD

LYMBROOK CL

Station Farm

Limb Brook

Warners

Moor Lane

STANTON HARCOURT RD

08

OX29

Blue Barn House

College Farm

2

Rushy Common

Tar Wood

07

Tar Farm

Tar Farm Cottages

Blue Barn

River Windrush

Friar's Farm

1

B4449

Hardwick Farm

Standlake Brook

06

38   A   39   B   40   C

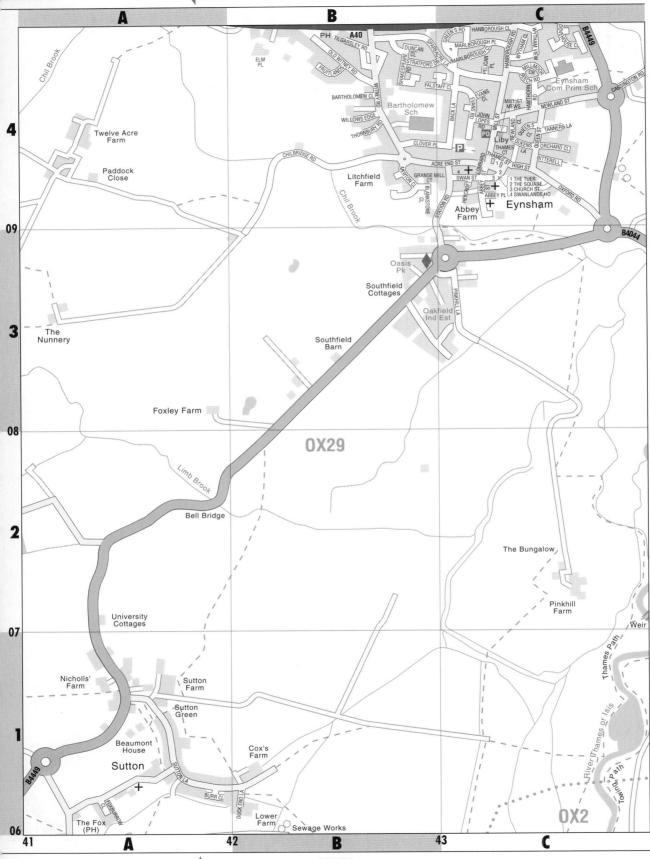

106

A B C

PH
A40
TILGARSLEY RD
OLD WITNEY RD
FRUITLANDS
ELM PL
WITNEY RD
DUNCAN CL
SHAKESPEARE RD
STRATFORD DR
SPAREACRE LA
GREEN'S RD
HANBOROUGH CL
MARLBOROUGH PL
MARLBOROUGH CL
PELICAN PL
HANBOROUGH RD
WYTHAM CL
WYTHAM VIEW
DOVEHOUSE CL
B4449
MILLMOOR CR
BEECH RD
Eynsham Com Prim Sch
CASSINGTON RD
FALSTAFF CL
BARTHOLOMEW CL
Bartholomew Sch
EVANS CL
EVANS RD
HAWTHORN RD
MILL ST MEWS
NEWLAND ST
WILLOWS EDGE
THORNBURY RD
BACK LA
JOHN LOPES RD
MILL ST
NEWLAND CL
QUEEN'S CL
TANNERS LA
PO
Liby
THAMES CT
QUEENS LA
QUEEN ST
ORCHARD CL
CLOVER PL
P
THAMES ST
BITTERELL
CHILBRIDGE RD
ACRE END ST
HIGH ST
Litchfield Farm
MERTON CL
GRANGE MILL CT
SWAN ST
LOMBARD ST
ABBEY ST
1 THE TUER
2 THE SQUARE
3 CHURCH ST
4 SWANLANDS HO
OXFORD RD
BLANKSTONE CL
HEYCROFT
ABBEY PL
Chil Brook
STATION RD
Abbey Farm
Eynsham
B4044
Chil Brook
Twelve Acre Farm
Paddock Close
Oasis Pk
Southfield Cottages
PINKHILL LA
Oakfield Ind Est
The Nunnery
Southfield Barn
Foxley Farm
OX29
Limb Brook
Bell Bridge
The Bungalow
Pinkhill Farm
University Cottages
Weir
Thames Path
Nicholls' Farm
Sutton Farm
Sutton Green
River Thames or Isis
Beaumont House
Cox's Farm
Sutton
SUTTON LA
B4449
BURR CL
FOXBURROW CL
DUCK END LA
Towing Path
The Fox (PH)
Lower Farm
Sewage Works
OX2

4
09
3
08
2
07
1
06

41 A 42 B 43 C

119

138

A
B
C

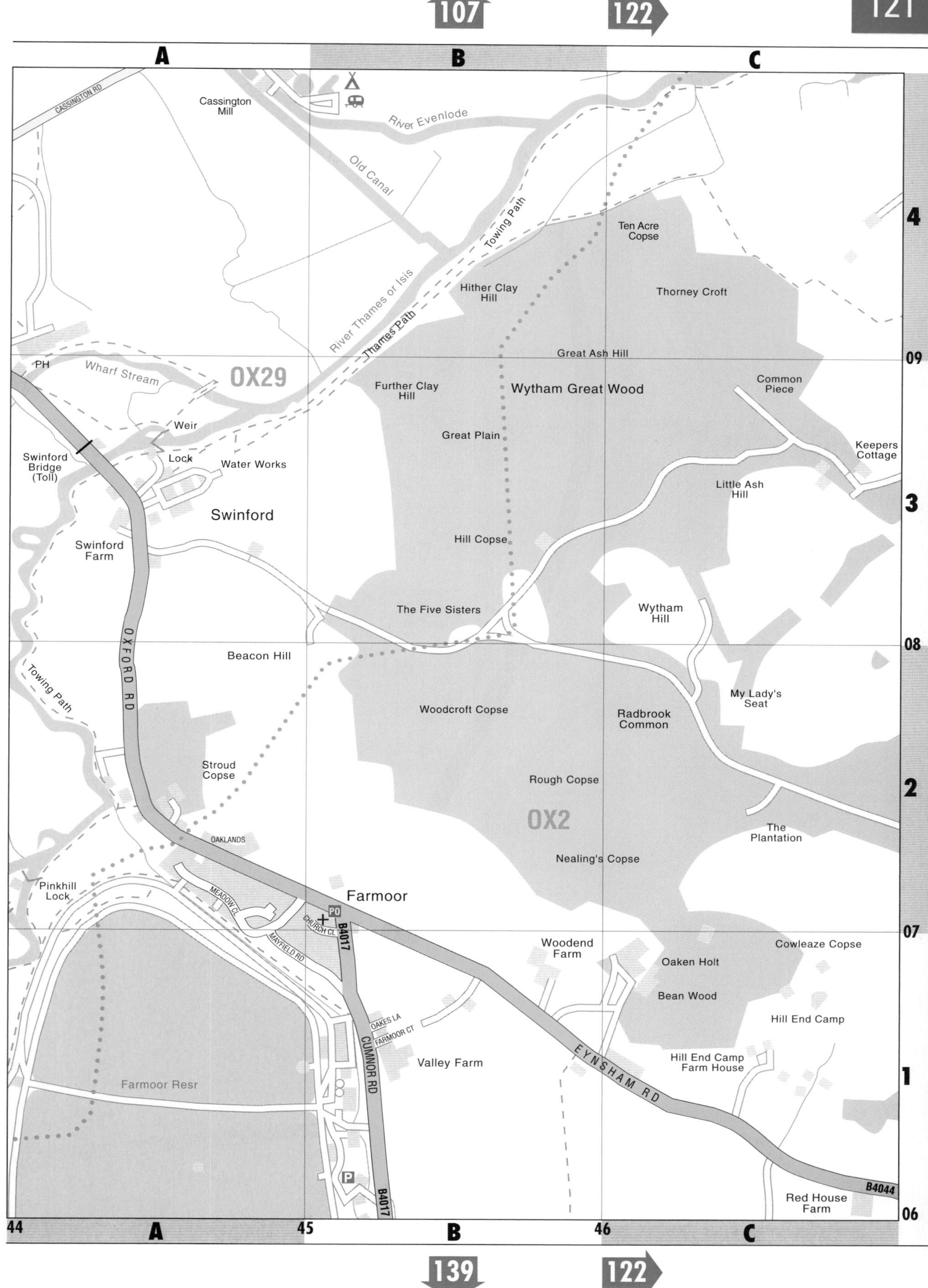

Cassington Mill
River Evenlode
Old Canal
Towing Path
Ten Acre Copse
4
Hither Clay Hill
Thorney Croft
River Thames or Isis
Thames Path
Great Ash Hill
09
PH
Wharf Stream
OX29
Further Clay Hill
Wytham Great Wood
Common Piece
Weir
Great Plain
Keepers Cottage
Swinford Bridge (Toll)
Lock
Water Works
Swinford
Little Ash Hill
3
Swinford Farm
Hill Copse
Oxford Rd
The Five Sisters
Wytham Hill
08
Towing Path
Beacon Hill
My Lady's Seat
Woodcroft Copse
Radbrook Common
Stroud Copse
Rough Copse
OX2
The Plantation
2
OAKLANDS
Nealing's Copse
Pinkhill Lock
MEADOW CL
Farmoor
PO
Woodend Farm
Cowleaze Copse
07
CHURCH CL
B4017
Oaken Holt
MAYFIELD RD
Bean Wood
Hill End Camp
OAKES LA
FARMOOR CT
CUMNOR RD
Valley Farm
Hill End Camp Farm House
EYNSHAM RD
1
Farmoor Resr
P
B4017
Red House Farm
B4044
06

44
A
45
B
46
C

121
108

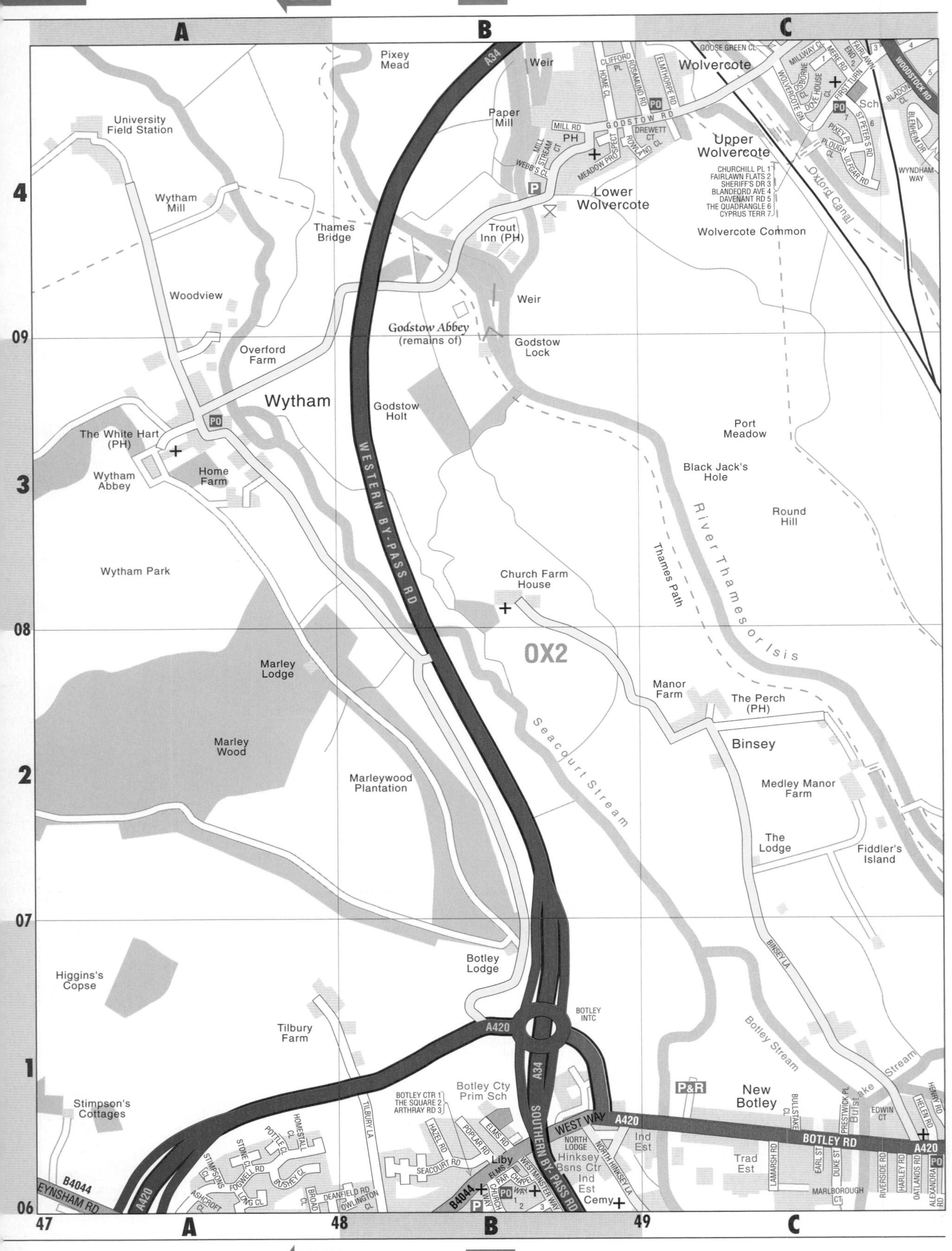
A
B
C
4
09
3
08
2
07
1
06
47
48
49
Pixey Mead
Weir
Wolvercote
University Field Station
Paper Mill
PH
Upper Wolvercote
Wytham Mill
Lower Wolvercote
Thames Bridge
Trout Inn (PH)
Wolvercote Common
Woodview
Weir
Godstow Abbey (remains of)
Godstow Lock
Overford Farm
Wytham
Godstow Holt
Port Meadow
The White Hart (PH)
Wytham Abbey
Home Farm
Black Jack's Hole
Round Hill
River Thames or Isis
Thames Path
WESTERN BY-PASS RD
Wytham Park
Church Farm House
OX2
Marley Lodge
Manor Farm
The Perch (PH)
Binsey
Marley Wood
Seacourt Stream
Marleywood Plantation
Medley Manor Farm
The Lodge
Fiddler's Island
Oxford Canal
Higgins's Copse
Botley Lodge
BOTLEY INTC
Tilbury Farm
A420
A34
Botley Stream
Bulstake Stream
New Botley
Stimpson's Cottages
Botley Cty Prim Sch
WEST WAY
BOTLEY RD
Ind Est
Trad Est
Liby
North Hinksey Bsns Ctr
Ind Est
Cemy
SOUTHERN BY-PASS RD
B4044
EYNSHAM RD
CHURCHILL PL 1
FAIRLAWN FLATS 2
SHERIFF'S DR 3
BLANDFORD AVE 4
DAVENANT RD 5
THE QUADRANGLE 6
CYPRUS TERR 7
BOTLEY CTR 1
THE SQUARE 2
ARTHRAY RD 3
GOOSE GREEN CL
GODSTOW RD
WOODSTOCK RD
BINSEY LA
TILBURY LA
SEACOURT RD
NORTH HINKSEY LA
WESTMINSTER WAY
WYNDHAM WAY

121
140

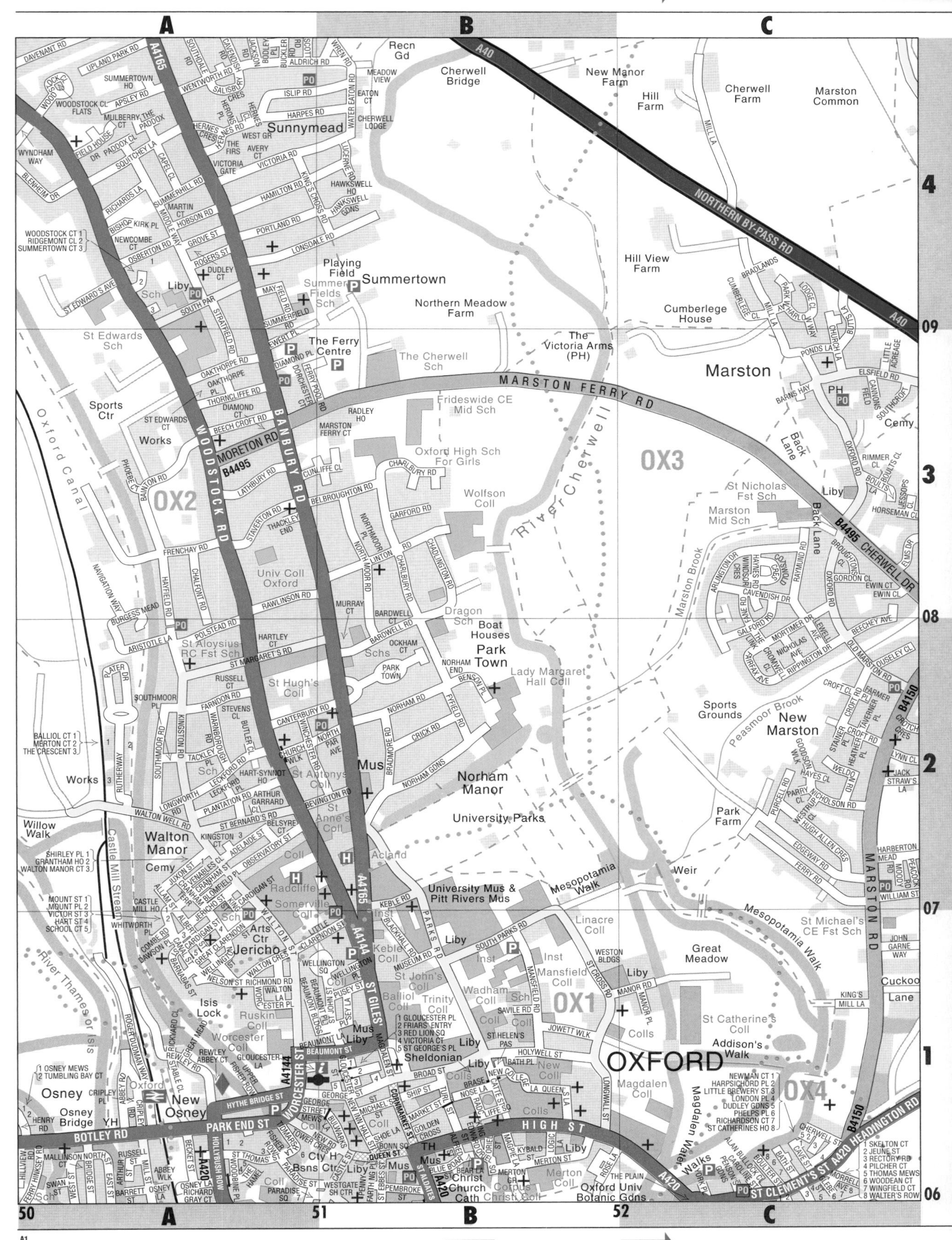

A1
1 CASTLE MEWS
2 THE OLD BAKERY
3 CLEMENT BURROWS HO
4 CHRIST CHURCH OLD BLDGS
5 JACKSON COLE HO
6 ST GEORGES GATE
7 SWAN CT

123
110

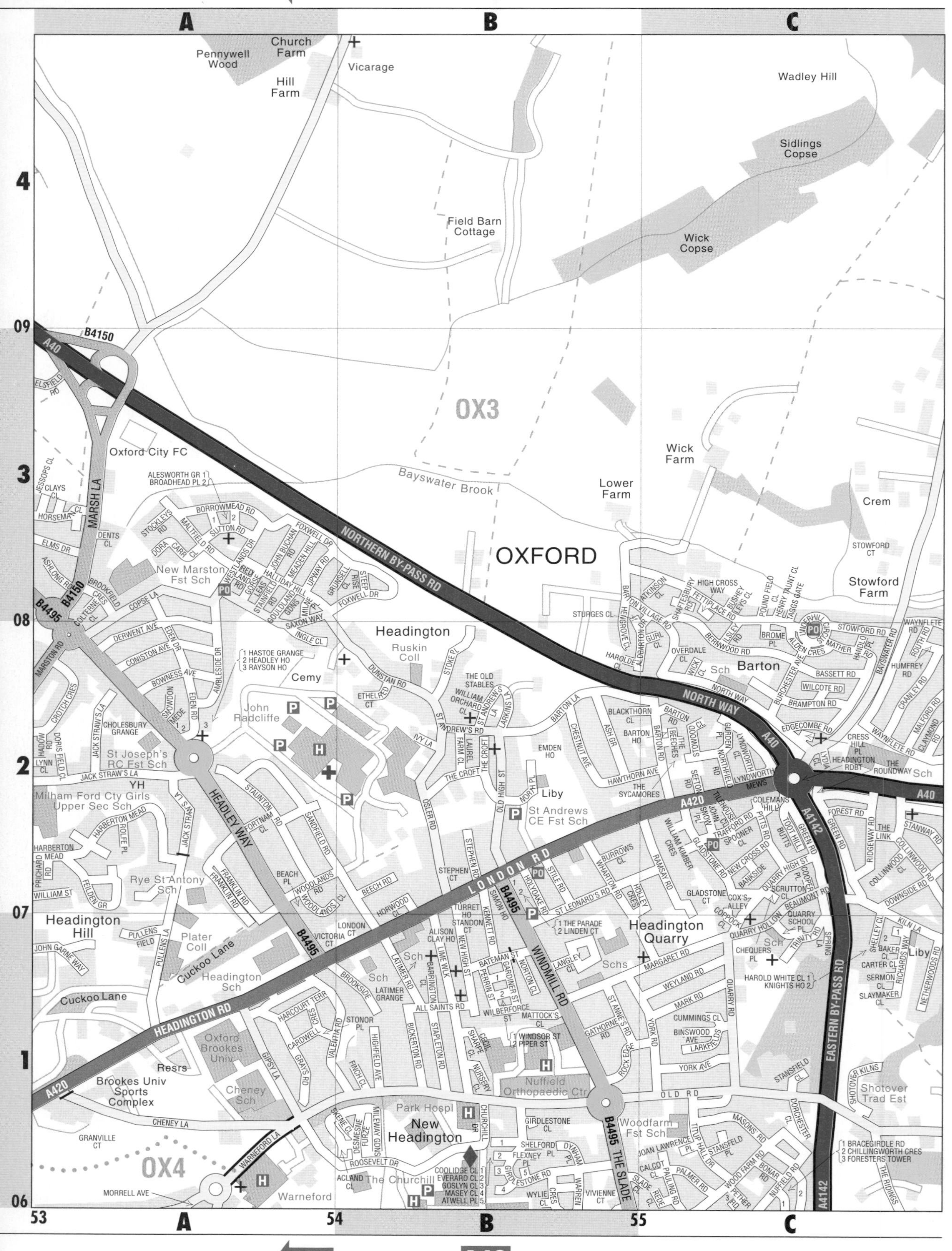
A
B
C
4
09
3
08
2
07
1
06
53
54
55
Church Farm
Pennywell Wood
Hill Farm
Vicarage
Wadley Hill
Sidlings Copse
Field Barn Cottage
Wick Copse
OX3
Wick Farm
Lower Farm
Crem
Oxford City FC
Bayswater Brook
OXFORD
Stowford Farm
NORTHERN BY-PASS RD
A40
B4150
MARSH LA
New Marston Fst Sch
Headington
Ruskin Coll
Cemy
Barton
NORTH WAY
John Radcliffe
St Joseph's RC Fst Sch
YH
Milham Ford Cty Girls Upper Sec Sch
HEADLEY WAY
B4495
A420
LONDON RD
Liby
St Andrews CE Fst Sch
A4142
EASTERN BY-PASS RD
Rye St Antony Sch
Headington Hill
Plater Coll
Cuckoo Lane
Headington Sch
Headington Quarry
HEADINGTON RD
Oxford Brookes Univ
Resrs
Brookes Univ Sports Complex
Cheney Sch
Nuffield Orthopaedic Ctr
Park Hospl
New Headington
Woodfarm Fst Sch
WINDMILL RD
THE SLADE
Shotover Trad Est
OX4
The Churchill
Warneford
CHENEY LA
OLD RD

123
142

111
126

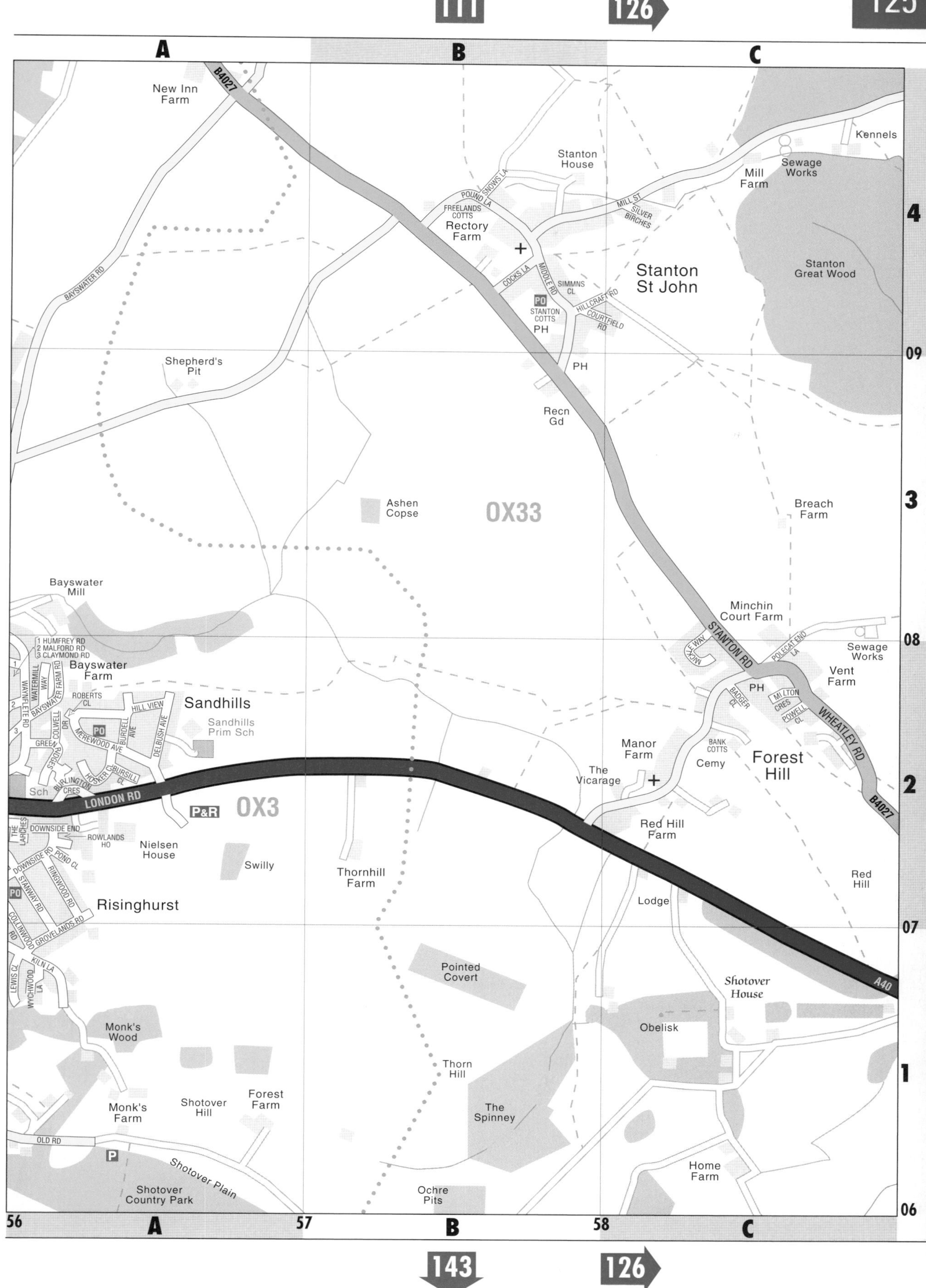
A
B
C
New Inn Farm
B4027
Stanton House
Kennels
Sewage Works
Mill Farm
POUND LA
SNOWS LA
FREELANDS COTTS
Rectory Farm
MILL ST
SILVER BIRCHES
4
Stanton St John
Stanton Great Wood
BAYSWATER RD
COCKS LA
MIDDLE RD
SIMMNS CL
HILLCRAFT RD
COURTFIELD RD
PO
STANTON COTTS
PH
09
Shepherd's Pit
PH
Recn Gd
Ashen Copse
OX33
3
Breach Farm
Bayswater Mill
Minchin Court Farm
1 HUMFREY RD
2 MALFORD RD
3 CLAYMOND RD
08
Sewage Works
Bayswater Farm
STANTON RD
POLECAT END LA
Vent Farm
NICKLE WAY
PH
BADGER CL
MILTON CRES
POWELL CL
WHEATLEY RD
Sandhills
ROBERTS CL
HILL VIEW
Sandhills Prim Sch
WATERMILL WAY
BAYSWATER FARM RD
WAYNFLETE RD
COLWELL DR
MEREWOOD AVE
BURDELL AVE
DELBUSH AVE
GREEN RIDGES
HOSKER CL
BURSILL CL
BURLINGTON CRES
BANK COTTS
Manor Farm
Cemy
Forest Hill
The Vicarage
2
Sch
LONDON RD
P&R
OX3
B4027
Red Hill Farm
THE LARCHES
DOWNSIDE END
ROWLANDS HO
Nielsen House
DOWNSIDE RD
POND CL
Swilly
STANWAY RD
RINGWOOD RD
PO
Thornhill Farm
Red Hill
Risinghurst
Lodge
COLLINWOOD RD
GROVELANDS RD
07
Pointed Covert
KILN LA
LEWIS CL
WYCHWOOD LA
Shotover House
A40
Monk's Wood
Obelisk
Thorn Hill
1
Monk's Farm
Shotover Hill
Forest Farm
The Spinney
OLD RD
P
Shotover Plain
Shotover Country Park
Ochre Pits
Home Farm
06
56
A
57
B
58
C

143
126

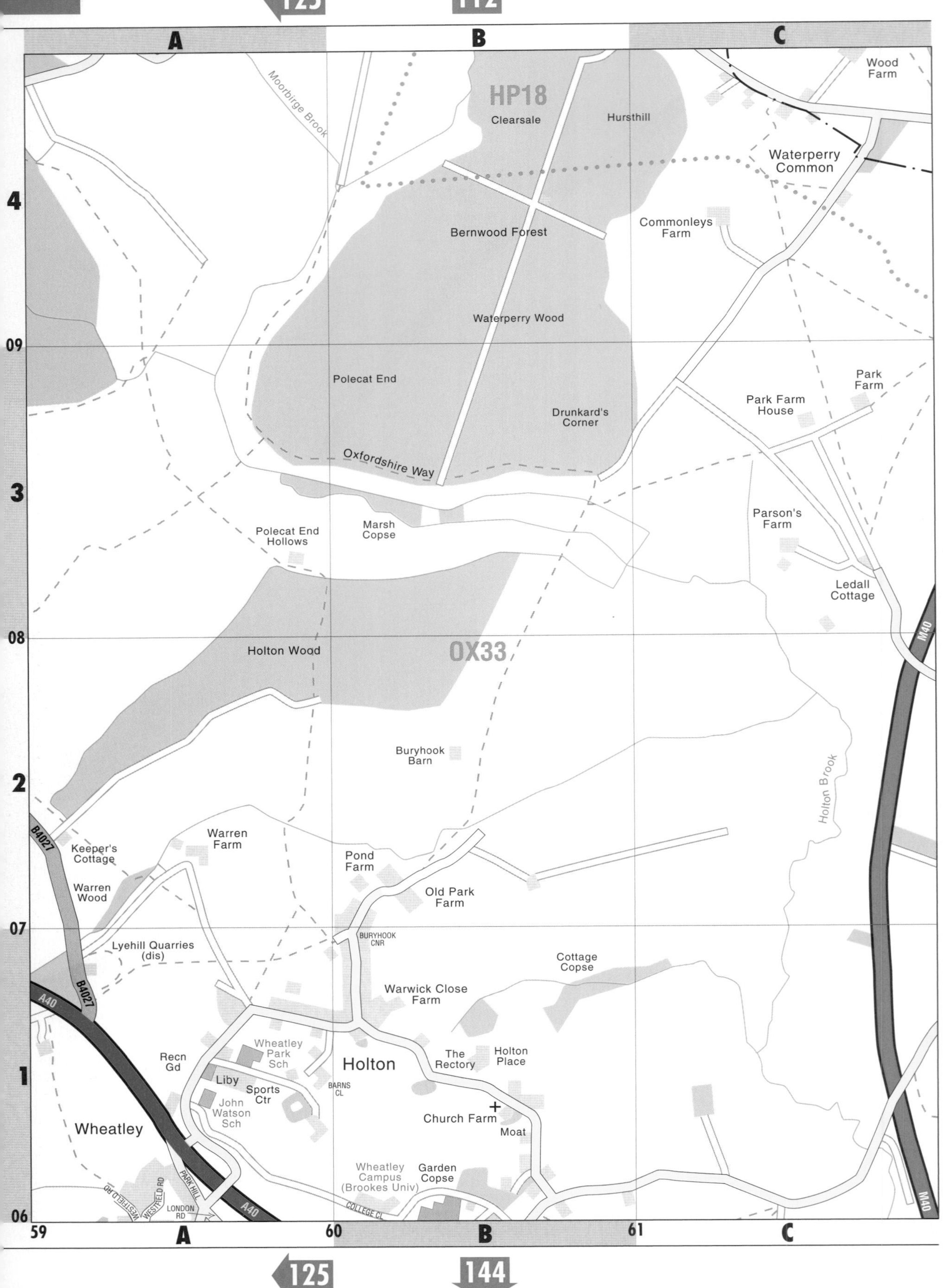

A   B   C

Moorbirge Brook

HP18
Clearsale   Hursthill

Wood Farm

Waterperry Common

4

Bernwood Forest

Commonleys Farm

Waterperry Wood

09

Polecat End

Park Farm House   Park Farm

Drunkard's Corner

Oxfordshire Way

3

Polecat End Hollows   Marsh Copse

Parson's Farm

Ledall Cottage

08

Holton Wood   OX33

M40

Buryhook Barn

Holton Brook

2

Keeper's Cottage   Warren Farm

Warren Wood   Pond Farm

B4027   Old Park Farm

07

A40   B4027   Lyehill Quarries (dis)   BURYHOOK CNR   Cottage Copse

Warwick Close Farm

Recn Gd   Wheatley Park Sch   The Rectory   Holton Place

1

Liby   Holton

Sports Ctr   BARNS CL

John Watson Sch   Church Farm

Wheatley   Moat

Garden Copse

Wheatley Campus (Brookes Univ)

WESTFIELD RD   PARK HILL   LONDON RD   A40   COLLEGE CL

06

59   A   60   B   61   C

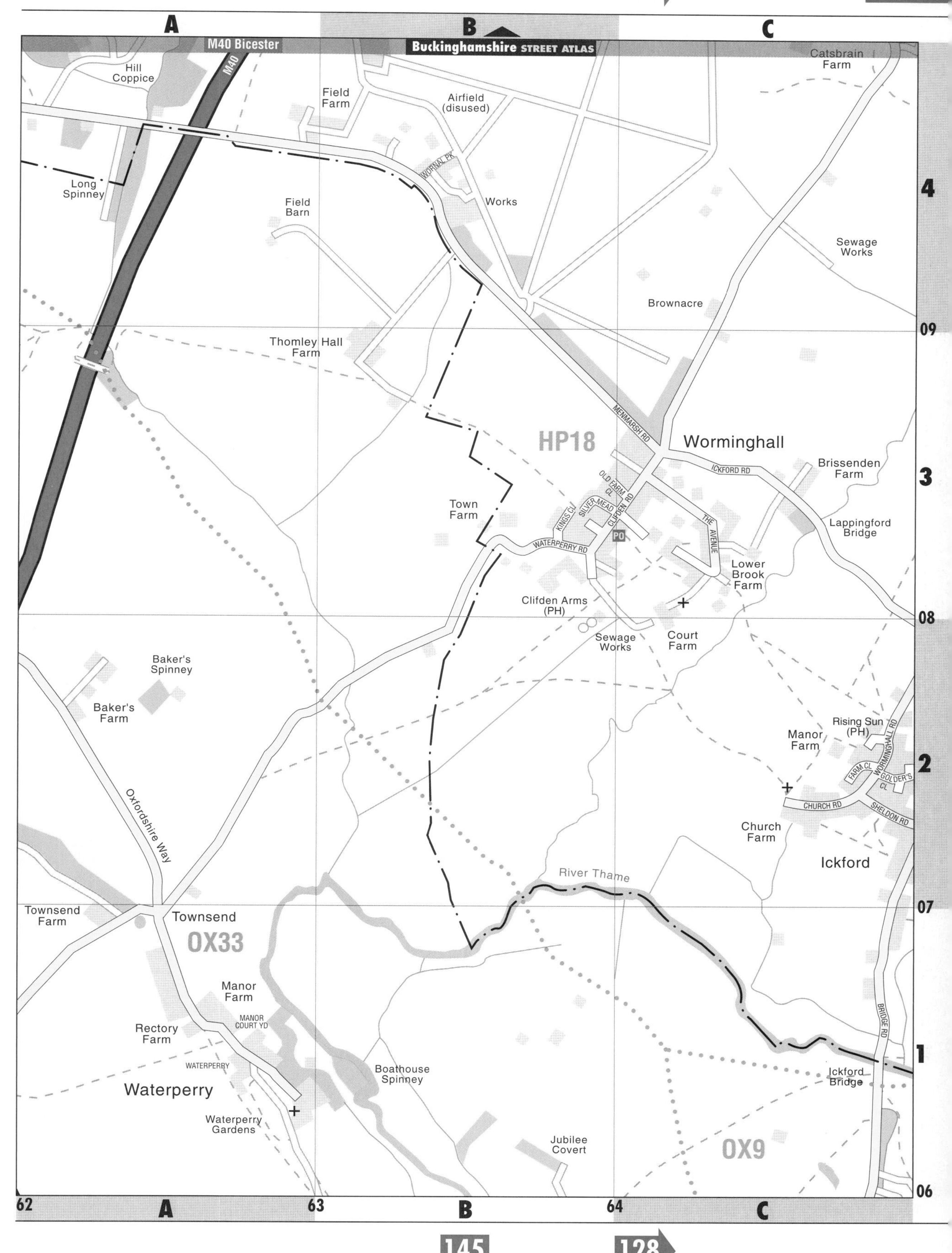

A — B — Buckinghamshire STREET ATLAS — C

M40 Bicester

Hill Coppice

Long Spinney

Field Farm

Airfield (disused)

WORNAL PK

Works

Catsbrain Farm

Sewage Works

Field Barn

Brownacre

Thomley Hall Farm

MENMARSH RD

09

HP18

Worminghall

ICKFORD RD

Brissenden Farm

Town Farm

OLD FARM RD

SILVER MEAD CL

KINGS CL

WATERPERRY RD

PO

THE AVENUE

Lappingford Bridge

3

Clifden Arms (PH)

Lower Brook Farm

✛

08

Sewage Works

Court Farm

Baker's Spinney

Baker's Farm

Manor Farm

Rising Sun (PH)

FARM CL

WORMINGHALL RD

GOLDER'S CL

✛

CHURCH RD

SHELDON RD

2

Oxfordshire Way

Church Farm

Ickford

River Thame

07

Townsend Farm

Townsend

OX33

BRIDGE RD

Manor Farm

MANOR COURT YD

WATERPERRY

Rectory Farm

1

Boathouse Spinney

Ickford Bridge

Waterperry

Waterperry Gardens

✛

Jubilee Covert

OX9

06

62 — A — 63 — B — 64 — C

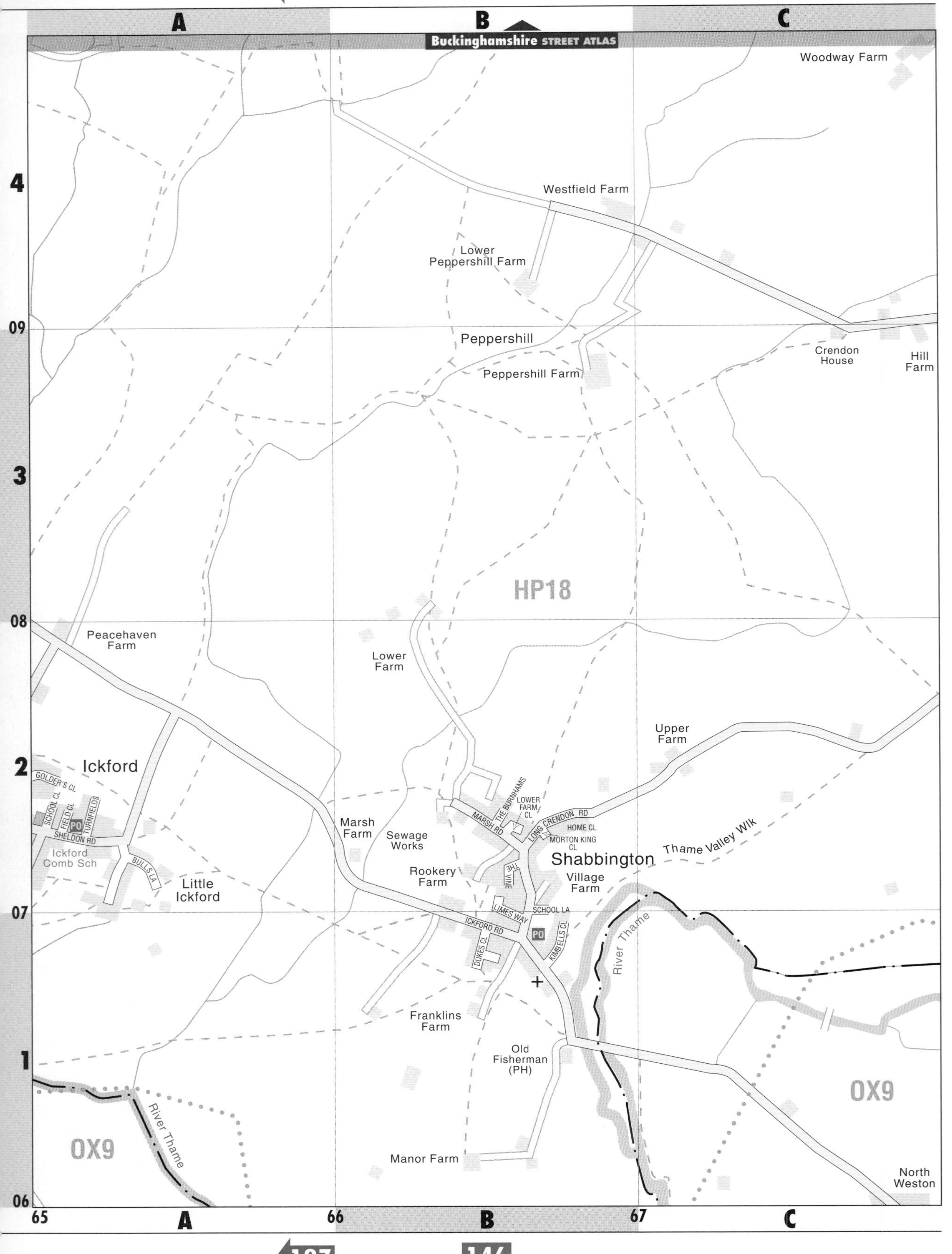

Buckinghamshire STREET ATLAS

A

B

C

Woodway Farm

4

Westfield Farm

Lower
Peppershill Farm

09

Peppershill

Crendon
House

Hill
Farm

Peppershill Farm

3

HP18

08

Peacehaven
Farm

Lower
Farm

Upper
Farm

2

Ickford

GOLDER'S CL

SCHOOL CL

FIELD CL

PO

TURNFIELDS

SHELDON RD

Ickford
Comb Sch

BULLS LA

Little
Ickford

Marsh
Farm

Sewage
Works

Rookery
Farm

Marsh Rd

THE BURNHAMS

LOWER
FARM
CL

LONG CRENDON RD

HOME CL

MORTON KING
CL

Shabbington

Village
Farm

THE VINE

Thame Valley Wlk

07

ICKFORD RD

LIMES WAY

DUKES CL

SCHOOL LA

PO

KIMBELLS CL

River Thame

+

Franklins
Farm

Old
Fisherman
(PH)

OX9

1

OX9

River Thame

Manor Farm

North
Weston

06

65

A

66

B

67

C

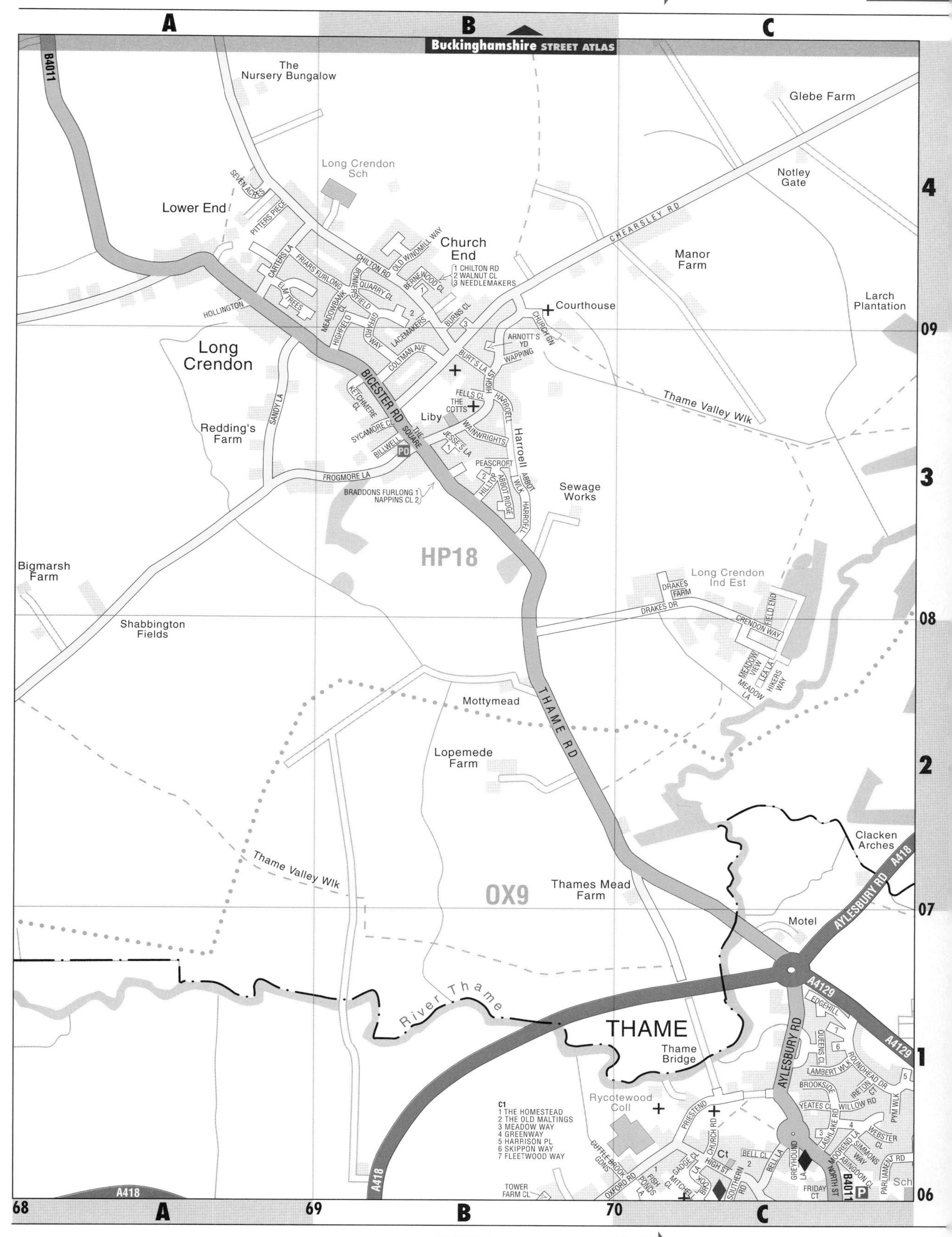

Buckinghamshire STREET ATLAS

The Nursery Bungalow

Glebe Farm

B4011

Notley Gate

Lower End

Long Crendon Sch

Chearsley Rd

Manor Farm

Larch Plantation

Church End

1 CHILTON RD
2 WALNUT CL
3 NEEDLEMAKERS

Courthouse

4

09

SEVEN ACRES

PITTERS PIECE

CARTERS LA

CHILTON RD

OLD WINDMILL WAY

BERNEWOOD CL

FRIARS FURLONG

QUARRY CL

BURNS CL

CHURCH GN

ARNOTT'S YD

WAPPING

Thame Valley Wlk

HOLLINGTON

ELM TREES

MEADOW BANK

HIGHFIELD

GIFFARD WAY

COLTMAN AVE

BURT'S LA

FELLS CL

HIGH ST

HARROELL

Long Crendon

BICESTER RD

KETCHMERE CL

LACEMAKERS

THE COTTS

Liby

WAINWRIGHTS

JESSE'S LA

Redding's Farm

SANDY LA

SYCAMORE CL

BILLWELL

PO

PEASCROFT

HARROELL ABBOT

3

FROGMORE LA

BRADDONS FURLONG 1
NAPPINS CL 2

HILLTOP

ABBOT RIDGE

TILLS

HARROELL

Sewage Works

HP18

Bigmarsh Farm

Long Crendon Ind Est

DRAKES FARM

FIELD END

Shabbington Fields

DRAKES DR

CRENDON WAY

08

MEADOW VIEW

LEA LA

HINKERS WAY

MEADOW LA

THAME RD

Mottymead

2

Lopemede Farm

Clacken Arches

A418

OX9

Thames Mead Farm

07

Motel

AYLESBURY RD

Thame Valley Wlk

A4129

River Thame

THAME

Thame Bridge

A4129

1

EDGEHILL

QUEENS CL

ROUNDHEAD DR

LAMBERT WLK

IRETON CT

BROOKSIDE

PYM WLK

AYLESBURY RD

YEATES CL

WILLOW RD

WEBSTER CL

C1
1 THE HOMESTEAD
2 THE OLD MALTINGS
3 MEADOW WAY
4 GREENWAY
5 HARRISON PL
6 SKIPPON WAY
7 FLEETWOOD WAY

Rycotewood Coll

PRIESTEND

CHINNOR RD

FISH PONDS LA

BELL CL

BELL LA

SIMMONS CL

ABINGDON RD

PARLIAMENT RD

Sch

GHATELE BROOK

OXFORD RD

CHURCH RD

Ct

HIGH ST

SOUTHERN RD

GREYHOUND LA

FRIDAY CT

B4011

NORTH ST

P

TOWER FARM CL

A418

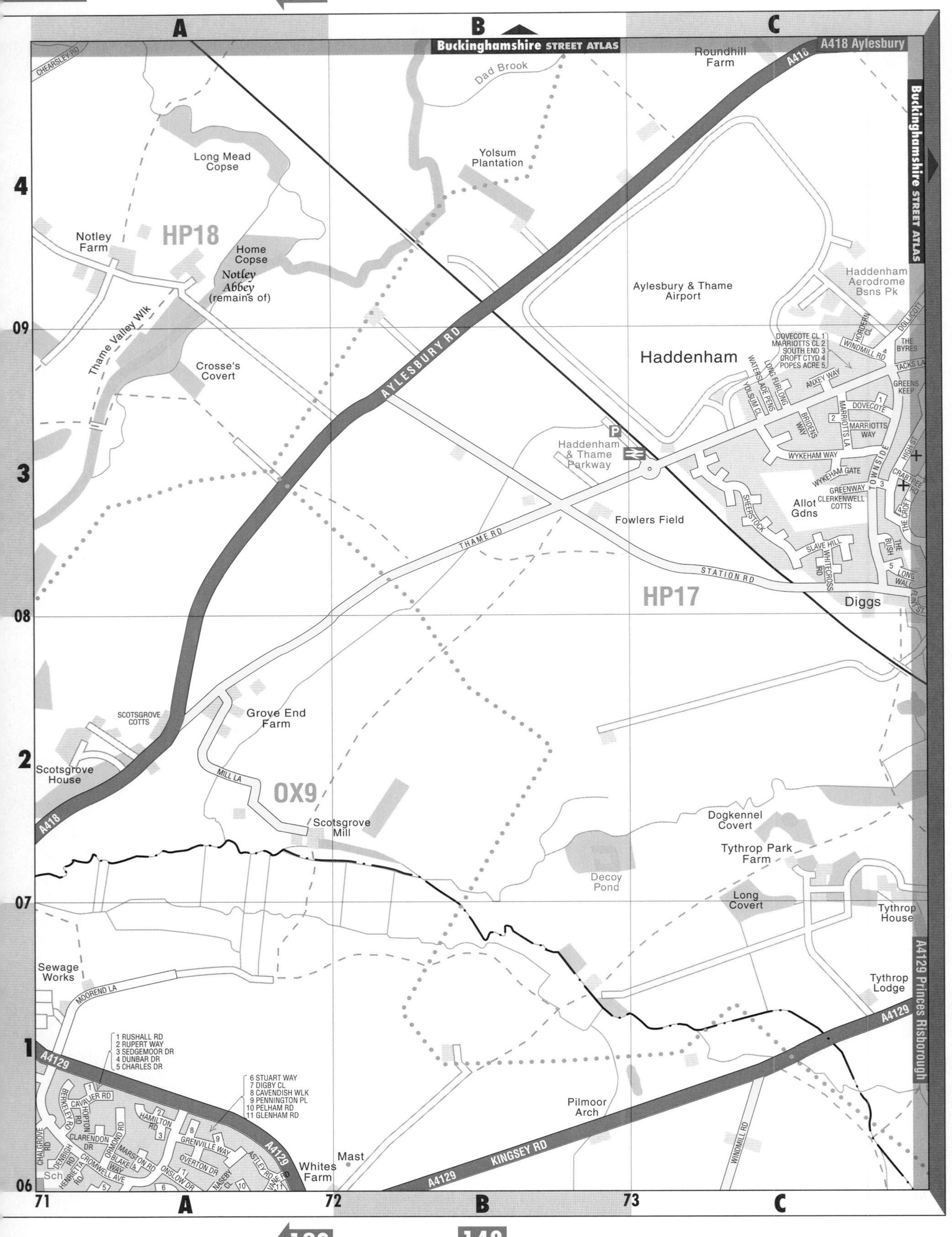

129

A   B   C

Buckinghamshire STREET ATLAS

A418 Aylesbury

Buckinghamshire STREET ATLAS

Dad Brook

Roundhill Farm

Yolsum Plantation

4

Long Mead Copse

HP18

Notley Farm

Home Copse

Notley Abbey (remains of)

Aylesbury & Thame Airport

Haddenham Aerodrome Bsns Pk

09

Thame Valley Wlk

Crosse's Covert

AYLESBURY RD

Haddenham

DOVECOTE CL 1
MARRIOTTS CL 2
SOUTH END 3
CROFT CTYD 4
POPES ACRE 5.

WATERS ACE PENS

LONG FURLONG

YOLSUM CL

ANKEY WAY

WINDMILL RD

MORDEN

TACKS LA

THE BYRES

GREENS KEEP

HIGH ST

BINDERS WAY

DOVECOTE

MARRIOTTS LA

MARRIOTTS WAY

3

Haddenham & Thame Parkway

WYKEHAM GATE

WYKEHAM WAY

TOWNSIDE

CRABTREE

THE GROFT

GREENWAY

CLERKENWELL COTTS

SHERBOURN

Allot Gdns

Fowlers Field

THAME RD

SLAVE HILL

WHITECROSS

THE BUSH

LONG WALL

5

08

STATION RD

HP17

Diggs

Scotsgrove Cotts

Grove End Farm

MILL LA

OX9

2

Scotsgrove House

A418

Scotsgrove Mill

Dogkennel Covert

Tythrop Park Farm

Decoy Pond

Long Covert

07

Tythrop House

Sewage Works

MOOREND LA

Tythrop Lodge

A4129 Princes Risborough

1

A4129

1 RUSHALL RD
2 RUPERT WAY
3 SEDGEMOOR DR
4 DUNBAR DR
5 CHARLES DR

6 STUART WAY
7 DIGBY CL
8 CAVENDISH WLK
9 PENNINGTON PL
10 PELHAM RD
11 GLENHAM RD

A4129

CAVALIER RD
HOPTON RD
BERKELEY RD
CLARENDON DR
DIAMOND RD
BLAKE LA
HAMILTON RD
MARSTON RD
GRENVILLE WAY
MASSEY CL
OVERTON DR
ONSLOW DR
ASTLEY RD
CROMWELL AVE
CHALGROVE RD
HORNET CL
RODNEY RD
School

Mast

Whites Farm

Pilmoor Arch

A4129 KINGSEY RD

WINDMILL RD

06

71   A   72   B   73   C

129   148

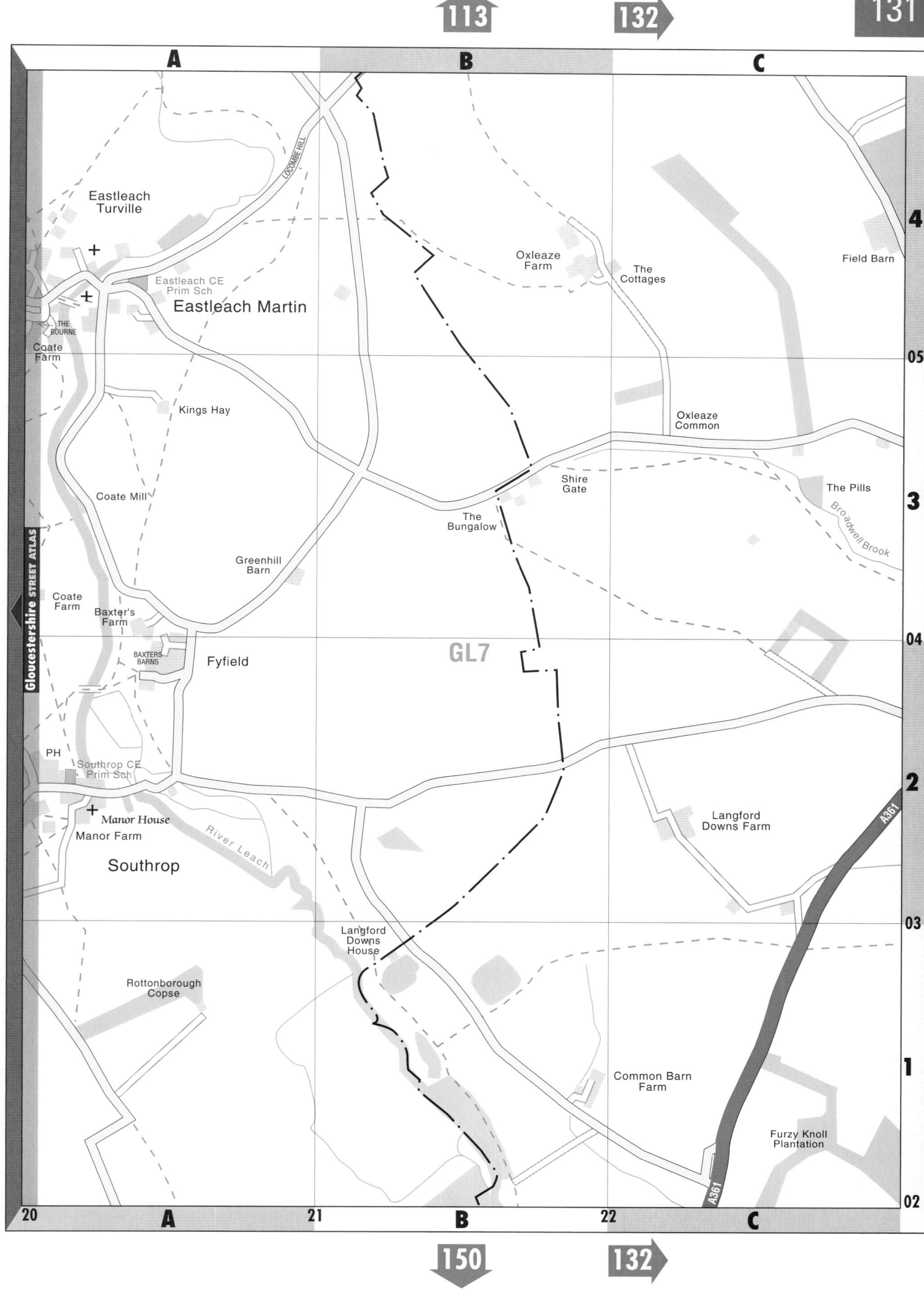

113
132

A   B   C

Gloucestershire STREET ATLAS

Eastleach
Turville

Eastleach CE
Prim Sch

Eastleach Martin

THE
BOURNE

Coate
Farm

Kings Hay

Coate Mill

Greenhill
Barn

Coate
Farm

Baxter's
Farm

BAXTERS
BARNS

Fyfield

PH

Southrop CE
Prim Sch

Manor House

Manor Farm

Southrop

River Leach

Rottonborough
Copse

Oxleaze
Farm

The
Cottages

Field Barn

Oxleaze
Common

Shire
Gate

The Pills

Broadwell Brook

The
Bungalow

GL7

Langford
Downs Farm

A361

Langford
Downs
House

Common Barn
Farm

Furzy Knoll
Plantation

A361

LOCOMBE HILL

4

05

3

04

2

03

1

02

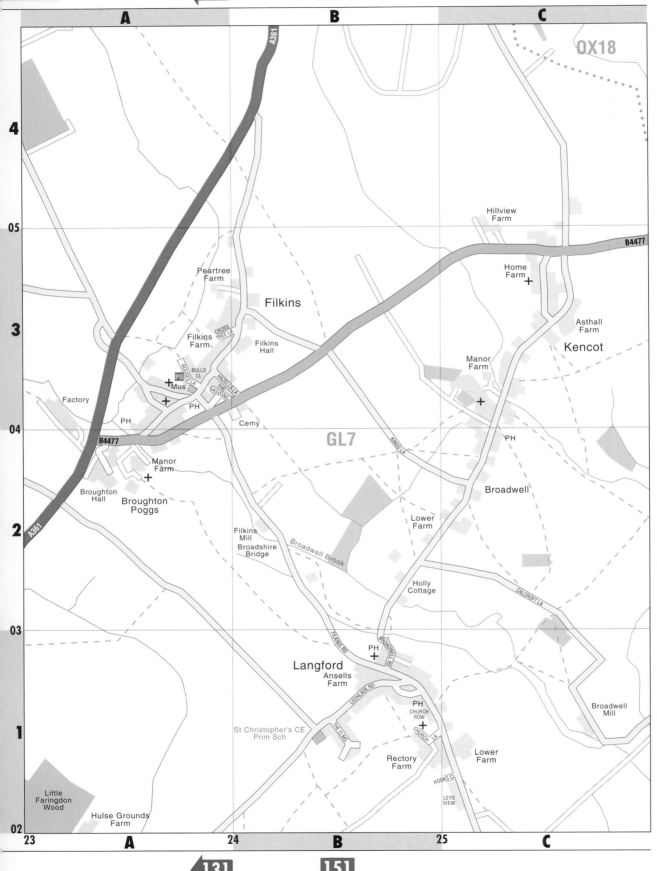

A B C

OX18

4

05

Hillview
Farm

B4477

Peartree
Farm

Home
Farm

Filkins

Asthall
Farm

3

Filkins
Farm

CROSS
TREE LA

Filkins
Hall

Kencot

Manor
Farm

BULLS
CL

ROUSES LA

PO
Mus

HAZELLS LA

THE
GASSONS

PH

Factory

PH

Cemy

GL7

KINGS LA

PH

04

B4477

Manor
Farm

Broughton
Hall

Manor
Farm

Broadwell

Broughton
Poggs

Lower
Farm

2

A361

Filkins
Mill

Broadshire
Bridge

Broadwell Brook

Holly
Cottage

CALCROFT LA

03

FILKINS RD

PH

BROADWELL RD

Langford

Ansells
Farm

LECHLADE RD

PH
CHURCH
ROW

Broadwell
Mill

1

St Christopher's CE
Prim Sch

THE ELMS

CHURCH LA

Rectory
Farm

Lower
Farm

HOOKS CL

LEYS
VIEW

Little
Faringdon
Wood

Hulse Grounds
Farm

02

23

A

24

B

25

C

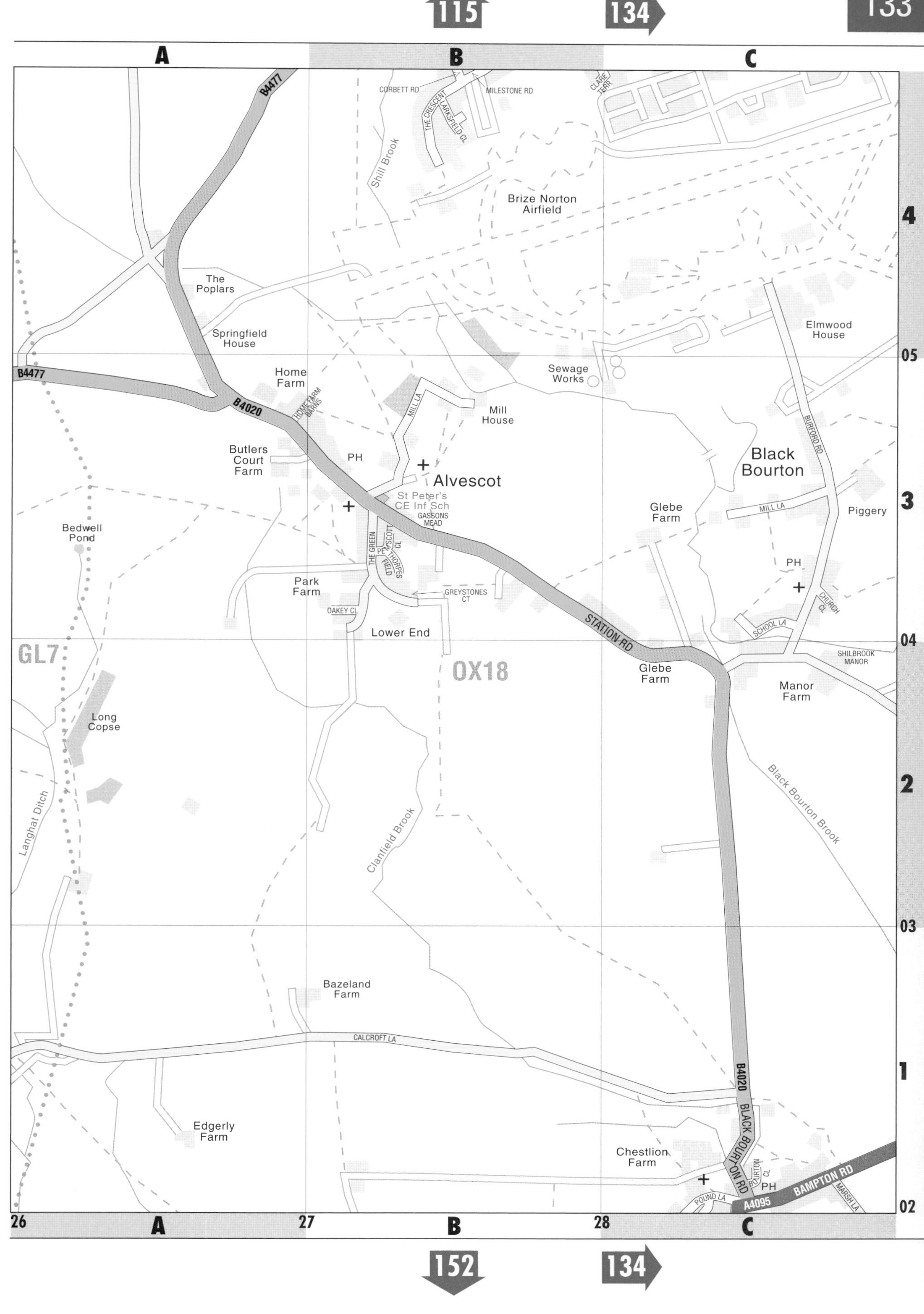

A
B
C

B4477

CORBETT RD
THE CRESCENT
ARKSFIELD CL
MILESTONE RD
CLARE TERR

Shill Brook

Brize Norton
Airfield

4

The Poplars

Springfield
House

Elmwood
House

B4477

Home
Farm

HOME FARM BARNS

Sewage
Works

05

B4020

MILL LA

Mill
House

Butlers
Court
Farm

PH

Alvescot

Black
Bourton

BURFORD RD

3

St Peter's
CE Inf Sch
GASSONS
MEAD

Glebe
Farm

MILL LA

Piggery

Bedwell
Pond

THE GREEN
PRESCOTT CL
PEN FIELD
THORPES

PH

CHURCH CL

Park
Farm

OAKEY CL

GREYSTONES
CT

SCHOOL LA

GL7

Lower End

STATION RD

04

SHILBROOK
MANOR

OX18

Glebe
Farm

Manor
Farm

Long
Copse

Black Bourton Brook

2

Langhat Ditch

Clanfield Brook

03

Bazeland
Farm

CALCROFT LA

B4020

1

Edgerly
Farm

BLACK BOURTON RD

Chestlion
Farm

BURTON CL
PH

BAMPTON RD
MARSH LA

POUND LA

A4095

02

26
A
27
B
28
C

133
116

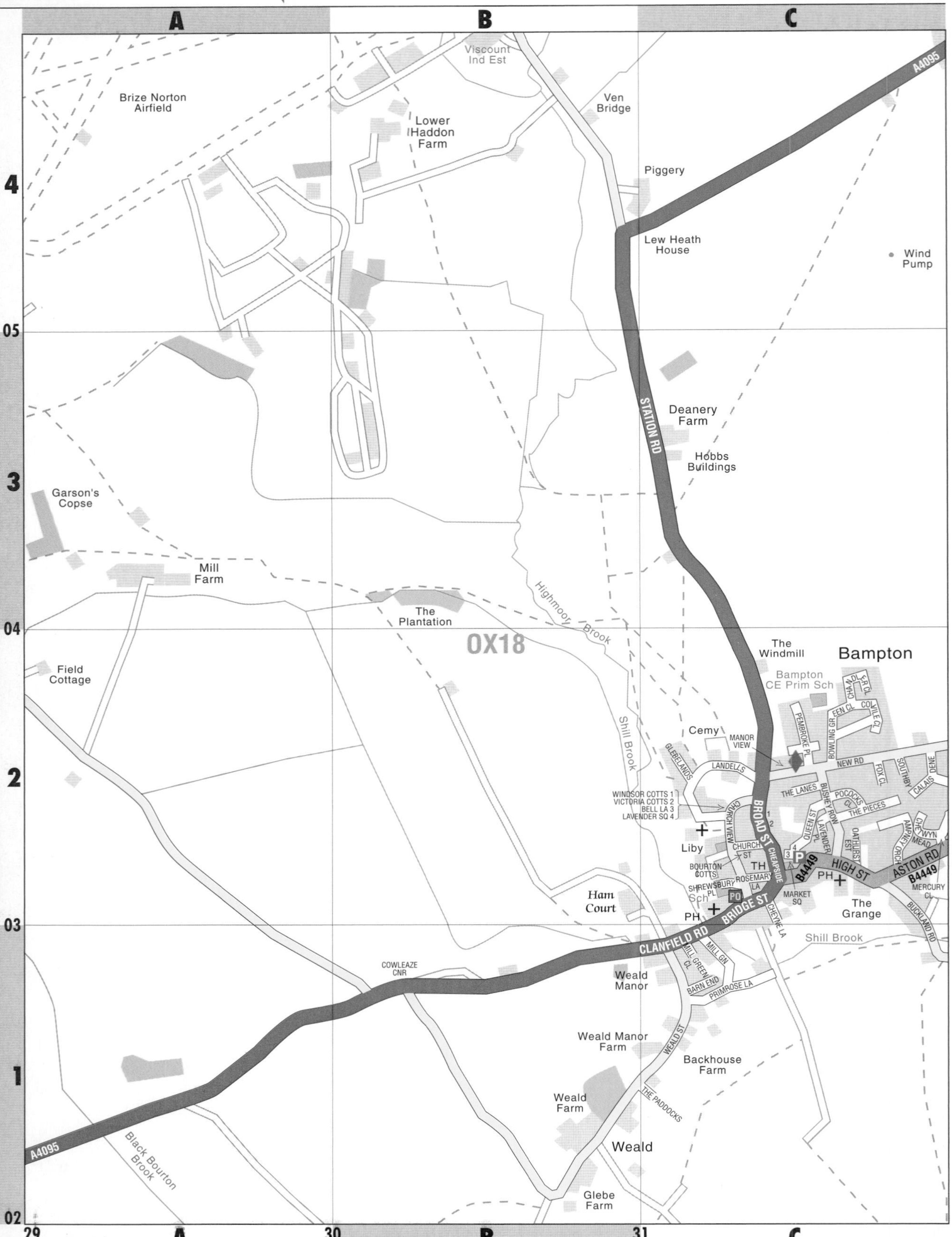

A   B   C

4

Brize Norton
Airfield

Viscount
Ind Est

Ven
Bridge

Lower
Haddon
Farm

Piggery

Lew Heath
House

Wind
Pump

05

STATION RD

Deanery
Farm

Hobbs
Buildings

3

Garson's
Copse

Highmoor Brook

Mill
Farm

The
Plantation

04

OX18

The
Windmill

Bampton

Field
Cottage

Shill Brook

Bampton
CE Prim Sch

Cemy

MANOR
VIEW

PEMBROKE PL

FEN CL
COLVILE CL

GLEBELANDS

LANDELL'S

THE LANES

NEW RD

FOX CL

SOUTHBY
DENE

CALAIS
DENE

2

WINDSOR COTTS 1
VICTORIA COTTS 2
BELL LA 3
LAVENDER SQ 4

CHURCH VIEW

BROAD ST CHEAPSIDE

BUSHEY ROW

POCOCK'S
THE PIECES

AMPNEY
MEAD

TWYN

DATHURST

Liby

+

Sch

BOURTON
COTTS

PL

CHURCH
ST

TH

QUEEN ST

ROSEMARY
LA

LAVENDER

B4449

HIGH ST

ASTON RD

B4449

MARKET
SQ

MERCURY
CL

03

Ham
Court

SHREWSBURY
PL

PO

PH +

BRIDGE ST

CHEYNE LA

P
B4449

PH +

The
Grange

Shill Brook

BUCKLAND RD

CLANFIELD RD

MILL
CL

MILL GREEN

COWLEAZE
CNR

Weald
Manor

BARN END

PRIMROSE LA

Weald
Manor
Farm

WEALD ST

Backhouse
Farm

1

THE PADDOCKS

Weald
Farm

Weald

A4095

Black Bourton
Brook

Glebe
Farm

02

29   A   30   B   31   C

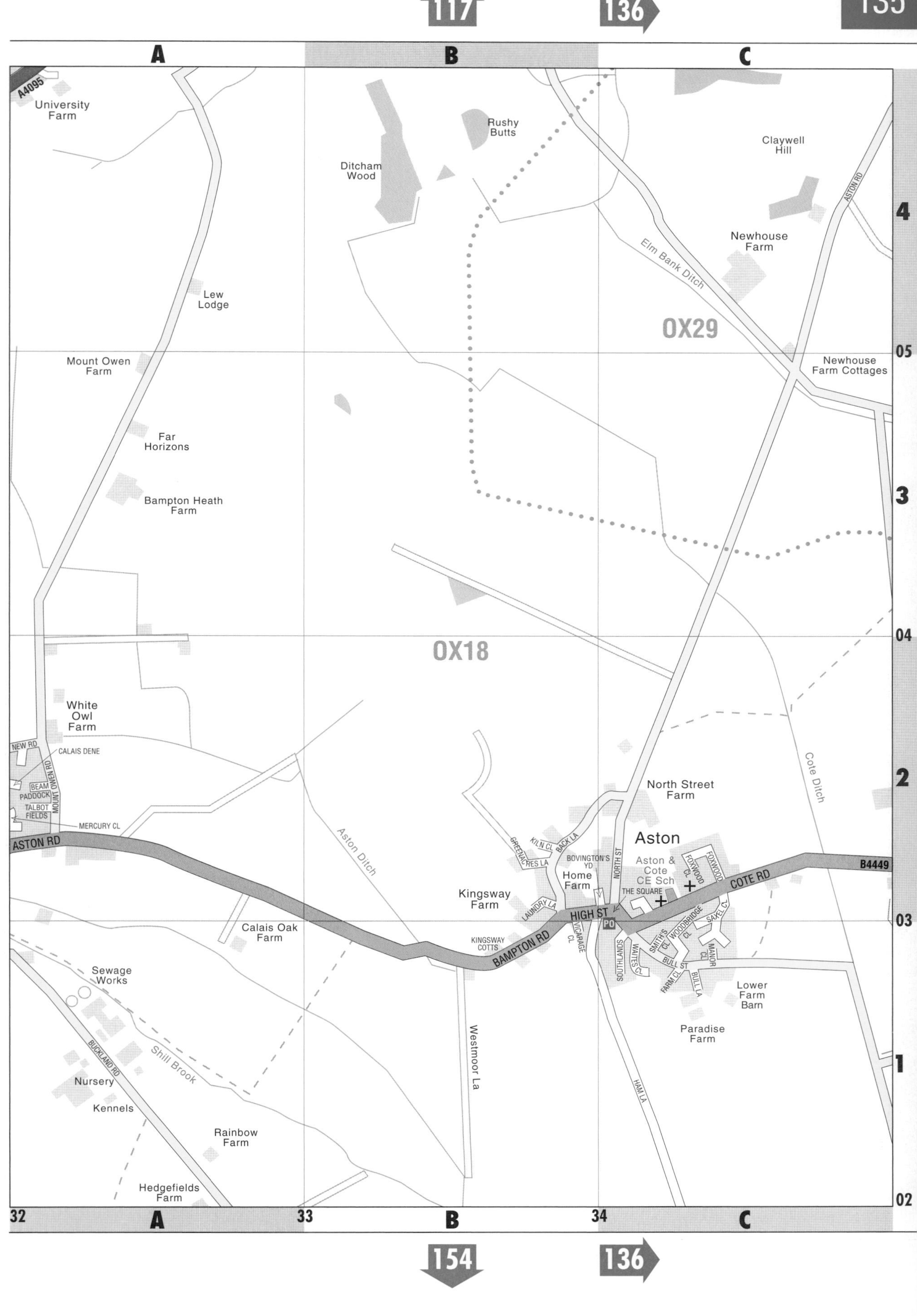

A4095

University
Farm

Rushy
Butts

Ditcham
Wood

Claywell
Hill

Elm Bank Ditch

Newhouse
Farm

Lew
Lodge

OX29

ASTON RD

05

Mount Owen
Farm

Newhouse
Farm Cottages

Far
Horizons

3

Bampton Heath
Farm

OX18

04

White
Owl
Farm

NEW RD
CALAIS DENE
OLD UNION RD
BEAM
PADDOCK
TALBOT
FIELDS
MERCURY CL

Cote Ditch

North Street
Farm

2

ASTON RD

GREENACRES LA
KILN CL
BACK LA
BOVINGTON'S
YD
NORTH ST

Aston

Aston &
Cote
CE Sch

FOXWOOD
CL
B4449

Aston Ditch

Kingsway
Farm

Home
Farm

THE SQUARE

COTE RD

03

Calais Oak
Farm

KINGSWAY
COTTS

LAUNDRY LA
HIGH ST
UGARAGE
PO
BAMPTON RD
CL

SMITH'S
CL
WOODBRIDGE
CL
SAXEL CL
SOUTHLANDS
WAITES CL
BULL ST
MANOR
CL
BULL LA

Lower
Farm
Barn

Sewage
Works

BUCKLAND RD

Shill Brook

Westmoor La

Paradise
Farm

HAM LA

1

Nursery

Kennels

Rainbow
Farm

Hedgefields
Farm

02

135
118

A   B   C

Boys Wood
Long Train
Cokethorpe Park
Home Wood
FAIRFIELDS
Hardwick
A415
B4449
STANDLAKE RD
ASTON RD
A415

4

Claywell Farm
Rickless Hill
Breach Farm Cottage

05

Manor Farm
Westfield Farm
Hawthorn Farm
Yelford
College Farm
CALAIS LA

3

OX29

04

Brighthampton Cut

Cote Lodge Farm

2

New Shifford Farm
B4449
Green Acres
New Shifford Cottages
ASTON RD

03

OX18
B4449
Cote
South Farm
Chicken Hatchery
New Cottages

1

Cote Bungalow
Cote House
Cote House Farm
Shifford

02

35   A   36   B   37   C

119
138

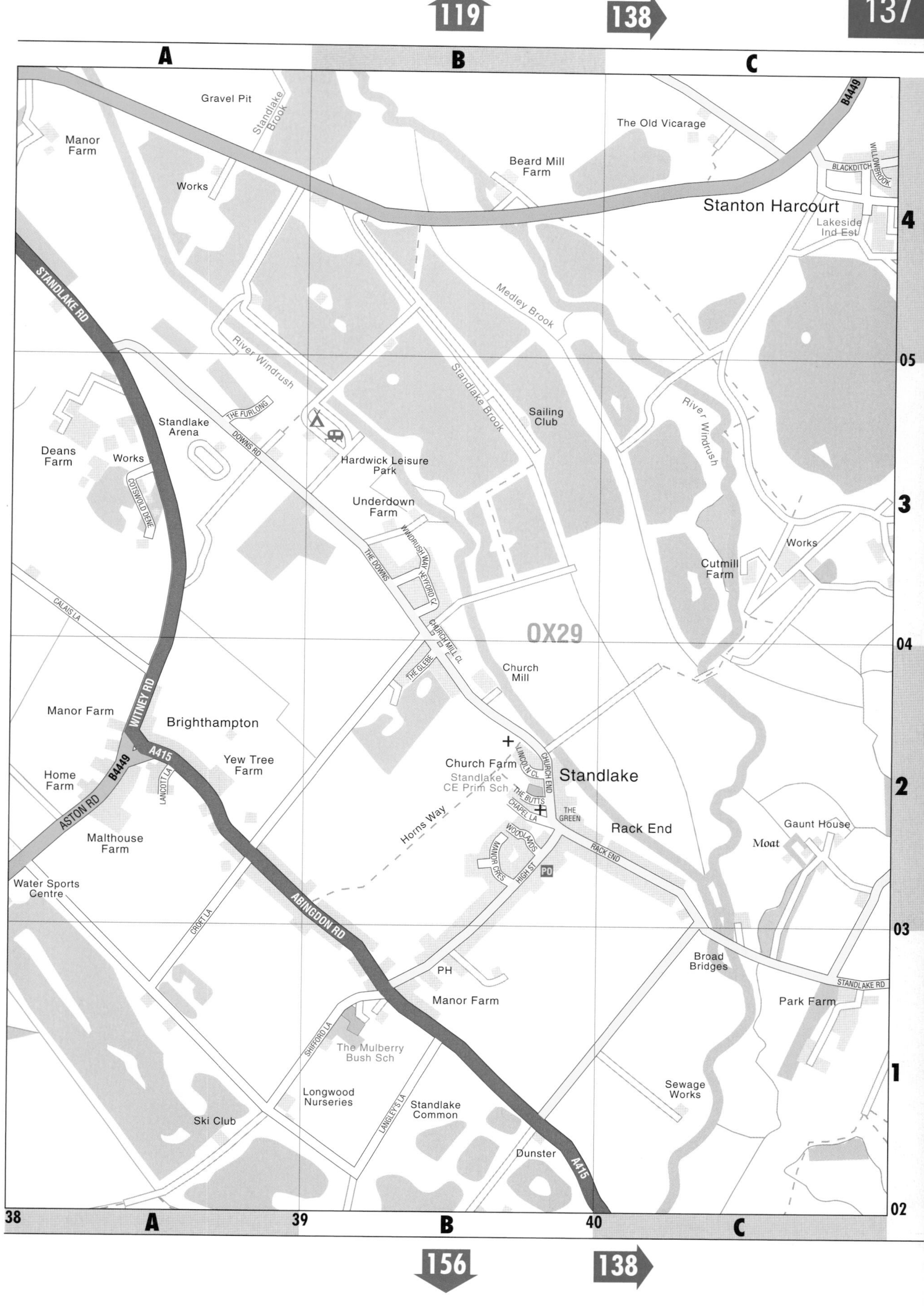
A
B
C
Gravel Pit
Standlake Brook
Manor Farm
Works
The Old Vicarage
B4449
Beard Mill Farm
BLACKDITCH
WILLOWBROOK
Stanton Harcourt
Lakeside Ind Est
STANDLAKE RD
Medley Brook
River Windrush
Standlake Brook
Sailing Club
THE FURLONG
Standlake Arena
DOWNS RD
Deans Farm
Works
COTSWOLD DENE
Hardwick Leisure Park
Underdown Farm
WINDRUSH WAY
HEYFORD CL
THE DOWNS
River Windrush
Cutmill Farm
Works
CALAIS LA
OX29
CHURCH MILL CL
THE GLEBE
Church Mill
Manor Farm
WITNEY RD
Brighthampton
A415
Yew Tree Farm
Church Farm
LINCOLN CL
CHURCH END
Standlake
Standlake CE Prim Sch
Home Farm
B4449
LANCOTT LA
THE BUTTS
CHAPEL LA
THE GREEN
ASTON RD
Horns Way
Rack End
Gaunt House
Moat
Malthouse Farm
WOODLANDS
MANOR CRES
HIGH ST
RACK END
PO
Water Sports Centre
ABINGDON RD
CROFT LA
Broad Bridges
PH
STANDLAKE RD
Manor Farm
Park Farm
SHIFFORD LA
The Mulberry Bush Sch
Longwood Nurseries
LANGLEY'S LA
Standlake Common
Sewage Works
Ski Club
Dunster
A415
4
05
3
04
2
03
1
02
38
39
40

156
138

137 120

A B C

4

Stanton Harcourt CE Prim Sch
Chapel & Pope's Tower
FLEXNEYS PADDOCK
BURT MEAD
THE CLOSE
THE ROW
BLACKDITCH CL
FARMHOUSE CL
PO
THE GREEN
Blackditch
Stanton Harcourt
Stanton Harcourt Ind Est
STEADY'S LA
Steady's Farm
MANOR COTTS
Cemy

OX2

05

Tawney's Farm
Pimm Farm

Gravel Pits

Linch Hill Cottages

3

Elms Farm
Payne's Farm
West End

The Ferryman Inn
Bablock Hythe
Whitley Copse

Linch Hill Leisure Park
Stoneacres Lake

04

OX29
Lower Farm

Thames Path
River Thames or Isis
BABLOCK HYTHE RD
Towing Path
Mast

2

Manor Farm
Mount Pleasant
CHAPEL LA
Watkins Farm
Pencots

Long Meadow

Pinnocks Farm
GRIFFITHS CL
Ferryman Farm

OX13

03

Brook Farm
The Dun Cow (PH)
Clarks Farm
Northmoor
STANDLAKE RD
The Red Lion (PH)
Church Farm
Rectory Farm
NORTHMOOR PK
Fairacre Farm

Eaton Plantation

1

Northmoor Lock
Ash Copse
Weir

02

41 A 42 B 43 C

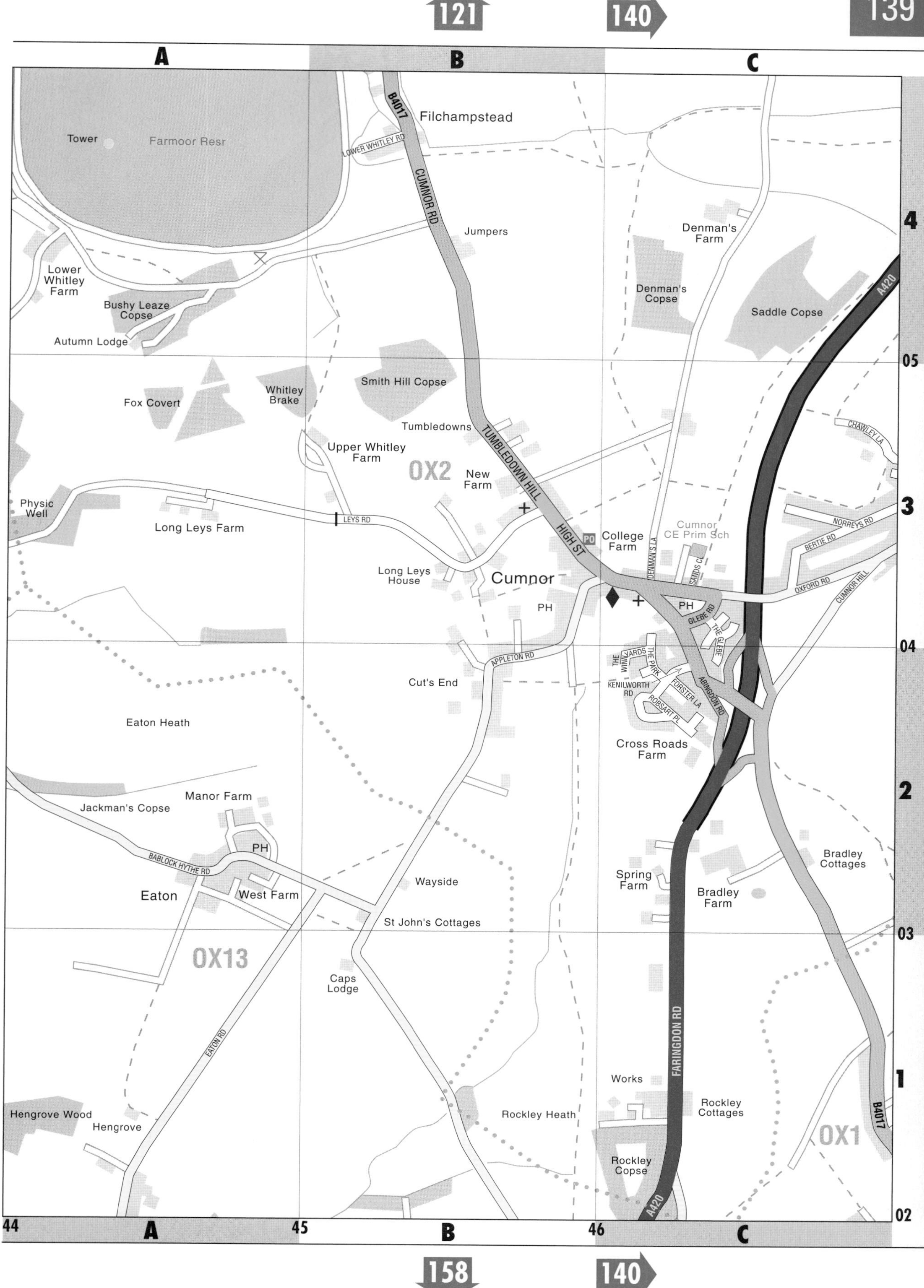

121
140

A   B   C

Tower
Farmoor Resr
B4017
Filchampstead
LOWER WHITLEY RD
CUMNOR RD
Jumpers
Denman's Farm
Denman's Copse
Saddle Copse
A420
4
Lower Whitley Farm
Bushy Leaze Copse
Autumn Lodge
Smith Hill Copse
CHAWLEY LA
05
Fox Covert
Whitley Brake
Tumbledowns
TUMBLEDOWN HILL
OX2
Upper Whitley Farm
New Farm
Cumnor CE Prim Sch
NORREYS RD
3
Physic Well
Long Leys Farm
LEYS RD
HIGH ST
PO
College Farm
BERTIE RD
SANDS CL
DENMAN'S LA
OXFORD RD
CUMNOR HILL
Long Leys House
Cumnor
PH
PH
GLEBE RD
THE GLEBE
Cut's End
APPLETON RD
THE WINDYARDS
THE PARK
ABINGDON RD
04
Eaton Heath
KENILWORTH RD
FORSTER LA
ROBSART PL
Cross Roads Farm
2
Jackman's Copse
Manor Farm
Bradley Cottages
BABLOCK HYTHE RD
PH
Wayside
Spring Farm
Bradley Farm
Eaton
West Farm
St John's Cottages
03
OX13
Caps Lodge
EATON RD
FARINGDON RD
1
Works
B4017
Hengrove Wood
Hengrove
Rockley Heath
Rockley Cottages
OX1
Rockley Copse
A420
02

44   A   45   B   46   C

158
140

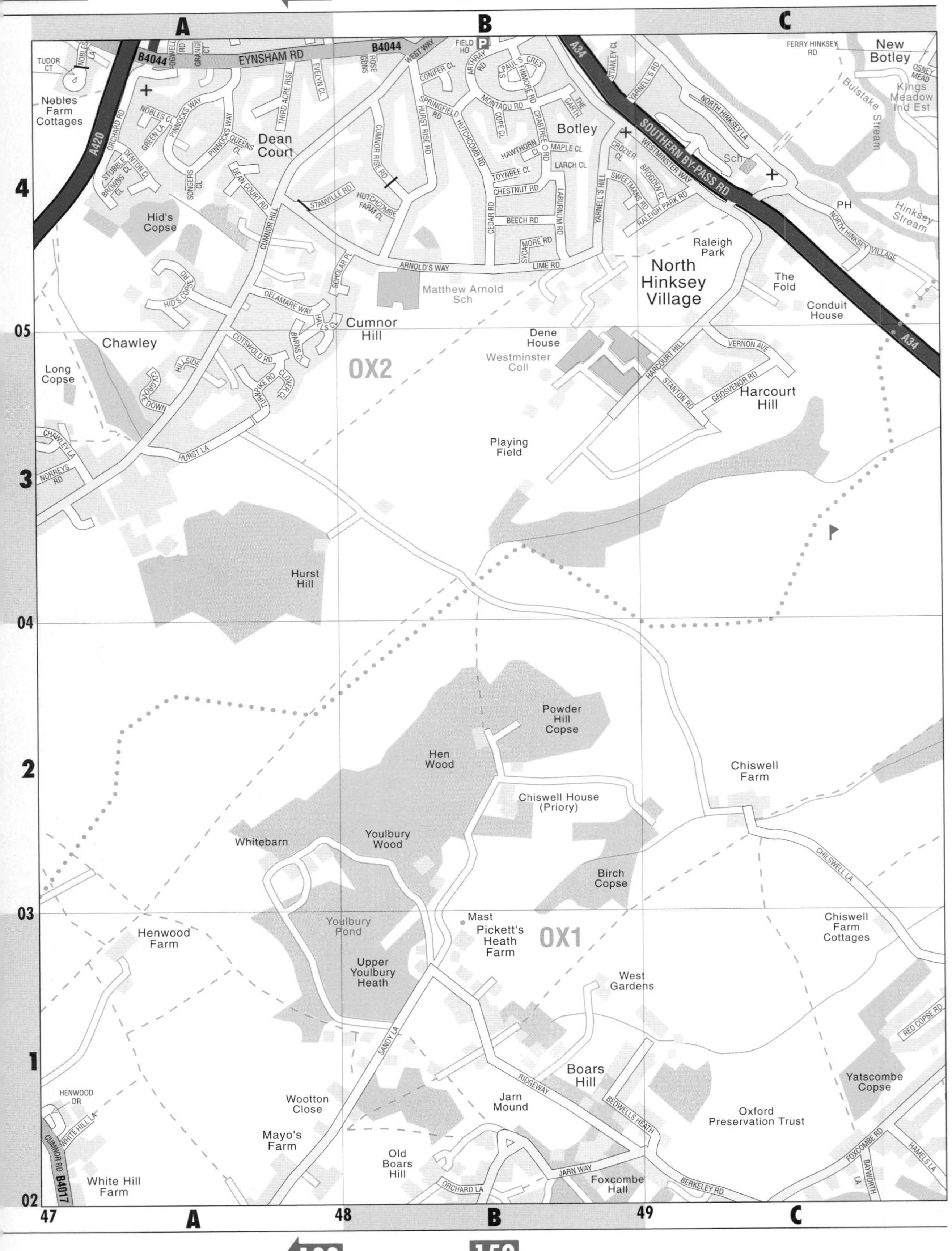

A
B
C

TUDOR CT
NOBLES
B4044
EYNSHAM RD
B4044
WEST WAY
FIELD HO
A34
STANLEY CL
FERRY HINKSEY RD
New Botley
OSNEY MEAD

Nebles Farm Cottages
ORCHARD RD
GRANGE CT
GREEN CL
ROSE GDNS
CONIFER CL
ARTIGRAY
ST PAUL'S CRES
FINMORE RD
VARNELL'S RD
NORTH HINKSEY LA
Kings Meadow Ind Est

A420
STUBBLE CL
DEXTON CL
BROWNS CL
NOBLES CL
PINNOCKS WAY
PINNICK QUEENS CL
Dean Court
EVELYN CL
SPRINGFIELD
MONTAGU RD
HUTCHCOMBE RD
CRABTREE RD
HAWTHORN
COPE CL
THE CARTER
Botley
CROZIER CL
WESTMINSTER WAY
BRIDGER CL
SOUTHERN BY-PASS RD
Bulstake Stream
Hinksey Stream

4
Hid's Copse
HID'S CLOSE RD
THIRD ACRE RISE
CUMNOR RISE RD
HURST RISE RD
MAPLE CL
LARCH CL
MORE RD
VARNELL'S HILL
SWEETMANS RD
RALEIGH PARK RD
Sch
PH

DEAN COURT RD
CUMNOR HILL
STANVILLE RD
HUTCHCOMBE FARM CL
CEDAR RD
CHESTNUT RD
BEECH RD
TOYNBEE CL
LABURNUM RD
Raleigh Park
Hinksey Village

Chawley
DELAMARE WAY
SCHOLAR PL
ARNOLD'S WAY
SYCAMORE
LIME RD
North Hinksey Village
The Fold
Conduit House

05
HID'S CLOSE
COTSWOLD RD
BARNS CL
HALLS CL
Cumnor Hill
Matthew Arnold Sch
Dene House
HARCOURT HILL
VERNON AVE
A34

Long Copse
HILL SIDE
CROSS DOWN
DYKE CL
OX2
Westminster Coll
STANTON RD
GROSVENOR RD
Harcourt Hill

3
CHAWLEY LA
NORREYS RD
HURST LA
Playing Field

Hurst Hill

04
Powder Hill Copse

Hen Wood
Chiswell Farm

2
Chiswell House (Priory)
CHILSWELL LA

Whitebarn
Youlbury Wood
Birch Copse
Chiswell Farm Cottages

03
Henwood Farm
Youlbury Pond
Mast
Pickett's Heath Farm
OX1
RED COPSE RD

Upper Youlbury Heath
West Gardens
Yatscombe Copse

1
SANDY LA
RIDGEWAY
Boars Hill
BEDWELLS HEATH
FOXCOMBE RD
BAYWORTH LA

HENWOOD DR
WHITE HILL LA
Wootton Close
Jarn Mound
Oxford Preservation Trust
HAMELS LA

CUMNOR RD
B4017
Mayo's Farm
Old Boars Hill
ORCHARD LA
JARN WAY
Foxcombe Hall
BERKELEY RD

02
White Hill Farm

47
A
48
B
49
C

B4
1 WESTGATE SH CTR
2 ROGER BACON LA
3 ST EBBES ST
4 PEMBROKE SQ
5 TURN AGAIN LA
6 PIKE TERR
7 FAULKNER ST
8 CAMBRIDGE TERR
9 CLARK'S ROW
10 BROOKS TAYLOR CT
11 BUTTERWYKE PL
12 CROMWELL ST
13 LUTHER CT
14 STEPHENSON HO
15 BLACKFRIARS RD
16 PREACHERS LA
17 FOLLY BRIDGE CT
18 THAMES CT
19 BUCKINGHAM ST
20 WATERMANS REACH
21 THE CLOISTERS
22 BURFORD LODGE
23 PEGASUS CT
24 STREATLEY LODGE
25 GORING LODGE
26 OLNEY CT

C4
1 DAWSON ST
2 JEUNE HALL
3 GRANTS MEWS
4 PEMBROKE CT
5 COLLINS ST
6 SOUTH PARK CT
7 EAST AVE
8 RANDOLPH ST
9 HAWKINS ST
10 MONARD TERR

123
142

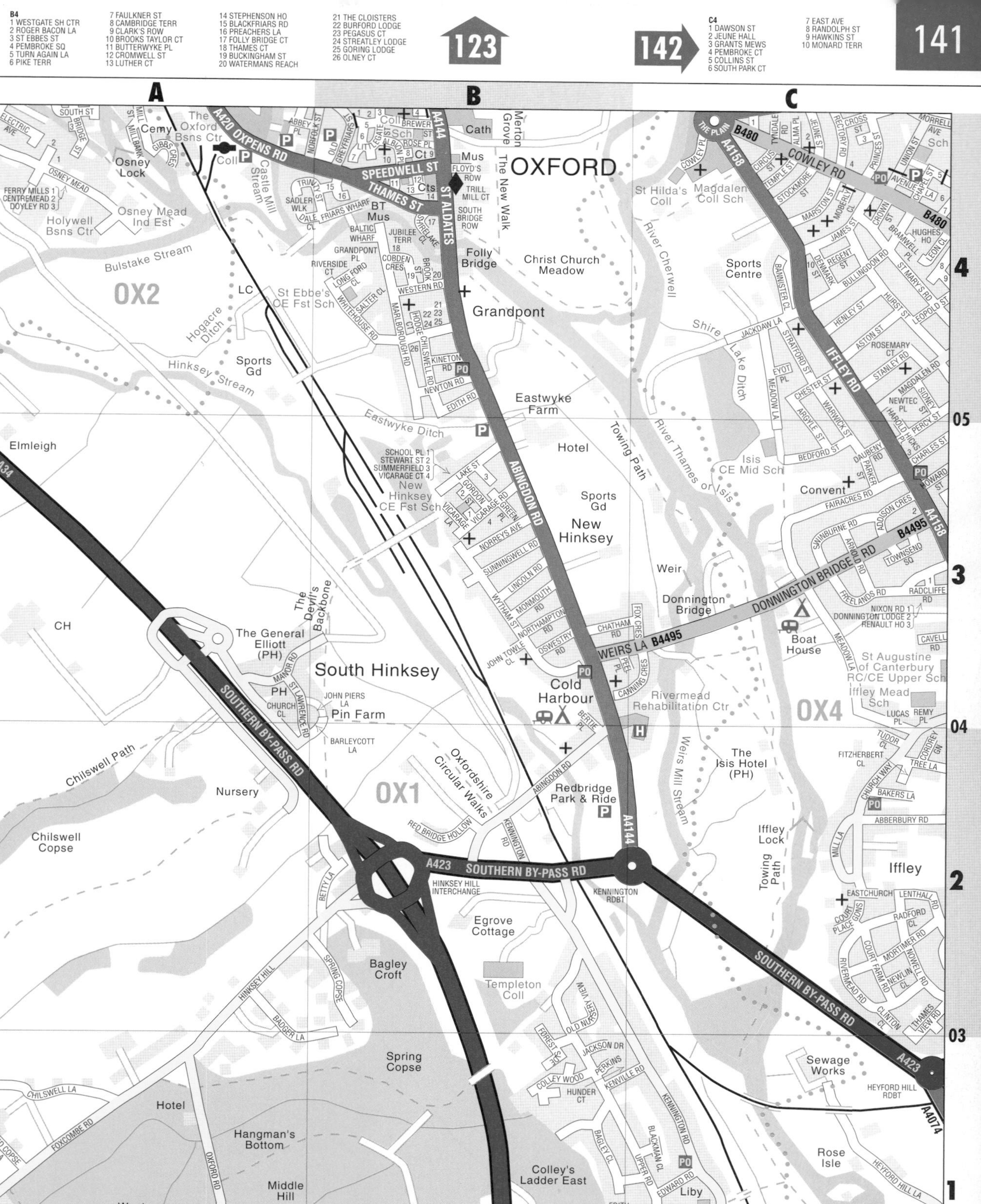

160
142

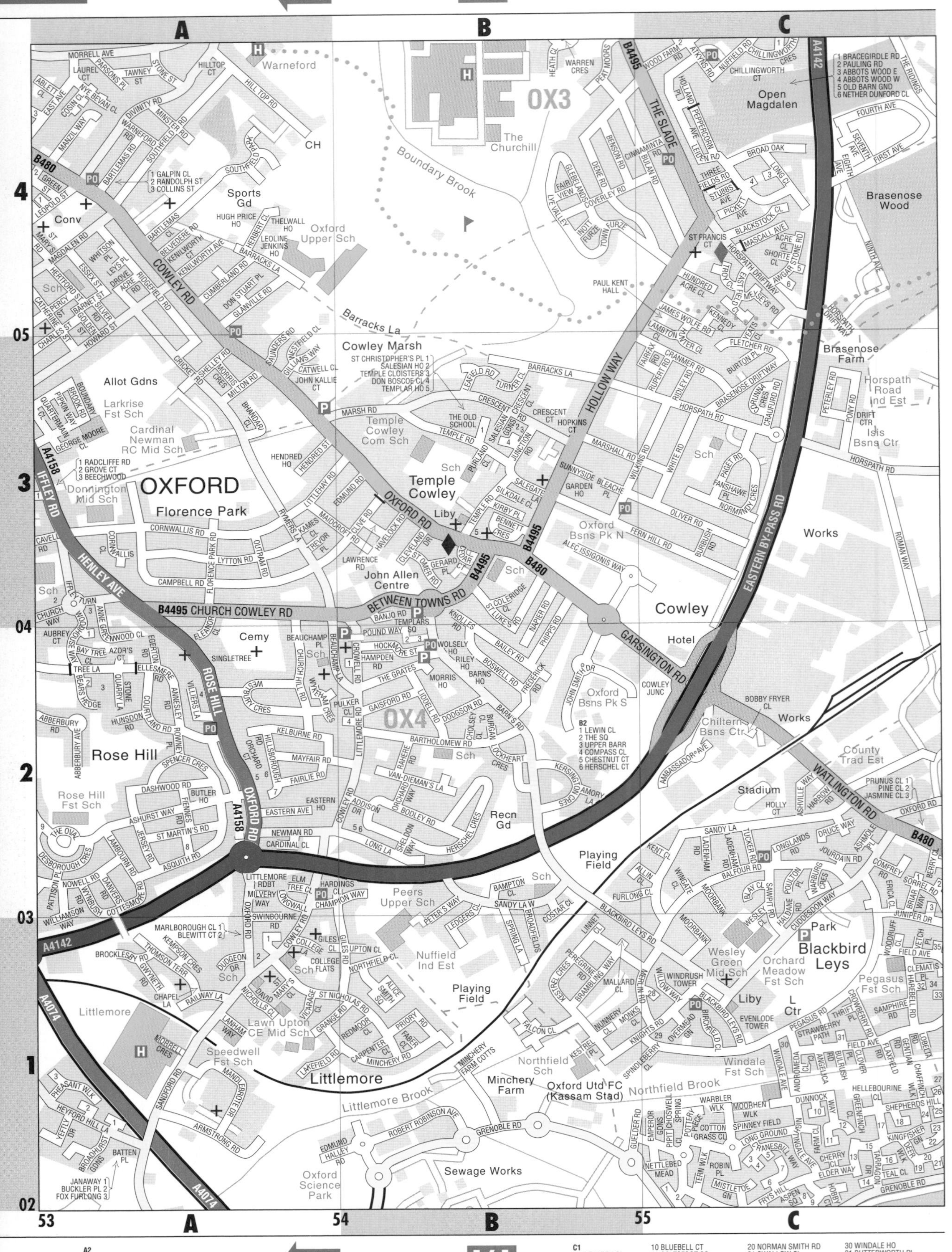

141 124

OX3

The Churchill

Open
Magdalen

Brasenose
Wood

1 BRACEGIRDLE RD
2 PAULING RD
3 ABBOTS WOOD E
4 ABBOTS WOOD W
5 OLD BARN GND
6 NETHER DUNFORD CT

Warneford

Boundary Brook

Sports
Gd

Cowley Rd

Oxford
Upper Sch

Barracks La

Cowley Marsh

ST CHRISTOPHER'S PL 1
SALESIAN HO 2
TEMPLE CLOISTERS 3
DON BOSCO CL 4
TEMPLAR HO 5

Brasenose
Farm

Horspath
Road
Ind Est

Isis
Bsns Ctr

Allot Gdns

Larkrise
Fst Sch

Cardinal
Newman
RC Mid Sch

Temple
Cowley Com Sch

THE OLD
SCHOOL

OXFORD

1 RADCLIFFE RD
2 GROVE CT
3 BEECHWOOD

Donnington
Mid Sch

Florence Park

Temple
Cowley

Liby

Oxford
Bsns Pk N

Works

Henley Ave

John Allen
Centre

Lawrence
Rd

Cowley

Between Towns Rd

Church Cowley Rd

Cemy

Wolsely
Ho

Hotel

OX4

Oxford
Bsns Pk S

Cowley
Junc

Works

Rose Hill

Rose Hill
Fst Sch

County
Trad Est

1 LEWIN CL
2 THE SQ
3 UPPER BARR
4 COMPASS CL
5 CHESTNUT CT
6 HERSCHEL CT

Chiltern
Bsns Ctr

Bobby Fryer
Cl

Stadium

Recn
Gd

Playing
Field

Peers
Upper Sch

Blackbird
Leys

Wesley
Green Mid Sch

Orchard
Meadow
Fst Sch

Pegasus
Fst Sch

Nuffield Ind Est

Playing
Field

Liby

L
Ctr

Windale
Fst Sch

Lawn Upton
CE Mid Sch

Speedwell
Fst Sch

Littlemore

Minchery
Farm

Northfield
Sch

Oxford Utd FC
(Kassam Stad)

Northfield Brook

Littlemore Brook

Sewage Works

Oxford
Science
Park

JANAWAY 1
BUCKLER PL 2
FOX FURLONG 3

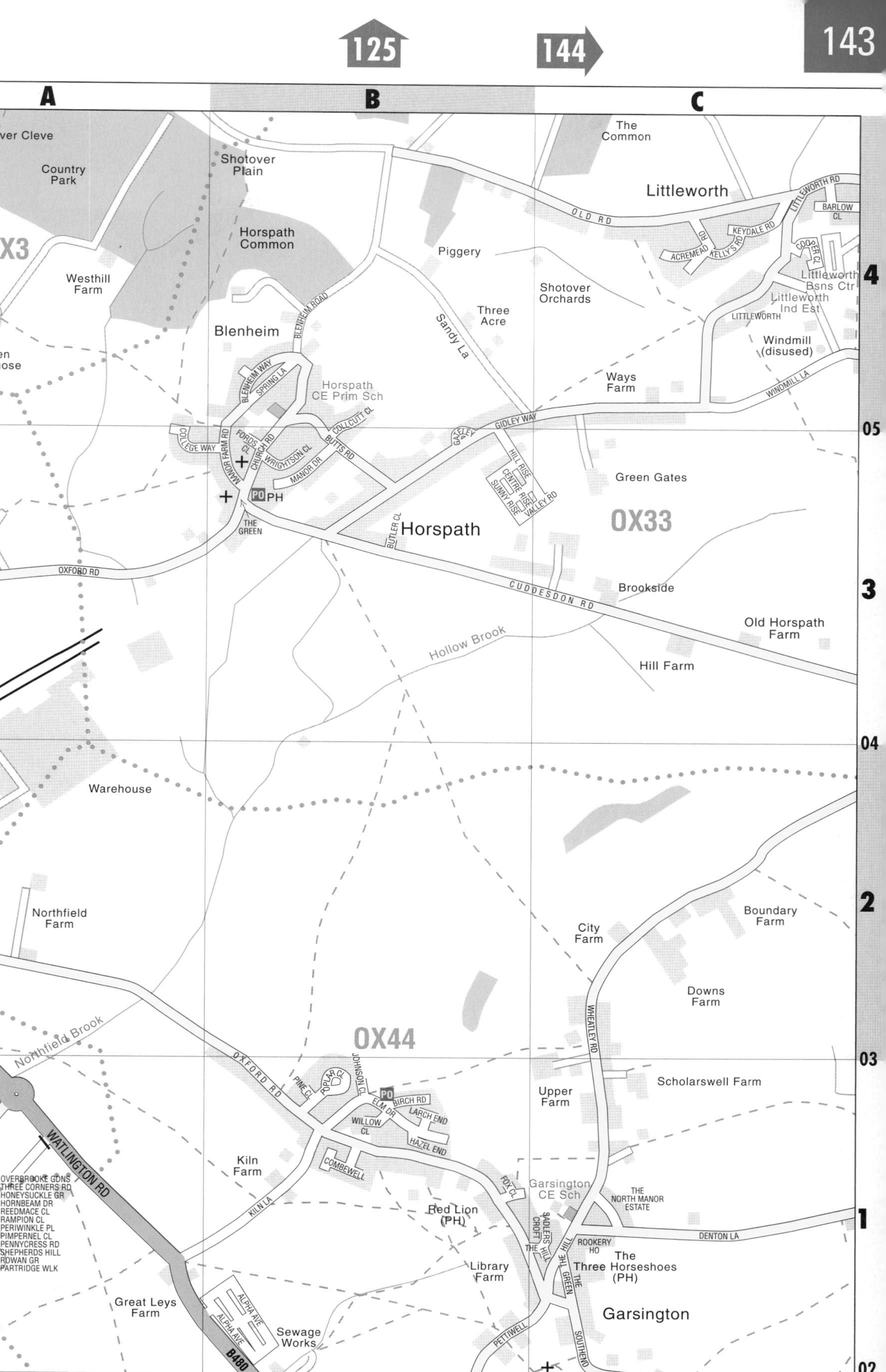
A
B
C
Shotover Cleve
Country Park
Shotover Plain
The Common
Littleworth
OX3
Horspath Common
Westhill Farm
Piggery
Shotover Orchards
Littleworth Bsns Ctr
Littleworth Ind Est
Three Acre
Blenheim
Open Brasnose
Windmill (disused)
Ways Farm
Horspath CE Prim Sch
Green Gates
OX33
Sports Ground
Horspath
Brookside
Old Horspath Farm
Hollow Brook
Hill Farm
Depot
Warehouse
OX4
Northfield Farm
Boundary Farm
City Farm
Guydens Farm
Downs Farm
OX44
Northfield Brook
Upper Farm
Scholarswell Farm
Kiln Farm
Garsington CE Sch
THE NORTH MANOR ESTATE
Red Lion (PH)
The Three Horseshoes (PH)
Library Farm
Depot
Great Leys Farm
Sewage Works
Garsington
OLD RD
LITTLEWORTH RD
BARLOW CL
KEYDALE RD
ACREMEAD RD
KELLY'S RD
COOPER CL
LITTLEWORTH
WINDMILL LA
Sandy La
BLENHEIM ROAD
BLENHEIM WAY
SPRING LA
COLLCUTT CL
BUTTS RD
GIDLEY WAY
GATELEY
HILL RISE
CENTRE RISE
SUNNY RISE
VALLEY RD
COLLEGE WAY
MANOR FARM RD
FORDS CL
CHURCH RD
WRIGHTSON CL
MANOR DR
PO PH
THE GREEN
BUTLER CL
OXFORD RD
CUDDESDON RD
THE RIDINGS
WHEATLEY RD
JOHNSON CL
POPLAR CL
PINE CL
ELM DR
BIRCH RD
LARCH END
WILLOW CL
HAZEL END
COMBEWELL
KILN LA
FOX CL
SADLERS CROFT
THE HILL
THE GREEN
ROOKERY HO
DENTON LA
PETTIWELL
SOUTHEND
WATLINGTON RD
B480
ALPHA AVE
BERRY CL
SORREL RD
SUNDEW CL
TREFOIL PL
BRYONY CL
CENTAURY PL
YEW CL
GREEN HILL
THISTLE DR
FIELD AVE
LITTLE BURY
BROOK VIEW
REDWOOD
MERCURY RD
MARJORAM CL
GRENOBLE RD
JANE SEAMAN CT
BRAKE HILL
BLACKBERRY LA
COLUMBINE GDNS
1 OVERBROOKE GDNS
2 THREE CORNERS RD
3 HONEYSUCKLE GR
4 HORNBEAM DR
5 REEDMACE CL
6 RAMPION CL
7 PERIWINKLE PL
8 PIMPERNEL CL
9 PENNYCRESS RD
10 SHEPHERDS HILL
11 ROWAN GR
12 PARTRIDGE WLK
05
04
03
02
4
3
2
1
56
57
58

143
126

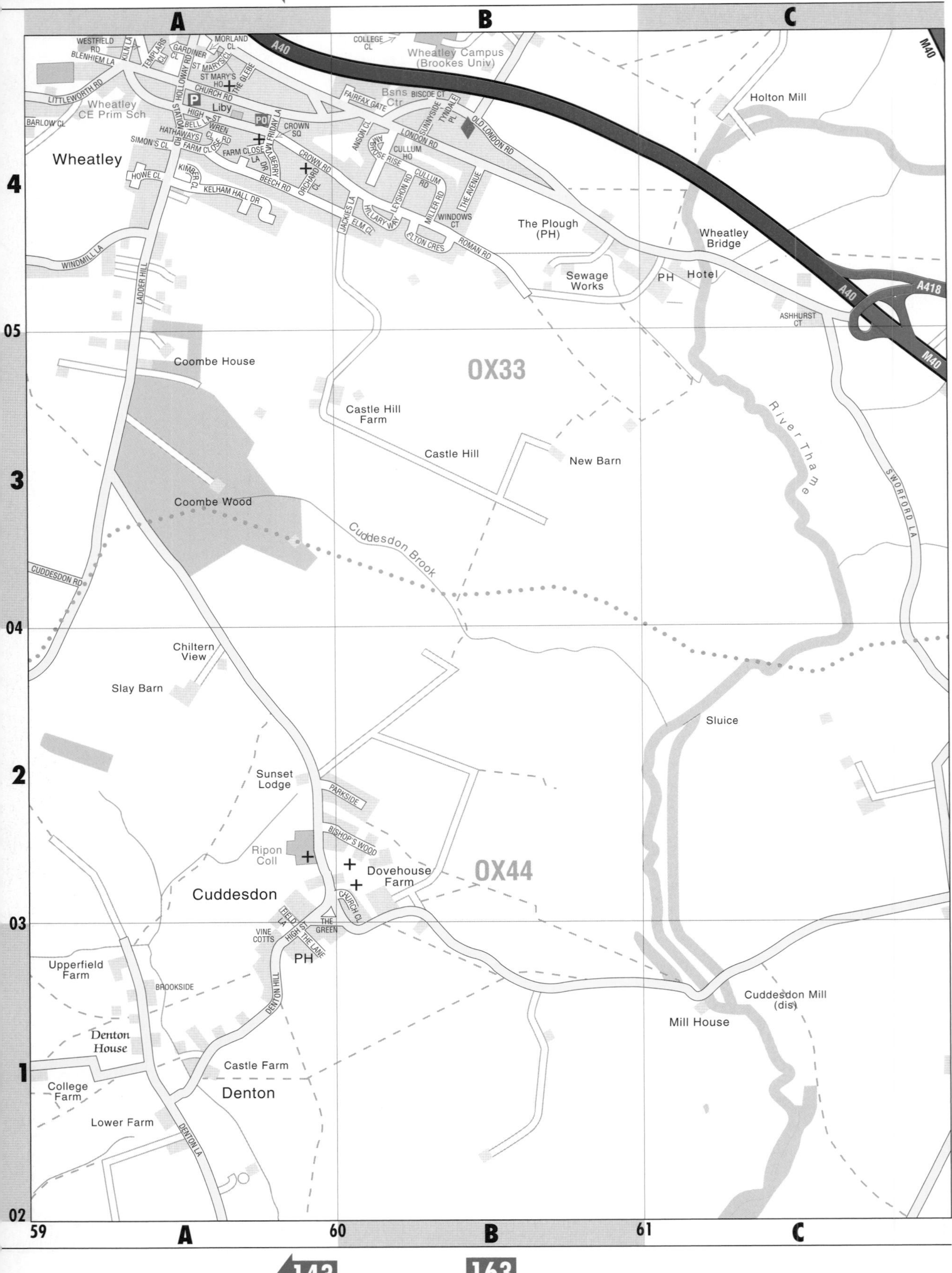
A
B
C
4
05
3
04
2
03
1
02
59
60
61
A40
M40
A418
Wheatley
Wheatley CE Prim Sch
Liby
Wheatley Campus (Brookes Univ)
Bsns Ctr
Holton Mill
The Plough (PH)
Wheatley Bridge
Sewage Works
PH
Hotel
OX33
Coombe House
Castle Hill Farm
Castle Hill
New Barn
River Thame
Coombe Wood
Cuddesdon Brook
Chiltern View
Slay Barn
Sluice
Sunset Lodge
Ripon Coll
Dovehouse Farm
OX44
Cuddesdon
Upperfield Farm
Denton House
Castle Farm
Denton
College Farm
Lower Farm
Cuddesdon Mill (dis)
Mill House
PH
WESTFIELD RD
BLENHIEM LA
LITTLEWORTH RD
BARLOW CL
HOWE CL
SIMON'S CL
HATHAWAYS
KIMBER CL
KELHAM HALL DR
WINDMILL LA
LADDER HILL
CUDDESDON RD
SWORFORD LA
DENTON HILL
DENTON LA
BROOKSIDE
VINE COTTS
FIELD LA
HIGH ST
THE LANE
THE GREEN
CHURCH CL
BISHOP'S WOOD
PARKSIDE
ASHHURST CT
ROMAN RD
ELTON CRES
WINDOWS CT
JACKIES LA
ELM CL
HILLARY WAY
LEYSHON RD
MILLER RD
CULLUM RD
THE AVENUE
OLD LONDON RD
LONDON RD
CULLUM HO
AMBROSE RISE
ANSON CL
SUNNYSIDE
TYNDALE PL
BISCOE CT
FAIRFAX GATE
COLLEGE CL
MORLAND CL
GARDINER CL
ST MARY'S CL
ST MARY'S HO
THE GLEBE
CHURCH RD
KILN LA
TEMPLARS CL
HOLLOWAY RD
STATION RD
HIGH ST
BELL LA
WREN RD
FARM CLOSE RD
FARM CLOSE LA
MULBERRY DR
FRIDAY LA
CROWN SQ
CROWN RD
ORCHARD CL
BEECH RD

143
163

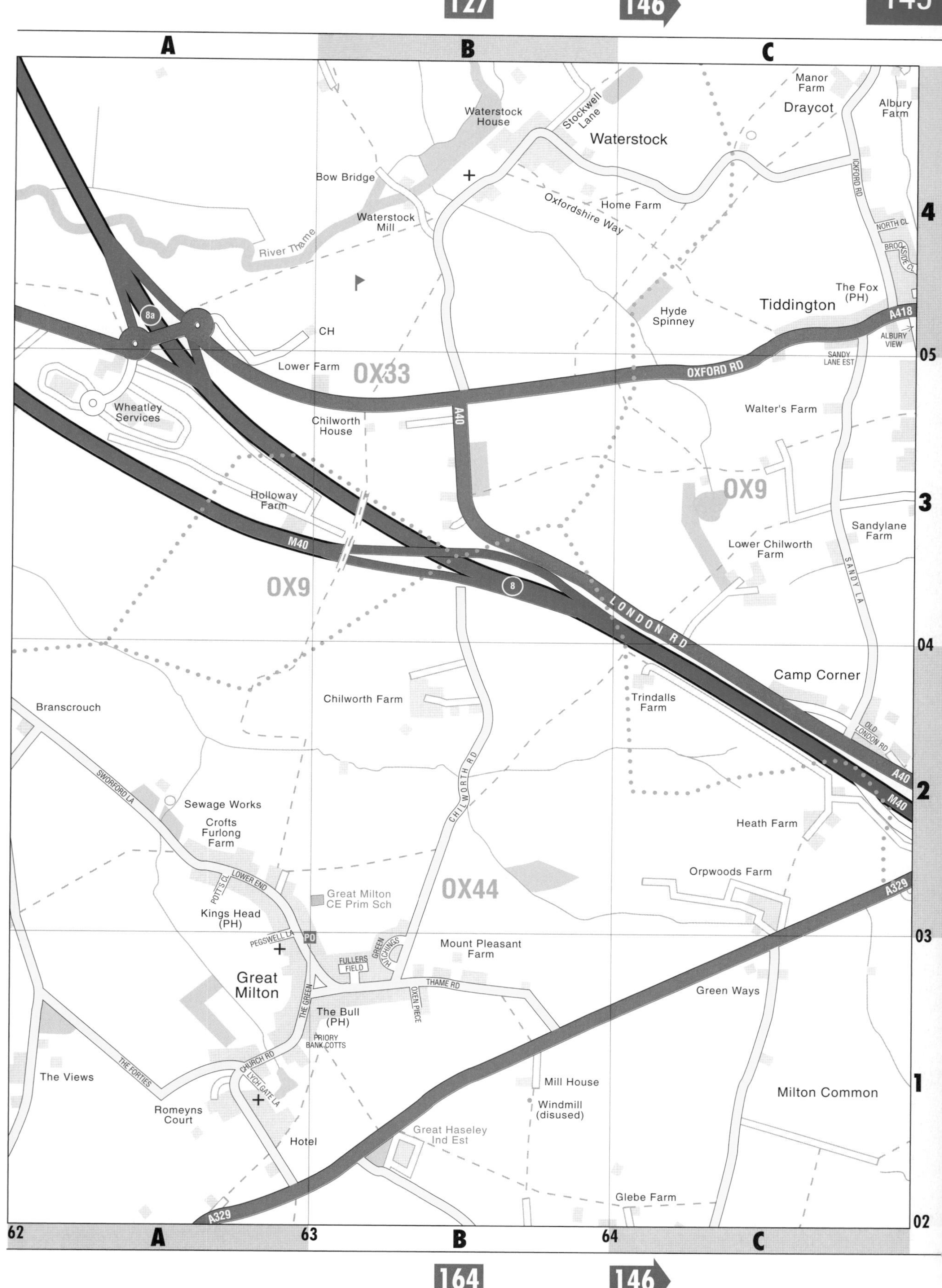

A   B   C

Manor Farm

Waterstock House

Stockwell Lane

Draycot

Albury Farm

Bow Bridge

Waterstock

ICKFORD RD

NORTH CL

Oxfordshire Way

Home Farm

4

River Thame

Waterstock Mill

BROOKSIDE CL

The Fox (PH)

A418

Tiddington

8a

CH

Hyde Spinney

ALBURY VIEW

Lower Farm

OX33

OXFORD RD

SANDY LANE EST

05

Wheatley Services

Chilworth House

A40

Walter's Farm

OX9

Holloway Farm

M40

Lower Chilworth Farm

Sandylane Farm

3

OX9

B

LONDON RD

SANDY LA

04

Camp Corner

Branscrouch

Chilworth Farm

Trindalls Farm

OLD LONDON RD

A40

SWORFORD LA

CHILWORTH RD

Heath Farm

M40

2

Sewage Works

Crofts Furlong Farm

POTTS CL

LOWER END

Orpwoods Farm

A329

Great Milton CE Prim Sch

OX44

Kings Head (PH)

PEGSWELL LA

PO

GREEN

THE CHAINS

Mount Pleasant Farm

03

FULLERS FIELD

Green Ways

Great Milton

THE GREEN

THAME RD

OXEN PIECE

The Bull (PH)

PRIORY BANK COTTS

The Views

THE FORTIES

CHURCH RD

Mill House

Milton Common

1

Romeyns Court

LYCH GATE LA

Windmill (disused)

Hotel

Great Haseley Ind Est

Glebe Farm

A329

02

62   A   63   B   64   C

145 128

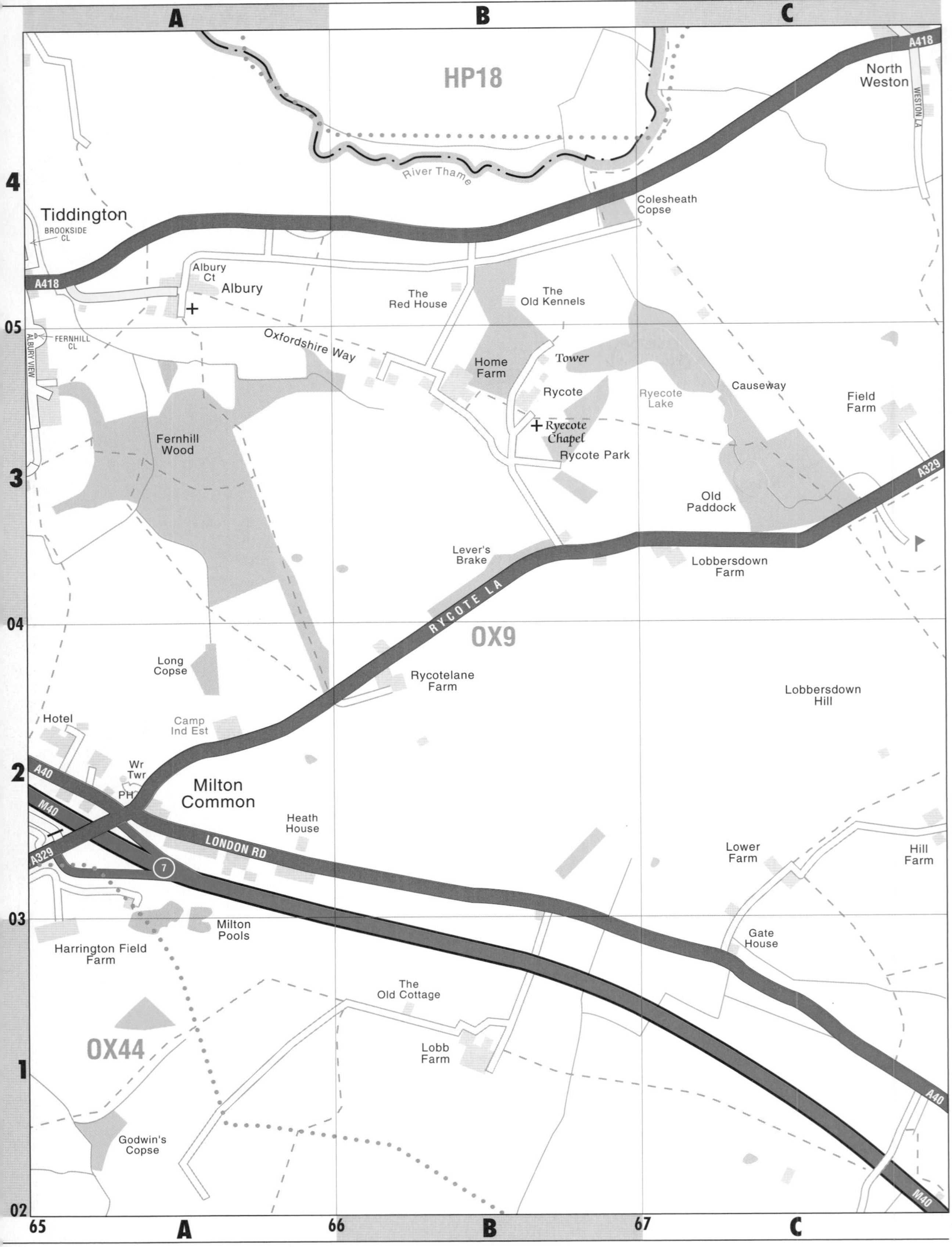

A · B · C

HP18

North Weston

A418

WESTON LA

River Thame

Colesheath Copse

4

Tiddington

BROOKSIDE CL

A418

Albury Ct

Albury

FERNHILL CL

ALBURY VIEW

The Red House

The Old Kennels

Oxfordshire Way

05

Home Farm

Tower

Rycote

Ryecote Lake

Causeway

Field Farm

Ryecote Chapel

Rycote Park

Fernhill Wood

Old Paddock

A329

3

Lever's Brake

Lobbersdown Farm

RYCOTE LA

04

OX9

Long Copse

Rycotelane Farm

Lobbersdown Hill

Hotel

Camp Ind Est

A40

Wr Twr

PH

2

Milton Common

Heath House

LONDON RD

Lower Farm

Hill Farm

M40

A329

7

03

Milton Pools

Gate House

Harrington Field Farm

The Old Cottage

OX44

1

Lobb Farm

Godwin's Copse

M40

A40

02

65 · A · 66 · B · 67 · C

145 165

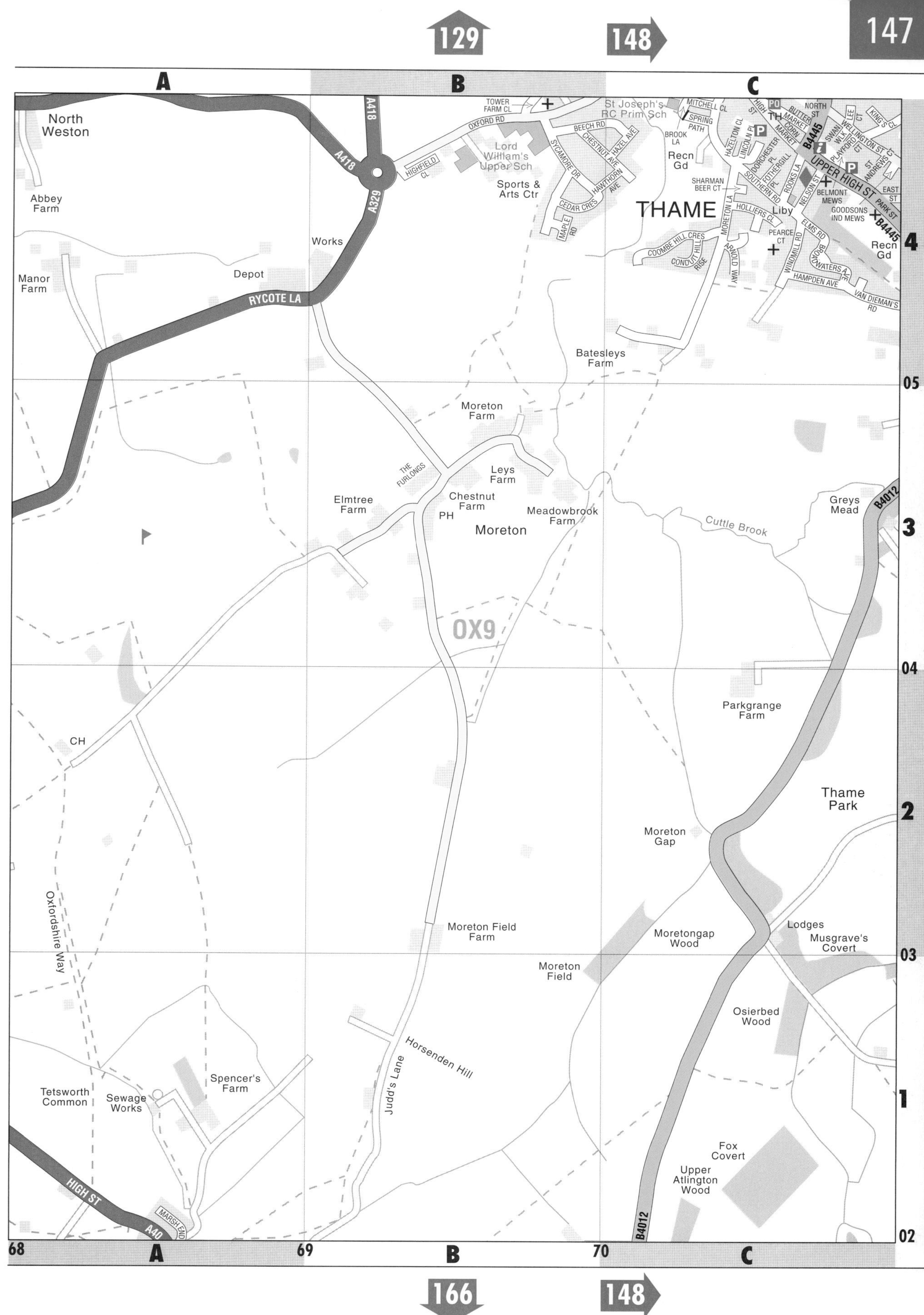

129
148
166
148

A **B** **C**

North
Weston

Abbey
Farm

A418

A329

TOWER
FARM CL

OXFORD RD

HIGHFIELD
CL

BEECH RD

CHESTNUT AVE

HAZEL AVE

SYCAMORE DR

HAWTHORN
AVE

St Joseph's
RC Prim Sch

MITCHELL CL

SPRING
PATH

BROOK
LA

Lord
William's
Upper Sch

Sports &
Arts Ctr

Recn
Gd

SHARMAN
BEER CT

HIGH ST

HAZELTON RD

LINCOLN PL

MARKET

BUTTER

NORTH
ST

KING'S

MITCHELL CL

SWAN WK

WELLINGTON ST

LEE

EAST
ST

PARK ST

ST ANDREWS

SOUTHERN RD

DORCHESTER
PL

LOTHERGILL

HOLLIERS CL

MORETON LA

ROOKS LA

NELSON ST

ELMS RD

BELMONT
MEWS

GOODSONS
IND MEWS

UPPER HIGH ST

B4445

B4445

THAME

Liby

Recn
Gd

4

CEDAR CRES

MAPLE
RD

Manor
Farm

Works

Depot

RYCOTE LA

COOMBE HILL CRES

CONDUIT
HILL
RISE

PEARCE
CT

WINDMILL RD

APSLEY
WAY

WATERS A

HAMPDEN AVE

VAN DIEMAN'S
RD

Batesleys
Farm

Moreton
Farm

05

THE
FURLONGS

Elmtree
Farm

Leys
Farm

Chestnut
Farm

PH

Meadowbrook
Farm

Moreton

Cuttle Brook

Greys
Mead

B4012

3

OX9

04

Parkgrange
Farm

Thame
Park

2

Moreton
Gap

CH

Moretongap
Wood

Lodges

Musgrave's
Covert

03

Moreton Field
Farm

Moreton
Field

Osierbed
Wood

Oxfordshire Way

Judd's Lane

Horsenden Hill

Tetsworth
Common

Sewage
Works

Spencer's
Farm

Fox
Covert

1

Upper
Atlington
Wood

HIGH ST

A40

MARSH END

B4012

02

147
130

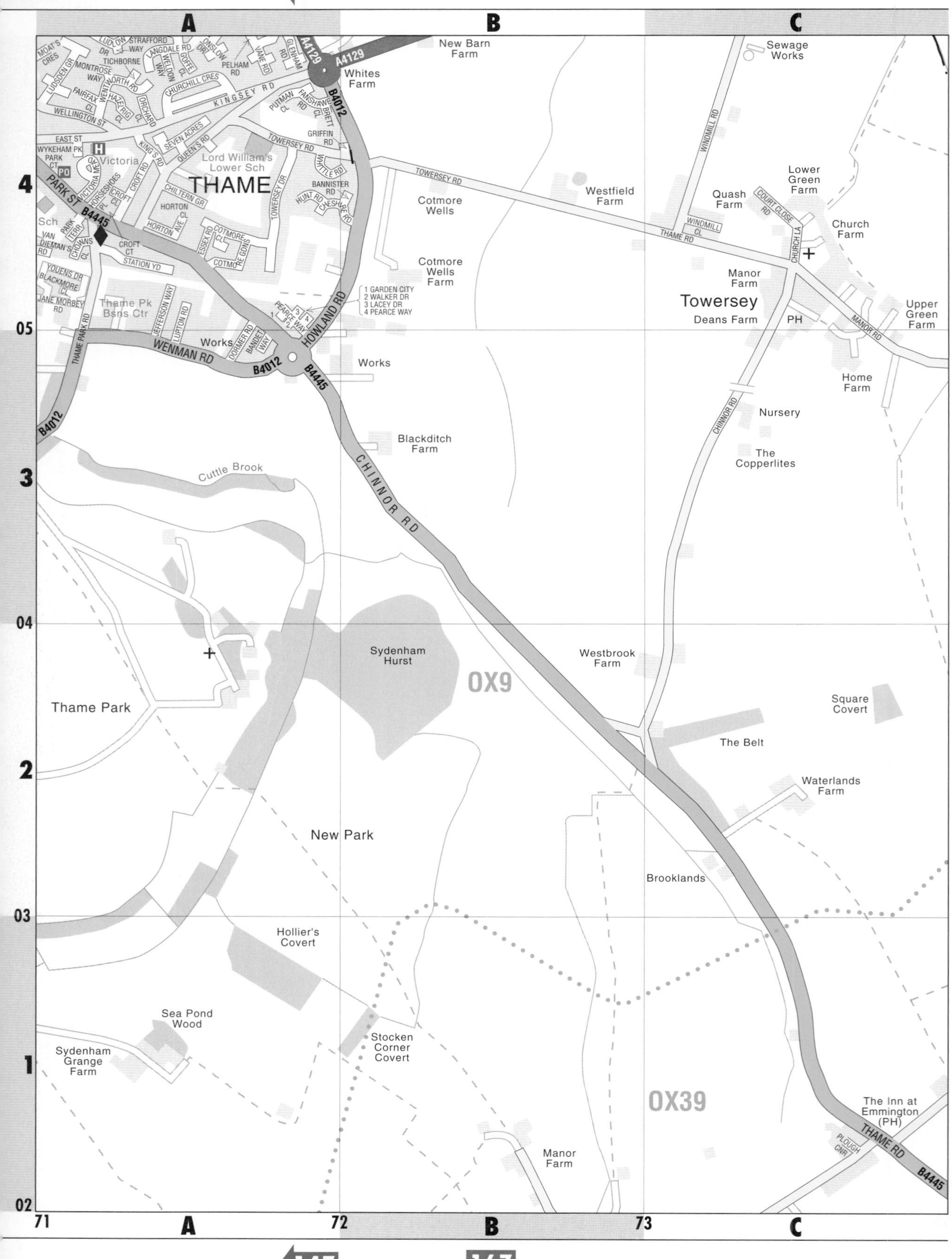
THAME
Towersey
Thame Park
New Park
Sydenham Hurst
OX9
OX39
New Barn Farm
Whites Farm
Sewage Works
Lord William's Lower Sch
Victoria
Cotmore Wells
Cotmore Wells Farm
Westfield Farm
Quash Farm
Lower Green Farm
Church Farm
Manor Farm
Deans Farm
PH
Upper Green Farm
Home Farm
Nursery
The Copperlites
Works
Blackditch Farm
Thame Pk Bsns Ctr
Cuttle Brook
Westbrook Farm
Square Covert
The Belt
Waterlands Farm
Brooklands
Hollier's Covert
Sea Pond Wood
Sydenham Grange Farm
Stocken Corner Covert
Manor Farm
The Inn at Emmington (PH)
TOWERSEY RD
THAME RD
CHINNOR RD
HOWLAND RD
WENMAN RD
KINGSEY RD
PARK ST
WINDMILL RD
MANOR RD
A4129
B4012
B4445
1 GARDEN CITY
2 WALKER DR
3 LACEY DR
4 PEARCE WAY
A
B
C
71
72
73
05
04
03
02

147
167

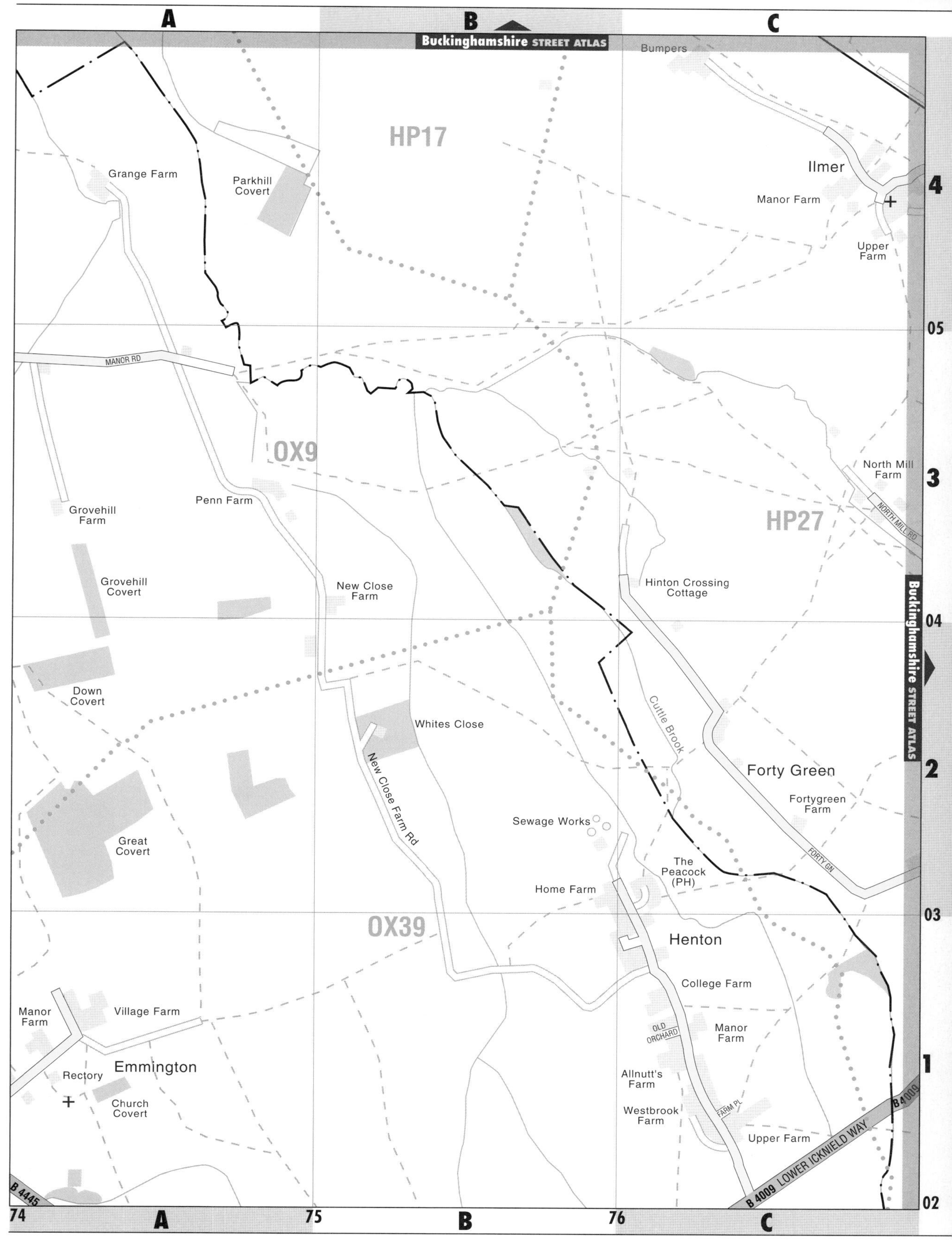

Buckinghamshire STREET ATLAS

Buckinghamshire STREET ATLAS

Bumpers

HP17

Ilmer

Manor Farm

Upper Farm

Grange Farm

Parkhill Covert

MANOR RD

05

OX9

North Mill Farm

NORTH MILL RD

3

Penn Farm

HP27

Grovehill Farm

Grovehill Covert

New Close Farm

Hinton Crossing Cottage

04

Down Covert

Whites Close

New Close Farm Rd

Cuttle Brook

Forty Green

Fortygreen Farm

FORTY GN

2

Great Covert

Sewage Works

Home Farm

The Peacock (PH)

03

OX39

Henton

College Farm

Manor Farm

Manor Farm

Village Farm

OLD ORCHARD

Rectory

Emmington

Allnutt's Farm

Westbrook Farm

FARM PL

1

Church Covert

Upper Farm

LOWER ICKNIELD WAY

B 4009

B 4009

B 4445

74   A   75   B   76   C

02

131

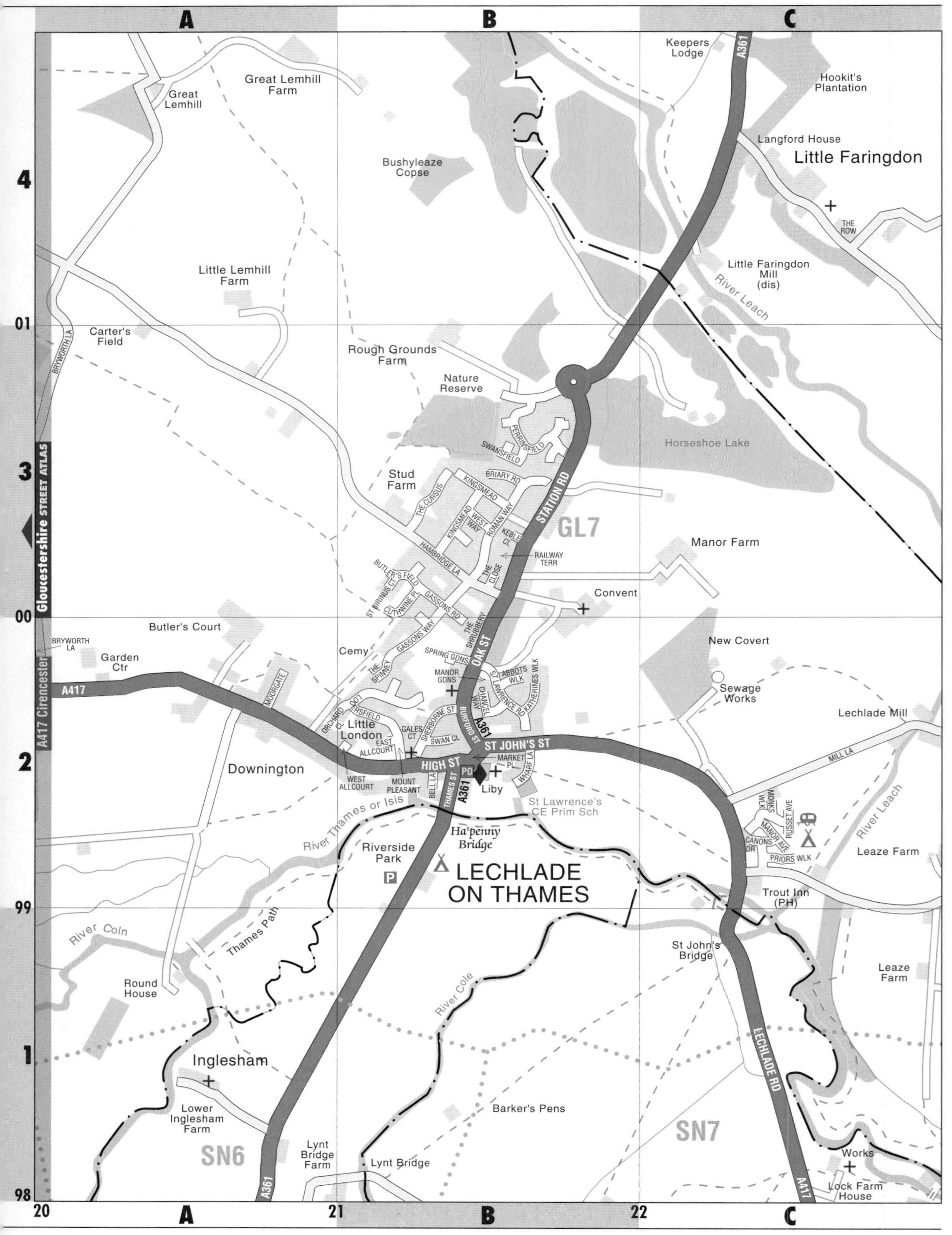
A
B
C
Keepers Lodge
A361
Hookit's Plantation
Great Lemhill Farm
Great Lemhill
Langford House
Little Faringdon
Bushyleaze Copse
4
THE ROW
Little Faringdon Mill (dis)
Little Lemhill Farm
River Leach
01
Carter's Field
BRYWORTH LA
Rough Grounds Farm
Nature Reserve
PERRINSFIELD
SWANSFIELD
Horseshoe Lake
3
Stud Farm
BRIARY RD
KINGSMEAD
THE CURSUS
STATION RD
GL7
ROMAN WAY
WEST WAY
KINGSMEAD
KEBLE CL
RAILWAY TERR
Manor Farm
HAMBRIDGE LA
BUTLER'S FIELD
THE CLOSE
Convent
ST BIRINUS CT
CUTHWINE PL
GASSONS RD
THE SHRUBBERY
00
Butler's Court
Gloucestershire STREET ATLAS
BRYWORTH LA
New Covert
Garden Ctr
Cemy
GASSONS WAY
THE SPINNEY
SPRING GDNS
OAK ST
MANOR GDNS
ABBOTS WLK
KATHERINES WLK
Sewage Works
A417
MOORGATE
ST LAWRENCE RD
CHANCEL WAY
A417 Cirencester
ORCHARD CL
Little London
GALES CT
SHERBORNE ST
BURFORD ST
A361
Lechlade Mill
EAST ALLCOURT
SWAN CL
ST JOHN'S ST
MILL LA
2
HIGH ST
MARKET PL
WHARF LA
Downington
WEST ALLCOURT
MOUNT PLEASANT
BELL LA
THAMES ST
A361
PO
Liby
St Lawrence's CE Prim Sch
MONKS WLK
RUSSET AVE
MANOR AVE
River Leach
River Thames or Isis
Ha'penny Bridge
CANONS DR
PRIORS WLK
Riverside Park
Leaze Farm
LECHLADE ON THAMES
P
99
Trout Inn (PH)
River Coln
Thames Path
St John's Bridge
Leaze Farm
Round House
River Cole
1
Inglesham
LECHLADE RD
Lower Inglesham Farm
Barker's Pens
SN7
SN6
Lynt Bridge Farm
Lynt Bridge
Works
A361
A417
Lock Farm House
98
20
A
21
B
22
C

170

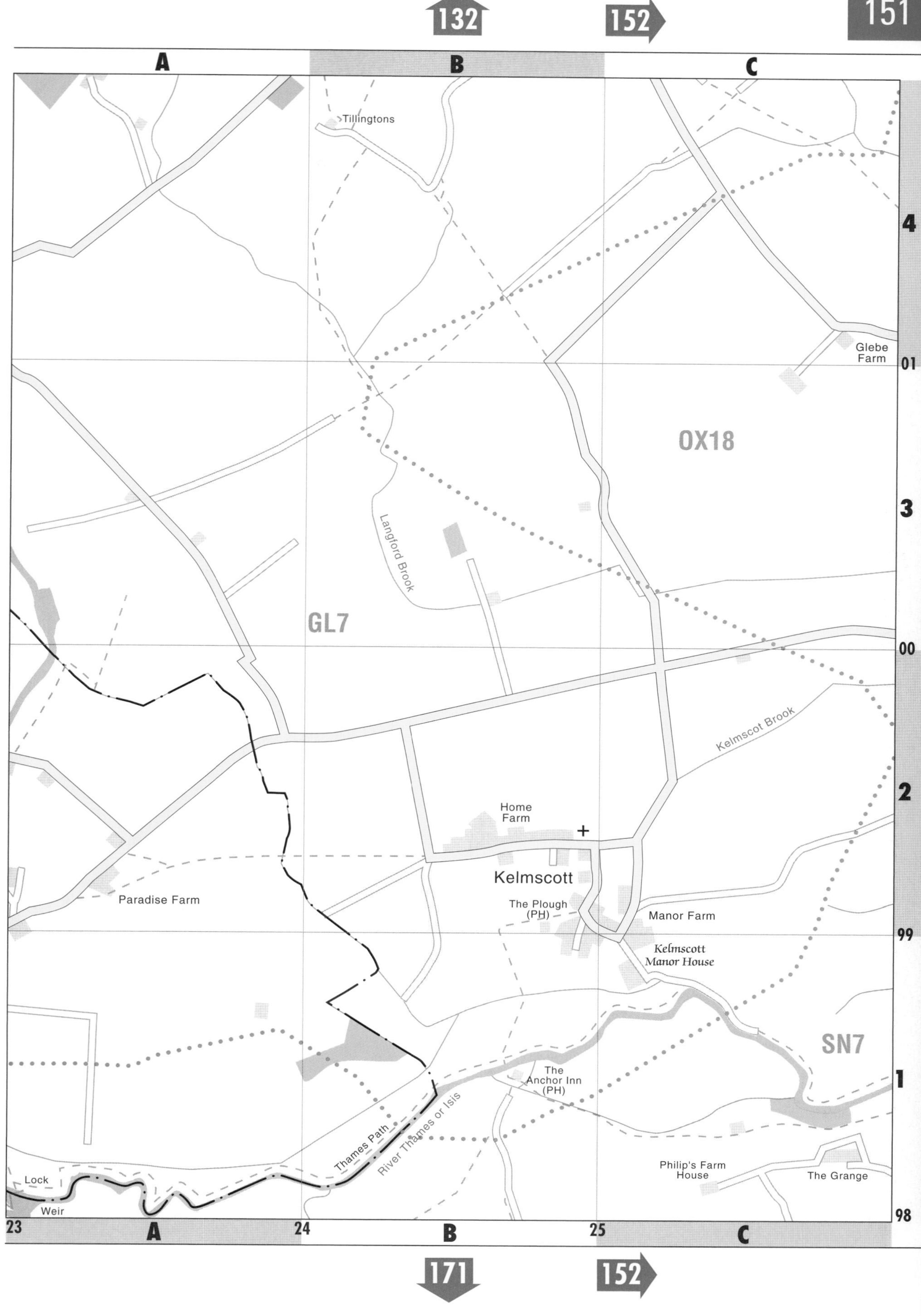

A B C

Tillingtons

4

Glebe
Farm

01

OX18

3

Langford Brook

GL7

00

Kelmscot Brook

2

Home
Farm

+

Kelmscott

99

The Plough
(PH)

Manor Farm

Kelmscott
Manor House

Paradise Farm

SN7

The
Anchor Inn
(PH)

1

Thames Path

River Thames or Isis

Philip's Farm
House

The Grange

Lock

Weir

98

23 A 24 B 25 C

151
133

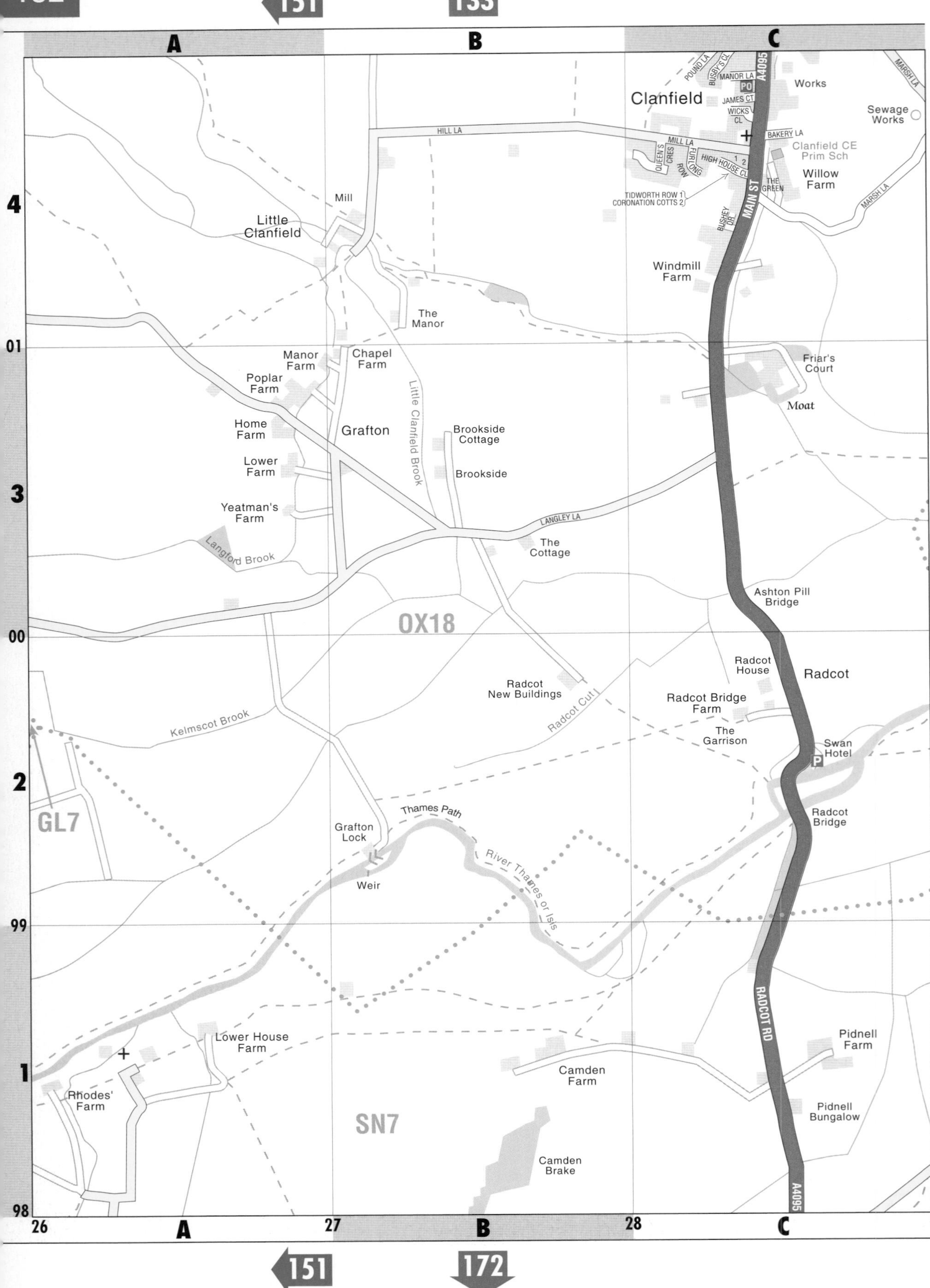
A
B
C
Clanfield
Works
Sewage Works
POUND LA
BUSBY'S CL
MANOR LA
PO
JAMES CT
WICKS CL
A4095
MARSH LA
HILL LA
MILL LA
BAKERY LA
QUEEN'S CRES
FURLONG ROW
HIGH HOUSE CL
THE GREEN
Clanfield CE Prim Sch
Willow Farm
TIDWORTH ROW 1
CORONATION COTTS 2
MAIN ST
BUSHEY DR
Mill
Little Clanfield
Windmill Farm
The Manor
Manor Farm
Chapel Farm
Poplar Farm
Friar's Court
Moat
Home Farm
Grafton
Little Clanfield Brook
Brookside Cottage
Brookside
Lower Farm
Yeatman's Farm
LANGLEY LA
The Cottage
Langford Brook
Ashton Pill Bridge
OX18
Radcot House
Radcot
Radcot New Buildings
Radcot Cut
Radcot Bridge Farm
The Garrison
Kelmscot Brook
Swan Hotel
P
GL7
Thames Path
Grafton Lock
Radcot Bridge
Weir
River Thames or Isis
RADCOT RD
Lower House Farm
Pidnell Farm
Camden Farm
Rhodes' Farm
Pidnell Bungalow
SN7
Camden Brake
A4095
4
01
3
00
2
99
1
98
26
27
28

151
172

134
154

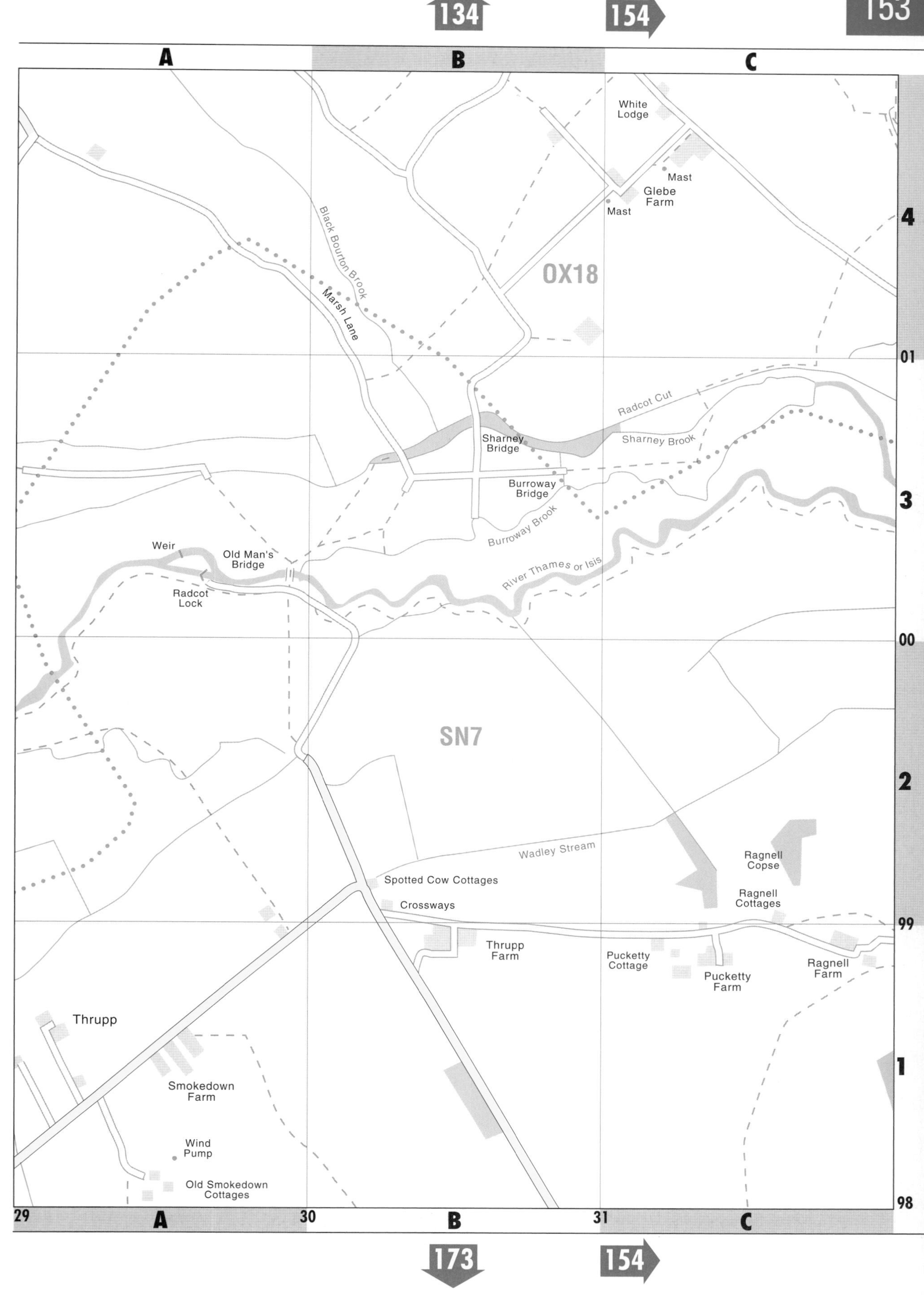
A
B
C
White Lodge
Mast
Glebe Farm
Mast
Black Bourton Brook
Marsh Lane
OX18
4
01
Radcot Cut
Sharney Bridge
Sharney Brook
Burroway Bridge
3
Burroway Brook
Weir
Old Man's Bridge
River Thames or Isis
Radcot Lock
00
SN7
2
Wadley Stream
Ragnell Copse
Spotted Cow Cottages
Ragnell Cottages
Crossways
99
Thrupp Farm
Pucketty Cottage
Pucketty Farm
Ragnell Farm
Thrupp
1
Smokedown Farm
Wind Pump
Old Smokedown Cottages
98
29
30
31

173
154

153
135

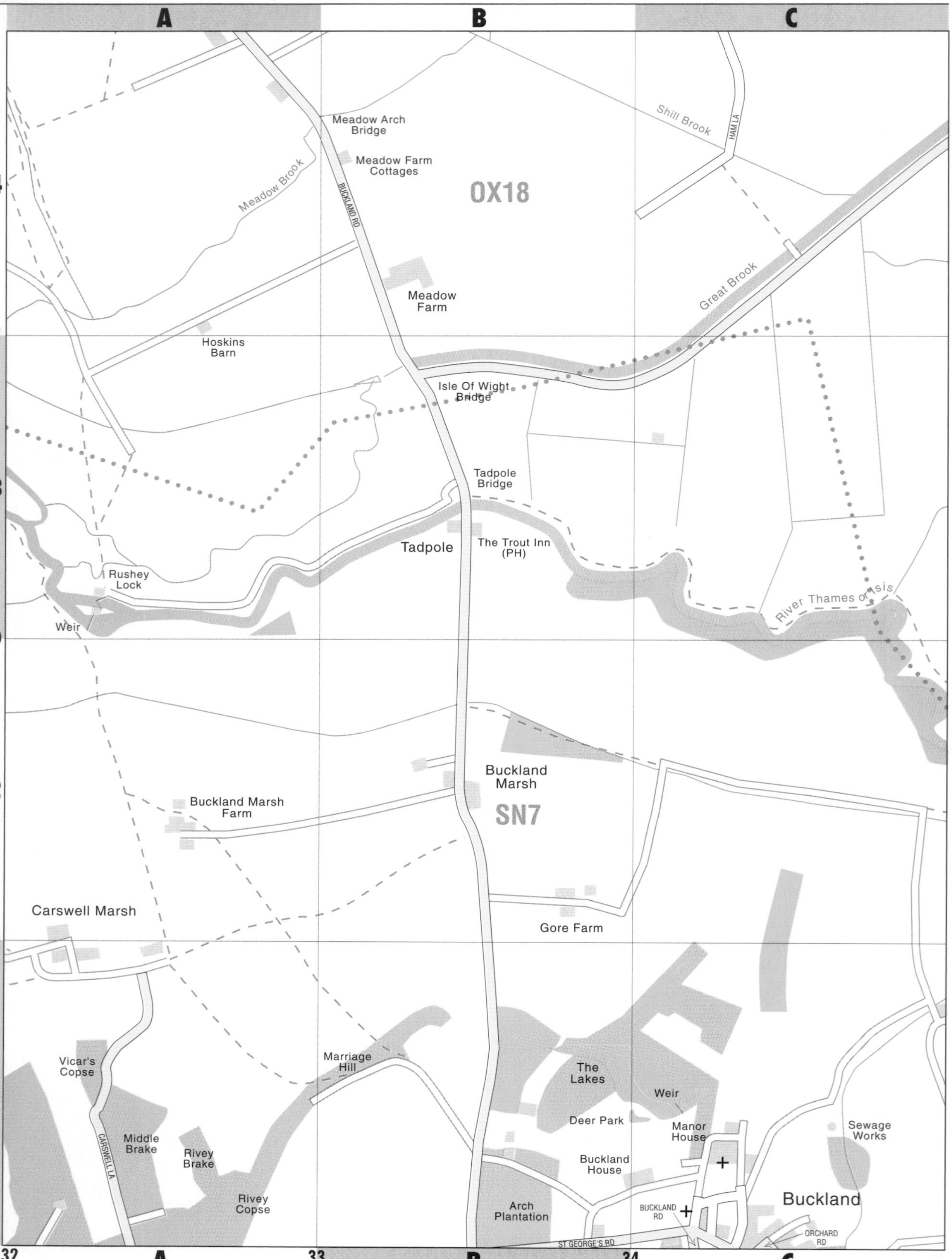

A **B** **C**

4

Meadow Arch Bridge

Meadow Farm Cottages

Shill Brook

HAM LA

OX18

Meadow Brook

BUCKLAND RD

Great Brook

01

Hoskins Barn

Meadow Farm

Isle Of Wight Bridge

3

Tadpole Bridge

Tadpole

The Trout Inn (PH)

Rushey Lock

River Thames or Isis

Weir

00

2

Buckland Marsh Farm

Buckland Marsh

SN7

Carswell Marsh

Gore Farm

99

Vicar's Copse

Marriage Hill

The Lakes

Weir

Sewage Works

1

CARSWELL LA

Middle Brake

Rivey Brake

Deer Park

Manor House

Buckland House

Rivey Copse

Arch Plantation

BUCKLAND RD

Buckland

ORCHARD RD

98

ST GEORGE'S RD

32 **A** **33** **B** **34** **C**

153
174

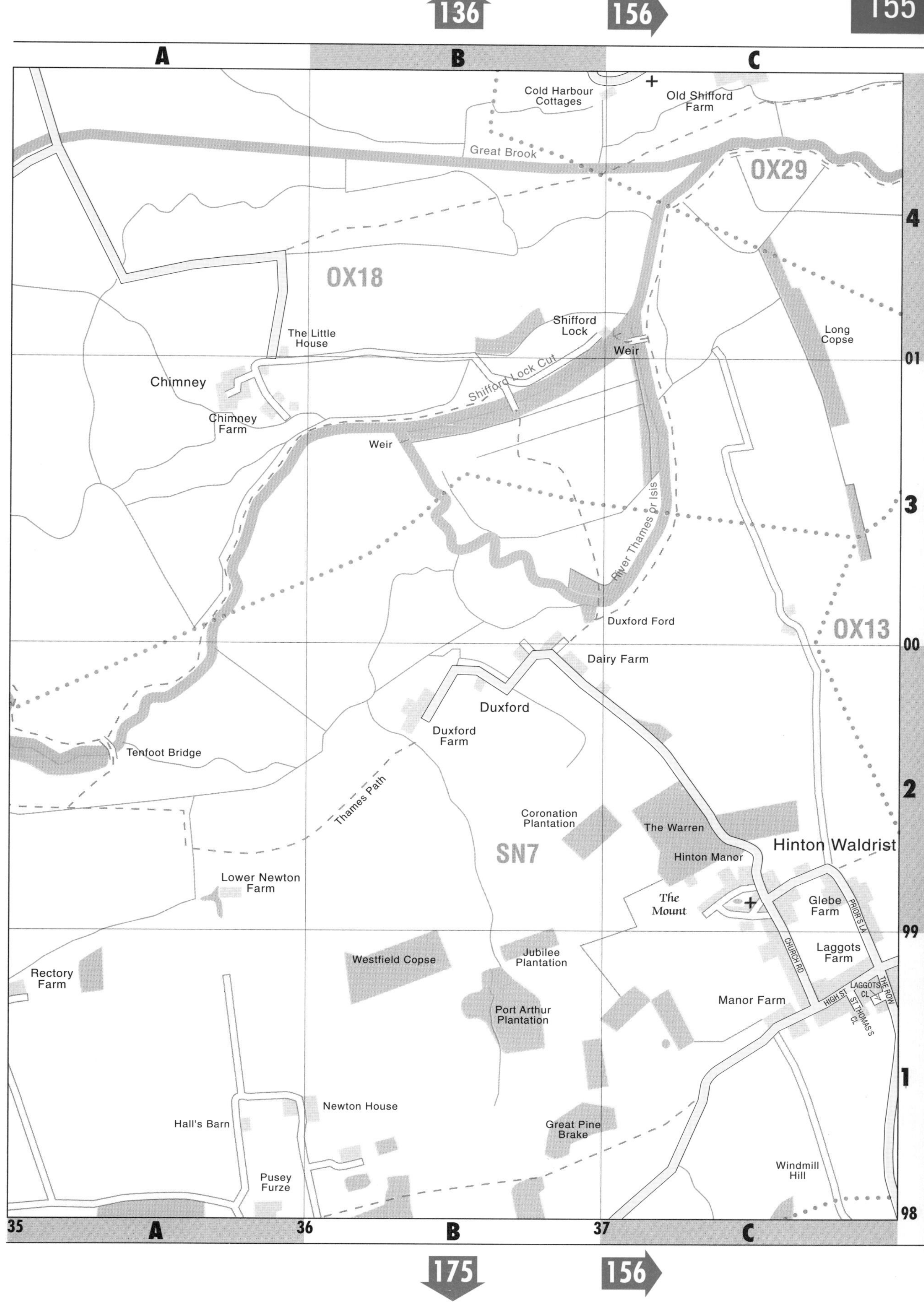
A
B
C
Cold Harbour Cottages
Old Shifford Farm
Great Brook
OX29
4
OX18
Shifford Lock
The Little House
Long Copse
Weir
01
Chimney
Shifford Lock Cut
Chimney Farm
Weir
River Thames or Isis
3
Duxford Ford
OX13
00
Dairy Farm
Duxford
Duxford Farm
Tenfoot Bridge
2
Thames Path
Coronation Plantation
The Warren
Hinton Waldrist
Hinton Manor
SN7
Lower Newton Farm
The Mount
Glebe Farm
PRIOR'S LA
99
CHURCH RD
Laggots Farm
Westfield Copse
Jubilee Plantation
Rectory Farm
LAGGOTS CL
THE ROW
HIGH ST
ST THOMAS'S CL
Manor Farm
Port Arthur Plantation
1
Newton House
Hall's Barn
Great Pine Brake
Windmill Hill
Pusey Furze
98
35
36
37

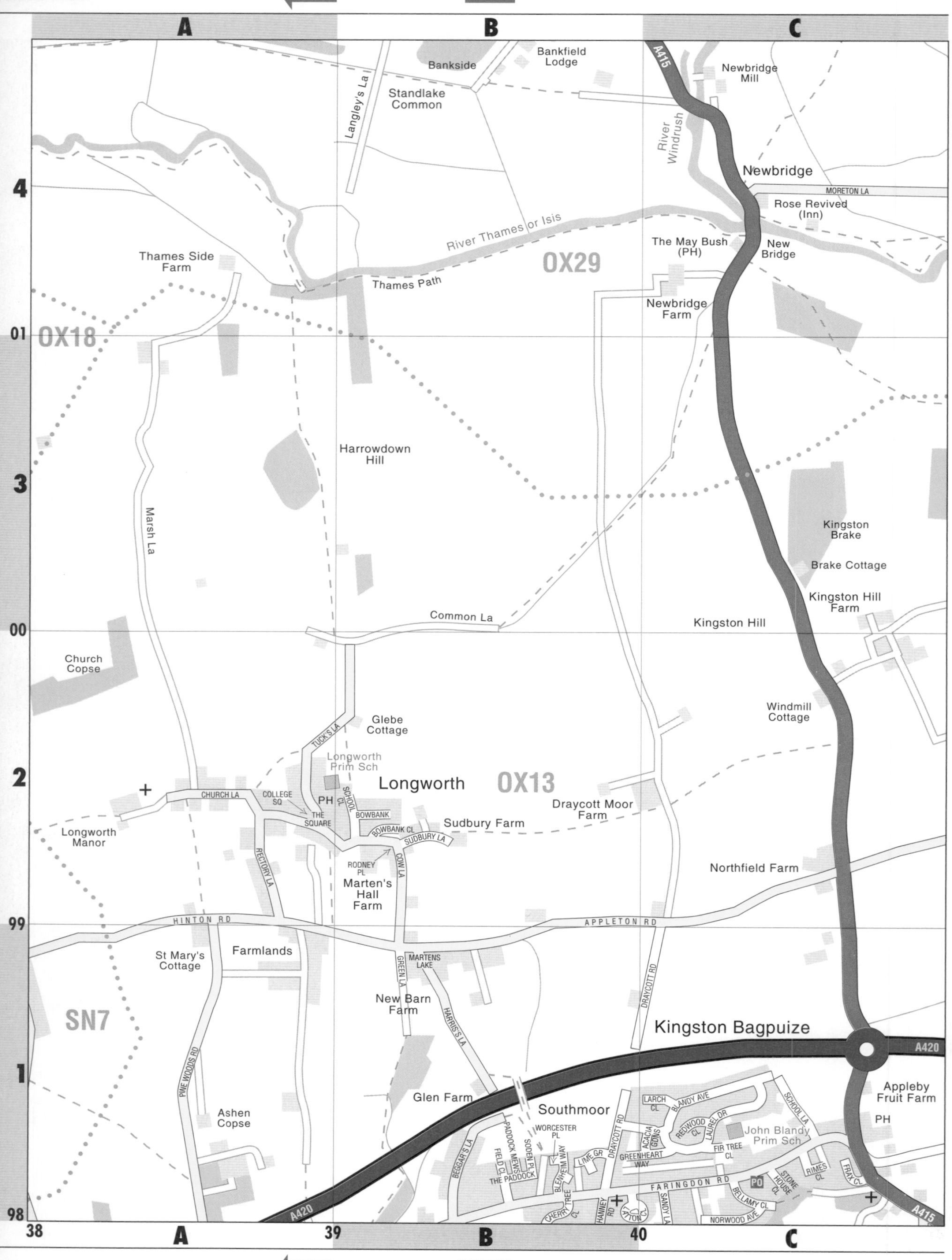

A | B | C

4

River Thames or Isis

OX29

01

OX18

Thames Side
Farm

Langley's La

Bankside

Standlake
Common

Bankfield
Lodge

A415

River
Windrush

Newbridge
Mill

Newbridge

MORETON LA

Rose Revived
(Inn)

The May Bush
(PH)

New
Bridge

Newbridge
Farm

Thames Path

Marsh La

Harrowdown
Hill

Kingston
Brake

Brake Cottage

3

Kingston Hill
Farm

00

Common La

Kingston Hill

Church
Copse

Windmill
Cottage

Glebe
Cottage

Longworth
Prim Sch

TUCK'S LA

SCHOOL LA

2

+

CHURCH LA

COLLEGE
SQ

PH

Longworth

OX13

Draycott Moor
Farm

BOWBANK

Sudbury Farm

THE
SQUARE

BOWBANK CL

RECTORY LA

Longworth
Manor

RODNEY
PL

SUDBURY LA

COW LA

Marten's
Hall
Farm

Northfield Farm

99

HINTON RD

APPLETON RD

St Mary's
Cottage

Farmlands

MARTENS
LAKE

GREEN LA

HARRIS'S LA

DRAYCOTT RD

SN7

New Barn
Farm

Kingston Bagpuize

A420

A420

Glen Farm

Southmoor

PINE WOODS RD

1

Appleby
Fruit Farm

PH

LARCH
CL

BLANDY AVE

SCHOOL LA

Ashen
Copse

BEGGAR'S LA

PADDOCK MEWS

SODEN RD

FIELD CL

THE PADDOCK

Worcester
PL

LIME GR

BLENHEIM WAY

ACACIA
GDNS

REDWOOD
CL

LAUREL DR

GREENHEART
WAY

FIR TREE
CL

John Blandy
Prim Sch

STONE
HOUSE
CL

RIMES
CL

FRAY CL

98

CHERRY
CL

HANNEY
RD

NEWTON
CL

SANDY LA

FARINGDON RD

BELLAMY CL

PO

NORWOOD AVE

+

A415

38 | 39 | 40

A | B | C

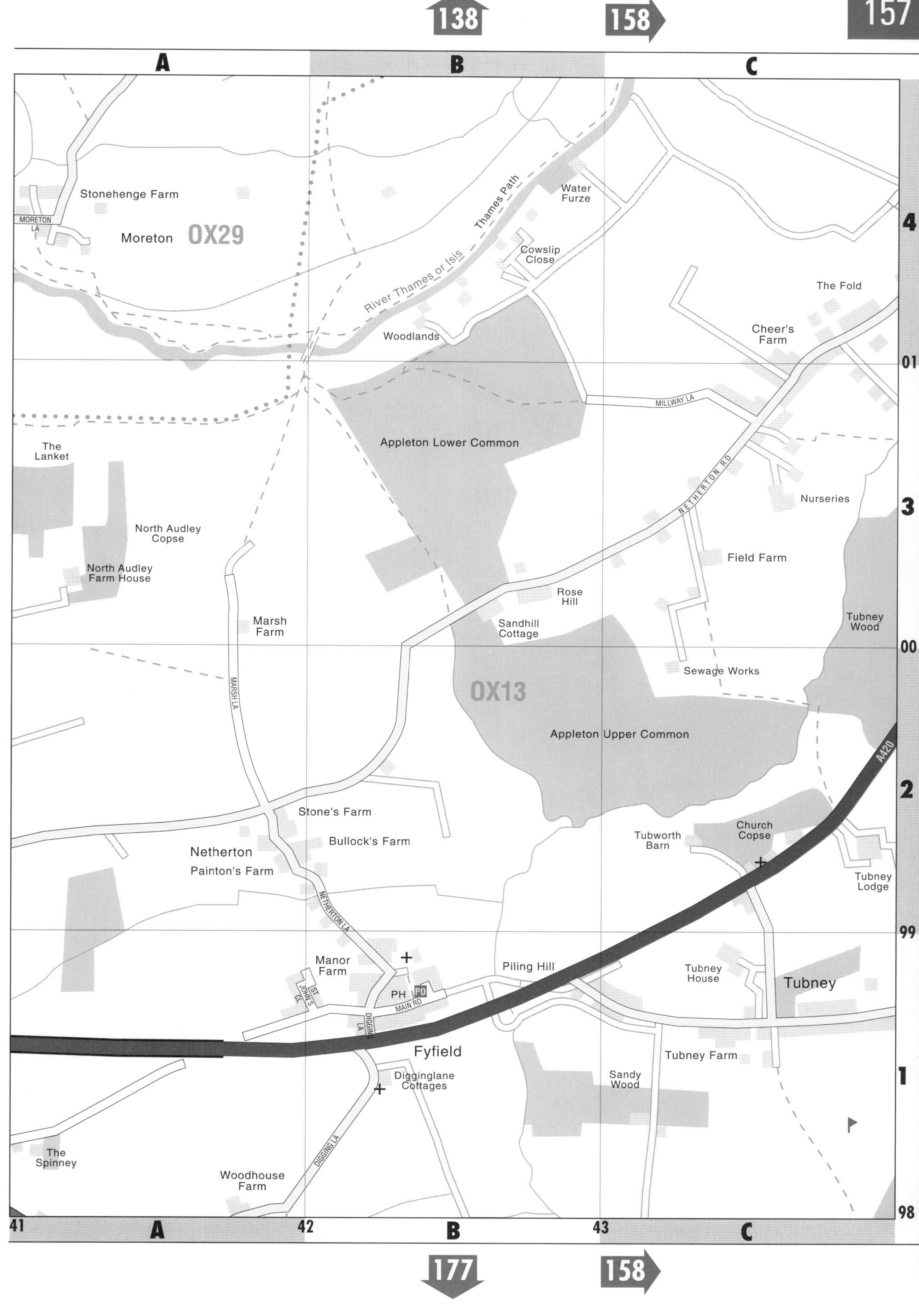

138
158

A   **B**   **C**

Stonehenge Farm

MORETON LA

Moreton **OX29**

Water Furze

Thames Path

Cowslip Close

River Thames or Isis

The Fold

Cheer's Farm

Woodlands

4

MILLWAY LA

01

The Lanket

Appleton Lower Common

NETHERTON RD

Nurseries

3

North Audley Copse

North Audley Farm House

Field Farm

Tubney Wood

Rose Hill

Marsh Farm

Sandhill Cottage

MARSH LA

OX13

00

Sewage Works

Appleton Upper Common

A420

2

Stone's Farm

Bullock's Farm

Tubworth Barn

Church Copse

Netherton

Painton's Farm

Tubney Lodge

NETHERTON LA

99

Manor Farm

Piling Hill

Tubney House

Tubney

ST JOHN'S CL

PH PO

DIGGING LA

MAIN RD

Tubney Farm

Fyfield

Digginglane Cottages

Sandy Wood

1

The Spinney

Woodhouse Farm

DIGGING LA

98

41   **A**   42   **B**   43   **C**

177
158

157
139

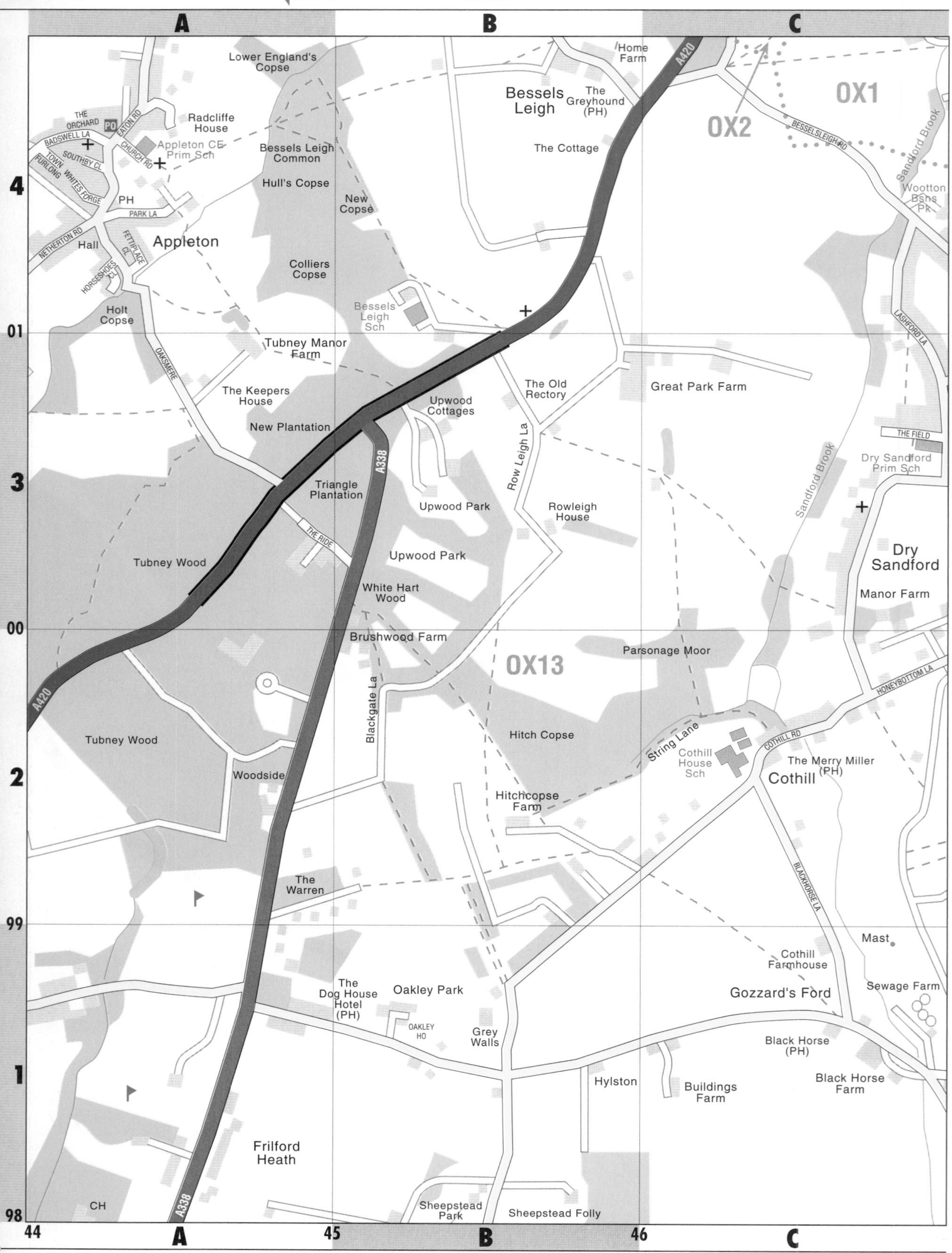
A
B
C
Lower England's Copse
Home Farm
Bessels Leigh
The Greyhound (PH)
OX1
OX2
Radcliffe House
Appleton CE Prim Sch
Bessels Leigh Common
The Cottage
Hull's Copse
New Copse
Wootton Bsns Pk
Appleton
Colliers Copse
Bessels Leigh Sch
Holt Copse
Tubney Manor Farm
The Old Rectory
Great Park Farm
The Keepers House
Upwood Cottages
New Plantation
Triangle Plantation
Upwood Park
Rowleigh House
Dry Sandford Prim Sch
Dry Sandford
Manor Farm
Tubney Wood
White Hart Wood
Brushwood Farm
Parsonage Moor
OX13
Hitch Copse
Cothill House Sch
The Merry Miller (PH)
Cothill
Woodside
Hitchcopse Farm
The Warren
Mast
Cothill Farmhouse
The Dog House Hotel (PH)
Oakley Park
Gozzard's Ford
Sewage Farm
Grey Walls
Black Horse (PH)
Hylston
Buildings Farm
Black Horse Farm
Frilford Heath
CH
Sheepstead Park
Sheepstead Folly
44
45
46
98
1
99
2
00
3
01
4
A420
A338
Row Leigh La
Blackgate La
String Lane
Sandford Brook
Hall
PH
PO

157
178

140
160

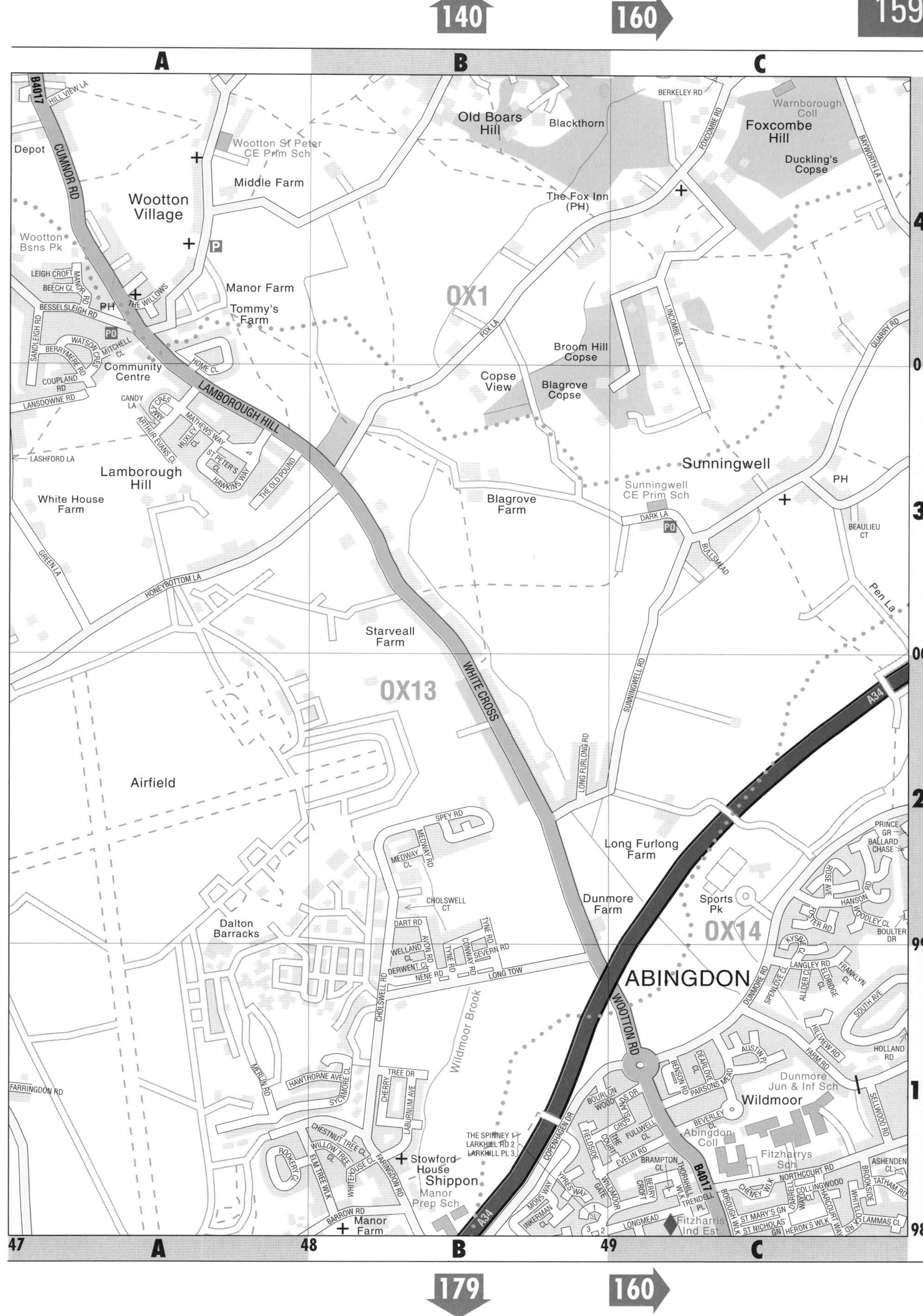
A
B
C
Old Boars Hill
Blackthorn
Foxcombe Hill
Warnborough Coll
Duckling's Copse
Wootton St Peter CE Prim Sch
Middle Farm
Wootton Village
Depot
Wootton Bsns Pk
Manor Farm
Tommy's Farm
Community Centre
The Fox Inn (PH)
OX1
Broom Hill Copse
Copse View
Blagrove Copse
Lamborough Hill
White House Farm
Sunningwell
Sunningwell CE Prim Sch
Blagrove Farm
Starveall Farm
OX13
Airfield
Long Furlong Farm
Dunmore Farm
Sports Pk
OX14
Dalton Barracks
ABINGDON
Wildmoor
Dunmore Jun & Inf Sch
Abingdon Coll
Fitzharrys Sch
Stowford House
Shippon
Manor Prep Sch
Manor Farm
Fitzharris Ind Est
Wildmoor Brook
CUMMOR RD
LAMBOROUGH HILL
WHITE CROSS
WOOTTON RD
FOX LA
HONEYBOTTOM LA
SUNNINGWELL RD
LONG FURLONG RD
B4017
A34
4
3
2
1
01
00
99
98
47
48
49

179
160

159 141

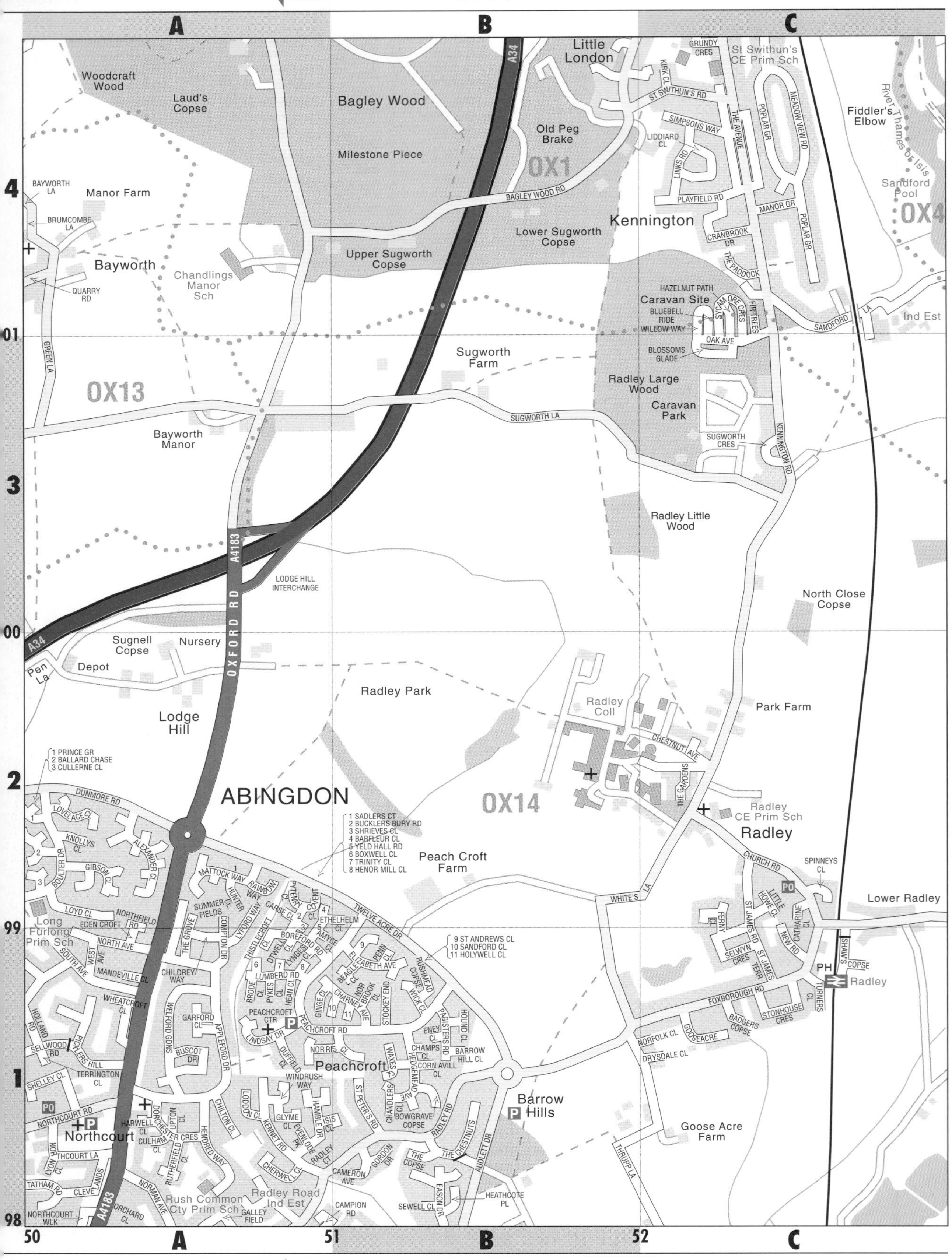

Woodcraft Wood
Laud's Copse
Bagley Wood
Milestone Piece
Little London
Old Peg Brake
OX1
St Swithun's CE Prim Sch
Fiddler's Elbow
River Thames or Isis
Sandford Pool
OX4
Manor Farm
Kennington
Lower Sugworth Copse
Upper Sugworth Copse
Bayworth
Chandlings Manor Sch
Caravan Site
Ind Est
Sugworth Farm
OX13
Radley Large Wood
Caravan Park
Bayworth Manor
Radley Little Wood
LODGE HILL INTERCHANGE
North Close Copse
Sugnell Copse
Nursery
Depot
Radley Park
Radley Coll
Park Farm
Lodge Hill
ABINGDON
OX14
Radley CE Prim Sch
Radley
Peach Croft Farm
Lower Radley
Long Furlong Prim Sch
Peachcroft
Barrow Hills
Goose Acre Farm
Northcourt
Rush Common Cty Prim Sch
Radley Road Ind Est
A34
A4183
OXFORD RD
1 PRINCE GR
2 BALLARD CHASE
3 CULLERNE CL
1 SADLERS CT
2 BUCKLERS BURY RD
3 SHRIEVES CL
4 BARFLEUR CL
5 YELD HALL RD
6 BOXWELL CL
7 TRINITY CL
8 HENOR MILL CL
9 ST ANDREWS CL
10 SANDFORD CL
11 HOLYWELL CL

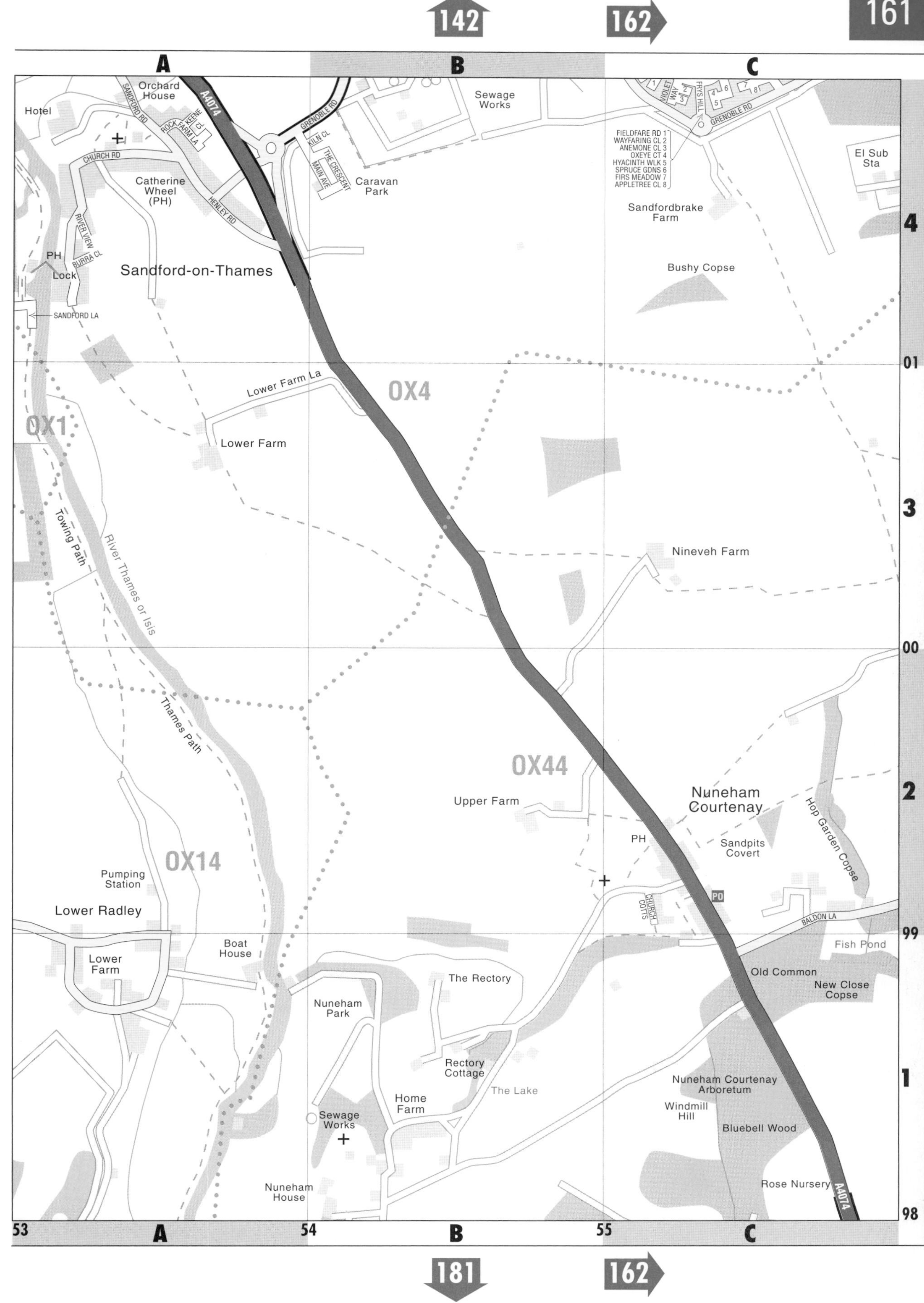

A

B

C

Hotel

Orchard House

SANDFORD RD

ROCK FARM LA

KEENE CL

A4074

GRENOBLE RD

KILN CL

THE CRESCENT

MAIN AVE

Caravan Park

Sewage Works

FIELDFARE RD 1
WAYFARING CL 2
ANEMONE CL 3
OXEYE CT 4
HYACINTH WLK 5
SPRUCE GDNS 6
FIRS MEADOW 7
APPLETREE CL 8

VIOLET WAY

PITTS HILL

GRENOBLE RD

El Sub Sta

+

CHURCH RD

Catherine Wheel (PH)

HENLEY RD

Sandfordbrake Farm

4

PH

RIVER VIEW

BURRA CL

Lock

Sandford-on-Thames

Bushy Copse

SANDFORD LA

01

OX1

Lower Farm La

OX4

Lower Farm

3

Towing Path

River Thames or Isis

Nineveh Farm

00

Thames Path

OX44

2

Upper Farm

Nuneham Courtenay

Hop Garden Copse

PH

Sandpits Covert

OX14

Pumping Station

+

CHURCH COTTS

PO

BALDON LA

Lower Radley

99

Boat House

Fish Pond

Lower Farm

The Rectory

Old Common

New Close Copse

Nuneham Park

1

Rectory Cottage

The Lake

Nuneham Courtenay Arboretum

Home Farm

Windmill Hill

Sewage Works

+

Bluebell Wood

Nuneham House

Rose Nursery

A4074

98

53

A

54

B

55

C

161
143

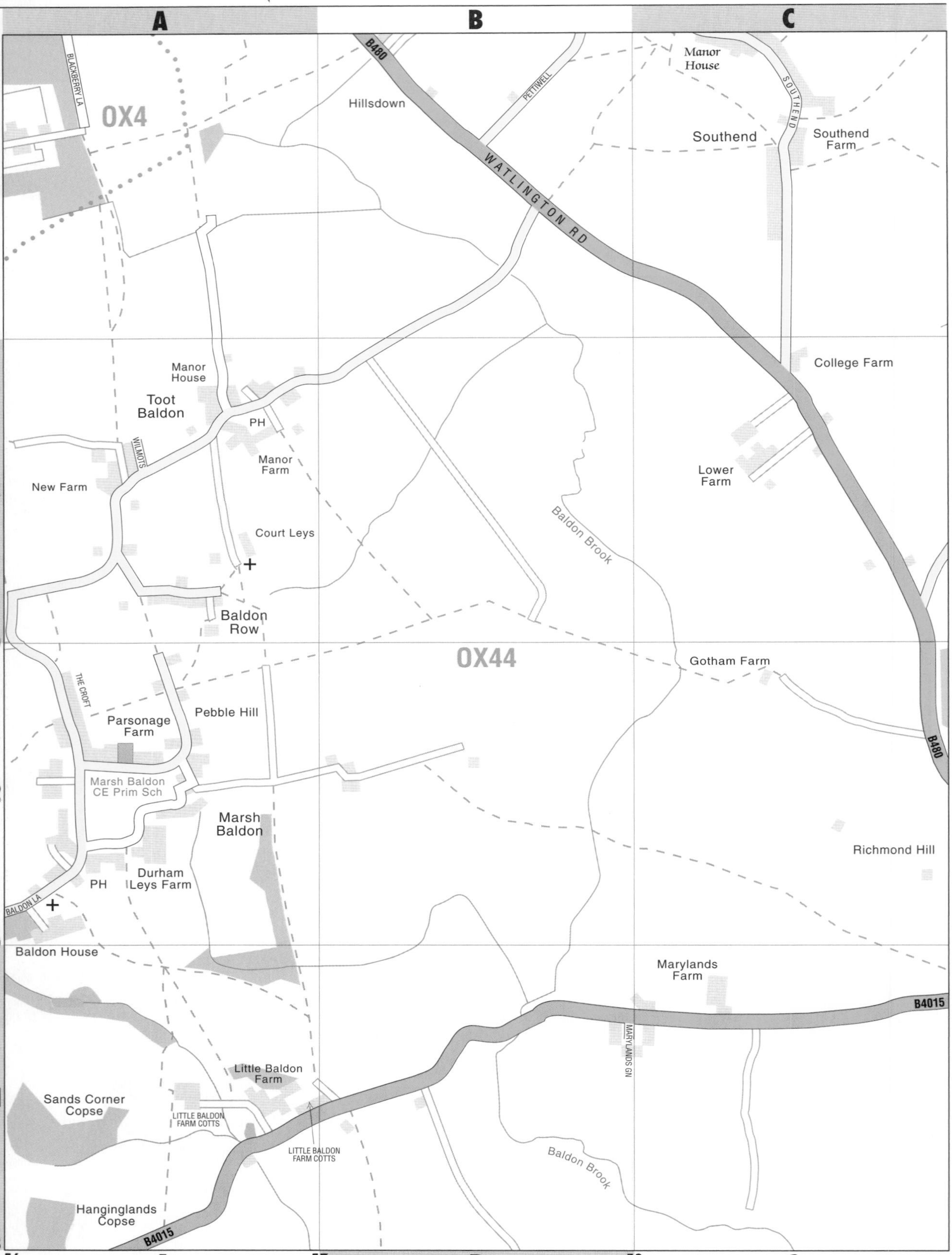

A | B | C

BLACKBERRY LA

OX4

Hillsdown

B480

PETTIWELL

Manor House

Southend

SOUTHEND

Southend Farm

B480

4

01

WATLINGTON RD

College Farm

Manor House

Toot Baldon

PH

WILMOTS

Manor Farm

Lower Farm

3

New Farm

Court Leys

+

Baldon Brook

Baldon Row

00

THE CROFT

OX44

Gotham Farm

Parsonage Farm

Pebble Hill

Marsh Baldon CE Prim Sch

2

Marsh Baldon

Richmond Hill

PH

Durham Leys Farm

BALDON LA

+

99

Baldon House

Marylands Farm

B4015

MARYLANDS GN

Sands Corner Copse

1

Little Baldon Farm

LITTLE BALDON FARM COTTS

LITTLE BALDON FARM COTTS

Baldon Brook

Hanginglands Copse

B4015

98

56 | 57 | 58

A | B | C

161
182

144
164

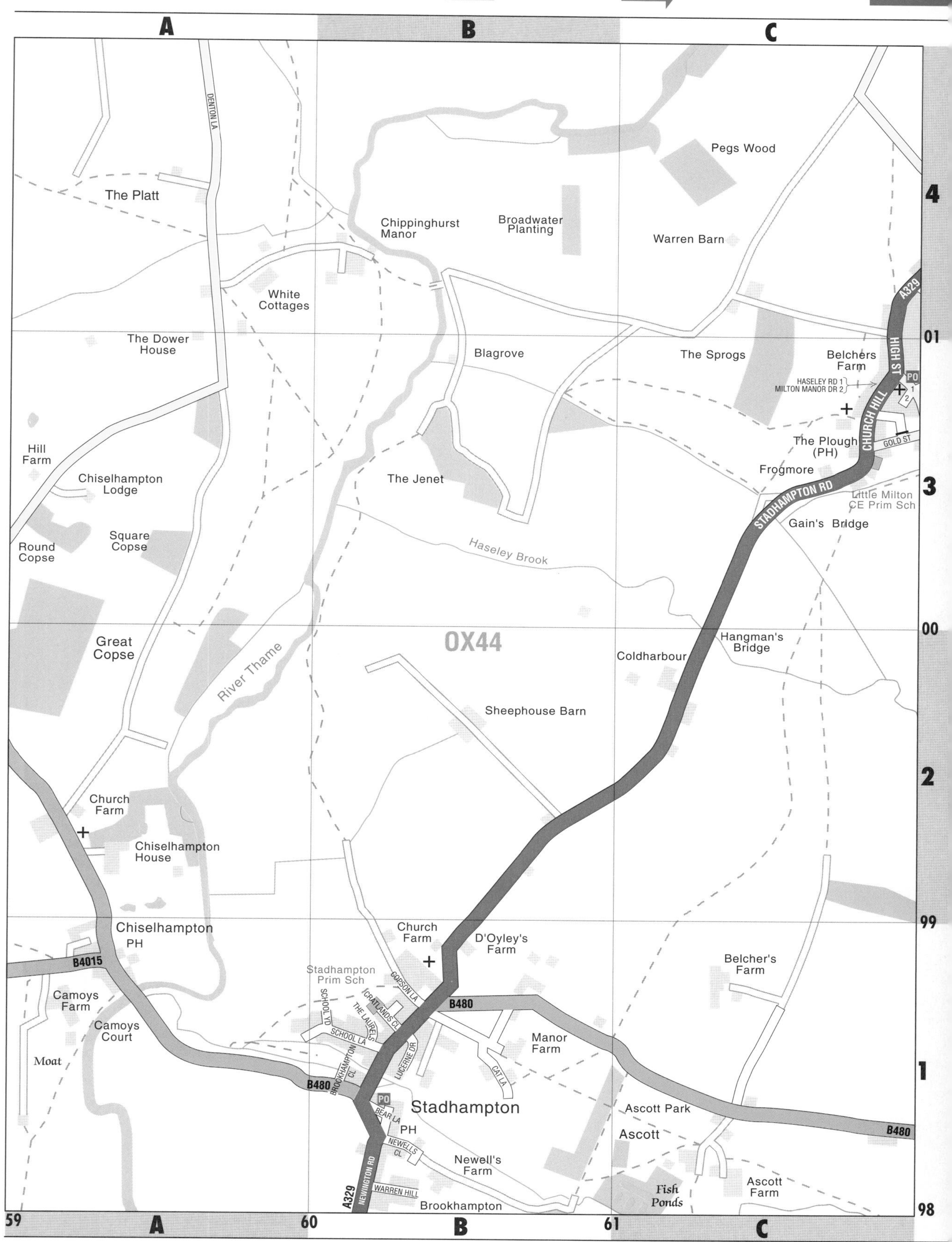
A
B
C
4
01
3
00
2
99
1
98
59
60
61
DENTON LA
The Platt
Chippinghurst Manor
Broadwater Planting
Pegs Wood
Warren Barn
White Cottages
The Dower House
Blagrove
The Sprogs
Belchers Farm
HASELEY RD 1
MILTON MANOR DR 2
HIGH ST
CHURCH HILL
A329
GOLD ST
The Plough (PH)
Frogmore
Hill Farm
Chiselhampton Lodge
The Jenet
STADHAMPTON RD
Little Milton CE Prim Sch
Gain's Bridge
Round Copse
Square Copse
Haseley Brook
Great Copse
River Thame
OX44
Hangman's Bridge
Coldharbour
Sheephouse Barn
Church Farm
Chiselhampton House
Chiselhampton
PH
B4015
Church Farm
D'Oyley's Farm
Stadhampton Prim Sch
Belcher's Farm
Camoys Farm
Camoys Court
Moat
SCHOOL YD
SCHOOL LA
THE LAURELS
CRATLANDS CL
COPSON LA
B480
LUCERNE DR
Manor Farm
CAT LA
BROOKHAMPTON CL
PO
BEAR LA
Stadhampton
PH
Ascott Park
Ascott
NEWELLS CL
Newell's Farm
NEWINGTON RD
WARREN HILL
Brookhampton
Fish Ponds
Ascott Farm

183
164

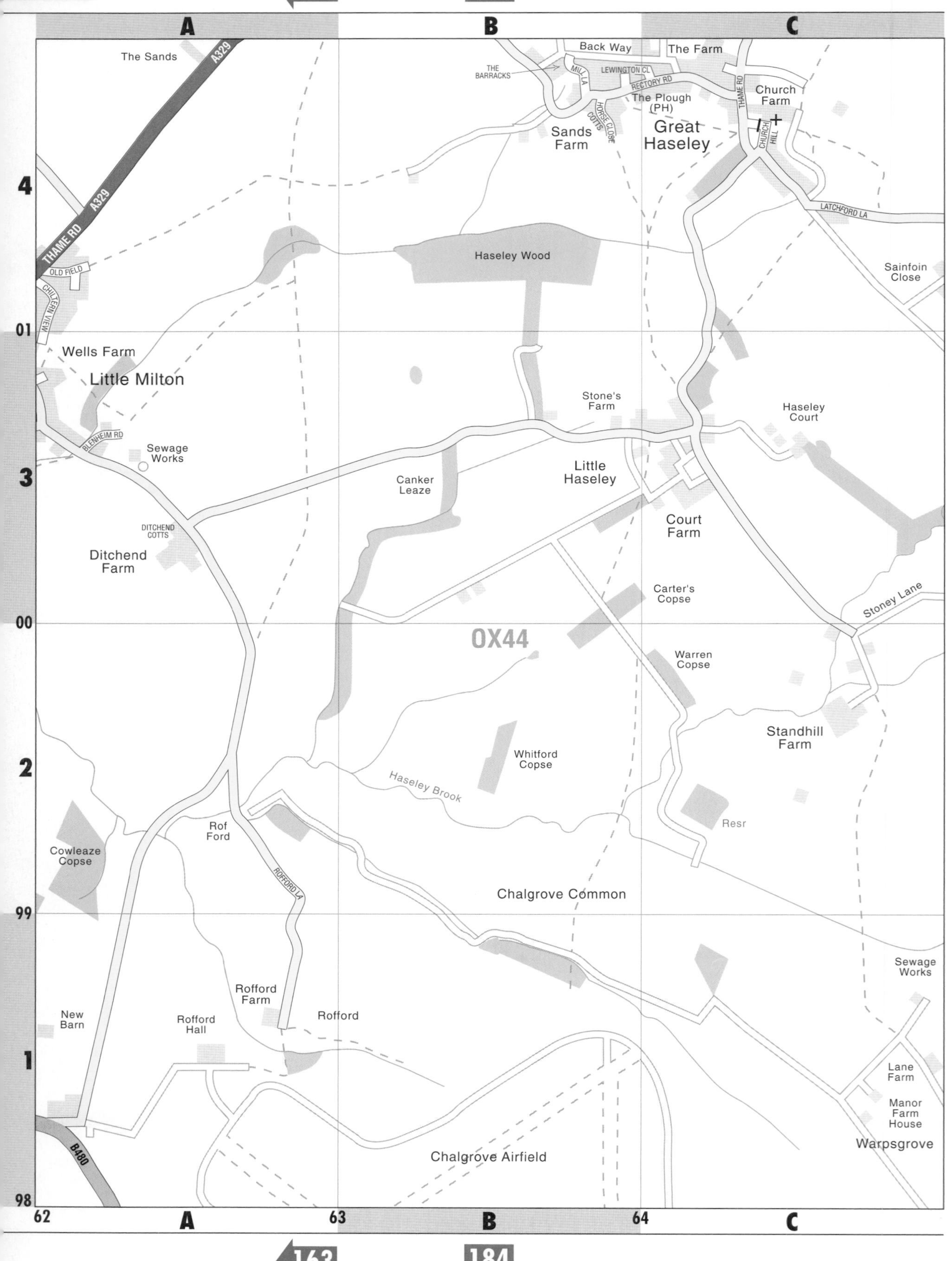

163
145

A
B
C

The Sands
THE BARRACKS
Back Way
The Farm
MILL LA
LEWINGTON CL
RECTORY RD
HORSE CLOSE COTTS
THAME RD
Church Farm
The Plough (PH)
Sands Farm
Great Haseley
CHURCH HILL

4

A329
THAME RD
Old Field
CHILTERN VIEW
Haseley Wood
Latchford La
Sainfoin Close

01

Wells Farm
Little Milton
Stone's Farm
Haseley Court

BLENHEIM RD
Sewage Works
Canker Leaze
Little Haseley

3

DITCHEND COTTS
Ditchend Farm
Court Farm
Carter's Copse

Stoney Lane

00

OX44
Warren Copse

Standhill Farm

2

Whitford Copse
Cowleaze Copse
Haseley Brook
Resr

Rof Ford

Chalgrove Common

99

ROFFORD LA
Sewage Works

Rofford Farm
New Barn
Rofford Hall
Rofford

1

Lane Farm
Manor Farm House

B480
Warpsgrove

98

62
A
63
B
64
C

Chalgrove Airfield

146
166

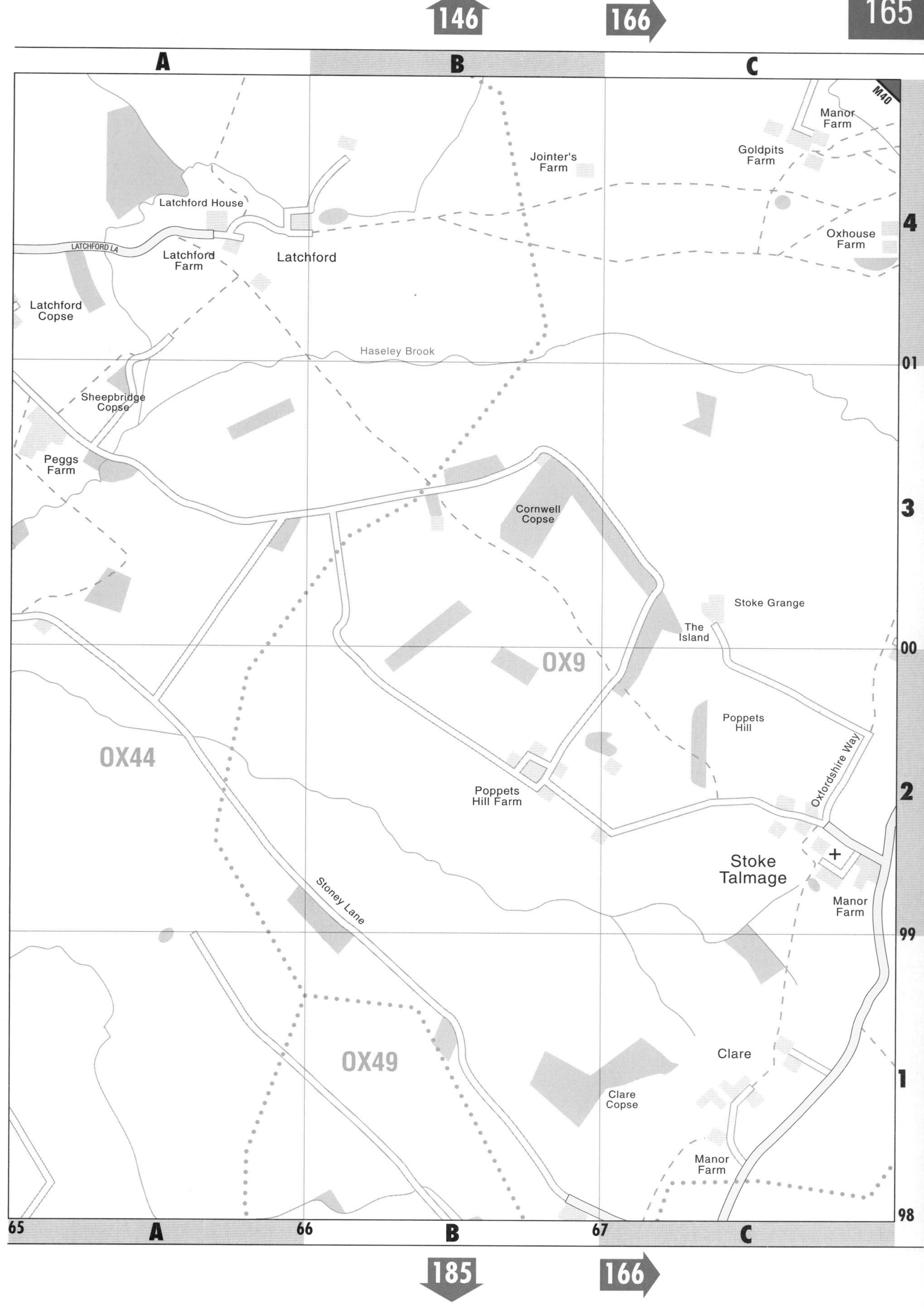
A
B
C
M40
Manor Farm
Goldpits Farm
Jointer's Farm
Latchford House
LATCHFORD LA
Latchford Farm
Latchford
Oxhouse Farm
Latchford Copse
Haseley Brook
Sheepbridge Copse
Peggs Farm
Cornwell Copse
Stoke Grange
The Island
OX9
OX44
Poppets Hill
Oxfordshire Way
Poppets Hill Farm
Stoke Talmage
Manor Farm
Stoney Lane
OX49
Clare
Clare Copse
Manor Farm
4
01
3
00
2
99
1
98
65
66
67

185
166

165
147

A B C

Red Lion (PH)
The Green
Tetsworth
PH
SWAN GDNS
Judd's Lane
SILVER ST
PO
ELM CL
BACK ST
YEW TREE CL
HIGH ST
CHILTERN VIEW
Tetsworth Prim Sch
Mount Hill Farm
MARSH END 1
CYGNET CL 2
THE MOUNT 3
PARKERS HILL 4
THE LAURELS 5
M40
A40
Dormers Leys
B4012
Attington Stud
Attington House
OAK FARM CL
Harlesford House
Copcourt
Harlesford Farm
Upper Copcourt Farm
Oxfordshire Way
Haseley Brook
Wheatfield Cottages
Square Covert
Lower Farm
Lower Farm
OX9
BOX TREE LA
LOWER RD
Glebe Farm
Adwell House Farm
Adwell Farm
Wheatfield House
Adwell House
PH
GLEBE COTTS
Wheatfield Park
Postcombe
Adwell
Red Lion (PH)
Wheatfield Wood
Upper Farm
Beech Farm
Park Farm
Wheatfield
The Warren
Adwell Cop
Gilton Hill
SALT LA
Mill House
Nethercote
The Salisbury Arms (PH)
Manor Farm
South Weston
OX49
RECTORY LA
WESTON RD
Sewage Works

4
01
3
00
2
99
1
98
68 69 70

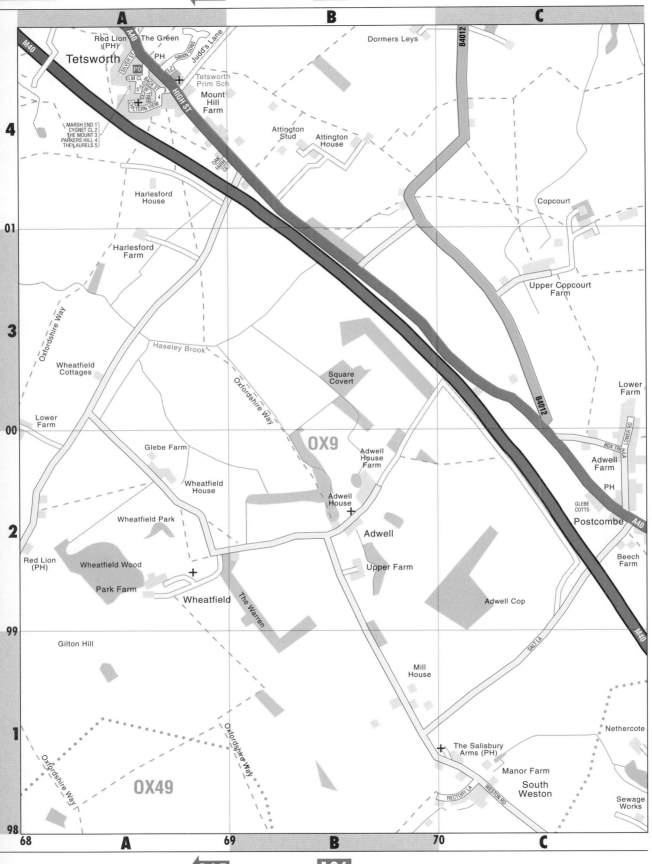

148
168

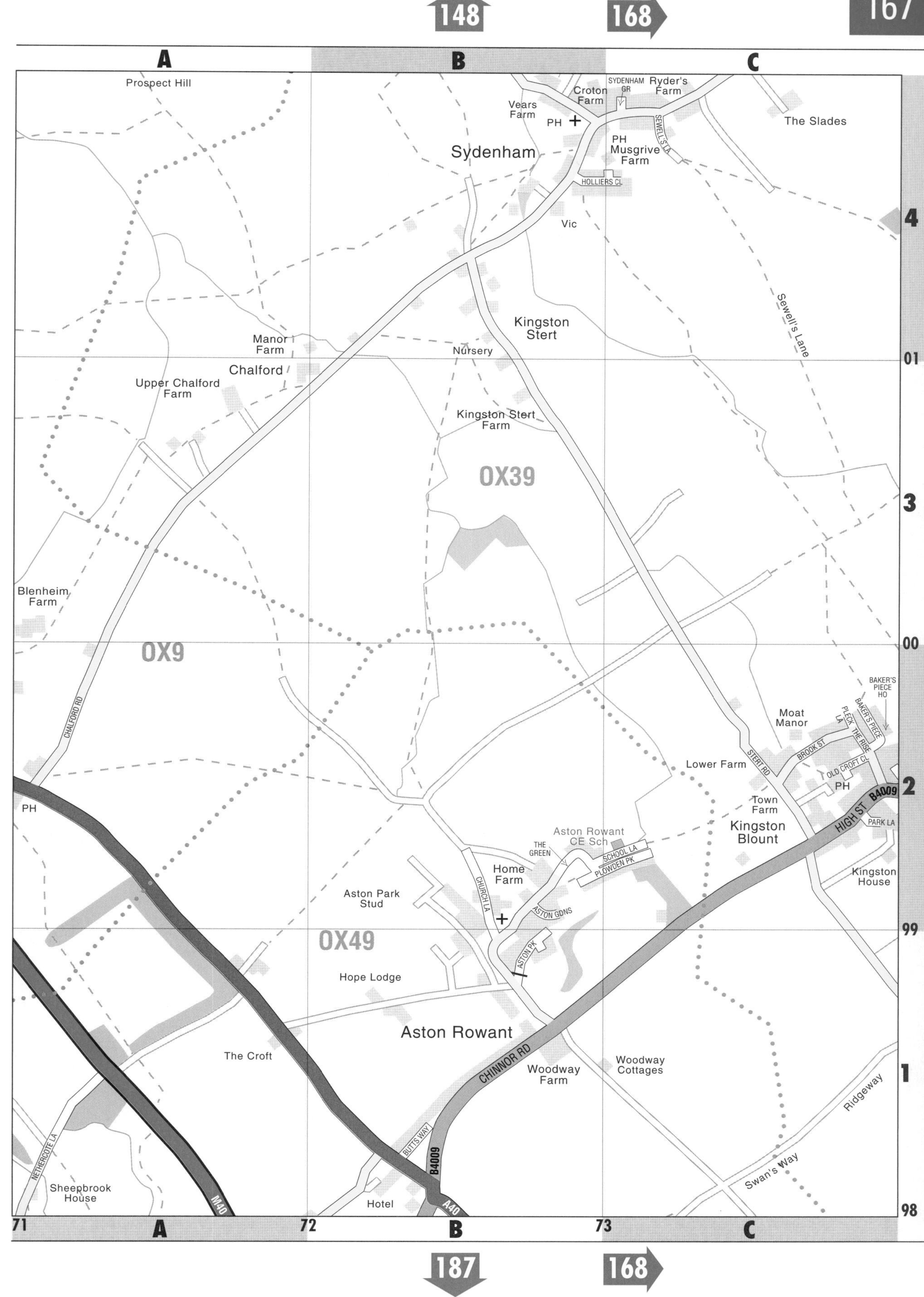
A
B
C
Prospect Hill
Vears Farm
Croton Farm
SYDENHAM GR
Ryder's Farm
The Slades
PH
Sydenham
PH
Musgrive Farm
SEWELL'S LA
HOLLIERS CL
Vic
4
Kingston Stert
Manor Farm
Nursery
Sewell's Lane
01
Chalford
Upper Chalford Farm
Kingston Stert Farm
OX39
3
Blenheim Farm
OX9
00
CHALFORD RD
BAKER'S PIECE HO
Moat Manor
PLECK LA
BAKER'S PIECE
THE RISE
BROOK ST
STERT RD
Lower Farm
OLD CROFT CL
PH
2
PH
Town Farm
B4009
HIGH ST
PARK LA
Aston Rowant CE Sch
Kingston Blount
THE GREEN
SCHOOL LA
PLOWDEN PK
Home Farm
Kingston House
Aston Park Stud
CHURCH LA
ASTON GDNS
99
OX49
ASTON PK
Hope Lodge
Aston Rowant
The Croft
Woodway Farm
Woodway Cottages
CHINNOR RD
1
Ridgeway
NETHERCOTE LA
BUTTS WAY
B4009
Swan's Way
Sheepbrook House
M40
A40
Hotel
98
71
A
72
B
73
C

187
168

167
149

A **B** **C**

B4445

THAME RD

B4009 LOWER ICKNIELD WAY

HP27

4

Lane Farm

ELDERDENE

HOLLAND CL

SPRINGFIELD GDNS

LEYBOURNE GDNS

New Farm

B4445

MALYNS CL

B4009 LOWER RD

DOVELEAT

GRAFTON HO

Lower Wainhill   LC

Mill Lane Cty Prim Sch

Mill Lane

P

BENTON DR

MUSGRAVE RD

Chinnor

Hempton Wainhill

01

PH

St Andrew's CE Prim Sch

Liby

DUCK SQ

DIEMENS

TWR WILLOW RD

STATION RD

CHERRY TREE

RECTORY MDW

HIGH ST

CHURCH RD

Icknield Line

LC

Bledlow Cross

Middle Farm

MILL LA

FORESTERS WAY

BEECH RD

HAILEY CFT

BENWELLS WAY

LEVERKUS CT 1
LEVERKUS HO 2

LIME CL

St Andrews Ho

KEENS LA

THE AVENUE

HILL FARM CT

CLEANERS

COWMORE

MILLERS TURN

EDGAR WAY

MIDDLE WAY

HEDGERLEY

RANNAL DR

PO

LC

HUNTERS POINT

FOX COVER

LACEMAKERS WAY

PH

CHURCH LA

THE HILL

3

ROBINS PLATT

ASHRIDGE

RIDERS

PENLEY

FLINT HOLLOW PL

OAKLEY LA

TIMBER WAY

DRUIDS WLK

ORCHARD WAY

WHEELER

GLYNSWOOD

RAVENSMEAD

GREENWOOD

GREENWOOD MDW

Saw Mill

WYKEHAM RISE

SOUTHER HILLS

MEADOW RD

Chinnor Hill Nature Reserve

OAKLEY RD

GLYNDERS GR

WOODVILLE

HILL RD

Oakley

ST ANDREW'S RD

ELM DR

ELM CL

GREENWOOD AVE

Chinnor

P

Crowell End Farm

Quarry

Chinnor Hill

OX39

Works

Woodlands Farm

00

Crowell Farm

Ridgeway

Quarry

HILL TOP LA

CHINNOR RD

CHINNOR RD

Crowell

PH

Quarry

Oakley Hill

Manor Farm

ICKNIELD CL

B4009

HIGH ST

2

Bledlow Circular Ride

Sunley Wood

99

Swan's Way

Race Course

Venus Wood

Venus Wood

1

Crowellhill Wood

Crowell Hill

Sprig's Alley

Grove Farm

Crowellhill Farm

SPRIGS HOLLY LA

KINGSTON HILL

Kingston Wood

HP14

98

74   **A**   75   **B**   76   **C**

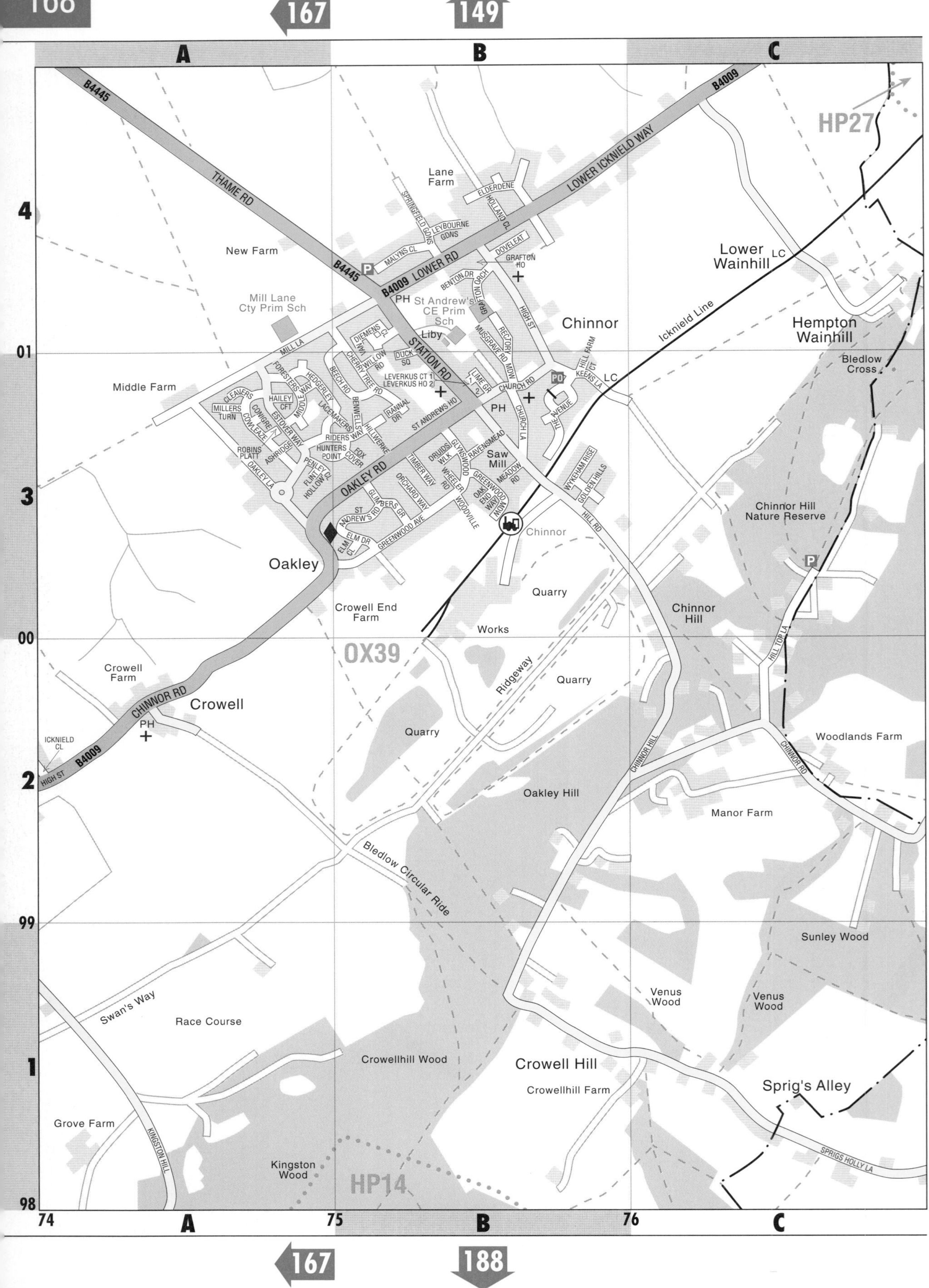

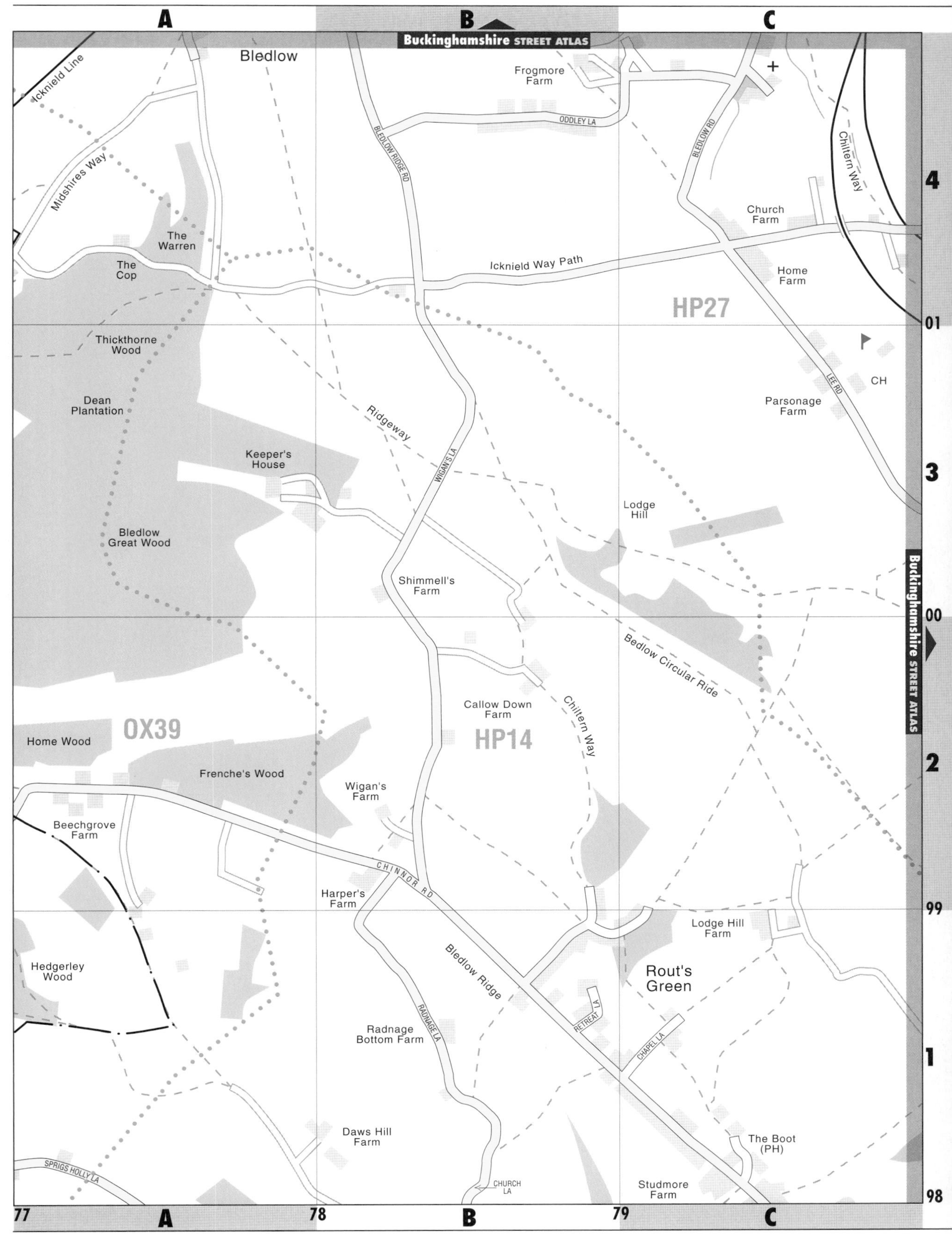

Bledlow

Buckinghamshire STREET ATLAS

Frogmore Farm

ODDLEY LA

BLEDLOW RIDGE RD

BLEDLOW RD

Chiltern Way

4

Church Farm

Home Farm

Icknield Line

Midshires Way

The Warren

The Cop

Icknield Way Path

HP27

01

Thickthorne Wood

LEE RD

CH

Dean Plantation

Ridgeway

Parsonage Farm

Keeper's House

WIGAN'S LA

3

Lodge Hill

Bledlow Great Wood

Shimmell's Farm

Bedlow Circular Ride

00

Home Wood

OX39

Frenche's Wood

Callow Down Farm

HP14

Chiltern Way

2

Wigan's Farm

Beechgrove Farm

CHINNOR RD

Lodge Hill Farm

99

Harper's Farm

Hedgerley Wood

Bledlow Ridge

Rout's Green

RADNAGE LA

RETREAT

CHAPEL LA

Radnage Bottom Farm

1

Daws Hill Farm

The Boot (PH)

SPRIGS HOLLY LA

CHURCH LA

Studmore Farm

98

77   A   78   B   79   C

Buckinghamshire STREET ATLAS

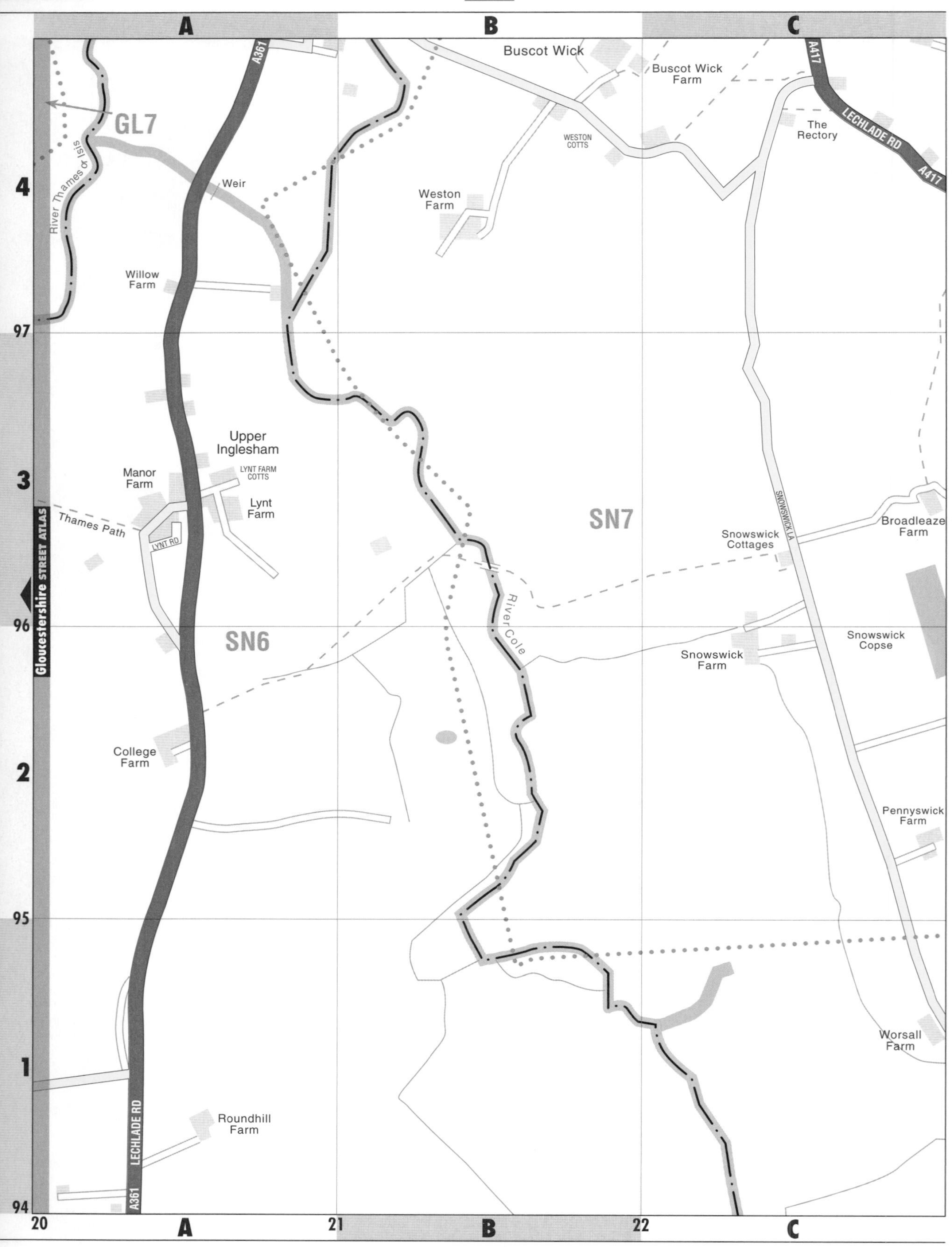

GL7

River Thames or Isis

Weir

Willow
Farm

Buscot Wick

Buscot Wick
Farm

WESTON
COTTS

The
Rectory

LECHLADE RD

A417

A417

Weston
Farm

A361

Upper
Inglesham

Manor
Farm

LYNT FARM
COTTS

Lynt
Farm

Thames Path

LYNT RD

SN7

SNOWSWICK LA

Snowswick
Cottages

Broadleaze
Farm

SN6

River Cole

Snowswick
Farm

Snowswick
Copse

College
Farm

Gloucestershire STREET ATLAS

Pennyswick
Farm

Worsall
Farm

LECHLADE RD

A361

Roundhill
Farm

151
172

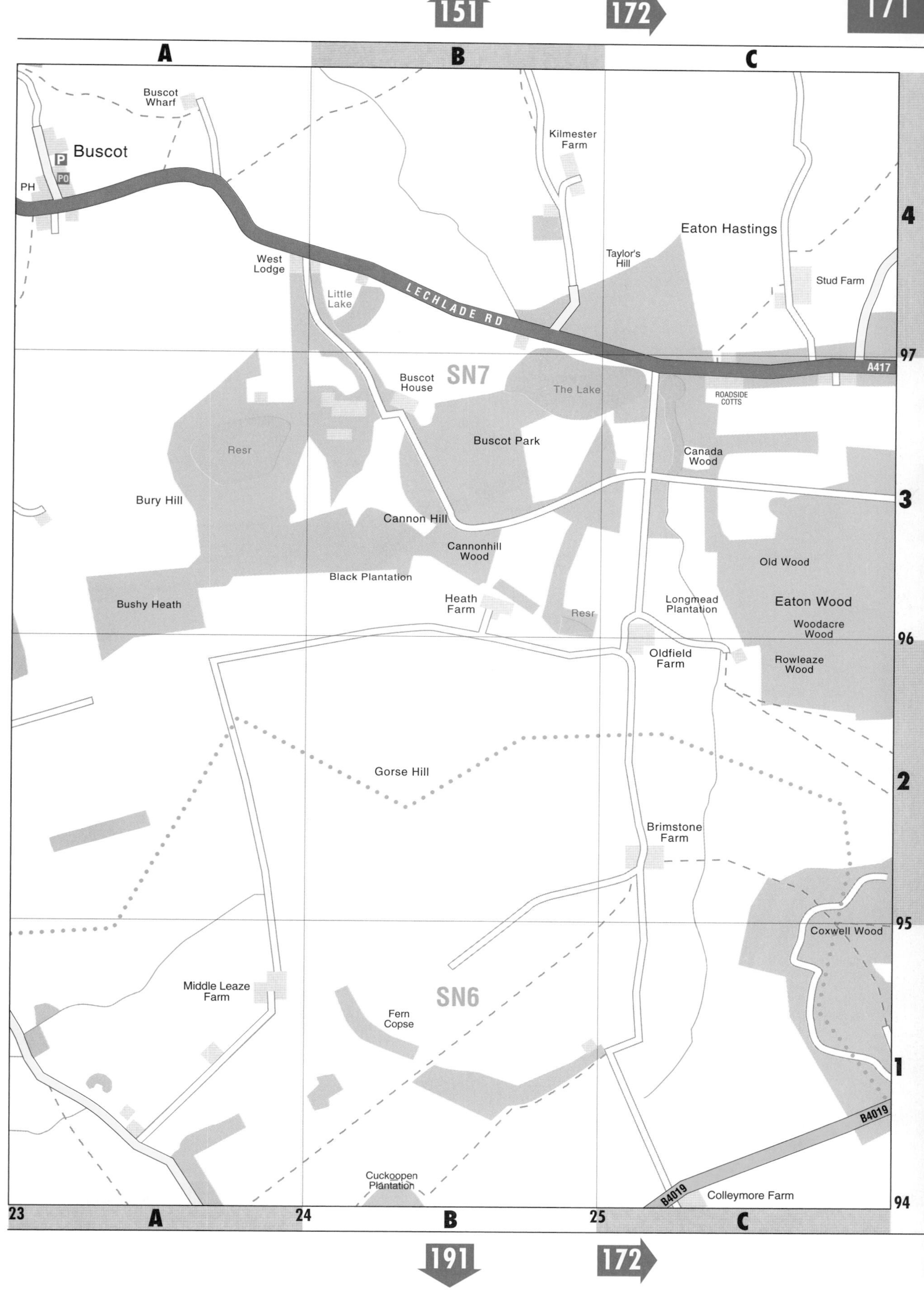
A
B
C
Buscot Wharf
Buscot
P
PO
PH
Kilmester Farm
Eaton Hastings
Taylor's Hill
Stud Farm
West Lodge
Little Lake
LECHLADE RD
Buscot House
SN7
The Lake
A417
ROADSIDE COTTS
Resr
Buscot Park
Canada Wood
Bury Hill
Cannon Hill
Cannonhill Wood
Old Wood
Black Plantation
Heath Farm
Longmead Plantation
Eaton Wood
Bushy Heath
Resr
Woodacre Wood
Oldfield Farm
Rowleaze Wood
Gorse Hill
Brimstone Farm
Coxwell Wood
Middle Leaze Farm
SN6
Fern Copse
B4019
Cuckoopen Plantation
Colleymore Farm
4
97
3
96
2
95
1
94
23
24
25

191
172

171 152

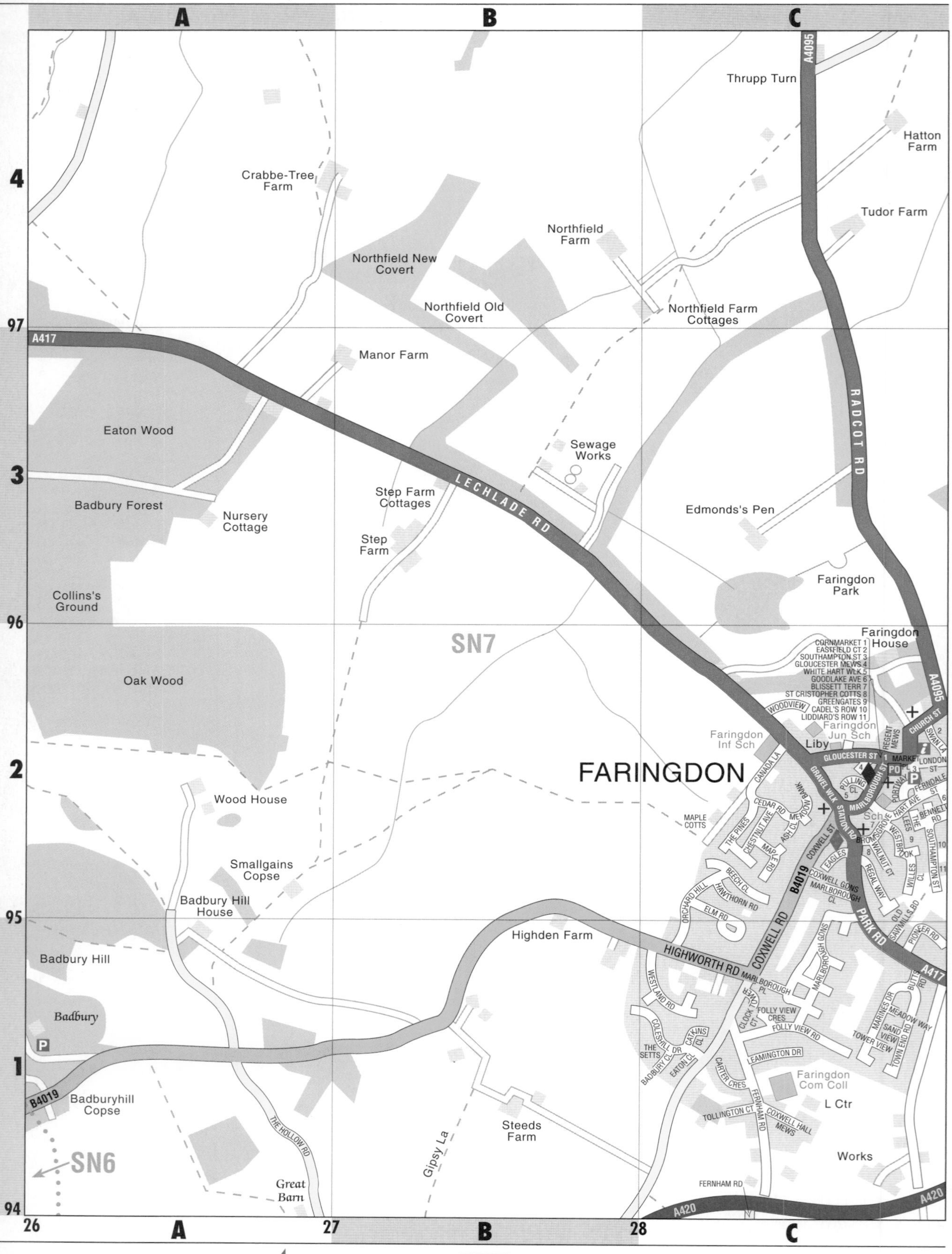

A B C

4

97

A417

Crabbe-Tree Farm

Northfield New Covert

Northfield Old Covert

Northfield Farm

Thrupp Turn

Hatton Farm

Tudor Farm

Northfield Farm Cottages

A4095

RADCOT RD

Manor Farm

3

Eaton Wood

Badbury Forest

Nursery Cottage

Step Farm Cottages

LECHLADE RD

Step Farm

Sewage Works

Edmonds's Pen

Faringdon Park

96

Collins's Ground

SN7

Faringdon House

Oak Wood

2

Wood House

Smallgains Copse

MAPLE COTTS

FARINGDON

Faringdon Inf Sch

Faringdon Jun Sch

Liby

Faringdon Com Coll

95

Badbury Hill House

Badbury Hill

Badbury

Highden Farm

HIGHWORTH RD

COXWELL RD

B4019

PARK RD

A417

1

B4019

Badburyhill Copse

THE HOLLOW RD

Gipsy La

Steeds Farm

L Ctr

Works

SN6

Great Barn

FERNHAM RD

A420

94

26 A 27 B 28 C

171 192

153 174

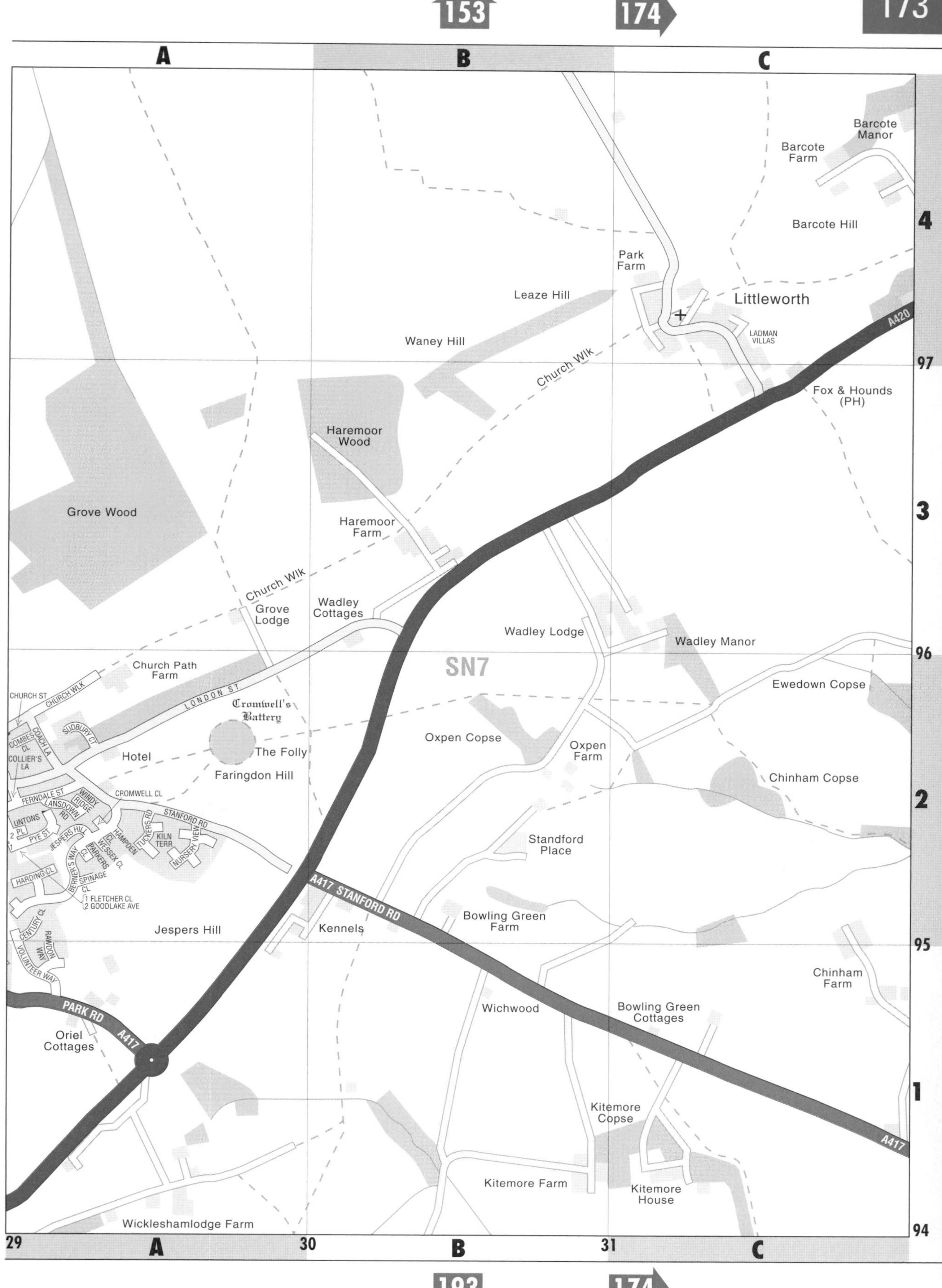
A
B
C
4
3
2
1
97
96
95
94
29
30
31
Barcote Manor
Barcote Farm
Barcote Hill
Park Farm
Leaze Hill
Littleworth
LADMAN VILLAS
A420
Waney Hill
Church Wlk
Fox & Hounds (PH)
Haremoor Wood
Haremoor Farm
Grove Wood
Church Wlk
Grove Lodge
Wadley Cottages
Wadley Lodge
Wadley Manor
SN7
Church Path Farm
CHURCH ST
CHURCH WLK
LONDON ST
Cromwell's Battery
Ewedown Copse
COACH LA
COMBES CL
SUDBURY CT
COLLIER'S LA
Hotel
The Folly
Faringdon Hill
Oxpen Copse
Oxpen Farm
Chinham Copse
FERNDALE ST
WINDY RIDGE
CROMWELL CL
LANSDOWN RD
STANFORD RD
UNTONS PL
PYE ST
JESPERS HILL
HAMPDEN CL
TUCKERS RD
KILN TERR
NURSERY VIEW
WESSEX CL
PARKERS CL
BERNEYS WAY
HARDING CL
SPINAGE CL
1 FLETCHER CL
2 GOODLAKE AVE
Standford Place
A417 STANFORD RD
CENTURY CL
RAWSON WAY
VOLUNTEER WAY
Jespers Hill
Kennels
Bowling Green Farm
PARK RD
A417
Chinham Farm
Wichwood
Bowling Green Cottages
Oriel Cottages
Kitemore Copse
Kitemore Farm
Kitemore House
Wickleshamlodge Farm

193 174

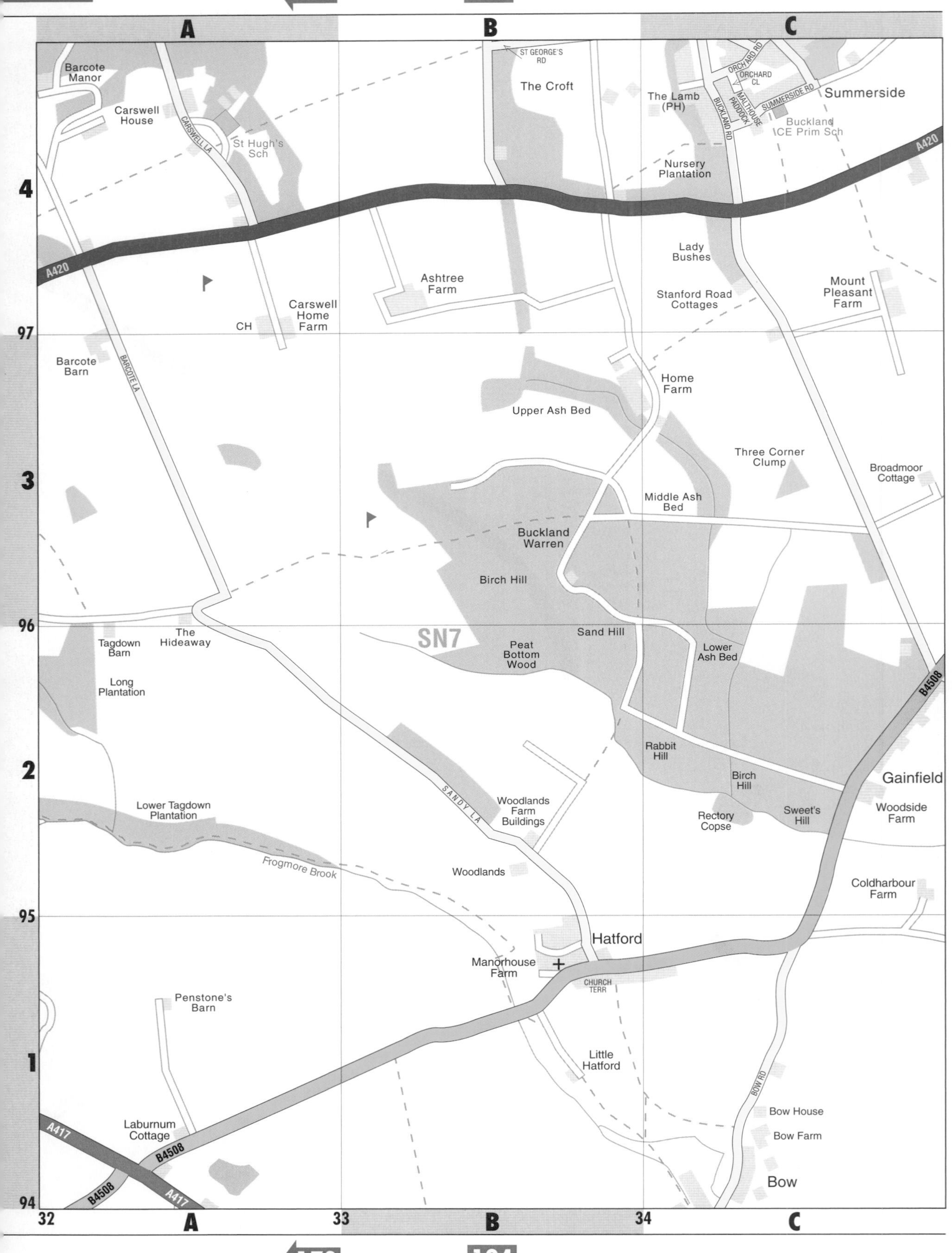

A B C

St George's Rd
The Croft
Barcote Manor
Carswell House
St Hugh's Sch
Carswell La

The Lamb (PH)
Orchard Rd
Orchard Cl
Summerside Rd
Malthouse Paddock
Buckland Rd
Buckland CE Prim Sch
Summerside

4

A420

Nursery Plantation

Lady Bushes

Ashtree Farm

Carswell Home Farm

CH

Stanford Road Cottages

Mount Pleasant Farm

97

Barcote Barn

Barcote La

Home Farm

Upper Ash Bed

Three Corner Clump

Broadmoor Cottage

3

Middle Ash Bed

Buckland Warren

Birch Hill

SN7

96

Tagdown Barn

The Hideaway

Sand Hill

Lower Ash Bed

B4508

Long Plantation

Peat Bottom Wood

Lower Tagdown Plantation

Sandy La

Rabbit Hill

Birch Hill

Gainfield

2

Woodlands Farm Buildings

Rectory Copse

Sweet's Hill

Woodside Farm

Frogmore Brook

Woodlands

Coldharbour Farm

95

Hatford

Manorhouse Farm

Church Terr

Penstone's Barn

1

Little Hatford

Bow Rd

A417

Laburnum Cottage

B4508

Bow House

Bow Farm

B4508

A417

Bow

94

32 A **33** B **34** C

155
176

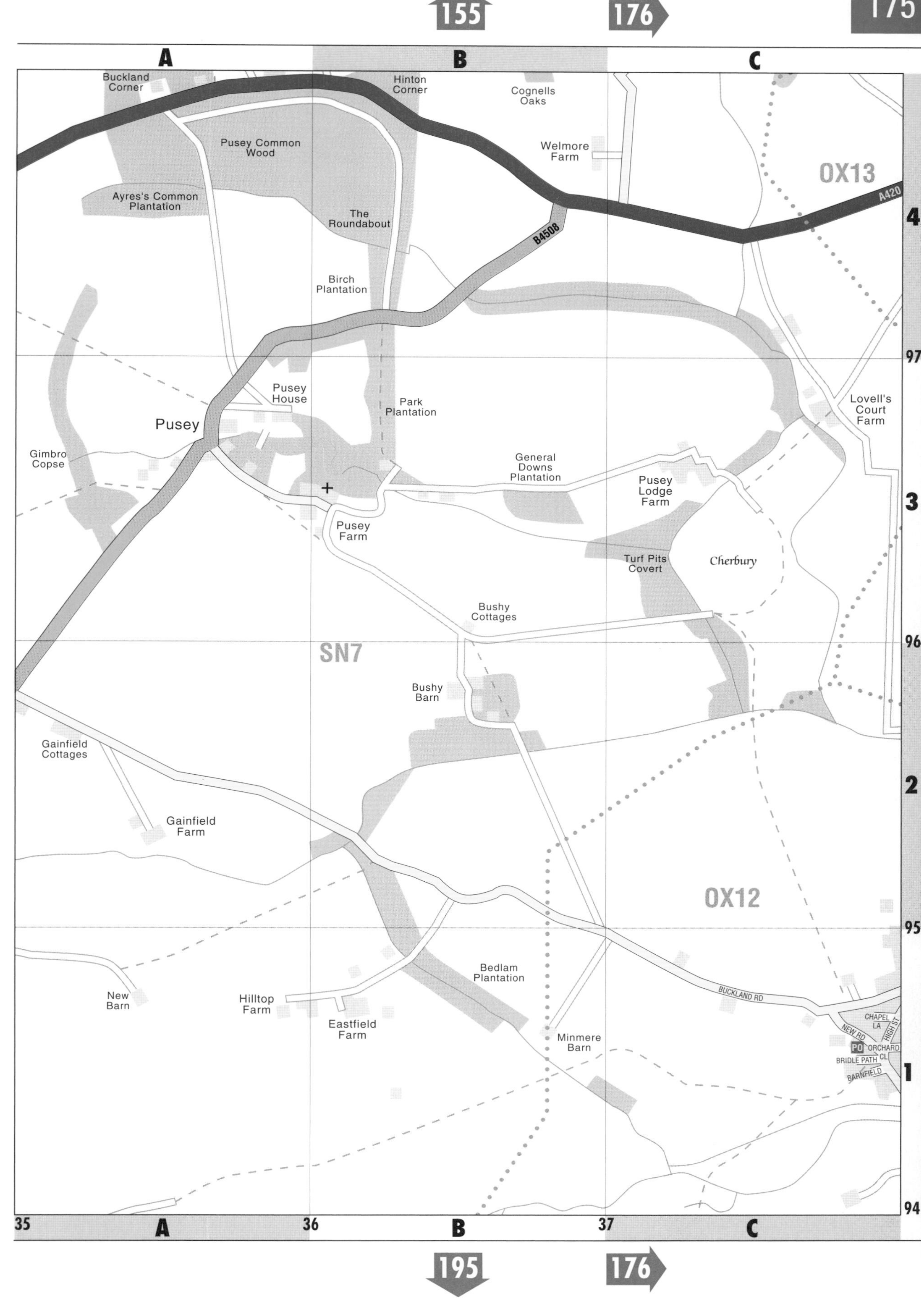
A
B
C
Buckland Corner
Hinton Corner
Cognells Oaks
Welmore Farm
Pusey Common Wood
Ayres's Common Plantation
The Roundabout
OX13
A420
4
B4508
Birch Plantation
97
Pusey House
Park Plantation
Lovell's Court Farm
Pusey
Gimbro Copse
General Downs Plantation
Pusey Lodge Farm
3
Pusey Farm
Turf Pits Covert
Cherbury
Bushy Cottages
96
SN7
Bushy Barn
Gainfield Cottages
2
Gainfield Farm
OX12
95
Bedlam Plantation
BUCKLAND RD
New Barn
Hilltop Farm
Eastfield Farm
Minmere Barn
CHAPEL LA
NEW RD
HIGH ST
PO
ORCHARD CL
BRIDLE PATH
BARNFIELD
1
94
35
36
37

195
176

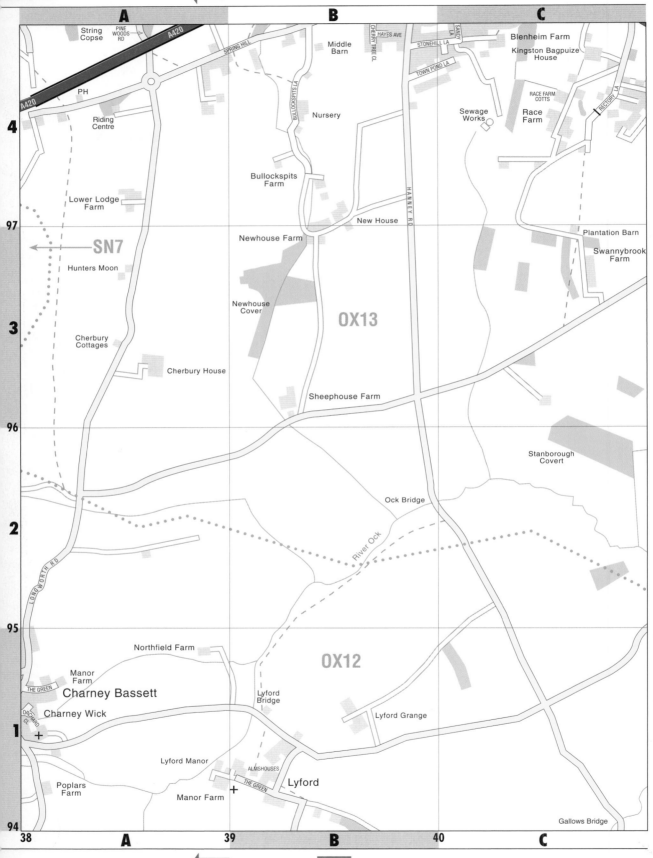

175
156

A
B
C
String Copse
PINE WOODS RD
A420
SPRING HILL
Middle Barn
CHERRY TREE CL
HAYES AVE
STONEHILL LA
SANDY LA
TOWN POND LA
Blenheim Farm
Kingston Bagpuize House
PH
Riding Centre
BULLOCKSPITS LA
Nursery
Sewage Works
RACE FARM COTTS
Race Farm
RECTORY LA
4
Bullockspits Farm
Lower Lodge Farm
HANNEY RD
New House
97
SN7
Newhouse Farm
Plantation Barn
Swannybrook Farm
Hunters Moon
Newhouse Cover
OX13
3
Cherbury Cottages
Cherbury House
Sheephouse Farm
96
Stanborough Covert
Ock Bridge
2
River Ock
LONGWORTH RD
95
Northfield Farm
OX12
Manor Farm
THE GREEN
Charney Bassett
Lyford Bridge
Charney Wick
ORCHARD CL
Lyford Grange
1
Lyford Manor
ALMSHOUSES
THE GREEN
Lyford
Poplars Farm
Manor Farm
Gallows Bridge
94
38
A
39
B
40
C

175
196

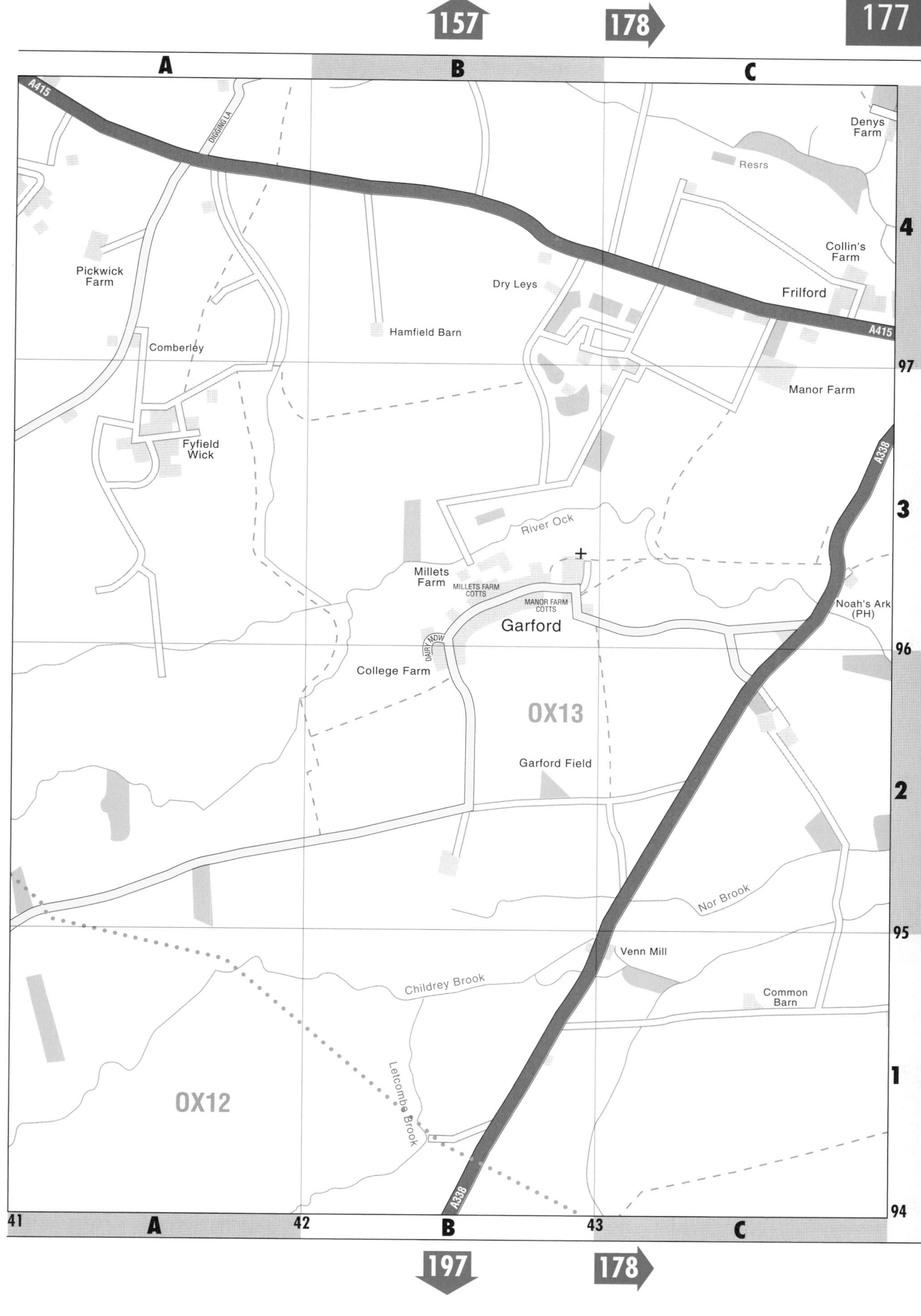

A
B
C

A415

Denys Farm

Resrs

DIGGING LA

Collin's Farm

4

Pickwick Farm

Dry Leys

Frilford

A415

Comberley

Hamfield Barn

97

Manor Farm

Fyfield Wick

A338

River Ock

3

Millets Farm

Noah's Ark (PH)

MILLETS FARM COTTS

MANOR FARM COTTS

Garford

96

DARK MDW

College Farm

OX13

Garford Field

2

Nor Brook

95

Venn Mill

Childrey Brook

Common Barn

1

Letcombe Brook

OX12

A338

94

41
A
42
B
43
C

177
158

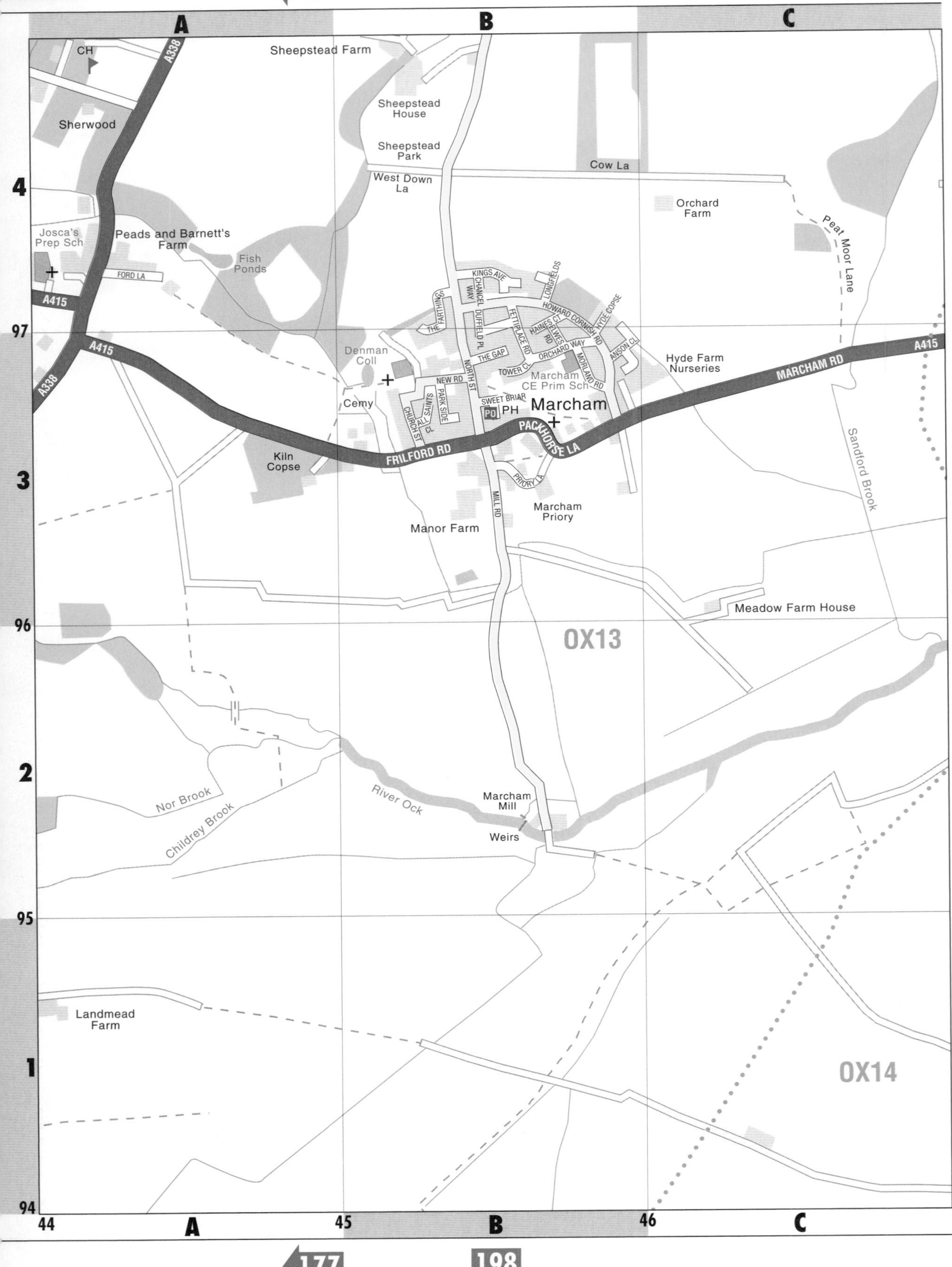
A
B
C
4
97
3
96
2
95
1
94
44
45
46
CH
A338
Sheepstead Farm
Sheepstead House
Sheepstead Park
Sherwood
West Down La
Cow La
Orchard Farm
Peat Moor Lane
Josca's Prep Sch
Peads and Barnett's Farm
Fish Ponds
FORD LA
A415
KINGS AVE
LONGFIELDS
THE FARTHINGS
CHANCEL WAY
HOWARD CORNISH RD
HYDE COPSE
FETTIPLACE RD
HAINES CT
ELWES RD
DUFFIELD PL
ANSON CL
THE GAP
ORCHARD WAY
MORLAND RD
Denman Coll
TOWER CL
Marcham CE Prim Sch
NEW RD
NORTH ST
Hyde Farm Nurseries
MARCHAM RD
SWEET BRIAR
PO
PH
Marcham
Cemy
CHURCH ST
ALL SAINTS CL
PARK SIDE
PACKHORSE LA
FRILFORD RD
Kiln Copse
PRIORY LA
MILL RD
Marcham Priory
Manor Farm
Sandford Brook
Meadow Farm House
OX13
Nor Brook
River Ock
Childrey Brook
Marcham Mill
Weirs
Landmead Farm
OX14

177
198

C3
1 MEADOWSIDE CT
2 BREWERS CT
3 WINSMORE LA
4 HIVE MEWS
5 ST EDMUND'S LA
6 ST HELEN'S MEWS
7 BRICK ALLEY
8 MILL PADDOCK
9 BAILIE CL
10 MUSSON CL
11 THURSTON CL
12 SYMPSON CL
13 GODFREY CL

159

C4
1 THORNHILL WLK
2 BOROUGH WLK
3 FINMORE CL
4 THE HOLT
5 STANFORD DR
6 MAYOTT'S RD

180

C4
7 CARSWELL CT
8 TOMKIN'S ALMSHOUSES
9 OCK MEWS
10 BANBURY CT
11 THE VINES
12 THE SQUARE
13 MARKET PL
14 HIGH ST
15 LOMBARD ST

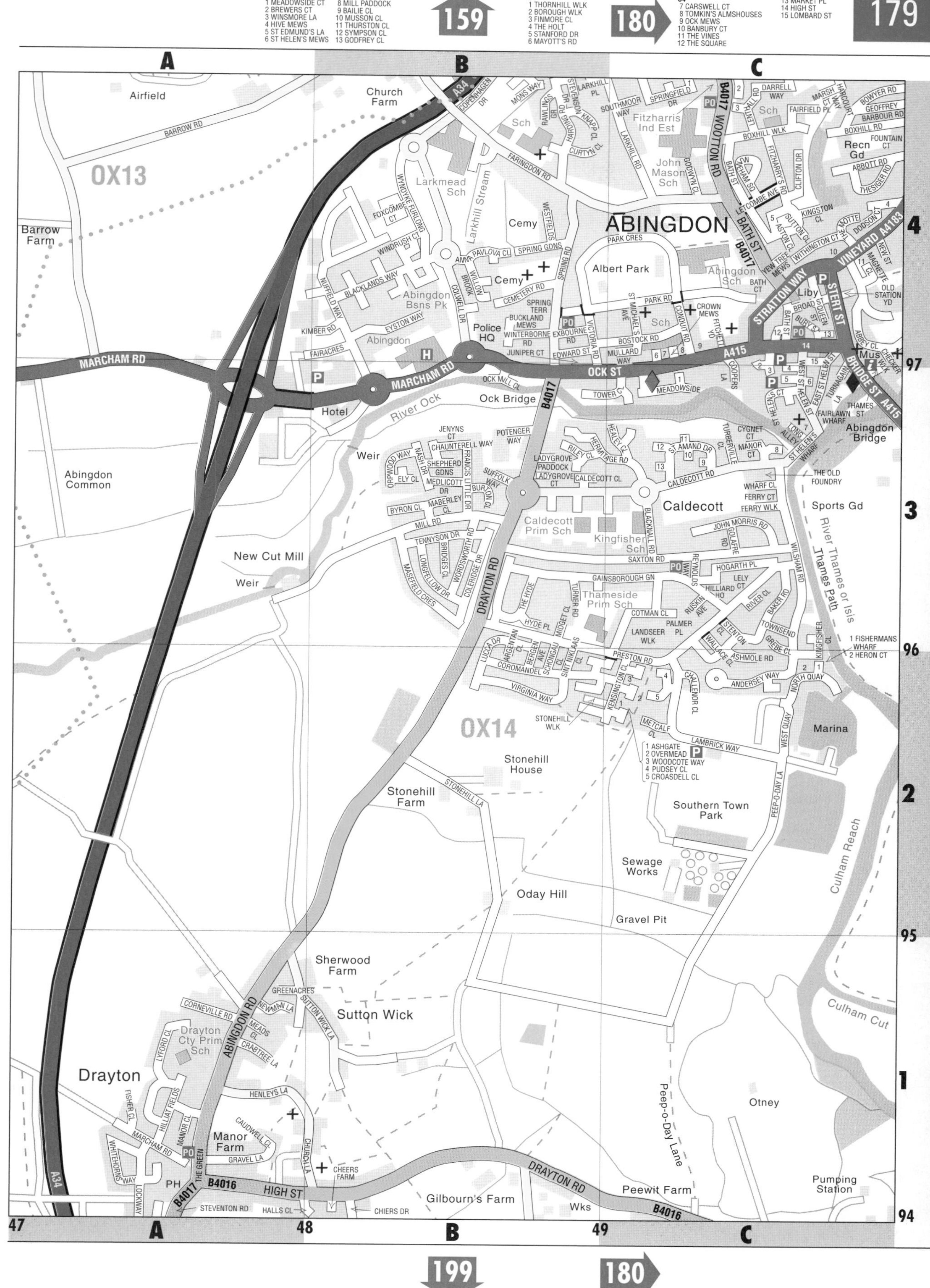

199

180

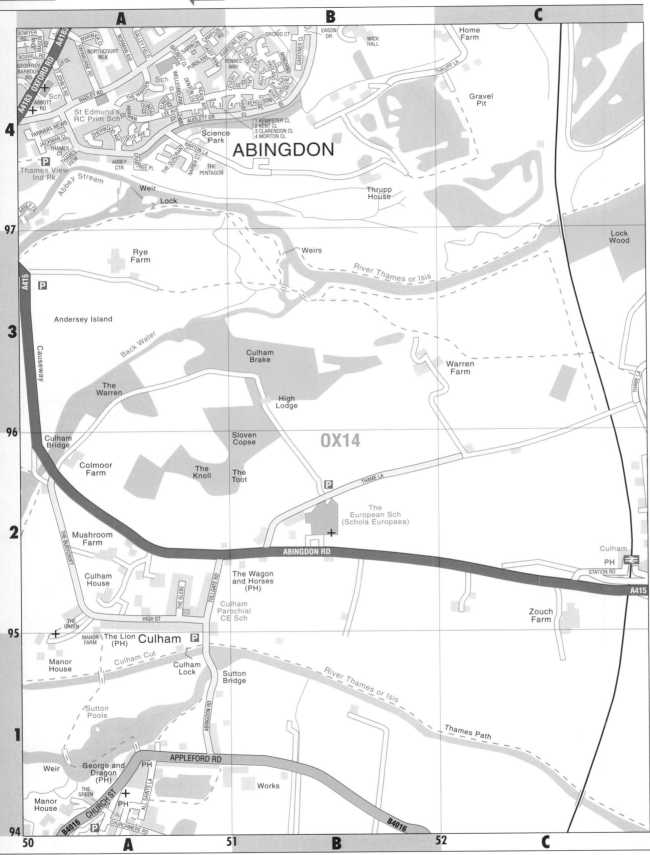
179
160

A B C

4 3 2 1 97 96 95 94

Home Farm
EASON DR
WICK HALL
ORCHID CT
BOWYER RD
JOHN MASON RD
A4183
WARWICK CL
NORMAN AVE
GALLEY FIELD
CAMPION RD
SAFFRON CT
GRUNDY CL
SWINBURNE RD
NORTHCOURT WLK
BOXHILL RD
GEOFFREY BARBOUR RD
OX CL
ST JOHN'S RD
OXFORD RD
A4183
PURSLANE
DAISY BANK
RAMSONS WAY
FENNEL WAY
VILLEBOIS CL
GALL CL
RIVY CL
HADLAND RD
MINCHINS CL
FARM CL
GARDINER CL
THRUPP LA
Gravel Pit
Sch
WELLESBOURNE CL
DENTON CL
READE AVE
LEVERY CL
FERGUSON PL
NYATT RD
HART CL
Sch
ABBOTT RD
RADLEY RD
THE WARREN
HERMAN CL
DUNDAS CL
FLINES CL
LEE AVE
HOBBS CL
St Edmund's RC Prim Sch
AUDLETT DR
1 KEMPSTER CL
2 KENT CL
3 CLARENDON CL
4 MORTON CL
FARRIERS MEWS
JACKMAN CL
SHERWOOD AVE
CURTIS AVE
Science Park
ABINGDON
THAMES CT
THAMES VIEW
ABBEY CTR
CRABTREE PL
THE QUADRANT
NAPIER CT
BARTON LA
THE PENTAGON
Thames View Ind Pk
Abbey Stream
Weir
Lock
Thrupp House
ABBEY CL
Lock Wood
Rye Farm
Weirs
River Thames or Isis
A415
Andersey Island
Back Water
Causeway
Culham Brake
Warren Farm
THAME LA
The Warren
High Lodge
OX14
Culham Bridge
Sloven Copse
Colmoor Farm
The Knoll
The Toot
THAME LA
The European Sch (Schola Europaea)
Mushroom Farm
THE BURYCROFT
ABINGDON RD
Culham
PH
STATION RD
A415
Culham House
TOLLGATE RD
THE GLEBE
The Wagon and Horses (PH)
Culham Parochial CE Sch
Zouch Farm
HIGH ST
THE GREEN
MANOR FARM
The Lion (PH)
Culham
Manor House
Culham Cut
Culham Lock
Sutton Bridge
River Thames or Isis
Sutton Pools
ABINGDON RD
Thames Path
APPLEFORD RD
Weir
George and Dragon (PH)
PH
THE GREEN
CHURCH ST
ALL SAINTS LA
PH
Works
Manor House
B4016
CHURCHMERE RD
B4016

50 A 51 B 52 C

179
200

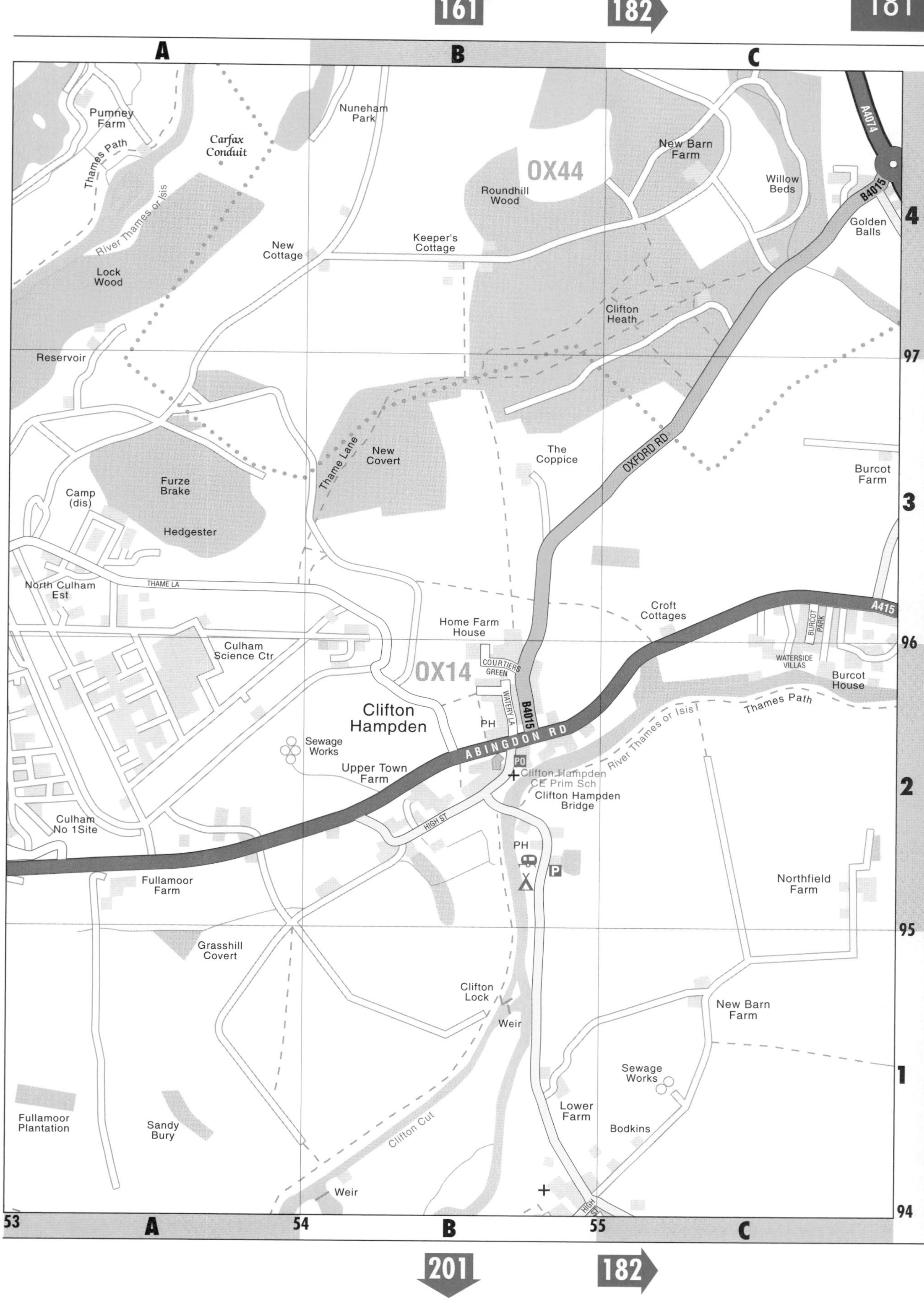

A
B
C

Pumney Farm

Thames Path

Carfax Conduit

Nuneham Park

New Barn Farm

OX44

Willow Beds

A4074

B4015

Golden Balls

4

River Thames or Isis

Lock Wood

New Cottage

Keeper's Cottage

Roundhill Wood

Clifton Heath

97

Reservoir

Thame Lane

New Covert

The Coppice

OXFORD RD

Burcot Farm

3

Furze Brake

Camp (dis)

Hedgester

Croft Cottages

A415

BURCOT PARK

96

North Culham Est

THAME LA

Culham Science Ctr

Home Farm House

WATERSIDE VILLAS

Burcot House

OX14

COURTIERS GREEN

WATERY LA

B4015

Clifton Hampden

PH

Sewage Works

Upper Town Farm

ABINGDON RD

PO

Clifton Hampden CE Prim Sch

River Thames or Isis

Thames Path

2

Culham No 1Site

HIGH ST

Clifton Hampden Bridge

PH

P

Northfield Farm

Fullamoor Farm

95

Grasshill Covert

Clifton Lock

Weir

New Barn Farm

1

Fullamoor Plantation

Sandy Bury

Clifton Cut

Lower Farm

Sewage Works

Bodkins

HIGH ST

Weir

94

53
A
54
B
55
C

A　　　**B**　　　**C**

Baldon Brook

OX44

B4015

Golden Balls

B4015

A4074

4

The Copse

97

Burcot Farm

PRITCHARD CL

TOWER RD

RUSSELL JACKSON CL

BARRINGTON CL

CHERWELL RD

HAME DR

GLYME DR

EVENLODE DR

COLNE DR

CRUTCH FURLONG

LAY AVE

OCK DR

WEST CROFT

CONKER

Berinsfield

3

GREEN FURLONG

LEACH RD

Liby Sports Ctr

WIMBLE STRAW

SHARNEL RD

WEY RD

BULLINGDON AVE

ABBEY WOODS CL

CHILTERN CL

Berinsfield Prim Sch

Mount Farm

LODEN AVE

Trad Est

Works

WINDRUSH RD

A415

BALFOUR COTTS

Berinsfield RDBT

KENNET CL

96

Burcot

PH

WIMBLE STRAW RD

A415

DORCHESTER RD

OX14

Wally Corner

OX10

BURCOT LA

CINNET CL

Weir

2

Water Sports Ctr

DRAYTON RD

Queenford Farm

ABINGDON RD

Thames Path

95

River Thames or Isis

THE LIMES

Queenford Bridge

OXFORD RD

River Thame

PH

DRAYTON RD

Bishop's Court

Cemy

PAGE FURLONG

1

HERRINGCOTE

BELCHER CT

MARTIN'S LA

JEMMETT'S CL

MANOR FARM RD

KIMBER CL

QUEEN ST

QUEEN'S CL

Dorchester

CROWN LA

ROMAN TOWN

BEECHCROFT

HIGH ST

PO

St Birinus Sch

MALTHOUSE LA

Weir

WATLING LA

PH

Mus

Abbey Bridge

BRIDGE END

ROTTEN ROW

Overy Farm

Overy

A4074

94

56　　　**A**　　　**57**　　　**B**　　　**58**　　　**C**

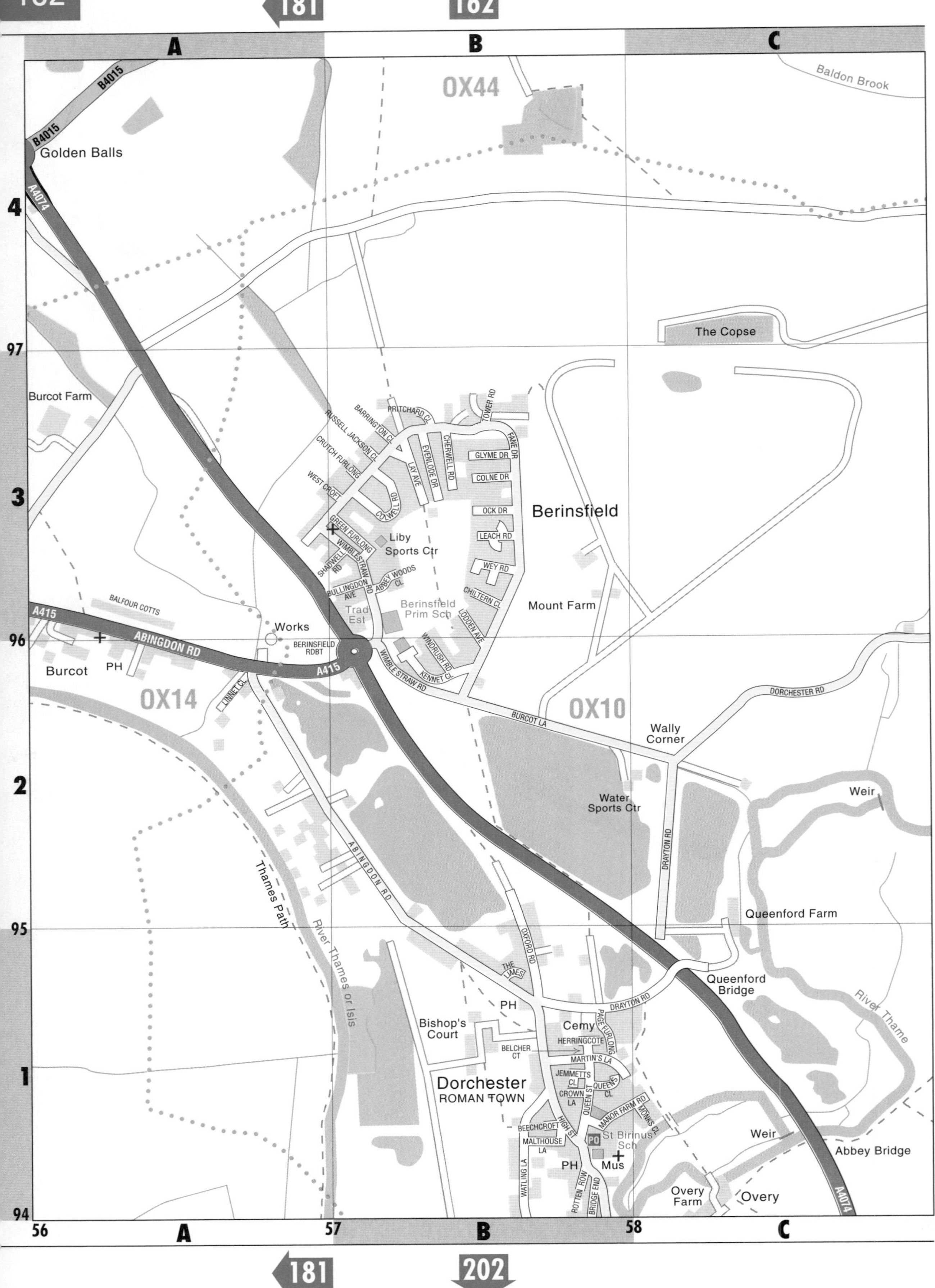

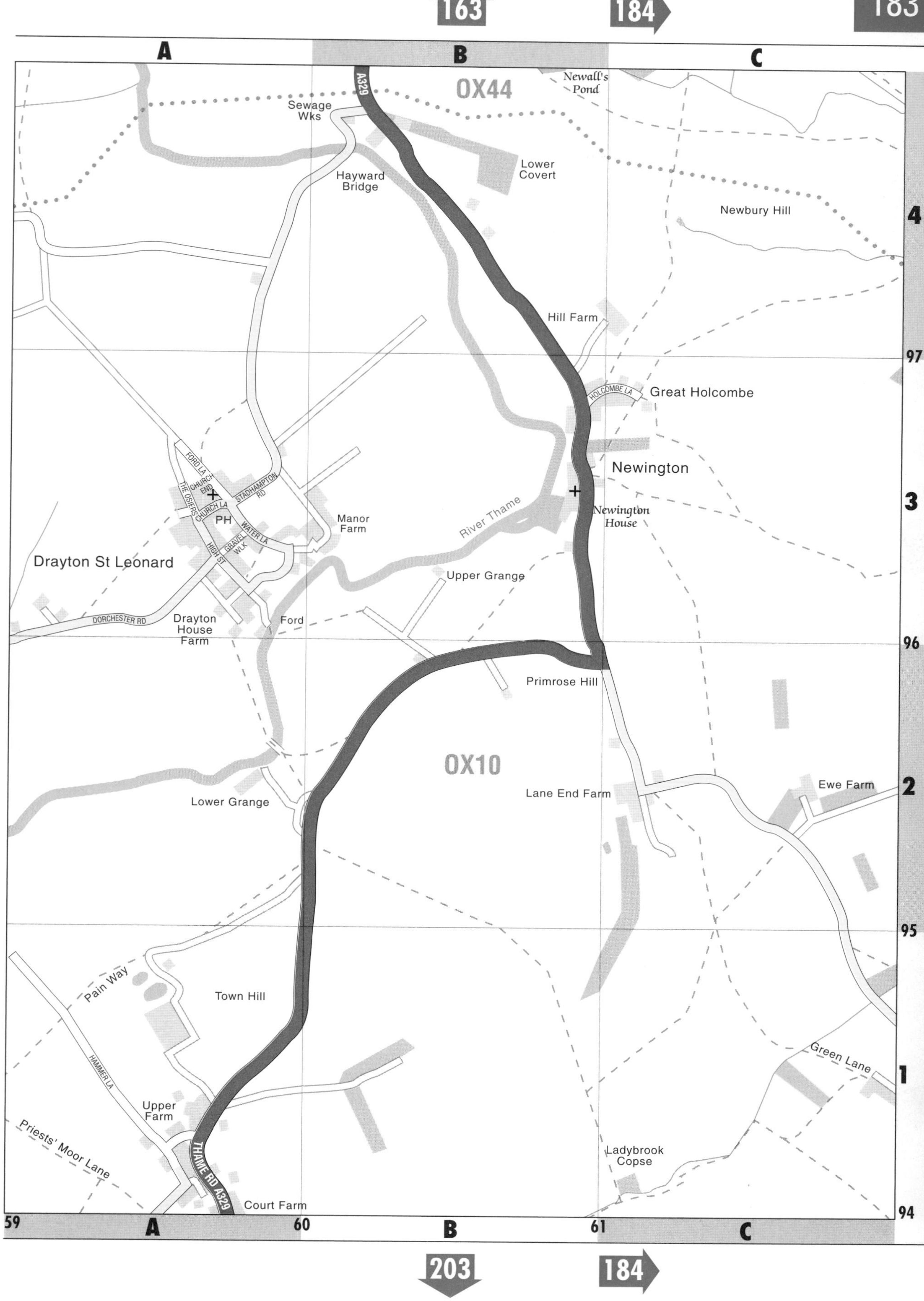

163
184

A   B   C

OX44

Newall's Pond

Sewage Wks

A329

Lower Covert

Newbury Hill

Hayward Bridge

4

Hill Farm

97

HOLCOMBE LA

Great Holcombe

Newington

FORD LA
CHURCH END
THE OSIERS
CHURCH LA
STADHAMPTON RD

+

3

River Thame

Newington House

PH

HIGH ST
GRAVEL WLK
WATER LA

Manor Farm

Drayton St Leonard

Upper Grange

DORCHESTER RD

Drayton House Farm

Ford

96

Primrose Hill

OX10

Lower Grange

Lane End Farm

Ewe Farm

2

95

Pain Way

Town Hill

Green Lane

1

HAMMER LA

Upper Farm

Priests' Moor Lane

THAME RD A329

Ladybrook Copse

Court Farm

94

59   A   60   B   61   C

203
184

183
164

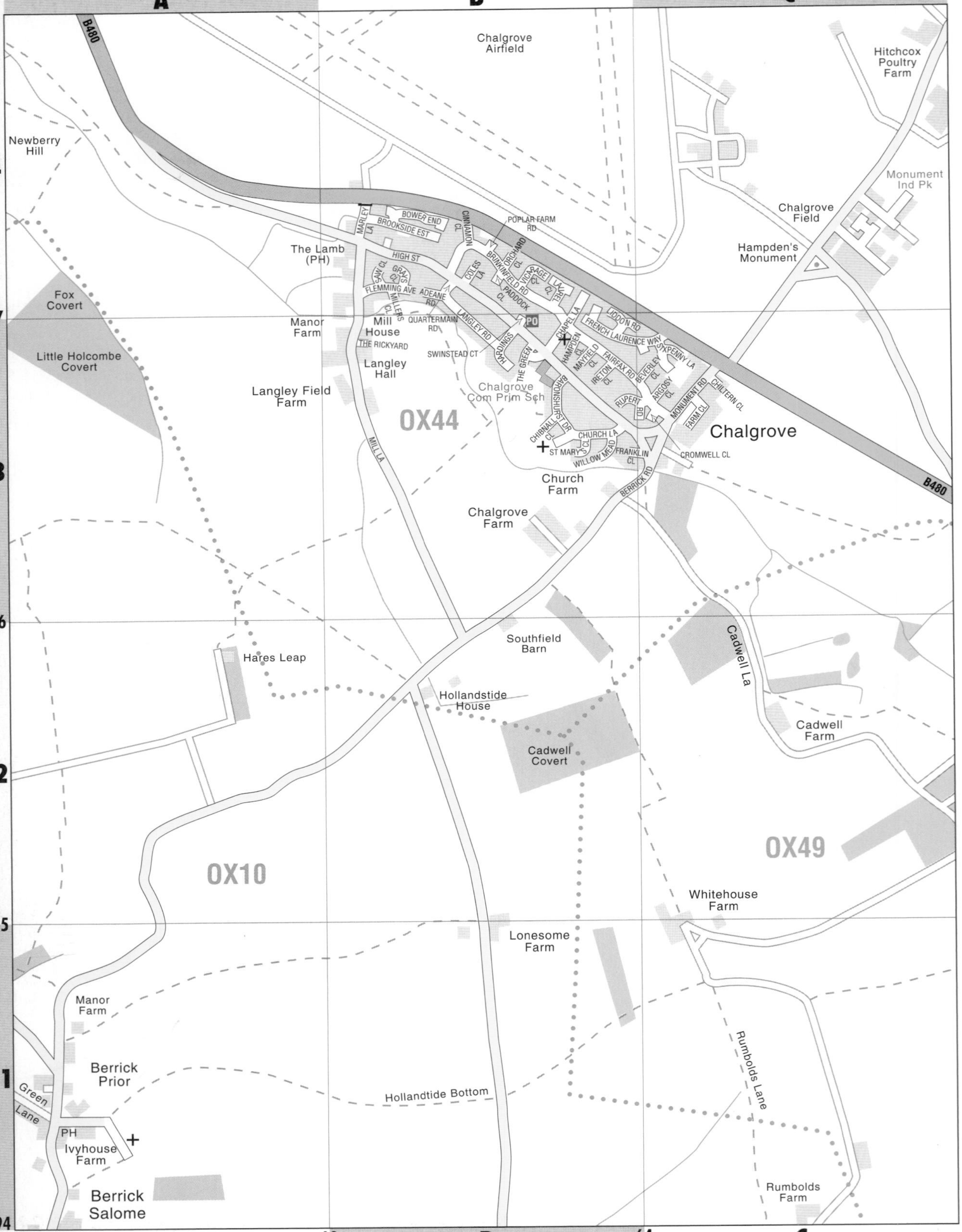

A   **B**   **C**

Chalgrove Airfield

Hitchcox Poultry Farm

Newberry Hill

Monument Ind Pk

4

Chalgrove Field

Hampden's Monument

Fox Covert

BOWER END

BROOKSIDE EST

The Lamb (PH)

HIGH ST

MARLEY LA

CINNAMON CL

RICHARD

POPLAR FARM RD

Little Holcombe Covert

97

LAW CL

GRAIL CL

FLEMMING AVE

ADEANE RD

MILLES

COLES LA

BRINKINFIELD RD

PADDOCK CL

VICKS CL

SAGE CL

IVY CL

LIDDON RD

Manor Farm

Mill House

THE RICKYARD

QUARTERMAIN RD

LANGLEY RD

PO

CHAPEL LA

FRENCH LAURENCE WAY

SIXPENNY LA

Langley Hall

SWINSTEAD CT

THE GREEN

HAMPDEN CL

MAYTIE CL

FAIRFAX RD

BEVERLEY CL

ARGOSY CL

MONUMENT RD

FARM CL

CHILTERN CL

Langley Field Farm

OX44

Chalgrove Com Prim Sch

WHARFINGHURST DR

IRETON CL

RUPERT RD

Chalgrove

3

CHIBNALL DR

CHRISTMAS DR

CHURCH LA

St MARY'S

WILLOW WD

FRANKLIN CL

BERRICK RD

CROMWELL CL

MILL LA

Church Farm

Chalgrove Farm

Southfield Barn

Cadwell La

96

Hares Leap

Hollandstide House

Cadwell Farm

Cadwell Covert

2

OX49

OX10

Whitehouse Farm

95

Lonesome Farm

Manor Farm

Rumbolds Lane

1

Berrick Prior

Green Lane

Hollandtide Bottom

PH

Ivyhouse Farm

Rumbolds Farm

Berrick Salome

94

62   **A**   63   **B**   64   **C**

183
204

165
186

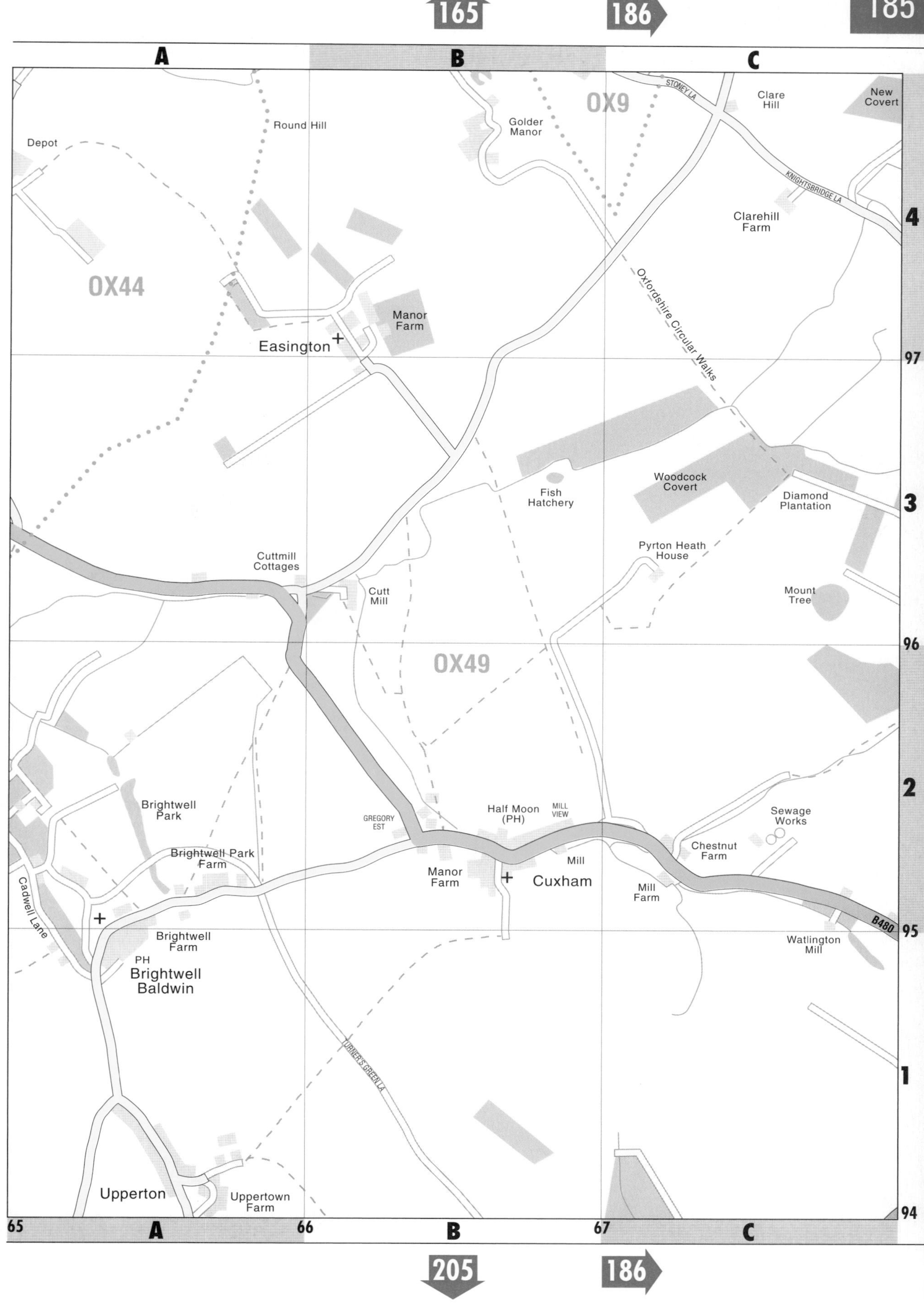
A
B
C
Round Hill
Depot
Golder Manor
OX9
STONEY LA
Clare Hill
New Covert
KNIGHTSBRIDGE LA
Clarehill Farm
4
OX44
Oxfordshire Circular Walks
Manor Farm
Easington
97
Woodcock Covert
Fish Hatchery
Diamond Plantation
3
Pyrton Heath House
Cuttmill Cottages
Cutt Mill
Mount Tree
96
OX49
2
Brightwell Park
GREGORY EST
Half Moon (PH)
MILL VIEW
Sewage Works
Brightwell Park Farm
Chestnut Farm
Mill
Manor Farm
Cuxham
Mill Farm
Cadwell Lane
B480
95
Brightwell Farm
PH
Brightwell Baldwin
Watlington Mill
TURNER'S GREEN LA
1
Upperton
Uppertown Farm
94
65
A
66
B
67
C

205
186

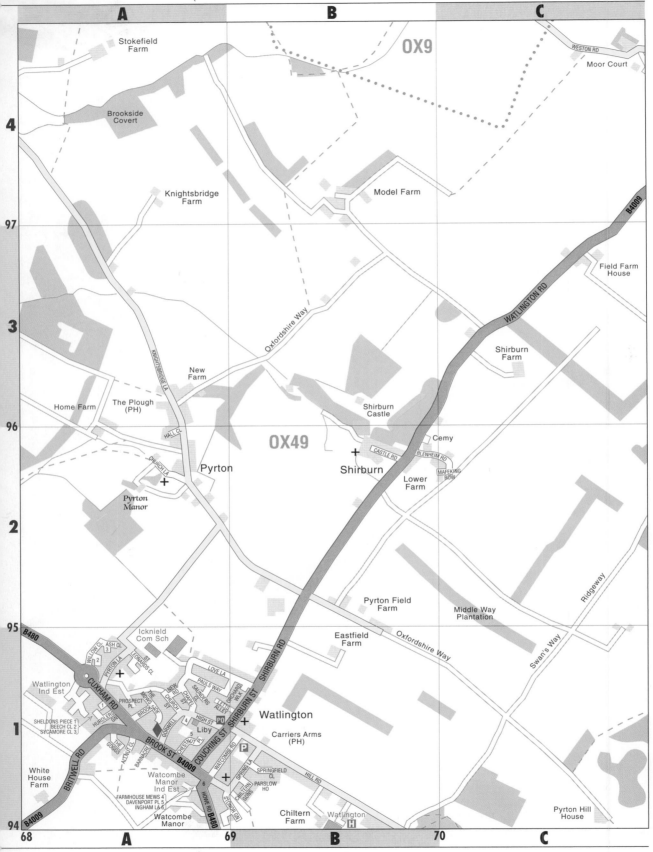

A B C

OX9

WESTON RD

Moor Court

Stokefield
Farm

Brookside
Covert

4

Knightsbridge
Farm

Model Farm

B4009

97

Field Farm
House

WATLINGTON RD

Oxfordshire Way

Shirburn
Farm

3

New
Farm

KNIGHTSBRIDGE LA

Home Farm

The Plough
(PH)

HALL CL

Shirburn
Castle

96

CHURCH LA

OX49

Cemy

Pyrton

CASTLE RD

Shirburn

BLENHEIM RD

MAFEKING
ROW

Lower
Farm

Pyrton
Manor

2

Ridgeway

Swan's Way

Pyrton Field
Farm

Middle Way
Plantation

95

B480

Icknield
Com Sch

Eastfield
Farm

Oxfordshire Way

WILLOW CL

ASH CL 3
BEECH CL 2
SYCAMORE CL 3

PYRTON LA

EDWARDS CL

LOVE LA

PAULS WAY

SHIRBURN RD

Watlington
Ind Est

CUXHAM RD

PROSPECT
PL

NEW
CHURCH
RD

CHAPEL
ST

SAUNDERS
CL

RICHARD
WLK

SHIRBURN ST

Watlington

SHELDONS PIECE 1
BEECH CL 2
SYCAMORE CL 3

HURDLERS
GDN

THE
GOGGS

BROOK DVE

GODWELL

HIGH ST

CHESTNUT PL

LETTS
ALLEY

PO

1

BRITWELL RD

BROOK ST

COUCHING ST

Liby

Carriers Arms
(PH)

WATCOMBE RD

P

SPRINGFIELD
CL

PARSLOW
HO

HILL RD

White
House
Farm

THE
ALLNUTT CL

BARNACRE

B4009

Watcombe Manor
Ind Est

HOME RD

B400

CHILTERN
GDNS

SPRING LA

STONOR LN

FARMHOUSE MEWS 4
DAVENPORT PL 5
INGHAM LA 6

Chiltern
Farm

Watlington

H

Pyrton Hill
House

94

B4009

Watcombe
Manor

68 A 69 B 70 C

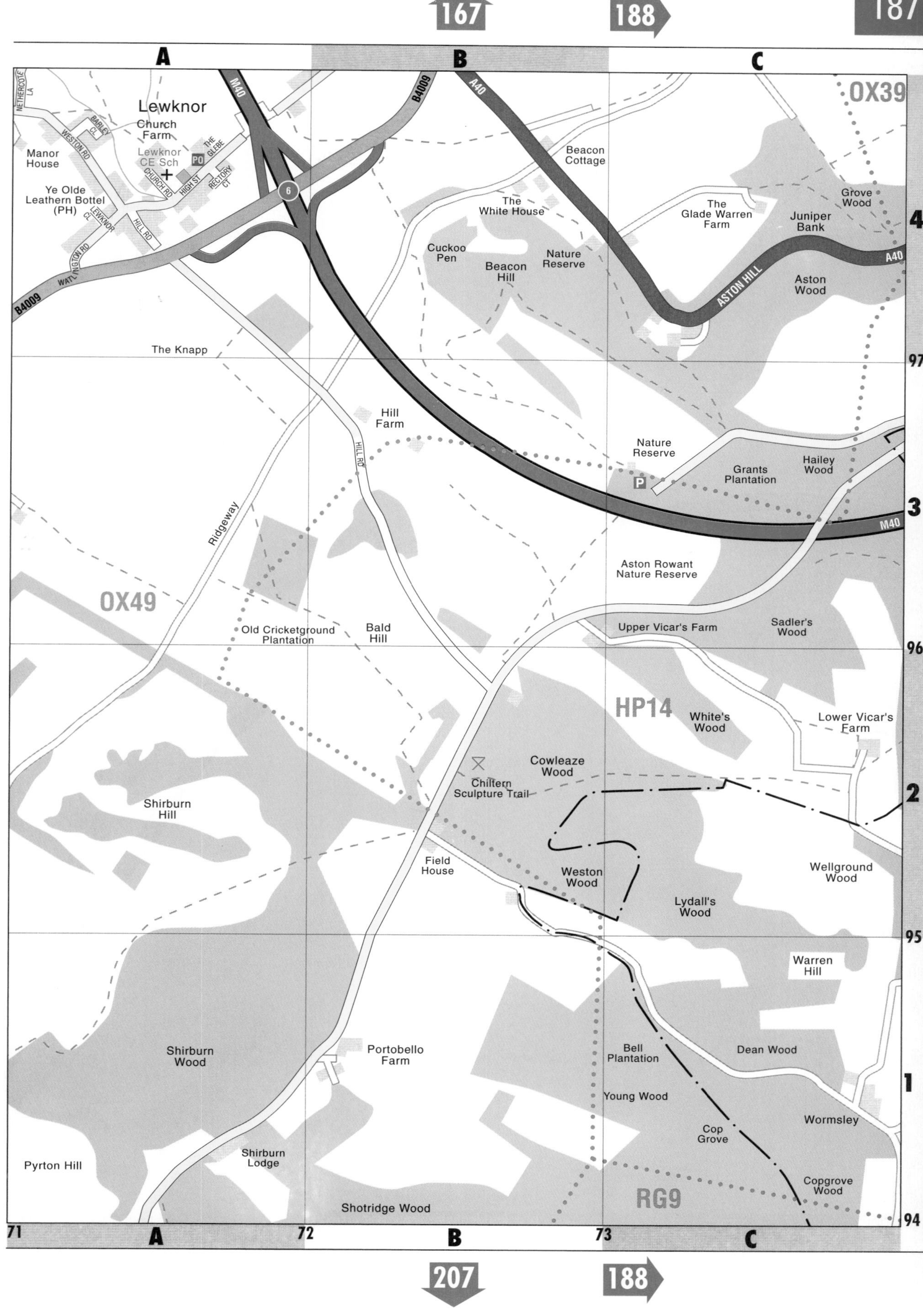

OX39

M40

B4009

A40

Lewknor

NETHERCOTE LA

Church Farm

Manor House

BARLEY

WESTON RD

Lewknor CE Sch

PO

THE GLEBE

Ye Olde Leathern Bottel (PH)

CHURCH RD

HIGH ST

RECTORY CT

LEWKNOR

HILL RD

WATLINGTON RD

6

B4009

The Knapp

Beacon Cottage

The White House

The Glade Warren Farm

Grove Wood

Juniper Bank

ASTON HILL

A40

Cuckoo Pen

Beacon Hill

Nature Reserve

Aston Wood

4

97

Hill Farm

HILL RD

Ridgeway

Nature Reserve

P

Grants Plantation

Hailey Wood

M40

3

OX49

Old Cricketground Plantation

Bald Hill

Aston Rowant Nature Reserve

Upper Vicar's Farm

Sadler's Wood

96

HP14

White's Wood

Lower Vicar's Farm

Shirburn Hill

Cowleaze Wood

Chiltern Sculpture Trail

2

Field House

Weston Wood

Lydall's Wood

Wellground Wood

95

Warren Hill

Shirburn Wood

Portobello Farm

Bell Plantation

Dean Wood

1

Young Wood

Wormsley

Cop Grove

Pyrton Hill

Shirburn Lodge

Shotridge Wood

RG9

Copgrove Wood

94

187
168

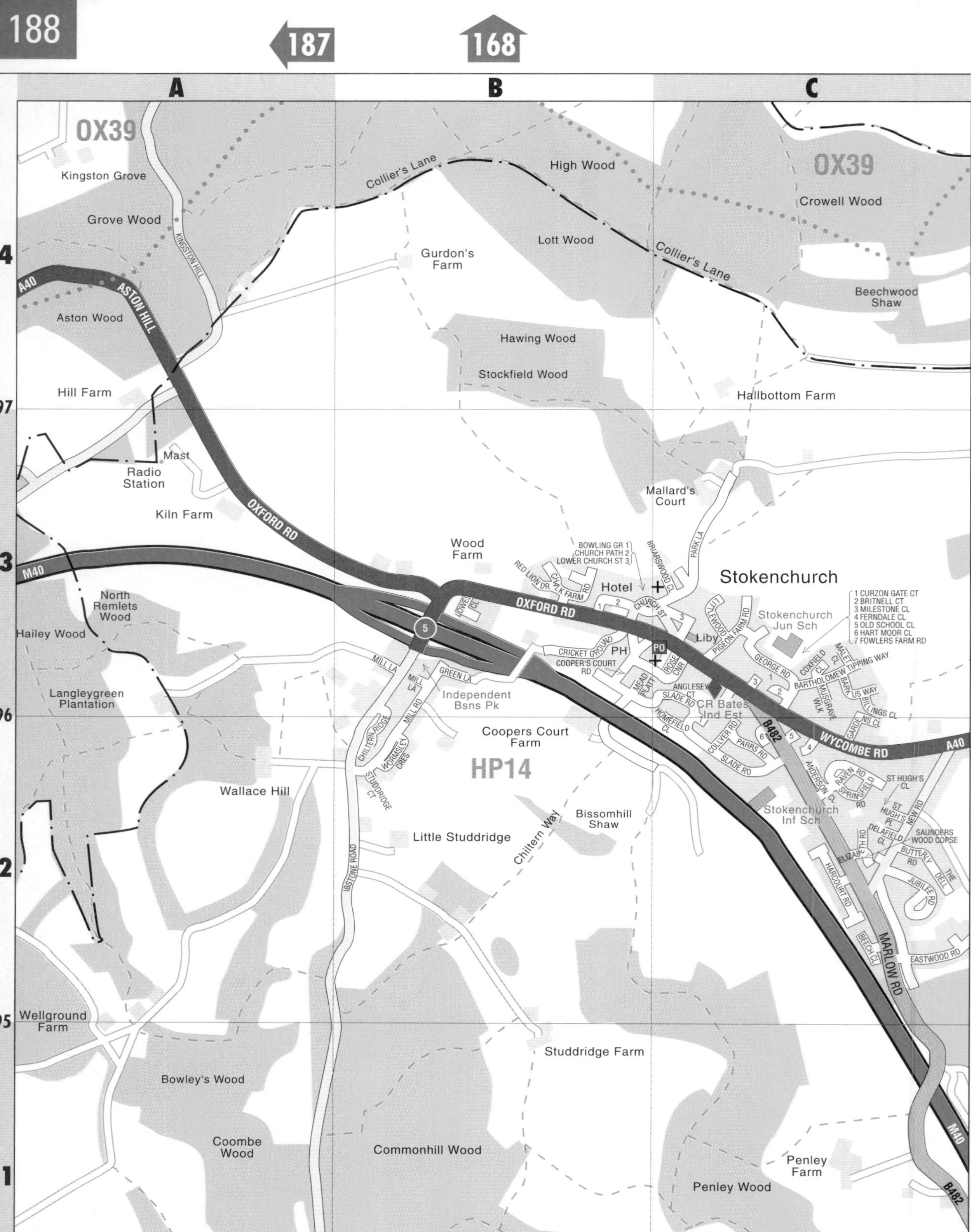
A
B
C
OX39
Kingston Grove
Grove Wood
Collier's Lane
High Wood
Crowell Wood
Lott Wood
Gurdon's Farm
KINGSTON HILL
A40
ASTON HILL
Aston Wood
Beechwood Shaw
Hawing Wood
Stockfield Wood
Hill Farm
Hallbottom Farm
Mast
Radio Station
Mallard's Court
Kiln Farm
OXFORD RD
Wood Farm
BOWLING GR 1
CHURCH PATH 2
LOWER CHURCH ST 3
BRIARSWOOD CL
PARK LA
Stokenchurch
M40
North Remlets Wood
Hotel
Stokenchurch Jun Sch
1 CURZON GATE CT
2 BRITNELL CT
3 MILESTONE CL
4 FERNDALE CL
5 OLD SCHOOL CL
6 HART MOOR CL
7 FOWLERS FARM RD
Hailey Wood
Liby
PH
PO
CRICKET GROUND
COOPER'S COURT RD
MILL LA
GREEN LA
Independent Bsns Pk
Langleygreen Plantation
CR Bates Ind Est
B482
WYCOMBE RD
Coopers Court Farm
HP14
Wallace Hill
Stokenchurch Inf Sch
Bissomhill Shaw
Chiltern Way
Little Studdridge
IBSTONE ROAD
HARCOURT RD
MARLOW RD
EASTWOOD RD
Wellground Farm
Studdridge Farm
Bowley's Wood
Coombe Wood
Commonhill Wood
Penley Farm
Penley Wood
Hartmoor Wood
4
97
3
96
2
95
1
94
74
75
76

187

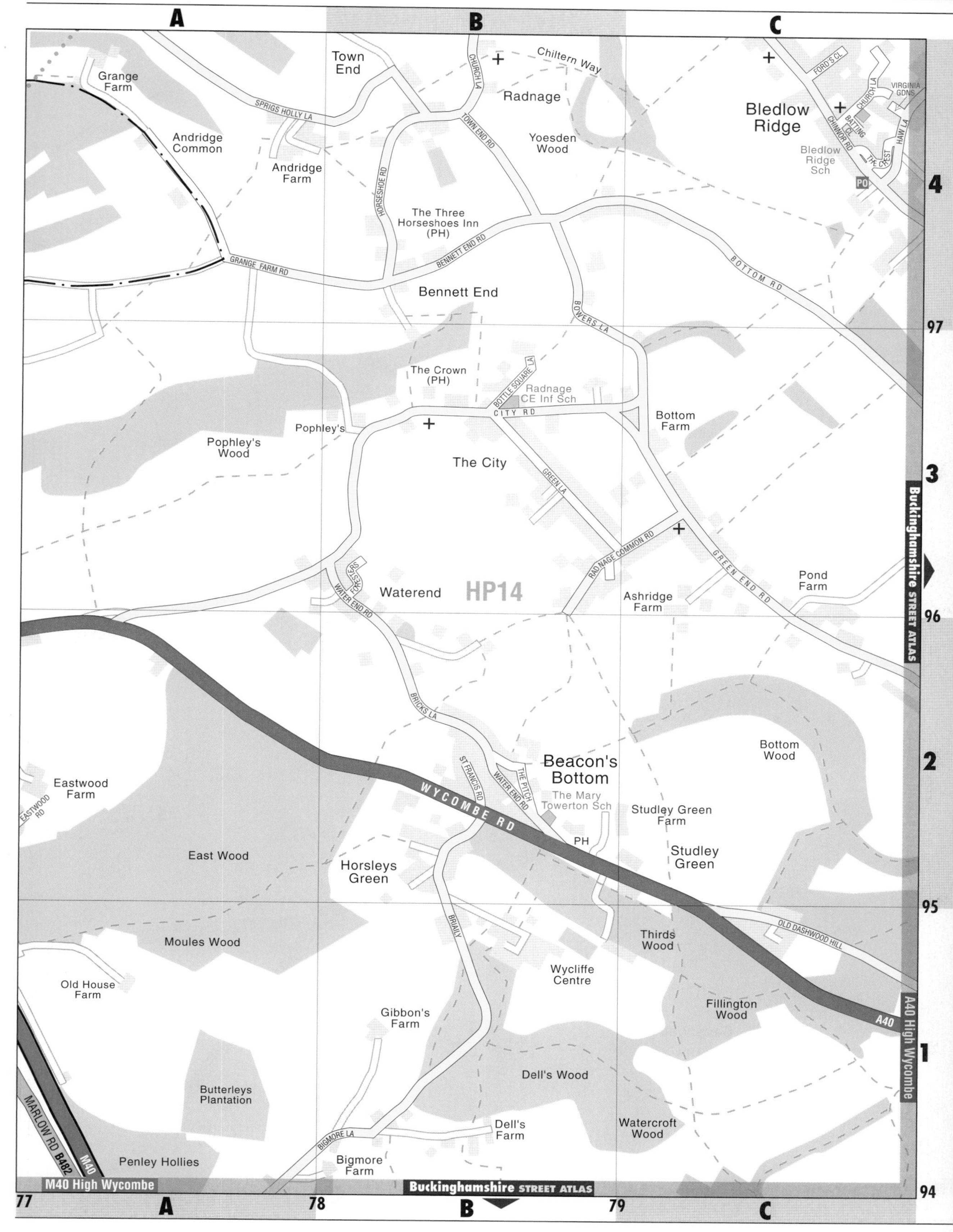

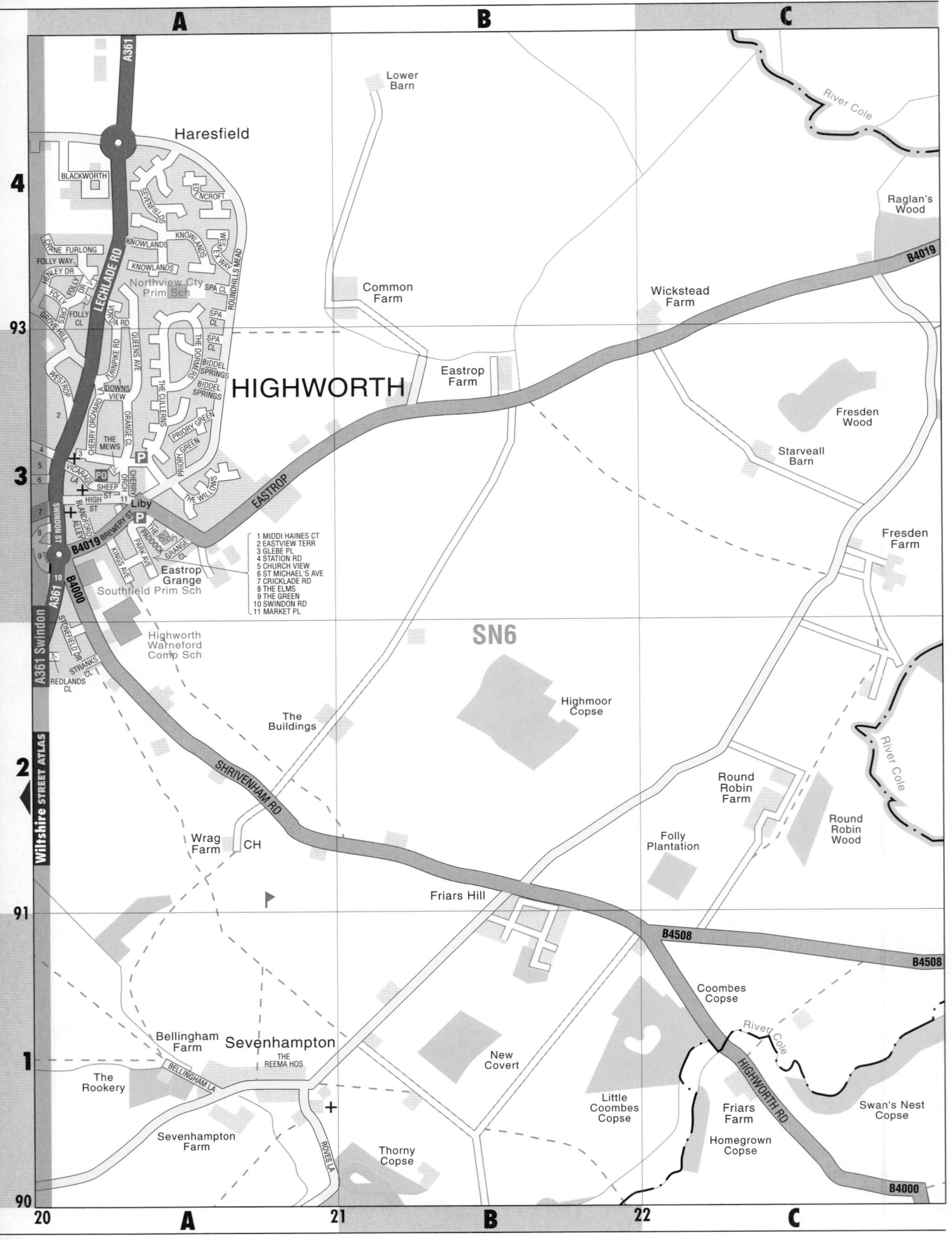

A

B

C

Lower
Barn

River Cole

Haresfield

BLACKWORTH

4

Raglan's
Wood

B4019

Common
Farm

Wickstead
Farm

93

HIGHWORTH

Eastrop
Farm

Fresden
Wood

Starveall
Barn

3

EASTROP

Liby

Fresden
Farm

1 MIDDI HAINES CT
2 EASTVIEW TERR
3 GLEBE PL
4 STATION RD
5 CHURCH VIEW
6 ST MICHAEL'S AVE
7 CRICKLADE RD
8 THE ELMS
9 THE GREEN
10 SWINDON RD
11 MARKET PL

Eastrop
Grange

Southfield Prim Sch

SN6

Highworth
Warneford
Comp Sch

Highmoor
Copse

2

The
Buildings

SHRIVENHAM RD

Round
Robin
Farm

River Cole

Round
Robin
Wood

Wrag
Farm   CH

Folly
Plantation

91

Friars Hill

B4508

B4508

Coombes
Copse

River Cole

Bellingham
Farm

Sevenhampton

THE
REEMA HOS

1

New
Covert

HIGHWORTH RD

The Rookery

BELLINGHAM LA

Little
Coombes
Copse

Friars
Farm

Swan's Nest
Copse

Sevenhampton
Farm

ROVES LA

Thorny
Copse

Homegrown
Copse

90

B4000

20

A

21

B

22

C

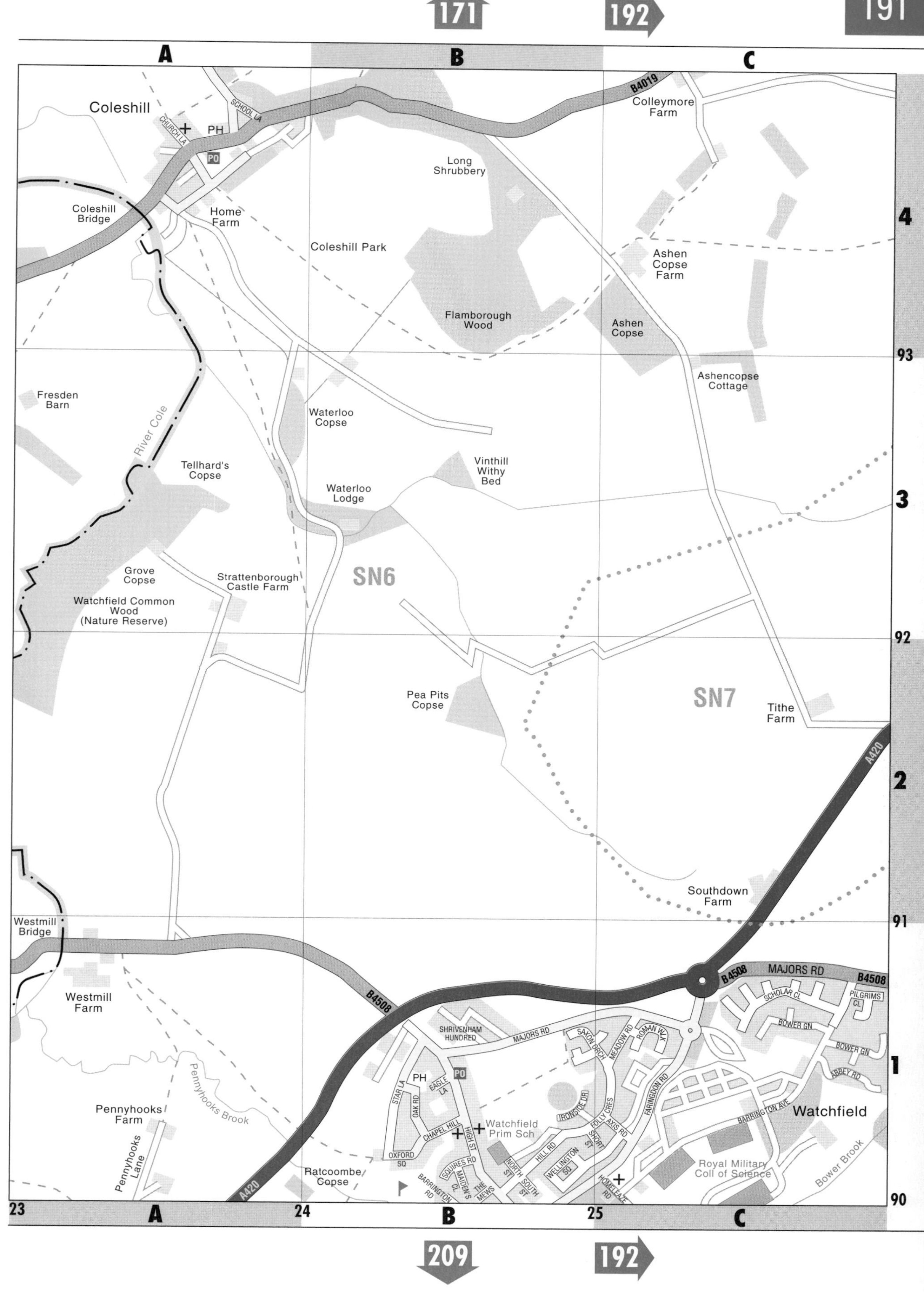
171
192
A
B
C
Coleshill
SCHOOL LA
CHURCH LA
PH
PO
B4019
Colleymore Farm
Long Shrubbery
Coleshill Bridge
Home Farm
Coleshill Park
Ashen Copse Farm
Flamborough Wood
Ashen Copse
Ashencopse Cottage
Fresden Barn
Waterloo Copse
River Cole
Tellhard's Copse
Vinthill Withy Bed
Waterloo Lodge
SN6
Grove Copse
Strattenborough Castle Farm
Watchfield Common Wood (Nature Reserve)
Pea Pits Copse
SN7
Tithe Farm
A420
Southdown Farm
Westmill Bridge
B4508
MAJORS RD
Westmill Farm
SCHOLAR CL
PILGRIMS CL
SHRIVENHAM HUNDRED
MAJORS RD
SAXON ORCH
MEADOW RD
ROMAN WLK
BOWER GN
ABBEY RD
Pennyhooks Brook
EAGLE LA
STAR LA
OAK RD
IRONSIDE DR
FOLLY CRES
AXIS RD
FARINGDON RD
BARRINGTON AVE
Watchfield
Pennyhooks Farm
CHAPEL HILL
HIGH ST
Watchfield Prim Sch
HILL RD
SHORT ST
Pennyhooks Lane
OXFORD SQ
SQUIRES RD
MAIDEN'S CL
THE MEWS
NORTH ST
SOUTH ST
WELLINGTON SQ
HOMELEAZE RD
Royal Military Coll of Science
Bower Brook
Ratcoombe Copse
BARRINGTON RD
4
93
3
92
2
91
1
90
23
24
25
209
192

191
172

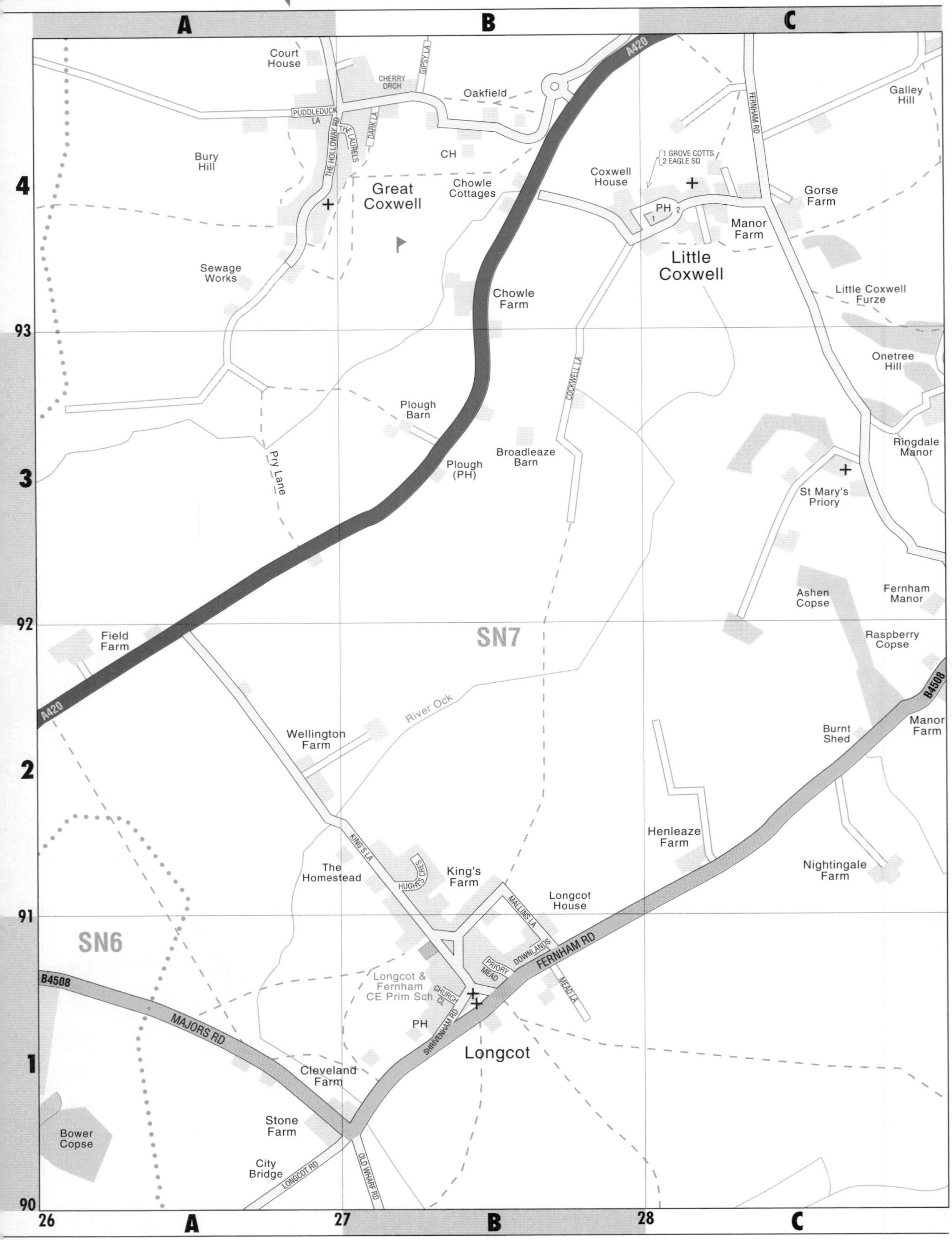
A
B
C
Court House
CHERRY ORCH
GIPSY LA
Oakfield
PUDDLEDUCK LA
THE HOLLOWAY RD
THE LAURELS
DARK LA
A420
FERNHAM RD
Galley Hill
Bury Hill
CH
1 GROVE COTTS
2 EAGLE SQ
Coxwell House
Great Coxwell
Chowle Cottages
PH
Manor Farm
Gorse Farm
Little Coxwell
Sewage Works
Chowle Farm
Little Coxwell Furze
Onetree Hill
COCKWELL LA
Plough Barn
Ringdale Manor
Broadleaze Barn
Pry Lane
Plough (PH)
St Mary's Priory
Ashen Copse
Fernham Manor
Field Farm
SN7
Raspberry Copse
River Ock
B4508
Wellington Farm
Burnt Shed
Manor Farm
Henleaze Farm
KING'S LA
The Homestead
HUGHES CRES
King's Farm
Nightingale Farm
Longcot House
MALLINS LA
SN6
DOWNLANDS
FERNHAM RD
PRIORY MEAD
B4508
Longcot & Fernham CE Prim Sch
CHURCH CL
MEAD LA
MAJORS RD
PH
SHRIVENHAM RD
Longcot
Cleveland Farm
Stone Farm
Bower Copse
City Bridge
LONGCOT RD
OLD WHARF RD
4
93
3
92
2
91
1
90
26
27
28

191
210

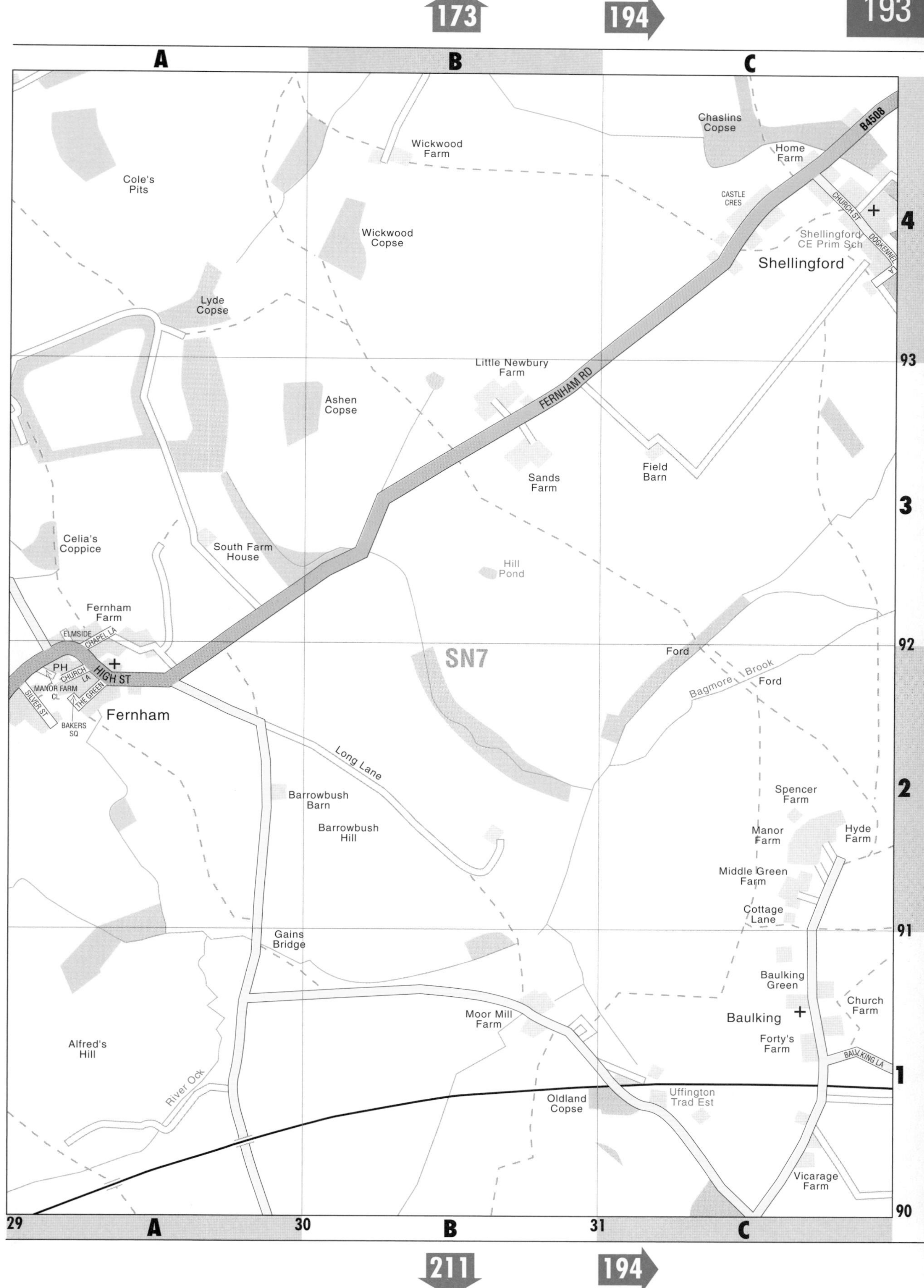

A
B
C

Cole's Pits

Wickwood Farm

Chaslins Copse

B4508

Home Farm

CASTLE CRES

Shellingford CE Prim Sch

Wickwood Copse

4

Shellingford

CHURCH ST

DOCKENNEL

Lyde Copse

93

Ashen Copse

Little Newbury Farm

FERNHAM RD

Celia's Coppice

Sands Farm

Field Barn

3

South Farm House

Hill Pond

Fernham Farm

Ford

ELMSIDE

CHAPEL LA

SN7

Bagmore Brook

Ford

92

PH

CHURCH LA

HIGH ST

MANOR FARM CL

SILVER ST

THE GREEN

Spencer Farm

BAKERS SQ

Fernham

Manor Farm

Hyde Farm

2

Long Lane

Middle Green Farm

Barrowbush Barn

Cottage Lane

Barrowbush Hill

91

Gains Bridge

Baulking Green

Baulking

Church Farm

Moor Mill Farm

Alfred's Hill

Forty's Farm

River Ock

Uffington Trad Est

1

BAULKING LA

Oldland Copse

Vicarage Farm

90

29
A
30
B
31
C

193
174

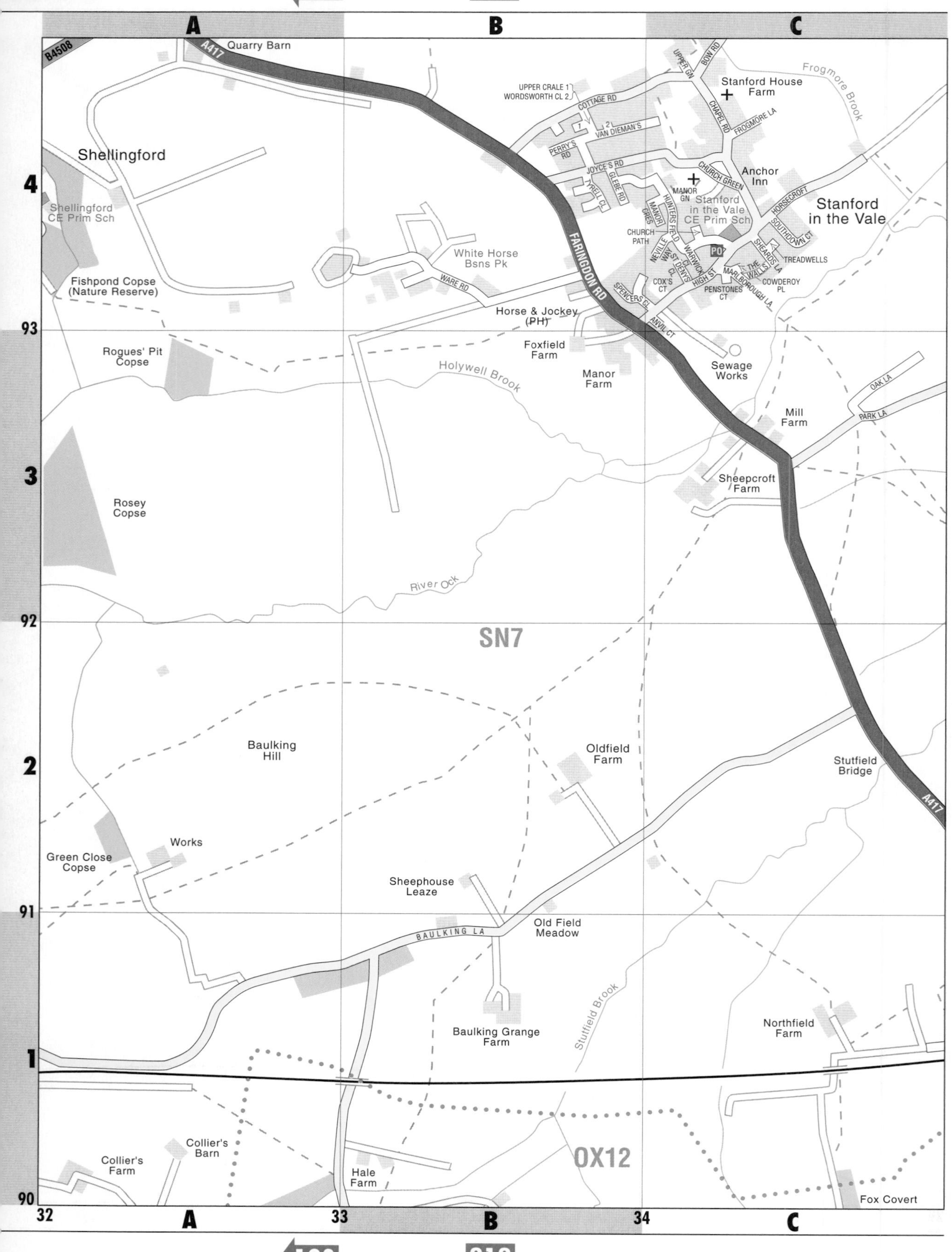
A
B
C
B4508
A417
Quarry Barn
Shellingford
Shellingford CE Prim Sch
Fishpond Copse (Nature Reserve)
Rogues' Pit Copse
Rosey Copse
White Horse Bsns Pk
WARE RD
Horse & Jockey (PH)
Foxfield Farm
Manor Farm
Holywell Brook
FARINGDON RD
UPPER CRALE 1
WORDSWORTH CL 2
COTTAGE RD
VAN DIEMAN'S
PERRY'S RD
JOYCE'S RD
TYRELL CL
GLEBE RD
MANOR GN
MANOR CRES
HUNTERS FIELD
CHURCH PATH
NEVILLE WAY
ST DENYS CL
WARWICK CL
COX'S CT
SPENCERS CL
ANVIL CT
HIGH ST
PENSTONES CT
MARLBOROUGH LA
COWDEROY PL
THE WALLS
SHEARDS LA
TREADWELLS
SOUTHDOWN CT
HORSECROFT
CHURCH GREEN
UPPER GN
BOW RD
CHAPEL RD
FROGMORE LA
Frogmore Brook
Stanford House Farm
Anchor Inn
Stanford in the Vale CE Prim Sch
Stanford in the Vale
PO
Sewage Works
Mill Farm
OAK LA
PARK LA
Sheepcroft Farm
River Ock
SN7
Baulking Hill
Oldfield Farm
Stutfield Bridge
A417
Works
Green Close Copse
Sheephouse Leaze
Old Field Meadow
BAULKING LA
Baulking Grange Farm
Stutfield Brook
Northfield Farm
Collier's Barn
Collier's Farm
Hale Farm
OX12
Fox Covert
4
93
3
92
2
91
1
90
32
33
34
A
B
C

193
212

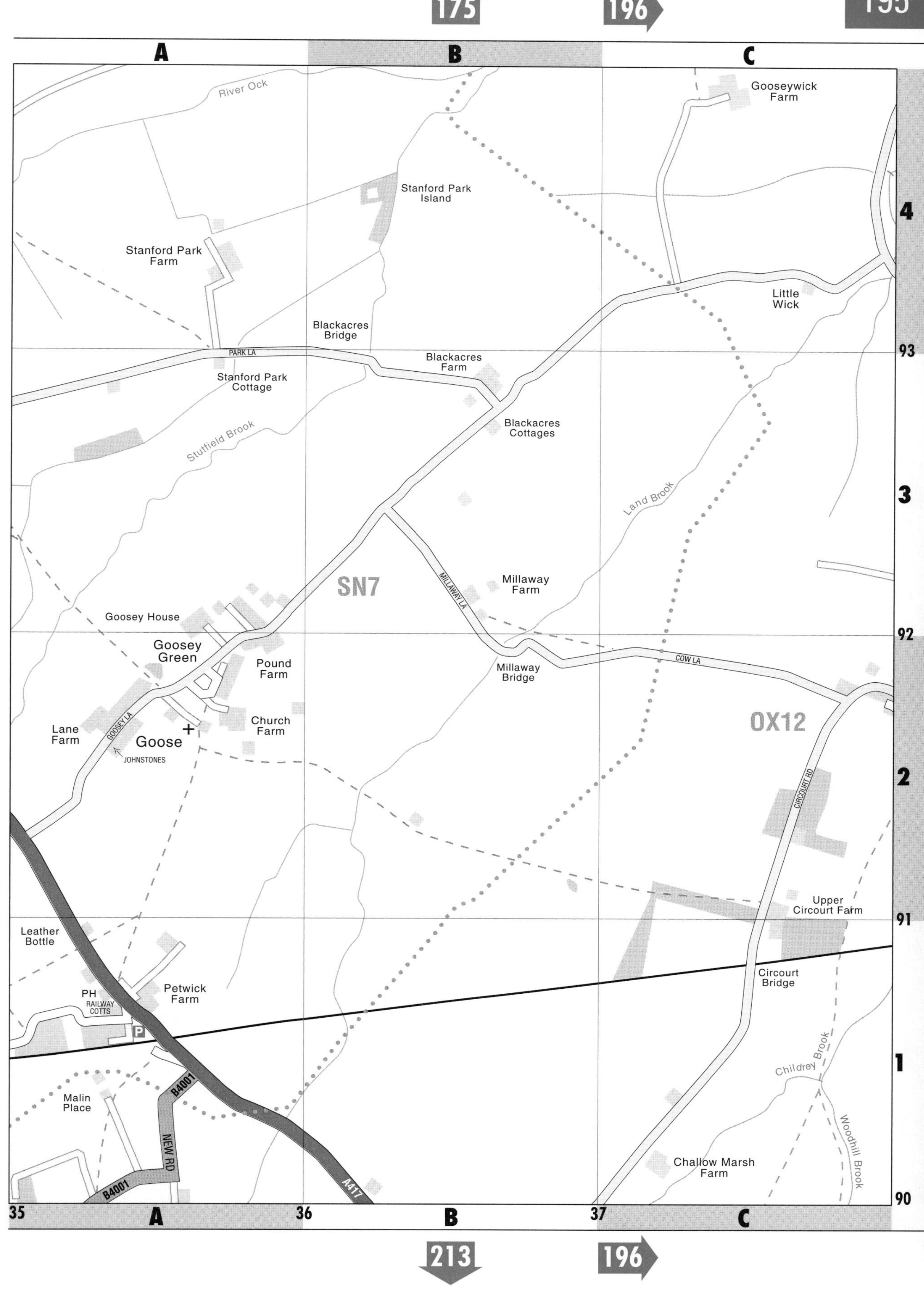

A B C

River Ock

Gooseywick Farm

Stanford Park Island

4

Stanford Park Farm

Little Wick

Blackacres Bridge

PARK LA

93

Stanford Park Cottage

Blackacres Farm

Stutfield Brook

Blackacres Cottages

Land Brook

3

SN7

MILLAWAY LA

Millaway Farm

Goosey House

92

Goosey Green

Pound Farm

Millaway Bridge

COW LA

Lane Farm

Church Farm

Goose

+

OX12

JOHNSTONES

GOOSEY LA

2

Upper Circourt Farm

CIRCOURT RD

91

Leather Bottle

Circourt Bridge

PH

RAILWAY COTTS

Petwick Farm

Childrey Brook

1

P

Woodhill Brook

Malin Place

B4001

NEW RD

Challow Marsh Farm

B4001

A417

90

A   B   C

4

Land Brook

Hedges Farm

Bailey's Mead Copse

Botney Meadows

NORTHMEAD LA

Flapp's Barn

RECTORY FARM CL

NORTH GN

WINTER LA

THE CROFT

THE MEADS

Lamb (PH)

93

Grange Farm

Hyde Farm

MONKS CL

THE GREEN

SCHOOL RD

MAIN ST

CHURCH ST

West Hanney

Lydbrook Farm

Childrey Brook

Pike's Barn

Manor Farm

3

HYDE RD

South Denchworth Farm

Cow La

92

KIMBERS CL

BROOK LA

Denchworth

Brooklane Bridge

Hill Barn

Sewage Works

COW LA

Bradfield Grove Farm

OX12

CIRCOURT RD

2

Hanney Bridge

Works

Grove Wick Farm

A338

91

Denchworth Road Bridge

DENCHWORTH RD

Monk's Farm

VESTRY CL

CHURCHWARD CL

THE MAPLES

Townsend

Grove CE Sch

TULWICK LA

STEPTOE CL

WICK GN

WESTBROOK

NORTH DR

The Green

OXFORD LA

1

FULMAR PL 1
HAWKSWORTH CL 2

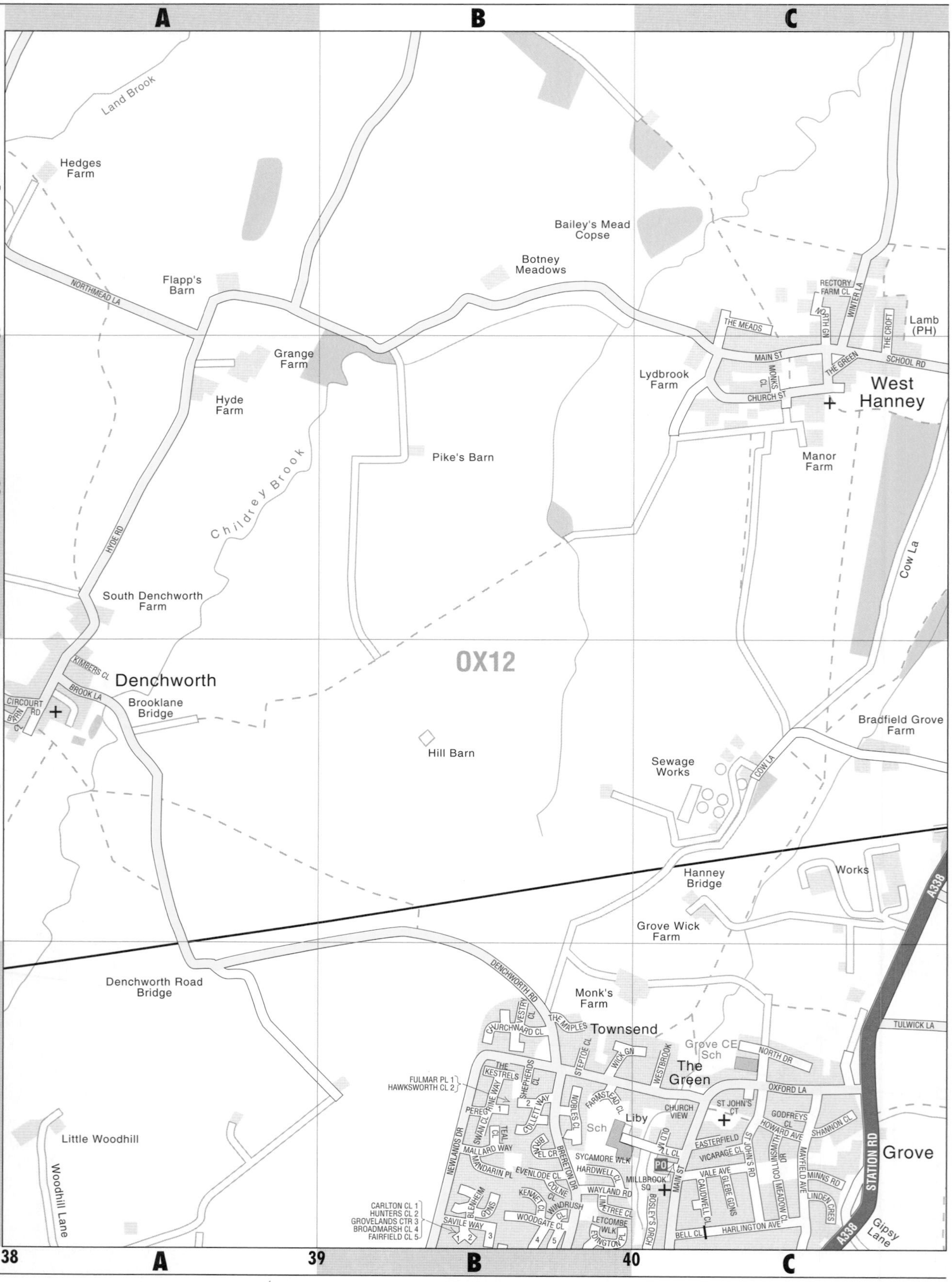

THE KESTRELS

SHEPHERDS CL

FARMSTEAD CL

ST JOHN'S CT

GODFREYS CL

SHANNON CL

CATHERINE WAY

COLLETT WAY

Sch

CHURCH VIEW

Liby

NOBLES CL

Grove

Little Woodhill

NEWLANDS DR

PEREGRINE

TEAL

GREEN CR

SYCAMORE WLK

Easterfield

HOWARD AVE

HURST(NICK) MEADOW

MAYFIELD RD

LINDEN CRES

MALLARD WAY

MANDARIN PL

EVENLODE CL

COLNE

HARDWELL CL

WAYLAND RD

VICARAGE CL

VALE AVE

CAUDWELL CL

GLEBE GDNS

MINNS RD

STATION RD

Woodhill Lane

BLENHEIM GDNS

SWAN CL

KENNET CL

WINDRUSH

BREWERTON

PO

MILLBROOK SQ

TREE CL

ST JOHN'S RD

ELLINGTON

BOSLEY'S ORCH

LETCOMBE WLK

BELL CL

HARLINGTON AVE

A338

Gipsy Lane

CARLTON CL 1
HUNTERS CL 2
GROVELANDS CTR 3
BROADMARSH CL 4
FAIRFIELD CL 5

SAVILE WAY

WOODGATE CL

90

38   A   39   B   40   C

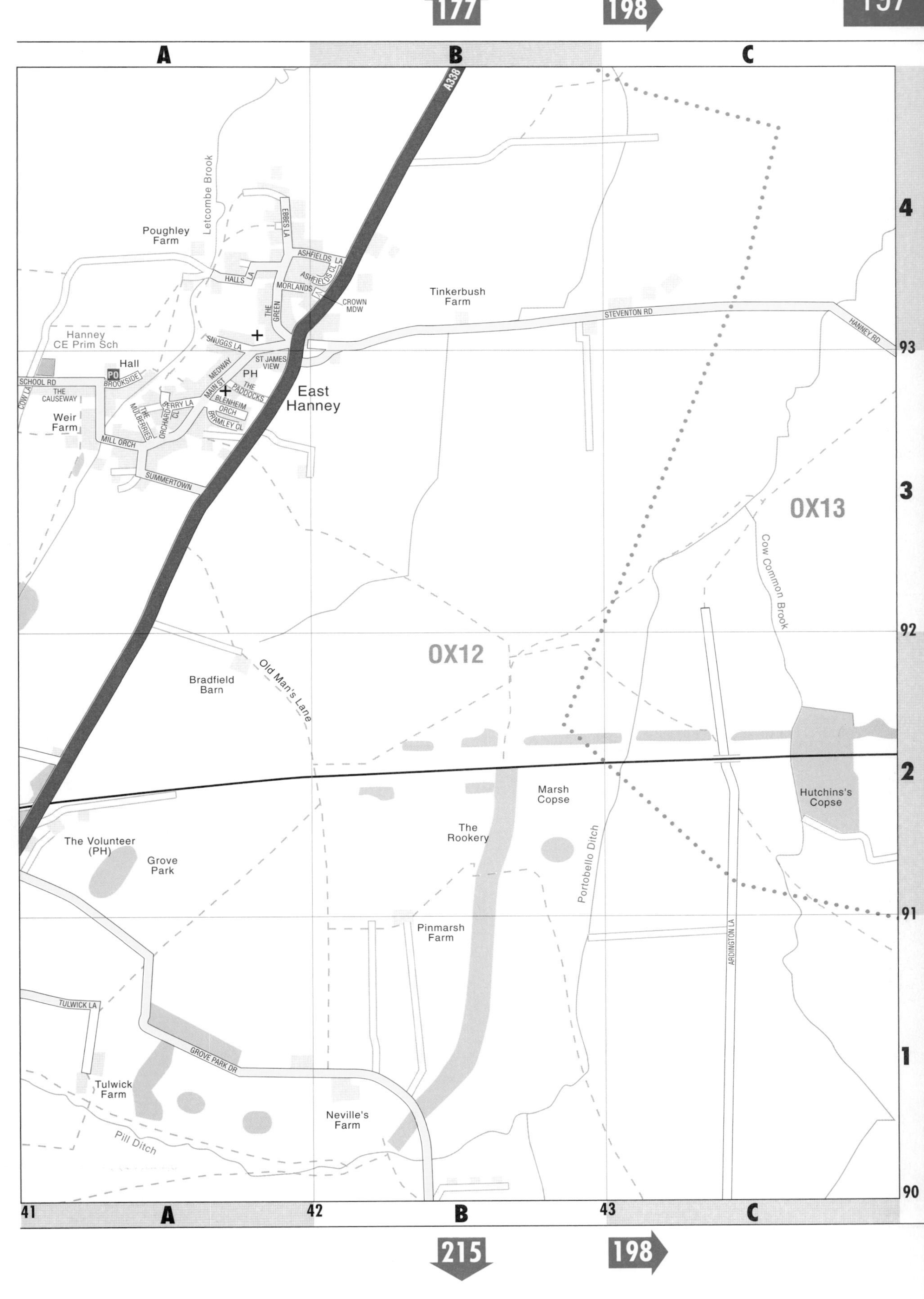

177
198
215
198

A B C

Poughley Farm

Letcombe Brook

A338

EBBS LA

ASHFIELDS LA

ASHFIELDS CL

HALLS LA

MORLANDS

CROWN MDW

Tinkerbush Farm

STEVENTON RD

HANNEY RD

Hanney CE Prim Sch

THE GREEN

SNUGGS LA

ST JAMES VIEW

PH

East Hanney

4

93

Hall

PO

SCHOOL RD

THE CAUSEWAY

COW LA

BROOKSIDE

MEDWAY

MAIN ST

BLENHEIM

ORCH

THE PADDOCKS

Weir Farm

THE MULBERRIES

ORCHARD CL

PERRY LA

BRAMLEY CL

MILL ORCH

SUMMERTOWN

OX13

Cow Common Brook

3

92

OX12

Bradfield Barn

Old Man's Lane

Marsh Copse

Hutchins's Copse

2

The Volunteer (PH)

Grove Park

The Rookery

Portobello Ditch

ARDINGTON LA

91

TULWICK LA

GROVE PARK DR

Pinmarsh Farm

1

Tulwick Farm

Neville's Farm

Pill Ditch

90

41 42 43

A B C

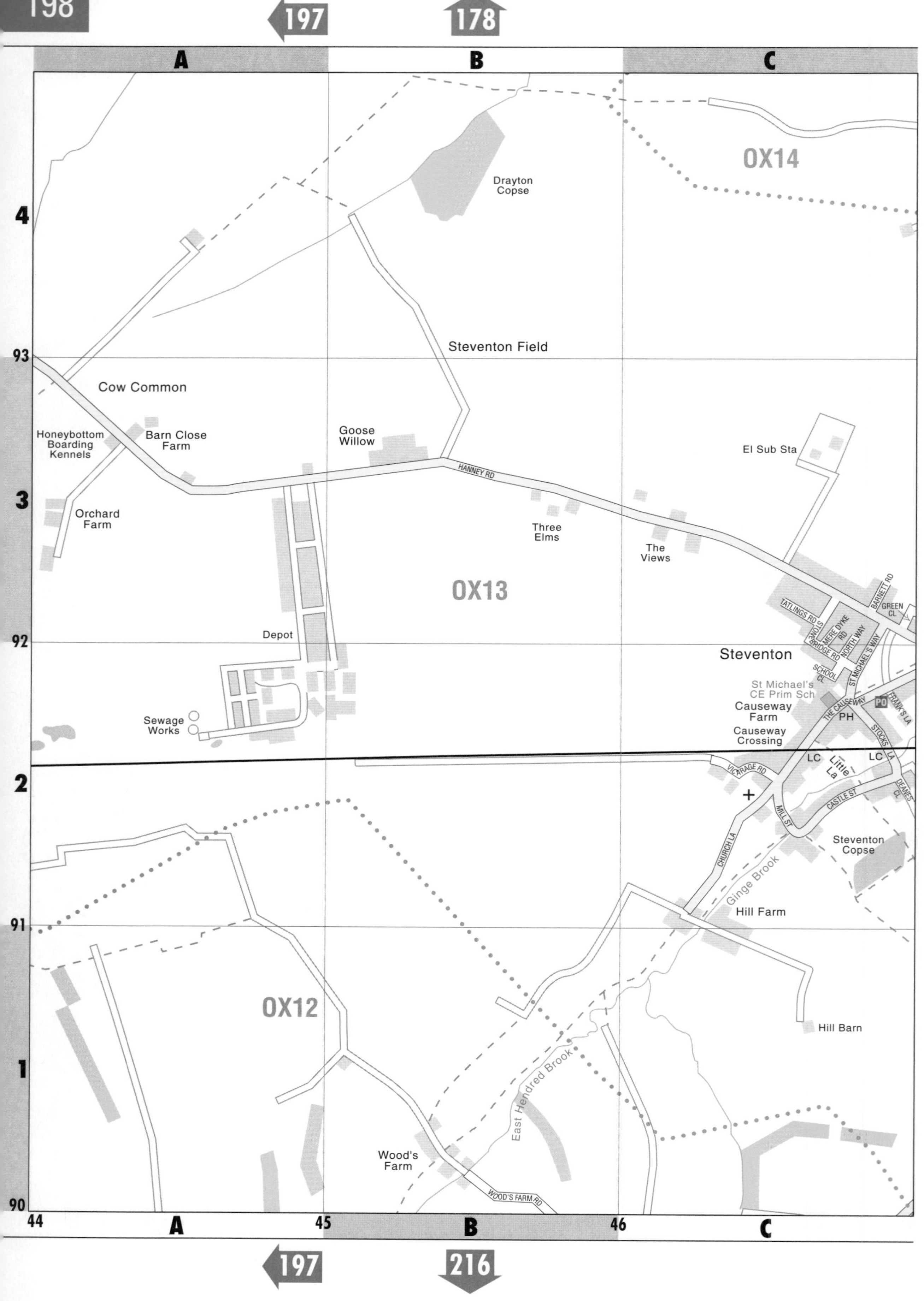

A B C

OX14

Drayton Copse

4

Steventon Field

93

Cow Common

Honeybottom Boarding Kennels

Barn Close Farm

Goose Willow

El Sub Sta

HANNEY RD

3

Orchard Farm

Three Elms

The Views

OX13

BARRETT RD

GREEN CL

TATLINGS RD

CRIDGE RD

MERE DYKE RD

NORTH WAY

Depot

92

Steventon

ST MICHAEL'S WAY

SCHOOL CL

FRANK'S LA

St Michael's CE Prim Sch

Causeway Farm

Causeway Crossing

THE CAUSEWAY

PO

PH

STOCKS LA

Sewage Works

LC

Little La

LC

DEARS?

VICARAGE RD

2

+

CASTLE ST

Steventon Copse

CHURCH LA

MILL ST

Ginge Brook

Hill Farm

91

OX12

Hill Barn

East Hendred Brook

1

Wood's Farm

WOOD'S FARM RD

90

44 A 45 B 46 C

179
200

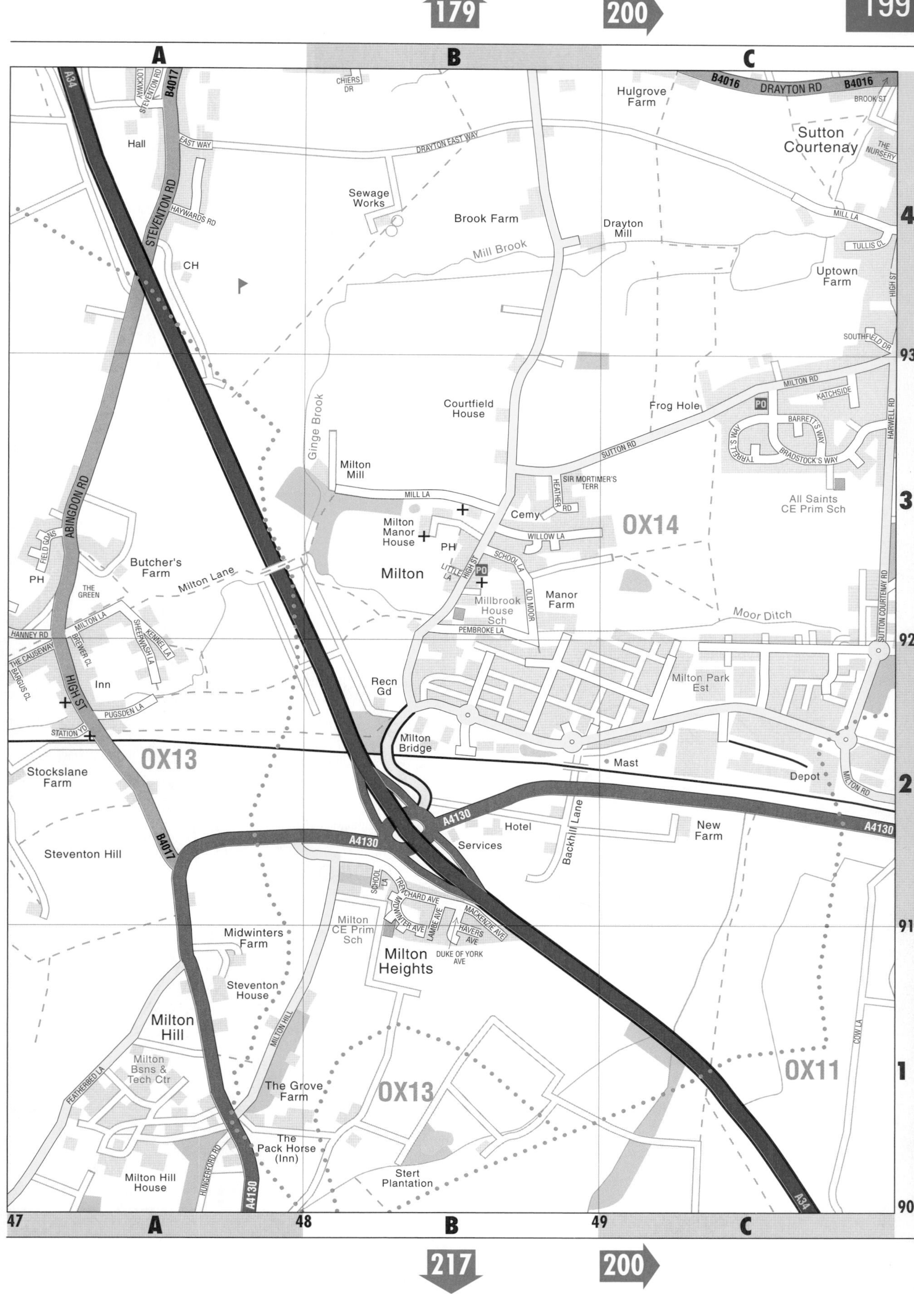
A
B
C
Hall
CH
Sewage Works
Brook Farm
Drayton Mill
Mill Brook
Hulgrove Farm
Sutton Courtenay
Uptown Farm
Courtfield House
Frog Hole
Milton Mill
Milton Manor House
PH
Cemy
OX14
Milton
Butcher's Farm
Milton Lane
Manor Farm
Millbrook House Sch
All Saints CE Prim Sch
Moor Ditch
Milton Park Est
Recn Gd
Inn
Milton Bridge
OX13
Stockslane Farm
Mast
Depot
Hotel
New Farm
Services
Steventon Hill
Midwinters Farm
Milton CE Prim Sch
Milton Heights
Steventon House
Milton Hill
Milton Bsns & Tech Ctr
The Grove Farm
OX13
OX11
The Pack Horse (Inn)
Stert Plantation
Milton Hill House
Ginge Brook
Backhill Lane
A34
A4130
B4017
B4016
DRAYTON RD
DRAYTON EAST WAY
EAST WAY
STEVENTON RD
HAYWARDS RD
ABINGDON RD
HIGH ST
MILL LA
SUTTON RD
MILTON RD
WILLOW LA
SCHOOL LA
PEMBROKE LA
TULLIS CL
HARWELL RD
SUTTON COURTENAY RD
COW LA
HUNGERFORD RD
FEATHERBED LA
MILTON HILL
4
3
2
1
93
92
91
90
47
48
49

217
200

199
180

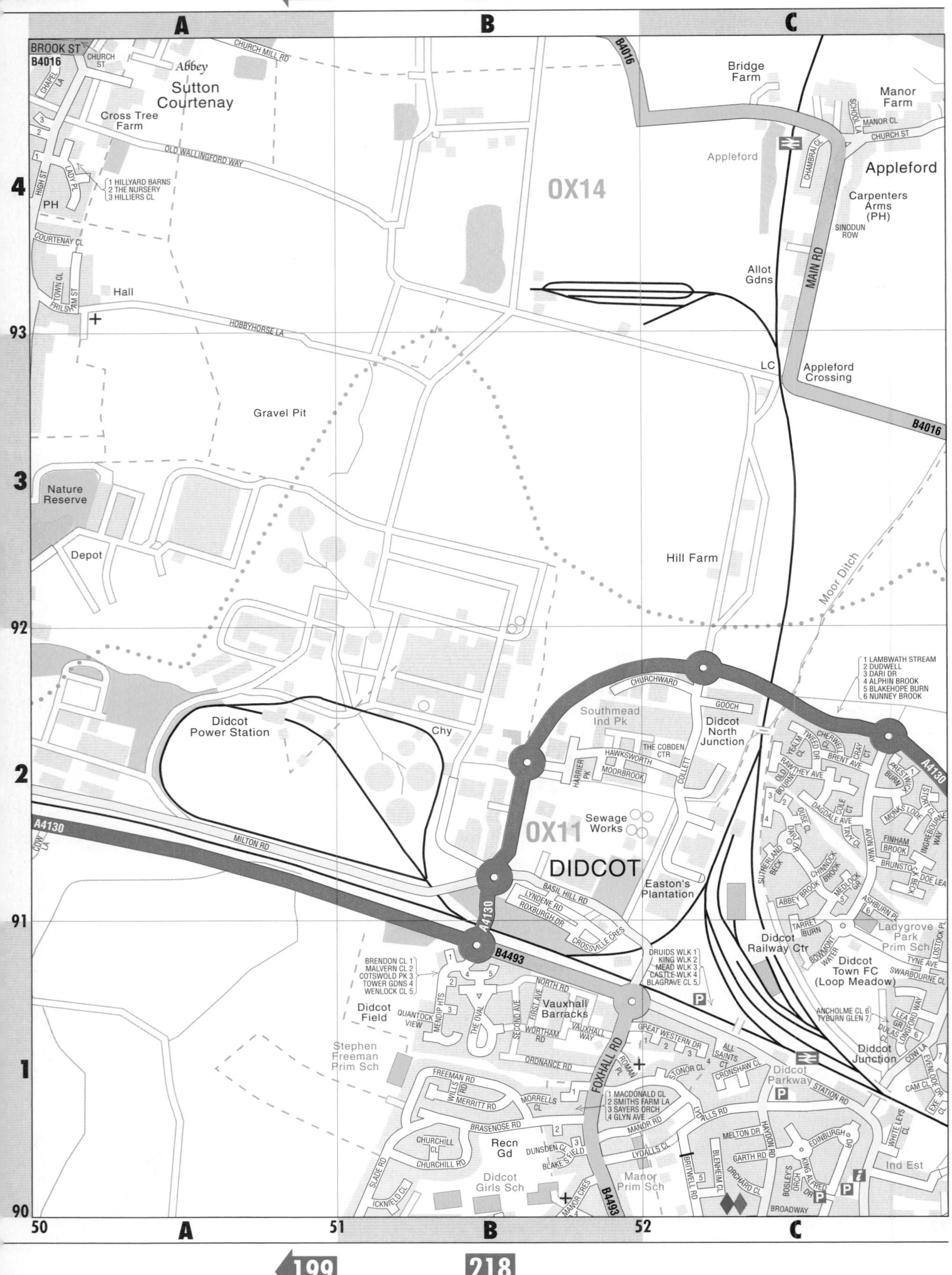
A
B
C
Sutton Courtenay
Abbey
Cross Tree Farm
Bridge Farm
Manor Farm
Appleford
Carpenters Arms (PH)
OX14
Allot Gdns
Hall
Appleford Crossing
LC
Gravel Pit
Nature Reserve
Depot
Hill Farm
Moor Ditch
Didcot Power Station
Chy
Southmead Ind Pk
Didcot North Junction
Sewage Works
OX11
DIDCOT
Easton's Plantation
Didcot Railway Ctr
Ladygrove Park Prim Sch
Didcot Town FC (Loop Meadow)
Didcot Field
Vauxhall Barracks
Stephen Freeman Prim Sch
Didcot Parkway
Didcot Junction
Recn Gd
Didcot Girls Sch
Manor Prim Sch
Ind Est
1 HILLYARD BARNS
2 THE NURSERY
3 HILLIERS CL
1 LAMBWATH STREAM
2 DUDWELL
3 DARI DR
4 ALPHIN BROOK
5 BLAKEHOPE BURN
6 NUNNEY BROOK
BRENDON CL 1
MALVERN CL 2
COTSWOLD PK 3
TOWER GDNS 4
WENLOCK CL 5
DRUIDS WLK 1
KING WLK 2
MEAD WLK 3
CASTLE WLK 4
BLAGRAVE CL 5
1 MACDONALD CL
2 SMITHS FARM LA
3 SAYERS ORCH
4 GLYN AVE
ANCHOLME CL 6
TYBURN GLEN 7
B4016
A4130
B4493
50
51
52
90
91
92
93
1
2
3
4

199
218

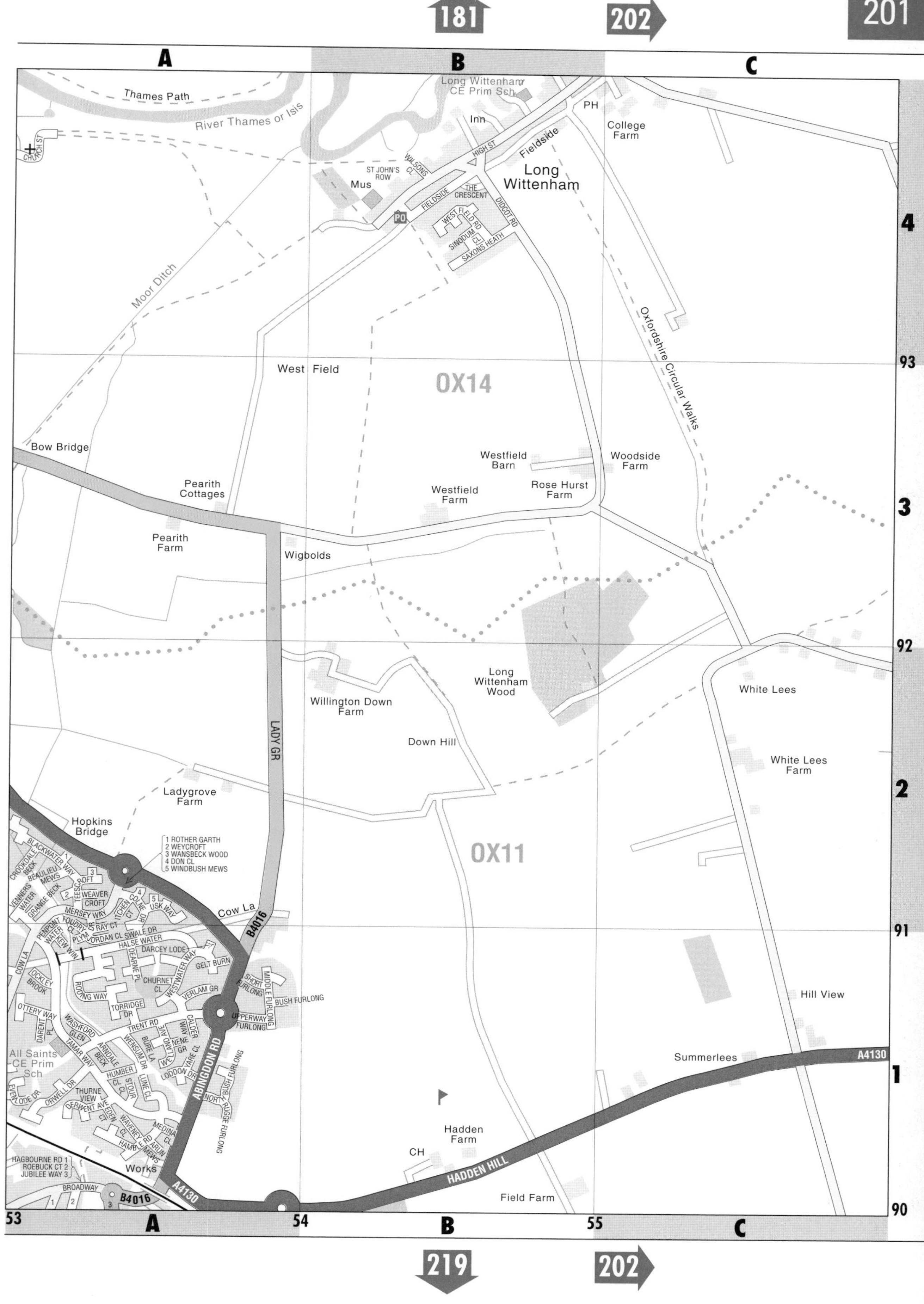

A B C

Thames Path

River Thames or Isis

CHURCH ST

Long Wittenham
CE Prim Sch

Inn

PH

High St

Fieldside

College
Farm

St John's
Row

WILSONS CL

Mus

FIELDSIDE

THE
CRESCENT

WEST FIELD RD

DIDCOT RD

Long
Wittenham

PO.

SINODUM CL

SAXONS HEATH

Moor Ditch

West Field

OX14

93

Bow Bridge

Westfield
Barn

Woodside
Farm

Oxfordshire Circular Walks

Pearith
Cottages

Westfield
Farm

Rose Hurst
Farm

3

Pearith
Farm

Wigbolds

LADY GR

92

Willington Down
Farm

Long
Wittenham
Wood

White Lees

Down Hill

White Lees
Farm

Hopkins
Bridge

Ladygrove
Farm

OX11

2

1 ROTHER GARTH
2 WEYCROFT
3 WANSBECK WOOD
4 DON CL
5 WINDBUSH MEWS

BLACKWATER WAY

CROXDALE

BEAULIEU
MEWS

WATER
BECK

CROFT

VERMERS
WATER

WEAVER
CROFT

GRANGE BECK

Cow La

B4016

MERSEY WAY

PIERPONT
WATER CL

ITCHEL
COURT

5 USK WAY

PLYM CL
JORDAN CL

RAY CT

SWALE DR

COLNE
CT

WAVENEY WYN

DARCEY LODE

Hill View

COW LA

LOCKLEY
BROOK

HALSE WATER

DEARNE PL

GELT BURN

SHORT
FURLONG

MIDDLE FURLONG

BUSH FURLONG

OTTERY WAY

WASHFORD
GLEN

CHURNET
CL

RIDING WAY

TORRIDGE
DR

WESTWATER WAY

VERLAM GR

UPPERWAY
FURLONG

ABINGDON RD

DARENT
PL

TAMAR WAY

TRENT RD

CALDER
WAY

NENE GR

DART CL

BIRLING FURLONG

OTHER FURLONG

AUGER FURLONG

All Saints
CE Prim
Sch

THURNE
VIEW

ORWELL DR

BRENDLE
CL

BURE LA

LODDON BR

HUMBER
CL

DERWENT AVE

STOUR CL

LINE CL

Summerlees

A4130

1

EXE LODE DR

WALENEY RD

MEDINA
CL

HAMB MEWS

Hadden
Farm

HAGBOURNE RD 1
ROEBUCK CT 2
JUBILEE WAY 3

Works

CH

BROADWAY

B4016

1 2 3

A4016

A4130

HADDEN HILL

Field Farm

53 54 55 90

A B C

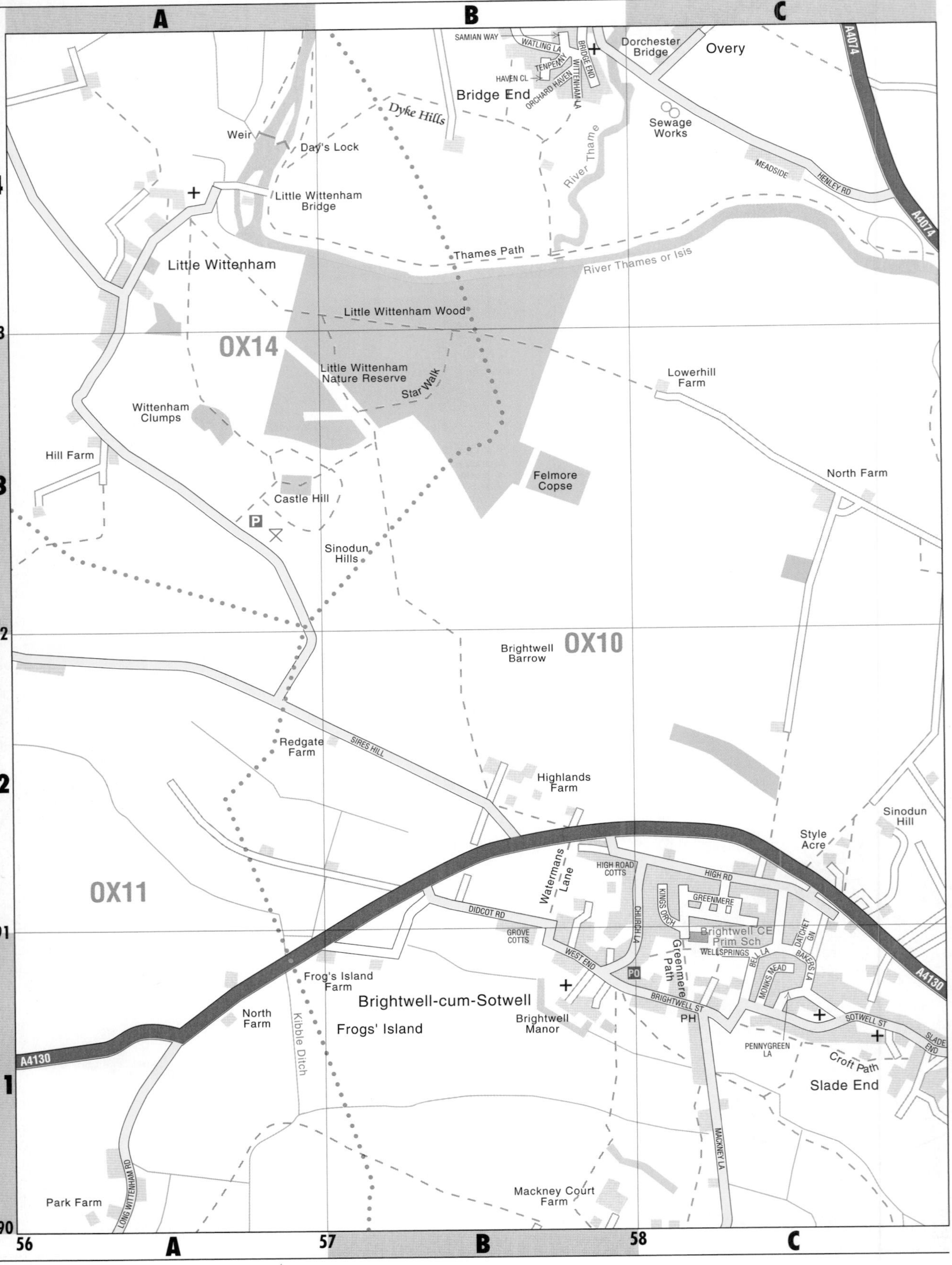

A B C

SAMIAN WAY
WATLING LA
TENPENY
HAVEN CL
ORCHARD HAVEN
WITTENHAM LA
BRIDGE END
Bridge End
Dorchester Bridge
Overy

Dyke Hills
Sewage Works

Weir
Day's Lock

River Thame

MEADSIDE
HENLEY RD
A4074

Little Wittenham Bridge

4

Little Wittenham

Thames Path
River Thames or Isis

OX14

Little Wittenham Wood

93

Little Wittenham Nature Reserve
Star Walk

Lowerhill Farm

Wittenham Clumps

Hill Farm

Felmore Copse

North Farm

3

Castle Hill
P

Sinodun Hills

Brightwell Barrow
OX10

92

Redgate Farm
SIRES HILL

Highlands Farm

Sinodun Hill

2

OX11

Style Acre

Watermans Lane
HIGH ROAD COTTS
HIGH RD
GREENMERE
KINGS DITCH
Brightwell CE Prim Sch
DATCHET GN

DIDCOT RD
GROVE COTTS
WEST END
CHURCH LA
Greenmere Path
WELLSPRINGS
BELL LA
MONKS MEAD
BAKERS LA

91

Frog's Island Farm
PO
BRIGHTWELL ST
PH
SOTWELL ST
SLADE END
A4130

North Farm
Brightwell-cum-Sotwell
Frogs' Island
Brightwell Manor
PENNYGREEN LA
Croft Path
Slade End

A4130
Kibble Ditch

1

LONG WITTENHAM RD

Park Farm

Mackney Court Farm

MACKNEY LA

90

56 A 57 B 58 C

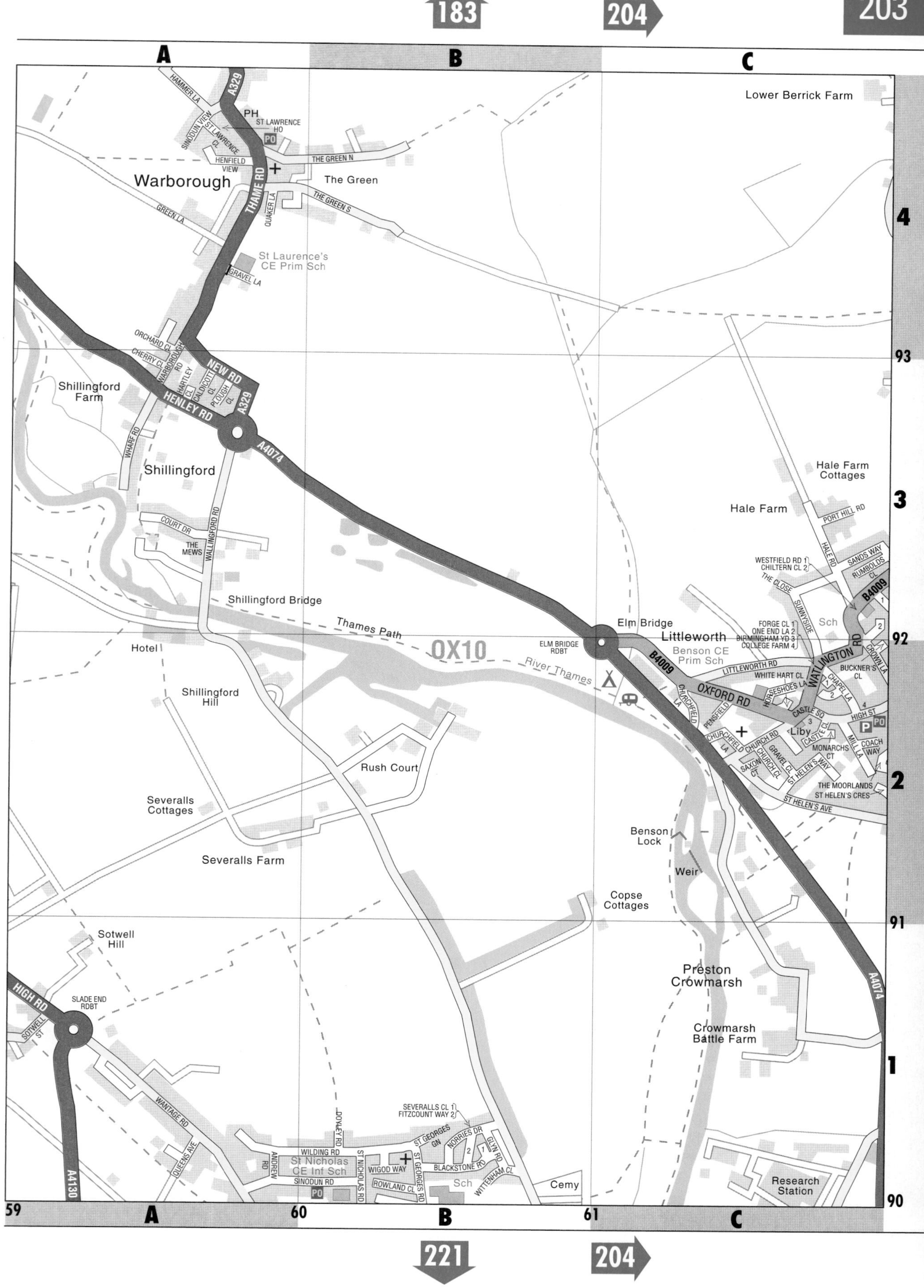

A B C

Lower Berrick Farm

4

HAMMER LA

A329

PH
ST LAWRENCE HO
PO
ST LAWRENCE CL

SINODUN VIEW

HENFIELD VIEW

Warborough

THE GREEN N

The Green

GREEN LA

THAME RD

QUAKER LA

THE GREEN S

St Laurence's
CE Prim Sch

GRAVEL LA

93

ORCHARD CL

CHERRY CL

HARTLEY CL

WARBOROUGH RD

CALDICOTT CL

PLOUGH CL

NEW RD

A329

Shillingford
Farm

HENLEY RD

WHARF RD

Shillingford

A4074

Hale Farm
Cottages

3

Hale Farm

PORT HILL RD

HALE RD

WESTFIELD RD 1
CHILTERN CL 2

THE CLOSE

SANDS WAY

RUMBOLDS CL

B4009

COURT DR

WALLINGFORD RD

THE MEWS

Shillingford Bridge

Thames Path

OX10

Elm Bridge

ELM BRIDGE
RDBT

River Thames

Littleworth

Benson CE
Prim Sch

SUNNYSIDE

Sch

FORGE CL 1
ONE END LA 2
BIRMINGHAM YD 3
COLLEGE FARM 4

WATLINGTON RD

CROWN LA

92

Hotel

Shillingford
Hill

Rush Court

Severalls
Cottages

Severalls Farm

B4009

OXFORD RD

CHURCHFIELD LA

PENSFIELD LA

CHURCHFIELD LA

SAXON RD

GRAVEL CL

CHURCH CL

ST HELEN'S WAY

LITTLEWORTH RD

WHITE HART CL

HORSESHOES LA

ST HELEN'S AVE

CASTLE SQ

CHAPEL LA

BUCKNER'S CL

HIGH ST

MONARCHS
CT

COACH
WAY

Liby

PO

THE MOORLANDS
ST HELEN'S CRES

2

Benson
Lock

Weir

Copse
Cottages

91

Sotwell
Hill

HIGH RD

SOTWELL ST

SLADE END
RDBT

A4074

Preston
Crowmarsh

WANTAGE RD

QUEENS AVE

A4130

DONKEY RD

WILDING RD

ANDREW RD

ST NICHOLAS RD

St Nicholas
CE Inf Sch

PO

SINODUN RD

WIGOD WAY

ROWLAND CL

ST GEORGES
GN

NORRIES DR

ST GEORGES RD

BLACKSTONE RD

GLEBE RD

WITTENHAM CL

SEVERALLS CL 1
FITZCOUNT WAY 2

Sch

Cemy

Crowmarsh
Battle Farm

Research
Station

1

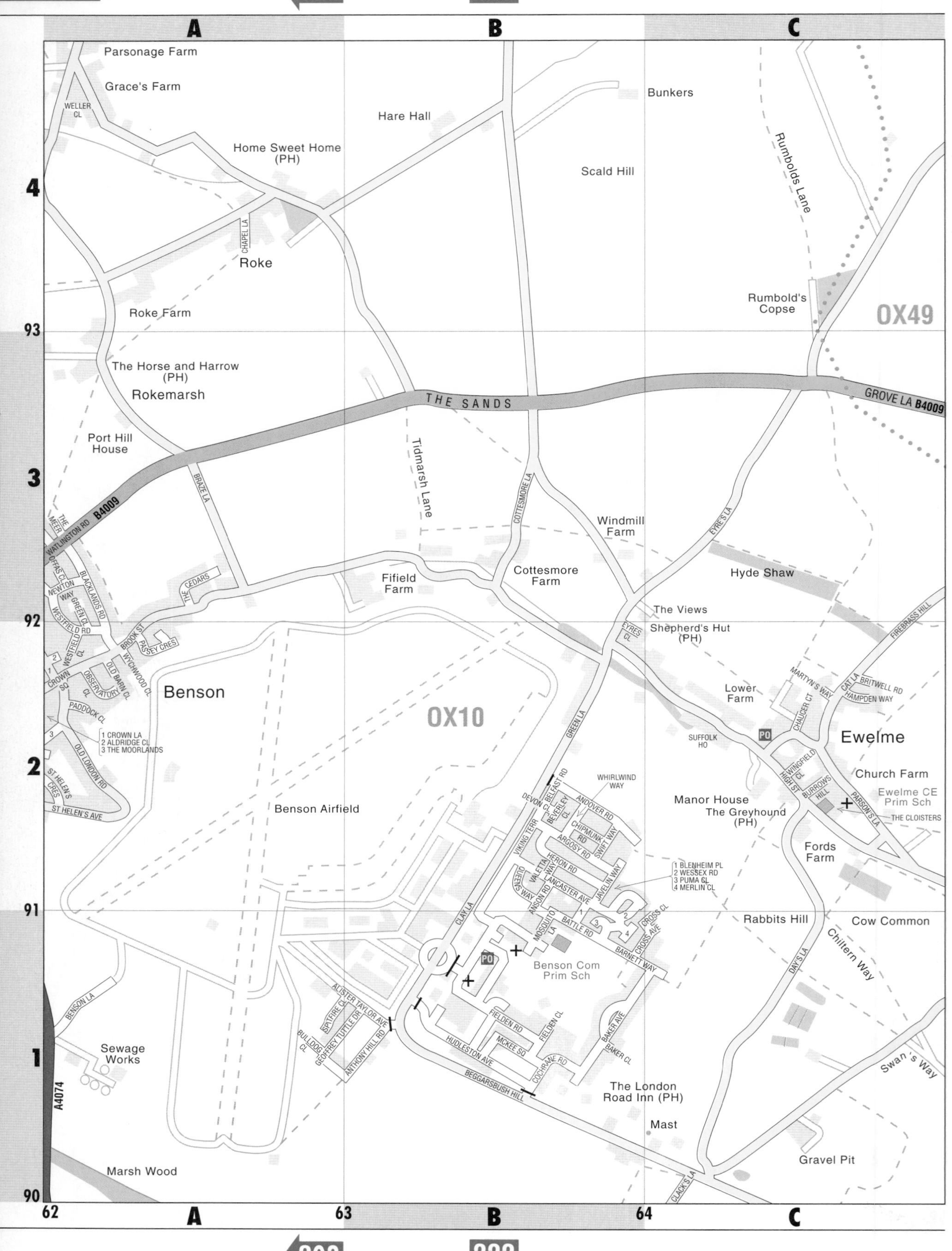

A   B   C

4

93

3

92

2

91

1

90

62   A   63   B   64   C

Parsonage Farm

Grace's Farm

WELLER CL

Home Sweet Home (PH)

Hare Hall

Bunkers

Scald Hill

Rumbolds Lane

CHAPEL LA

Roke

OX49

Rumbold's Copse

Roke Farm

The Horse and Harrow (PH)

Rokemarsh

THE SANDS

GROVE LA B4009

Port Hill House

Tidmarsh Lane

BRAZIL LA

COTTESMORE LA

Windmill Farm

EYRES LA

B4009

THE MEER

WATLINGTON RD

THE CEDARS

Fifield Farm

Cottesmore Farm

Hyde Shaw

DOUGLAS CL

NEWTON WAY

BLACKLANDS RD

GREEN CL

BROOK ST

PASSEY CRES

WYCHWOOD CL

OLD BARN CL

The Views

Shepherd's Hut (PH)

WESTFIELD RD

OBSERVATORY

Benson

OX10

EYRES CL

Lower Farm

MARTYN'S WAY

CL4

BRITWELL RD

HAMPDEN WAY

CROWN SQ

PADDOCK CL

1 CROWN LA
2 ALDRIDGE CL
3 THE MOORLANDS

GREEN LA

SUFFOLK HO

PO

CHAUCER CT

Ewelme

Church Farm

Ewelme CE Prim Sch

THE CLOISTERS

OLD LONDON RD

ST HELEN'S CRES

ST HELEN'S AVE

Benson Airfield

WHIRLWIND WAY

BELFAST RD

DEVON CL

BEVERLEY

ANDOVER RD

CHIPMUNK RD

SWIFT WAY

Manor House
The Greyhound (PH)

HIGH ST

BURROWS HILL

PARSON'S LA

WINGFIELD

Fords Farm

VIKING TERR

VALETTA WAY

HERON RD

ARGOSY RD

LANCASTER AVE

JAVELIN WAY

1 BLENHEIM PL
2 WESSEX RD
3 PUMA CL
4 MERLIN CL

QUEENS AVE

ANSON RD

MOSQUITO LA

BATTLE RD

CROSS CL

CROSS AVE

Rabbits Hill

Cow Common

DAY'S LA

Chiltern Way

CLAY LA

PO

Benson Com Prim Sch

BARNETT WAY

BAKER AVE

BAKER CL

AUSTER TAYLOR AVE

SPITFIRE CL

GEOFFREY TUTTLE DR

BULLDOG CL

ANTHONY HILL RD

FIELDEN RD

MCKEE SQ

FIELDEN CL

Swan's Way

Sewage Works

A4074

BENSON LA

HUDLESTON AVE

COCHRANE RD

BEGGARSBUSH HILL

The London Road Inn (PH)

Mast

Gravel Pit

CLACK'S LA

Marsh Wood

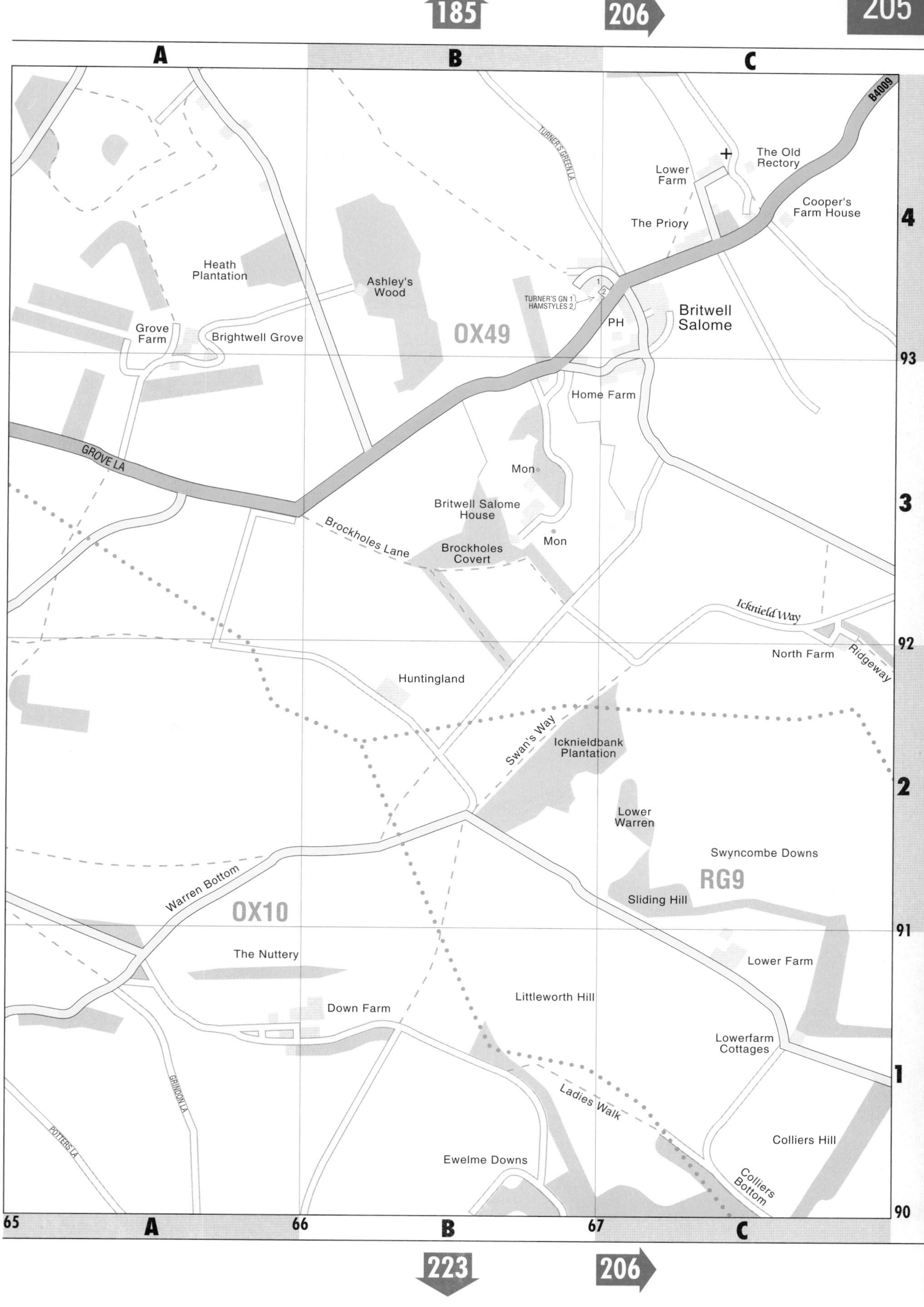

A B C

B4009

The Old Rectory

Lower Farm

Cooper's Farm House

The Priory

TURNER'S GREEN LA

Heath Plantation

Ashley's Wood

OX49

TURNER'S GN 1
HAMSTYLES 2

1
2

PH

Britwell Salome

Grove Farm

Brightwell Grove

Home Farm

GROVE LA

Mon

Britwell Salome House

Mon

Brockholes Lane

Brockholes Covert

Icknield Way

North Farm

Ridgeway

Huntingland

Swan's Way

Icknieldbank Plantation

Lower Warren

Swyncombe Downs

RG9

Sliding Hill

Warren Bottom

OX10

The Nuttery

Lower Farm

Littleworth Hill

Down Farm

Lowerfarm Cottages

GRINDON LA

Ladies Walk

Colliers Hill

POTTERS LA

Ewelme Downs

Colliers Bottom

205
186

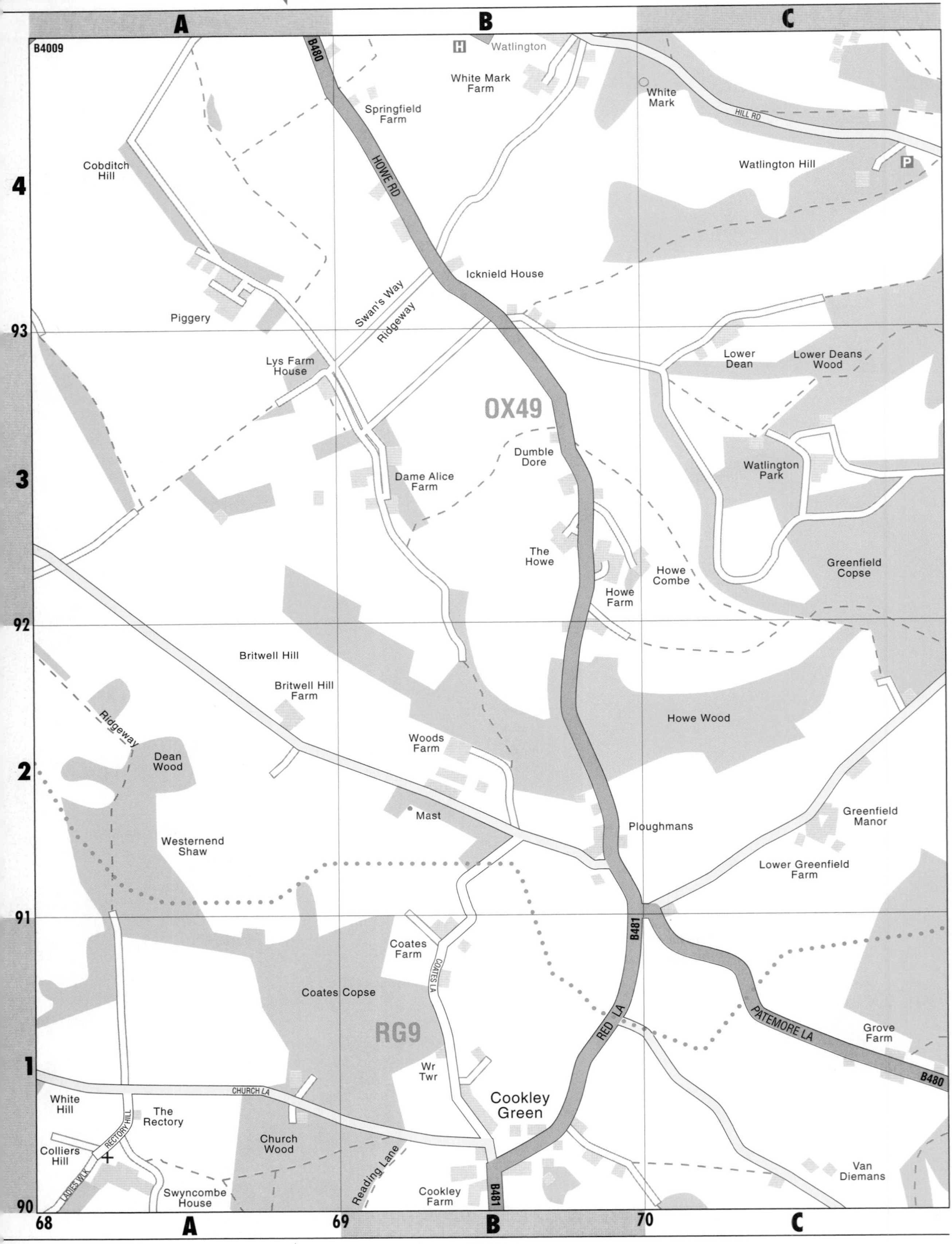

B4009

A   B   C

H Watlington

White Mark Farm

White Mark

B480

Springfield Farm

HILL RD

Watlington Hill

Cobditch Hill

4

P

Piggery

HOWE RD

Swan's Way

Ridgeway

Icknield House

93

Lys Farm House

Lower Dean

Lower Deans Wood

OX49

Dumble Dore

Dame Alice Farm

Watlington Park

3

The Howe

Howe Combe

Howe Farm

Greenfield Copse

92

Britwell Hill

Britwell Hill Farm

Howe Wood

Ridgeway

Dean Wood

Woods Farm

2

Mast

Ploughmans

Greenfield Manor

Westernend Shaw

Lower Greenfield Farm

91

B481

Coates Farm

COATES LA

PATEMORE LA

Coates Copse

RED LA

Grove Farm

RG9

Wr Twr

Cookley Green

B480

1

CHURCH LA

White Hill

The Rectory

RECTORY HILL

Church Wood

Van Diemans

Colliers Hill

+

LADIES WLK

Swyncombe House

Reading Lane

Cookley Farm

B481

90

68   A   69   B   70   C

205
224

187

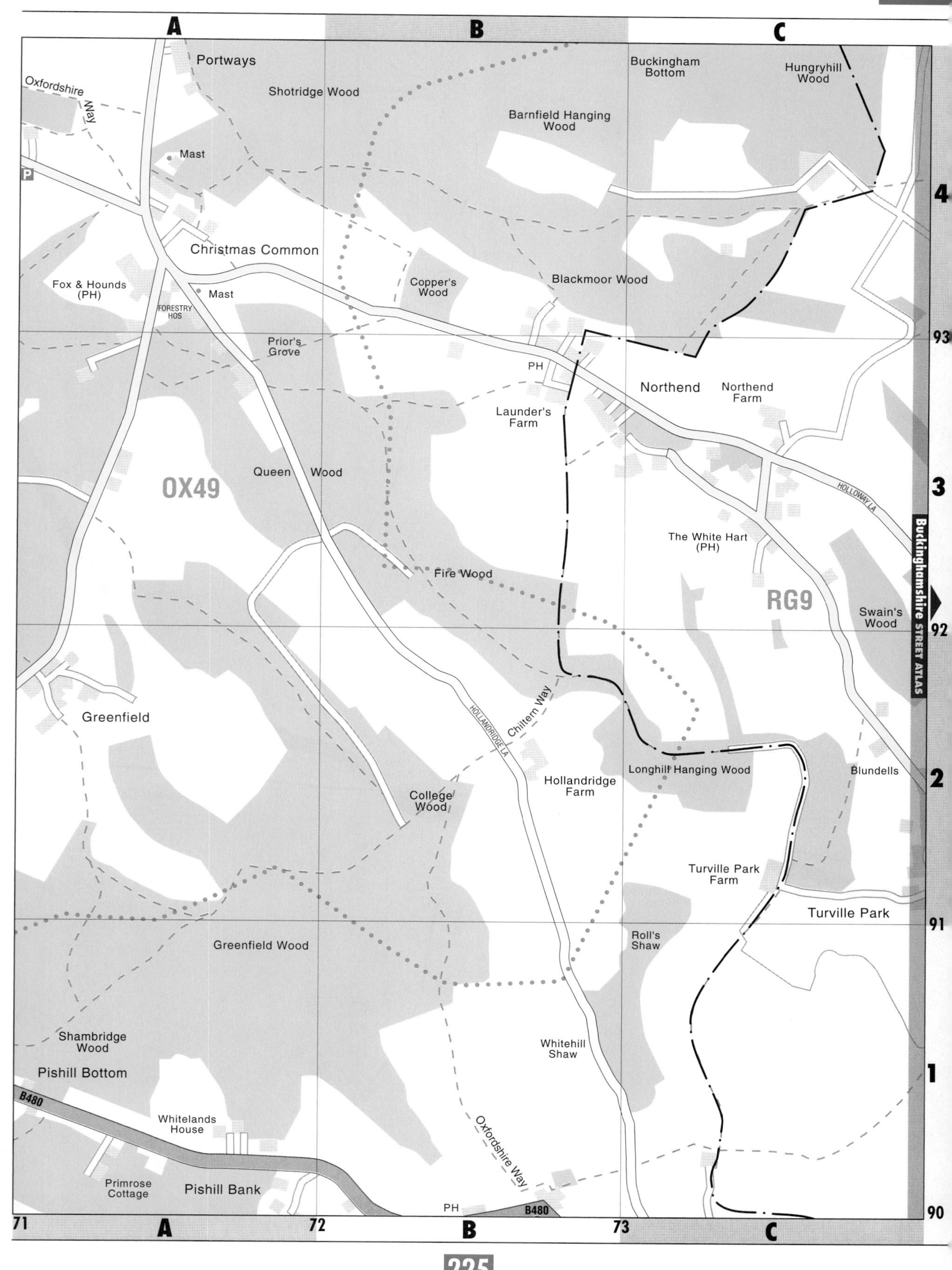

A
B
C
Portways
Oxfordshire Way
Shotridge Wood
Buckingham Bottom
Hungryhill Wood
Barnfield Hanging Wood
Mast
Christmas Common
Fox & Hounds (PH)
Mast
FORESTRY HOS
Copper's Wood
Blackmoor Wood
Prior's Grove
PH
Northend
Northend Farm
Launder's Farm
Queen Wood
OX49
HOLLOWAY LA
The White Hart (PH)
Fire Wood
RG9
Swain's Wood
Greenfield
Chiltern Way
HOLLANDRIDGE LA
Longhill Hanging Wood
Blundells
Hollandridge Farm
College Wood
Turville Park Farm
Turville Park
Greenfield Wood
Roll's Shaw
Shambridge Wood
Whitehill Shaw
Pishill Bottom
B480
Whitelands House
Oxfordshire Way
Primrose Cottage
Pishill Bank
PH
B480
4
93
3
92
2
91
1
90
71
72
73
Buckinghamshire STREET ATLAS

225

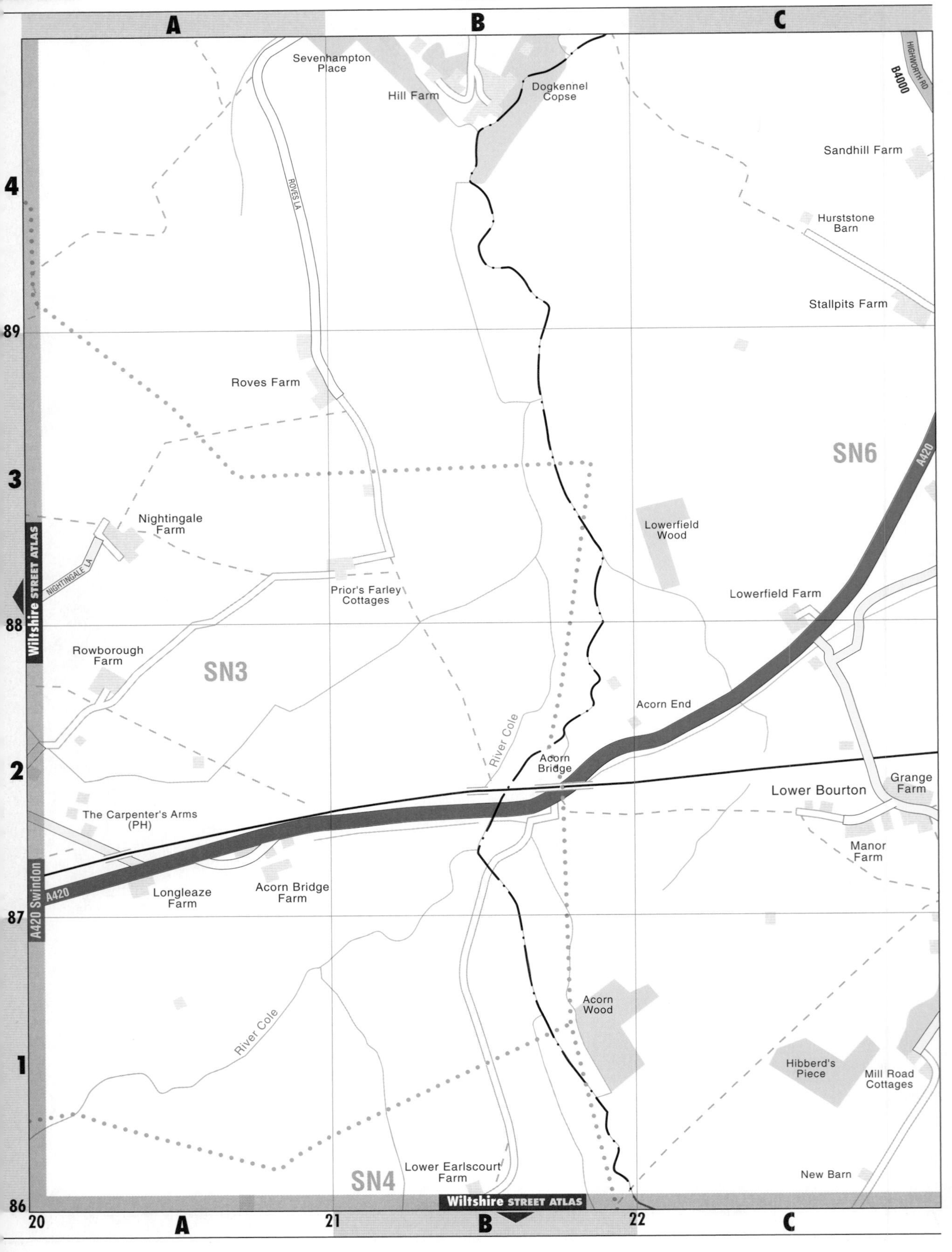

A   **B**   **C**

Sevenhampton Place

Hill Farm

Dogkennel Copse

B4000

HIGHWORTH RD

Sandhill Farm

Hurststone Barn

4

Stallpits Farm

89

Roves Farm

ROVES LA

SN6

A420

3

Nightingale Farm

NIGHTINGALE LA

Lowerfield Wood

Prior's Farley Cottages

Lowerfield Farm

88

Rowborough Farm

SN3

Acorn End

River Cole

Acorn Bridge

2

The Carpenter's Arms (PH)

Lower Bourton

Grange Farm

A420 Swindon

A420

Manor Farm

Longleaze Farm

Acorn Bridge Farm

87

Acorn Wood

Hibberd's Piece

Mill Road Cottages

River Cole

1

New Barn

SN4

Lower Earlscourt Farm

86

20   **A**   21   **B**   22   **C**

Wiltshire STREET ATLAS

191
210

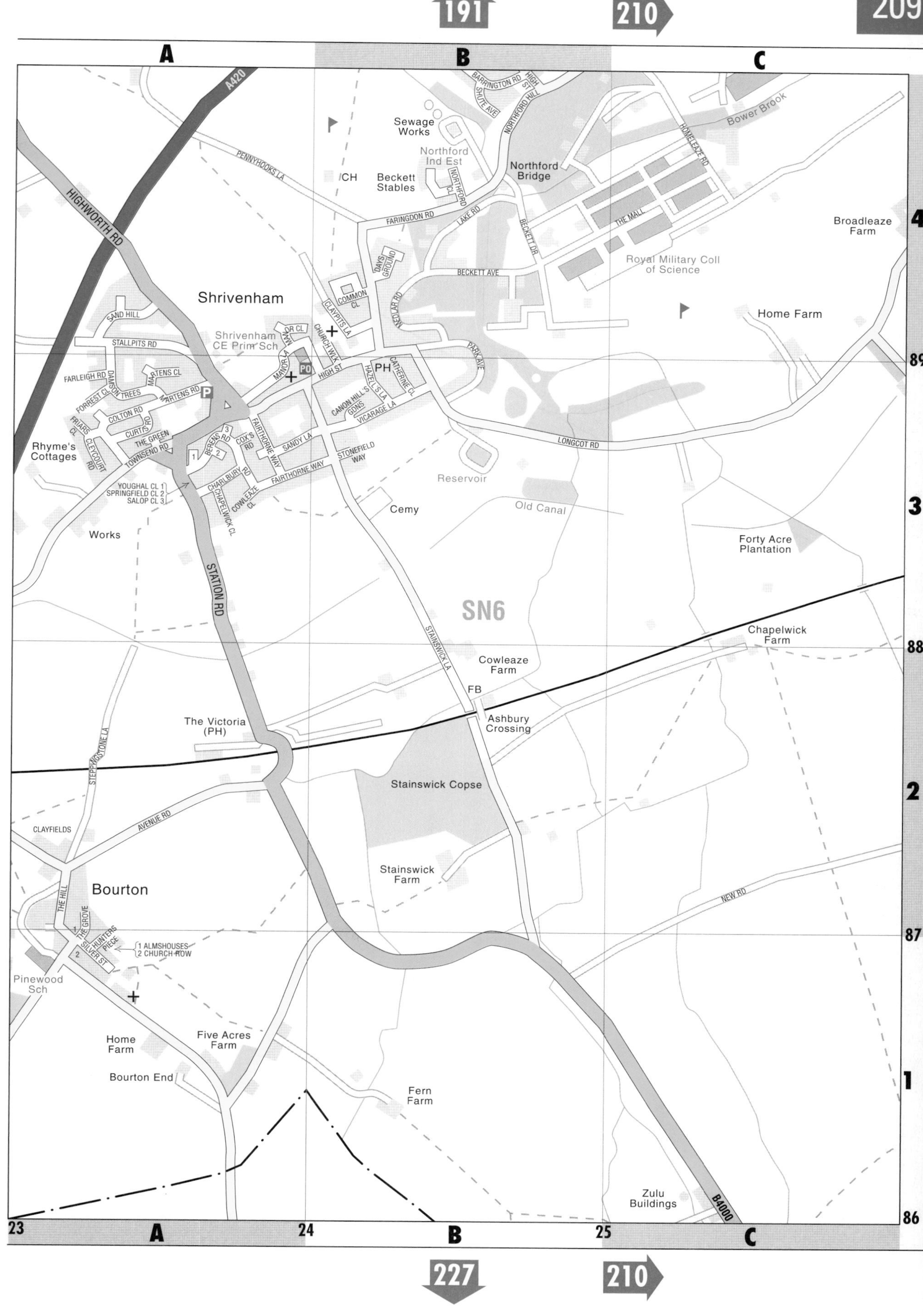
A
B
C
A420
HIGHWORTH RD
PENNYHOOKS LA
BARRINGTON RD
HIGH ST
SHUTE AVE
NORTHFORD HILL
Bower Brook
HOMELEAZE RD
Sewage Works
Northford Ind Est
NORTHFORD CL
CH
Beckett Stables
Northford Bridge
FARINGDON RD
LAKE RD
BECKETT DR
THE MALL
Broadleaze Farm
4
DAYS GROUND
BECKETT AVE
Royal Military Coll of Science
Shrivenham
COMMON CL
CLAYPITS LA
NEDLAR RD
SAND HILL
Home Farm
Shrivenham CE Prim Sch
MANOR CL
CHURCH WLK
STALLPITS RD
MANOR LA
PO
HIGH ST
PH
HAZELL'S LA
CATHERINE CL
PARK AVE
89
FARLEIGH RD
DAMSON TREES
MARTENS CL
MARTENS RD
FORREST CL
P
FRIARS CL
COLTON RD
CURTIS RD
CANON HILL'S GDNS
VICARAGE LA
LONGCOT RD
Rhyme's Cottages
CLEYCOURT RD
THE GREEN
TOWNSEND RD
BERENS RD
COX'S RD
FAIRTHORNE WAY
SANDY LA
STONEFIELD WAY
Reservoir
YOUGHAL CL 1
SPRINGFIELD CL 2
SALOP CL 3
CHARLBURY RD
CHAPELWICK CL
COWLEAZE CL
Cemy
Old Canal
3
Works
Forty Acre Plantation
STATION RD
SN6
STAINSWICK LA
Chapelwick Farm
88
Cowleaze Farm
FB
The Victoria (PH)
Ashbury Crossing
STEPPINGSTONE LA
Stainswick Copse
2
CLAYFIELDS
AVENUE RD
Stainswick Farm
Bourton
THE HILL
NEW RD
THE GROVE
HUNTERS PIECE
SILVER ST
1 ALMSHOUSES
2 CHURCH ROW
87
Pinewood Sch
Home Farm
Five Acres Farm
Bourton End
Fern Farm
1
Zulu Buildings
B4000
86
23
A
24
B
25
C

227
210

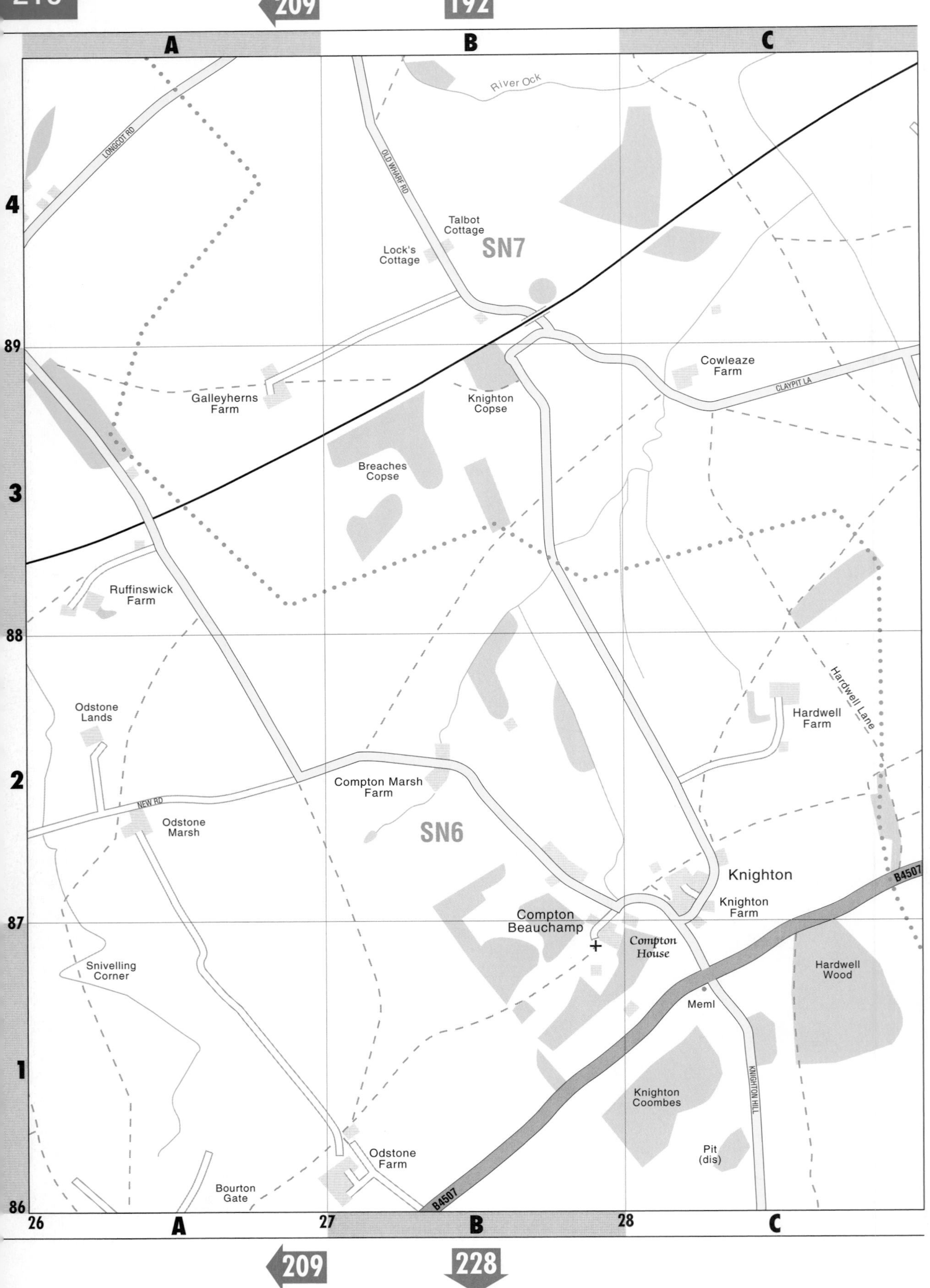

209
192

A   B   C

4

River Ock

LONGCOT RD

OLD WHARF RD

Talbot
Cottage

Lock's
Cottage

SN7

89

Cowleaze
Farm

CLAYPIT LA

Galleyherns
Farm

Knighton
Copse

3

Breaches
Copse

Ruffinswick
Farm

88

Odstone
Lands

Hardwell Lane

Hardwell
Farm

2

Compton Marsh
Farm

SN6

NEW RD

Odstone
Marsh

Knighton

B4507

Knighton
Farm

87

Compton
Beauchamp

Compton
House

Hardwell
Wood

Snivelling
Corner

Meml

1

B4507

Knighton
Coombes

KNIGHTON HILL

Pit
(dis)

Odstone
Farm

86

Bourton
Gate

B4507

26   A   27   B   28   C

209
228

193
212

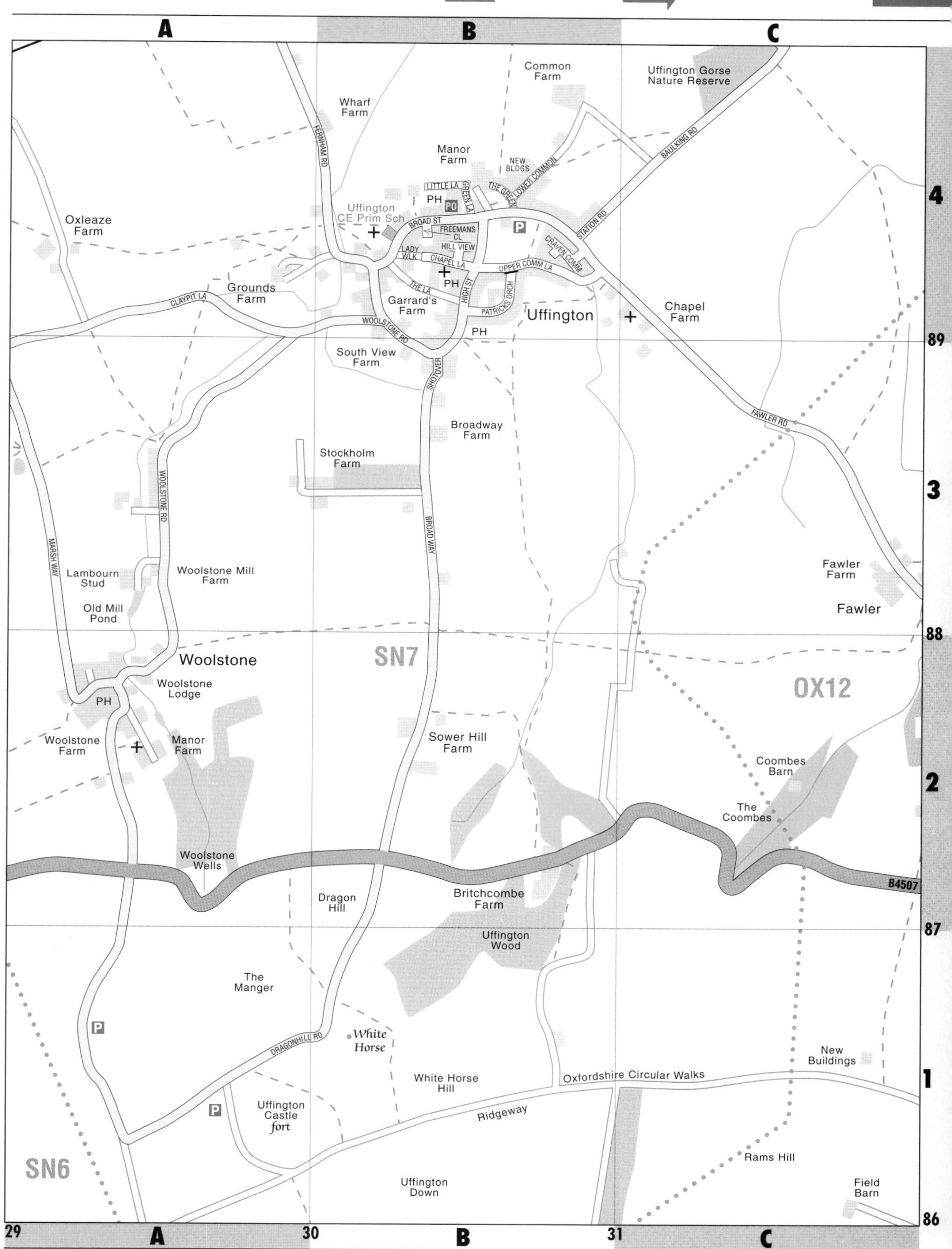

A **B** **C**

4

Uffington Gorse
Nature Reserve

Common
Farm

Wharf
Farm

BAULKING RD

Manor
Farm

NEW
BLDGS

LITTLE LA

PH

PO

GREEN LA

THE GREEN

LOWER COMMON

Uffington
CE Prim Sch

STATION RD

BROAD ST

FREEMANS
CL

HILL VIEW

P

CRAVEN COMM

Oxleaze
Farm

LADY
WLK

CHAPEL LA

UPPER COMM LA

Grounds
Farm

THE LA

PH

HIGH ST

Chapel
Farm

CLAYPIT LA

WOOLSTONE RD

Garrard's
Farm

PATRICKS ORCH

Uffington

89

South View
Farm

PH

SHOTOVER

WOOLSTONE RD

Broadway
Farm

Stockholm
Farm

BROAD WAY

3

FERNHAM RD

MARSH WAY

Lambourn
Stud

Woolstone Mill
Farm

Fawler
Farm

Fawler

Old Mill
Pond

Woolstone

SN7

88

Woolstone
Lodge

OX12

PH

Manor
Farm

Woolstone
Farm

Sower Hill
Farm

Coombes
Barn

The
Coombes

2

Woolstone
Wells

B4507

Dragon
Hill

Britchcombe
Farm

87

Uffington
Wood

The
Manger

P

DRAGONHILL RD

*White
Horse*

New
Buildings

1

White Horse
Hill

Oxfordshire Circular Walks

P

Uffington
Castle *fort*

Ridgeway

Rams Hill

SN6

Uffington
Down

Field
Barn

86

29 **A** 30 **B** 31 **C**

229
212

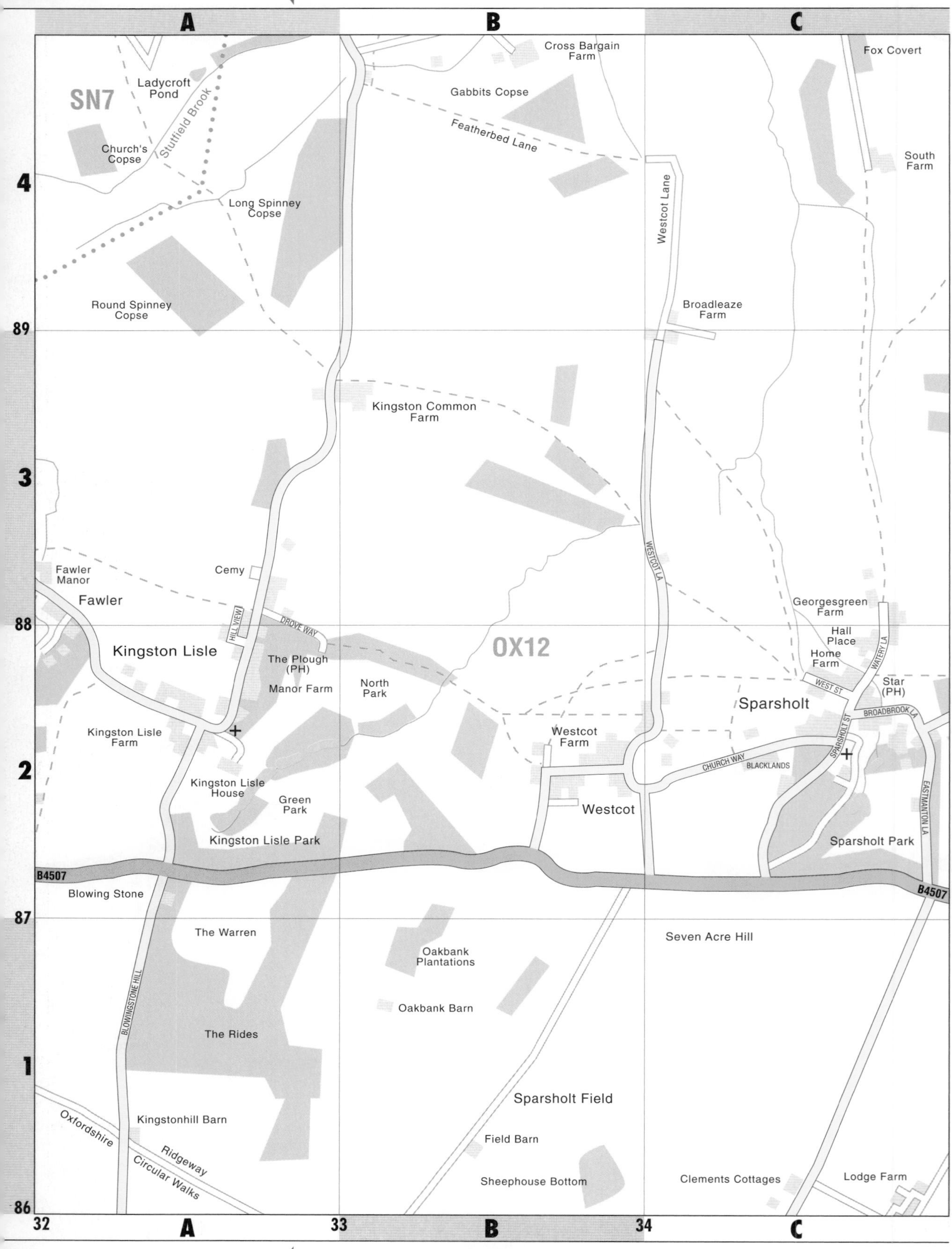

A   B   C

SN7

Ladycroft Pond

Church's Copse

Stutfield Brook

Long Spinney Copse

4

Cross Bargain Farm

Gabbits Copse

Featherbed Lane

Fox Covert

Westcot Lane

South Farm

Round Spinney Copse

Broadleaze Farm

89

Kingston Common Farm

3

Fawler Manor

Fawler

Cemy

WEST COT LA

Georgesgreen Farm

Hall Place Home Farm

Star (PH)

88

HILL VIEW

DROVE WAY

Kingston Lisle

The Plough (PH)

Manor Farm

North Park

OX12

Sparsholt

Kingston Lisle Farm

Westcot Farm

WEST ST

SPARSHOLT ST

BROADBROOK LA

2

Kingston Lisle House

Green Park

CHURCH WAY

BLACKLANDS

Sparsholt Park

Kingston Lisle Park

Westcot

EASTMANTON LA

B4507

Blowing Stone

B4507

87

The Warren

BLOWINGSTONE HILL

Oakbank Plantations

Seven Acre Hill

Oakbank Barn

The Rides

1

Sparsholt Field

Kingstonhill Barn

Field Barn

Oxfordshire

Ridgeway

Circular Walks

Sheephouse Bottom

Clements Cottages

Lodge Farm

86

32   A   33   B   34   C

195
214

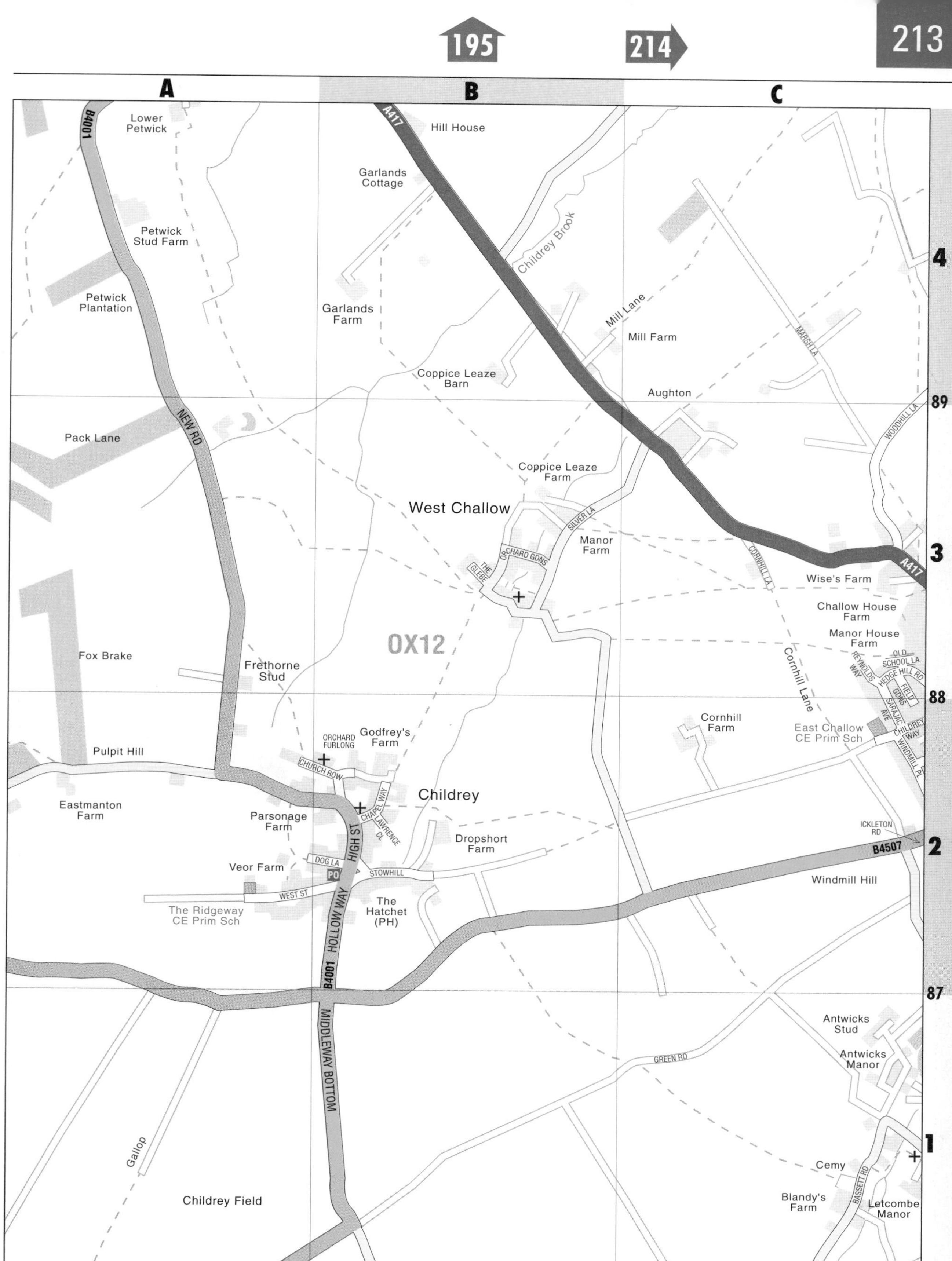
A
B
C
Lower Petwick
Hill House
Garlands Cottage
Petwick Stud Farm
Childrey Brook
Petwick Plantation
Garlands Farm
Mill Lane
Mill Farm
Coppice Leaze Barn
Aughton
NEW RD
Pack Lane
Coppice Leaze Farm
West Challow
SILVER LA
Manor Farm
ORCHARD GDNS
THE GLEBE
CORNHILL LA
Wise's Farm
Challow House Farm
Manor House Farm
OX12
Fox Brake
Frethorne Stud
Cornhill Lane
Cornhill Farm
East Challow CE Prim Sch
ORCHARD FURLONG
Godfrey's Farm
Pulpit Hill
CHURCH ROW
Childrey
Eastmanton Farm
Parsonage Farm
CHAPEL WAY
LAWRENCE CL
Dropshort Farm
ICKLETON RD
B4507
DOG LA
HIGH ST
Veor Farm
STOWHILL
Windmill Hill
WEST ST
The Ridgeway CE Prim Sch
The Hatchet (PH)
HOLLOW WAY
B4001
MIDDLEWAY BOTTOM
Antwicks Stud
Antwicks Manor
GREEN RD
Gallop
Cemy
Childrey Field
Blandy's Farm
BASSETT RD
Letcombe Manor
Letcombe Bassett Field
A417
MARSH LA
WOODHILL LA
REYNOLDS WAY
OLD SCHOOL LA
HEDGE HILL RD
FIELD GDNS
SARAJAC AVE
CHILDREY WAY
WINDMILL PL
4
89
3
88
2
87
1
86
35
36
37

231
214

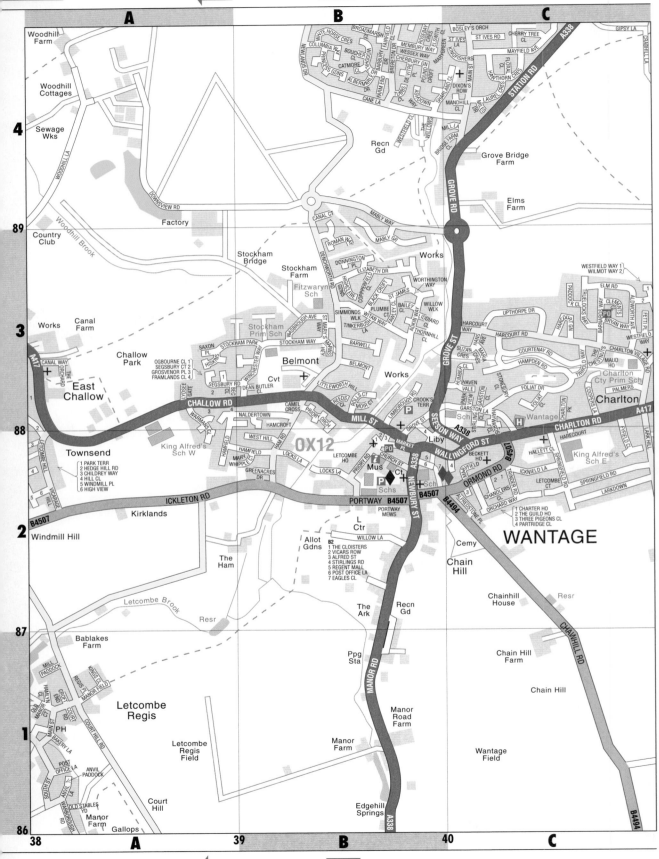
213

196

A B C

Woodhill Farm
Woodhill Cottages
Sewage Wks
WOODHILL LA
Country Club
Woodhill Brook
Factory
DOWNSVIEW RD
4
89
3
88
2
87
1
86

BROADMARSH CL
WHITE HORSE CRES
COLUMBIA WAY
NEWLANDS DR
PRINCESS GDNS
BOUCHER CL
CATMORE CL
ALBERMARLE DR
BARBURY DR
FAIRFIELD
BRERETON DR
MEMBURY WAY
WESSEX WAY
CHERBURY GN
DE VITRE PL
POUND CROFT
ROSEBAY CRES
ELSWITH CL
MARYGREEN CL
ST IVES LA
KINGFISHERS
BOSLEY'S ORCH
ST IVES RD
CHERRY TREE CL
MAYFIELD AVE
FLORAL CL
HAWTHORN CRES
LAUREL CRES
MAIN ST
DIXON'S ROW
MANDHILL CL
SHARLAND CL
ASHDOWN WAY
TUBBS CL
FARM END
CANE LA
MILES DR
STATION RD
A338
GIPSY LA
CRABHILL LA
WESTFIELD CL
THE WILLOWS
MILL LA
BRIDGE FARM CL
Recn Gd
Grove Bridge Farm
GROVE RD
Elms Farm
CANAL CT
MABLY WAY
MABLY GR
ROMAN WAY
DONNINGTON PL
ELIZABETH DR
Works
WORTHINGTON WAY
Stockham Bridge
Stockham Farm
Fitzwaryn Sch
DENCHWORTH RD
HIGHCLERE GDNS
COPPERFIELD CL
BLACK CROFT
ST JAMES
PLUMBE CT
FAWLEY CL
BAILEY CL
WILLOW WLK
LIDDIARD CL
ADKIN WAY
THORNHILL CL
SIMMONDS WLK
TINKERBUSH LA
WITAN WAY
BARWELL
BELMONT
WASBROUGH AVE
ST MARY'S WAY
MARNS HEY
Stockham Prim Sch
STOCKHAM PARK
STOCKHAM WAY
SAXON PL
HISKINS
WINCHESTER WAY
Belmont
Cvt
SEGSBURY RD
BEC CL
DEAN BUTLER CL
LITTLEWORTH HILL
REEDS CL
ROLLS CT
MOIR CT
Works
LIMBOROUGH RD
CROOK'S TERR
Works
Canal Farm
Challow Park
OGBOURNE CL 1
SEGSBURY CT 2
GROSVENOR PL 3
FRAMLANDS CL 4
CANAL WAY
THE ORCHARD
A417
East Challow
LYDSEE GATE
CHALLOW RD
WARMANS CL
NALDERTOWN
CAMEL CROSS
PRIORY ORCH
HAMCROFT
MILL ST
WEST HILL
HAMFIELD
HAM RD
OX12
LOCKS LA
MARY WHIPPLE CT
GREENACRES DR
King Alfred's Sch W
Townsend
1 PARK TERR
2 HEDGE HILL RD
3 CHILDREY WAY
4 HILL CL
5 WINDMILL PL
6 HIGH VIEW
LETCOMBE HILL
VICARAGE HILL
ICKLETON RD
B4507
Kirklands
Windmill Hill
LETCOMBE HO
PRIORY RD
CHURCH ST
MARKET PL
Mus
Ct
P
Schs
GROVE ST
Liby
A338
SEESON WAY
WALLINGFORD ST
BECKETT HO
MAYFIELD
ORMOND RD
B4507
Sch
PORTWAY B4507
PORTWAY MEWS
NEWBURY ST
L Ctr
WILLOW LA
Allot Gdns
B2
1 THE CLOISTERS
2 VICARS ROW
3 ALFRED ST
4 STIRLINGS RD
5 REGENT MALL
6 POST OFFICE LA
7 EAGLES CL
The Ham
WESTFIELD WAY 1
WILMOT WAY 2
ELM RD
PADDOCK CL
TRUELOCKS WAY
BARNARDS WAY
CLEMENTS CL
ALDWORTH AVE
FETTI PL
UPTHORPE DR
BRYAN WAY
HARCOURT WAY
HARCOURT GN
HARCOURT RD
WESTFIELD WAY
SUZAN CRES
HANS AVE
MARIA CRES
COURTENAY RD
CHARLTON VILLAGE RD
HAMPDEN RD
THE CHESTNUTS
MAUD HO
TIRROLD WAY
Charlton Cty Prim Sch
PALMERS
Charlton
HUMBER CL
HAVEN VALE
PARK VIEW
GARSTON CL
STONEBURY CL
FOLIAT DR
FOLIAT CL
COOPERS LA
STIRLING CL
GARSTON LA
HAYWARDS CL
CHARLTON PK
Sch
Wantage
H
CHARLTON RD
A417
HARECOURT
FYFIELD CL
LARK HILL
HALLETT CL
King Alfred's Sch E
ICKNIELD LA
SPRINGFIELD RD
LETCOMBE CT
SPRINGFIELD RD
LARKDOWN
TRINDER RD
CHANDLERS CL
ORCHARD WAY
ALFREDSTONE PL
B4494
1 CHARTER HO
2 THE GUILD HO
3 THREE PIGEONS CL
4 PARTRIDGE CL
WANTAGE
Cemy
Chain Hill
Letcombe Brook
Resr
The Ark
Recn Gd
Chainhill House
Resr
Ppg Sta
CHAINHILL RD
Chain Hill Farm
Chain Hill
MANOR RD
Bablakes Farm
MILL PADDOCK
KINGS CL
REGIS PL
MANOR FIELD
HAMLYN CL
CROFT END
OLD MANOR CT
COURT RD
MAIN ST
PH
Letcombe Regis
COURT HILL RD
BAKERY LA
POST OFFICE LA
ANVIL PADDOCK
SOUTH ST
ANVIL LA
OLD STABLES YD
WARBOROUGH RD
Manor Farm
Gallops
Letcombe Regis Field
Court Hill
Manor Road Farm
Manor Farm
Edgehill Springs
A338
Wantage Field
B4494

38 A 39 B 40 C

213
232

197
216

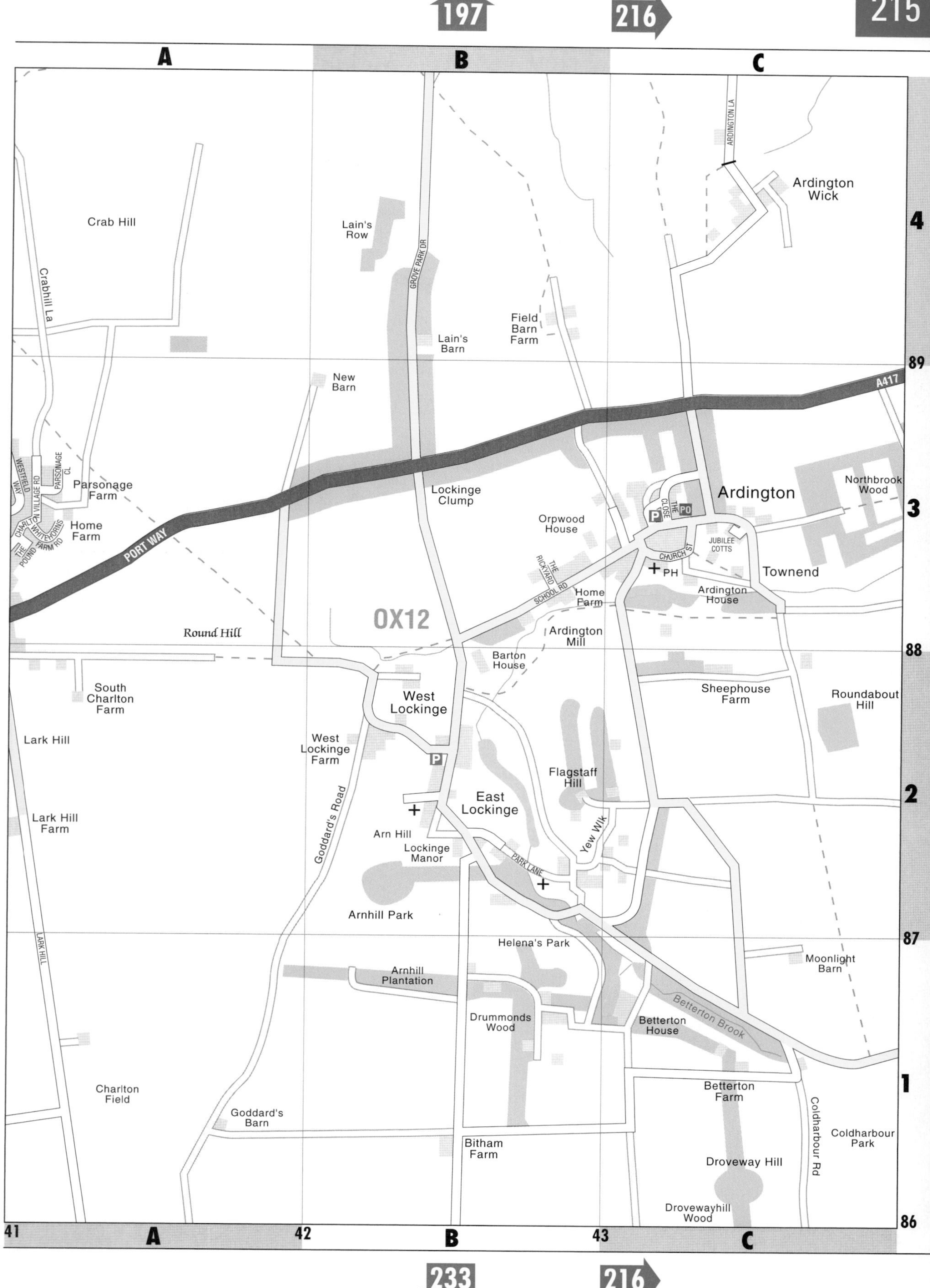
A
B
C
Crab Hill
Crabhill La
Lain's Row
GROVE PARK DR
Lain's Barn
Field Barn Farm
ARDINGTON LA
Ardington Wick
4
89
A417
New Barn
Parsonage Farm
PARSONAGE CL
WESTFIELD WAY
VILLAGE RD
CHARLTON
WHITEHORNS
POUND FARM RD
THE
Home Farm
PORT WAY
Lockinge Clump
Orpwood House
THE CLOSE
PO
P
Ardington
Northbrook Wood
3
JUBILEE COTTS
CHURCH ST
PH
Townend
THE RICKYARD
SCHOOL RD
Home Farm
Ardington House
OX12
Round Hill
Ardington Mill
88
Barton House
South Charlton Farm
West Lockinge
Sheephouse Farm
Roundabout Hill
Lark Hill
West Lockinge Farm
P
Flagstaff Hill
Goddard's Road
East Lockinge
2
Lark Hill Farm
Arn Hill
Lockinge Manor
Yew Wlk
PARK LANE
Arnhill Park
87
LARK HILL
Helena's Park
Moonlight Barn
Arnhill Plantation
Drummonds Wood
Betterton House
Betterton Brook
1
Charlton Field
Betterton Farm
Coldharbour Rd
Coldharbour Park
Goddard's Barn
Bitham Farm
Droveway Hill
Drovewayhill Wood
86
41
42
43

233
216

215
198

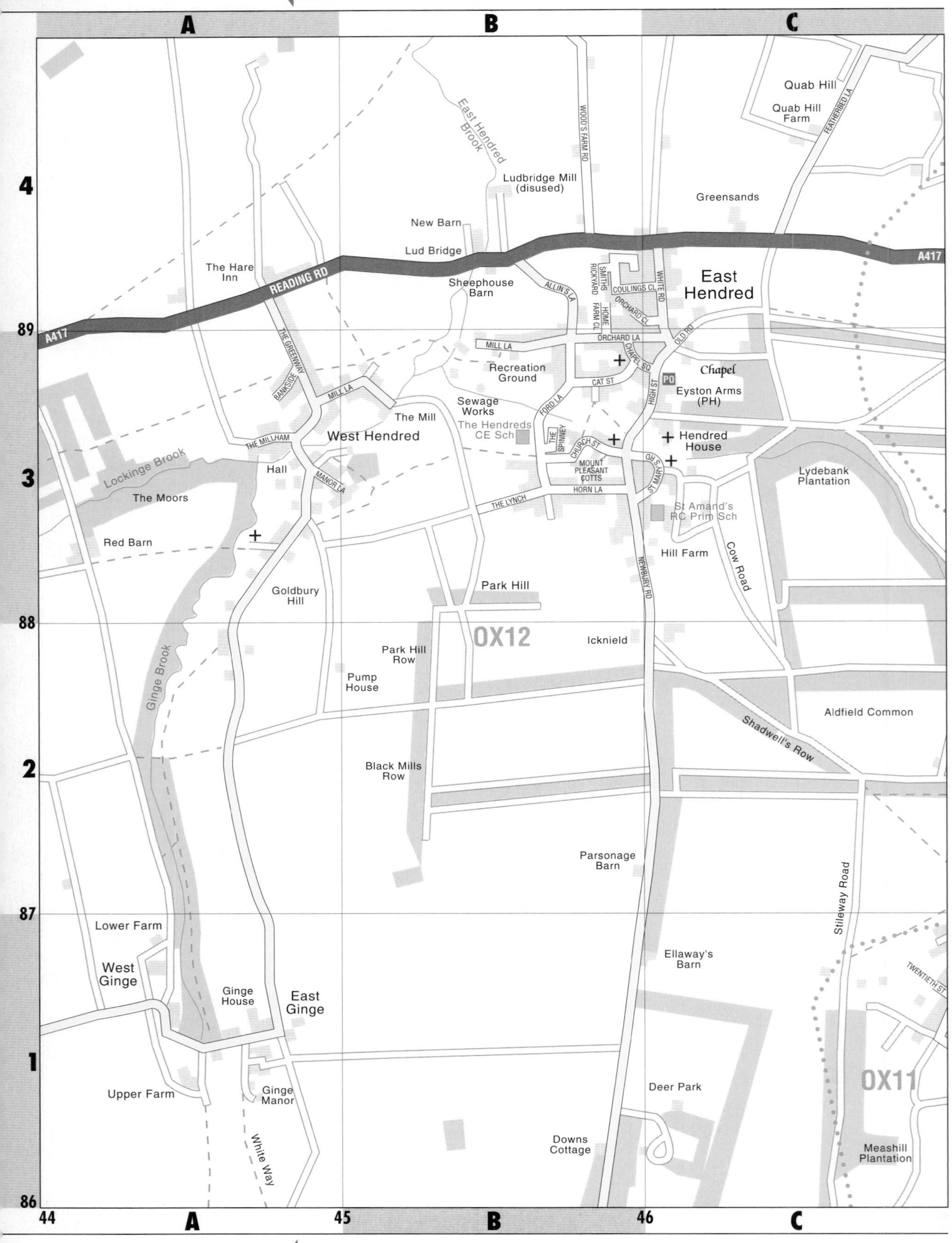
A
B
C
Quab Hill
Quab Hill Farm
FEATHERBED LA
WOOD'S FARM RD
East Hendred Brook
Ludbridge Mill (disused)
Greensands
New Barn
Lud Bridge
A417
The Hare Inn
READING RD
Sheephouse Barn
ALLIN'S LA
RICKYARD
SMITHS
COULINGS CL
WHITE RD
East Hendred
FARM CL
HOME
ORCHARD CL
A417
THE GREENWAY
MILL LA
ORCHARD LA
OLD RD
Recreation Ground
CHAPEL SQ
Chapel
BANKSIDE
MILL LA
CAT ST
HIGH ST
Eyston Arms (PH)
Sewage Works
FORD LA
The Mill
The Hendreds CE Sch
West Hendred
THE MILLHAM
THE SPINNEY
CHURCH ST
Hendred House
Lockinge Brook
Hall
MANOR LA
MOUNT PLEASANT COTTS
ST MARY'S RD
Lydebank Plantation
The Moors
HORN LA
THE LYNCH
St Amand's RC Prim Sch
Red Barn
Hill Farm
Cow Road
NEWBURY RD
Goldbury Hill
Park Hill
OX12
Icknield
Park Hill Row
Ginge Brook
Pump House
Aldfield Common
Shadwell's Row
Black Mills Row
Parsonage Barn
Stileway Road
Lower Farm
Ellaway's Barn
TWENTIETH ST
West Ginge
Ginge House
East Ginge
OX11
Upper Farm
Ginge Manor
Deer Park
White Way
Downs Cottage
Meashill Plantation
4
89
3
88
2
87
1
86
44
45
46

215
234

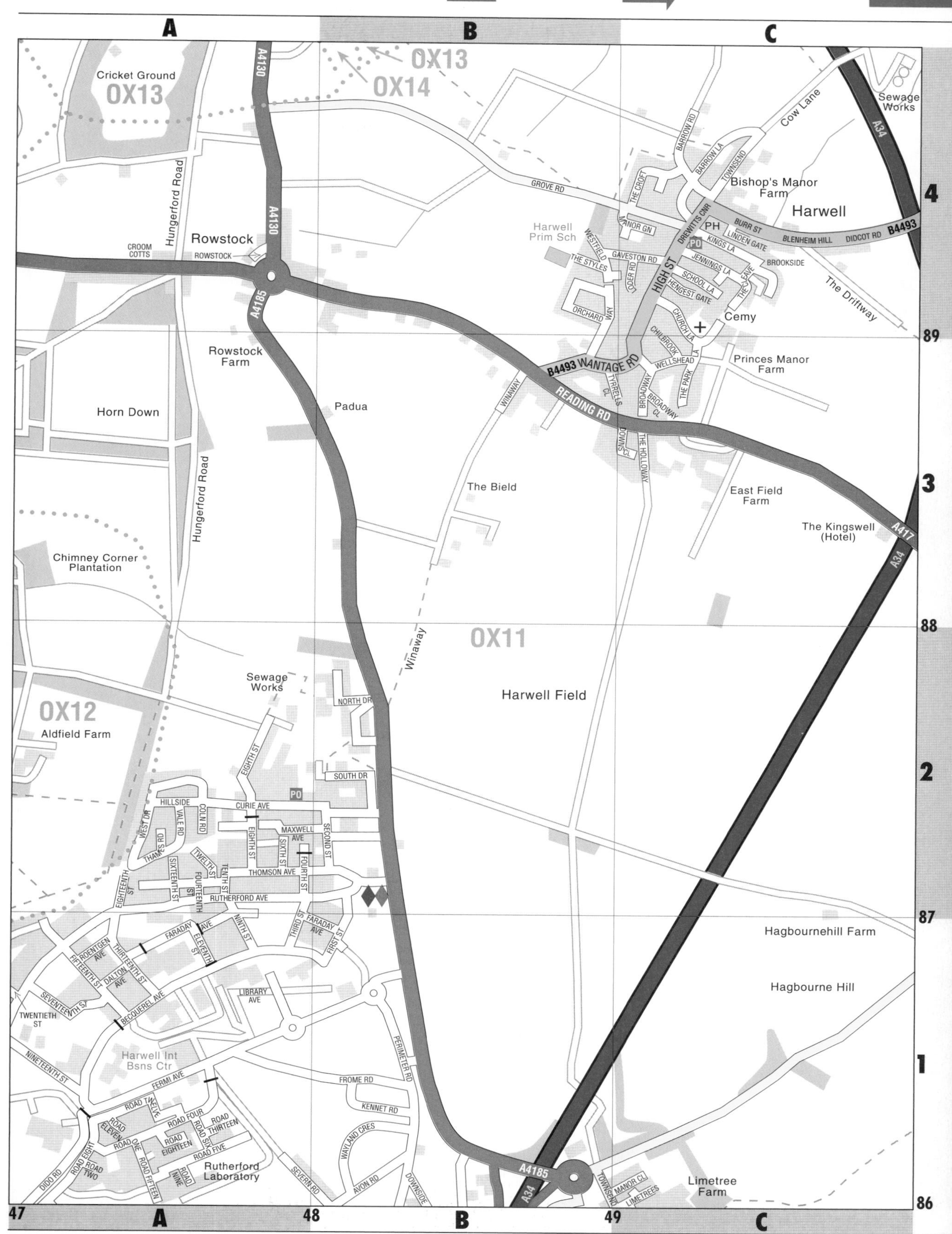
A
B
C
Cricket Ground
OX13
OX14
Sewage Works
Cow Lane
Hungerford Road
Rowstock
CROOM COTTS
ROWSTOCK
GROVE RD
Bishop's Manor Farm
Harwell
Harwell Prim Sch
HIGH ST
BLENHEIM HILL
DIDCOT RD
B4493
BROOKSIDE
The Driftway
Cemy
Rowstock Farm
B4493 WANTAGE RD
READING RD
Princes Manor Farm
Horn Down
Padua
The Bield
East Field Farm
The Kingswell (Hotel)
Chimney Corner Plantation
OX11
Harwell Field
Winaway
Sewage Works
OX12
Aldfield Farm
NORTH DR
SOUTH DR
CURIE AVE
THOMSON AVE
RUTHERFORD AVE
Hagbournehill Farm
Hagbourne Hill
Harwell Int Bsns Ctr
FERMI AVE
FROME RD
KENNET RD
Rutherford Laboratory
A4185
A34
A4130
A417
Limetree Farm
4
3
2
1
89
88
87
86
47
48
49

217
200

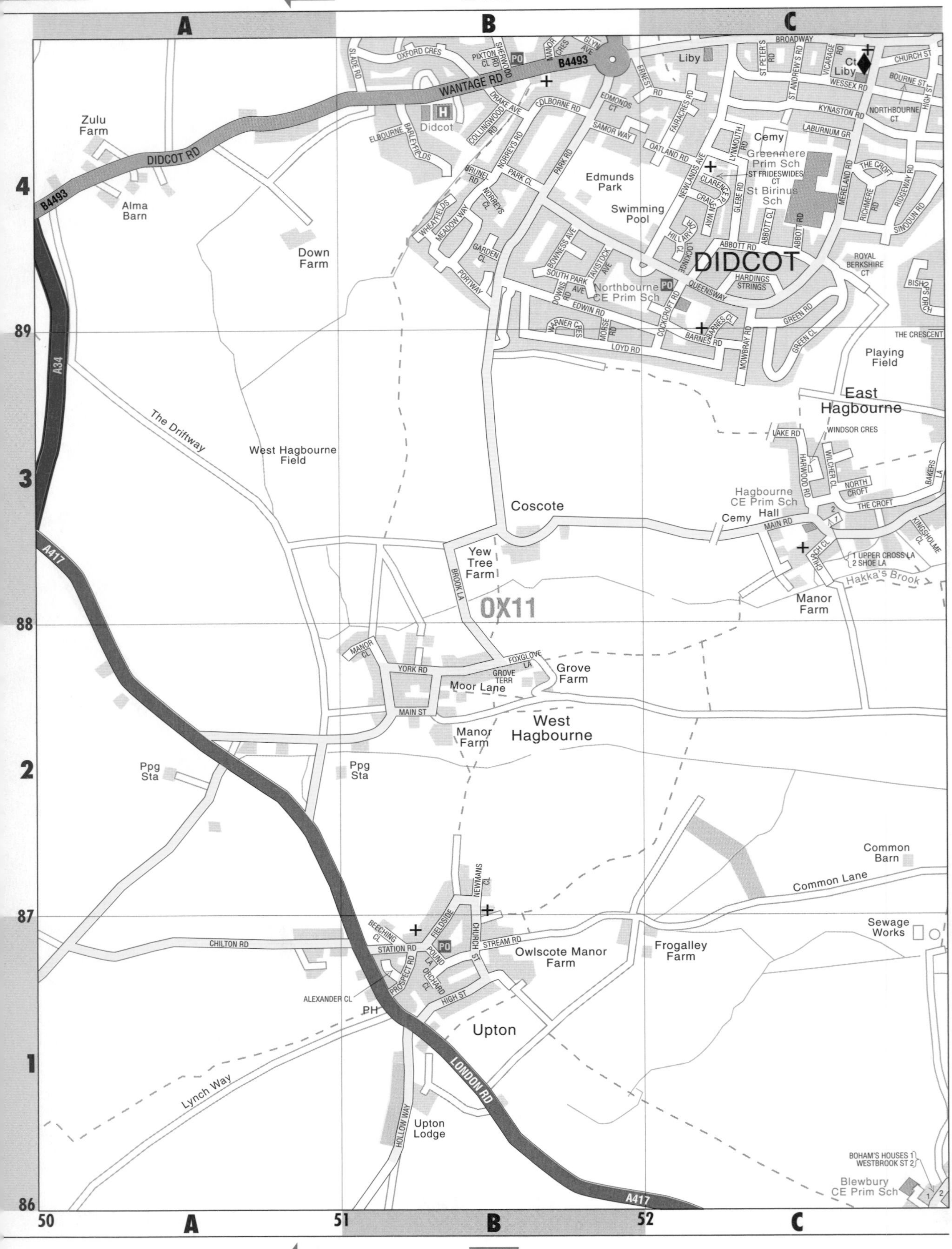
A
B
C
DIDCOT
Didcot
Zulu Farm
Alma Barn
Down Farm
DIDCOT RD
B4493
WANTAGE RD
Edmunds Park
Swimming Pool
Northbourne CE Prim Sch
Greenmere Prim Sch
St Birinus Sch
Cemy
Liby
Playing Field
East Hagbourne
The Driftway
West Hagbourne Field
A34
A417
Coscote
Yew Tree Farm
OX11
Hagbourne CE Prim Sch
Hall
Manor Farm
Hakka's Brook
Grove Farm
Moor Lane
West Hagbourne
Ppg Sta
Common Barn
Common Lane
Sewage Works
Frogalley Farm
Owlscote Manor Farm
Upton
Lynch Way
LONDON RD
Upton Lodge
HOLLOW WAY
Blewbury CE Prim Sch
CHILTON RD
STATION RD
HIGH ST
CHURCH ST
STREAM RD
MAIN ST
YORK RD
BROOK LA
MAIN RD
4
89
3
88
2
87
1
86
50
51
52

217
236

201
220

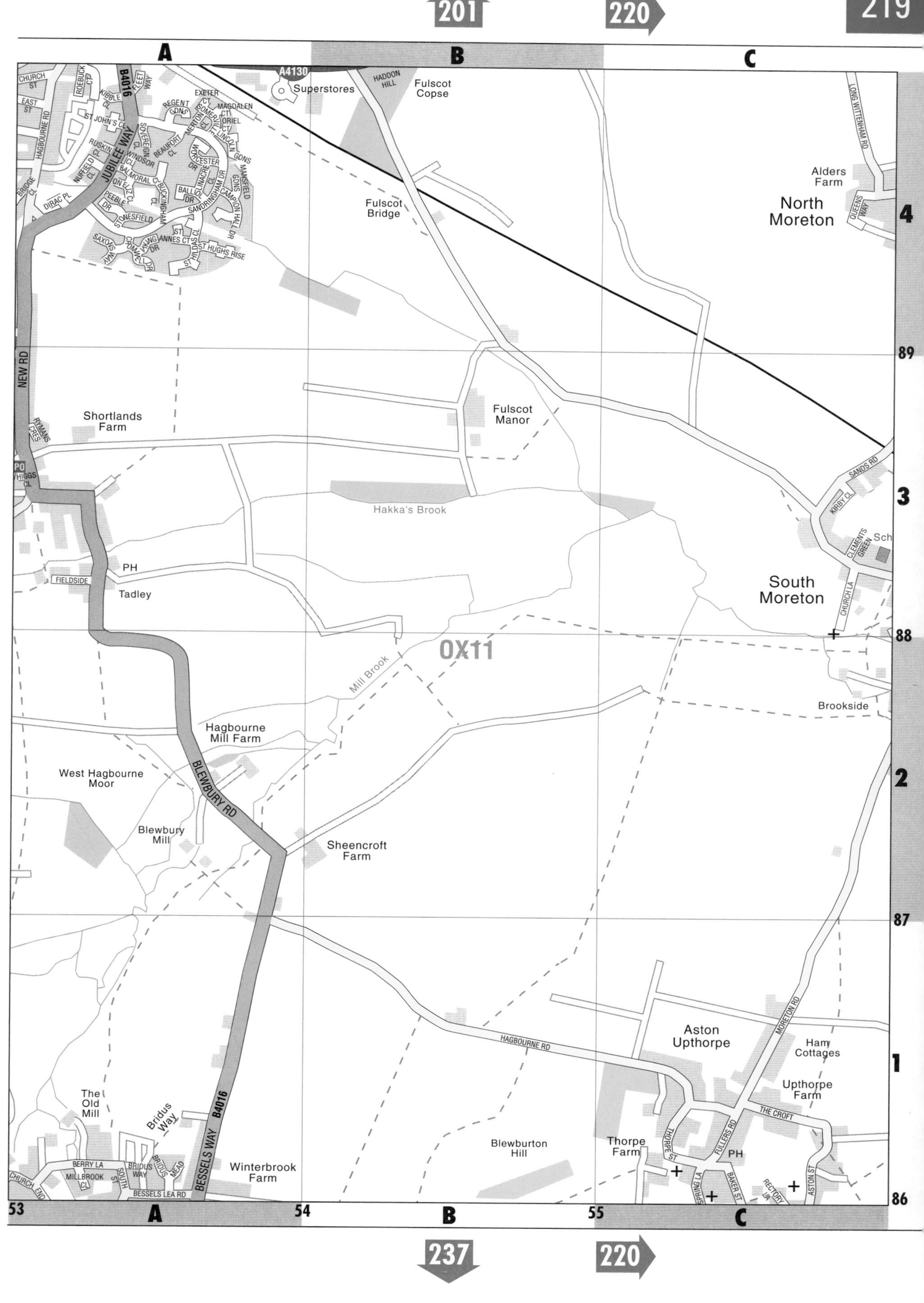
A
B
C
A4130
Superstores
HADDON HILL
Fulscot Copse
Fulscot Bridge
JUBILEE WAY
B4016
NEW RD
Alders Farm
North Moreton
Shortlands Farm
Fulscot Manor
Hakka's Brook
PH
Tadley
FIELDSIDE
South Moreton
OX11
Mill Brook
Brookside
Hagbourne Mill Farm
West Hagbourne Moor
BLEWBURY RD
Blewbury Mill
Sheencroft Farm
HAGBOURNE RD
Aston Upthorpe
MOREton RD
Ham Cottages
Upthorpe Farm
THE CROFT
The Old Mill
Bridus Way
BESSELS WAY
Blewburton Hill
Thorpe Farm
Winterbrook Farm
BERRY LA
MILLBROOK CL
BESSELS LEA RD
89
88
87
86
4
3
2
1
53
54
55

237
220

219 202

A   **B**   **C**

MACKNEY LA

Mackney

Sherwood
Farm

ELM RD

LONG WITTENHAM RD

Kibble Ditch

HIGH ST

4

The Bear
(PH)

BEAR LA

DUNSOMER HILL

89

Mill Brook

Glebe
Cottage

Hithercroft
Farm

HITHERCROFT

3

The Crown
(PH)

OX11

CROWN LA

PAPER MILL LA

Pumping
Station

MILL LA

88

Cholsey Hill

OX10

MORETON RD

ANCHOR LA

Hillgreen
Farm

2

Poultry
Farm

The Manor

Sewage
Works

Manor
Farm

Cholsey and Wallingford Rly

87

CHURCH RD

GOLDFINCH LA

The
Lees

Red Lion
(PH)

WALLINGFORD RD

CROSS RD

Cholsey
Prim Sch

THE
POUND

CHEQUERS
PL

ILGES LA

Lees
Cottages

MARYMEAD

THE FORTY

PO

POUND LA

1

West
End

STATION RD

DROVESIDE

BROOKSIDE

PATERNOSTER

COLLEGE CL

QUEENS RD

FAIR FIELD

SANDY LA

ST GEORGE'S RD

HONEY LA

CRESCENT WAY

KENTWOOD CL

THE
ROWANS

BUCKTHORN
LA

Pancroft
Farm

WEST END

FORD CL

WESTFIELD
RD

PAPIST WAY

86

The Elms

Cholsey

219 238

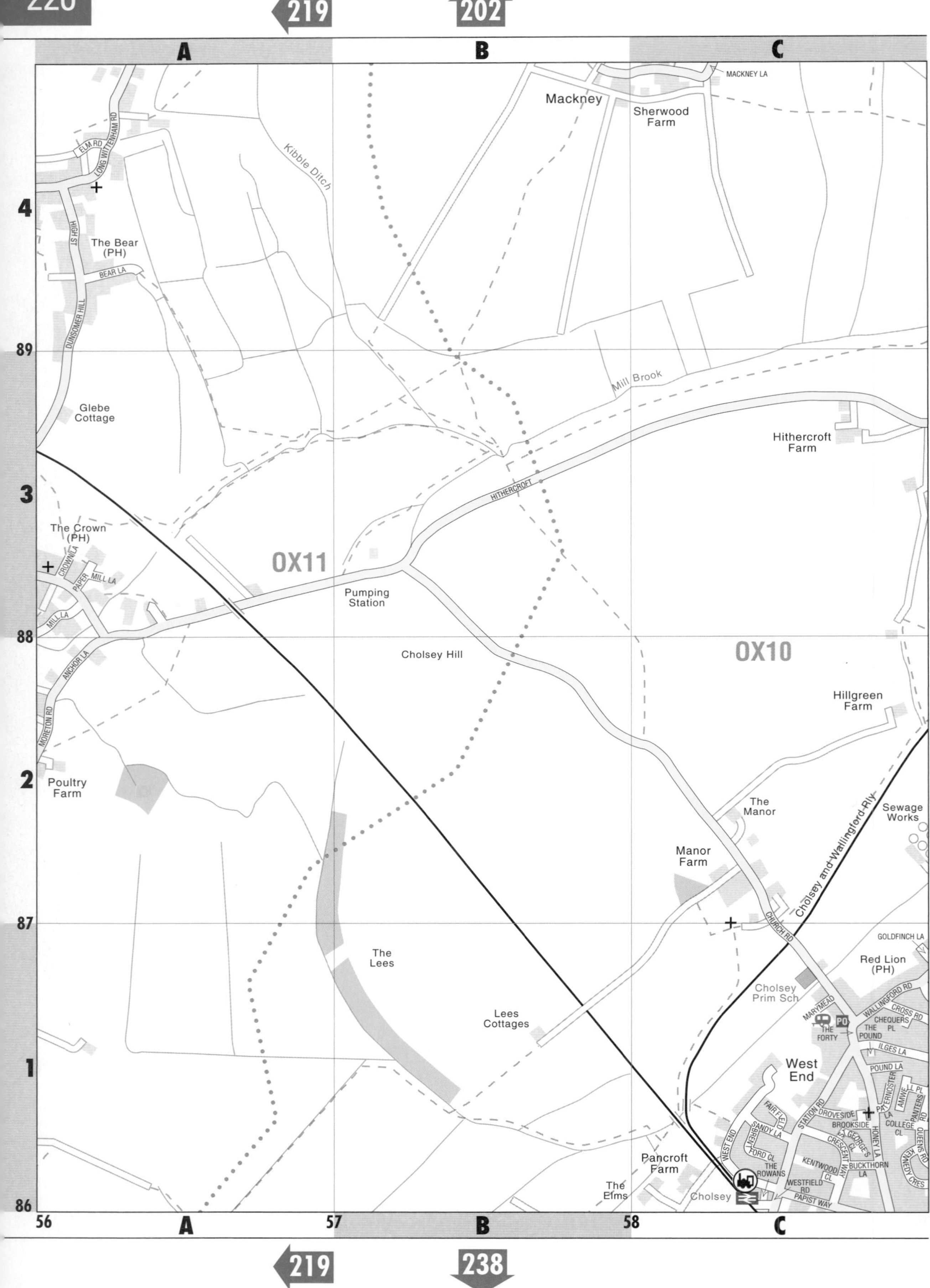

B4
1 WEEDON CT
2 COMPTON TERR
3 CROFT VILLAS
4 SOUTH VIEW
5 OAKDALE CT
6 ST JOHN'S TERR

7 BROOKSIDE
8 CROFT TERR
9 BEANSHEAF TERR
10 ST RUALD'S CL
11 MARIOT CT
12 GOLDSMITH'S TERR
13 ST ALBAN'S CT

14 THE MINT
15 MARKET PL
16 THE ARCADE
17 ST LEONARD'S SQ
18 OLD BLDGS
19 JOHNSTONE PL
20 HART ST

21 MOUSEY LA
22 ST PETER'S PL
23 PRIORY MEWS
24 SEYER MILWARD TERR

203   222

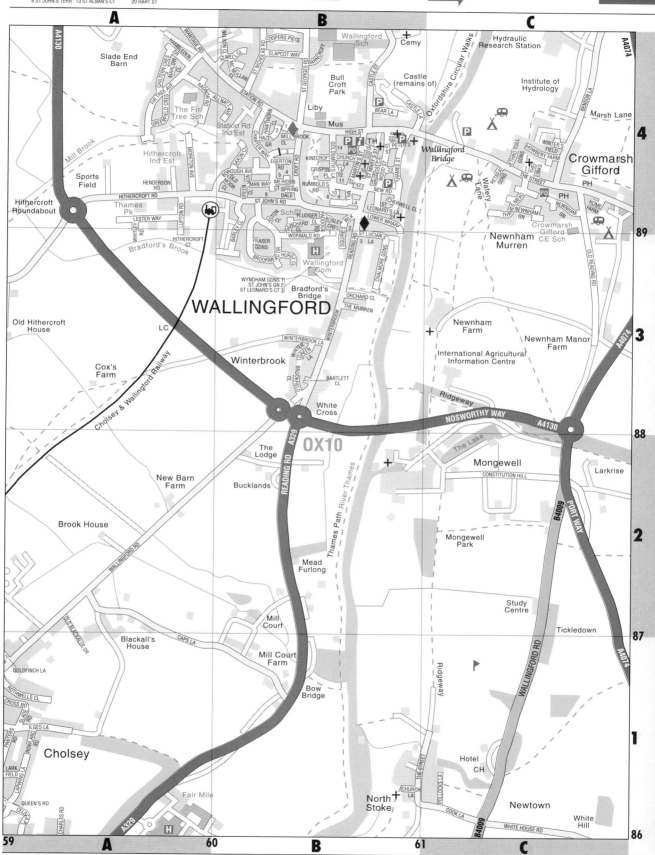

239   222

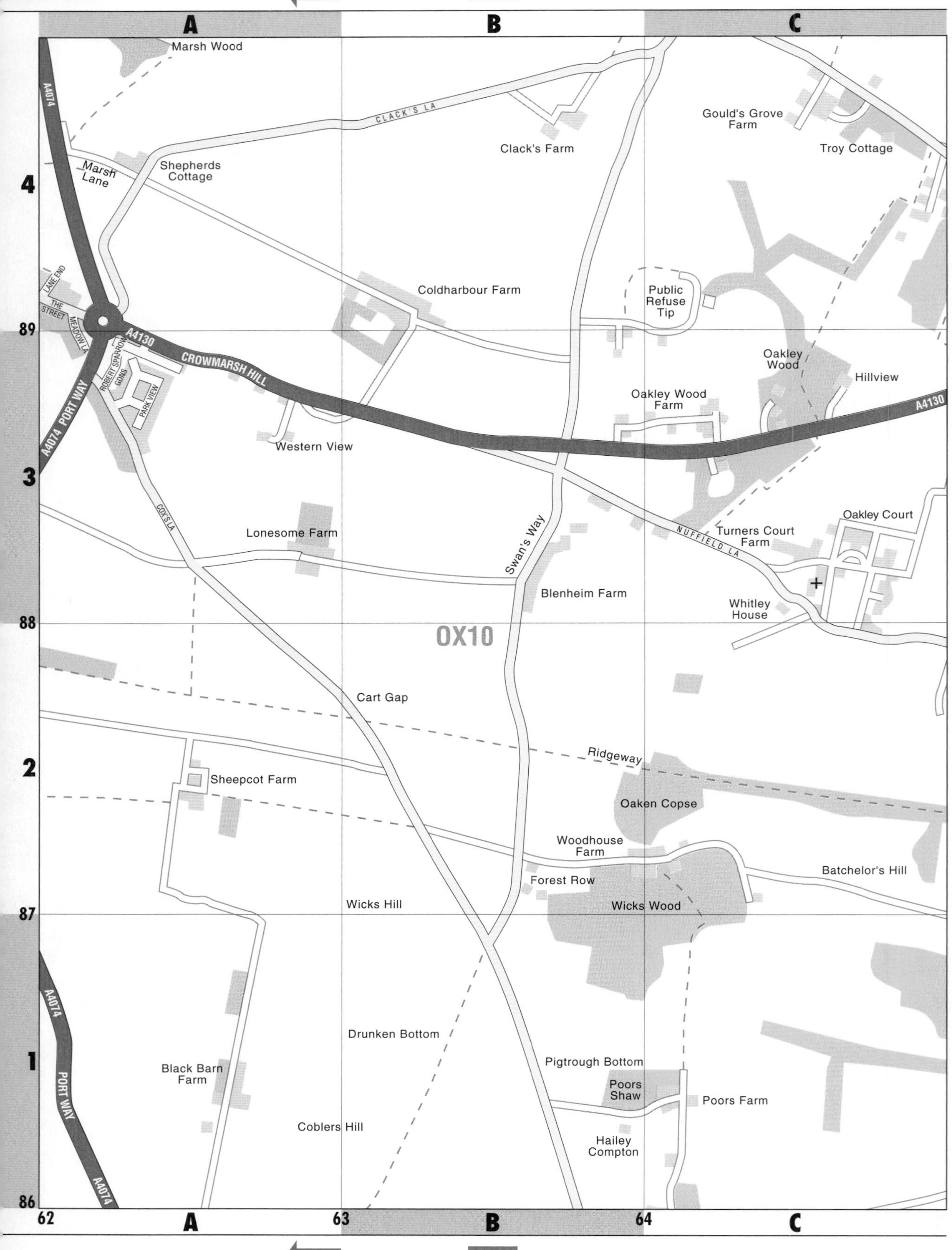

Marsh Wood

CLACK'S LA

Clack's Farm

Gould's Grove Farm

Troy Cottage

Marsh Lane

Shepherds Cottage

4

LANE END

THE STREET

MEADOW LA

A4130

A4074 PORT WAY

89

ROBERT SPARROW GDNS

PARK VIEW

CROWMARSH HILL

Coldharbour Farm

Public Refuse Tip

Oakley Wood

Hillview

Oakley Wood Farm

A4130

Western View

3

COX'S LA

Lonesome Farm

Swan's Way

Turners Court Farm

NUFFIELD LA

Oakley Court

Blenheim Farm

Whitley House

+

88

OX10

Cart Gap

Ridgeway

2

Sheepcot Farm

Oaken Copse

Batchelor's Hill

Woodhouse Farm

Forest Row

Wicks Wood

Wicks Hill

87

A4074

PORT WAY

1

Drunken Bottom

Pigtrough Bottom

Black Barn Farm

Poors Shaw

Poors Farm

Coblers Hill

Hailey Compton

86

A4074

205
224

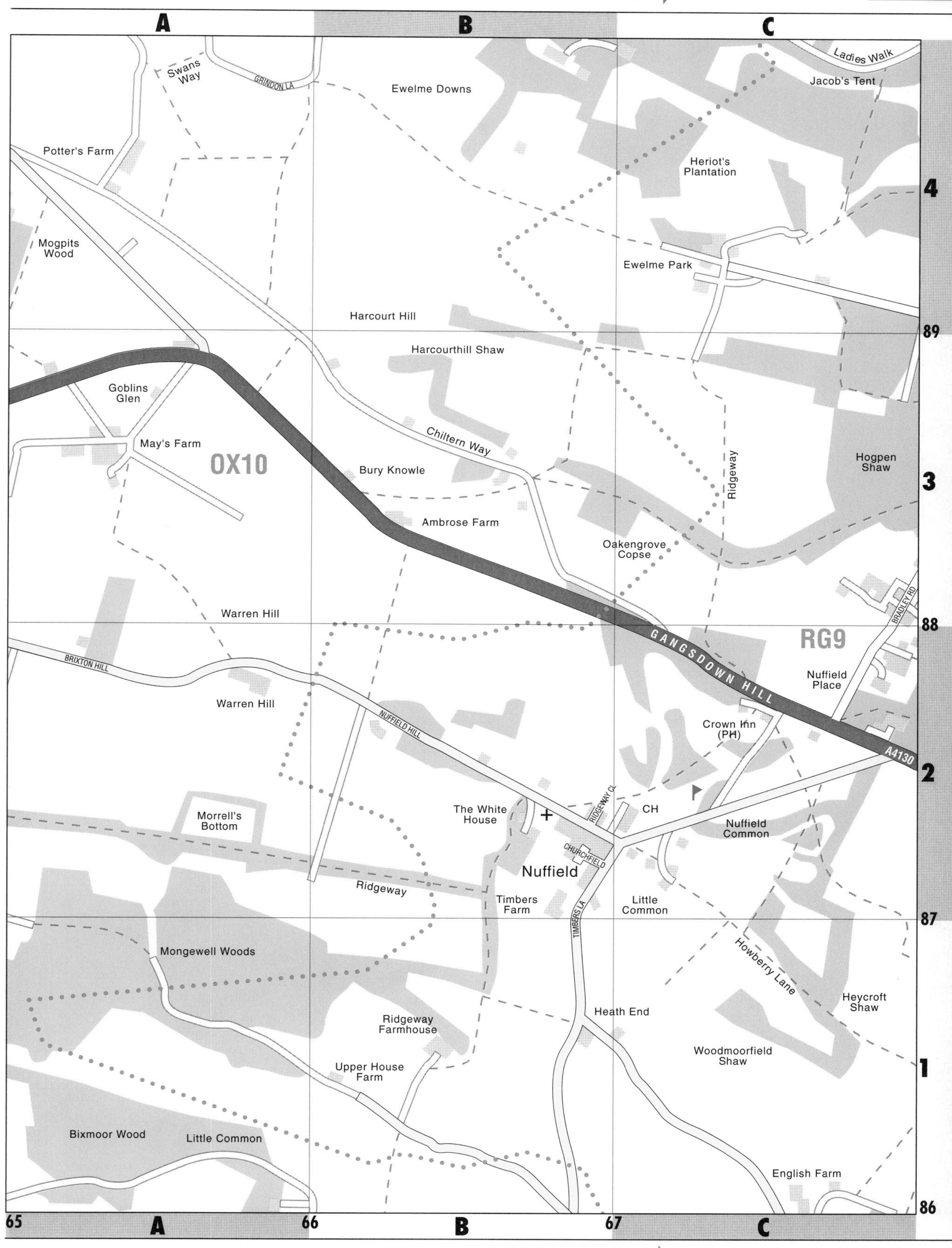
A
B
C
Swans Way
GRINDON LA
Ewelme Downs
Ladies Walk
Jacob's Tent
Potter's Farm
Heriot's Plantation
4
Mogpits Wood
Ewelme Park
Harcourt Hill
89
Harcourthill Shaw
Goblins Glen
May's Farm
OX10
Chiltern Way
Bury Knowle
Ridgeway
Hogpen Shaw
3
Ambrose Farm
Oakengrove Copse
BRADLEY RD
Warren Hill
88
GANGSDOWN HILL
RG9
BRIXTON HILL
Nuffield Place
Warren Hill
NUFFIELD HILL
Crown Inn (PH)
A4130
2
The White House
RIDGEWAY CL
CH
Morrell's Bottom
Nuffield Common
CHURCHFIELD
Nuffield
Ridgeway
Timbers Farm
TIMBERS LA
Little Common
87
Mongewell Woods
Howberry Lane
Heycroft Shaw
Heath End
Ridgeway Farmhouse
Woodmoorfield Shaw
1
Upper House Farm
Bixmoor Wood
Little Common
English Farm
86
65
A
66
B
67
C

241
224

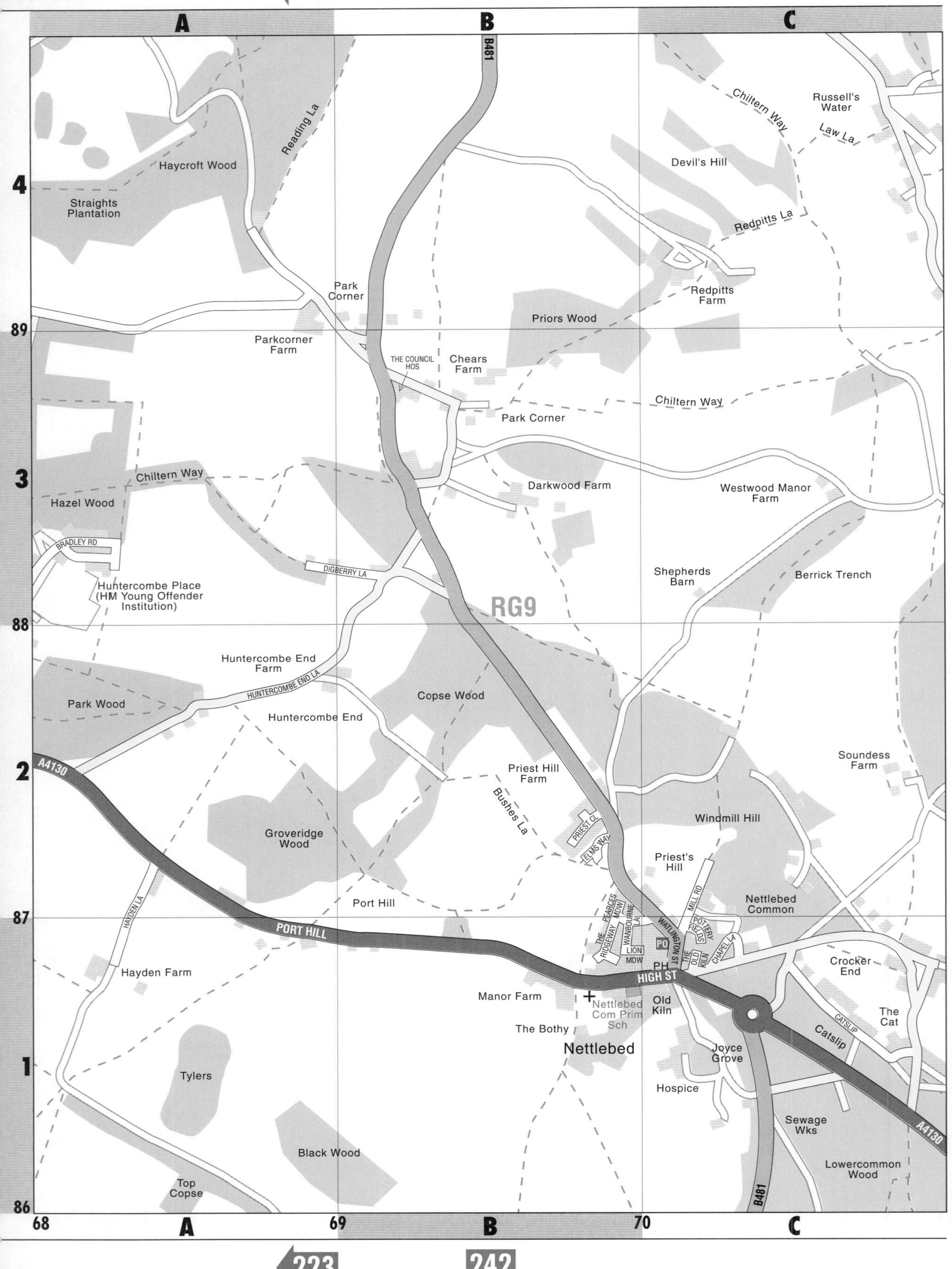
A   B   C

4

Straights
Plantation

Haycroft Wood

Reading La

Russell's
Water

Chiltern Way

Law La

Devil's Hill

Redpitts La

Park
Corner

89

Parkcorner
Farm

THE COUNCIL
HOS

Chears
Farm

Priors Wood

Redpitts
Farm

Chiltern Way

Park Corner

3

Chiltern Way

Hazel Wood

BRADLEY RD

DIGBERRY LA

Darkwood Farm

Westwood Manor
Farm

Huntercombe Place
(HM Young Offender
Institution)

Shepherds
Barn

Berrick Trench

88

RG9

Huntercombe End
Farm

HUNTERCOMBE END LA

Copse Wood

Park Wood

Huntercombe End

Soundess
Farm

2

A4130

Priest Hill
Farm

Bushes La

Windmill Hill

Groveridge
Wood

Priest's
Hill

PRIEST CL

ELMS WAY

Nettlebed
Common

87

HAYDEN LA

Port Hill

PORT HILL

THE RIDGEWAY
PEARCES MDW
WANBOURNE LA
LION MDW
PO
WATLINGTON ST
THE OLD KILN
POTTERY FIELDS
CHAPEL LA

Crocker
End

Hayden Farm

PH

HIGH ST

Manor Farm

MILL RD

Nettlebed
Com Prim
Sch

Old
Kiln

CATSLIP

The
Cat

The Bothy

Nettlebed

Joyce
Grove

Catslip

1

Tylers

Hospice

Sewage
Wks

B481

A4130

Black Wood

Lowercommon
Wood

86

Top
Copse

68   A   69   B   70   C

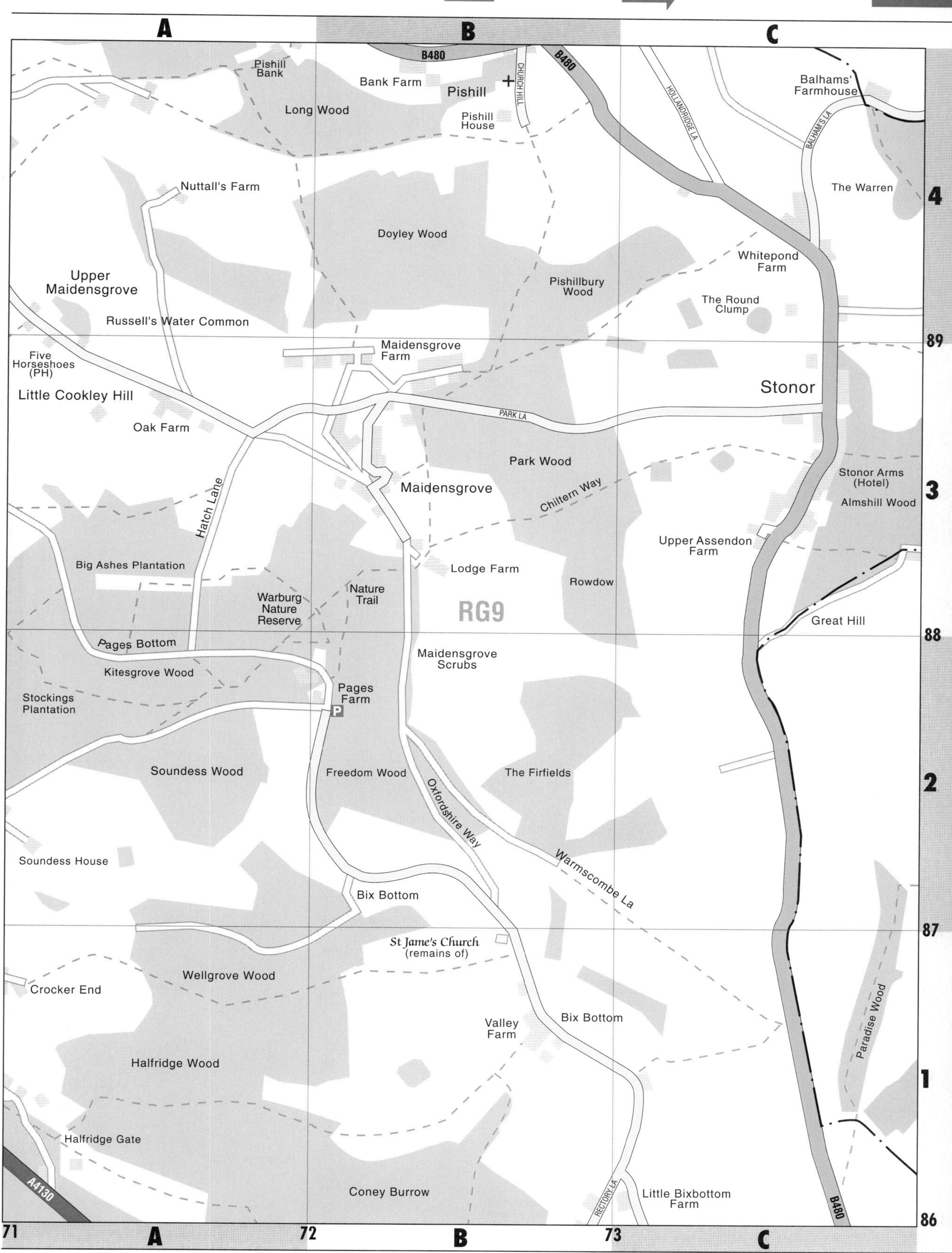

Pishill Bank

Bank Farm

Pishill

B480

B480

Long Wood

Pishill House

Balhams' Farmhouse

HOLLANDRIDGE LA

BALHAM'S LA

CHURCH HILL

The Warren

4

Nuttall's Farm

Doyley Wood

Pishillbury Wood

Whitepond Farm

The Round Clump

Upper Maidensgrove

Russell's Water Common

Maidensgrove Farm

89

Five Horseshoes (PH)

Little Cookley Hill

Oak Farm

PARK LA

Park Wood

Stonor

Maidensgrove

Chiltern Way

Stonor Arms (Hotel)

Almshill Wood

3

Hatch Lane

Big Ashes Plantation

Lodge Farm

Rowdow

Upper Assendon Farm

Nature Trail

Warburg Nature Reserve

RG9

Great Hill

88

Pages Bottom

Kitesgrove Wood

Maidensgrove Scrubs

Stockings Plantation

Pages Farm

P

Soundess Wood

Freedom Wood

The Firfields

Oxfordshire Way

2

Soundess House

Bix Bottom

Warmscombe La

87

Crocker End

Wellgrove Wood

St Jame's Church (remains of)

Bix Bottom

Paradise Wood

Halfridge Wood

Valley Farm

1

Halfridge Gate

A4130

Coney Burrow

RECTORY LA

Little Bixbottom Farm

B480

86

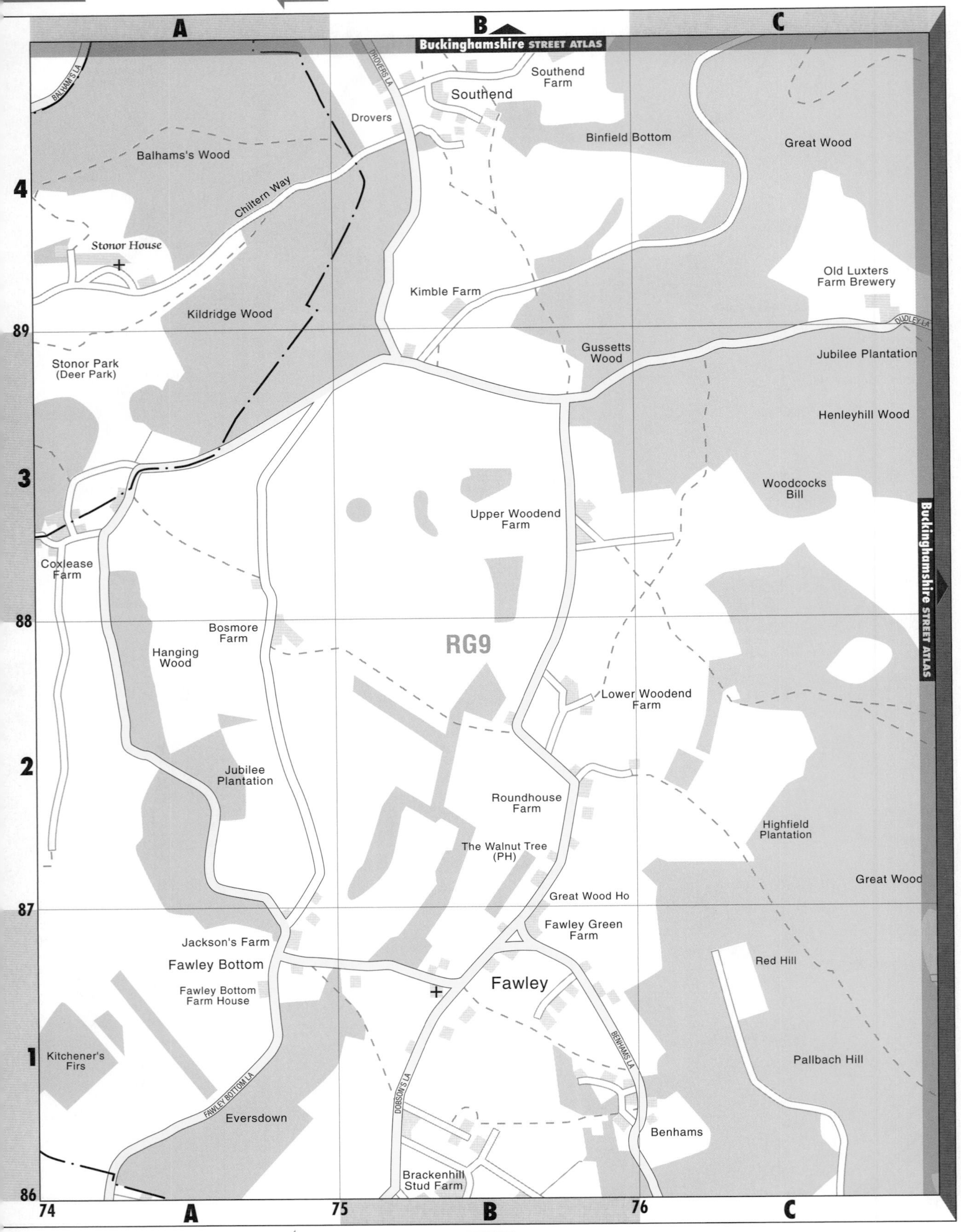

Buckinghamshire STREET ATLAS

A B C

Southend
Southend Farm
Drovers
Binfield Bottom
Great Wood

Balhams's Wood

Chiltern Way

4

Stonor House
+

Old Luxters
Farm Brewery

Kildridge Wood

Kimble Farm

89

Gussetts
Wood

DUDLEY LA

Jubilee Plantation

Stonor Park
(Deer Park)

Henleyhill Wood

Woodcocks
Bill

3

Coxlease
Farm

Upper Woodend
Farm

Buckinghamshire STREET ATLAS

88

Bosmore
Farm

RG9

Hanging
Wood

Lower Woodend
Farm

2

Jubilee
Plantation

Highfield
Plantation

Roundhouse
Farm

The Walnut Tree
(PH)

Great Wood

Great Wood Ho

87

Fawley Green
Farm

Jackson's Farm

Red Hill

Fawley Bottom

Fawley Bottom
Farm House

+

Fawley

BENHAMS LA

1

Kitchener's
Firs

Pallbach Hill

FAWLEY BOTTOM LA

DOBSON S LA

Eversdown

Benhams

86

Brackenhill
Stud Farm

74 A 75 B 76 C

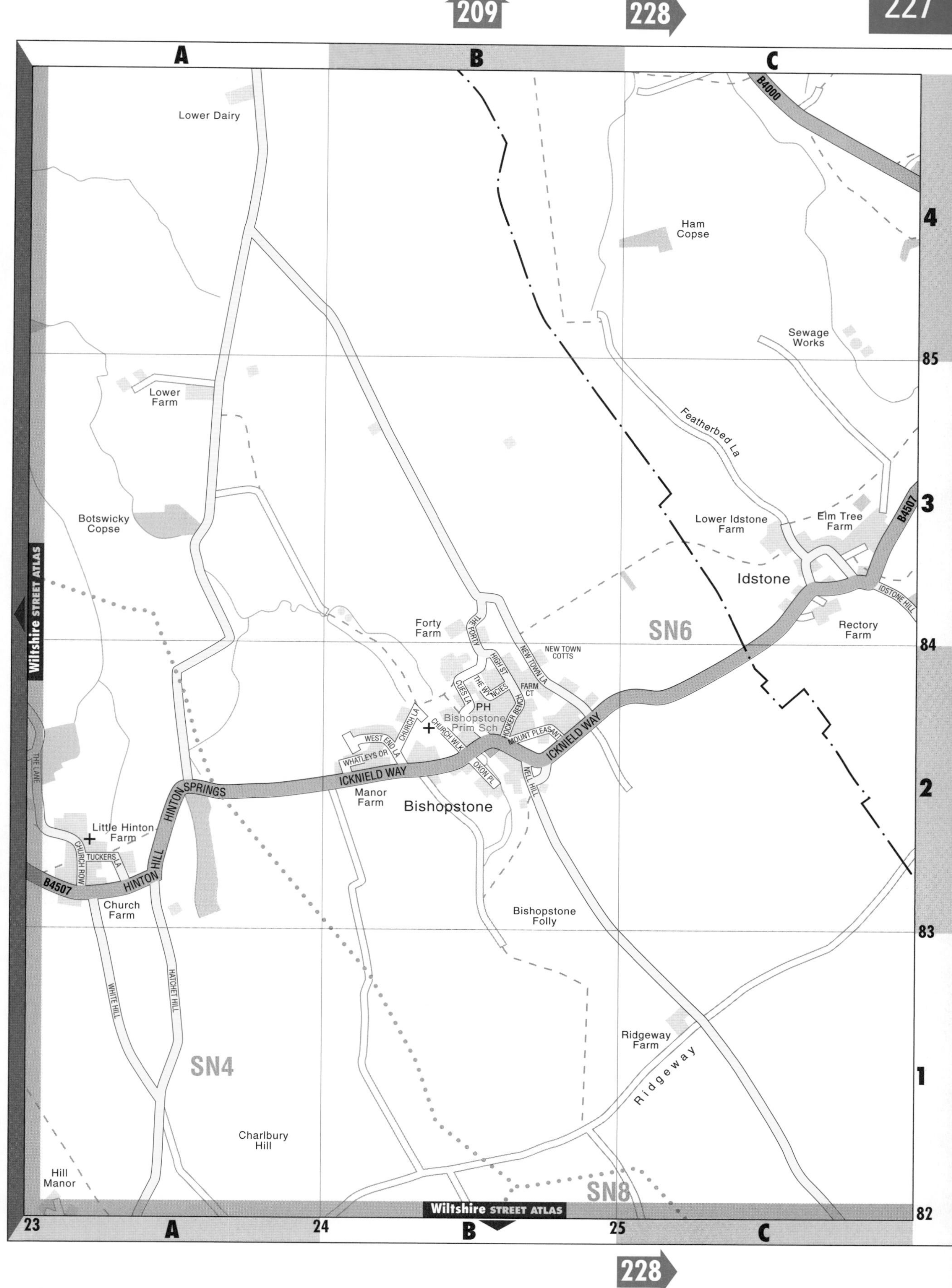

209

228

A

B

C

Lower Dairy

Ham
Copse

4

Sewage
Works

85

Lower
Farm

Featherbed La

Botswicky
Copse

Lower Idstone
Farm

Elm Tree
Farm

3

B4507

Idstone

SN6

Rectory
Farm

84

Forty
Farm

NEW TOWN
COTTS

PH

Bishopstone
Prim Sch

ICKNIELD WAY

Wiltshire STREET ATLAS

HINTON SPRINGS

ICKNIELD WAY

Manor
Farm

Bishopstone

2

Little Hinton
Farm

HINTON HILL

TUCKERS

CHURCH ROW

B4507

Church
Farm

Bishopstone
Folly

83

WHITE HILL

HATCHET HILL

SN4

Ridgeway
Farm

Ridgeway

1

Charlbury
Hill

Hill
Manor

SN8

82

227
210

A **B** **C**

4

Kingstone
Winslow

B4507

Odstone Hill

Wayland's
Smithy

Ridgeway

B4000

Ashbury

Kingstone
Farm

Winslow
Bank

Odstone
Coombes

Knighton
Barn

STATION RD

POUND
PIECE

MALTHOUSE CL

WALNUT TREES HILL

Berrycroft

BERRYCROFT RD

KINGS
CL

Sch

MALTHOUSE

THE
MALTHOUSES

Kingstone Coombes

Odstone Barn

85

HIGH ST

PO

PH
P

Lértwell

ASHBURY HILL

Resr

Kingstone
Barn

Odstone Barn

IDSTONE RD

B4507

Ashbury
Folly

Down
Folly

Compton
Bottom

3

SN6

Ridgeway

Idstone
Plantation

84

IDSTONE HILL

Tower Hill

Honeybunch
Corner

2

Odstone Down

83

Hailey Wood

RG17

Crowberry
Tump

Kingstone Down

1

Middle Wood

P

B4000

Alfred's Castle

Ashdown
House

Starveall
Farm

82

26 **A** 27 **B** 28 **C**

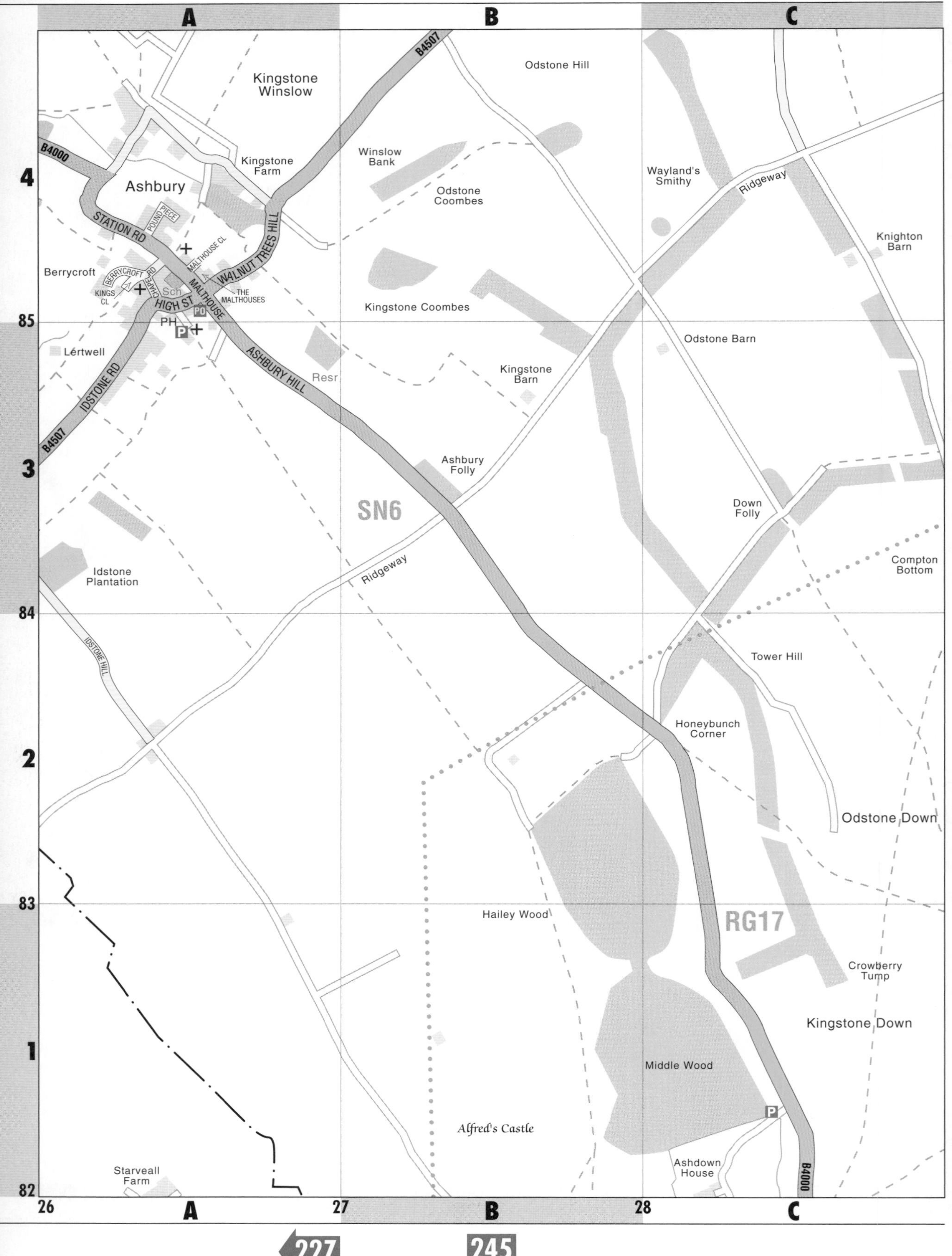

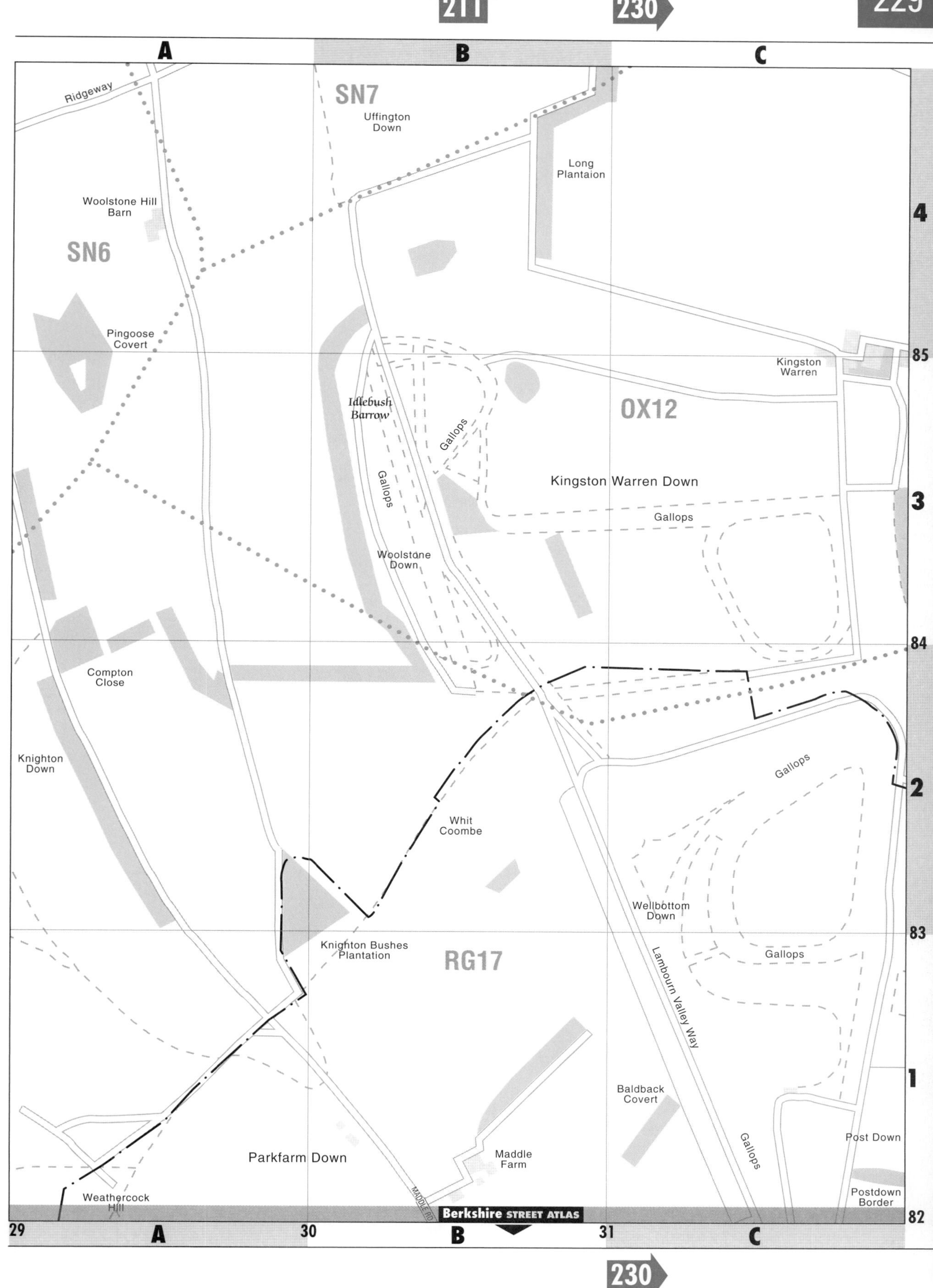

SN7
Uffington
Down

Long
Plantaion

Ridgeway

Woolstone Hill
Barn

SN6

Pingoose
Covert

Kingston
Warren

85

Idlebush
Barrow

OX12

Gallops

Gallops

Kingston Warren Down

Gallops

3

Gallops

Woolstone
Down

84

Compton
Close

Gallops

Knighton
Down

Whit
Coombe

Gallops

2

Wellbottom
Down

83

Knighton Bushes
Plantation

RG17

Gallops

Lambourn Valley Way

Baldback
Covert

1

Post Down

Parkfarm Down

Maddle
Farm

Gallops

Postdown
Border

Weathercock
Hill

MADDLE RD

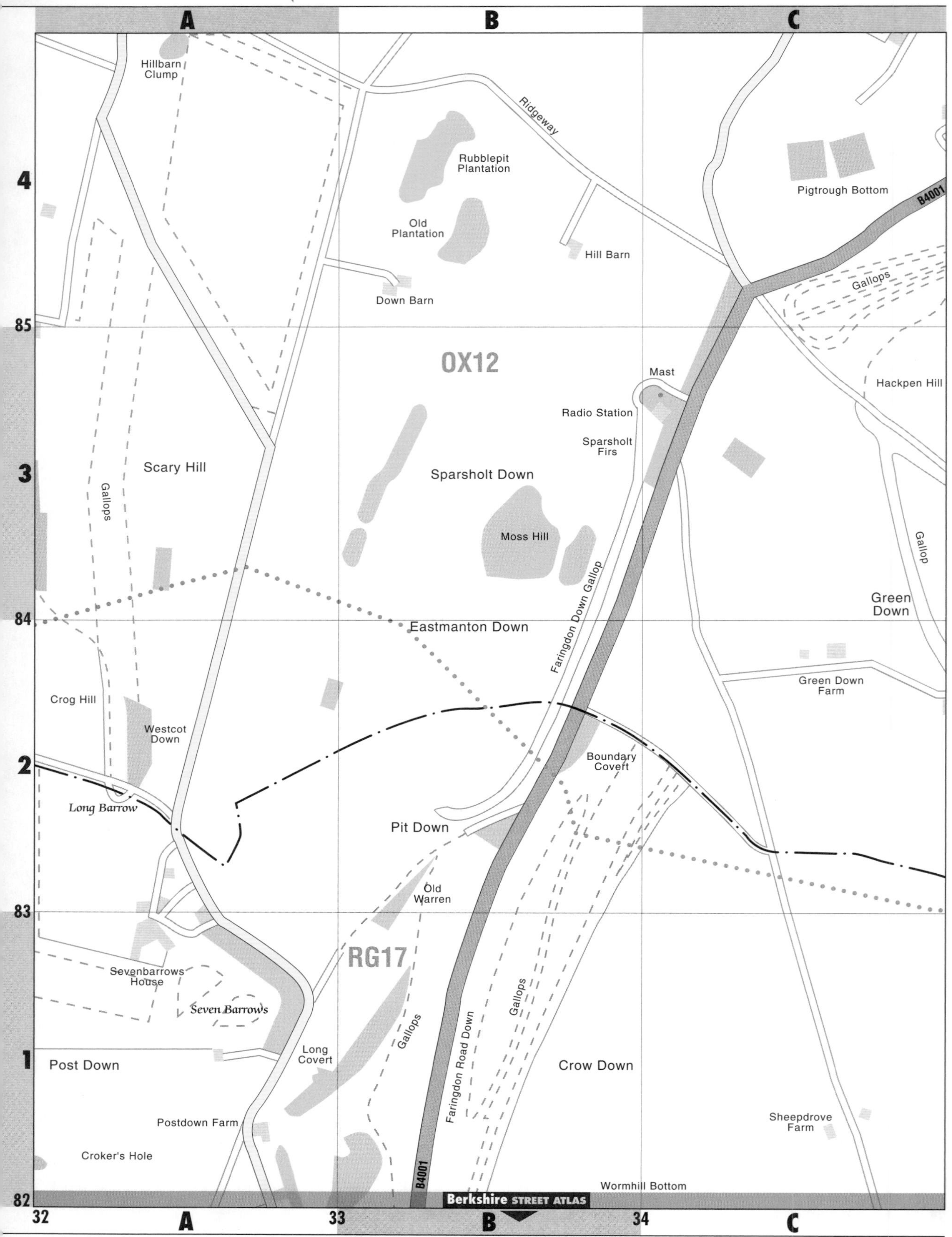

A B C

4

Hillbarn Clump

Ridgeway

Rubblepit Plantation

Old Plantation

Pigtrough Bottom

B4001

Hill Barn

Down Barn

Gallops

85

OX12

Mast

Radio Station

Hackpen Hill

Scary Hill

Sparsholt Firs

3

Gallops

Sparsholt Down

Moss Hill

Faringdon Down Gallop

Green Down

Gallop

84

Eastmanton Down

Crog Hill

Green Down Farm

Westcot Down

2

Boundary Covert

Long Barrow

Pit Down

Old Warren

83

RG17

Sevenbarrows House

Seven Barrows

Gallops

Gallops

Gallops

1

Post Down

Long Covert

Faringdon Road Down

Crow Down

Sheepdrove Farm

Postdown Farm

Croker's Hole

B4001

Wormhill Bottom

82

32 A 33 B 34 C

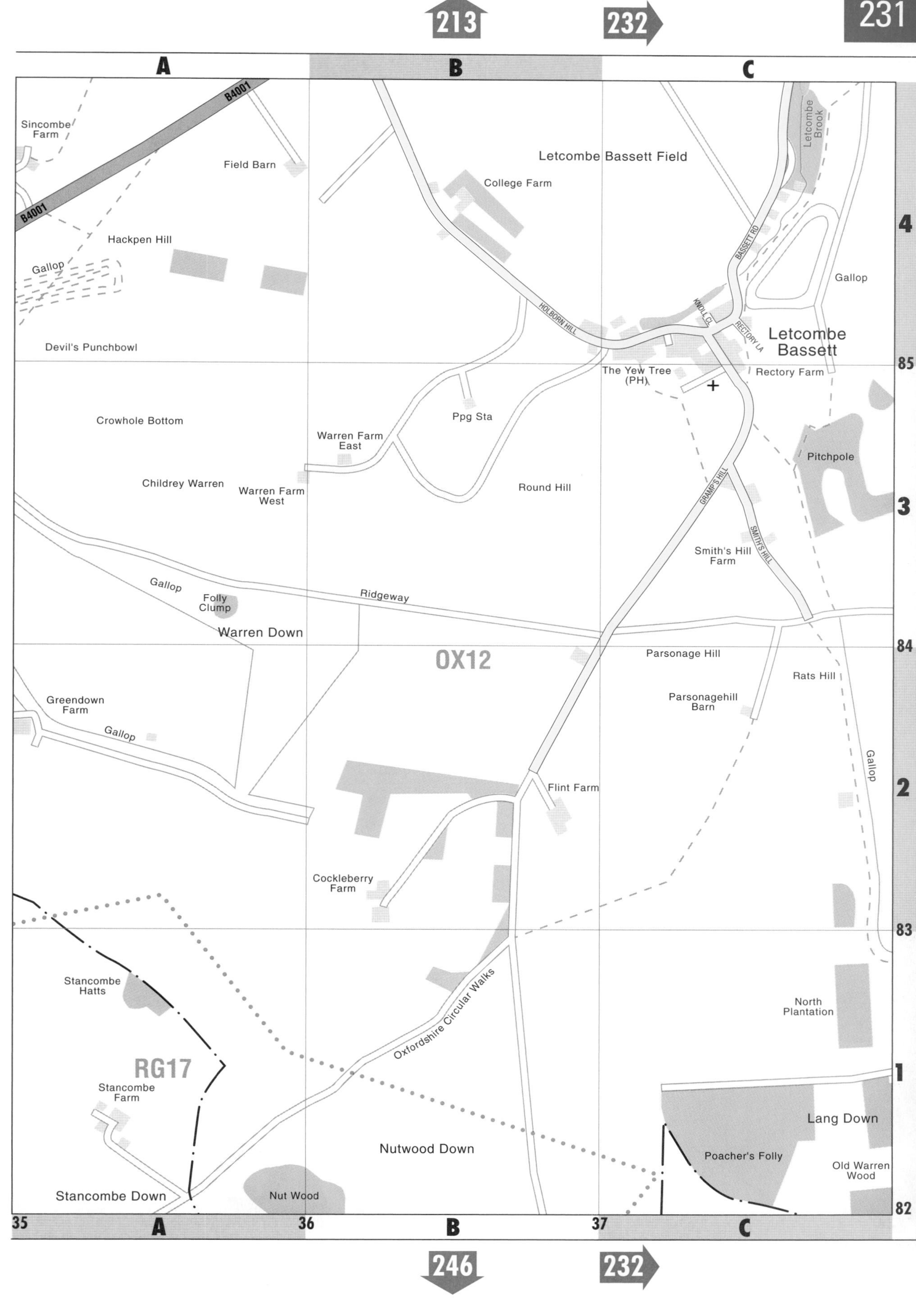

A
B
C

Sincombe Farm

B4001

Field Barn

Hackpen Hill

Gallop

B4001

Devil's Punchbowl

Letcombe Bassett Field

College Farm

Letcombe Brook

HOLBORN HILL

BASSETT RD

KNOLL CL

RECTORY LA

Letcombe Bassett

Gallop

4

The Yew Tree (PH)

Rectory Farm

85

Crowhole Bottom

Warren Farm East

Ppg Sta

Round Hill

GRAMP'S HILL

SMITH'S HILL

Pitchpole

Childrey Warren

Warren Farm West

Smith's Hill Farm

3

Gallop

Folly Clump

Ridgeway

Warren Down

OX12

Parsonage Hill

84

Rats Hill

Greendown Farm

Gallop

Parsonagehill Barn

Gallop

2

Flint Farm

Cockleberry Farm

83

Stancombe Hatts

Oxfordshire Circular Walks

North Plantation

RG17

Stancombe Farm

1

Lang Down

Poacher's Folly

Old Warren Wood

Nutwood Down

Stancombe Down

Nut Wood

82

35
A
36
B
37
C

231
214

A
B
C
A338
Spike Lodge Farm
B4494 CHAINHILL RD
Field Barn
Gallop
4
The Downs
Warborough Farm
WARBOROUGH RD
COURT HILL RD
Warborough Bottom
Furzewick Farm
Wantage Down
85
Furzewick Down
Castle Hill
The Ridgeway (YH)
Gallops
Pewit Farm
3
MANOR RD
Black Bushes Barn
Whitehouse Farm
THE RIDGEWAY
Segsbury Down
Ridgeway
Angeldown Farm
Upper Black Bushes
Segsbury Farm
Angeldown Cottages
84
New Warren
OX12
Ashen Pen
Greenhill Down
2
Lattindown Farm
Black Bushes
83
Corpse Copse
Little Hall
Letcombe Bowers Farm
The Wilderness
Sparrow's Copse
Pinal Wood
Gallop
1
Bowers Wood
South Plantation
Winterdown Bottom
A338
The Beeches
82
Berkshire STREET ATLAS
A338 Hungerford
38
A
39
B
40
C

231

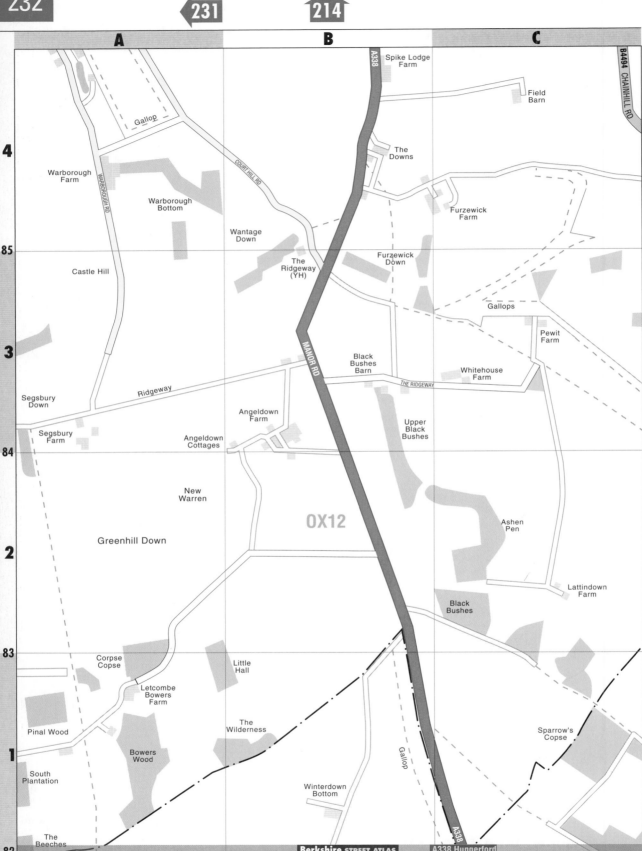

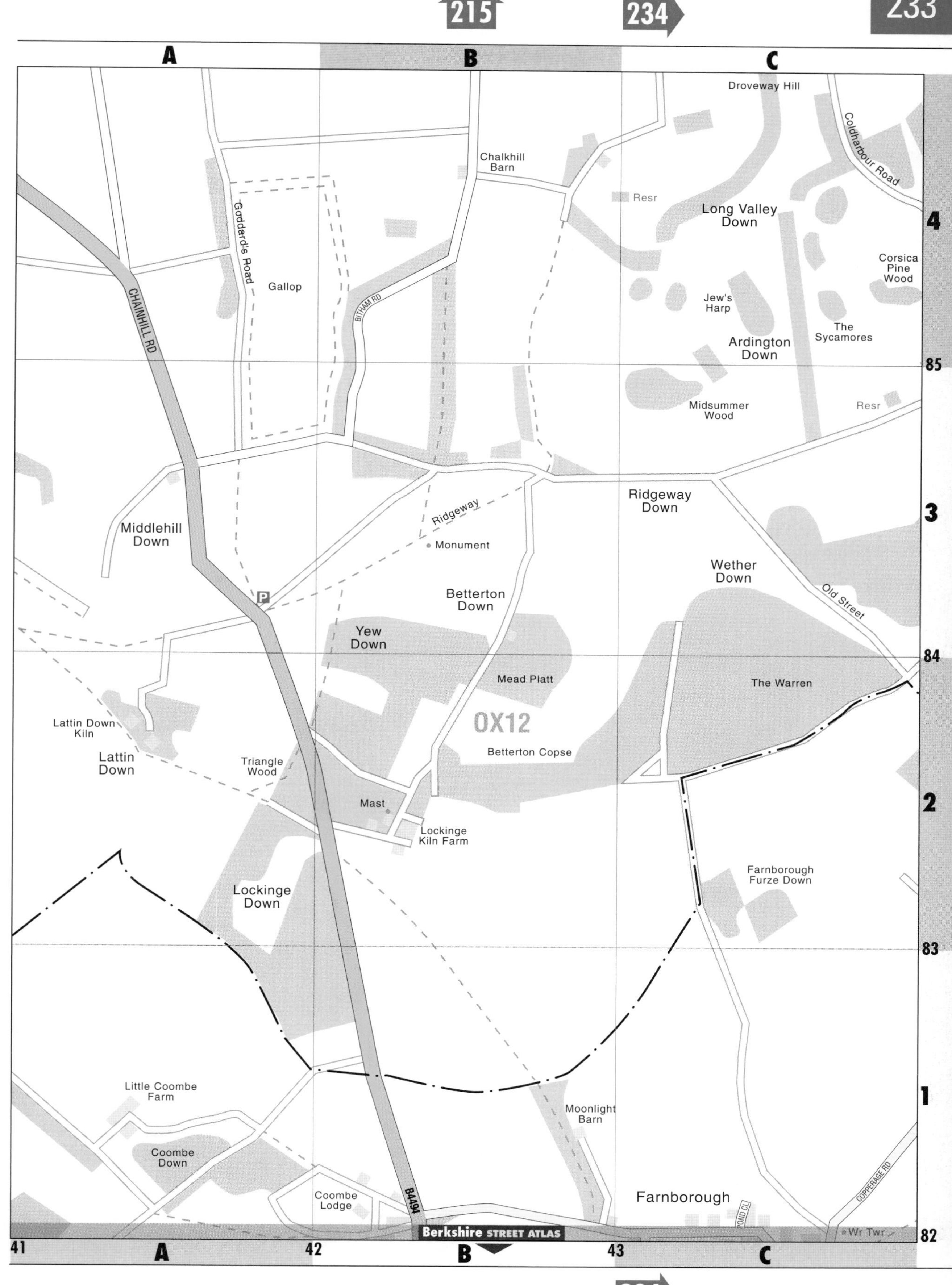

A B C

Droveway Hill

Coldharbour Road

Chalkhill Barn

Resr

Long Valley Down

Corsica Pine Wood

Goddard's Road

Gallop

Jew's Harp

The Sycamores

BITHAM RD

Ardington Down

CHAINHILL RD

Midsummer Wood

Resr

Ridgeway

Ridgeway Down

Middlehill Down

Monument

Wether Down

Old Street

P

Betterton Down

Yew Down

Mead Platt

The Warren

OX12

Lattin Down Kiln

Betterton Copse

Lattin Down

Triangle Wood

Mast

Lockinge Kiln Farm

Farnborough Furze Down

Lockinge Down

Little Coombe Farm

Moonlight Barn

Coombe Down

Farnborough

Coombe Lodge

B4494

POND CL

COPPERAGE RD

Wr Twr

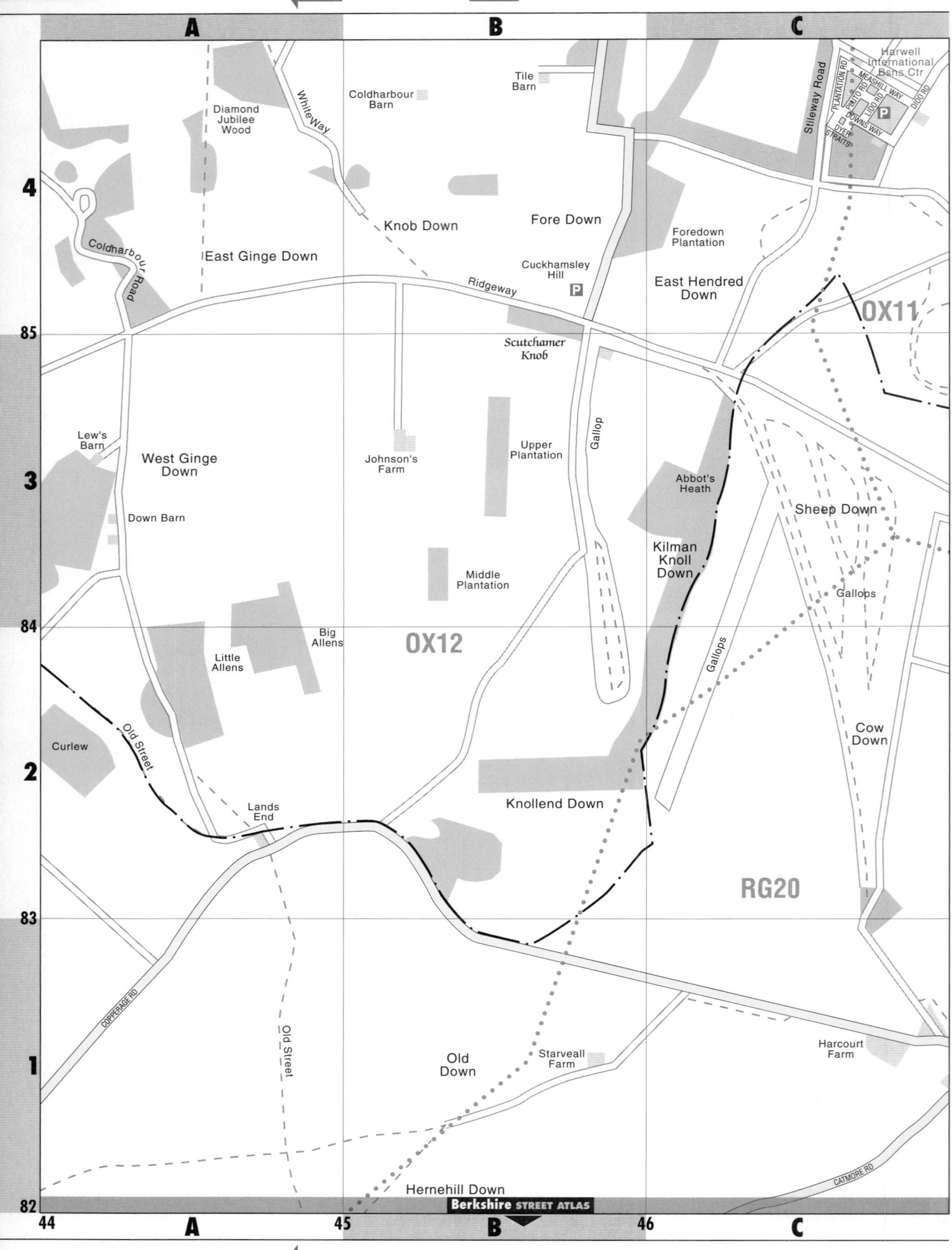

A B C

4

Diamond Jubilee Wood

WhiteWay

Coldharbour Barn

Tile Barn

Harwell International Bsns Ctr

Stileway Road

PLANTATION RD
PRIOR TO RD
LLOYD RD
DIDO RD
MEASHILL WAY
DOWNS WAY
DYER
STRAITS

P

Knob Down

Fore Down

Foredown Plantation

East Ginge Down

Coldharbour Road

Ridgeway

Cuckhamsley Hill

P

East Hendred Down

OX11

85

Scutchamer Knob

Lew's Barn

West Ginge Down

Johnson's Farm

Upper Plantation

Gallop

Abbot's Heath

Sheep Down

3

Down Barn

Kilman Knoll Down

Gallops

Middle Plantation

84

Big Allens

OX12

Little Allens

Gallops

Cow Down

Curlew

Old Street

2

Lands End

Knollend Down

RG20

83

COPPERAGE RD

Old Street

1

Old Down

Starveall Farm

Harcourt Farm

CATMORE RD

82

Hernehill Down

44 A 45 B 46 C

217
236

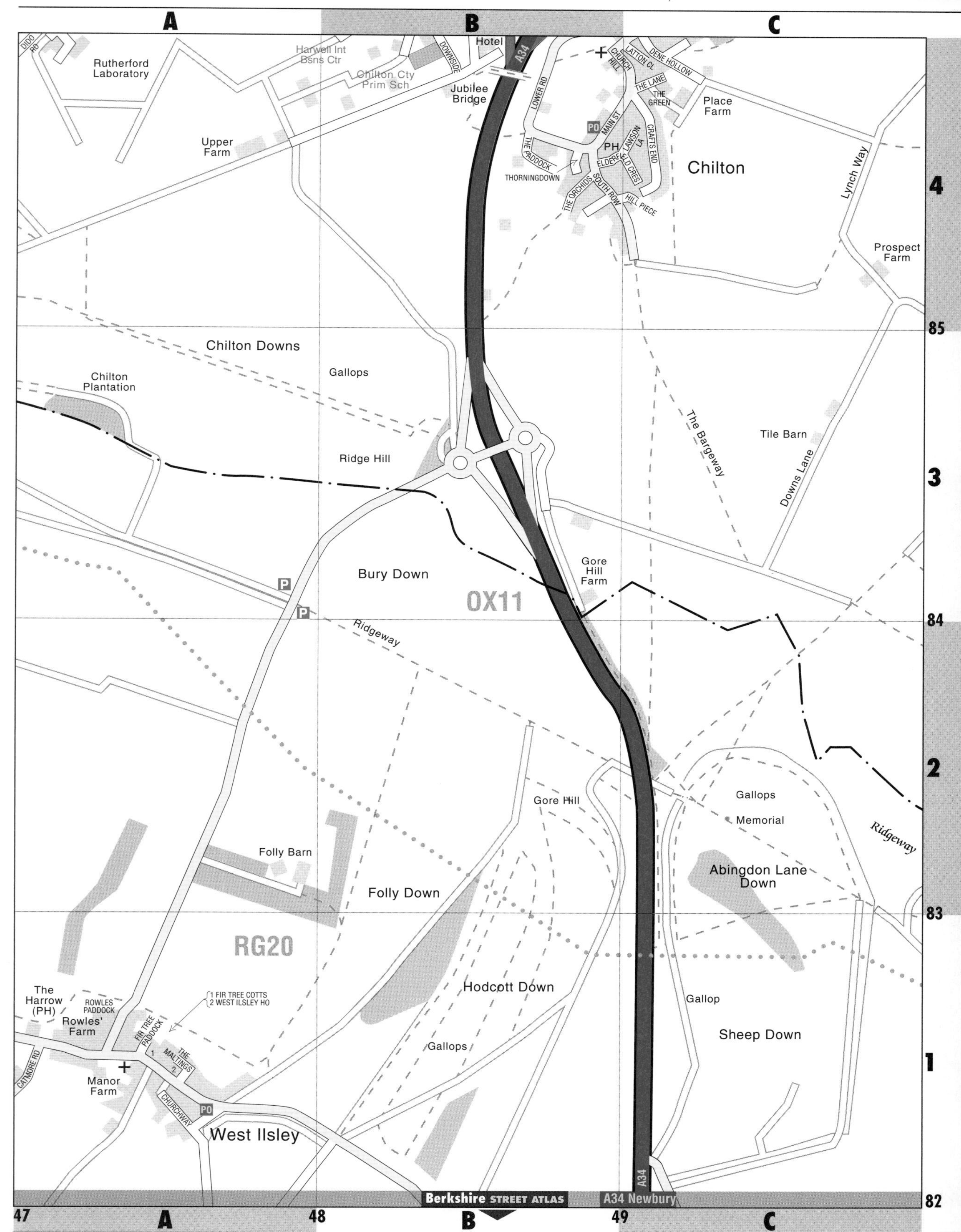
A
B
C
Rutherford Laboratory
Harwell Int Bsns Ctr
Chilton Cty Prim Sch
Hotel
DOWNSIDE
Jubilee Bridge
A34
LOWER RD
CHURCH HILL
LATTON CL
DENE HOLLOW
THE LANE
THE GREEN
Place Farm
MAIN ST
LAWSON LA
CRAFTS END
PO
PH
THE PADDOCK
THORNINGDOWN
ELDERFIELD CRES
THE ORCHIDS
SOUTH ROW
HILL PIECE
Chilton
Lynch Way
Upper Farm
Prospect Farm
4
85
Chilton Downs
Gallops
Chilton Plantation
The Bargeway
Tile Barn
Ridge Hill
Downs Lane
3
Bury Down
Gore Hill Farm
OX11
P
Ridgeway
84
2
Gore Hill
Gallops
Memorial
Ridgeway
Folly Barn
Abingdon Lane Down
Folly Down
83
RG20
Hodcott Down
The Harrow (PH)
ROWLES PADDOCK
Rowles' Farm
1 FIR TREE COTTS
2 WEST ILSLEY HO
FIR TREE PADDOCK
THE MALTINGS
Gallop
Sheep Down
Gallops
CATMORE RD
Manor Farm
CHURCHWAY
West Ilsley
1
A34
82
47
48
49

235
218

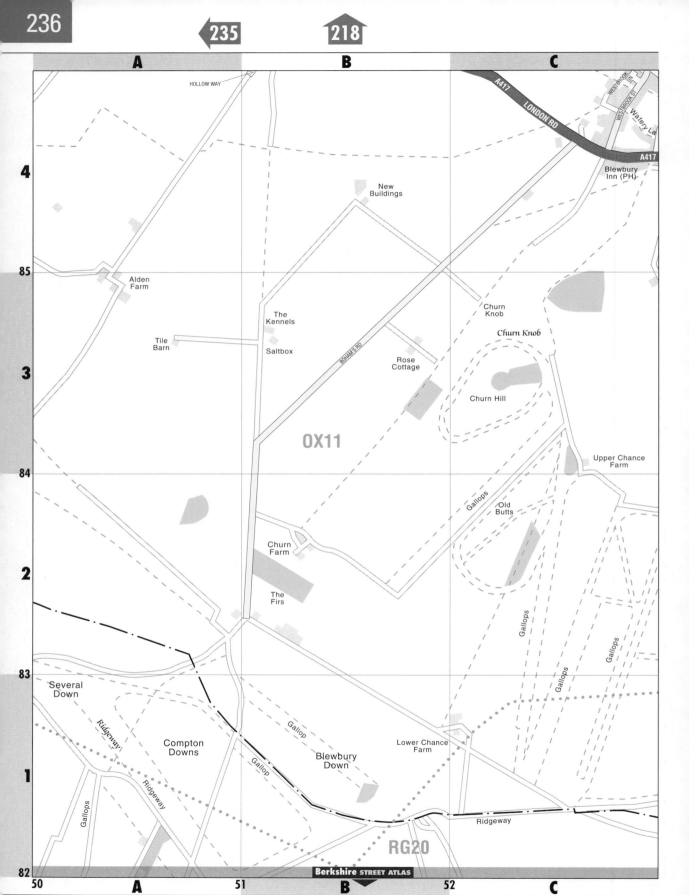
A
B
C
HOLLOW WAY
A417
LONDON RD
WESTBROOK GN
WESTBROOK ST
Watery La
A417
Blewbury Inn (PH)
4
New Buildings
85
Alden Farm
Churn Knob
The Kennels
Churn Knob
Tile Barn
Saltbox
BOHAM'S RD
Rose Cottage
3
Churn Hill
OX11
Upper Chance Farm
84
Gallops
Old Butts
Churn Farm
2
The Firs
Gallops
Gallops
83
Several Down
Gallops
Gallop
Ridgeway
Compton Downs
Lower Chance Farm
Blewbury Down
1
Gallop
Ridgeway
Gallops
Ridgeway
RG20
82
50
51
52
A
B
C

235

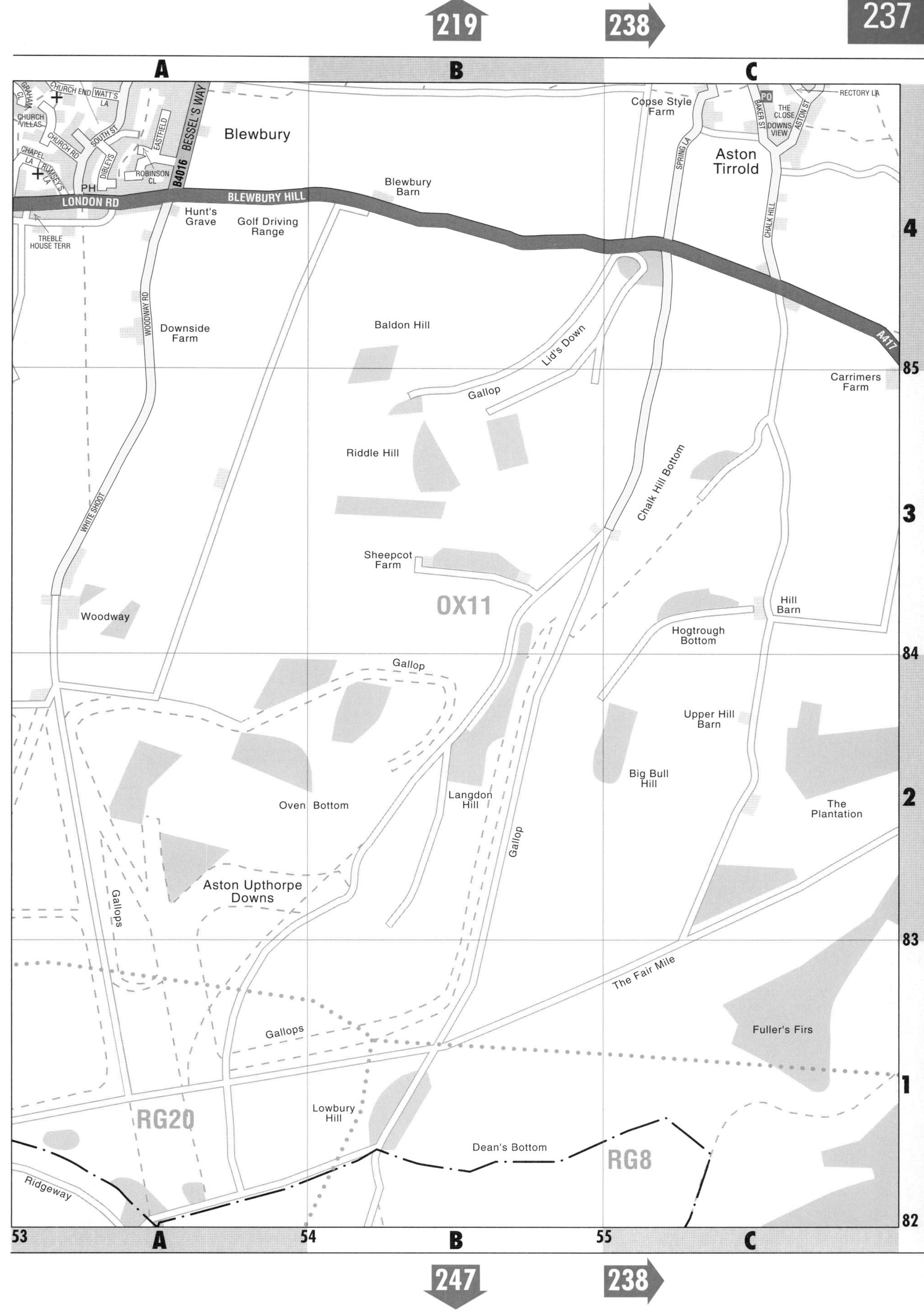

A **B** **C**

Blewbury

GRAHAM LA
CHURCH END
WATT'S LA
CHURCH VILLAS
CHURCH RD
SOUTH ST
DUBLEYS
EASTFIELD
BESSEL'S WAY
B4016
CHAPEL LA
RUSSET'S LA
PH
ROBINSON CL
LONDON RD
BLEWBURY HILL

Copse Style Farm

RECTORY LA
PO
THE CLOSE
DOWNS VIEW
BAKER ST
ASTON ST

Aston Tirrold

TREBLE HOUSE TERR

Hunt's Grave

Blewbury Barn

SPRING LA
CHALK HILL

Golf Driving Range

4

WOODWAY RD
Downside Farm

Baldon Hill

Lid's Down

A417

Carrimers Farm

85

WHITE SHOOT

Gallop

Chalk Hill Bottom

Riddle Hill

Hill Barn

3

Woodway

Sheepcot Farm

OX11

Hogtrough Bottom

84

Gallop

Upper Hill Barn

Oven Bottom

Langdon Hill

Big Bull Hill

The Plantation

2

GALLOPS
Aston Upthorpe Downs

Gallop

83

The Fair Mile

Gallops

Fuller's Firs

1

RG20

Lowbury Hill

Dean's Bottom

RG8

Ridgeway

82

53 **A** **54** **B** **55** **C**

A B C

4

Westfield
Farm

Lollingdon
Farm

The
Lynch

85

A417

Lollingdon
Hill

Bowslade

WESTFIELD RD

Offlands
Farm

OX11

Sheephouse
Farm

HALFPENNY LA

3

Breach
House

Breach
Farm

Cranford
House Sch

WILLOW COURT LA

A329

THE STREET

Stormerbank
Kennels

OX10

WILLOW
COTTS

GLEBE CL

84

Westfield
Stables

Moulsford

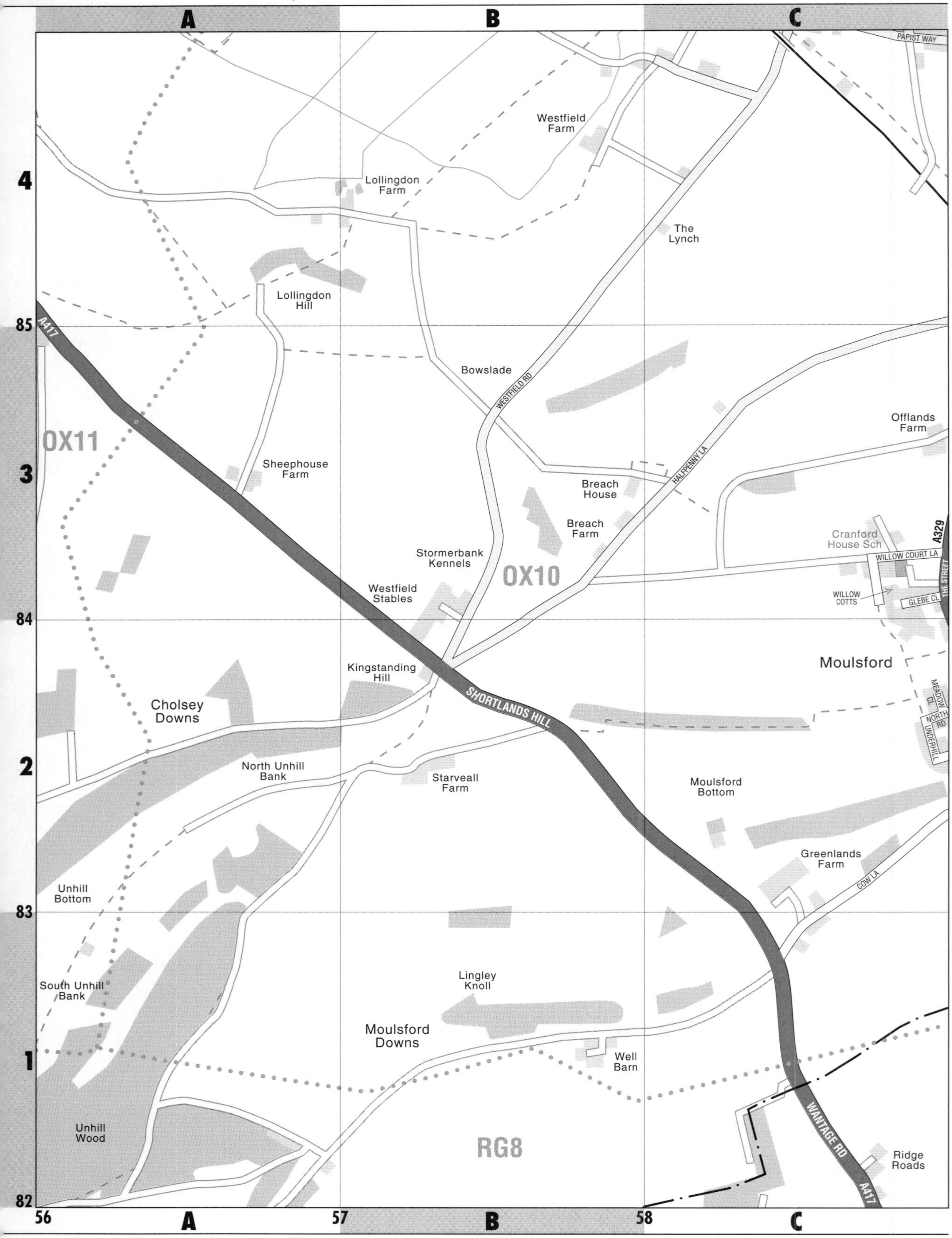

Kingstanding
Hill

SHORTLANDS HILL

MEADOW CL

NORTH RD

UNDERHILL

Cholsey
Downs

North Unhill
Bank

Starveall
Farm

Moulsford
Bottom

2

Greenlands
Farm

COW LA

Unhill
Bottom

83

Lingley
Knoll

South Unhill
Bank

Moulsford
Downs

Well
Barn

WANTAGE RD

1

Unhill
Wood

RG8

Ridge
Roads

A417

82

56

A

57

B

58

C

221
240

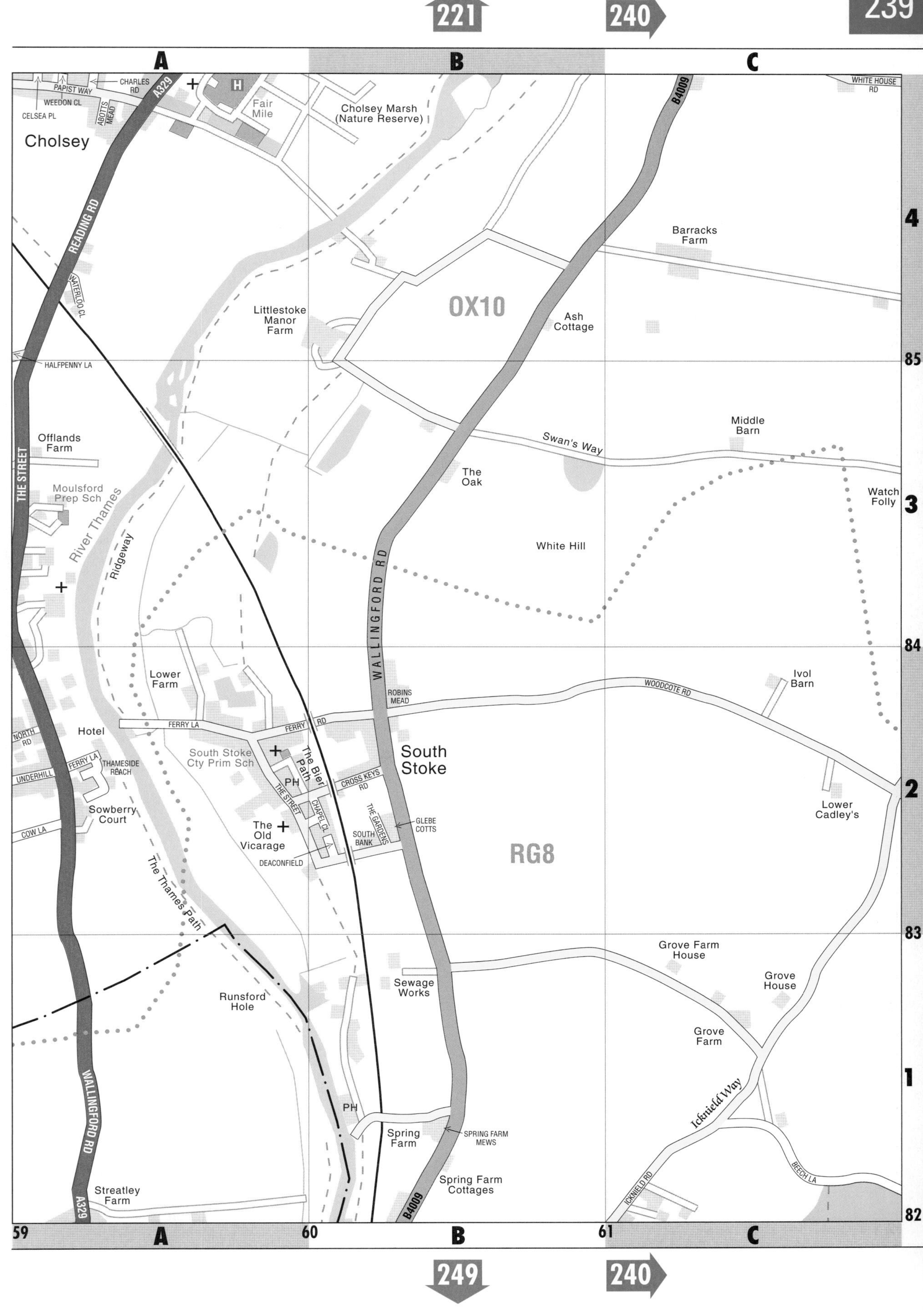
A
B
C
CHARLES RD
PAPIST WAY
WEEDON CL
CELSEA PL
ABOTTS MEAD
A329
Fair Mile
Cholsey Marsh (Nature Reserve)
B4009
WHITE HOUSE RD
Cholsey
READING RD
Barracks Farm
WATERLOO CL
Littlestoke Manor Farm
OX10
Ash Cottage
HALFPENNY LA
Middle Barn
Offlands Farm
Swan's Way
THE STREET
The Oak
Moulsford Prep Sch
River Thames
Watch Folly
Ridgeway
White Hill
WALLINGFORD RD
Lower Farm
ROBINS MEAD
WOODCOTE RD
Ivol Barn
FERRY LA
FERRY RD
NORTH RD
Hotel
South Stoke Cty Prim Sch
The Bier Path
South Stoke
FERRY LA
THAMESIDE REACH
UNDERHILL
PH
CROSS KEYS RD
THE STREET
CHAPEL CL
Sowberry Court
THE GARDENS
GLEBE COTTS
Lower Cadley's
COW LA
The Old Vicarage
SOUTH BANK
RG8
DEACONFIELD
The Thames Path
Grove Farm House
Sewage Works
Grove House
Runsford Hole
Grove Farm
Icknield Way
PH
Spring Farm
SPRING FARM MEWS
WALLINGFORD RD
BEECH LA
ICKNIELD RD
Spring Farm Cottages
Streatley Farm
A329
B4009
4
85
3
84
2
83
1
82
59
60
61

249
240

239
222

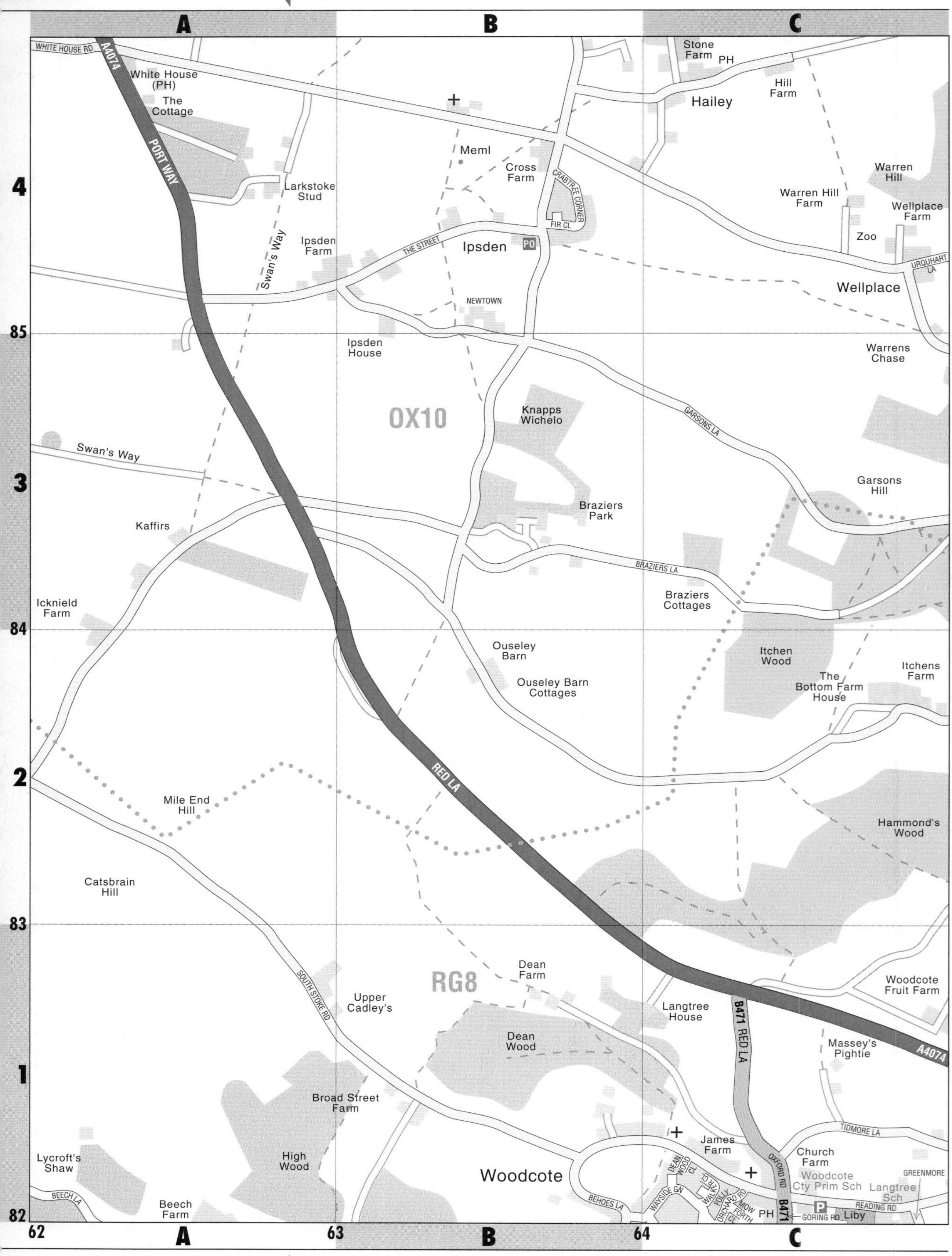
A
B
C
WHITE HOUSE RD
A4074
White House (PH)
The Cottage
PORT WAY
Stone Farm
PH
Hailey
Hill Farm
Meml
Cross Farm
CRABTREE CORNER
FIR CL
Larkstoke Stud
Swan's Way
Ipsden Farm
THE STREET
Ipsden
PO
Warren Hill
Warren Hill Farm
Wellplace Farm
Zoo
URQUHART LA
Wellplace
NEWTOWN
Ipsden House
Warrens Chase
OX10
Knapps Wichelo
GARSONS LA
Swan's Way
Garsons Hill
Kaffirs
Braziers Park
BRAZIERS LA
Icknield Farm
Braziers Cottages
Ouseley Barn
Itchen Wood
Itchens Farm
Ouseley Barn Cottages
The Bottom Farm House
RED LA
Mile End Hill
Hammond's Wood
Catsbrain Hill
Dean Farm
RG8
SOUTH STOKE RD
Upper Cadley's
Langtree House
B471 RED LA
Woodcote Fruit Farm
Dean Wood
Massey's Pightie
A4074
Broad Street Farm
TIDMORE LA
James Farm
Church Farm
High Wood
Lycroft's Shaw
Woodcote
DEAN WOOD CL
WAYSIDE GN
OXFORD RD
Woodcote Cty Prim Sch
Langtree Sch
GREENMORE
BEECH LA
Beech Farm
BEHOES LA
ORCHARD RD
MOW FORTH
READING RD
PH
B471
P
GORING RD
Liby
4
85
3
84
2
83
1
82
62
63
64

239
250

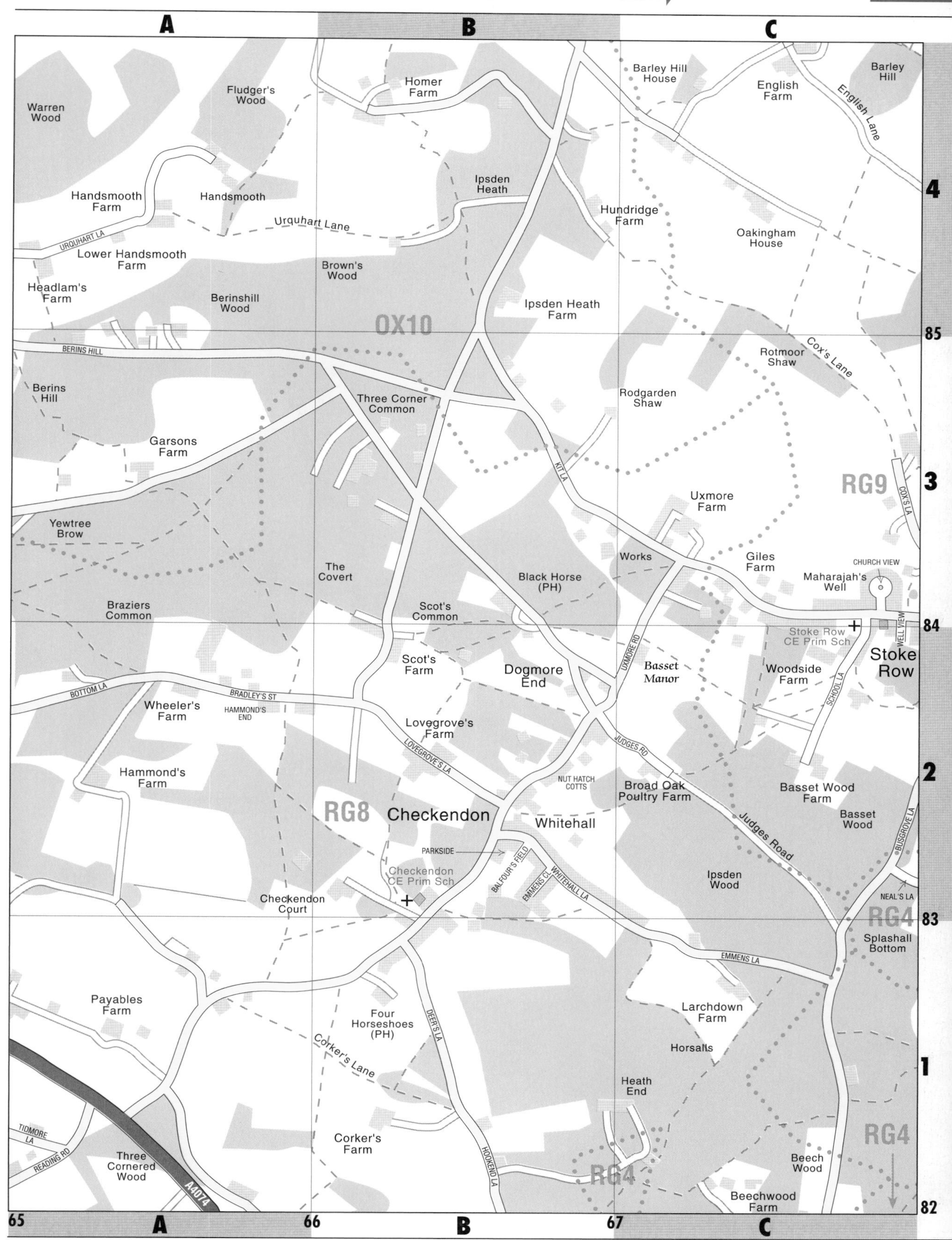

A B C

Warren Wood

Fludger's Wood

Homer Farm

Barley Hill House

English Farm

Barley Hill

English Lane

Handsmooth Farm

Handsmooth

Ipsden Heath

Hundridge Farm

Oakingham House

4

Urquhart Lane

Urquhart La

Lower Handsmooth Farm

Brown's Wood

Ipsden Heath Farm

Headlam's Farm

Berinshill Wood

OX10

85

Berins Hill

BERINS HILL

Berins Hill

Three Corner Common

Rotmoor Shaw

Cox's Lane

Rodgarden Shaw

Garsons Farm

NUT LA

RG9

3

Yewtree Brow

Uxmore Farm

COX'S LA

The Covert

Works

Giles Farm

CHURCH VIEW

Maharajah's Well

Braziers Common

Scot's Common

Black Horse (PH)

Stoke Row CE Prim Sch

WELL VIEW

84

Scot's Farm

Dogmore End

Basset Manor

Woodside Farm

Stoke Row

Bottom La

BOTTOM LA

BRADLEY'S ST

Wheeler's Farm

HAMMOND'S END

Lovegrove's Farm

UXMORE RD

SCHOOL LA

Hammond's Farm

LOVEGROVE'S LA

NUT HATCH COTTS

JUDGES RD

Broad Oak Poultry Farm

Basset Wood Farm

Basset Wood

2

RG8

Checkendon

Whitehall

Judges Road

BUGGROVE LA

PARKSIDE

Checkendon CE Prim Sch

BALFOUR'S FIELD

EMMENS CL

WHITEHALL LA

Ipsden Wood

NEAL'S LA

Checkendon Court

RG4

83

Splashall Bottom

Payables Farm

Four Horseshoes (PH)

DEER'S LA

EMMENS LA

Larchdown Farm

Corker's Lane

Horsalls

1

TIDMORE LA

READING RD

A4074

Three Cornered Wood

Corker's Farm

HOOKEND LA

Heath End

RG4

Beech Wood

RG4

Beechwood Farm

82

65 66 A 67 B C

241
224

A   **B**   **C**

4

Kate's Copse

Howberrywood Farm

Upper Shaw

Devil's Hill

Deadman's Lane

Swan Wood

B481

Oxlands Bottom

Highmoor Trench

Highmoor Common Wood

English Lane

Oakingham Bottom

Nott Wood

Hall Farm

Merrimoles

Newnham Hill

85

Newnhamhill Farm

Highmoor

Lower Highmoor

Bush Wood

Little Farm

Highmoor Farm

The Dog & Duck (PH)

Holly Grove

Stokerow Farm

NEWNHAMHILL BOTTOM

3

The Crooked Billet (PH)

THE GLEBE

HOLLY CL

Highmoor Cross

Scotland

Church Farm

COX'S LA

NOTTWOOD LA

CHERRY TREE CL

NEWLAN DS LA

ISHREE COTTS

PH

PO

BENARES GR

ALMA GN

Witheridge Hill

Rising Sun (PH)

Stonehouse Farm

ROCKY LA

84

Vanalloys Bsns Pk

BUSGROVE LA

RG9

Bear Wood

Padnell's Wood

Orchard Copse

Busgrove Wood

Clayhill Wood

Satwell

Stag Hall

Greyhone Wood

Satwell House Farm

2

Oveys Wood

PH

Burnt Platt

Greyhone Plantation

RG4

Neal's Shaw

NEAL'S LA

Coldmoor Wood

Greatbottom Wood

83

Neal's Farm

Barn Farm

Great David's

Kibes

B481

Neal's Wood

HAZEL GR

The Grouse & Claret (PH)

Kingwood Common

Kingwood Kennels

1

ASHDOWN WAY

HAWTHORN DR

WYFOLD CT

LIME AVE

Hazel Grove

Cheriton House

RG4

Littlebottom Wood

82

68   **A**   **69**   **B**   **70**   **C**

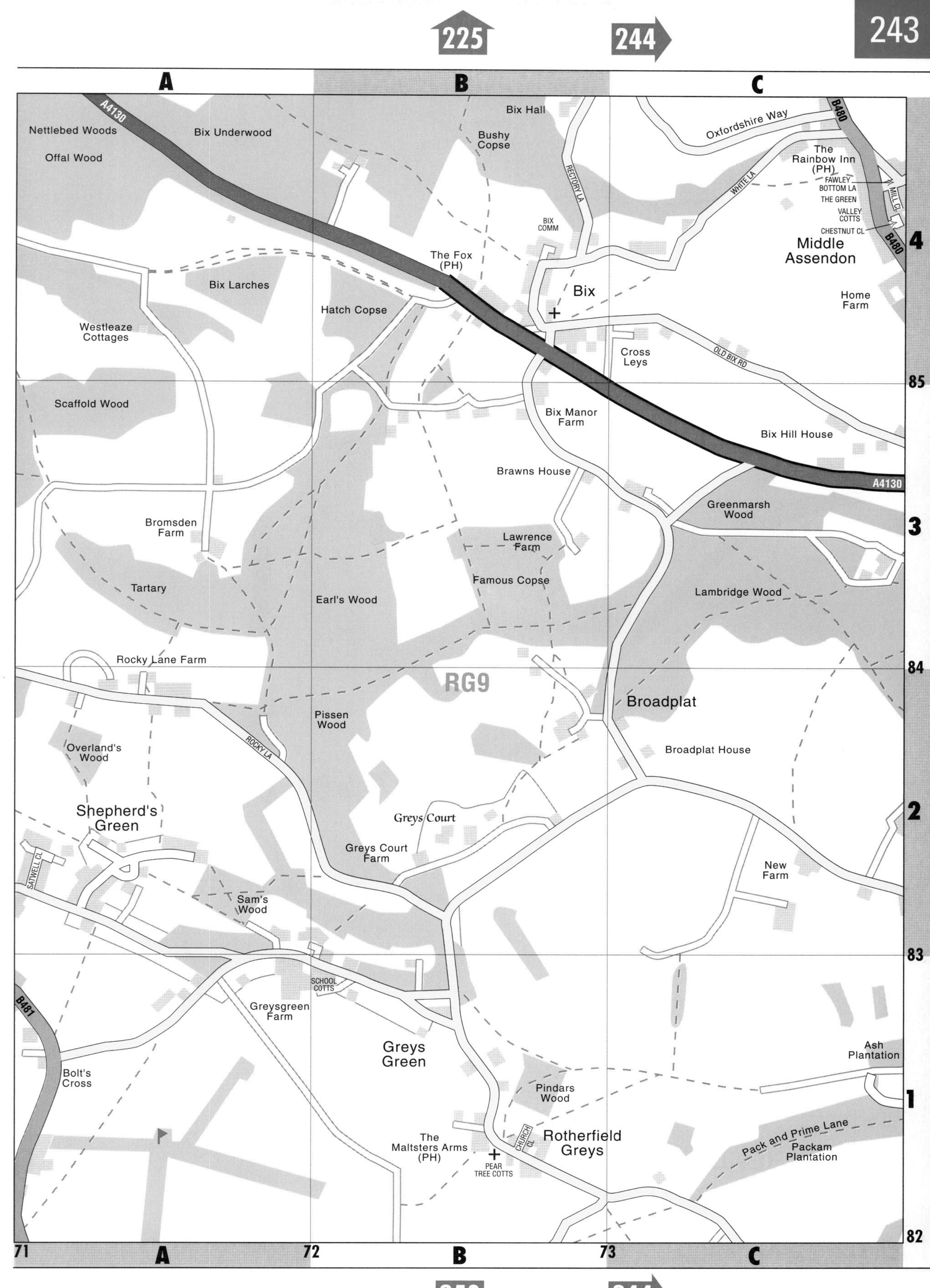

A B C

A4130

Nettlebed Woods

Bix Underwood

Bix Hall

Bushy Copse

Oxfordshire Way

B480

The Rainbow Inn (PH)

Offal Wood

RECTORY LA

WHITE LA

FAWLEY BOTTOM LA
THE GREEN
VALLEY COTTS

MILL CL

The Fox (PH)

BIX COMM

CHESTNUT CL

Middle Assendon

B480

4

Bix Larches

Hatch Copse

Bix

Home Farm

Westleaze Cottages

Cross Leys

OLD BIX RD

85

Scaffold Wood

Bix Manor Farm

Bix Hill House

Brawns House

Greenmarsh Wood

A4130

Bromsden Farm

Lawrence Farm

3

Tartary

Famous Copse

Lambridge Wood

Earl's Wood

Rocky Lane Farm

RG9

84

Pissen Wood

Broadplat

Overland's Wood

ROCKY LA

Broadplat House

Shepherd's Green

Greys Court

2

SATWELL CL

Greys Court Farm

New Farm

Sam's Wood

83

SCHOOL COTTS

Greysgreen Farm

Ash Plantation

B481

Greys Green

Bolt's Cross

Pindars Wood

Pack and Prime Lane

Packam Plantation

1

The Maltsters Arms (PH)

CHURCH CL

Rotherfield Greys

PEAR TREE COTTS

82

71 A 72 B 73 C

243
226

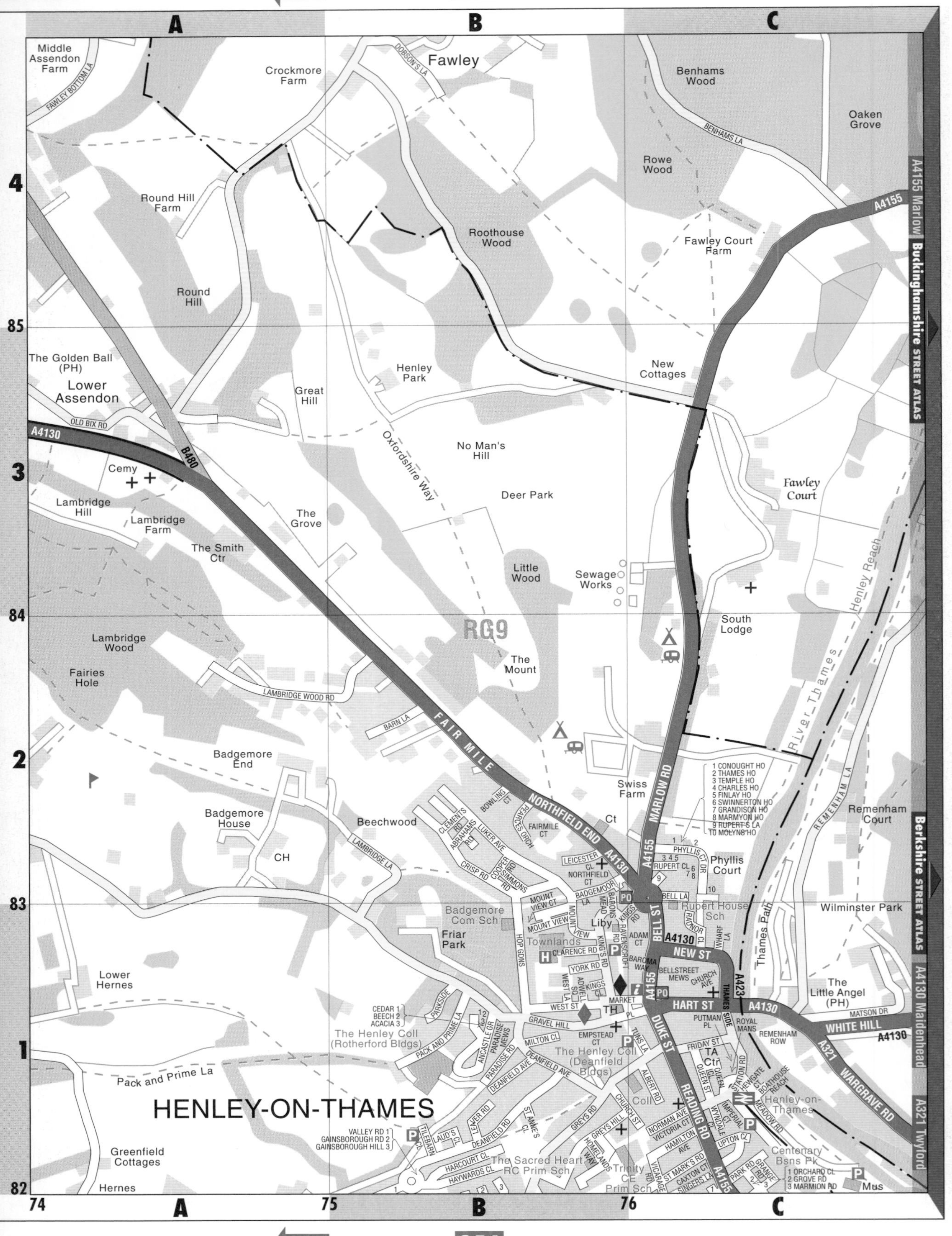
Fawley
Crockmore Farm
Middle Assendon Farm
Benhams Wood
Oaken Grove
Rowe Wood
Round Hill Farm
Roothouse Wood
Fawley Court Farm
Round Hill
The Golden Ball (PH)
Lower Assendon
Henley Park
Great Hill
New Cottages
No Man's Hill
Oxfordshire Way
Cemy
Lambridge Hill
Lambridge Farm
The Grove
Deer Park
Fawley Court
The Smith Ctr
Little Wood
Sewage Works
Lambridge Wood
Fairies Hole
RG9
The Mount
South Lodge
Badgemore End
Swiss Farm
Badgemore House
Beechwood
CH
Remenham Court
Phyllis Court
Rupert House Sch
Badgemore Com Sch
Friar Park
Townlands
Wilminster Park
Lower Hernes
The Henley Coll (Rotherford Bldgs)
The Henley Coll (Deanfield Bldgs)
The Little Angel (PH)
Pack and Prime La
HENLEY-ON-THAMES
Henley-on-Thames
Greenfield Cottages
The Sacred Heart RC Prim Sch
Trinity CE Prim Sch
Centenary Bsns Pk
Hernes
Mus
River Thames
Henley Reach
Thames Path
FAIR MILE
NORTHFIELD END
MARLOW RD
BELL ST
NEW ST
HART ST
DUKE ST
READING RD
WHITE HILL
WARGRAVE RD
REMENHAM LA
A4130
A4155
B480
A423
A321
A4155 Marlow
A4130 Maidenhead
A321 Twyford
Buckinghamshire STREET ATLAS
Berkshire STREET ATLAS
1 CONOUGHT HO
2 THAMES HO
3 TEMPLE HO
4 CHARLES HO
5 FINLAY HO
6 SWINNERTON HO
7 GRANDISON HO
8 MARMYON HO
9 RUPERT'S LA
10 MOLYNS HO
CEDAR 1
BEECH 2
ACACIA 3
VALLEY RD 1
GAINSBOROUGH RD 2
GAINSBOROUGH HILL 3
1 ORCHARD CL
2 GROVE RD
3 MARMION RD
A B C
74 75 76
82 83 84 85 1 2 3 4

243
254

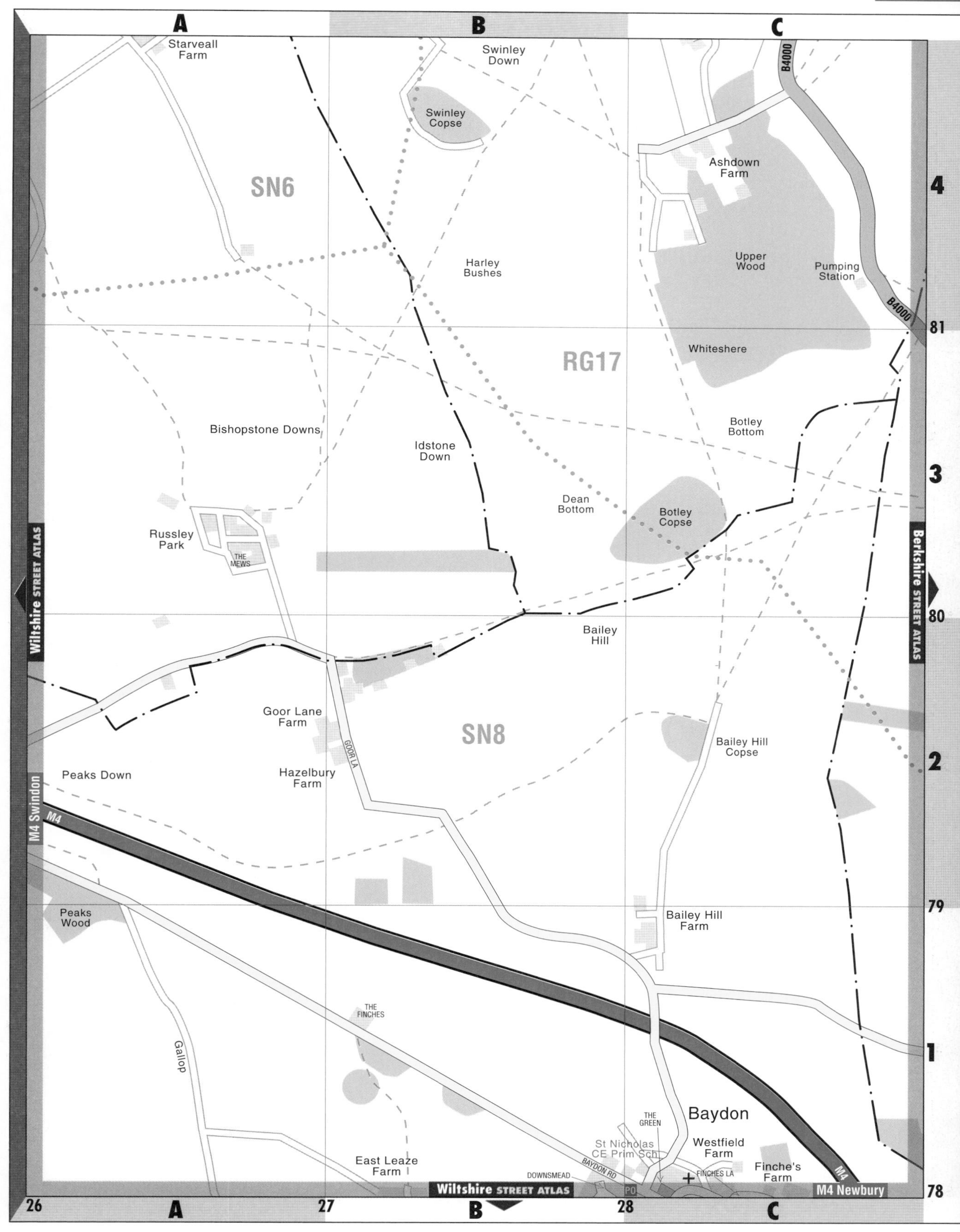

Starveall Farm

Swinley Down

Swinley Copse

SN6

Ashdown Farm

Upper Wood

Pumping Station

B4000

4

Harley Bushes

RG17

Whiteshere

81

Bishopstone Downs

Idstone Down

Botley Bottom

Dean Bottom

Botley Copse

3

Russley Park

THE MEWS

Bailey Hill

80

Goor Lane Farm

SN8

Bailey Hill Copse

GOOR LA

2

Peaks Down

Hazelbury Farm

Peaks Wood

Bailey Hill Farm

79

M4 Swindon

M4

THE FINCHES

Gallop

1

THE GREEN

Baydon

Westfield Farm

Finche's Farm

St Nicholas CE Prim Sch

FINCHES LA

East Leaze Farm

DOWNSMEAD

BAYDON RD

PO

M4

M4 Newbury

78

26 A 27 B 28 C

Wiltshire STREET ATLAS

Berkshire STREET ATLAS

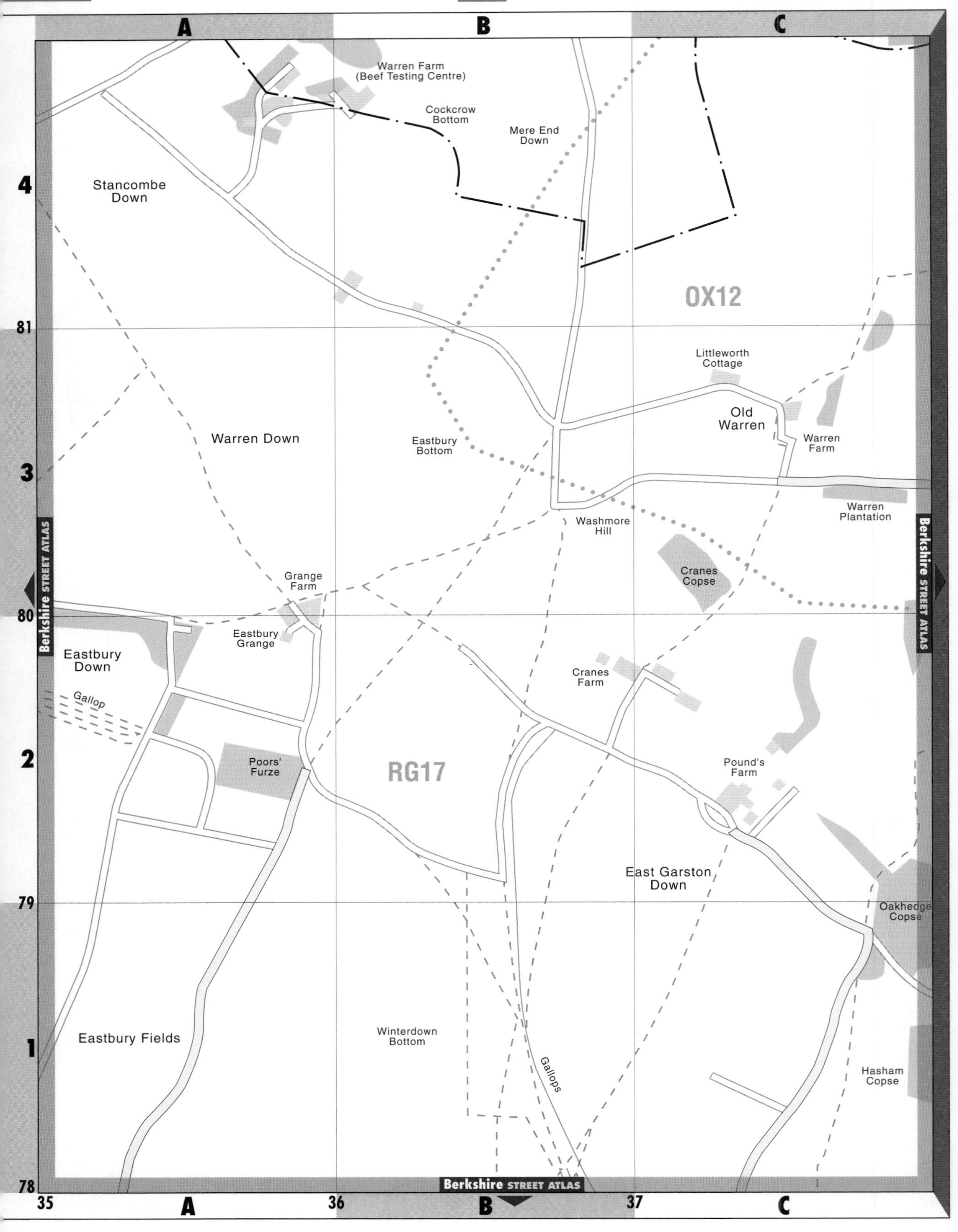

A　　　**B**　　　**C**

Warren Farm
(Beef Testing Centre)

Cockcrow
Bottom

Mere End
Down

4

Stancombe
Down

OX12

81

Littleworth
Cottage

Warren Down

Old
Warren

Eastbury
Bottom

Warren
Farm

3

Washmore
Hill

Warren
Plantation

Cranes
Copse

Grange
Farm

80

Eastbury
Grange

Eastbury
Down

Cranes
Farm

Gallop

Poors'
Furze

RG17

Pound's
Farm

2

East Garston
Down

79

Oakhedge
Copse

1

Eastbury Fields

Winterdown
Bottom

Gallops

Hasham
Copse

78

35　　**A**　　36　　**B**　　37　　**C**

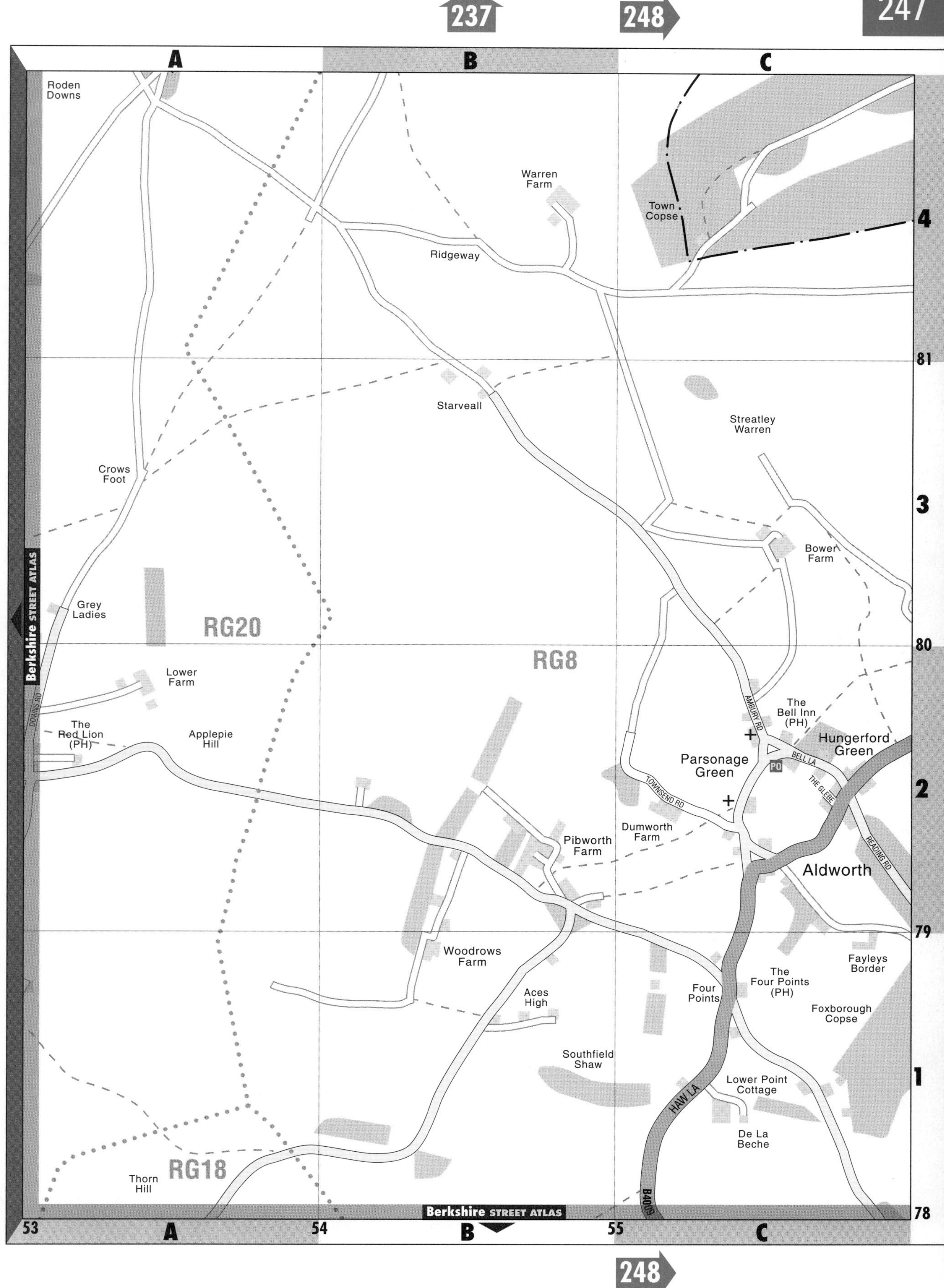

Roden Downs

Warren Farm

Town Copse

Ridgeway

4

81

Starveall

Streatley Warren

Crows Foot

3

Bower Farm

Berkshire STREET ATLAS

Grey Ladies

RG20

80

RG8

Lower Farm

The Bell Inn (PH)

AMBURY RD

The Red Lion (PH)

Applepie Hill

Parsonage Green

Hungerford Green

BELL LA

PO

DOWNS RD

TOWNSEND RD

THE GLEBE

2

Dumworth Farm

Aldworth

READING RD

Pibworth Farm

79

Woodrows Farm

Fayleys Border

Aces High

Four Points

The Four Points (PH)

Foxborough Copse

Southfield Shaw

1

HAW LA

Lower Point Cottage

De La Beche

RG18

Thorn Hill

B4009

78

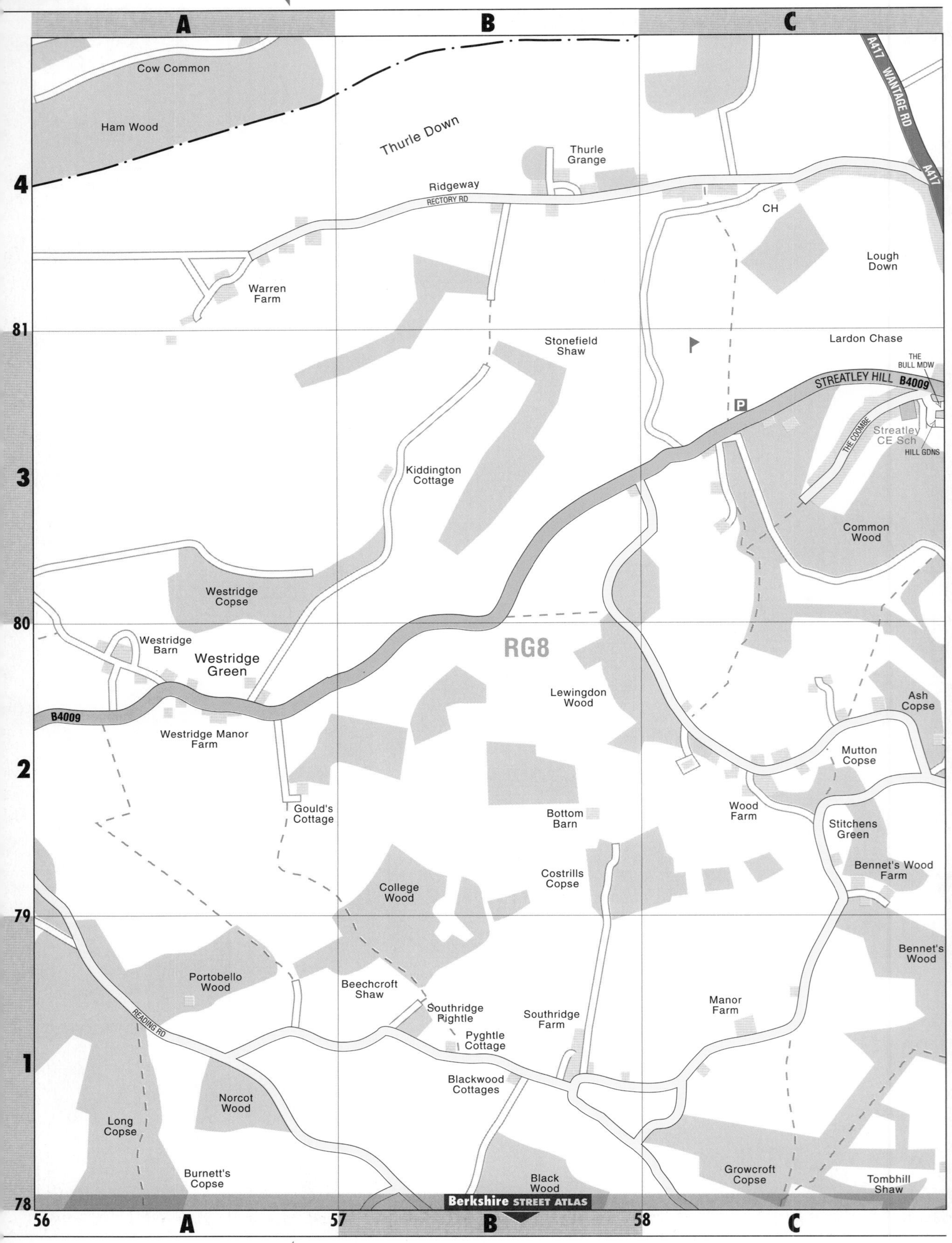

A B C

Cow Common

Ham Wood

Thurle Down

Thurle Grange

Ridgeway

RECTORY RD

CH

Lough Down

4

Warren Farm

81

Stonefield Shaw

Lardon Chase

THE BULL MDW

STREATLEY HILL **B4009**

P

Streatley CE Sch

HILL GDNS

Kiddington Cottage

3

Common Wood

Westridge Copse

80

Westridge Barn

Westridge Green

RG8

Lewingdon Wood

Ash Copse

B4009

Westridge Manor Farm

Mutton Copse

Wood Farm

Stitchens Green

2

Gould's Cottage

Bottom Barn

Bennet's Wood Farm

Costrills Copse

College Wood

79

Bennet's Wood

Portobello Wood

Beechcroft Shaw

Southridge Rightle

Southridge Farm

Manor Farm

READING RD

Pyghtle Cottage

1

Blackwood Cottages

Norcot Wood

Long Copse

Growcroft Copse

Tombhill Shaw

Burnett's Copse

Black Wood

Berkshire STREET ATLAS

78

56   A   57   B   58   C

239
250

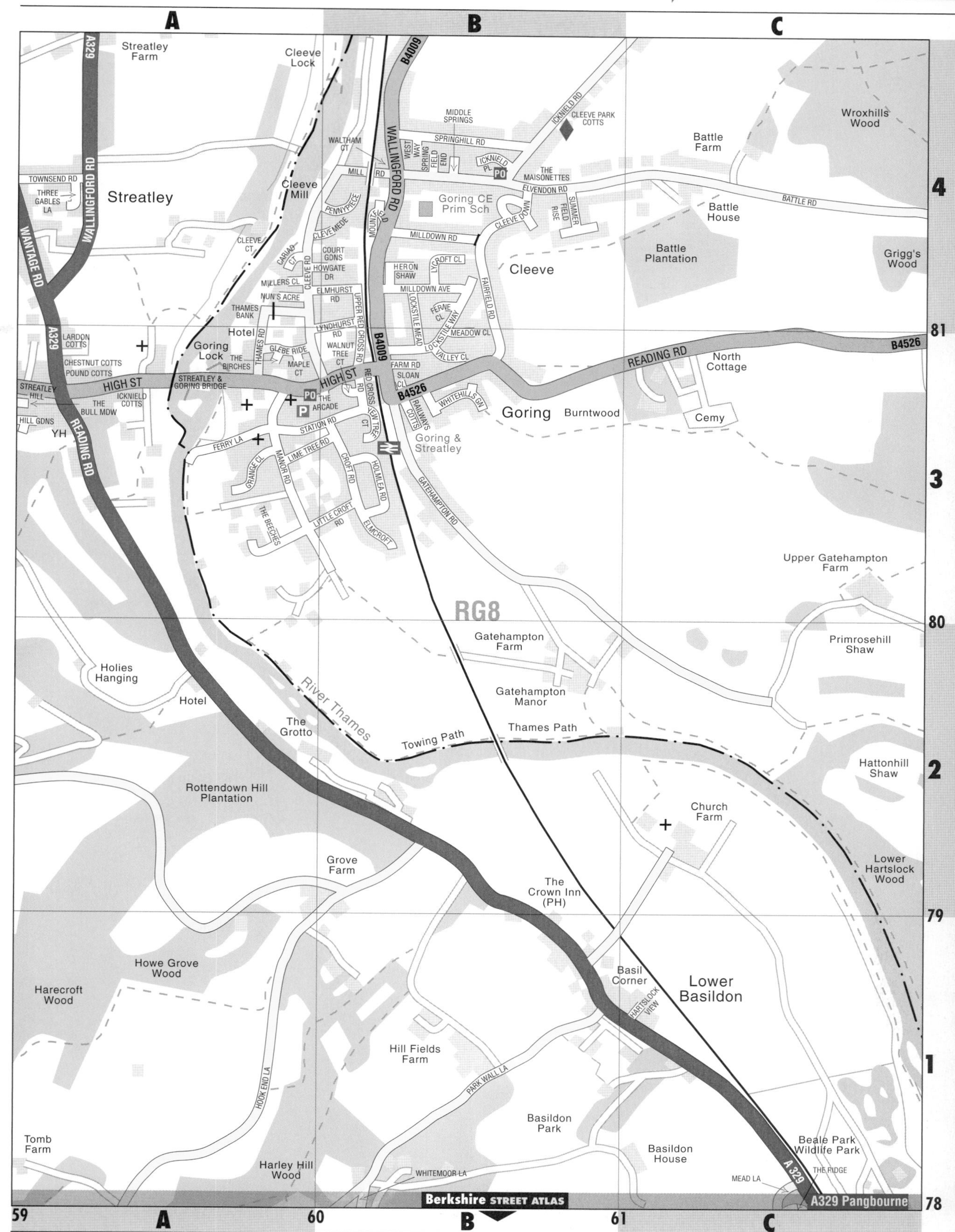
Streatley
Cleeve
Goring
Goring & Streatley
Lower Basildon
Streatley Farm
Cleeve Lock
Cleeve Mill
Goring Lock
Battle Farm
Battle House
Battle Plantation
Wroxhills Wood
Grigg's Wood
North Cottage
Cemy
Burntwood
Goring CE Prim Sch
RG8
River Thames
Towing Path
Thames Path
Gatehampton Farm
Gatehampton Manor
Upper Gatehampton Farm
Primrosehill Shaw
Hattonhill Shaw
Lower Hartslock Wood
Church Farm
Holies Hanging
Hotel
The Grotto
Rottendown Hill Plantation
Grove Farm
The Crown Inn (PH)
Basil Corner
Howe Grove Wood
Harecroft Wood
Hill Fields Farm
Basildon Park
Basildon House
Beale Park Wildlife Park
Tomb Farm
Harley Hill Wood
WALLINGFORD RD
WANTAGE RD
READING RD
HIGH ST
A329
B4009
B4526
BATTLE RD
ELVENDON RD
SPRINGHILL RD
GATEHAMPTON RD
STATION RD
HOOK END LA
PARK WALL LA
WHITEMOOR LA
MEAD LA
THE RIDGE
HARTSLOCK VIEW
A329 Pangbourne
Berkshire STREET ATLAS

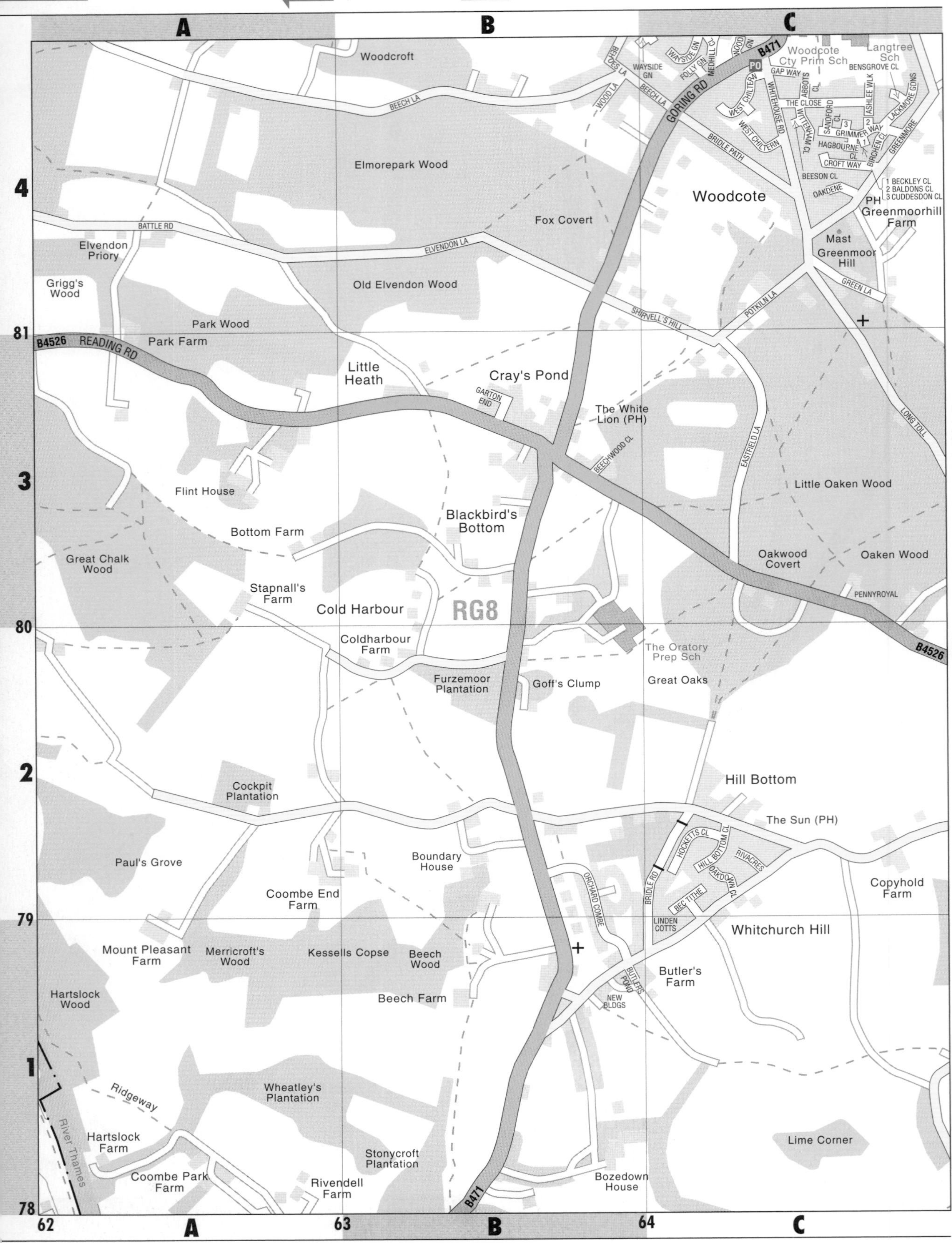

249
240

A   **B**   **C**

Woodcroft

BEECH LA

Elmorepark Wood

BELKS LA

WAYSIDE GN

WOOD LA

BEECH LA

WAY SIDE GN

FOLLY GN

MEDHILL CT

NEWTON RD

GOTON RD

B471

PO

Woodcote Cty Prim Sch

Langtree Sch

Bensgrove CL

GAP WAY

WEST CHILTERN

WHITEHOUSE RD

THE CLOSE

ABBOTS CL

WITTENHAM CL

SANDFORD CL

ASHLEE WLK

LACKMORE GDNS

GREENMORE

3

GRIMMER CL

HAGBOURNE CL

BIRCHEN CL

4

Fox Covert

GORING RD

BRIDLE PATH

WEST CHILTERN

CROFT WAY

BEESON CL

OAKDENE

Woodcote

PH Greenmoorhill Farm

1 BECKLEY CL
2 BALDONS CL
3 CUDDESDON CL

Elvendon Priory

BATTLE RD

ELVENDON LA

Old Elvendon Wood

SHIRNELL'S HILL

Mast Greenmoor Hill

POTKILN LA

GREEN LA

Grigg's Wood

Park Wood

81

B4526 READING RD

Park Farm

Little Heath

GARTON END

Cray's Pond

The White Lion (PH)

BEECHWOOD CL

EASTFIELD LA

LONG TOLL

Flint House

3

Bottom Farm

Blackbird's Bottom

Little Oaken Wood

Great Chalk Wood

Stapnall's Farm

Cold Harbour

RG8

Oakwood Covert

Oaken Wood

PENNYROYAL

80

Coldharbour Farm

Furzemoor Plantation

Goff's Clump

The Oratory Prep Sch

Great Oaks

B4526

2

Cockpit Plantation

Hill Bottom

The Sun (PH)

HOCKETTS CL

HILL BOTTOM CL

OAKDOWN

RIVACRES

Paul's Grove

Boundary House

BRIDLE RD

Coombe End Farm

BEC TITHE

Copyhold Farm

79

LINDEN COTTS

Whitchurch Hill

Mount Pleasant Farm

Merricroft's Wood

Kessells Copse

Beech Wood

ORCHARD COMBE

BUTLERS POND

Butler's Farm

Hartslock Wood

Beech Farm

NEW BLDGS

1

Ridgeway

Wheatley's Plantation

Lime Corner

River Thames

Hartslock Farm

Stonycroft Plantation

Coombe Park Farm

Rivendell Farm

Bozedown House

B471

78

62   **A**   **63**   **B**   **64**   **C**

249
256

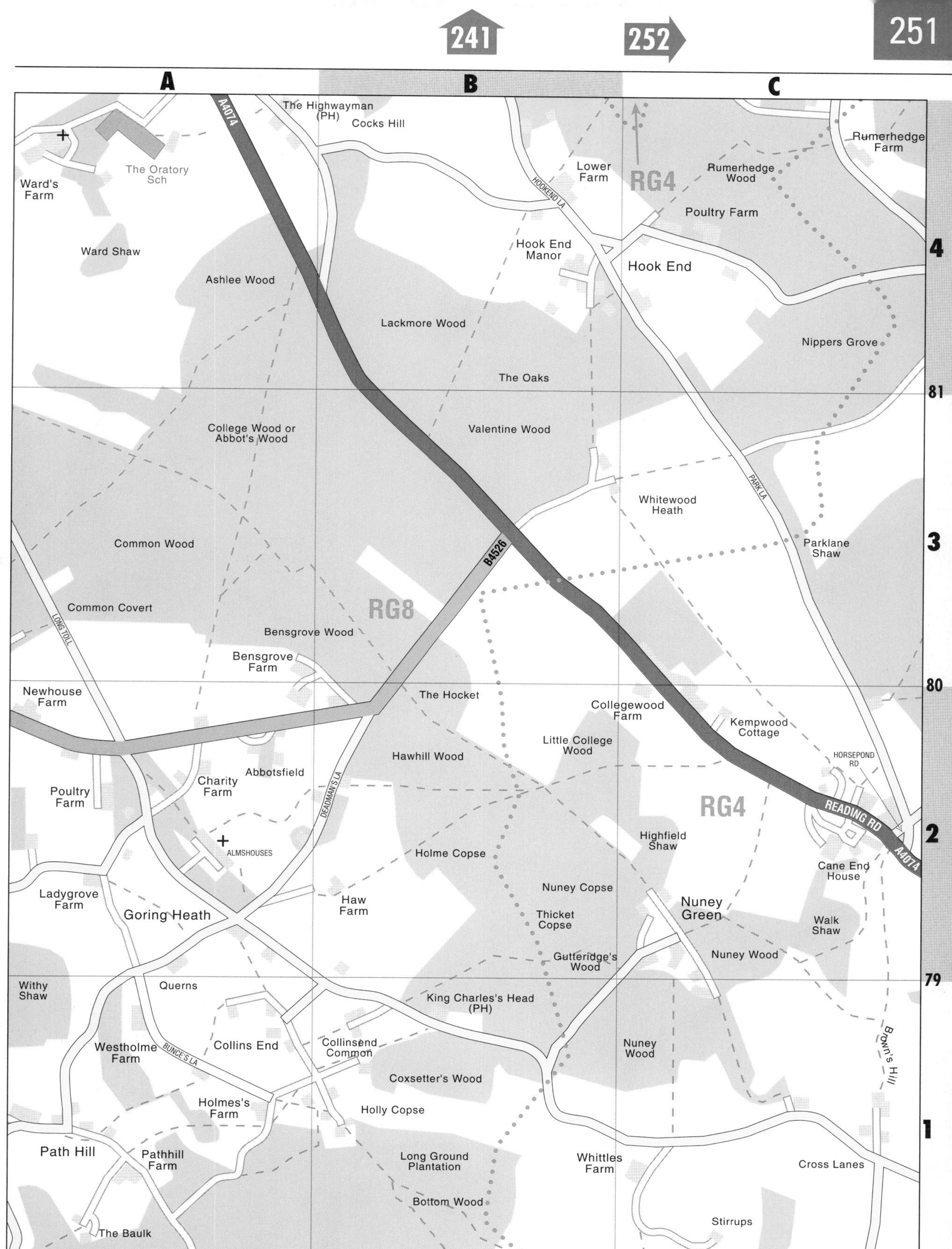

The Highwayman (PH)
Cocks Hill
Lower Farm
RG4
Rumerhedge Farm
Rumerhedge Wood
Poultry Farm
Hook End Manor
Hook End
Ward's Farm
The Oratory Sch
Ward Shaw
Ashlee Wood
Lackmore Wood
Nippers Grove
A4074
HOOKEND LA

81

The Oaks
Valentine Wood
College Wood or Abbot's Wood
Whitewood Heath
PARK LA
Parklane Shaw

3

Common Wood
RG8
B4526
Common Covert
LONG TOLL
Bensgrove Wood
Bensgrove Farm
The Hocket
Collegewood Farm
Kempwood Cottage

80

Newhouse Farm
Hawhill Wood
Little College Wood
HORSEPOND RD
Abbotsfield
Charity Farm
DEADMAN'S LA
Highfield Shaw
RG4
READING RD
Cane End House
A4074

2

Poultry Farm
ALMSHOUSES
Holme Copse
Nuney Copse
Nuney Green
Walk Shaw
Ladygrove Farm
Haw Farm
Thicket Copse
Nuney Wood
Goring Heath
Gutteridge's Wood

79

Withy Shaw
Querns
King Charles's Head (PH)
Nuney Wood
Brown's Hill
Westholme Farm
BUNCE'S LA
Collins End
Collinsend Common
Coxsetter's Wood
Holmes's Farm
Holly Copse

1

Path Hill
Pathhill Farm
Long Ground Plantation
Whittles Farm
Cross Lanes
Bottom Wood
Stirrups
The Baulk

78

A B C

4

Park
Farm

COLMORE LA

Manor
Farm

STEVENS LA

ESTER
CARLING
LA

DOVE LA

COLLIERS LA

Peppard
Hill

B481

CHURCH
LA

Peppard
Common

WYFOLD LA

RG9

Wyfold
Grange

CHILTERN RD

STOKE ROW RD

PEPPARD HILL

SPRINGWOOD
LA

81

Wyfold
Wood

New Copse

CHILTERN
BANK

GALLOWSTREE RD

Shiplake
Bottom

SHIPLAKE BOTTOM CRES

GRAVEL HILL

HILLCREST LA

BLOUNTS COURT RD

PRIORY COPSE

GRAVEL HILL

CHURCH
CRES

Bishopswood
Sch

OLD COPSE
GDNS

CARLING RD

BEECH RISE

NEWFIELD RD

PEPPARD RD B481

SEDGEWELL RD

JOSEY CL

WOOD LANE

WOODLANDS RD

SMITH

INGLEWOOD
CL

WOOD CL

Sonning
Common

APPLETREE
CL

HAZEL GDNS

3

Withy
Copse

WYFOLD RD

Common
Farm

WOODSIDE LA

HEARNS LA

Gallowstree
Common

Bishopswood
Farm

LAMBOURNE RD

ORCHARD AVE

BRIAR CL

WALNUT CL

GREEN LA

RUSSEL CL

BASKERVILLE

WYCHWOOD CL

WOOD RD

PO

Liby

THE HAMLET

ORCHARD FIELD

ASHFORD AVE

CROWSLEY WAY

PAGES ORCH

FARM CL

ELSEL F.

Sonning
Common
Prim Sch

ELM CT

COUNCIL
COTTS

HORSEPOND RD

The Crown &
Anchor
(PH)

READE'S LA

RG4

GROVE RD

CHERITON PL

SCH CL

WESTLEIGH DR

LEA RD

ROWAN CL

ILEX CL

80

Coldnorton
Wood

HAZELMOOR LA

Chiltern Edge
Com Sch

KIDMORE LA

KEANTS LANDS RD

Coldnorton
Shaw

Oakridge
Farm

WOOD LA

Holly Tree
Farm

2

Cane End
Farm

READING RD A4074

CROWSLEAZE

Kidmore End
CE Prim Sch

Kidmore
End

PH

Vines
Farm

79

Madge Gray's
Wood

Highland
Wood

Curtis
Farm

BUTLERS ORCH

COOPERS
PIGHTLE

Cemy

Stocking
Shaw

CHALKHOUSE GREEN RD

Cross
Farm

Kidmore
House

1

Green Dean
Wood

GREEN DEAN HILL

Tankers Table
Farm

MILL LA

Bardolph's
Wood

TOKERS GREEN RD

Hodmore
Farm

SHEEPWAYS LA

The Pack Horse
(PH)

Dyson's
Wood

DYSONS WOOD LANE

CHALKHOUSE
GREEN LA

Hodmore Farm
Cottage

A4074

Tinker's
Green

TANNERS
LA

KIDMORE
END RD

78

68 A 69 B 70 C

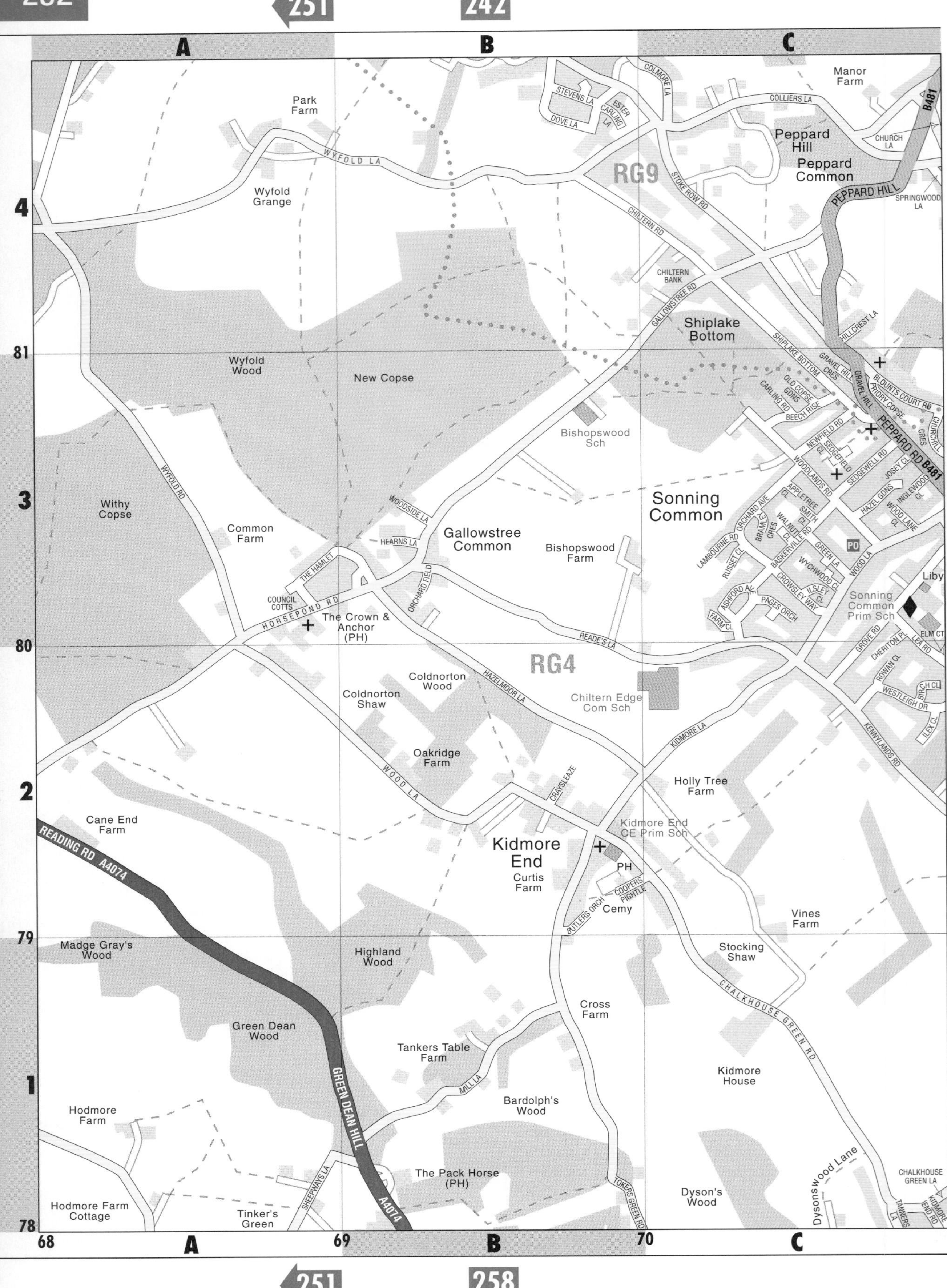

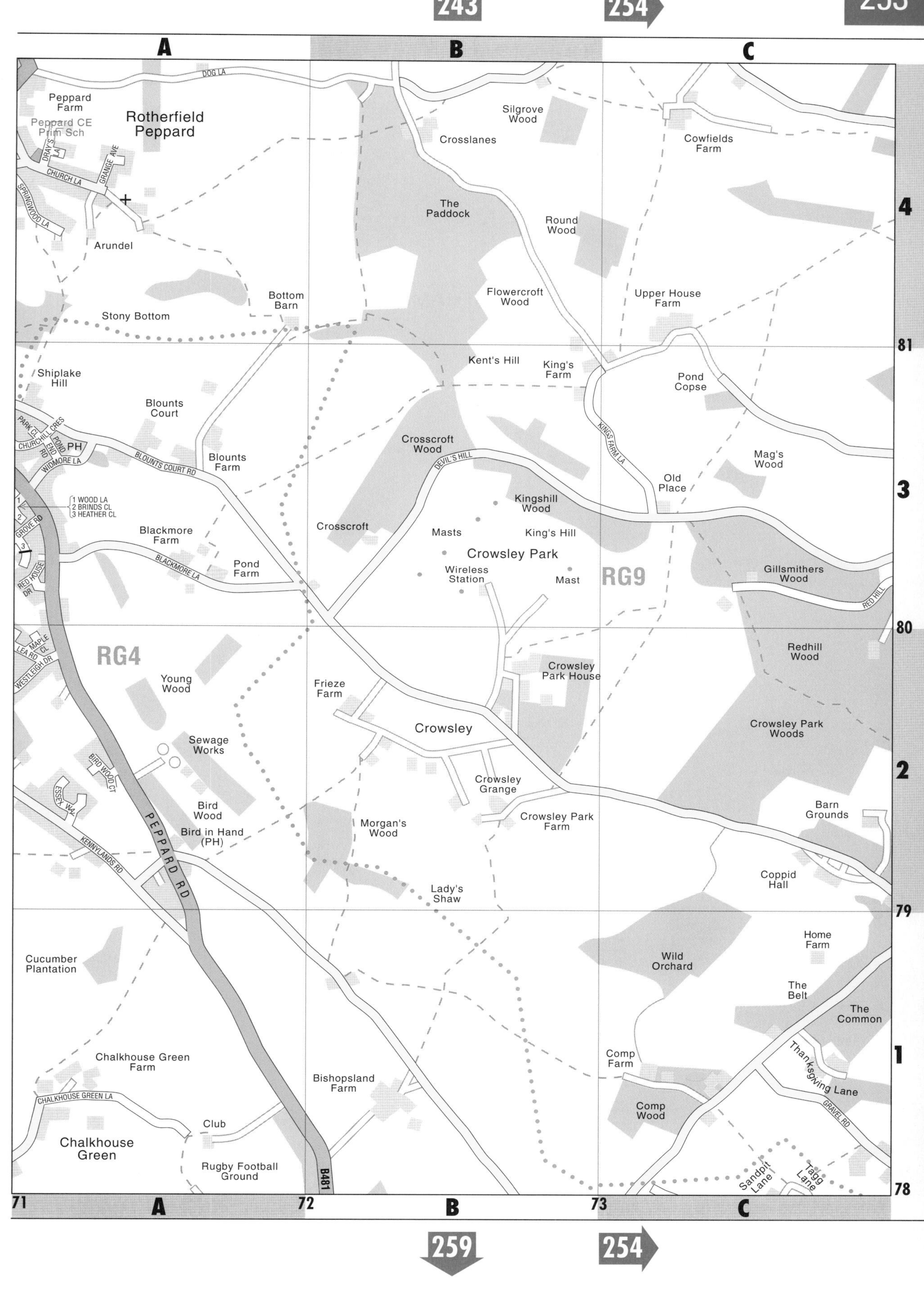
A
B
C
DOG LA
Peppard Farm
Rotherfield Peppard
Peppard CE Prim Sch
DRAY'S LA
GRANGE AVE
CHURCH LA
SPRINGWOOD LA
Arundel
Silgrove Wood
Crosslanes
Cowfields Farm
The Paddock
Round Wood
Flowercroft Wood
Upper House Farm
Bottom Barn
Stony Bottom
Shiplake Hill
Kent's Hill
King's Farm
Pond Copse
Blounts Court
PARK CL
CHURCHILL CRES
POND END RD
PH
WIDMORE LA
BLOUNTS COURT RD
Blounts Farm
Crosscroft Wood
DEVIL'S HILL
KINGS FARM LA
Mag's Wood
Old Place
1 WOOD LA
2 BRINDS CL
3 HEATHER CL
GROVE RD
Kingshill Wood
Blackmore Farm
Crosscroft
Masts
King's Hill
Crowsley Park
BLACKMORE LA
Pond Farm
Wireless Station
Mast
RG9
Gillsmithers Wood
RED HILL
RED HOUSE DR
MAPLE CL
LEA RD
WESTLEIGH DR
RG4
Young Wood
Frieze Farm
Crowsley Park House
Redhill Wood
Crowsley
Crowsley Park Woods
Sewage Works
BIRD WOOD CT
ESSEX WAY
Crowsley Grange
Bird Wood
Bird in Hand (PH)
Morgan's Wood
Crowsley Park Farm
Barn Grounds
KENNYLANDS RD
PEPPARD RD
Lady's Shaw
Coppid Hall
Home Farm
Cucumber Plantation
Wild Orchard
The Belt
The Common
Chalkhouse Green Farm
Comp Farm
Thanksgiving Lane
Bishopsland Farm
CHALKHOUSE GREEN LA
GRAVEL RD
Comp Wood
Club
Chalkhouse Green
Rugby Football Ground
B481
Sandpit Lane
Tagg Lane
4
81
3
80
2
79
1
78
71
72
73

253
244

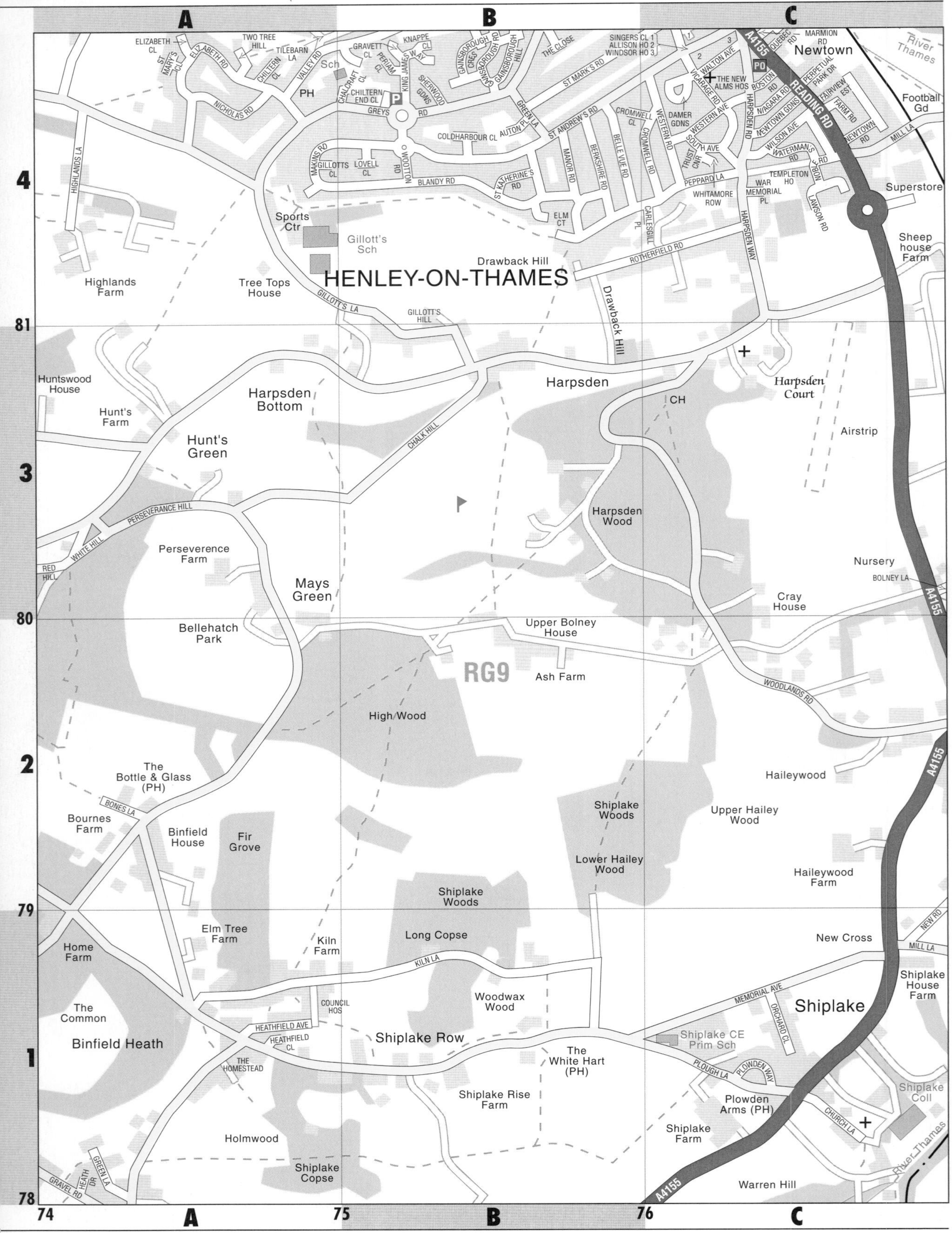
A
B
C
4
81
3
80
2
79
1
78
74
75
76
HENLEY-ON-THAMES
Newtown
River Thames
Football Gd
Superstore
Sheep house Farm
Sports Ctr
Gillott's Sch
Drawback Hill
Highlands Farm
Tree Tops House
Huntswood House
Hunt's Farm
Harpsden Bottom
Harpsden
Harpsden Court
Airstrip
CH
Hunt's Green
Harpsden Wood
Perseverence Farm
Mays Green
Nursery
Cray House
Bellehatch Park
Upper Bolney House
RG9
Ash Farm
High Wood
Haileywood
The Bottle & Glass (PH)
Shiplake Woods
Upper Hailey Wood
Bournes Farm
Binfield House
Fir Grove
Lower Hailey Wood
Haileywood Farm
Shiplake Woods
Elm Tree Farm
Home Farm
Kiln Farm
Long Copse
New Cross
Shiplake House Farm
Woodwax Wood
The Common
Shiplake
Binfield Heath
Shiplake Row
Shiplake CE Prim Sch
The White Hart (PH)
Shiplake Rise Farm
Plowden Arms (PH)
Shiplake Coll
Holmwood
Shiplake Farm
Shiplake Copse
Warren Hill
River Thames
A4155
READING RD
GREYS RD
NICHOLAS RD
HIGHLANDS LA
GILLOTT'S LA
GILLOTT'S HILL
CHALK HILL
PERSEVERANCE HILL
WHITE HILL
RED HILL
BONES LA
KILN LA
HEATHFIELD AVE
HEATHFIELD CL
THE HOMESTEAD
COUNCIL HOS
MEMORIAL AVE
ORCHARD CL
PLOUGH LA
PLOWDEN WAY
CHURCH LA
GRAVEL RD
HEATH DR
GREEN LA
WOODLANDS RD
BOLNEY LA
MILL LA
NEW RD
ROTHERFIELD RD
HARPSDEN WAY
HARPSDEN RD
BLANDY RD
ST ANDREW'S RD
ST MARK'S RD
ST KATHERINE'S RD
MANOR RD
BERKSHIRE RD
BELLE VUE RD
CROMWELL RD
CROMWELL CL
WESTERN RD
WESTERN AVE
VICARAGE RD
WALTON AVE
DAMER GDNS
SOUTH AVE
TRUST CNR
PEPPARD LA
WHITAMORE ROW
WAR MEMORIAL PL
TEMPLETON HO
LAWSON RD
ELM CT
CARLESGILL PL
COLDHARBOUR CL
AUTON PL
GREEN LA
WOOTTON RD
MAKINS RD
GILLOTTS CL
LOVELL CL
ELIZABETH CL
ELIZABETH RD
ST MARY'S CL
TWO TREE HILL
TILEBARN LA
CHILTERN CL
VALLEY RD
GRAVETT CL
PERIAM CL
KNAPPE CL
KING JAMES WAY
CHALCRAFT CL
CHILTERN END CL
SHERWOOD GDNS
GAINSBOROUGH CRES
GAINSBOROUGH RD
GAINSBOROUGH HILL
THE CLOSE
SINGERS CL 1
ALLISON HO 2
WINDSOR HO 3
THE NEW ALMS HOS
BOSTON RD
QUEBEC RD
MARMION RD
PERPETUAL PARK DR
FAIRVIEW EST
FARM RD
NIAGARA RD
NEWTOWN GDNS
NEWTOWN RD
WILSON AVE
WATERMAN'S RD
JOHN ST RD
Sch
PH
PO
P

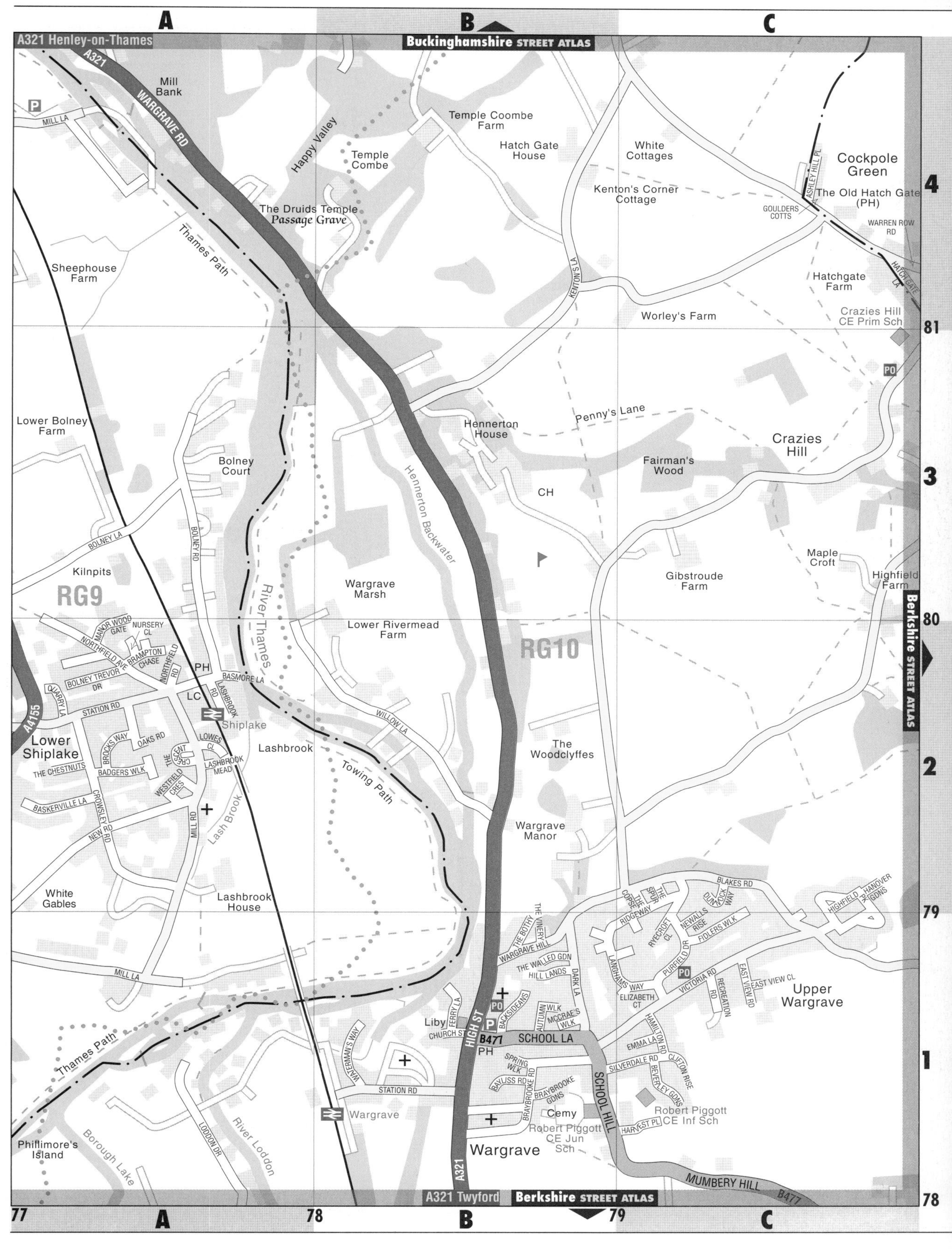

A   **B**   **C**

A321

MILL LA

WARGRAVE RD

Mill
Bank

Happy Valley

Temple
Combe

Temple Coombe
Farm

Hatch Gate
House

White
Cottages

Cockpole
Green

ASHLEY HILL PL

The Old Hatch Gate
(PH)

GOULDERS
COTTS

WARREN ROW
RD

Thames Path

The Druids Temple
Passage Grave

Kenton's Corner
Cottage

4

HATCHGATE LA

Sheephouse
Farm

Worley's Farm

Hatchgate
Farm

Crazies Hill
CE Prim Sch

81

Lower Bolney
Farm

Bolney
Court

Hennerton
House

Penny's Lane

Crazies
Hill

PO

BOLNEY LA

River Thames

Hennerton Backwater

CH

Fairman's
Wood

Maple
Croft

Highfield
Farm

3

Kilnpits

RG9

Wargrave
Marsh

Gibstroude
Farm

Berkshire STREET ATLAS

BOLNEY RD

MANOR WOOD
GATE

NURSERY
CL

Lower Rivermead
Farm

80

A4155

NORTHFIELD AVE

NORTHFIELD RD

BRAMPTON
CHASE

PH

RG10

BOLNEY TREVOR
DR

QUARRY LA

STATION RD

LC

BASMORE LA

LASHBROOK RD

Shiplake

WILLOW LA

The
Woodclyffes

2

Lower
Shiplake

BROCKS WAY

OAKS RD

THE CRESCENT

LOWER RD

Lashbrook

Towing Path

THE CHESTNUTS

WESTFIELD CRES

LASHBROOK
MEAD

BADGERS WLK

BASKERVILLE LA

CROWSLEY WAY

MILL RD

Lash Brook

Wargrave
Manor

79

NEW RD

White
Gables

Lashbrook
House

BLAKES RD

KNOCK WAY

QUINS
WAY

HANOVER
GDNS

Highfield

THE SPUR

RIDGEWAY

RYECROFT
CL

HEWALLS
RISE

FIDLERS WLK

Upper
Wargrave

MILL LA

THE BOTTY

WARGRAVE HILL

THE VINERY

PURFIELD DR

LARKSPUR
WAY

ELIZABETH
CT

VICTORIA RD

RECREATION
RD

EAST VIEW CL

EAST VIEW RD

PO

Thames Path

THE WALLED GDN

HILL LANDS

DARK LA

Liby

FERRY LA

BACKSIDEANS

AUTUMN
WLK

McCRAE'S
WLK

EMMA LA

HAMILTON RD

1

WATERMAN'S WAY

PO

HIGH ST

CHURCH ST

B477

PH

SCHOOL LA

SPRING
WLK

SILVERDALE RD

CLIFTON RISE

BEVERLEY GDNS

Phillimore's
Island

Borough Lake

LODDON DR

River Loddon

STATION RD

Wargrave

BAYLISS ROAD

BRAYBROOKE
GDNS

Cemy

SCHOOL HILL

Robert Piggott
CE Inf Sch

HART-ST PL

Robert Piggott
CE Jun Sch

A321

Wargrave

MUMBERY HILL

B477

78

250

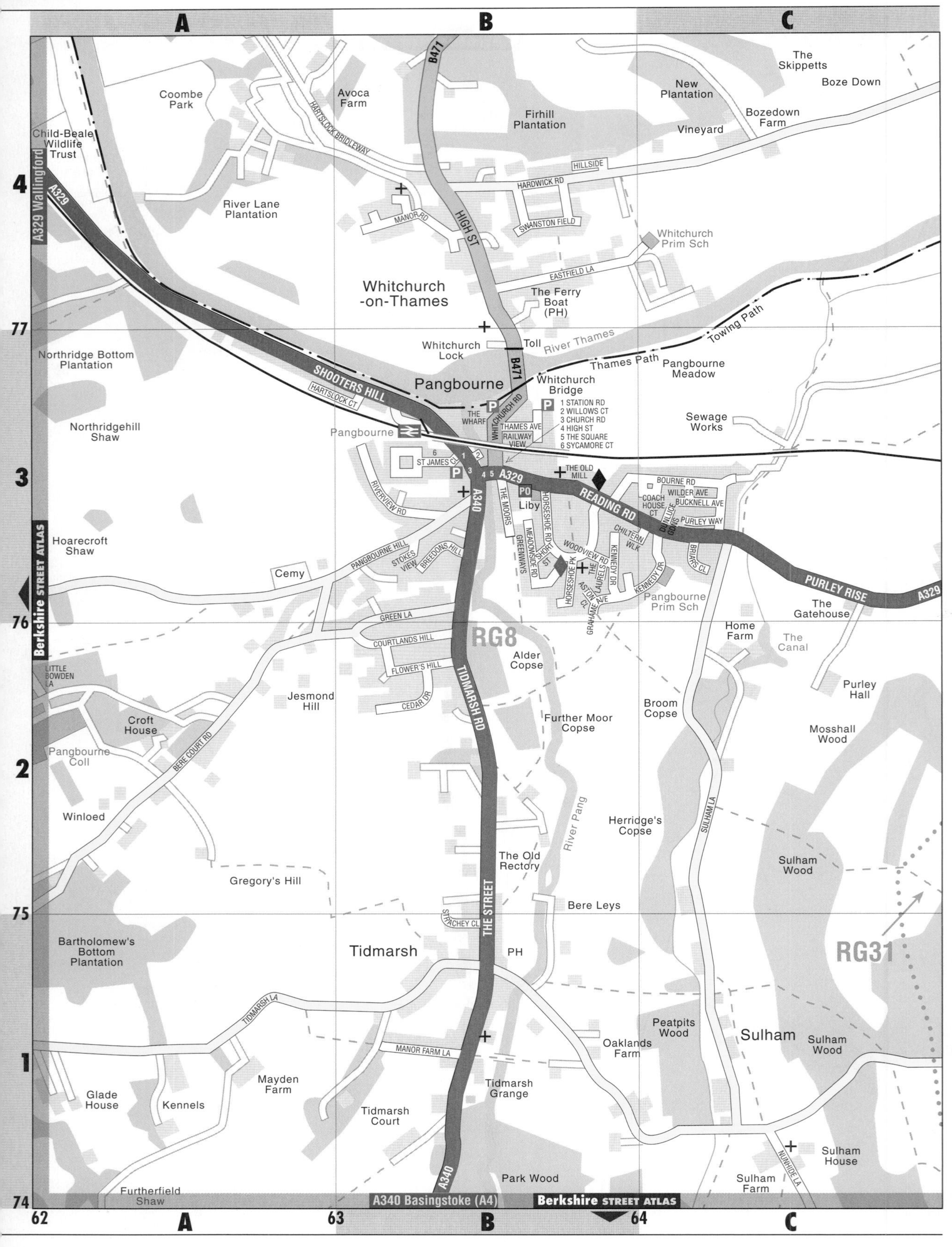
A
B
C
4
77
3
76
2
75
1
74
62
63
64
Coombe Park
Avoca Farm
Firhill Plantation
New Plantation
The Skippetts
Boze Down
Bozedown Farm
Vineyard
Child-Beale Wildlife Trust
A329 Wallingford
River Lane Plantation
HARTSLOCK BRIDLEWAY
B471
HIGH ST
HILLSIDE
HARDWICK RD
MANOR RD
SWANSTON FIELD
Whitchurch Prim Sch
EASTFIELD LA
Whitchurch -on-Thames
The Ferry Boat (PH)
Whitchurch Lock
Toll
River Thames
Towing Path
Thames Path
Pangbourne Meadow
Northridge Bottom Plantation
SHOOTERS HILL
HARTSLOCK CT
Pangbourne
Whitchurch Bridge
WHITCHURCH RD
THE WHARF
1 STATION RD
2 WILLOWS CT
3 CHURCH RD
4 HIGH ST
5 THE SQUARE
6 SYCAMORE CT
THAMES AVE
RAILWAY VIEW
Sewage Works
Northridgehill Shaw
ST JAMES CL
THE OLD MILL
A329
READING RD
PO
Liby
THE MOORS
A340
RIVERVIEW RD
BOURNE RD
WILDER AVE
COACH HOUSE CT
BUCKNELL AVE
DUNLUCE GDNS
PURLEY WAY
CHILTERN WLK
BRIARS CL
HORSESHOE RD
SHORT ST
MEADOWSIDE RD
GREENWAYS
WOODVIEW RD
KENNEDY DR
HORSESHOE PK
THE LAURELS
ASTON CL
GRAHAME AVE
Pangbourne Prim Sch
PURLEY RISE
The Gatehouse
Hoarecroft Shaw
Cemy
PANGBOURNE HILL
STOKES VIEW
BREEDONS HILL
GREEN LA
COURTLANDS HILL
FLOWER'S HILL
CEDAR DR
RG8
Alder Copse
Home Farm
The Canal
LITTLE BOWDEN LA
Jesmond Hill
TIDMARSH RD
Broom Copse
Purley Hall
Croft House
Further Moor Copse
Mosshall Wood
Pangbourne Coll
BERE COURT RD
Winloed
River Pang
Herridge's Copse
SULHAM LA
The Old Rectory
Gregory's Hill
Sulham Wood
Bere Leys
STRACHEY CL
THE STREET
Bartholomew's Bottom Plantation
Tidmarsh
PH
RG31
TIDMARSH LA
Peatpits Wood
Sulham
Oaklands Farm
MANOR FARM LA
Mayden Farm
Tidmarsh Grange
Glade House
Kennels
Tidmarsh Court
Sulham House
NUNHIDE LA
Park Wood
Sulham Farm
Furtherfield Shaw
A340 Basingstoke (A4)
Berkshire STREET ATLAS

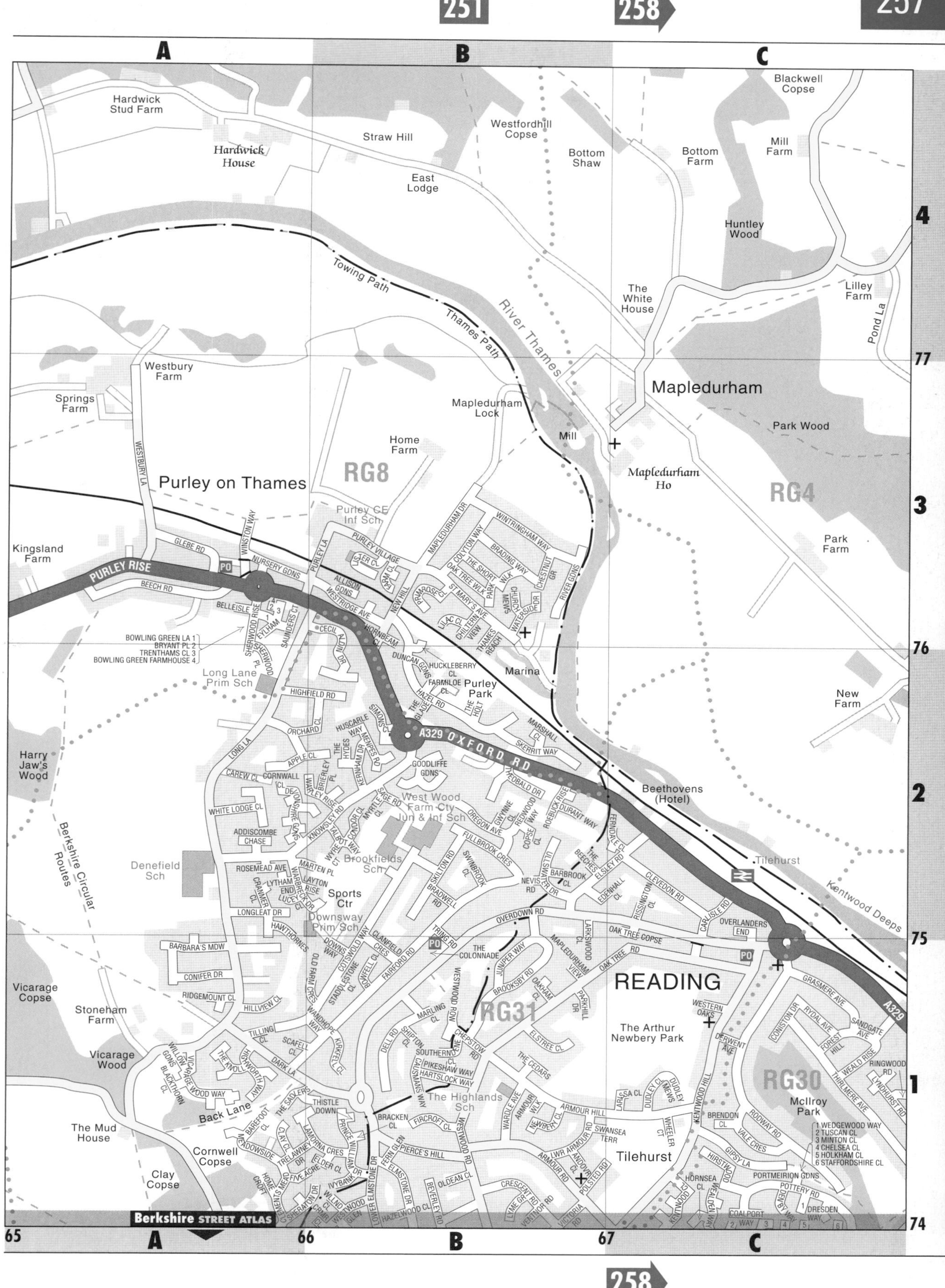
Hardwick Stud Farm
Hardwick House
Straw Hill
Westfordhill Copse
Bottom Shaw
Bottom Farm
Blackwell Copse
Mill Farm
East Lodge
Huntley Wood
Towing Path
Thames Path
River Thames
The White House
Lilley Farm
Pond La
Westbury Farm
Springs Farm
Mapledurham
Mapledurham Lock
Park Wood
Home Farm
Mill
Mapledurham Ho
RG8
RG4
Purley on Thames
Purley CE Inf Sch
Kingsland Farm
Park Farm
PURLEY RISE
Marina
Purley Park
New Farm
Long Lane Prim Sch
A329 OXFORD RD
Harry Jaw's Wood
Beethovens (Hotel)
West Wood Farm Cty Jun & Inf Sch
Berkshire Circular Routes
Denefield Sch
Brookfields Sch
Tilehurst
Sports Ctr
Downsway Prim Sch
Kentwood Deeps
READING
Vicarage Copse
Stoneham Farm
RG31
The Arthur Newbery Park
Vicarage Wood
The Highlands Sch
RG30
McIlroy Park
Back Lane
The Mud House
Cornwell Copse
Tilehurst
Clay Copse
1 WEDGEWOOD WAY
2 TUSCAN CL
3 MINTON CL
4 CHELSEA CL
5 HOLKHAM CL
6 STAFFORDSHIRE CL
BOWLING GREEN LA 1
BRYANT PL 2
TRENTHAMS CL 3
BOWLING GREEN FARMHOUSE 4
A
B
C
4
77
3
76
2
75
1
74
65
66
67

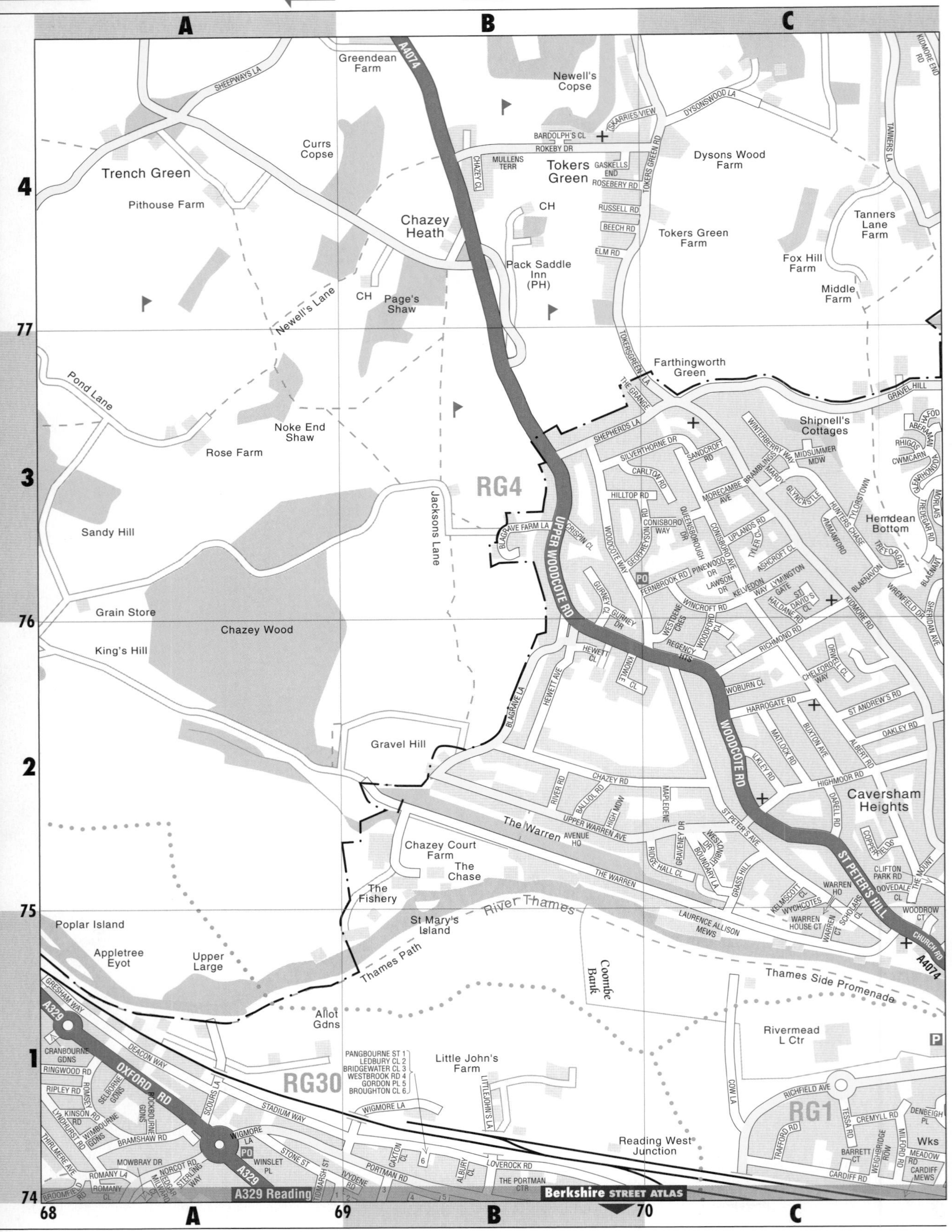

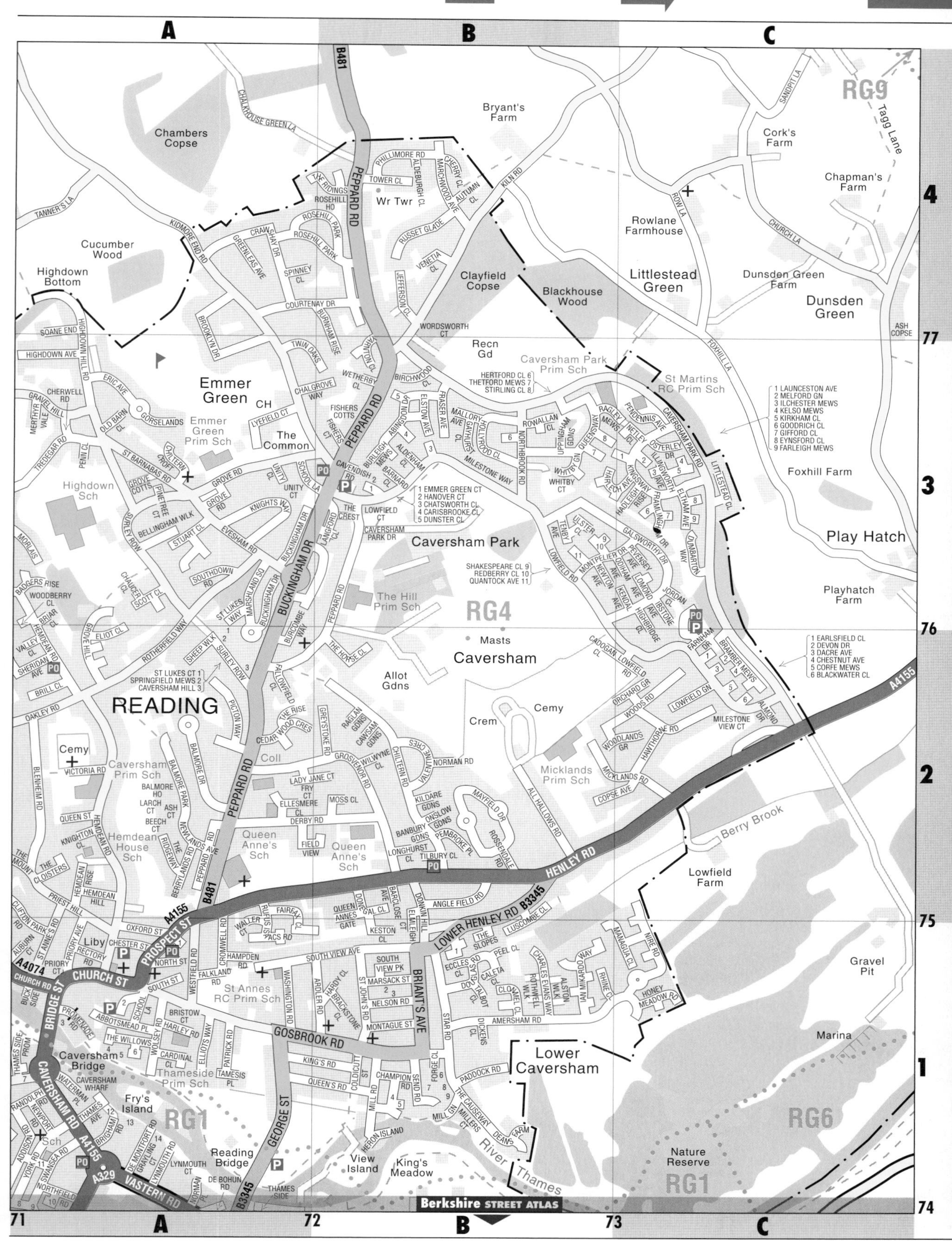

A1
1 SHORT ST
2 ARCHWAY RD
3 RIVERSIDE CT
4 CRENDON CT
5 CLAYDON CT
6 ST STEPHENS CL
7 RICHFIELD AVE
8 CARDIFF RD
9 BARRY PL
10 MONMOUTH CT
11 ROSS RD
12 THAMES SIDE
13 REGENTS RIVERSIDE
14 HALLSMEAD CT

B1
1 FLAMBARDS
2 RICHARD NEVILL CT
3 WALEYS PL
4 PIGGOTT'S RD
5 MONKLEY CT
6 GOSBROOK HO
7 BROOK LEA
8 GLIFFARD HO
9 PEMBROKE HO

259
254

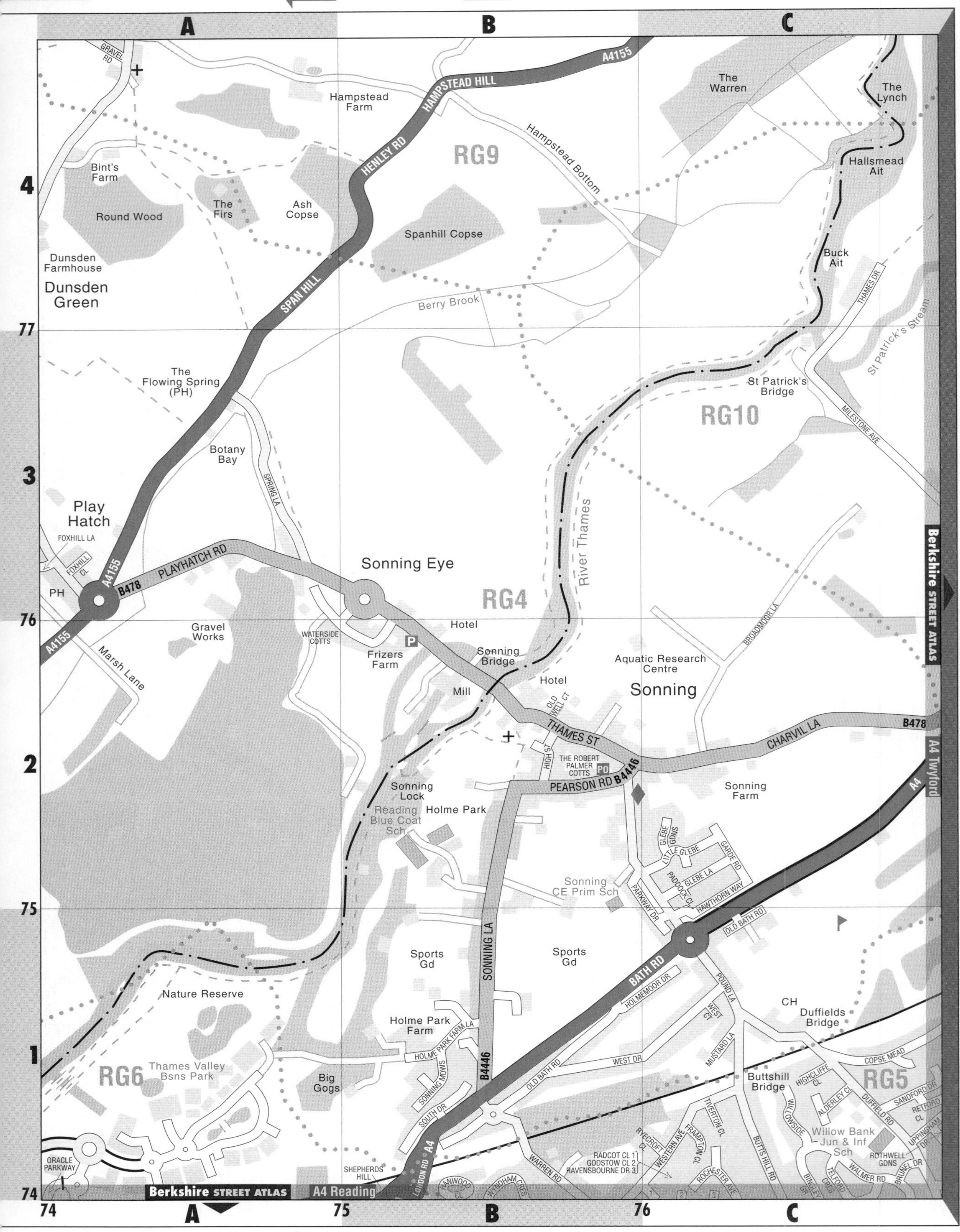
A
B
C
4
3
2
1
77
76
75
74
A4155
HAMPSTEAD HILL
Hampstead Farm
HENLEY RD
RG9
Hampstead Bottom
The Warren
The Lynch
Hallsmead Ait
Bint's Farm
Round Wood
The Firs
Ash Copse
Spanhill Copse
Dunsden Farmhouse
Dunsden Green
SPAN HILL
Berry Brook
Buck Ait
THAMES DR
St Patrick's Stream
St Patrick's Bridge
RG10
MILESTONE AVE
The Flowing Spring (PH)
Botany Bay
SPRING LA
Play Hatch
FOXHILL LA
FOXHILL CL
PH
B478
PLAYHATCH RD
Sonning Eye
River Thames
RG4
BROADMOOR LA
Berkshire STREET ATLAS
Gravel Works
Marsh Lane
WATERSIDE COTTS
Frizers Farm
Hotel
Sonning Bridge
Mill
Aquatic Research Centre
Sonning
OLD WELL CT
THAMES ST
CHARVIL LA
HIGH ST
THE ROBERT PALMER COTTS
PO
PEARSON RD
B4446
A4 Twyford
Sonning Lock
Reading Blue Coat Sch
Holme Park
Sonning Farm
GLEBE GDNS
LITTLE GLEBE
GARDE RD
GLEBE LA
PADDOCK CL
HAWTHORN WAY
PARKWAY DR
Sonning CE Prim Sch
OLD BATH RD
SONNING LA
Sports Gd
BATH RD
HOLMEMOOR DR
POUND LA
WEST CL
Nature Reserve
Holme Park Farm
HOLME PARK FARM LA
CH
Duffields Bridge
MUSTARD LA
COPSE MEAD
WEST DR
Thames Valley Bsns Park
RG6
Big Gogs
SONNING MDWS
SOUTH DR
Buttshill Bridge
HIGHCLIFFE CL
RG5
DUFFIELD RD
SANDFORD DR
RETFORD CL
ALDERLEY CL
WILLOWSIDE
Willow Bank Jun & Inf Sch
UPPINGHAM DR
TIVERTON CL
FRAMPTON CL
RYECROFT CL
WESTERN AVE
RADCOT CL 1
GODSTOW CL 2
RAVENSBOURNE DR 3
ROCHESTER AVE
BUTTS HILL RD
ROTHWELL GDNS
WALMER RD
BRUNEL DR
TELFORD CRES
BINGLEY GR
ORACLE PARKWAY
SHEPHERDS HILL
LONDON RD
A4
HANWOOD CL
WYNDHAM CRES
WARREN RD
A4 Reading
74
75
76

259

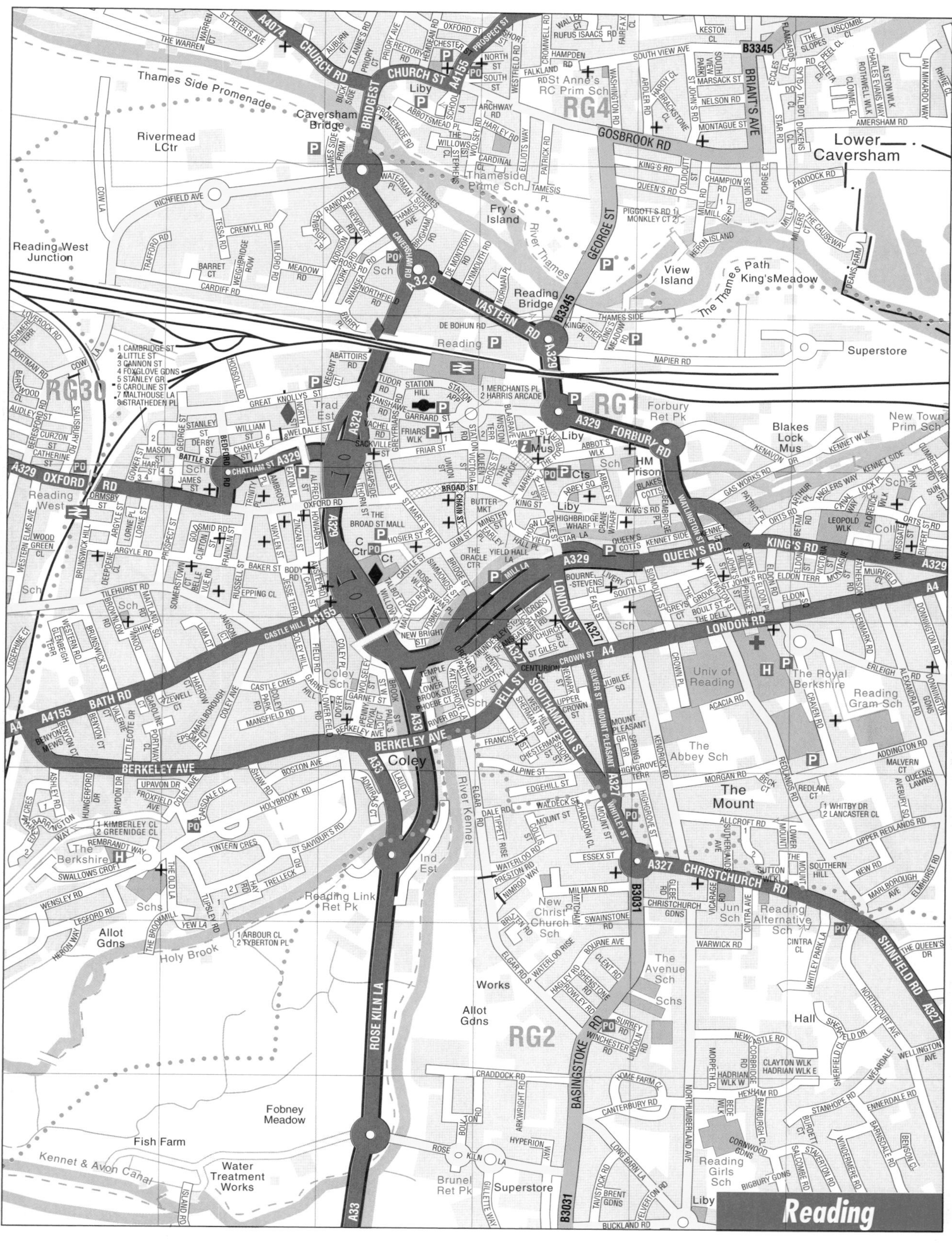

Reading
RG1
RG2
RG4
RG30
Lower Caversham
Caversham Bridge
Rivermead LCtr
Reading West Junction
Thames Side Promenade
Fry's Island
River Thames
View Island
King's Meadow
The Thames Path
Reading Bridge
Reading
Superstore
Forbury Ret Pk
New Town Prim Sch
Blakes Lock Mus
HM Prison
Reading West
The Broad St Mall
The Oracle Ctr
Univ of Reading
The Royal Berkshire
Reading Gram Sch
The Abbey Sch
The Mount
Coley
River Kennet
Ind Est
Reading Link Ret Pk
The Berkshire
Holy Brook
Allot Gdns
Works
The Avenue Sch
New Christ Church Sch
Reading Alternative Sch
Fobney Meadow
Fish Farm
Kennet & Avon Canal
Water Treatment Works
Brunel Ret Pk
Superstore
Reading Girls Sch
Thameside Prim Sch
St Anne's RC Prim Sch
OXFORD RD
CHURCH RD
CHURCH ST
BRIDGE ST
GOSBROOK RD
GEORGE ST
VASTERN RD
CAVERSHAM RD
FORBURY RD
KING'S RD
QUEEN'S RD
LONDON RD
LONDON ST
CASTLE HILL
BATH RD
BERKELEY AVE
SOUTHAMPTON ST
CHRISTCHURCH RD
SHINFIELD RD
BASINGSTOKE RD
ROSE KILN LA
A4
A33
A329
A327
A4155
A4074
B3345
B3031

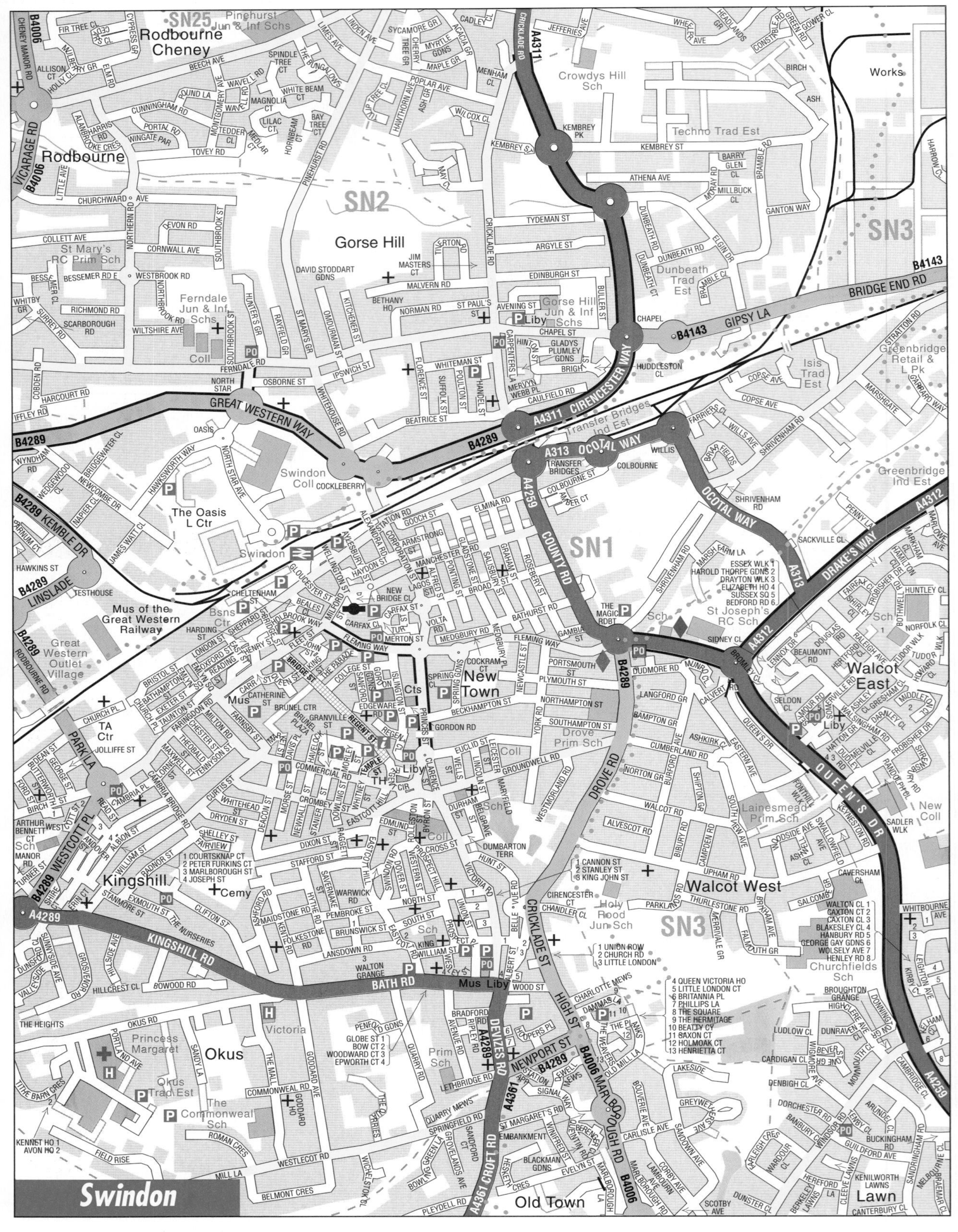
Swindon
SN25
SN2
SN3
SN1
Rodbourne Cheney
Rodbourne
Pinehurst Jun & Inf Schs
Gorse Hill
Crowdys Hill Sch
Techno Trad Est
Works
St Mary's RC Prim Sch
Ferndale Jun & Inf Schs
Coll
Gorse Hill Jun & Inf Schs
Liby
Dunbeath Trad Est
Isis Trad Est
Greenbridge Retail & L Pk
Transfer Bridges Ind Est
Greenbridge Ind Est
Swindon Coll
The Oasis L Ctr
Swindon
Mus of the Great Western Railway
Great Western Outlet Village
Bsns Ctr
New Town
Cts
Mus
TA Ctr
St Joseph's RC Sch
Walcot East
Drove Prim Sch
Lainesmead Prim Sch
New Coll
Kingshill
Cemy
Walcot West
Holy Rood Jun Sch
Churchfields Sch
Victoria
Princess Margaret
Okus
Okus Trad Est
The Commonweal Sch
Prim Sch
Mus Liby
Old Town
Lawn
GREAT WESTERN WAY
CIRCENCESTER WAY
OCOTAL WAY
COUNTY RD
DRAKE'S WAY
QUEEN'S DR
GIPSY LA
BRIDGE END RD
KINGSHILL RD
BATH RD
DEVIZES RD
CROFT RD
HIGH ST
CRICKLADE ST
CRICKLADE RD
DROVE RD
MARLBOROUGH RD
KEMBLE DR
LINSLADE
WESTCOTT PL
PARK LA
VICARAGE RD
CHENEY MANOR RD
A4311
A4289
A4259
A4312
A313
A4361
B4289
B4143
B4006

Church Rd **6** Beckenham BR2..........**53** C6

Place name — May be abbreviated on the map

Location number — Present when a number indicates the place's position in a crowded area of mapping

Locality, town or village — Shown when more than one place has the same name

Postcode district — District for the indexed place

Page and grid square — Page number and grid reference for the standard mapping

Public and commercial buildings are highlighted in magenta   **Places of interest** are highlighted in blue with a star★

Abbreviations used in the index

Acad	Academy	Comm	Common	Gd	Ground	L	Leisure
App	Approach	Cott	Cottage	Gdn	Garden	La	Lane
Arc	Arcade	Cres	Crescent	Gn	Green	Liby	Library
Ave	Avenue	Cswy	Causeway	Gr	Grove	Mdw	Meadow
Bglw	Bungalow	Ct	Court	H	Hall	Meml	Memorial
Bldg	Building	Ctr	Centre	Ho	House	Mkt	Market
Bsns, Bus	Business	Ctry	Country	Hospl	Hospital	Mus	Museum
Bvd	Boulevard	Cty	County	HQ	Headquarters	Orch	Orchard
Cath	Cathedral	Dr	Drive	Hts	Heights	Pal	Palace
Cir	Circus	Dro	Drove	Ind	Industrial	Par	Parade
Cl	Close	Ed	Education	Inst	Institute	Pas	Passage
Cnr	Corner	Emb	Embankment	Int	International	Pk	Park
Coll	College	Est	Estate	Intc	Interchange	Pl	Place
Com	Community	Ex	Exhibition	Junc	Junction	Prec	Precinct

(continued)

Prom	Prom
Rd	Road
Recn	Recreation
Ret	Retail
Sh	Shopping
Sq	Square
St	Street
Sta	Station
Terr	Terrace
TH	Town Hall
Univ	University
Wk, Wlk	Walk
Wr	Water
Yd	Yard

Index of localities, towns and villages

Abingdon . . .179 C4
Adderbury . . .23 A2
Adlestrop . . .40 B1
Aldworth . . .247 C2
Alvescot . . .133 B3
Ambrosden . . .81 B2
Appleford . . .200 C4
Appleton . . .158 A4
Ardington . . .215 C3
Ardley . . .50 B2
Ascott-under-Wychwood 71 B1
Ashbury . . .228 A4
Aston . . .135 C2
Aston Rowant . . .167 B1
Aston Tirrold . . .237 C4
Avon Dassett . . .2 C4
Aynho . . .35 B4
Bampton . . .134 C2
Banbury . . .16 C3
Barford St Michael . . .32 C3
Barton-on-the-Heath . . .26 C3
Baydon . . .245 C1
Beacon's Bottom . . .189 B2
Beckley . . .111 A2
Begbroke . . .108 A4
Benson . . .204 A2
Berinsfield . . .182 B3
Berrick Salome . . .184 A1
Bicester . . .65 B2
Bishopstone . . .227 B2
Bix . . .243 B4
Black Bourton . . .133 C3
Blackthorn . . .82 A3
Bladon . . .91 B1
Bledington . . .54 B1
Bledlow . . .169 A4
Bledlow Ridge . . .189 C4
Bletchingdon . . .93 A4
Blewbury . . .237 A4
Bloxham . . .21 B3
Bodicote . . .22 B4
Bourton . . .209 A2
Brackley . . .24 A4
Brightwell-cum-Sotwell . . .202 B1
Brill . . .98 A1
Britwell Salome . . .205 C4
Brize Norton . . .116 B2
Broughton . . .15 B1
Buckland . . .154 C1
Bucknell . . .65 A4
Burford . . .100 B3
Buscot . . .171 A4
Carterton . . .115 C2
Cassington . . .107 B1
Chacombe . . .10 C2
Chadlington . . .57 A1
Chalgrove . . .184 C3
Charlbury . . .73 B2
Charlton-on-Otmoor . . .95 A2
Charney Bassett . . .176 A1
Chastleton . . .40 B4
Checkendon . . .241 B2
Chesterton . . .79 C4

Childrey . . .213 B2
Chilson . . .71 C2
Chilton . . .235 C4
Chinnor . . .168 B4
Chipping Norton . . .42 C1
Chipping Warden . . .5 C3
Cholsey . . .221 A1
Church Westcote . . .68 B3
Churchill . . .55 C3
Clanfield . . .152 C4
Claydon . . .1 B1
Clifton Hampden . . .181 B2
Cockpole Green . . .255 C4
Coleshill . . .191 A4
Combe . . .90 A3
Compton Wynyates . . .12 B4
Cottisford . . .37 C2
Crawley . . .103 C2
Cropredy . . .4 C1
Croughton . . .36 B4
Crowmarsh Gifford . . .221 C4
Cuddesdon . . .144 A2
Culham . . .180 A1
Cumnor . . .139 B3
Curbridge . . .117 B3
Cutteslowe . . .109 A1
Cuxham . . .185 B2
Deddington . . .33 C2
Denchworth . . .196 A2
Didcot . . .200 B2
Dorchester . . .182 B1
Drayton . . .179 A1
Drayton (Banbury) . . .15 B4
Drayton St Leonard . . .183 A3
Ducklington . . .118 A2
Duns Tew . . .47 B3
East Challow . . .214 A3
East Hagbourne . . .218 C3
East Hanney . . .197 A3
East Hendred . . .216 C4
Eastleach Martin . . .131 A4
Enstone . . .58 C3
Epwell . . .13 A3
Ewelme . . .204 C2
Eynsham . . .120 C4
Faringdon . . .172 C2
Farnborough (Berks) . . .233 C1
Farnborough (Warks) . . .3 C4
Fawley . . .226 B1
Fernham . . .193 A2
Fifield . . .69 B1
Filkins . . .132 B3
Finmere . . .39 B4
Finstock . . .88 B3
Forest Hill . . .125 C2
Freeland . . .106 A4
Fringford . . .52 B3
Fritwell . . .49 C4
Fulbrook . . .100 C4
Fyfield . . .157 B1
Garford . . .177 B3
Garsington . . .143 C1
Goring . . .249 B3
Great Bourton . . .9 B4

Great Coxwell . . .192 B4
Great Haseley . . .164 C4
Great Milton . . .145 A1
Great Rissington . . .83 A4
Great Rollright . . .29 A2
Great Tew . . .45 B4
Grove . . .196 C1
Haddenham . . .130 C3
Hailey . . .104 A3
Hampton Poyle . . .93 A2
Hanwell . . .8 C2
Hardwick . . .51 B4
Harwell . . .217 C4
Henley-on-Thames . . .244 A1
Hethe . . .52 A4
Highworth . . .190 A3
Hinton Waldrist . . .155 C2
Holton . . .126 B1
Hook Norton . . .30 A4
Horley . . .8 A2
Hornton . . .7 B4
Horspath . . .143 B3
Horton-cum-Studley . . .112 A3
Ickford . . .128 A2
Idbury . . .69 A2
Ipsden . . .240 B4
Islip . . .109 C4
Kelmscott . . .151 B2
Kencot . . .132 C3
Kennington . . .160 C4
Kidlington . . .108 B4
Kidmore End . . .252 B2
Kingham . . .55 A2
Kings Sutton . . .23 C3
Kingston Bagpuize . . .156 C1
Kingston Lisle . . .212 A2
Kirtlington . . .77 C2
Langford . . .132 B1
Launton . . .66 B1
Leafield . . .86 C2
Lechlade . . .150 B2
Letcombe Bassett . . .231 C4
Lewknor . . .187 A4
Little Compton . . .26 C1
Little Coxwell . . .192 C4
Little Milton . . .164 A3
Little Tew . . .45 A3
Long Compton . . .27 C3
Long Crendon . . .129 A3
Long Hanborough . . .90 B1
Long Wittenham . . .201 B4
Longcot . . .192 B1
Longworth . . .156 B2
Lower Basildon . . .249 C1
Lower Heyford . . .62 B3
Lower Odington . . .54 A4
Ludgershall . . .98 B4
Lyneham . . .70 C3
Mapledurham . . .257 C2
Marcham . . .178 B3
Marsh Gibbon . . .67 C2
Marston . . .123 C3
Merton . . .95 B4
Middle Barton . . .60 C4

Middleton Cheney . . .11 A1
Middleton Stoney . . .64 A2
Milcombe . . .21 A1
Milton . . .199 B3
Milton (Banbury) . . .22 B2
Milton Common . . .146 A2
Milton-under-Wychwood 70 B1
Minster Lovell . . .102 C1
Mixbury . . .38 B4
Mollington . . .4 A2
Moulsford . . .238 C2
Murcott . . .95 C2
Nettlebed . . .224 B1
North Aston . . .48 A3
North Hinksey Village . . .140 C4
North Leigh . . .105 A4
North Moreton . . .219 C4
North Newington . . .15 A2
Northend . . .207 C3
Northmoor . . .138 B1
Nuneham Courtenay . . .161 C2
Oddington . . .94 C1
Over Norton . . .42 C3
Oxford . . .123 C1
Pangbourne . . .256 B3
Piddington . . .97 C4
Poundon . . .67 C4
Purley on Thames . . .257 A3
Radley . . .160 C2
Ramsden . . .88 A2
Ratley . . .2 A2
Reading . . .259 A2
Rotherfield Greys . . .243 B1
Rotherfield Peppard . . .253 A4
Salford . . .41 C3
Sandford-on-Thames . . .161 A4
Shabbington . . .128 B2
Shalstone . . .25 C3
Shellingford . . .193 C4
Shenington . . .6 C1
Shepherd's Green . . .243 A2
Shilton . . .115 A3
Shiplake . . .254 C1
Shipton-on-Cherwell . . .92 A3
Shipton-under-Wychwood . . .85 C4
Shotteswell . . .8 B4
Shrivenham . . .209 A4
Shutford . . .14 A3
Sibford Ferris . . .19 A4
Sibford Gower . . .19 A4
Somerton . . .48 C3
Sonning . . .260 C2
Sonning Common . . .252 C3
Souldern . . .35 C2
South Hinksey . . .141 B3
South Leigh . . .119 B3
South Moreton . . .219 C3
South Newington . . .31 C4
South Stoke . . .239 B2
Southend . . .226 B4
Southrop . . .131 A2
Sparsholt . . .212 C2
Spelsbury . . .72 C3

Stadhampton . . .163 B1
Standlake . . .137 B2
Stanford in the Vale . . .194 C4
Stanton Harcourt . . .138 A4
Stanton St John . . .125 C4
Steeple Aston . . .62 A4
Steventon . . .198 C2
Stoke Lyne . . .51 A3
Stoke Row . . .241 C2
Stoke Talmage . . .165 C2
Stokenchurch . . .188 C3
Stonesfield . . .89 B4
Stonor . . .225 C3
Stratton Audley . . .52 B1
Streatley . . .249 A4
Sunningwell . . .159 C3
Sutton Courtenay . . .200 A4
Swalcliffe . . .19 C4
Swerford . . .30 C2
Swinbrook . . .101 C3
Sydenham . . .167 B4
Tackley . . .77 B3
Tadmarton . . .20 B4
Tetsworth . . .166 A4
Thame . . .148 A4
Tiddington . . .145 C4
Tidmarsh . . .256 B1
Towersey . . .148 C4
Turweston . . .24 B4
Uffington . . .211 B4
Upper Arncott . . .96 C4
Upper Heyford . . .62 C4
Upper Inglesham . . .170 A3
Upper Rissington . . .68 B2
Upton . . .218 B1
Wallingford . . .221 B3
Wantage . . .214 C2
Warborough . . .203 A4
Wardington . . .5 C1
Wargrave . . .255 B1
Warmington . . .3 A2
Watchfield . . .191 C1
Waterperry . . .127 A1
Watlington . . .186 B1
Wendlebury . . .80 A2
West Hagbourne . . .218 B2
West Hanney . . .196 C3
West Ilsley . . .235 A1
Westbury . . .25 A2
Weston-on-the-Green . . .79 A1
Wheatley . . .144 A4
Whichford . . .18 A1
Whitchurch-on-Thames 256 B4
Wigginton . . .31 A4
Witney . . .118 B4
Woodcote . . .250 C4
Woodstock . . .91 A3
Woolstone . . .211 A2
Wootton . . .75 C3
Wootton (Oxford) . . .159 A4
Worminghall . . .127 C3
Wroxton . . .15 A4
Wytham . . .122 A1
Yarnton . . .108 A3

Church St *continued*
Barford St M OX15 ....32 C3
Beckley OX3 ....111 A2
Bicester OX26 ....65 C1
Bladon OX20 ....91 A1
Bledington OX7 ....54 B1
Bloxham OX15 ....21 B2
Bodicote OX15 ....22 C4
Charlbury OX7 ....73 A2
Chipping Norton OX7 ......42 C2
Deddington OX15 ....33 C2
Didcot OX11 ....218 C4
Ducklington OX29 ....118 A2
East Hendred OX12 ......216 B3
Eynsham OX29 ....120 C4
Faringdon SN7 ....172 C2
Fifield OX7 ....69 A1
Henley-on-T RG9 ....244 B1
Idbury OX7 ....69 A2
Kidlington OX5 ....92 C1
Kingham OX7 ....55 A2
Marcham OX13 ....178 B3
Marsh Gibbon OX27 ....67 C2
Reading RG4 ....259 A1
Shellingford SN7 ....193 C4
Shipton-u-W OX7 ....85 B4
Somerton OX25 ....48 C3
Stokenchurch HP14 ......188 B3
Stonesfield OX29 ....89 B4
Sutton Courtenay OX14 ..180 A1
Upton OX11 ....218 B1
Wantage OX12 ....214 B2
Wargrave RG10 ....255 B1
Watlington OX49 ....186 A1
West Hanney OX12 ......196 C3
Wootton OX20 ....75 C2
Wroxton OX15 ....15 A4
Church Terr
Bicester OX26 ....65 C1
Stanford in the V SN7 ....174 B1
Church View
Ascott-u-W OX7 ....71 B1
Bampton OX18 ....134 C2
Banbury OX16 ....16 A2
Brackley NN13 ....24 A4
Carterton OX18 ....115 C1
Charlton-on-O OX5 ....95 A3
Freeland OX29 ....106 A3
Grove OX12 ....196 C1
Highworth SN6 ....190 A3
Stoke Row RG9 ....241 C3
Church View Rd OX28 ..117 C4
Church Villas OX11 .....237 A4
Church Way
N Hinksey Village OX2 ...122 B1
Oxford OX4 ....141 C2
Sparsholt OX12 ....212 C2
Church Wlk Banbury OX16 16 B3
Bishopstone SN6 ....227 B2
Combe OX29 ....90 A2
Faringdon SN7 ....173 A2
Oxford OX2 ....123 A2
Shipton-u-W OX7 ....70 B1
Shrivenham SN6 ....209 B4
Upper Heyford OX25 ......62 C4
Churchfield RG9 ....223 B2
Churchfield La OX10 ....203 C2
Churchfields OX29 ......89 B4
Churchill Cl Didcot OX11 200 B1
Woodstock OX20 ....91 A3
Churchill Cres
Sonning Common RG4 ...252 C3
Thame OX9 ....148 A4
Churchill Dr OX3 ......124 B1
Churchill Gate OX20 .....91 B3
Churchill Hospl The
OX3 ....142 B4
Churchill Pl OX2 ....122 C4
Churchill Rd
Bicester OX26 ....65 C2
Chipping Norton OX7 .....42 B1
Didcot OX11 ....200 B1
Kidlington OX5 ....108 C4
Kingham OX7 ....55 A4
Churchill Way OX29 ....106 A4
Churchlea OX17 ....4 A2
Churchmere Rd OX14 ..180 A1
Churchward OX11 ......200 C2
Churchward Cl OX12 ...196 B1
Churchway RG20 ....235 A1
Chure The OX5 ....95 A2
Churnet Cl OX11 ....201 A1
Cinnaminta Rd OX3 ....142 C4
Cinnamon Cl OX44 ......184 B4
Circourt Rd OX12 ......195 C2
Circular Rd OX26 ....81 A3
Circus St OX4 ....141 C4
City Rd HP14 ....189 B3
Clack's La Benson OX10 .222 B4
Crowmarsh G OX10 .....222 B4
Clanfield CE Prim Sch
OX18 ....152 C4
Clanfield Cres RG31 ....257 B1
Clanfield Rd OX18 ......134 C1
Clapcot Way OX10 ......221 B4
Clare Terr OX18 ....115 B1
Clarence Pl OX11 ....218 C4
Clarence Rd RG9 ....244 B1
Clarendon Cl OX14 .....180 A4
Clarendon Dr OX9 ......130 A1
Clark's Row 9 OX1 .....141 B4
Clarks La CV36 ....28 A3
Clarkston Rd OX18 ......115 B1
Clay Bank OX15 ....30 A4
Clay Cl RG31 ....257 A1
Clay Hut Cl OX7 ....58 C3
Clay La OX10 ....204 B1
Claydon Ct 5 RG4 ......259 A1
Claydon Rd OX17 ....4 C2
Clayfields SN6 ....209 A2
Claymond Rd OX3 ......124 C2
Claypit La SN7 ....211 A4
Claypits La SN6 ....209 B4
Clays Cl OX3 ....124 A3
Cleave The OX11 ....217 C4
Cleavers OX39 ....168 A3
Cleavers Sq 4 OX4 .....142 C1
Cleeve Ct RG8 ....249 A4
Cleeve Down RG8 ......249 B4
Cleeve Park Cotts RG8 .249 B4
Cleeve Rd RG8 ....249 A4
Cleeves Ave OX7 ....42 C2
Cleeves Cnr OX7 ....42 C3
Clematis Pl OX4 ....142 C1
Clement Burrows Ho 3
OX1 ....123 A1
Clements Cl OX12 ......214 C3
Clements Gn OX11 .....219 C3
Clements La OX27 ....67 C1
Clements Mead RG31 ...257 A1
Clements Rd RG9 ....244 B2
Clerkenwell Cotts HP17 130 C3
Clevedon Ct 3 OX5 .....108 C4
Clevedon Rd RG31 ......257 C2
Cleveland Cl OX5 ......109 A4
Cleveland Dr OX4 ......142 B3
Clevelands OX14 ....160 A1
Cleveley Rd OX7 ....58 C3
Clevemede RG8 ....249 B4
Cleycourt Rd SN6 ......209 A3
Clifden Rd HP18 ....127 B3
Clifford Pl OX2 ....122 B4
Clifton Dr OX14 ....179 C4
Clifton Hampden CE Prim
Sch OX14 ....181 B2
Clifton Park Rd RG4 ....258 C2
Clifton Rd OX15,OX17 ....34 B2
Clifton Rise RG10 ......255 C1
Clinton Cl OX4 ....141 C2
Clive Rd OX4 ....142 B3
Clock Tower Ct SN7 ....172 C1
Cloisters The
Ewelme OX10 ....204 C2
21 Oxford OX1 ....141 B4
Reading RG4 ....259 A2
1 Wantage OX12 ....214 B2
Clonmel Cl RG4 ....259 B1
Close The
Ardington OX12 ....215 C3
Aston Tirrold OX11 ......237 C4
Benson OX10 ....203 C3
Chipping Warden OX17 .....5 C3
Great Bourton OX17 ....9 B4
Henley-on-T RG9 ....254 B4
Lechlade GL7 ....150 B3
Stanton Harcourt OX29 ..138 A4
Stoke Lyne OX27 ....51 A3
Woodcote RG8 ....250 C4
Closes The OX5 ....92 C1
Clover Cl OX2 ....140 A3
Clover Mead OX26 ....65 C3
Clover Pl Eynsham OX29 .120 B4
Oxford OX4 ....142 C1
Coach House Ct RG8 ....256 C3
Coach La SN7 ....173 A2
Coach Way OX10 ....203 C2
Coalport Way RG30 .....257 C1
Coates La RG9 ....206 B1
Cobden Cres OX1 ....141 B4
Cobden Ctr The OX11 ....200 C2
Cochrane Rd OX10 ......204 B1
Cockcroft Rd OX11 .....218 C4
Cockington Gn OX16 .....16 C4
Cockpit Cl OX20 ....91 A3
Cocks La OX33 ....125 B4
Cockshoot Cl OX29 ....89 B4
Cockwell La SN7 ....192 B3
Cogges Farm Mus★
OX28 ....118 B4
Cogges Hill Rd OX28 ....118 B4
Coghill OX5 ....93 A4
Coker Cl OX26 ....65 C1
Colborne Rd OX11 ......218 B4
Coldharbour Cl RG9 ....254 B4
Coldicutt St RG4 ....259 B1
Cole Ct OX11 ....200 C2
Colegrave Rd OX15 ....21 C3
Colemans Hill OX3 ......124 C2
Coleridge Cl
1 Bicester OX26 ....65 B2
Oxford OX4 ....142 B3
Coleridge Dr OX14 ......179 B3
Colerne Rd OX18 ....115 C2
Coles La OX44 ....184 B4
Colesbourne Rd OX15 ....21 B2
Coleshill Dr SN7 ....172 C1
Colgrove Down OX2 .....140 A3
Collcutt Cl OX33 ....143 B4
College Cl Cholsey OX10 .220 C1
Holton OX33 ....126 B1
College Farm
Benson OX10 ....203 C2
Chadlington OX7 ....57 A1
College Farm Cl OX5 ....94 C1
College Flats OX4 ......142 A1
College La
Long Compton CV36 ....28 A2
Oxford OX4 ....142 A1
College Sq OX13 ....156 A2
College The OX18 ......101 C2
College Way OX33 ......143 A3
Collett OX11 ....200 C2
Collett Way OX12 ......196 B1
Colley Wood OX1 ....141 B1
Collice St OX5 ....109 C4
Collier's La SN7 ....173 A2
Colliers La RG9 ....252 C4
Collingwood Cl OX14 ...159 C1
Collingwood Rd OX11 ..218 B4
Collins St 5 OX4 ....141 C4
Collinsmith Dr OX12 ....196 C1
Collinsons Row OX7 ......73 A2
Collinwood Cl OX3 .....124 C2
Collinwood Rd OX3 .....124 C2
Collyer Rd HP14 ....188 C2
Colmore La RG9 ....252 C4
Coln Rd OX11 ....217 A2
Colne Cl Bicester OX26 ...65 B1
Grove OX12 ....196 B1
Colne Dr
Berinsfield OX10 ....182 B3
Didcot OX11 ....201 A2
Colonnade The RG31 ...257 B1
Colony Rd OX15 ....19 A4
Colterne Cl OX3 ....124 A3
Coltman Ave HP18 .....129 B3
Colton Rd SN6 ....209 A3
Coltsfoot Sq 11 OX4 ....142 C1
Columbia Way OX12 ....214 B4
Columbine Gdns OX4 ...143 A1
Colvile Cl OX18 ....134 C2
Colville Wlk OX16 ....16 C4
Colwell Dr
Abingdon OX14 ....179 B4
Oxford OX3 ....125 A2
Witney OX28 ....117 C3
Colwell Rd OX10 ....182 B3
Colyton Way RG8 ....257 B3
Combe CE Prim Sch
OX29 ....90 A2
Combe Gate OX29 ....90 A2
Combe Rd Oxford OX2 ..123 A1
Stonesfield OX29 ....89 B4
Combe Sta OX29 ....90 A2
Combes Cl SN7 ....173 A2
Combewell OX44 ....143 B1
Comfrey Rd OX4 ....142 C2
Common Cl
North Leigh OX29 ....105 A3
Shrivenham SN6 ....209 B4
Common La OX7 ....42 B1
Common Rd Beckley OX3 110 C2
North Leigh OX29 ....105 A3
Compass Cl 4 OX4 .....142 B2
Compton Ct CV36 ....27 C4
Compton District Prim Sch
The CV36 ....27 C3
Compton Dr OX14 ......160 A1
Compton Terr 2 OX10 ..221 B4
Condor Cl RG31 ....257 B2
Conduit Hill Rise OX9 ..147 C4
Conduit House★ OX2 ....140 C4
Conduit Rd OX14 ....179 C4
Conifer Cl OX2 ....140 B4
Conifer Dr Bicester OX26 .65 C3
Reading RG31 ....257 A1
Conifer Rise OX16 ....9 A1
Conigre OX39 ....168 A3
Conisboro Ave RG4 .....258 C3
Conisboro Way RG4 .....258 C3
Coniston Ave OX3 ....124 A2
Coniston Dr RG30 ......257 C1
Connaught Ho RG9 .....244 C2
Connolly Dr OX18 ....115 B2
Constable's Croft OX25 ..96 C4
Constitution Hill OX10 ..221 C2
Convent The OX7 ....68 B3
Conway Dr OX16 ....15 C3
Conway Rd OX13 ....159 B1
Conyger Cl OX5 ....93 C1
Conygree Terr OX7 ....42 C2
Cook La OX10 ....221 C1
Cook's Hill OX15 ....14 A3
Cooks La OX7 ....41 C3
Coolidge Cl OX3 ....124 B1
Coombe Hill Cres OX9 ..147 C4
Coombe The RG8 ....248 C3
Coombes Cl OX7 ....85 B4
Cooper Cl
Chipping Norton OX7 .....42 C2
Wheatley OX33 ....143 C4
Cooper Pl OX3 ....124 C2
Cooper Rd RG9 ....244 B2
Cooper Sch OX26 ....65 C2
Cooper's Court Rd HP14 188 B3
Coopers Gate OX16 ......16 B4
Coopers Gn OX26 ....65 C3
Coopers La
Abingdon OX14 ....179 C3
Wantage OX12 ....214 C3
Coopers Piece OX10 ....221 B4
Coopers Pightle RG4 ....252 B2
Cope Cl OX2 ....140 B4
Cope Rd OX16 ....16 B3
Copenhagen Dr OX14 ...159 B1
Copperage Rd OX12 .....234 A1
Copperfields RG4 ....258 C2
Coppice Cl OX16 ....16 C2
Coppock Cl OX3 ....124 C1
Coppperfield Cl OX12 ...214 B3
Copse Ave RG4 ....259 C2
Copse Cl RG31 ....257 B2
Copse La OX3 ....124 A3
Copse Mead RG5 ....260 C1
Copse The
Abingdon OX14 ....160 B1
Wargrave RG10 ....255 C2
Copson La OX44 ....163 B1
Copthorne Rd OX5 ......108 C4
Corbett Rd OX18 ....115 B1
Cordrey Gn OX4 ....141 C2
Corfe Mews RG4 ....259 C2
Coriander Way 15 OX4 ..142 C1
Corn Avill Cl OX14 .....160 B1
Corn Bar OX28 ....117 C4
Corn St OX28 ....118 A4
Corncrake Way OX26 .....66 A1
Corndell Gdns OX28 ....118 A4
Corner Cl The OX15 ......13 A3
Corneville Rd OX14 .....179 A1
Cornfield Cl OX28 ......117 C4
Cornhill La OX12 ....213 C3
Cornish Rd OX7 ....42 B1
Cornmarket
Faringdon SN7 ....172 C2
Thame OX9 ....147 C4
Cornmarket St OX1 .....123 B1
Cornwall Cl RG31 ....257 A2
Cornwallis Cl OX4 ......142 A3
Cornwallis Rd OX4 .....142 A3
Cornwell OX7 ....41 B2
Coromandel OX14 ....179 B2
Coronation Cotts OX18 .152 C4
Coronation La OX17 ......8 B4
Corpus Christi Coll OX1 123 B1
Corunna Cres OX4 ......142 C3
Cosford Gdns OX26 ......66 A2
Cosin Cl OX4 ....142 A4
Costar Cl OX4 ....142 B2
Cot's Gn OX5 ....92 B1
Cote Rd OX18 ....135 C2
Cothill House Sch OX13 158 C2
Cothill Rd OX13 ....158 C2
Cotman Cl OX14 ....179 C3
Cotmore Cl OX9 ....148 A4
Cotmore Gdns OX9 .....148 A4
Cotshill Gdns OX7 ....42 C2
Cotswold Cl
Minster Lovell OX29 .....102 C1
Sibford Ferris OX15 ....19 A4
Cotswold Cnr OX7 ....29 A2
Cotswold Cres
Chipping Norton OX7 .....42 C1
Marston OX3 ....123 C3
Cotswold Cres Bungs
OX7 ....42 C1
Cotswold Dene OX29 ...137 A3
Cotswold Mdw OX28 ....117 B4
Cotswold Pk OX11 ......200 B1
Cotswold Rd OX2 ....140 A3
Cotswold Terr OX7 ....42 C1
Cotswold View OX7 ......73 A2
Cotswold Way
Carterton OX18 ....115 B2
Reading RG31 ....257 B1
Cotswold Wildlife Pk★
OX18 ....114 B3
Cotswold Woollen Weavers
Mus★ GL7 ....132 A3
Cottage Rd SN7 ....194 B4
Cottages The OX18 .....114 A3
Cottesmore La OX10 ....204 B3
Cottesmore Rd OX4 ....142 A2
Cotton Grass Cl OX4 ...142 C1
Cotts The HP18 ....129 B3
Couching St OX49 ......186 A1
Coulings Cl OX12 ....216 B4
Council Cotts RG4 ......252 A3
Council Hos
Bloxham OX15 ....21 B2
Great Tew OX7 ....45 B4
Shiplake RG9 ....254 A1
Council Hos The
Barford St M OX15 ....32 C3
Charlbury OX7 ....73 A2
Hanwell OX17 ....8 C2
Nettlebed RG9 ....224 B3
Council Houses OX7 .....72 C4
Council Houses The
OX17 ....10 C4
Country Pk OX28 ....118 A3
County Rd NN13 ....24 A3
County Trading Est OX4 142 C2
County View OX15 ....34 B2
Coupland Rd OX13 .....159 A3
Court Cl Kidlington OX5 ..108 B4
Shipton-u-W OX7 ....85 B4
Warmington OX17 ....3 A2
Court Close Rd OX9 ....148 C4
Court Dr OX10 ....203 A3
Court Farm Rd OX4 ....141 C2
Court Gdns RG8 ....249 B4
Court Hill Rd OX12 .....214 A1
Court Place Gdns OX4 ..141 C2
Court Rd OX12 ....214 A1
Court The OX14 ....159 C1
Courtenay Cl OX14 .....200 A4
Courtenay Dr RG4 ......259 A4
Courtenay Rd OX12 .....214 C3
Courtfield Rd OX33 .....125 B4
Courthouse★ HP18 ......129 B4
Courtiers Gn OX14 .....181 B2
Courtington La OX15 .....21 B3
Courtland Rd OX4 ......142 A2
Courtlands Hill RG8 ....256 B2
Courtlands Rd OX7 ....85 B4
Courts Gdns OX28 ......118 B4
Courtyard The
Banbury OX17 ....17 B3
Crawley OX29 ....103 B3
Tadmarton OX15 ....21 A3
Covent Cl OX14 ....160 A2
Coverley Rd OX3 ....142 B4
Covert The OX20 ....91 B3
Cow La Denchworth OX12 195 C2
Didcot OX11 ....201 A1
Grove OX12 ....196 C2
Kennington OX1 ....141 C1
Longworth OX13 ....156 B2
Cow La *continued*
Moulsford OX10 ....238 C2
Reading RG1 ....258 C1
Steeple Aston OX25 ....62 A4
Sutton Courtenay OX11 ..199 C1
Cowderoy Pl SN7 ....194 C4
Cowleaze OX39 ....168 A3
Cowleaze Cl SN6 ....209 A3
Cowleaze Cnr OX18 ....134 B1
Cowley Junc OX4 ....142 C2
Cowley Pl OX4 ....141 C4
Cowley Rd Oxford OX4 ..142 A4
Oxford, Littlemore OX4 ..142 A1
Cowper Cl 2 OX26 ....65 B2
Cox La OX7 ....42 A1
Cox's Alley OX3 ....124 C2
Cox's Ct SN7 ....194 C4
Cox's La
Crowmarsh G OX10 .....222 A3
Stoke Row RG9 ....241 C3
Cox's Rd SN6 ....209 A3
Coxfield Cl HP14 ....188 C3
Coxmoor Cl OX7 ....54 C2
Coxwell Gdns SN7 ....172 C2
Coxwell Hall Mews SN7 172 C1
Coxwell Rd SN7 ....172 C1
Coxwell St SN7 ....172 C2
Cozens La OX7 ....54 C2
CR Bates Ind Est HP14 .188 C3
Crabtree Cnr OX10 .....240 B4
Crabtree La OX14 ....179 A1
Crabtree Pl OX14 ....180 A4
Crabtree Rd
Haddenham HP17 ....130 C3
N Hinksey Village OX2 ...140 B4
Crafts End OX11 ....235 C4
Cranbourne Gdns RG30 258 A1
Cranbrook Ct OX28 .....118 A3
Cranbrook Dr OX1 ......160 C4
Crane Furlong SN6 ......190 A4
Cranesbill Dr OX26 ....65 B3
Cranesbill Way OX4 ....142 C1
Cranford House Sch
OX10 ....238 C3
Cranham St OX2 ....123 A2
Cranham Terr OX2 ......123 A2
Cranleigh Cl OX16 ....16 A2
Cranley Rd OX3 ....124 C2
Cranmer Cl RG31 ....257 A2
Cranmer Rd OX4 ....142 C3
Cranston Ct 5 OX4 .....142 A2
Cranwell Ave OX18 .....115 C1
Craster Cl OX16 ....16 B2
Cratlands Cl OX44 ......163 B1
Craufurd Rd OX4 ....142 C3
Craven Comm SN7 ......211 B4
Craven Way OX11 ....218 C4
Crawborough Rd OX7 ....73 B2
Crawborough Villas OX7 .73 B2
Crawley Mill Ind Est
OX29 ....103 B2
Crawley Rd OX28 ....104 A1
Crawshay Dr RG4 ....259 A4
Cray Ct OX11 ....200 C2
Craysleaze RG4 ....252 B2
Crazies Hill CE Prim Sch
RG10 ....255 C3
Creampot Cl OX17 ....4 C1
Creampot Cres OX17 ......4 C1
Creampot La OX17 ....4 C1
Crecy Wlk OX20 ....91 B3
Cremyll Rd RG1 ....258 C1
Crendon Ct 4 RG4 ......259 A1
Crendon Way HP18 .....129 C2
Crescent Cl OX4 ....142 B3
Crescent Ct OX4 ....142 B3
Crescent Rd Oxford OX4 .142 B3
Reading RG31 ....257 B1
Crescent The
Adderbury OX17 ....23 A3
Bicester OX26 ....65 B2
Carterton OX18 ....133 B4
East Hagbourne OX11 ...218 C3
Long Wittenham OX14 ...201 B4
Oxford OX2 ....123 A2
Sandford-on-T OX4 ......161 B4
Shiplake RG9 ....255 A2
Steeple Aston OX25 ......62 A4
Witney OX28 ....104 B1
Crescent Way OX10 .....220 C1
Cress Hill Pl OX3 ....124 C2
Crest The
Bledlow Ridge HP14 .....189 C4
Reading RG4 ....259 B3
Crick Rd OX2 ....123 B2
Cricket Ground HP14 ...188 B3
Cricket Rd OX4 ....142 A3
Cricklade Rd SN6 ....190 A3
Cripley Pl OX2 ....123 A1
Cripley Rd OX2 ....123 A1
Crisp Rd RG9 ....244 B2
Crispin Cl RG4 ....258 B3
Crispin Pl OX10 ....221 B4
Croasdell Cl OX14 ......179 C2
Crockwell Cl OX26 ....65 C1
Crockwell St CV36 ....27 C4
Croft Ave OX5 ....108 C4
Croft Cl Merton OX25 .....95 B4
Oxford OX3 ....123 C2
Thame OX9 ....148 A4
Croft Ct OX9 ....148 A4
Croft Ctyd HP17 ....130 C3
Croft End OX12 ....214 A1
Croft La OX17 ....23 A2
Croft Rd Goring RG8 ....249 B3
Oxford OX3 ....123 C2
Thame OX9 ....148 A4
Wallingford OX10 ....221 B4

Edmund Halley Rd OX4 142 A1
Edmund Rd OX4 142 B3
Edmunds Rd OX16 15 C3
Edward Feild Cty Prim Sch OX5 108 C4
Edward Rd OX1 141 C1
Edward St
Abingdon OX14 179 B4
Banbury OX16 16 C3
Edward Stone Rise OX7 42 B1
Edwin Ct OX2 122 C1
Edwin Rd OX11 218 B4
Egerton Cl NN13 24 A4
Egerton Rd Oxford OX4 142 A2
Wallingford OX10 221 B4
Eglin St OX25 63 A4
Eighteenth St OX11 217 A2
Eighth Ave OX3 142 C4
Eighth St OX11 217 A2
Elbourne OX11 218 B4
Elder Cl RG31 257 B1
Elder Way OX4 142 C1
Elderdene OX39 168 B4
Elderfield Cres OX11 235 B4
Elderfield Rd OX27 65 C4
Eldridge Cl OX14 159 C1
Eleanor Cl OX4 142 A2
Electric Ave OX2 141 A4
Eleventh St OX11 217 A1
Eliot Cl RG4 259 A2
Elizabeth Ave OX14 160 B1
Elizabeth Cl RG9 254 A4
Elizabeth Ct RG10 255 C1
Elizabeth Dr OX12 214 B3
Elizabeth Rd
Henley-on-T RG9 254 A4
Stokenchurch HP14 188 C2
Elizabeth Rise OX16 16 A2
Ell's La OX15 21 B4
Ellesmere Cl RG4 259 A2
Ellesmere Rd OX4 142 A2
Elliots Way RG4 259 A1
Ellison Dr OX17 8 C1
Elm Bridge Rdbt OX10 203 C2
Elm Cl Ambrosden OX25 81 B2
Bicester OX26 65 C2
Chinnor OX39 168 B3
Tetsworth OX9 166 A4
Wheatley OX33 144 B4
Witney OX28 117 C4
Elm Cres OX7 73 B2
Elm Ct Henley-on-T RG9 254 B4
Sonning Common RG4 252 C2
Elm Dr Chinnor OX39 168 B3
Garsington OX44 143 B1
Elm Gr Kidlington OX5 108 C3
Milton-u-W OX7 70 A1
Elm La OX25 81 B2
Elm Pl OX29 120 B4
Elm Rd Faringdon SN7 172 C2
Mapledurham RG4 258 B4
North Moreton OX11 220 A4
Wantage OX12 214 C3
Elm Tree Cl OX4 142 A2
Elm Tree Wlk OX13 159 B1
Elm Trees HP18 129 A4
Elmcroft RG8 249 B3
Elmhurst Rd RG8 249 B4
Elmleigh Ct RG4 259 B2
Elms Dr OX3 124 A3
Elms Par OX2 122 B1
Elms Rd Cassington OX29 107 B1
N Hinksey Village OX2 122 B1
Thame OX9 147 C4
Elms The Highworth SN6 190 A3
Langford GL7 132 B1
Elms Way RG9 224 B2
Elmscote Rd OX16 16 B1
Elmsfield Farm Ind Est OX7 42 B2
Elmside SN7 193 A3
Elmstone Dr RG31 257 B1
Elmthorpe Rd OX2 122 C4
Elsfield Rd OX3 123 C3
Elsfield Way OX2 109 A1
Elsley Rd RG31 257 C2
Elstow Ave RG4 259 B3
Elstree Cl RG31 257 B1
Elswith Cl OX12 214 B4
Eltham Ave RG4 259 C3
Elton Cres OX33 144 B4
Elton Rd OX16 16 C1
Elvendon La RG8 250 B4
Elvendon Rd RG8 249 B4
Elwes Cl OX14 180 A4
Elwes Rd OX13 178 B3
Ely Cl Abingdon OX14 179 B3
Carterton OX18 115 C2
Emden Ho OX3 124 B2
Emma La RG10 255 C1
Emmanuel Christian Sch OX4 142 A1
Emmens Cl RG8 241 B2
Emmer Green Ct RG4 259 B3
Emmer Green Prim Sch RG4 259 A3
Emperor Gdns OX4 142 C1
Empstead Ct RG9 244 B1
Eney Cl OX14 160 B1
Enstone Airfield Complex (Ind Est) OX7 59 B4
Enstone Cty Prim Sch OX7 58 C3
Enstone Rd Charlbury OX7 73 A2
Little Tew OX7 45 A3
Enstone Rd *continued*
Middle Barton OX7 60 C4
EP Collier Prim Sch RG1 259 A1
Epwell Rd OX15 13 C3
Eric Ave RG4 259 A3
Erica Cl Banbury OX16 9 A1
Oxford OX4 142 C2
Ermont Way OX16 16 C4
Ernest Rd OX11 218 C4
Ernicote Cl OX25 81 C2
Essex Rd OX9 148 A4
Essex St OX4 142 A4
Essex Way RG4 253 A2
Ester Carling La RG9 252 B4
Estover Way OX39 168 A3
Ethelhelm Cl OX14 160 B2
Ethelred Ct OX3 124 B2
Eton Cl OX28 118 B4
European Sch The OX14 180 B2
Evans Cl OX29 120 C4
Evans Ct OX5 108 C4
Evans La OX5 108 C4
Evans Rd OX29 120 C4
Evans Yd 9 OX26 65 C1
Evelin Rd OX14 159 C1
Evelyn Cl OX2 140 A4
Evenlode OX16 16 A4
Evenlode Cl Bicester OX26 65 B1
Charlbury OX7 73 A2
Grove OX12 196 B1
North Leigh OX29 105 A3
Evenlode Cres OX5 92 A1
Evenlode Ct OX28 118 A4
Evenlode Dr
Berinsfield OX10 182 B3
Didcot OX11 200 C1
Long Hanborough OX29 90 A1
Evenlode Ho OX26 65 B1
Evenlode Pk OX14 160 A1
Evenlode Twr OX4 142 C1
Everard Cl OX3 124 B1
Eversley Cl OX7 57 A1
Evesham Rd RG4 259 A3
Ewart Cl OX26 65 B2
Ewelme CE Prim Sch OX10 204 C2
Ewert Pl OX2 123 A3
Ewin Cl OX3 123 C3
Ewin Ct OX3 123 C3
Exbourne Rd OX14 179 B4
Exe Cl OX11 200 C1
Exeter Coll OX1 123 B1
Exeter Ct Didcot OX11 219 A4
5 Kidlington OX5 108 C4
Eylham RG8 257 A3
Eynsford Cl RG4 259 C3
Eynsham Com Prim Sch OX29 120 C4
Eynsham Ct OX29 105 B3
Eynsham Rd
Cassington OX29 107 B1
Cumnor OX2 121 C1
N Hinksey Village OX2 140 A4
Eyot Pl OX4 141 C4
Eyre's La OX10 204 C3
Eyres Cl OX10 204 B2
Eyston Way OX14 179 B4

F

Faber Cl OX4 142 B1
Fair Cl OX26 65 C2
Fair Mile RG9 244 B2
Fair Mile Hopsl OX10 221 A1
Fair View OX3 142 B4
Fairacres OX14 179 B4
Fairacres Rd
Didcot OX11 218 C4
Oxford OX4 141 C3
Fairfax Ave OX3 123 C2
Fairfax Cl Banbury OX16 16 A3
Reading RG4 259 A2
Thame OX9 148 A4
Fairfax Ctr OX5 108 C3
Fairfax Gate OX33 144 B4
Fairfax Rd
Chalgrove OX44 184 B3
Kidlington OX5 108 C3
Oxford OX4 142 C3
Fairfield OX10 220 C1
Fairfield Cl OX12 214 B4
Fairfield Dr OX28 117 C4
Fairfield Pl OX14 179 C4
Fairfield Rd RG8 249 B4
Fairfields OX29 136 C4
Fairford Rd RG31 257 B1
Fairford Way OX26 66 A2
Fairhaven Rd OX27 65 C4
Fairlawn End OX2 122 C4
Fairlawn Flats OX2 122 C4
Fairlawn Wharf OX14 179 C3
Fairlie Rd OX4 142 A2
Fairmile Ct RG9 244 B2
Fairspear Rd OX29 86 C2
Fairthorne Way SN6 209 A3
Fairview Est RG9 254 C4
Fairview Rd OX16 16 B2
Fairway The OX16 16 A3
Falcon Cl Banbury OX16 16 A2
Carterton OX18 115 B2
Oxford OX4 142 B1
Falcon Mead OX26 81 A4
Falcon Villas OX7 73 B3
Falkland Ho OX18 115 C1
Falkland Rd RG4 259 A1
Falkner's Cl OX17 23 A2
Fallow Way OX16 16 C1
Fallowfield Cl RG4 259 A2
Fallowfields OX26 65 C1
Falstaff Cl OX29 120 C4
Fane Cl OX26 65 B2
Fane Dr OX10 182 B3
Fane Ho 2 OX26 65 C1
Fane Rd OX3 123 C3
Fanshawe Pl OX4 142 C3
Fanshawe Rd OX9 148 A4
Faraday Ave OX11 217 A1
Faringdon Com Coll SN7 172 C1
Faringdon Inf Sch SN7 172 C2
Faringdon Jun Sch SN7 172 C2
Faringdon Rd
Appleton OX2 139 C1
Kingston Bagpuize OX13 156 C1
Shrivenham SN6 209 B4
Stanford in the V SN7 194 B4
Watchfield SN6 191 C1
Farleigh Mews RG4 259 C3
Farleigh Rd SN6 209 A3
Farley Cl OX29 89 B4
Farm Cl Aston OX18 135 C1
Chalgrove OX44 184 C3
Ickford HP18 127 C2
Kidlington OX5 92 C1
Purley on T RG8 257 B3
Sandford-on-T OX4 142 C1
Sonning Common RG4 252 C3
Farm Close La OX33 144 A4
Farm Close Rd OX33 144 A4
Farm Cotts OX5 93 A4
Farm Ct SN6 227 B2
Farm End Grove OX12 214 B4
Woodstock OX20 91 A4
Farm La OX29 103 B3
Farm Mill La OX28 118 A4
Farm Pl OX39 149 C1
Farm Rd Abingdon OX14 159 C1
Brackley NN13 24 A3
Goring RG8 249 B3
Henley-on-T RG9 254 C4
Farm Way OX16 16 C2
Farman Cres GL54 68 A2
Farmer Pl OX3 123 C2
Farmers Cl OX28 104 A1
Farmfield Rd OX16 16 B2
Farmhouse Cl OX29 138 A4
Farmhouse Mdw OX28 117 C4
Farmhouse Mews OX49 186 A1
Farmiloe Cl RG8 257 B2
Farmington Dr OX28 117 C4
Farmoor Ct OX2 121 B1
Farmstead Cl OX12 196 B1
Farnborough Hall★ OX17 3 C4
Farndon Rd OX2 123 A2
Farnham Ct 6 OX5 108 C4
Farnham Dr RG4 259 C2
Farrier's Mead OX26 80 A2
Farriers Cl OX27 52 B3
Farriers Mews OX14 180 A4
Farriers Rd OX7 60 C4
Farringdon Rd OX13 159 A1
Farthings The OX13 178 B4
Faulder Ave OX18 115 B2
Faulkner St 7 OX1 141 B4
Fawler La OX7 88 B4
Fawler Rd Charlbury OX7 73 B1
Uffington SN7,OX12 211 C3
Fawley Bottom La RG9 226 A1
Fawley Cl OX12 214 B3
Fawley Ct★ RG9 244 C3
Featherbed La
East Hendred OX12 216 C4
Milton OX14 199 A1
Mixbury NN13 38 B3
Feilden Cl OX29 118 A2
Feilden Gr OX3 124 A2
Fells Cl HP18 129 B3
Feltwell Cl OX18 115 C2
Fencott Rd OX5 95 A2
Fenlock Ct OX29 90 C1
Fenlock Rd OX29 90 C1
Fennel Way OX14 180 B4
Fenny Compton Rd OX17 1 B1
Fenway OX25 48 A1
Ferguson Pl OX14 180 B4
Fergusson Rd OX16 16 C4
Fermi Ave OX11 217 A1
Fern Glen RG31 257 B1
Fern Hill Rd OX4 142 C3
Fernbrook Rd RG4 258 C3
Ferndale Cl
Reading RG31 257 B2
Stokenchurch HP14 188 C2
Ferndale Prep Sch SN7 172 C2
Ferndale Rd OX16 15 C4
Ferndale St SN7 173 A2
Ferne Cl RG8 249 B4
Fernham Rd
Faringdon SN7 172 C1
Little Coxwell SN7 192 C4
Longcot SN7 192 B1
Shellingford SN7 193 B3
Fernhill Cl Kidlington OX5 108 B4
Milcombe OX15 21 A1
Tiddington OX9 146 A3
Fernhill Rd OX5 108 A4
Ferny Cl OX14 160 C2
Ferriston OX16 9 A1
Ferry Ct OX14 179 C3
Ferry Hinksey Rd OX2 123 A1
Ferry La Goring RG8 249 A3
Moulsford OX10 239 A2
South Stoke OX10,RG8 239 A2
Ferry La *continued*
Wargrave RG10 255 B1
Ferry Mills OX2 141 A4
Ferry Pool Rd OX2 123 A3
Ferry Rd Oxford OX3 123 C2
South Stoke RG8 239 B2
Ferry Wlk OX14 179 C3
Fetti Pl OX12 214 C3
Fettiplace OX7 70 A1
Fettiplace Cl OX13 158 A4
Fettiplace Rd
Marcham OX13 178 B3
Oxford OX3 124 C3
Witney OX28 117 C4
Fewcott Rd OX27 49 C4
Fiddlers Hill OX7 85 C3
Fidlers Wlk RG10 255 C1
Field Ave OX4 142 C1
Field Cl Ickford HP18 128 A2
Kidlington OX5 108 C4
Kingston Bagpuize OX13 156 B1
Stonesfield OX29 89 B4
Yarnton OX5 108 A3
Field Ct OX25 47 B3
Field End
Long Crendon HP18 129 C3
Wargrave RG10 255 C1
Field Gdns
East Challow OX12 213 C3
Steventon OX13 199 A3
Field Ho OX2 140 B4
Field House Dr OX2 123 A4
Field La OX44 144 A2
Field Rd Kingham OX7 54 C2
Murcott OX5 96 A3
Field St OX26 65 C1
Field The OX13 158 C3
Field View RG4 259 A2
Fielden Cl OX10 204 B1
Fielden Rd OX10 204 B1
Fieldfare Rd OX4 161 C4
Fieldmere Cl OX28 117 C4
Fieldside Abingdon OX14 159 B1
East Hagbourne OX11 219 A3
Long Wittenham OX14 201 B4
Upton OX11 218 B1
Fiennes Rd Banbury OX16 16 A3
Oxford OX4 142 A2
Fifteenth St OX11 217 A1
Fifth Ave NN13 36 C4
Fifth St NN13 36 C4
Fifth St E NN13 36 C4
Filkins Rd GL7 132 B1
Finch Cl OX3 124 B1
Finchdale Cl OX18 115 B2
Finches La SN8 245 C1
Finches The SN8 245 B1
Finchley La OX26 65 B1
Finham Brook OX11 200 C2
Finlay Ho RG9 244 C2
Finmere CE Prim Sch MK18 39 B3
Finmore Cl 3 OX14 179 C4
Finmore Rd OX2 140 B4
Finsbury Pl OX7 42 C2
Finstock CE Prim Sch OX7 88 B3
Finstock Sta OX7 88 B4
Fir Cl OX10 240 B4
Fir La OX25 48 A1
Fir Tree Ave OX10 221 A4
Fir Tree Cl OX13 156 C1
Fir Tree Cotts RG20 235 A1
Fir Tree Paddock RG20 235 A1
Fir Tree Sch The OX10 221 A4
Fir Trees OX1,OX14 160 C4
Fircroft Banbury OX16 16 B2
Bicester OX26 65 C3
Fircroft Cl RG31 257 B1
Firebrass Hill OX10 204 C3
Firs Cl OX7 54 B1
Firs Mdw 9 OX4 142 C1
Firs The Cutteslowe OX2 123 A4
Wroxton OX15 15 A4
First Ave Didcot OX11 200 B1
Oxford OX3 142 C4
First St Croughton NN13 36 C3
Harwell OX11 217 B1
First Turn OX2 122 C4
Firtree Cl OX16 8 C1
Fish Ponds La OX9 129 C1
Fisher Cl Banbury OX16 16 C4
Drayton OX14 179 A1
Fisher Row OX1 123 A1
Fisher's La OX7 73 A2
Fishermans Wharf OX14 179 C2
Fishers Cl OX29 104 A3
Fishers Cotts RG4 259 B3
Fishers Ct RG4 259 B3
Fitchett Yd OX14 179 C4
Fitzcount Way OX10 203 B1
Fitzharris Ind Est OX14 179 C4
Fitzharry's Rd OX14 179 C4
Fitzharrys Sch OX14 159 C1
Fitzherbert Cl OX4 141 C2
Fitzwaryn Sch OX12 214 B3
Five Acre RG31 257 B1
Five Acres Cty Prim Sch OX25 81 B2
Five Mile Dr OX2 109 A1
Fiveacres OX5 95 C2
Flambards 1 RG4 259 B1
Flatford Pl OX5 92 B1
Flavius Gate NN13 24 A4
Flaxfield Rd OX4 142 C1
Fleet Way OX11 219 A4
Fleetwood Way 7 OX9 129 C1
Fleming Cl OX26 65 B2
Fleming Dr OX7 60 C4
Flemings Rd OX20 91 B3
Flemming Ave OX44 184 B4
Fletcher Cl
Faringdon SN7 173 A2
Yarnton OX5 108 A3
Fletcher Rd OX4 142 C3
Flexney Pl OX3 124 B1
Flexneys Paddock OX29 138 A4
Flint Hollow OX39 168 A3
Flint St HP17 130 C3
Floral Cl OX12 214 C4
Florence Cl OX5 108 C4
Florence Park Rd OX4 142 A3
Florey's Cl OX29 104 A3
Flowers Hill RG8 256 B2
Floyd's Row OX1 141 B4
Fludger Cl OX10 221 B4
Fogwell Rd OX2 122 A1
Foliat Cl OX12 214 C3
Foliat Dr OX12 214 C3
Folland Cl OX7 42 C2
Follets Cl OX5 108 A3
Followfields Ct 16 OX26 65 C1
Folly Bridge Ct 17 OX1 141 B4
Folly Cl SN6 190 A4
Folly Cres Highworth SN6 190 A4
Watchfield SN6 191 C1
Folly Ct OX15 19 B4
Folly Dr SN6 190 A4
Folly Gn RG8 250 C4
Folly Orchard Rd RG8 240 C1
Folly View Cres SN7 172 C1
Folly View Rd SN7 172 C1
Folly Way SN6 190 A4
Ford La
Drayton St L OX10 183 A3
East Hendred OX12 216 B3
Garford OX13 178 A4
Ford's Cl HP14 189 C4
Fords Cl OX33 143 B3
Forest Cl Launton OX26 66 B1
Milton-u-W OX7 70 A1
Forest Hill RG30 257 C1
Forest Rd OX3 124 C2
Forest Side OX1 141 B1
Foresters
Beacon's Bottom HP14 189 B3
Chinnor OX39 168 A3
Foresters Twr OX3 124 C1
Forestry Hos OX49 207 A4
Forge Cl Benson OX10 203 C2
Horton-cum-S OX33 112 A3
Marsh Gibbon OX27 67 C2
Merton OX25 95 B4
Reading RG4 259 B1
Forge Pl OX27 49 C4
Forgeway OX16 9 A1
Forrest Cl SN6 209 A3
Forster La OX2 139 C2
Forsythia Cl OX26 65 C3
Forsythia Wlk OX16 9 A1
Fortescue Dr OX26 80 A4
Forties The OX44 145 A1
Fortnam Cl OX3 124 A2
Forty Gn HP27 149 C2
Forty The
Bishopstone SN6 227 B3
Cholsey OX10 220 C1
Foscote Private Hospl OX16 16 B2
Foscote Rise OX16 16 C2
Fosseway The OX18 116 B2
Foster Rd OX14 159 C2
Fothergill Pl OX9 147 C4
Foudry Cl OX11 201 A1
Foundry St OX16 16 B3
Fountain Ct OX14 179 C4
Fourteenth St OX11 217 A2
Fourth Ave
Croughton NN13 36 C3
Oxford OX3 142 C4
Fourth St Croughton NN13 36 C3
Harwell OX11 217 A2
Fowler Rd OX16 16 C4
Fowler's Rd OX7 55 A2
Fowlers Farm Rd HP14 188 C2
Fox Cl Bampton OX18 134 C2
Chipping Norton OX7 42 C1
Garsington OX44 143 B1
Hailey OX29 104 A2
Fox Cover OX39 168 B3
Fox Cres OX1 141 C3
Fox Furlong OX4 142 A1
Fox La Bicester OX26 65 B1
Middle Barton OX7 60 C4
Souldern OX6 35 C2
Wootton (Oxford) OX1, OX13 159 B4
Foxborough Rd OX14 160 C1
Foxburrow Cl OX29 120 A1
Foxburrow La OX29 103 C2
Foxcombe Ct OX14 179 B4
Foxcombe La OX1 141 A1
Foxcombe Rd OX1 140 C1
Foxcroft Dr OX18 115 B1
Foxdown Cl OX5 92 C1
Foxfield OX7 42 C1
Foxglove Cl Bicester OX26 65 C2
7 Sandford-on-T OX4 142 C1
Foxglove La OX11 218 B2
Foxglove Rd OX5 108 A4
Foxhall Rd OX11 200 B1
Foxhill Cl RG4 260 A3
Foxhill La Reading RG4 259 C3
Souldern OX6 35 C2

Foxholes Nature Reserve★ OX7 69 C3
Foxton Cl OX2 108 C1
Foxtowns Gn OX5 78 A3
Foxwell Dr OX3 124 A3
Foxwood OX18 135 C2
Foxwood Cl Aston OX18 135 C2
Banbury OX16 16 B1
Framlands Cl OX12 214 A3
Framlingham Dr RG4 259 C3
Frampton Cl RG5 260 C1
Frances Rd OX7 60 C4
Francis Little Dr OX14 179 B3
Frank Cook Ct OX5 92 C1
Frank Wise Specl Sch OX16 16 A3
Frank's La OX13 198 C2
Franklin Cl
Chalgrove OX44 184 B3
Kidlington OX5 92 C1
Franklin Rd OX3 124 A2
Franklyn Cl OX14 159 C1
Fraser Ave RG4 259 B3
Fraser Cl OX16 16 C3
Fraser Gdns OX10 221 B3
Frax Cl OX13 156 C1
Frederick Rd OX4 142 B2
Freeborn Cl OX5 92 C2
Freehold St OX25 62 B3
Freeland CE Prim Sch OX29 106 A4
Freelands Cotts OX33 125 B4
Freelands Rd OX4 141 C3
Freeman Rd OX11 200 B1
Freemans Cl SN7 211 B4
Freemans Rd OX15 22 C4
French Cl OX28 117 C4
French Laurence Way OX44 184 B3
Frenchay Rd OX2 123 A3
Frensham Cl OX16 9 A1
Frethern Cl OX18 100 C2
Friar's Well OX17 35 B4
Friars Cl SN6 209 A3
Friars Furlong HP18 129 A4
Friars Wharf OX1 141 B4
Friars' Entry OX1 123 B1
Friday Ct OX9 129 C1
Friday La OX33 144 A4
Friday St RG9 244 C1
Frideswide CE Mid Sch OX2 123 B3
Friends Cl OX29 89 B4
Frieze Way OX2,OX5 108 C2
Friford Rd OX13 178 B3
Frilsham St OX14 200 A4
Fringford CE Prim Sch OX27 52 B3
Fritwell CE Prim Sch OX27 49 C4
Fritwell Rd OX27 50 A2
Frog La OX7 70 A1
Frogmore La SN7 194 C4
Frome Rd OX11 217 B1
Fruitlands OX29 120 B4
Fry Ct RG4 259 A2
Frys Hill OX4 142 C1
Fuchsia Wlk OX16 9 A1
Fullbrook Cres RG31 257 B2
Fullers Field OX44 145 B1
Fullers Rd OX11 219 C1
Fullwell Cl OX14 159 C1
Fulmar Ct OX26 66 A2
Fulmar Pl OX12 196 B1
Fulwell Rd Finmere MK18 39 B4
Westbury NN13 25 A2
Furlong Cl OX4 142 B2
Furlong Row OX18 152 C4
Furlong The OX29 137 A3
Furlongs The OX9 147 B3
Fyfield Cl OX12 214 C2
Fyfield Rd OX2 123 B2

G

Gadge Cl OX9 129 C1
Gainsborough Cres RG9 254 B4
Gainsborough Gn OX14 179 C3
Gainsborough Hill RG9 254 B4
Gainsborough Rd RG9 254 B4
Gaisford Rd OX4 142 B2
Gales Ct GL7 150 B2
Gall Cl OX14 180 B4
Galley Field OX14 180 A4
Gallowstree Rd RG9 252 C4
Galpin Cl OX4 142 A4
Galsworthy Dr RG4 259 C3
Gangsdown Hill RG9 223 C2
Gap The OX13 178 B3
Gap Way RG8 250 C4
Garde Rd RG4 260 C2
Garden City OX9 148 A4
Garden Cl Banbury OX16 16 B4
Didcot OX11 218 B4
Garden Ho OX4 142 B3
Gardens Cl HP14 188 C2
Gardens The
Radley OX14 160 C2
South Stoke RG8 239 B2
Gardiner Cl
Abingdon OX14 180 B4
Wheatley OX33 144 A4
Gardiner St OX3 124 B1
Garford Cl OX14 160 A1
Garford Rd OX2 123 B3
Garne's La OX18 100 C3
Garner Cl OX18 115 B3
Garsington CE Sch OX44 143 C1
Garsington Rd OX4 142 C2
Garsons La OX10,RG8 240 C3
Garston Cl OX12 214 C3
Garston Ct OX18 116 A3
Garston La OX12 214 C3
Garth Rd OX11 200 C1
Garth The
N Hinksey Village OX2 140 B4
Yarnton OX5 108 A3
Garton End RG8 250 B3
Gas La OX7 85 B4
Gascoigne Way OX15 21 C1
Gaskells End RG4 258 B4
Gassons Mead OX18 133 B3
Gassons Rd GL7 150 B3
Gassons The GL7 132 A3
Gassons Way GL7 150 B2
Gatehampton Rd RG8 249 B3
Gateley OX33 143 B3
Gateway Prim Sch OX18 115 C1
Gathorne Rd OX3 124 B1
Gatteridge St OX16 16 B3
Gauntlets Cl OX15 21 C3
Gaveston Gdns OX15 33 C2
Gaveston Rd OX11 217 C4
Gavray Dr OX26 66 A1
Gaydon Cl OX18 115 C2
Gaydon Wlk 2 OX26 66 A2
Gayhurst Cl RG4 259 B3
Gelt Burn OX11 201 A1
Gentian Cl OX26 65 B3
Gentian Rd OX4 142 C1
Geoffrey Barbour Rd OX14 179 C4
Geoffrey Tuttle Dr OX10 204 B1
Geoffreyson Rd RG4 258 C3
George Moore Cl OX4 142 A3
George Rd HP14 188 C3
George St Banbury OX16 16 B3
Bicester OX26 65 B2
Oxford OX1 123 B1
Reading RG4 259 A1
George Street Mews OX1 123 A1
Gerard Pl OX4 142 B3
Germander Way OX26 65 B3
Gibbs Cres OX2 141 A4
Gibbs Rd OX16 16 C4
Gibson Cl OX14 160 A2
Gibson Dr OX25 63 B4
Gidley Way OX33 143 B4
Giernalls Rd OX29 104 A3
Giffard Way HP18 129 B4
Gifford Cl RG4 259 C3
Giles Cl OX4 142 A1
Giles Rd OX4 142 B1
Gilkes Yd OX16 16 A3
Gillett Cl OX16 16 A3
Gillett Rd OX16 16 A3
Gillians Way OX4 142 A3
Gillott's Hill RG9 254 B4
Gillott's Sch RG9 254 A4
Gillotts Cl RG9 254 A4
Gillotts La RG9 254 B4
Ginge Cl OX14 160 A1
Gipsy La
Great Coxwell SN7 192 B4
Grove OX12 214 C4
Oxford OX3 124 A1
Reading RG30 257 C1
Girdlestone Cl OX3 124 B1
Girdlestone Rd OX3 124 B1
Glade The RG8 257 B2
Glades The OX26 66 B1
Gladstone Ct OX3 124 C2
Gladstone Rd OX3 124 C2
Glamis Pl OX16 15 C3
Glanville Gdns OX16 16 A3
Glanville Rd OX4 142 A4
Glebe Cl Ambrosden OX25 81 B2
Moulsford OX10 238 C3
Glebe Cotts
Aston Rowant OX9 166 C2
South Stoke RG8 239 B2
Glebe Ct OX25 47 B3
Glebe Dr NN13 24 A4
Glebe Gdns Grove OX12 196 C1
Sonning RG4 260 C2
Glebe House Dr MK18 25 C3
Glebe La RG4 260 C2
Glebe Pl SN6 190 A3
Glebe Rd Cumnor OX2 139 C3
Didcot OX11 218 C4
Purley on T RG8 257 A3
Stanford in the V SN7 194 B4
Glebe Ride RG8 249 A3
Glebe St OX4 123 C1
Glebe The Aldworth RG8 247 C2
Aynho OX17 35 B4
Culham OX14 180 A2
Cumnor OX2 139 C3
East Challow OX12 213 B3
Hook Norton OX15 30 A4
Lewknor OX49 187 A4
Rotherfield Peppard RG9 242 C3
Standlake OX29 137 B2
Wheatley OX33 144 A4
Glebelands
Bampton OX18 134 C2
Oxford OX3 142 B4
Glen Cl OX27 52 B1
Glenham Rd OX9 148 A4
Glenmore Rd OX18 115 B2
Glenrhondda RG4 258 C3
Glifford Ho 8 RG4 259 B1
Glimbers Gr OX39 168 B3
Glissard Way OX18 114 B3
Glory Farm Sch OX26 66 A2
Gloucester Court Mews OX28 104 A1
Gloucester La OX1 123 A1
Gloucester Mews SN7 172 C2
Gloucester Pl
Oxford OX8 123 B1
Witney OX28 104 A1
Gloucester St
Faringdon SN7 172 C2
Oxford OX1 123 B1
Glover's Cl OX7 42 C1
Glovers Cl OX20 91 B3
Glovers La OX17 10 C1
Glyme Cl Abingdon OX14 160 A1
Woodstock OX20 91 A4
Glyme Dr OX10 182 B3
Glyme Way OX29 106 A4
Glympton Rd OX20 75 C3
Glyn Ave OX11 218 B4
Glyn Rd OX10 203 B1
Glyncastle RG4 258 C3
Glyndebourne Gdns OX16 9 A1
Glynswood OX39 168 B3
Gobles Ct OX26 65 C1
Goddard's La OX7 42 C2
Godfrey Cl 13 OX14 179 C3
Godfreys Cl Brill HP18 98 A1
Grove OX12 196 C1
Godstow Cl RG5 260 C1
Godstow Rd OX2 122 C4
Godwyn Cl OX14 179 C4
Goffe Cl OX9 148 A4
Goggs The OX49 186 A1
Golafre Rd OX14 179 C3
Gold St OX44 163 C3
Goldcrest Way OX26 81 A4
Golden Cross OX1 123 B1
Golden Hills OX39 168 B3
Golden Rd OX4 142 A4
Golden Villa Cl OX16 16 A3
Golder's Cl HP18 127 C2
Goldfinch La OX10 221 A1
Goldsmith Cl 3 OX26 65 B2
Goldsmith's La OX10 221 B4
Goldsmith's Terr 12 OX10 221 B4
Gooch OX11 200 C2
Goodlake Ave SN7 172 C2
Goodliffe Gdns RG31 257 B2
Goodrich Cl RG4 259 C3
Goodrington Cl OX16 16 A3
Goodson Wlk OX3 123 C2
Goodsons Ind Mews OX9 147 C4
Goor La SN8 245 B2
Goose Gn OX15 33 C2
Goose Green Cl OX2 122 C4
Goose La OX15 22 B4
Goose Wlk OX15 21 B2
Gooseacre OX14 160 C1
Goosey La SN7 195 A2
Gordon Cl OX3 123 C3
Gordon Dr OX14 160 B1
Gordon Pl RG30 258 B1
Gordon Rd OX25 63 B4
Gordon St OX1 141 B3
Goring & Streatley Sta RG8 249 B3
Goring CE Prim Sch RG8 249 B4
Goring Lodge 25 OX1 141 B4
Goring Rd RG8 250 C4
Gorse Leas OX3 124 A3
Gorselands RG4 259 A3
Gorton Playne OX7 70 B1
Gorwell OX49 186 A1
Gosbrook Ho 6 RG4 259 B1
Gosbrook Rd RG4 259 A1
Gosford Cl OX5 108 C3
Gosford Hill Ct OX5 108 C4
Gosford Hill Sch OX5 108 C4
Goslyn Cl OX3 124 B1
Gossway Fields OX5 78 A2
Gott Cl OX27 66 A3
Goulders Cotts RG10 255 C4
Gouldland Gdns OX3 124 A3
Goulds Villas OX16 16 A3
Grafton Ho OX39 168 B4
Grafton Lodge 26 OX16 16 B3
Grafton Orch OX39 168 B4
Graham Cl OX11 237 A4
Graham Rd OX26 65 B2
Grahame Ave RG8 256 B3
Grammar School Hill OX7 73 A2
Gramp's Hill OX12 231 C3
Grandison Ho RG9 244 C2
Grandpont Pl OX1 141 B4
Grange Ave RG9 253 A4
Grange Beck OX11 201 A2
Grange Cl Goring RG8 249 A3
Highworth SN6 190 A3
Grange Ct OX2 140 A4
Grange Farm Rd HP14 189 A4
Grange La OX15 19 B4
Grange Mill Ct OX29 120 B4
Grange Pk OX25 48 A1
Grange Prim Sch The OX16 16 B2
Grange Rd Banbury OX16 16 B2
Henley-on-T RG9 244 C1
Oxford OX4 142 A1
Grange The Kingham OX7 55 A2
Reading RG4 258 B3
Grangers Pl OX28 104 A1
Grantham Ho OX2 123 A2
Grants Mews 3 OX4 141 C4
Granville Ct OX3 124 A1
Granville Way OX26 66 A1
Grasmere Ave RG30 257 C1
Grass Hill RG4 258 C2
Grates The OX4 142 B2
Gravel Cl OX10 203 C2
Gravel Hill
Henley-on-T RG9 244 B1
Reading RG4 259 A3
Sonning Common RG9 252 C3
Gravel Hill Cres RG9 252 C3
Gravel La Drayton OX14 179 A1
Warborough OX10 203 A4
Gravel Pits La OX5 108 A3
Gravel Rd RG9 253 C1
Gravel Wlk
Drayton St L OX10 183 A3
Faringdon SN7 172 C2
Graveney Dr RG4 258 C2
Gravenhill Rd N OX26 81 A4
Gravett Cl RG9 254 B4
Grays Cl OX44 184 B4
Grays Rd OX3 124 A1
Great Barn★ SN7 172 A1
Great Clarendon St OX2 123 A1
Great Close Rd OX5 108 B3
Great Haseley Ind Est OX44 145 B1
Great Mead OX1 123 A1
Great Milton CE Prim Sch OX44 145 B2
Great Rissington Prim Sch GL54 83 A4
Great Rollright CE Prim Sch OX7 29 A2
Great Tew Prim Sch OX7 45 B4
Great Western Dr OX11 200 C1
Grebe Cl OX14 179 C3
Grebe Rd Banbury OX16 16 C2
Bicester OX26 66 A1
Grebe Sq GL54 68 A2
Green Cl Benson OX10 204 A3
Bicester OX26 65 C1
Didcot OX11 218 C3
Steventon OX13 198 C3
Wallingford OX10 221 B4
Green Cnr OX28 104 B1
Green Coll OX2 123 A2
Green Dean Hill RG4 252 B1
Green End Rd HP14 189 C3
Green Farm OX17 23 A2
Green Furlong OX10 182 B3
Green Hill OX4 143 A1
Green Hitchings OX44 145 B1
Green La Banbury OX16 16 B2
Bledlow Ridge HP14 189 B3
Chesterton OX26 79 C4
Ewelme OX10 204 B2
Henley-on-T RG9 254 B4
Little Tew OX7 44 B3
Longworth OX13 156 B1
Milton-u-W OX7 70 A1
N Hinksey Village OX2 140 A4
North Leigh OX29 105 A4
Pangbourne RG8 256 B3
Shiplake RG9 254 A1
Sonning Common RG4 252 C3
South Newington OX15 31 C4
Stokenchurch HP14 188 B3
Sunningwell OX13 160 A3
Swalcliffe OX15 14 A1
Uffington SN7 211 B4
Upper Arncott OX25 96 C4
Warborough OX10 203 A4
Woodcote RG8 250 C4
Woodstock OX20 91 A4
Wootton (Oxford) OX13 159 A3
Green N The OX10 203 B4
Green Pl OX1 141 B3
Green Rd Didcot OX11 218 C4
Kidlington OX5 108 C4
Oxford OX3 124 C2
Green Ridges OX3 125 A2
Green S The OX10 203 B4
Green St OX4 142 A4
Green The
Adderbury OX17 23 A2
Alvescot OX18 133 B3
Ascott-u-W OX7 71 B1
Aston Rowant OX49 167 B2
Barford St M OX15 32 C3
Baydon SN8 245 C1
Bix RG9 243 C4
Bladon OX20 91 A1
Cassington OX29 107 B1
Chalgrove OX44 184 B3
Charlbury OX7 73 B2
Charney Bassett OX12 176 A1
Charney Bassett, Lyford OX12 176 B1
Chesterton OX26 79 C4
Chilton OX11 235 C4
Chipping Norton OX7 42 C1
Clanfield OX18 152 C4
Culham OX14 180 A2
Drayton OX14 179 A1
East Hanney OX12 197 A4
Fernham SN7 193 A2
Fifield OX7 69 B1
Fringford OX27 52 B3
Garsington OX44 143 C1
Great Bourton OX17 9 B4
Great Milton OX44 145 A1
Great Rollright OX7 29 A2
Green The *continued*
Great Tew OX7 45 B4
Highworth SN6 190 A3
Hook Norton OX15 30 A4
Hornton OX15 7 B3
Horspath OX33 143 B3
Horton-cum-S OX33 112 A3
Launton OX26 66 C1
Milcombe OX15 20 C1
North Leigh OX29 89 B1
Shrivenham SN6 209 A3
Standlake OX29 137 B2
Stanton Harcourt OX29 138 A4
Steventon OX13 199 A3
Sutton Courtenay OX14 180 A1
Swalcliffe OX15 19 C4
Tackley OX5 77 A3
Uffington SN7 211 B4
West Hanney OX12 196 C3
Green's Rd OX29 120 C4
Greenacres OX14 179 A1
Greenacres Dr OX12 214 B2
Greenacres La OX18 135 B2
Greenfield Cres
Stonesfield OX29 89 B4
Wallingford OX10 221 A4
Greenfield Rd OX29 89 B4
Greenfields OX25 96 B4
Greenfinch Cl OX4 142 C1
Greengates SN7 172 C2
Greenheart Way OX13 156 C1
Greenhill Ct OX16 16 B2
Greenhills Pk OX15 21 B2
Greenlands OX7 70 A1
Greenleas Ave RG4 259 A4
Greenmere OX10 202 C2
Greenmere Prim Sch OX11 218 C4
Greenmore RG8 250 C4
Greens Garth OX15 21 C3
Greens Keep HP17 130 C3
Greensward The OX17 5 C1
Greenway
Haddenham HP17 130 C3
Lower Heyford OX25 63 A2
4 Thame OX9 129 C1
Greenway The OX12 216 A3
Greenways RG8 256 B3
Greenwich La OX29 87 A2
Greenwood Ave OX39 168 B3
Greenwood Dr OX26 65 A2
Greenwood Mdw OX39 168 B3
Gregory Est OX49 185 B2
Grenoble Rd Oxford OX4 143 A1
Sandford-on-T OX4 142 B1
Grenville Way OX9 130 A1
Gresham Way RG30 258 A1
Greycotes Sch OX2 123 B2
Greygoose La GL56 41 A3
Greyhound La OX9 129 C1
Greys Cl OX16 15 C3
Greys Ct RG9 243 B2
Greys Hill RG9 244 B1
Greys Rd RG9 254 B4
Greystoke Rd RG4 259 B2
Greystones Ct
Alvescot OX18 133 B3
Kidlington OX5 92 B1
Griffin Rd OX9 148 B4
Griffiths Cl OX29 138 B2
Griffiths Gdns OX27 66 A4
Grimmer Way RG8 250 C4
Grimsbury Dr OX16 16 C4
Grimsbury Gn OX16 16 C4
Grimsbury Sq OX16 16 C4
Grindon La OX10 205 A1
Grosvenor Pl OX12 214 A3
Grosvenor Rd
16 Banbury OX16 16 B3
N Hinksey Village OX2 140 C3
Reading RG4 259 B2
Grove CE Sch OX12 196 C1
Grove Cotts
Brightwell-cum-S OX10 202 B1
Little Coxwell SN7 192 C4
Reading RG4 259 A3
Grove Ct Deddington OX15 33 C2
Oxford OX4 142 A3
Grove Hill Highworth SN6 190 A4
Reading RG4 259 A2
Woodstock OX20 91 A3
Grove La Ewelme OX10 205 A3
Spelsbury OX7 72 C4
Grove Park Dr
Ardington OX12 215 B4
Grove OX12 197 A1
Grove Rd Bladon OX20 91 B2
Grove OX12 214 C4
Harwell OX11 217 B4
Henley-on-T RG9 244 C1
Reading RG4 259 A3
Sonning Common RG4 252 C3
Grove St Banbury OX16 16 B3
Cutteslowe OX2 123 A4
Wantage OX12 214 C3
Grove Terr OX11 218 B2
Grove The
Abingdon OX14 160 A1
Bourton SN6 209 A2
Deddington OX15 33 C2
Grovelands OX5 108 B4
Grovelands Ctr OX12 196 B1
Grovelands Rd OX3 125 A1
Grundy Cl OX14 180 A4
Grundy Cres OX1 141 C1

Grunsell Cl OX3 ....124 B3
Guardian Ct 3 OX16 ....16 C3
Guelder Rd OX4 ....142 B1
Guernsey Way OX16 ......9 A1
Guild Ho The OX12 .....214 C2
Guildenford OX18 ......100 C3
Guildford Ct 7 OX5 ....108 C4
Gulley Row OX25 ....95 B4
Gullicote La OX17 ....8 C2
Gulliver's Cl OX15 ....8 A2
Gurden Pl OX3 ....124 C2
Gurl Cl OX3 ....124 C2
Gurney Cl RG4 ....258 B3
Gurney Dr RG4 ....258 B3
Gwyneth Rd OX4 ....142 A1
Gwynne Cl RG31 ....257 B2

H

Hack La CV36 ....27 C4
Hackers La OX7 ....55 C2
Hadden Hill OX11 ....201 B1
Haddenham & Thame Parkway Sta HP17 ....130 C3
Haddenham Aerodrome Bsns Pk HP17 ....130 C4
Hadland Rd OX14 ....180 B4
Hadleigh Rise RG4 .....259 C3
Hadow Rd OX3 ....124 A2
Hadrians Gate NN13 .....24 A4
Hafod RG4 ....258 C3
Hagbourne CE Prim Sch OX11 ....218 C3
Hagbourne Cl RG8 .....250 C4
Hagbourne Rd
Aston Tirrold OX11 ......219 B1
Didcot OX11 ....219 A4
East Hagbourne OX11 ....219 B1
Hailey Ave OX7 ....42 C1
Hailey CE Prim Sch OX29 ....104 A3
Hailey Cft OX39 ....168 A3
Hailey Cres OX7 ....42 C1
Hailey Rd
Chipping Norton OX7 ......42 B1
Witney OX28,OX29 ......104 A2
Haines Ct OX13 ....178 B4
Haldane Rd Oxford OX4 .142 C1
Reading RG4 ....258 C3
Hale Rd OX10 ....203 C3
Halfpenny La OX10 .....238 C3
Halifax Rd OX26 ....66 A2
Hall Cl OX49 ....186 A2
Hall Cl The OX25 ....48 A3
Hallett Cl OX12 ....214 C2
Halliday Hill OX3 ......124 A3
Halls Cl Drayton OX14 ...179 B1
N Hinksey Village OX2 ...140 A4
Halls La OX12 ....197 A4
Hallsmead Ct 14 RG1 ...259 A1
Halse Water OX11 .....201 A1
Halton Rd OX18 ....115 C1
Ham La OX18 ....135 C1
Ham Rd OX12 ....214 B2
Hamble Dr OX14 ....160 A1
Hamble Rd OX11 ....201 A1
Hambleden Dr OX10 ....221 A4
Hambleside OX26 ....65 A1
Hambridge La GL7 .....150 B3
Hamcroft OX12 ....214 B3
Hamel The OX1 ....123 A1
Hamels La OX1 ....140 C1
Hamfield OX12 ....214 A2
Hamilton Ave RG9 .....244 C1
Hamilton Cl Banbury OX16 16 C4
Bicester OX26 ....65 C2
Hamilton Rd
Cutteslowe OX2 ....123 A4
Thame OX9 ....130 A1
Wargrave RG10 ....255 C1
Hamlet The RG4 ....252 A3
Hamlyn Cl OX12 ....214 A1
Hammer La OX10 ......183 A1
Hammett Pl OX18 ......115 B1
Hammond's End RG8 ...241 A2
Hampden Ave OX9 .....147 C4
Hampden Cl
Banbury OX16 ....15 C3
Bicester OX26 ....66 A2
Chalgrove OX44 ....184 B3
Faringdon SN7 ....173 A2
Hampden Dr OX5 ......108 C3
Hampden Rd Oxford OX4 142 B2
Reading RG4 ....259 A1
Wantage OX12 ....214 C3
Hampden Way OX10 ...204 C2
Hamplands OX7 ....29 A2
Hampstead Hill RG9 ...260 B4
Hampton Dr OX17 ....23 C3
Hamstyles OX49 ....205 C4
Hanborough Bsns Pk OX29 ....90 C1
Hanborough Cl OX29 ...120 C4
Hanborough Rd OX29 ...120 C4
Hanborough Sta OX29 ....90 C1
Handlo Pl OX3 ....124 C2
Hanney CE Prim Sch OX12 ....197 A3
Hanney Rd
Kingston Bagpuize OX13 ..176 B4
Steventon OX13 ....198 B3
Hannis Rd OX7 ....42 B1
Hanover Cl OX7 ....73 B2
Hanover Ct RG4 ....259 B3
Hanover Gdns
Bicester OX26 ....65 C1
Wargrave RG10 ....255 C2
Hans Ave OX12 ....214 C3
Hanson Rd OX14 ....159 C2
Hanwell Ct OX17 ....8 C2
Hanwood Cl RG5 ....260 B1
Harberton Mead OX3 ...123 C2
Harbord Rd OX2 ....109 A1
Harborne Rd OX5 ....77 B3
Harcourt Cl RG9 ......244 B1
Harcourt Gn OX12 .....214 C3
Harcourt Hill OX2 .....140 C3
Harcourt Ho 5 OX26 ....65 C1
Harcourt Rd
Stokenchurch HP14 .....188 C2
Wantage OX12 ....214 C3
Harcourt Terr OX3 .....124 A1
Harcourt Way
Abingdon OX14 ....159 C1
Wantage OX12 ....214 C3
Harding Cl SN7 ....173 A2
Harding Rd OX14 ......179 B4
Hardings OX44 ....184 B3
Hardings Cl OX4 ....142 A2
Hardings Strings OX11 .218 C4
Hardwell Cl OX12 .....196 B1
Hardwick Ave OX5 .....108 C4
Hardwick Pk OX16 ....8 C1
Hardwick Prim Sch OX16 16 A4
Hardwick Rd Hethe OX27 .52 A4
Whitchurch RG8 ....256 B4
Hardy Cl RG4 ....259 B1
Harebell Rd OX4 ......142 C1
Harecourt OX12 ....214 C2
Harefields OX2 ....109 A1
Harewood Rd OX16 ......16 C1
Harlech Ave RG4 ......259 B3
Harlech Cl OX16 ....15 C3
Harlequin Way OX16 .....9 A1
Harley Rd Oxford OX2 ...122 C1
Reading RG4 ....259 A1
Harlington Ave OX12 ...196 C1
Harlow Way OX3 ....123 C4
Harmon Cl OX27 ....66 A3
Harold Hicks Pl OX4 ...141 C3
Harold White Cl OX3 ...124 C1
Harolde Cl OX3 ....124 B2
Harolds Cl OX29 ....87 A2
Harper Cl OX25 ....96 B4
Harpes Rd OX2 ....123 A4
Harpsden Rd RG9 ......254 C4
Harpsden Way RG9 .....254 C4
Harpsichord Pl OX4 ....123 C1
Harrier Pk OX11 ......200 B2
Harrier Way OX26 ....66 A2
Harriers Ground Sch OX16 ....16 B2
Harriers View OX16 .....16 B2
Harris Gdns GL54 ....68 A2
Harris Rd OX25 ....63 B4
Harris's La OX13 ....156 B1
Harrison Pl 5 OX9 .....129 C1
Harrison's La OX20 .....91 A3
Harrisville OX25 ....62 A4
Harroell HP18 ....129 B3
Harrogate Rd RG4 .....258 C2
Harrow Rd OX4 ....142 C2
Harrowby Rd OX16 ......16 B1
Hart Ave SN7 ....172 C2
Hart Cl OX14 ....180 B4
Hart Moor Cl HP14 .....188 C2
Hart Pl OX26 ....66 A2
Hart St Henley-on-T RG9 .244 C1
Oxford OX2 ....123 A1
20 Wallingford OX10 .....221 B4
Hart-synnot Ho OX2 ...123 A2
Hartley Cl OX10 ......203 A3
Hartley Ct OX2 ....123 A2
Harts Cl OX5 ....108 B4
Hartslock Bridleway RG8 ....256 B4
Hartslock Ct RG8 ......256 A3
Hartslock View RG8 ....249 C1
Hartslock Way RG31 ...257 B1
Harvest Pl RG10 ......255 C1
Harwell Cl OX14 ......160 A1
Harwell Int Bsns Ctr OX11 ....217 A1
Harwell International Bsns Ctr OX11,OX12 ....234 C4
Harwell Prim Sch OX11 217 B4
Harwell Rd OX14 ......199 C3
Harwood Rd OX11 .....218 C3
Haslemere Gdns OX2 ...109 A1
Haslemere Tramway Est OX16 ....16 C3
Haslemere Way OX16 ....16 C3
Hastings Cl OX16 ....15 C3
Hastings Dr OX18 ......115 C1
Hastings Hill OX7 ....55 C3
Hastings Rd OX16 ....15 C4
Hastoe Grange OX3 ....124 A2
Hatch Cl OX5 ....77 C2
Hatch End OX5 ....77 C2
Hatch Gate La RG10 ...255 C4
Hatch Way OX5 ....77 C2
Hatchet Hill SN4 ......227 A1
Hatching La OX29 ....87 A2
Hatfield Pits La OX29 ..104 B4
Hathaways OX33 ....144 A4
Havelock Rd OX4 ......142 B3
Haven Cl OX10 ....202 B4
Haven Vale OX12 ......214 C3
Havers Ave OX14 ......199 B1
Haw La Aldworth RG8 ...247 C1
Bledlow Ridge HP14 .....189 C4
Hawke La OX15 ....21 B2
Hawke's La OX15 ....19 B4
Hawker Sq GL54 ....68 A2
Hawkins St 9 OX4 .....141 C4
Hawkins Way OX13 .....159 A3
Hawksmead OX26 ....81 A4
Hawksmoor Rd OX2 ....109 A1
Hawkswell Gdns OX2 ...123 B4
Hawkswell Ho OX2 .....123 B4
Hawksworth OX11 .....200 B2
Hawksworth Cl OX12 ...196 B1
Hawthorn Ave
Oxford OX3 ....124 B2
Thame OX9 ....147 B4
Hawthorn Cl
N Hinksey Village OX2 ...140 B4
Wallingford OX10 ....221 B4
Hawthorn Cres OX12 ...214 C4
Hawthorn Dr OX18 .....114 B4
Hawthorn Gr OX18 .....115 B1
Hawthorn Rd
Eynsham OX29 ....120 C4
Faringdon SN7 ....172 C2
Hawthorn Way
Kidlington OX5 ....108 C4
Sonning RG4 ....260 C2
Hawthorn Wlk 2 OX26 ...65 C2
Hawthorne Ave OX13 ...159 B1
Hawthorne Rd RG4 ....259 C2
Hawthornes RG31 ......257 A2
Hawthorns The OX16 ....16 B2
Hayden La RG9 ....224 A2
Haydon Rd OX11 ......200 C1
Hayes Ave OX13 ....176 B4
Hayes Cl OX3 ....123 C2
Hayfield Rd OX2 ......123 A3
Hayford Ho 7 OX16 .....16 C3
Hayfords Cty Prim Sch The OX25 ....62 C4
Haynes Rd OX3 ....123 C3
Hayward Dr OX18 .....115 B1
Hayward Rd OX2 ......109 A1
Haywards Cl
Henley-on-T RG9 ....244 B1
Wantage OX12 ....214 C3
Haywards Rd OX14 .....199 A4
Hazel Ave OX9 ....147 C4
Hazel Cres OX5 ....108 C3
Hazel End OX44 ....143 B1
Hazel Gdns RG4 ....252 C3
Hazel Gr Bicester OX26 ...65 C2
Stoke Row RG9 ....242 A1
Wallingford OX10 ....221 B4
Hazel Rd
N Hinksey Village OX2 ...122 B1
Purley on T RG8 ....257 B2
Hazel Wlk OX5 ....108 C3
Hazeldene Cl OX29 ....105 A3
Hazeldene Gdns OX16 ...16 B2
Hazell's La SN6 ....209 B3
Hazells La GL7 ....132 A3
Hazelmoor La RG4 .....252 B2
Hazelnut Path OX1,OX14 160 C4
Hazelrig Cl OX9 ....148 A4
Hazelton Cl OX9 ....147 C4
Hazelwood Cl RG31 ....257 B1
Headington Mid Sch OX3 ....124 B1
Headington Quarry CE Fst Sch OX3 ....124 C1
Headington Rd OX3 ....124 A1
Headington Rdbt OX3 ..124 C2
Headington Sch OX3 ...124 A1
Headley Ho OX3 ....124 A2
Headley Way OX3 .....124 A2
Healey Cl OX14 ....179 C3
Hean Cl OX14 ....160 A1
Hearns La RG4 ....252 B3
Hearthway OX16 ....9 A1
Heath Cl Milcombe OX15 ..20 C1
Oxford OX3 ....142 B4
Heath Dr RG9 ....254 A1
Heath La OX20 ....91 A1
Heathcote Ave OX16 .....16 C1
Heathcote Pl OX14 ....160 B1
Heather Cl
Carterton OX18 ....115 B3
Sonning Common RG4 ...253 A3
Heather Pl OX3 ....123 C2
Heather Rd Bicester OX26 65 C3
Milton OX14 ....199 B3
Heathfield Ave RG9 ....254 A1
Heathfield Cl RG9 .....254 A1
Hedge End OX20 ....91 B3
Hedge Hill Rd OX12 ...213 C3
Hedgemead Ave OX14 ..160 B1
Hedgerley OX39 ....168 A3
Hedges The OX15 ....14 A4
Helen Rd OX2 ....122 C1
Hellebourine Cl OX4 ...142 C1
Helwys Pl OX5 ....92 B1
Hemdean Hill RG4 .....259 A2
Hemdean House Sch RG4 ....259 A2
Hemdean Rd RG4 ......259 A2
Hemdean Rise RG4 ....259 A2
Hemingway Dr OX26 .....65 B1
Hemplands OX29 ......104 A3
Hempton Rd OX15 ....33 C2
Henderson Ho OX10 ...221 A4
Hendon Pl OX26 ....66 A2
Hendred Ho OX4 ....142 A3
Hendred St OX4 ....142 A3
Hendred Way OX14 ....160 A1
Hendreds CE Sch The OX12 ....216 B3
Henfield View OX10 ...203 A4
Hengest Gate OX11 ....217 C4
Hengrove Cl OX3 ......124 B2
Henley Ave OX4 ....142 A3
Henley Coll (Deanfield Bldgs) The RG9 ....244 B1
Henley Coll (Rotherfield Bldgs) The RG9 ....244 B1
Henley Dr SN6 ....190 A4
Henley Gdns 18 OX26 ....65 C1
Henley Rd
Dorchester OX10 ....202 C4
Reading RG4,RG9 ....260 B4
Sandford-on-T OX4 ......161 A4
Henley St OX4 ....141 C4
Henley-on-Thames Sta RG9 ....244 C1
Henleys La OX14 ......179 A1
Hennef Way OX16 ....16 C4
Henor Mill Cl OX14 ....160 A1
Henrietta Rd OX9 .....130 A1
Henry Box Cl OX28 ....118 A4
Henry Box Sch The OX28 ....118 A4
Henry Rd OX2 ....122 C1
Henry Taunt Cl OX3 ...124 C3
Hensington Cl OX20 .....91 B3
Hensington Rd OX20 ....91 A3
Hensington Wlk OX20 ...91 B3
Henwood Dr OX1 ......140 A1
Herald Way 3 OX26 .....66 A2
Herbert Cl OX4 ....142 A4
Hereford Way OX16 ......9 A1
Heritage La OX7 ....71 A1
Herman Cl OX14 ....180 A4
Hermitage Rd OX14 ....179 C3
Hernes Cl OX2 ....123 A4
Hernes Cres OX2 ......123 A4
Hernes Rd OX2 ....123 A4
Heron Cl OX18 ....115 B2
Heron Ct Abingdon OX14 .179 C2
Bicester OX26 ....66 A1
Heron Island RG4 .....259 B1
Heron Rd OX10 ....204 B2
Heron Shaw RG8 ......249 B4
Heron Way OX16 ....16 A2
Heron's Wlk OX14 .....159 C1
Herons Pl OX2 ....123 A4
Herringcote OX10 .....182 B1
Herschel Cres OX4 .....142 B2
Herschel Ct 6 OX4 ....142 B2
Hertford Cl Bicester OX26 .65 C2
Reading RG4 ....259 B3
Hertford Coll OX1 .....123 B1
Hertford Ct 8 OX5 .....108 C4
Hertford St OX4 ....142 A4
Hethe Rd Cottisford NN13 .38 A2
Hardwick OX27 ....51 B4
Hewett Ave RG4 ....258 B2
Hewett Cl RG4 ....258 B2
Hewetts Cl OX29 ....87 A2
Hewgate Ct RG9 ....244 C1
Heycroft OX29 ....120 C4
Heydons Terr OX17 ......3 C4
Heyford Cl OX29 ......137 B3
Heyford Hill La OX4 ...141 C1
Heyford Hill Rdbt OX4 ..141 C1
Heyford Mead OX5 ......92 B1
Heyford Rd
Kirtlington OX5 ....77 C2
Middleton Stoney OX25 ....64 A2
Steeple Aston OX25 ......62 A4
Heyford Sta OX25 ....62 B3
Hicks Cl OX29 ....104 A3
Hid's Copse Rd OX2 ...140 A4
Higgs Cl OX11 ....219 A3
High Acres OX16 ....16 C2
High Cross Way OX3 ...124 C3
High Furlong OX16 ......16 A4
High House Cl OX18 ...152 C4
High Land Cl HP18 ......98 A1
High Mdw Reading RG4 ..258 B2
Sibford Gower OX15 ......13 A1
High Rd Beckley OX3 ...111 A2
Brightwell-cum-S OX10 ...202 C2
Brightwell-cum-S, Slade End OX10 ....203 A1
High Road Cotts OX10 ..202 B2
High St
14 Abingdon OX14 ......179 C4
Adderbury OX17 ....23 A2
Ascott-u-W OX7 ....71 B1
Ashbury SN6 ....228 A4
Aston OX18 ....135 B2
Aston Rowant OX39 .....167 C2
Bampton OX18 ....134 C2
Banbury OX16 ....16 B3
Barford St M OX15 ....32 C3
Benson OX10 ....203 C2
Bishopstone SN6 ....227 B2
Bloxham OX15 ....21 C3
Bodicote OX15 ....22 B4
Burford OX18 ....100 C3
Chalgrove OX44 ....184 B4
Charlton-on-O OX5 ....95 A2
Charney Bassett OX12 ...175 C1
Childrey OX12 ....213 B2
Chinnor OX39 ....168 B4
Chipping Norton OX7 .....42 C2
Clifton Hampden OX14 ...181 B2
Cropredy OX17 ....4 C1
Croughton NN13 ....36 B4
Cuddesdon OX44 ....144 A1
Culham OX14 ....180 A2
Cumnor OX2 ....139 B3
Deddington OX15 ....33 C2
Didcot OX11 ....218 C4
Dorchester OX10 ....182 B1
Drayton OX14 ....179 A1
Drayton St L OX10 ......183 A3
East Hendred OX12 .....216 C3
High St *continued*
Ewelme OX10 ....204 C2
Eynsham OX29 ....120 C4
Fernham SN7 ....193 A2
Fifield OX7 ....69 A1
Finstock OX7 ....88 A3
Goring RG8 ....249 B3
Great Rollright OX7 ....29 A2
Haddenham HP17 ....130 C3
Harwell OX11 ....217 C4
Highworth SN6 ....190 A3
Hinton Waldrist SN7 .....155 C1
Hook Norton OX15 ....30 A4
Islip OX5 ....93 C1
Kidlington OX5 ....92 C1
Lechlade GL7 ....150 B2
Lewknor OX49 ....187 A4
LIttle Milton OX44 ......163 C3
Long Crendon HP18 .....129 B3
Long Wittenham OX14 ...201 B4
Ludgershall HP18 ....98 A4
Middleton Cheney OX17 ...17 C4
Milton OX14 ....199 B3
Milton-u-W OX7 ....70 A1
Nettlebed RG9 ....224 B1
North Moreton OX11 ....220 A4
Oxford OX1,OX4 ....123 B1
Pangbourne RG8 ....256 B3
Ramsden OX7 ....88 A2
Ratley OX15 ....2 A2
Shipton-u-W OX7 ....85 B4
Shrivenham SN6 ....209 B3
Shutford OX15 ....14 A3
Sonning RG4 ....260 B2
Souldern OX6 ....35 C2
South Newington OX15 ....31 C4
Standlake OX29 ....137 B2
Stanford in the V SN7 ...194 C4
Steventon OX13 ....199 A2
Stonesfield OX29 ....89 B4
Streatley RG8 ....249 A3
Sutton Courtenay OX14 ..200 A4
Tetsworth OX9 ....166 A4
Thame OX9 ....129 C1
Uffington SN7 ....211 B4
Upper Heyford OX25 ......48 C1
Upton OX11 ....218 B1
Wallingford OX10 ....221 B4
Wargrave RG10 ....255 B1
Watchfield SN6 ....191 B1
Watlington OX49 ....186 A1
Wheatley OX33 ....144 A4
Whitchurch RG8 ....256 B4
Witney OX28 ....118 A4
Woodstock OX20 ....91 A3
Wootton OX20 ....75 C2
High View OX12 ....214 A2
Highbridge Cl RG4 ....259 C3
Highclere Gdns
Banbury OX16 ....15 C3
Wantage OX12 ....214 B3
Highdown Ave RG4 ....259 A3
Highdown Hill Rd RG4 .259 A3
Highdown Sch RG4 ....259 A3
Highfield HP18 ....129 B4
Highfield Ave OX3 .....124 B1
Highfield Cl OX9 ......147 B4
Highfield Pk RG10 .....255 C1
Highfield Rd RG31 ....257 B2
Highlands OX16 ....9 A1
Highlands La RG9 .....254 A4
Highlands Sch The RG31 ....257 B1
Highmoor Rd RG4 .....258 C2
Hightown Gdns OX16 ....16 B2
Hightown Leyes OX16 ...16 B2
Hightown Rd OX16 ......16 B2
Highworth Pl OX28 ....118 A4
Highworth Rd
Faringdon SN7 ....172 C1
Shrivenham SN6 ....209 A4
Highworth Warneford Comp Sch SN6 ....190 A2
Highworth Way RG31 ..257 A1
Hikers Way HP18 ......129 C2
Hill Bottom Cl RG8 ....250 C2
Hill Cl Charlbury OX7 .....73 B2
Chipping Norton OX7 .....42 C1
East Challow OX12 ......214 A2
Hill Cres OX7 ....88 B3
Hill Farm Ct OX39 .....168 B3
Hill Farm La OX25 ....47 B3
Hill Gdns RG8 ....249 A3
Hill La OX18 ....152 B4
Hill Lands RG10 ....255 B1
Hill Piece OX11 ....235 C4
Hill Prim Sch The RG4 .259 B3
Hill Rd Chinnor OX39 ....168 B3
Lewknor OX49 ....187 A4
Lewknor OX49,HP14 .....187 B3
Watchfield SN6 ....191 B1
Watlington OX49 ....206 C4
Hill Rise
Great Rollright OX7 ....29 A2
Horspath OX33 ....143 B3
Woodstock OX20 ....91 A4
Hill The Aynho OX17 .....35 B4
Bourton SN6 ....209 A2
Burford OX18 ....100 C2
Burford, Westwell OX18 ....99 C1
Garsington OX44 ....143 C1
Hill Top La OX39 ......168 C2
Hill Top Rd OX4 ....142 A4
Hill View Carterton OX18 .115 B2
Kingston Lisle OX12 .....212 A2
Oxford OX3 ....125 A2
Uffington SN7 ....211 B4
Hill View Cres OX16 .....16 A4

Hill View La OX1 ....159 A4
Hill View Prim Sch OX16 .16 A4
Hillary Dr OX11 ....218 C4
Hillary Way OX33 ......144 B4
Hillcraft Rd OX33 ......125 B4
Hillcrest La RG9 ....252 C4
Hilliard Ho OX14 ....179 C3
Hilliat Fields OX14 .....179 A1
Hilliers Cl OX14 ....200 A4
Hillsborough Cl 7 OX4 .142 A2
Hillsborough Rd OX4 ...142 A2
Hillside Cumnor OX2 ....140 A3
Harwell OX11 ....217 A2
Whitchurch RG8 ....256 B4
Hillside Cl Banbury OX16 .16 C2
Upper Arncott OX25 ......96 C4
Hillside Rd OX7 ....46 C1
Hilltop HP18 ....129 B3
Hilltop Ct OX4 ....142 A4
Hilltop Gdns OX5 ....93 C1
Hilltop Rd RG4 ....258 B3
Hillview Cl RG31 ....257 A1
Hillview Rd
Abingdon OX14 ....159 C1
Oxford OX2 ....123 A1
Hillwerke OX39 ....168 B3
Hilly Lawn Ct OX7 ......42 C2
Hillyard Barns OX14 ....200 A4
Hilton Rd OX16 ....16 A3
Hinksey Bsns Ctr OX2 ..122 B1
Hinksey Hill OX1 ....141 A2
Hinksey Hill Intc OX1 ..141 B2
Hinton Hill SN4 ....227 A2
Hinton Rd OX13 ....156 A2
Hinton Springs SN4 .....227 A2
Hirstwood RG30 ....257 C1
Hiskins OX12 ....214 A3
Hitchman Dr OX7 ....42 C2
Hithercroft Cholsey OX10 220 B3
South Moreton OX11 .....220 B3
Hithercroft Ct OX10 ....221 A3
Hithercroft Ind Est
OX10 ....221 A4
Hithercroft Rd OX10 ...221 A4
Hive Mews 4 OX14 ....179 C3
Hixet Wood OX7 ....73 A2
HM Prison (Bullingdon)
OX25,HP18 ....97 A4
Hobbs Cl OX14 ....180 A4
Hobby Ct OX4 ....142 C1
Hobbyhorse La OX14 ...200 A4
Hobson Rd OX2 ....123 A4
Hocker Bench SN6 .....227 B2
Hocketts Cl RG8 ....250 C2
Hockmore St OX4 ......142 B2
Hodge Ct OX1 ....141 B4
Hodgson Cl OX27 ......49 C4
Hogarth Pl OX14 ....179 C3
Hogg End Bloxham OX15 ..21 C2
Chipping Warden OX17 .....5 C3
Holborn Hill OX12 ......231 B4
Holcombe La OX10 .....183 B3
Holford Rd OX28 ....117 C4
Holis Cl OX28 ....118 B4
Holkham Cl RG30 ......257 C1
Holland Cl OX39 ....168 B4
Holland Pl OX3 ....142 C4
Holland Rd OX14 ....160 A1
Hollandridge La OX49,
RG9 ....207 B2
Hollands Rise OX17 .....23 C2
Holley Cres OX3 ....124 C2
Holliers Cl
Sydenham OX39 ....167 B4
Thame OX9 ....147 C4
Holliers Cres OX7 ....60 C4
Hollies Ct The 18 OX16 ..16 B3
Hollington HP18 ....129 A4
Hollow Furlong OX29 ...107 B1
Hollow Way Aynho OX17 ..35 B4
Childrey OX12 ....213 B2
Oxford OX3,OX4 ....142 B3
Holloway Hill OX15 ......12 A1
Holloway La
Compton Wynyates OX15 ..12 A1
Northend RG9 ....207 C3
Holloway Rd OX33 .....144 A4
Holloway Rd The SN7 ..192 A4
Holloway The
Harwell OX11 ....217 C3
Mollington OX17 ....4 A2
Holloway Way OX11 ....218 B1
Holly Cl Bicester OX26 ...65 C3
Kidlington OX5 ....108 C4
Rotherfield Peppard RG9 .242 C3
Holly Ct OX4 ....142 C2
Hollybush Rd
Carterton OX18 ....115 B1
Hook Norton OX15 ....30 A4
Hollybush Row OX1 ....123 A1
Holm Sq OX26 ....65 C3
Holm Way OX26 ....65 C3
Holme Park Farm La
RG4 ....260 B1
Holmemoor Dr RG4 ....260 C1
Holmlea Rd RG8 ....249 B3
Holoway Rd OX28 ......118 A4
Holt The
4 Abingdon OX14 ......179 C4
Mollington OX17 ....3 C2
Purley on T RG8 ....257 B2
Holt Weer Cl OX2 ......109 A1
Holy Trinity RC Sch OX7 .42 C2
Holyoake Rd OX3 ......124 B2
Holyrood Cl RG4 ....259 B3
Holywell Bsns Ctr OX2 .141 A4
Holywell Cl OX14 ......160 B1
Holywell St OX1 ....123 B1
Home Cl Carterton OX18 .115 B1
Cutteslowe OX2 ....122 B4
Kidlington OX5 ....92 C1
Shabbington HP18 ......128 B2
Wootton (Oxford) OX13 ..159 A3
Home Croft RG31 ......257 A1
Home Farm OX10 ......221 C4
Home Farm Barns OX18 133 A3
Home Farm Cl
Ambrosden OX25 ....81 B2
East Hendred OX12 ......216 B4
Shipton-u-W OX7 ....85 B4
Home Farm Cotts OX29 102 C4
Home Farm Ct OX17 .....23 A2
Homefield Cl HP14 .....188 C2
Homelands Way RG9 ...244 B1
Homeleaze Rd SN6 .....209 C4
Homestall Cl OX2 ......122 A1
Homestead Cres OX25 ...63 A4
Homestead Rd OX16 .....16 C1
Homestead The
Bladon OX20 ....91 B2
Kidlington OX5 ....108 B4
Shiplake RG9 ....254 A1
1 Thame OX9 ....129 C1
Hone Ct OX7 ....73 A2
Honey La OX10 ....220 C1
Honey Meadow Rd RG4 259 C1
Honeybottom La OX13 .159 A3
Honeyham Cl OX18 .....116 B2
Honeysuckle Cl OX26 ...65 C3
Honeysuckle Gr OX4 ...143 A1
Honor Cl OX5 ....108 C4
Hook End La RG8 ......249 A1
Hook Norton CE Sch
OX15 ....30 A4
Hook Norton Rd
Great Rollright OX7 ....29 A2
Sibford Ferris OX15 ....19 A4
Hookend La RG8 ....251 B4
Hooks Cl GL7 ....132 C1
Hop Gdns RG9 ....244 B1
Hopcraft Cl OX25 ....96 C4
Hopcraft La OX15 ....33 C2
Hopkins Ct OX4 ....142 B3
Hopton Rd OX9 ....130 A1
Hordern Cl HP17 ....130 C3
Horley Path Rd OX15 .....8 A1
Horn Hill OX15 ....32 C3
Horn Hill Rd OX17 ......22 C2
Horn La Adlestrop GL56 ...40 A3
East Hendred OX12 ......216 B3
Hornbeam Cl
Banbury OX16 ....16 A3
Purley on T RG8 ....257 B3
Hornbeam Dr OX4 .....143 A1
Hornbeam Rd OX26 .....65 C3
Horne OX27 ....66 A4
Hornsea Cl RG30 ......257 C1
Hornton Hollow OX15 ...21 B2
Horse Cl The RG4 ......259 B2
Horse Close Cotts OX44 164 B4
Horse Fair Banbury OX16 .16 B3
Chipping Norton OX7 ......42 C2
Deddington OX15 ....33 C2
Horse Shoe La OX7 .....72 A4
Horsecroft SN7 ....194 C4
Horseman Cl OX3 ......124 A3
Horsemere La OX29 ....107 B1
Horsepond Rd RG4 .....252 A3
Horseshoe La OX20 .....75 C2
Horseshoe Pk RG8 .....256 B3
Horseshoe Rd
Bledlow Ridge HP14 .....189 B4
Pangbourne RG8 ....256 B3
Horseshoes Cl OX13 ...158 A4
Horseshoes La OX10 ...203 C2
Horseshoes Pl OX9 ....148 A4
Horsham Cl OX16 ....8 C1
Horspath CE Prim Sch
OX33 ....143 B4
Horspath Driftway OX4 .142 C4
Horspath Rd OX4 ......142 C3
Horspath Rd Ind Est
OX4 ....142 C3
Horton Ave OX9 ....148 A4
Horton Cl OX9 ....148 A4
Horton General Hospl
OX16 ....16 B2
Horton La OX15 ....21 A1
Horton View OX16 ......16 B2
Horwood Cl OX3 ....124 B2
Hosker Cl OX3 ....125 A2
Hound Cl OX14 ....160 B1
Howard Ave OX12 ......196 C1
Howard Cornish Rd
OX13 ....178 B4
Howard Rd OX16 ....16 C3
Howard St OX4 ....142 A4
Howbery Farm OX10 ...221 C4
Howe Cl OX33 ....144 A4
Howe Rd OX49 ....206 B4
Howes La OX26 ....65 A2
Howgate Dr RG8 ....249 B4
Howland Rd OX9 ....148 A4
Hoyle Cl OX28 ....104 A2
Huckleberry Cl RG8 ....257 B2
Hudleston Ave OX10 ...204 B1
Hudson Ct OX15 ....33 C2
Hudson St Bicester OX26 ..65 B2
Deddington OX15 ....33 C2
Hugh Allen Cres OX3 ...123 C4
Hugh Price Ho OX4 ....142 A4
Hughes Cl OX7 ....73 B1
Hughes Cres SN7 ......192 B2
Hughes Ho OX4 ....141 C4
Humber Cl Didcot OX11 .201 A1
Wantage OX12 ....214 C3
Humber St OX15 ....21 C2
Humber Wlk OX16 ......15 C4
Humfrey Rd OX3 ....124 C2
Humphries Cl OX18 ....115 C2
Hunder Ct OX1 ....141 B1
Hundred Acre Cl OX3 ..142 C4
Hungerford Rd OX13 ...199 A1
Hunsdon Rd OX4 ......142 A2
Hunt Cl OX26 ....65 C1
Hunt Rd OX9 ....148 A4
Hunt's Cl OX29 ....89 B4
Hunter Cl Abingdon OX14 160 A2
Oxford OX4 ....142 C3
Huntercombe End La
RG9 ....224 A2
Hunters Chase RG4 ....258 C3
Hunters Cl OX12 ....196 B1
Hunters Field SN7 ......194 C4
Hunters Piece SN6 .....209 A1
Hunters Point OX39 ....168 B3
Hunts Cl OX18 ....100 C2
Hurdeswell OX29 ....90 A1
Hurdlers Gn OX49 .....186 A1
Hurst Cl OX10 ....221 B3
Hurst La Cumnor OX2 ...140 A3
Freeland OX29 ....106 A4
Hurst Rise Rd OX2 .....140 B4
Hurst St OX4 ....141 C4
Huscarle Way RG31 ....257 B2
Hutchcomb Rd OX2 ....140 B4
Hutchcombe Farm Cl
OX2 ....140 B4
Huxley Cl Bicester OX26 ..65 B2
Wootton (Oxford) OX13 ..159 A3
Hyacinth Wlk OX4 .....161 C4
Hyde Copse OX13 ......178 B4
Hyde Gr OX15 ....21 B2
Hyde Pl OX14 ....179 B3
Hyde Rd OX12 ....196 A3
Hyde The OX14 ....179 B3
Hydes The RG31 ....257 B2
Hydrangea Wlk OX16 .....9 A1
Hythe Bridge St OX1 ...123 A1

I

Ian Mikardo Way RG4 ..259 B1
Ibstone Ave RG4 ......259 C3
Ibstone Rd HP14 ....188 B2
Ickford Comb Sch HP18 128 A2
Ickford Rd
Shabbington HP18 ......128 B1
Tiddington OX9 ....145 C4
Worminghall HP18 ......127 C3
Ickleton Rd OX12 ......214 A2
Icknield Cl Chinnor OX39 168 A2
Didcot OX11 ....200 B1
Icknield Com Sch OX49 186 A1
Icknield Cotts RG8 .....249 A3
Icknield La OX12 ....214 C2
Icknield Pl RG8 ....249 B4
Icknield Rd RG8 ....249 B4
Icknield Way SN6 ......227 B2
Idbury Cl OX28 ....117 B4
Idstone Hill SN6 ....228 A2
Idstone Rd SN6 ....228 A3
Iffley Mead Sch OX4 ...141 C3
Iffley Rd OX4 ....141 C4
Iffley Turn OX4 ....142 A3
Ilchester Mews RG4 ...259 C3
Ilex Cl RG4 ....252 C2
Ilges La OX10 ....221 A1
Ilkley Rd RG4 ....258 C2
Illingworth Ave RG4 ...259 C3
Ilsley Cl RG4 ....252 C3
Imperial Ct RG9 ....244 C1
Independent Bsns Pk
HP14 ....188 B3
Ingham La OX49 ....186 A1
Ingle Cl OX3 ....124 A2
Inglewood Cl RG4 .....252 C3
Ingrebourne Way OX11 .200 C2
Inkerman Cl OX14 .....159 B1
Innsworth Rd OX18 ....115 C2
Inott Furze OX3 ....142 B4
Insall Rd OX7 ....42 C2
Inst Of Virology &
Experimental Microbiology
OX1 ....123 B1
Ireton Cl OX44 ....184 B3
Ireton Ct OX9 ....129 C1
Iron Down Hill
Barford St M OX7,OX15 ....32 B2
South Newington OX7,OX15 31 C2
Ironside Dr SN6 ....191 B1
Ironstone Hollow OX15 ..30 B4
Ironstones OX16 ....16 A4
Ishree Cotts RG9 ......242 A3
Isis Ave OX26 ....65 A1
Isis Bsns Ctr OX4 .....142 C3
Isis CE Mid Sch OX4 ...141 C3
Isis Cl Abingdon OX14 ..160 B1
Long Hanborough OX29 ..106 A4
Islip Rd Bletchingdon OX5 .93 A4
Cutteslowe OX2 ....123 A4
Islip Sta OX5 ....93 C1
Islsley Rd OX3 ....124 C2
Itchen Ct OX11 ....201 A2
Ivatt Wlk OX16 ....16 C4
Ivy La Mollington OX17 .....4 A2
Oxford OX3 ....124 B2
Shutford OX15 ....14 A3
Ivybank RG31 ....257 B1
Ivydene Rd RG30 ......258 B1

J

Jack Argent Cl 22 OX4 .142 C1
Jack Straw's La OX3 ...124 A2
Jackdaw La OX4 ....141 C4
Jackies La OX33 ....144 B4
Jackman Cl OX14 ......180 A4
Jackson Cl OX18 ......115 B1
Jackson Cole Ho 5
OX1 ....123 A1
Jackson Dr OX1 ....141 B1
Jackson Rd
Bledington OX7 ....54 B1
Cutteslowe OX2 ....109 A1
Jacobs Cl OX28 ....104 A1
Jacobs Yd OX7 ....60 C4
James Ct OX18 ....152 C4
James St OX4 ....141 C4
James Wolfe Rd OX4 ...142 C4
Janaway OX4 ....142 A1
Jane Morbey Rd OX9 ...148 A4
Jane Seaman Ct OX4 ...143 A1
Japonica Cl OX26 ....65 C3
Japonica Wlk OX16 ......9 A1
Jarn Way OX1 ....140 B1
Jarvis La OX26 ....66 A1
Jasmine Cl OX4 ....142 C2
Jasmine Pl OX26 ....65 C3
Jasmine Wlk OX16 ....9 A1
Javelin Way OX10 .....204 B2
Jay Cl OX26 ....81 A4
Jaynes Cl OX16 ....16 B1
Jeff's Terr OX7 ....73 A2
Jefferson Cl RG4 ......259 B4
Jefferson Way OX9 ....148 A4
Jeffersons Piece OX7 ...73 B3
Jemmetts Cl OX10 .....182 B1
Jennings La OX11 .....217 C4
Jenyns Ct OX14 ....179 B3
Jericho St OX2 ....123 A2
Jerome Way OX5 ....92 B3
Jersey Dr OX16 ....9 A1
Jersey Rd OX4 ....142 A2
Jervis Cl OX7 ....60 C4
Jespers Hill SN7 ......173 A2
Jesse's La HP18 ....129 B3
Jessops Cl Marston OX3 .123 C3
Oxford OX3 ....124 A3
Jesus Coll OX1 ....123 B1
Jethro Tull Gdns OX10 ..221 C4
Jetty The OX17 ....5 C1
Jeune Hall 2 OX4 .....141 C4
Jeune St OX4 ....141 C4
Joan Lawrence Pl OX3 .124 C1
John Blandy Prim Sch
OX13 ....156 C1
John Buchan Rd OX3 ..124 A3
John Garne Way OX3 ..124 A1
John Hampen Prim Sch
OX9 ....148 A4
John Kallie Ho OX4 ....142 A3
John Lopes Rd OX29 ...120 C4
John Mason Sch
OX14 ....179 C4
John Mason Rd OX14 ..180 A4
John Morris Rd OX14 ..179 C3
John Piers La OX1 .....141 B3
John Radcliffe Hospl
OX3 ....124 A2
John Smith Dr OX4 ....142 B2
John Snow Pl OX3 .....124 C2
John Towle Cl OX1 .....141 B3
John Watson Sch OX33 126 A1
Johnson Cl OX44 ....143 B1
Johnston's Way OX7 ....42 C1
Johnstone Pl 19 OX10 ..221 B4
Johnstones SN7 ....195 A2
Jordan Cl Didcot OX11 ..201 A1
Reading RG4 ....259 C3
Jordan Hill OX2 ....109 A1
Jordans Cl OX7 ....88 A2
Josca's Prep Sch OX13 .178 A4
Josey Cl RG4 ....252 C3
Jourdain Rd OX4 ......142 C2
Jowett Wlk OX1 ....123 B1
Joyce's Rd SN7 ....194 B4
Jubilee Cl OX25 ....62 A4
Jubilee Cotts OX12 .....215 C3
Jubilee Ct OX16 ....16 B3
Jubilee Rd HP14 ....188 C2
Jubilee Terr OX1 ....141 B4
Jubilee Way OX11 .....219 A4
Jubillee La OX7 ....85 A4
Judd's Cl OX28 ....118 B4
Judges Cl OX5 ....108 C4
Judges Rd RG8 ....241 C2
Junction Rd
Banbury OX16 ....16 C3
Churchill OX7 ....55 C2
Oxford OX4 ....142 B3
Juniper Cl OX16 ....9 A1
Juniper Ct
Abingdon OX14 ....179 B4
18 Banbury OX16 ....16 B3
Juniper Dr OX4 ....142 C1
Juniper Gdns OX26 .....65 C3
Juniper Way RG31 .....257 B1
Juxon St OX2 ....123 A2

K

Kames Cl OX4 ....142 A3
Katchside OX14 ....199 C3
Katherine's Wlk GL7 ...150 B2
Keats Cl 4 OX26 ....65 B2
Keats Rd OX16 ....16 A2
Keble Cl GL7 ....150 B3
Keble Coll OX1 ....123 B1
Keble Rd Bicester OX26 ...65 C2
Oxford OX1 ....123 B2
Kedleston Rise OX16 ....16 C1
Keene Cl OX4 ....161 A4
Keens Cl OX7 ....58 C3
Keens La OX39 ....168 B3
Keeys Cl OX27 ....50 B2
Kelburne Rd OX4 ......142 A2
Kelham Hall Dr OX33 ...144 A4
Kelly's Rd OX33 ....143 C4
Kelmscott Cl RG4 .....258 C2
Kelmscott Manor Ho*
GL7 ....151 C1
Kelso Mews RG4 ......259 C3
Kelvedon Way RG4 ....258 C3
Kemps Rd OX17 ....23 A3
Kempson Cres OX4 ....142 A1
Kempster Cl OX14 .....180 A4
Kendal Ave RG4 ......259 C3
Kendal Cres OX2 ....109 A1
Kendal Piece OX7 ......73 B2
Kenhill Rd OX15 ....6 C1
Kenilworth Ave OX4 ...142 A4
Kenilworth Ct OX4 .....142 A4
Kenilworth Rd OX2 ....139 C2
Kenilworth Way OX16 ...15 C3
Kenley Ave OX18 ......115 C2
Kennedy Cl OX4 ....142 C4
Kennedy Cres OX10 ...220 C1
Kennedy Dr RG8 ....256 C3
Kennedy Ho OX16 ....16 A3
Kennedy Rd OX26 ....65 B1
Kennel La
Chipping Norton OX7 ......42 A1
Steventon OX13 ....199 A3
Kennet Cl
Berinsfield OX10 ....182 B2
Bicester OX26 ....65 B1
Grove OX12 ....196 B1
Kennet Rd
Abingdon OX14 ....160 A1
Harwell OX11 ....217 B1
Kennett Rd OX3 ....124 B1
Kennetts Hos OX15 ......21 B2
Kennington Rd
Kennington OX1 ....141 C1
Kennington OX1 ....160 C3
Radley OX14 ....160 C3
Kennington Rdbt OX1 ..141 B2
Kennylands Rd RG4 ....253 A2
Kensington Cl
Abingdon OX14 ....179 C2
Kings Sutton OX17 ....23 C3
Kent Cl Abingdon OX14 ..180 A4
Oxford OX4 ....142 C2
Kentons La RG10 ......255 B4
Kentwood Cl
Cholsey OX10 ....220 C1
Reading RG30 ....257 C1
Kentwood Hill RG31 ...257 C1
Kenville Rd OX1 ....141 B1
Kernham Dr RG31 .....257 B2
Kerry Cl OX16 ....9 A1
Kersington Cres OX4 ..142 B2
Kerwood Cl OX20 ....91 A4
Keston Cl RG4 ....259 B1
Kestrel Cl OX18 ....115 B2
Kestrel Cres OX4 ......142 B1
Kestrel Pl OX4 ....142 B1
Kestrel Way OX26 ....81 A4
Kestrels The OX12 .....196 B1
Ketchmere Cl HP18 ....129 B3
Kew Win OX11 ....201 A1
Keydale Rd OX33 ......143 C4
Keyser Rd OX15 ....22 C4
Keyte's Cl OX17 ....23 A2
Kibble Cl OX11 ....219 A4
Kiddington Rd OX7 .....60 C4
Kidlington Ctr OX5 ......92 C1
Kidlington Rd OX5 ......93 C1
Kidmore End CE Prim Sch
RG4 ....252 B2
Kidmore End Rd RG4 ..259 A4
Kidmore La RG4 ......252 C2
Kidmore Rd RG4 ......258 C3
Kilbale Cres OX16 ....16 B2
Kildare Gdns RG4 .....259 B2
Kilkenny La OX18 .....115 C3
Kiln Cl Aston OX18 .....135 B2
Sandford-on-T OX4 ......161 B4
Kiln La Garsington OX44 .143 B1
Oxford OX3 ....124 C1
Shiplake RG9 ....254 B1
Wheatley OX33 ....144 A4
Kiln Rd RG4 ....259 B4
Kiln Terr SN7 ....173 A2
Kimbells Cl HP18 ......128 B1
Kimber Cl OX33 ....144 A4
Kimber Rd OX14 ......179 B4
Kimberley Villas 21 OX16 .16 B3
Kimbers Cl OX12 ......196 A2
Kinecroft OX10 ....221 B4
Kineton Rd OX1 ....141 B4
King Alfred Dr OX11 ...200 C1
King Alfred's Sch OX12 .214 B2
King Alfred's Sch E
OX12 ....214 C2
King Alfred's Sch W
OX12 ....214 A2
King Edward St OX1 ...123 B1
King James Way RG9 ..254 B4
King St OX2 ....123 A2
King Wlk OX11 ....200 C1

Lovelace Cl OX14 ...160 A2
Lovelace Dr OX5 ...109 A4
Lovelace Rd OX2 ...109 A1
Lovelace Sq 8 OX2 ...109 A1
Lovell Cl
Ducklington OX29 ...118 A2
Henley-on-T RG9 ...254 B4
Minster Lovell OX18 ...102 C1
Loverock Rd RG30 ...258 B1
Lowell Pl OX28 ...118 A4
Lower Armour Rd RG31 257 B1
Lower Cherwell St OX16 .16 B3
Lower Church St HP14 .188 C3
Lower Cl OX15 ...22 C4
Lower Comm SN7 ...211 B4
Lower Cres OX29 ...102 C2
Lower Elmstone Dr
RG31 ...257 B1
Lower End
Great Milton OX44 ...145 A2
Piddington OX25 ...97 C4
Salford OX7 ...41 C2
Shutford OX15 ...14 A3
Lower Farm Cl HP18 ...128 B2
Lower Farm La OX17 ...3 C2
Lower Hades Rd OX5 ...77 A3
Lower Henley Rd RG4 ...259 B2
Lower Heyford Rd OX25 .63 A3
Lower High St OX18 ...100 C3
Lower Icknield Way
OX39 ...168 B4
Lower Rd
Aston Rowant OX9 ...166 C2
Blackthorn OX25 ...82 A2
Chilton OX11 ...235 B4
Chinnor OX39 ...168 B4
Long Hanborough OX29 ...90 C1
Lower St
Barford St M OX15 ...32 C3
Islip OX5 ...93 C1
Lower Wharf OX10 ...221 B4
Lower Whitley Rd OX2 .139 B4
Lowes Cl Shiplake RG9 ...255 A2
Stokenchurch HP14 ...188 B3
Lowfield Gn RG4 ...259 C2
Lowfield Rd RG4 ...259 B3
Loyd Cl OX14 ...160 A2
Loyd Rd OX11 ...218 B3
Lucas Pl OX4 ...141 C3
Lucca Dr OX14 ...179 B3
Lucerne Ave OX26 ...65 B2
Lucerne Dr OX44 ...163 B1
Lucerne Rd OX2 ...123 B4
Lucey Cl RG31 ...257 A2
Lucky La OX16 ...16 B3
Ludford Gdns OX15 ...21 B2
Ludgershall Rd OX25 ...97 C4
Ludlow Dr Banbury OX16 .15 C4
Thame OX9 ...148 A4
Ludsden Gr OX9 ...148 A4
Luker Ave RG9 ...244 B2
Lumberd Rd OX14 ...160 A1
Lune Cl OX11 ...201 A1
Lupton Rd Thame OX9 ...148 A4
Wallingford OX10 ...221 A4
Luscombe Cl RG4 ...259 B1
Luther Ct 13 OX1 ...141 B4
Lych Gate La OX44 ...145 A1
Lycroft Cl RG8 ...249 B4
Lydalls Cl OX11 ...200 C1
Lydalls Rd OX11 ...200 C1
Lydia Cl OX3 ...124 C2
Lydsee Gate OX12 ...214 A3
Lye Valley OX3 ...142 B4
Lyefield Ct RG4 ...259 A3
Lyford Cl OX14 ...179 A1
Lyford Way OX14 ...160 A1
Lymbrook Cl OX29 ...119 B3
Lyme Gr RG31 ...257 B1
Lymington Gate RG4 ...258 C3
Lynch The OX12 ...216 B3
Lyndene Rd OX11 ...200 B2
Lyndhurst Rd
Goring RG8 ...249 B3
Reading RG30 ...258 A1
Lyndworth Cl OX3 ...124 C2
Lyndworth Mews OX3 ...124 C2
Lyne Rd OX5 ...92 B1
Lyneham Cl
Carterton OX18 ...115 C2
Witney OX28 ...103 C1
Lyneham Rd
Bicester OX26 ...66 A2
Milton-u-W OX7 ...70 A2
Lynges Cl OX14 ...160 A1
Lynmouth Ct RG1 ...259 A1
Lynmouth Rd
Didcot OX11 ...218 C4
Reading RG1 ...259 A1
Lynn Cl OX3 ...123 C2
Lynt Farm Cotts SN6 ...170 A3
Lynt Rd SN6 ...170 A3
Lynton La OX29 ...107 B1
Lyon Cl OX14 ...160 A1
Lysander Cl 5 OX26 ...66 A2
Lytham End RG31 ...257 A2
Lytton Rd OX4 ...142 A3

M

Mabel Prichard Sch
OX4 ...142 A1
Maberley Cl OX14 ...179 B3
Mably Gr OX12 ...214 B3
Mably Way OX12 ...214 B4
Macaulay Cl 13 OX26 ...65 B2
Macdonald Cl OX11 ...200 B1
MacKenzie Ave OX14 ...199 B2
Mackenzie Cl 12 OX26 ...65 B2
Mackley Cl OX15 ...33 C2
Macray Rd OX29 ...118 A2
Mafeking Row OX49 ...186 C2
Magdalen Cl OX26 ...65 C2
Magdalen Coll OX1 ...123 C1
Magdalen Coll Sch OX4 141 C4
Magdalen Ct OX11 ...219 A4
Magdalen Pl OX18 ...115 B1
Magdalen Rd OX4 ...142 A4
Magdalen St OX1 ...123 B1
Magnette Cl OX14 ...179 C4
Magnolia Cl OX5 ...108 C4
Magnolias The
Banbury OX16 ...9 A1
Bicester OX26 ...65 C3
Magpie La OX1 ...123 B1
Maidcroft Rd OX4 ...142 B3
Maiden's Cl SN6 ...191 B1
Maidley Cl OX28 ...104 B1
Main Ave OX4 ...161 B4
Main Rd Appleford OX14 .200 C4
Broughton OX15 ...15 B1
Curbridge OX29 ...117 B3
East Hagbourne OX11 ...218 C3
Fyfield OX13 ...157 B1
Long Hanborough OX29 ...90 B1
Middleton Cheney OX17 ...17 C4
Main St Adlestrop GL56 ...40 B2
Bledington OX7 ...54 B1
Chilton OX11 ...235 B4
Clanfield OX18 ...152 C4
Claydon OX17 ...1 B1
Duns Tew OX25 ...47 B3
East Hanney OX12 ...197 A3
Finstock OX7 ...88 C4
Fringford OX27 ...52 B3
Grove OX12 ...196 C1
Hanwell OX17 ...8 C2
Hethe OX27 ...52 A4
Letcombe Bassett OX12 ...214 A1
Mollington OX17 ...4 A2
North Newington OX15 ...15 A2
Over Norton OX7 ...42 C3
Shalstone MK18 ...25 C3
Sibford Gower OX15 ...19 A4
Tadmarton OX15 ...20 B4
Turweston NN13 ...24 B4
West Hagbourne OX11 ...218 B2
West Hanney OX12 ...196 C3
Westbury NN13 ...25 A2
Wroxton OX15 ...15 A4
Maisonettes The RG8 ...249 B4
Majors Rd SN6 ...191 C1
Makins Rd RG9 ...254 A4
Malet Cl HP14 ...188 C3
Malford Rd OX3 ...124 C2
Mall The SN6 ...209 C4
Mallard Cl OX4 ...142 B1
Mallard Way OX12 ...196 B1
Mallards Way OX26 ...66 A1
Mallins La SN7 ...192 B2
Mallinson Ct OX2 ...123 A1
Mallory Ave RG4 ...259 B3
Maltfield Rd OX3 ...124 A3
Malthouse SN6 ...228 A4
Malthouse Cl SN6 ...228 A4
Malthouse La
Bodicote OX15 ...22 B4
Dorchester OX10 ...182 B1
Long Compton CV36 ...27 C3
Shutford OX15 ...14 A3
Malthouse Paddock
SN7 ...174 C4
Malthouse Wlk 8 OX16 ...16 B3
Malthouses The SN6 ...228 A4
Maltings Ct OX15 ...21 B2
Maltings The RG20 ...235 A1
Maltsters OX29 ...89 B4
Malvern Cl Banbury OX16 .16 B1
Didcot OX11 ...200 B1
Malyns Cl OX39 ...168 B4
Managua Cl RG4 ...259 C1
Manchester Coll OX1 ...123 B1
Manchester Terr 15
OX26 ...65 C1
Mandarin Pl OX12 ...196 B1
Mandeville Cl OX14 ...160 A1
Mandhill Cl OX12 ...214 C4
Mandlebrote Dr OX4 ...142 A1
Manning Cl OX15 ...21 C1
Mannings Cl OX15 ...19 A4
Manor Ave GL7 ...150 C2
Manor Cl Appleford OX14 200 C4
Aston OX18 ...135 C1
Cassington OX29 ...107 B1
Chilton OX11 ...217 C1
Drayton OX14 ...179 A1
Enstone OX7 ...58 C3
Great Bourton OX17 ...9 B4
Shrivenham SN6 ...209 A4
West Hagbourne OX11 ...218 B2
Manor Cotts OX29 ...138 A4
Manor Court Yd OX33 ...127 A1
Manor Cres Didcot OX11 .200 B1
Standlake OX29 ...137 B2
Stanford in the V SN7 ...194 C4
Manor Ct Abingdon OX14 179 C3
Banbury OX16 ...16 C4
Carterton OX18 ...115 B1
Chadlington OX7 ...57 B1
Manor Cty Prim Sch The
OX29 ...90 B1
Manor Dr OX33 ...143 B3
Manor Farm OX14 ...180 A1
Manor Farm Barns OX5 .95 A2
Manor Farm Cl
Fernham SN7 ...193 A2
Kingham OX7 ...54 C3
Merton OX25 ...95 B4
Manor Farm Cotts OX13 177 B3
Manor Farm Ct OX20 ...75 C2
Manor Farm La RG8 ...256 B1
Manor Farm Rd
Dorchester OX10 ...182 B1
Horspath OX33 ...143 B3
Manor Field OX12 ...214 A1
Manor Gdns GL7 ...150 B2
Manor Gn Harwell OX11 .217 C4
Stanford in the V SN7 ...194 C4
Manor Gr OX1 ...160 C4
Manor Ho★ OX5 ...108 A2
Manor La Clanfield OX18 .152 C4
East Hendred OX12 ...216 A3
Shrivenham SN6 ...209 A3
Manor Orch OX15 ...8 A2
Manor Pk OX17 ...1 B1
Manor Pl OX1 ...123 C1
Manor Prep Sch OX13 ...159 B1
Manor Prim Sch OX11 ...200 B1
Manor Rd Adderbury OX17 22 C2
Banbury OX16 ...16 C4
Bladon OX20 ...91 A1
Brize Norton OX18 ...116 A2
Carterton OX18 ...115 B3
Chinnor OX9 ...149 A3
Didcot OX11 ...200 B1
Ducklington OX29 ...118 A2
Fringford OX27 ...52 B4
Goring RG8 ...249 A3
Great Bourton OX17 ...9 B4
Henley-on-T RG9 ...254 B4
Middle Barton OX7 ...46 B1
Oxford OX1 ...123 C1
South Hinksey OX1 ...141 A3
Wantage OX12 ...232 B3
Whitchurch RG8 ...256 B4
Witney OX28 ...118 B4
Woodstock OX20 ...91 A4
Wootton (Oxford) OX13 ...159 A4
Manor View OX18 ...134 C2
Manor Way OX5 ...92 C1
Manor Wood Gate RG9 .255 A2
Manorsfield Rd OX26 ...65 C1
Mansell Cl OX29 ...106 B3
Mansfield Coll OX1 ...123 B1
Mansfield Gdns OX11 ...219 A4
Mansfield Rd OX1 ...123 B1
Mansion Hill OX17 ...17 C4
Mansmoor Rd OX5 ...94 C4
Manston Cl OX26 ...66 A2
Manzel Rd OX27 ...66 A3
Manzil Way OX4 ...142 A4
Maple Ave OX5 ...108 C4
Maple Cl Banbury OX16 ...16 C1
N Hinksey Village OX2 ...140 B4
Sonning Common RG4 ...253 A2
Maple Cotts SN7 ...172 C2
Maple Ct Goring RG8 ...249 A3
Kidlington OX5 ...108 C4
Maple Rd Bicester OX26 ...65 C1
Faringdon SN7 ...172 C2
Thame OX9 ...147 B4
Maple Way OX7 ...71 A1
Maple Well OX29 ...89 B4
Mapledene RG4 ...258 C2
Mapledurham Dr RG8 ...257 B3
Mapledurham Ho★
RG4 ...257 C3
Mapledurham View
RG31 ...257 B1
Maples The
Carterton OX18 ...115 B1
Grove OX12 ...196 B1
Maplewell Ho OX29 ...89 B4
March Rd OX17 ...3 B2
Marcham CE Prim Sch
OX13 ...178 B3
Marcham Rd
Abingdon OX14,OX13 ...179 A4
Drayton OX14 ...179 A1
Marchwood Ave RG4 ...259 B4
Mardy RG4 ...258 C3
Margaret Cl Banbury OX16 16 A3
Bicester OX26 ...65 B2
Margaret Rd
Adderbury OX17 ...23 A3
Oxford OX3 ...124 C1
Maria Cres OX12 ...214 C3
Marie Cl OX27 ...67 C4
Marigold Cl 18 OX4 ...142 C1
Marigold Wlk OX26 ...65 C3
Marines Dr SN7 ...172 C1
Mariot Ct 11 OX10 ...221 B4
Marjoram Cl OX4 ...143 A1
Mark Rd OX3 ...124 C1
Market End Way OX26 ...65 B2
Market Pl
13 Abingdon OX14 ...179 C4
Banbury OX16 ...16 B3
Deddington OX15 ...33 C2
Faringdon SN7 ...172 C2
Henley-on-T RG9 ...244 B1
Highworth SN6 ...190 A3
Lechlade GL7 ...150 B2
15 Wallingford OX10 ...221 B4
Wantage OX12 ...214 B2
Woodstock OX20 ...91 A3
Market Sq
Bampton OX18 ...134 C2
Bicester OX26 ...65 C1
Witney OX28 ...118 A4
Market St Charlbury OX7 ...73 A2
Chipping Norton OX7 ...42 C2
Market St *continued*
Oxford OX1 ...123 B1
Woodstock OX20 ...91 A3
Marlborough Ave OX5 ...92 B1
Marlborough CE Sch
OX20 ...91 B3
Marlborough Cl
Carterton OX18 ...115 C1
Eynsham OX29 ...120 C4
Faringdon SN7 ...172 C2
Kidlington OX5 ...92 B1
Kings Sutton OX17 ...23 C3
Oxford OX4 ...142 A1
Marlborough Cr OX20 ...91 A4
Marlborough Cres
OX29 ...106 A4
Marlborough Ct OX2 ...122 C1
Marlborough Dr OX29 ...107 B1
Marlborough Gdns SN7 172 C1
Marlborough La
Stanford in the V SN7 ...194 C4
Witney OX28 ...118 A4
Marlborough Pl
10 Banbury OX16 ...16 B3
Charlbury OX7 ...73 A2
Eynsham OX29 ...120 C4
Faringdon SN7 ...172 C1
Marlborough Rd
Banbury OX16 ...16 B3
Chipping Norton OX7 ...42 C2
Oxford OX1 ...141 B4
Marlborough St SN7 ...172 C2
Marley Ind Est OX16 ...16 B4
Marley La OX44 ...184 B4
Marley Way OX16 ...16 B4
Marling Cl RG31 ...257 B1
Marlow Cl OX10 ...221 A4
Marlow Rd RG9 ...244 C2
Marlowe Cl OX16 ...15 C3
Marmyon Ho RG9 ...244 C2
Marns Hey OX12 ...214 B3
Marriott Cl
Cutteslowe OX2 ...109 A1
Wootton OX20 ...76 A2
Marriotts Cl HP17 ...130 C3
Marriotts La HP17 ...130 C3
Marriotts Way HP17 ...130 C3
Marsack St RG4 ...259 B1
Marsh Baldon CE Prim Sch
OX44 ...162 A2
Marsh Cl OX5 ...108 B3
Marsh Ct OX14 ...179 C4
Marsh End OX9 ...147 A1
Marsh Gibbon CE Sch
OX27 ...67 C2
Marsh La Clanfield OX18 .152 C4
East Challow OX12 ...213 C4
Fyfield OX13 ...157 A2
Marston OX3 ...124 A3
Marsh Rd Oxford OX4 ...142 B3
Shabbington HP18 ...128 B2
Marsh Way SN7 ...211 A3
Marshall Cl
Chipping Norton OX7 ...42 C1
Reading RG8 ...257 B2
Marshall Cres OX7 ...46 C1
Marshall Rd OX4 ...142 B3
Marshalls Cl OX15 ...6 C1
Marshland Sq RG4 ...259 A3
Marston Ferry Ct OX2 ...123 B3
Marston Ferry Rd OX2,
OX3 ...123 B3
Marston Mid Sch OX3 ...123 C3
Marston Rd
Oxford OX3,OX4 ...123 C2
Thame OX9 ...130 A1
Marston St OX4 ...141 C4
Marten Gate OX16 ...16 B2
Marten Pl RG31 ...257 A2
Martens Cl SN6 ...209 A3
Martens Lake OX13 ...156 B1
Martens Rd SN6 ...209 A3
Martin Cl OX26 ...80 C4
Martin Ct OX2 ...123 A4
Martin's La OX10 ...182 B1
Martyn's Way OX10 ...204 C2
Mary Towerton Sch The
HP14 ...189 B2
Mary Whipple Ct OX12 .214 B2
Maryfield OX12 ...214 C2
Marygreen OX12 ...214 B4
Marylands Gn OX44 ...162 B1
Marymead OX10 ...220 C1
Mascall Ave OX3 ...142 C4
Mascord Cl OX16 ...16 A3
Mascord Rd OX16 ...16 A3
Masefield Cl 10 OX26 ...65 B2
Masefield Cres OX14 ...179 B3
Masefield Rd OX16 ...16 A2
Masey Cl OX3 ...124 B1
Masons' Rd OX3 ...124 C1
Mathematical Inst OX1 .123 B1
Mather Rd OX3 ...124 C2
Mathews Way OX13 ...159 A3
Matlock Rd RG4 ...258 C2
Matson Dr RG9 ...244 C1
Matthew Arnold Sch
OX2 ...140 B4
Mattock Way OX14 ...160 A2
Mattock's Cl OX3 ...124 B1
Maud Cl OX26 ...65 B2
Maud Ho OX12 ...214 C3
Maule Cl OX15 ...21 C1
Maunds The OX15 ...33 C2
Mavor Cl OX20 ...91 A4
Mawle Ct 9 OX16 ...16 B3
Mawles La OX7 ...85 B4
Maxwell Ave OX11 ...217 A2
May's Cl OX27 ...49 C4
Maycroft 4 OX26 ...65 C2
Mayfair Rd OX4 ...142 A2
Mayfield Ave OX12 ...196 C1
Mayfield Cl
Carterton OX18 ...115 B1
Chalgrove OX44 ...184 B3
Mayfield Dr RG4 ...259 B2
Mayfield Rd Banbury OX16 16 B1
Cumnor OX2 ...121 A1
Cutteslowe OX2 ...123 A4
Mayott's Rd 6 OX14 ...179 C4
Mc Mullan Cl OX10 ...221 B4
McCrae's Wlk RG10 ...255 B1
McKay Trad Est OX26 ...80 C4
McKee Sq OX10 ...204 B1
Mckeever Pl 5 OX16 ...16 C3
Mdws The OX49 ...186 A1
Mead La Longcot SN7 ...192 B1
Lower Basildon RG8 ...249 C1
Mead Platt HP14 ...188 B3
Mead Rd
Barford St M OX15 ...32 C4
Yarnton OX5 ...108 B2
Mead The OX17 ...3 C2
Mead Way OX5 ...92 C1
Mead Wlk OX11 ...200 C1
Meaden Hill OX3 ...124 A3
Meadow Bank SN7 ...172 C2
Meadow Cl Cumnor OX2 .121 A2
Goring RG8 ...249 B3
Grove OX12 ...196 C1
Moulsford OX10 ...238 C2
Shipton-u-W OX7 ...70 B1
Meadow End OX18 ...100 C3
Meadow La
Crowmarsh G OX10 ...222 A3
Fulbrook OX18 ...100 C3
Long Crendon HP18 ...129 C2
Oxford OX4 ...141 C4
Shipton-u-W OX7 ...70 B1
Meadow Pl OX7 ...55 B3
Meadow Prospect OX2 .122 B4
Meadow Rd
Chinnor OX39 ...168 B3
Henley-on-T RG9 ...244 C1
Reading RG1 ...258 C1
Watchfield SN6 ...191 C1
Meadow View
Adderbury OX17 ...23 A2
Banbury OX16 ...16 C2
Cutteslowe OX2 ...123 B4
Kidlington OX5 ...92 C1
Long Crendon HP18 ...129 C2
Wendlebury OX25 ...79 C2
Witney OX28 ...118 B4
Meadow View Rd OX1 ...160 C4
Meadow Way
Didcot OX11 ...218 B4
Faringdon SN7 ...172 C1
Kingham OX7 ...54 C2
3 Thame OX9 ...129 C1
Yarnton OX5 ...108 B3
Meadow Wlk OX20 ...91 B3
Meadowbank Cl
Ascott-u-W OX7 ...71 A1
Long Crendon HP18 ...129 B4
Meadowside
Abingdon OX14 ...179 C3
Reading RG31 ...257 A1
Meadowside Ct 1
OX14 ...179 C3
Meadowside Rd RG8 ...256 B3
Meads Cl OX14 ...179 A1
Meads The OX12 ...196 C4
Meadside OX10 ...202 C4
Meashill Way OX11 ...234 C4
Medcroft Rd OX5 ...77 A3
Medhill Cl RG8 ...250 C4
Medina Cl OX11 ...201 A1
Medina Gdns OX26 ...65 A1
Medlar Rd SN6 ...209 B4
Medlicott Dr OX14 ...179 B3
Medlock Gr OX11 ...200 C2
Medway OX12 ...197 A3
Medway Cl OX13 ...159 B2
Medway Rd OX13 ...159 B2
Meer The OX10 ...204 A3
Melbourne Cl OX16 ...16 C2
Melford Gn RG4 ...259 C3
Melton Dr OX11 ...200 C1
Melville Cl OX26 ...65 A1
Membury Way OX12 ...214 B4
Memorial Ave RG9 ...254 C1
Mendip Hts OX11 ...200 B1
Menmarsh Rd HP18 ...127 C3
Menpes Rd RG31 ...257 B2
Mercury Cl OX18 ...134 C2
Mercury Rd OX4 ...143 A1
Mere Dyke Rd OX13 ...198 C3
Mere Rd Cutteslowe OX2 .122 C4
Finmere MK18 ...39 B3
Meredith Cl OX26 ...65 B2
Mereland Rd OX11 ...218 C4
Merewood Ave OX3 ...125 A2
Merganser Dr OX26 ...81 A4
Meriden Ct OX10 ...221 B4
Merlin Cl Benson OX10 ...204 B1
Carterton OX18 ...115 B2
Merlin Rd Abingdon OX13 159 A1
Oxford OX4 ...142 C1
Merlin Way OX26 ...81 A4
Merritt Rd OX11 ...200 B1
Merrivale's La OX15 ...21 C2
Merrymouth Rd OX7 ...69 A1

Mersey Way OX11 ....201 A2
Merthyr Vale RG4 ....259 A3
Merton Cl Didcot OX11 ..219 A4
Eynsham OX29 ....120 B4
Merton Coll OX1 ....123 B1
Merton Ct OX2 ....123 A2
Merton Gr OX1 ....123 B1
Merton Rd OX25 ....81 B2
Merton St Banbury OX16 ..16 C3
Oxford OX1 ....123 B1
Merton Way OX5 ....108 A3
Merton Wlk 7 OX26 ....65 C2
Metcalf Cl OX14 ....179 C2
Metcalfe Cl OX15 ....15 B4
Meteor Cl OX26 ....66 A2
Mewburn Rd OX16 ....16 A3
Mews The Baydon SN8 ..245 A3
Highworth SN6 ....190 A3
Warborough OX10 ....203 A3
Watchfield SN6 ....191 B1
Meyseys Rd OX3 ....142 C4
Micklands Prim Sch RG4 ....259 B2
Micklands Rd RG4 ....259 C2
Mickle Way OX33 ....125 C2
Middi Haines Ct SN6 ..190 A3
Middle Aston La OX25 ..48 A3
Middle Barton Cty Prim Sch OX7 ....61 A4
Middle Furlong OX11 ..201 A1
Middle Hill OX15 ....30 A4
Middle La Shotteswell OX17 .8 B4
Wroxton OX15 ....14 B4
Middle Orch OX7 ....54 B1
Middle Rd Burford OX18 ..99 A3
Stanton St John OX33 ....125 B4
Middle Row
Chipping Norton OX7 ....42 C2
Great Rollright OX7 ....29 A2
Middle Springs RG8 ....249 B4
Middle St OX5 ....93 C1
Middle Way
Chinnor OX39 ....168 A3
Cutteslowe OX2 ....123 A4
Islip OX5 ....93 C1
Middleton Cheney Com Prim Sch OX17 ....17 C4
Middleton Cl OX16 ....17 A4
Middleton Rd
Banbury OX16, OX17 ....16 C4
Bucknell OX27 ....64 C4
Chacombe OX17 ....10 C2
Middleton Stoney Rd OX26 ....65 B1
Middleway Bottom OX12 ....213 B1
Midget Cl OX14 ....179 B3
Midsummer Mdw RG4 .258 C3
Midway OX17 ....11 A1
Midwinter Ave OX14 ..199 B2
Miles Dr OX12 ....214 C4
Milestone Cl HP14 ....188 C3
Milestone Rd OX18 ....115 B1
Milestone View Ct RG4 .259 C2
Milestone Way RG4 ....259 B3
Mileway Gdns OX3 ....124 B1
Milford Rd Reading RG1 .258 C1
Wootton OX20 ....76 A2
Milham Ford Cty Girls Upper Sec Sch OX3 ....124 A2
Milking La OX28,OX29 ..104 A2
Mill Cl Bix RG9 ....243 C4
Chadlington OX7 ....57 A1
Charlton-on-O OX5 ....95 A3
Deddington OX15 ....33 C2
Mill End OX5 ....93 A1
Mill Gn Bampton OX18 ..134 C1
Reading RG4 ....259 B1
Mill Green Cl OX18 ....134 C1
Mill La Adderbury OX17 ..23 A2
Alvescot OX18 ....133 B3
Ascott-u-W OX7 ....71 B1
Benson OX10 ....203 C2
Black Bourton OX18 ....133 C3
Brackley NN13 ....24 A3
Chalgrove OX44 ....184 B3
Chinnor OX39 ....168 A4
Chipping Warden OX17 ....5 C3
Clanfield OX18 ....152 C4
Croughton NN13 ....36 B4
Drayton (Banbury) OX15 ....15 B4
East Hendred OX12 ....216 B3
East Hendred, West Hendred OX12 ....216 A3
Great Haseley OX44 ....164 B4
Grove OX12 ....214 C4
Haddenham OX9 ....130 A2
Henley-on-T RG9 ....254 C4
Horton-cum-S OX33 ....112 A3
Kidmore End RG4 ....252 B1
Kings Sutton OX17 ....23 C2
Kirtlington OX5 ....77 C2
Lechlade GL7 ....150 C2
Lower Heyford OX25 ....62 B3
Marston OX3 ....123 C4
Middle Barton OX7 ....60 C4
Milton OX14 ....199 B3
Oxford OX4 ....141 C2
Shiplake RG9 ....255 A1
South Moreton OX11 ....220 A3
Stokenchurch HP14 ....188 B3
Sutton Courtenay OX14 ..199 C4
Upper Arncott OX25 ....96 C4
Upper Heyford OX25 ....48 C1
Wallingford OX10 ....221 B4
Mill La *continued*
Westbury NN13 ....25 A2
Weston-on-the-G OX25 ....79 A1
Wootton OX20 ....75 C2
Mill Lane Cty Prim Sch OX39 ....168 A4
Mill Orch OX12 ....197 A3
Mill Paddock
8 Abingdon OX14 ....179 C3
Letcombe Bassett OX12 ..214 A1
Mill Rd Abingdon OX14 ..179 B3
Cutteslowe OX2 ....122 B4
Goring RG8 ....249 B4
Marcham OX13 ....178 B3
Nettlebed RG9 ....224 C2
Reading RG4 ....259 B1
Shiplake RG9 ....255 A2
Stokenchurch HP14 ....188 B3
Stratton Audley OX27 ....52 C1
Mill St Eynsham OX29 ..120 C4
Islip OX5 ....109 C4
Kidlington OX5 ....92 C1
Oxford OX2 ....123 A1
Stanton St John OX33 ....125 C4
Steventon OX13 ....198 C2
Wantage OX12 ....214 B3
Witney OX28 ....104 A1
Mill St Mews OX29 ....120 C4
Mill The OX7 ....42 B1
Mill View OX49 ....185 B2
Millaway La SN7 ....195 B3
Millbank OX2 ....141 A4
Millbrook Cl
Blewbury OX11 ....219 A1
Wallingford OX10 ....221 B4
Millbrook Cty Prim Sch OX12 ....196 B1
Millbrook House Sch OX14 ....199 B3
Millbrook Sq OX12 ....196 C1
Milldown Ave RG8 ....249 B4
Milldown Rd RG8 ....249 B4
Miller Ho OX16 ....16 A3
Miller Rd Banbury OX16 ..16 A3
Wheatley OX33 ....144 B4
Miller's Acre 1 OX2 ..109 A1
Millers Cl
Chalgrove OX44 ....184 B4
Goring RG8 ....249 A4
Millers Ct RG4 ....259 B1
Millers La OX15 ....7 B4
Millers Mews OX28 ....104 A1
Millers Turn OX39 ....168 A3
Millets Farm Cotts OX13 ....177 B3
Millfield Ave OX27 ....67 C2
Millfield Cl OX27 ....67 C2
Millham The OX12 ....216 A3
Millmoor Cres OX29 ..120 C4
Mills La OX15 ....15 A4
Millstream Ct OX2 ....122 B4
Millview OX7 ....42 C1
Millway Cl OX2 ....122 C4
Millway La OX13 ....157 C3
Millwood End OX29 ....90 A1
Millwood Farm Barns OX29 ....90 A1
Millwood Vale OX29 ....90 A1
Millwright Cl 3 OX16 ....16 A3
Milne Pl OX3 ....124 A3
Milton Bsns & Tech Ctr OX13 ....199 A1
Milton CE Prim Sch OX13 ....199 B2
Milton Cl 11 Bicester OX26 65 B2
Henley-on-T RG9 ....244 B1
Milton Cres OX33 ....125 C2
Milton Hill OX14 ....199 A1
Milton La OX13 ....199 A3
Milton Manor Dr OX44 .163 C3
Milton Manor Ho★ OX14 ....199 B3
Milton Park Est OX14 ..199 C2
Milton Rd Bloxham OX15 ..21 C2
Didcot OX11 ....200 A2
Milton (Banbury) OX15 ....22 B1
Oxford OX4 ....142 A3
Shipton-u-W OX7 ....70 B1
Sutton Courtenay OX14 ..199 C3
Milton St OX16 ....16 B3
Milvery Way OX4 ....142 A2
Minchery Farm Cotts OX4 ....142 B1
Minchery Rd OX4 ....142 B1
Minchins Cl OX14 ....180 B4
Minnow La OX18 ....99 B3
Minns Rd OX12 ....196 C1
Minster Ind Pk OX29 ....103 A1
Minster Lovell Hall★ OX29 ....103 A2
Minster Rd
Brize Norton OX18 ....116 A3
Oxford OX4 ....142 A4
Minster Riding OX29 ..102 C2
Mint The 14 OX10 ....221 B4
Minton Cl RG30 ....257 C1
Minty Cl OX18 ....115 B1
Mirfield Rd OX28 ....117 C4
Mistletoe Gn OX4 ....142 C1
Mitchell Cl Thame OX9 ..147 C4
Wootton (Oxford) OX13 ..159 A4
Mixbury NN13 ....38 B4
Moat Cl OX18 ....116 A2
Moat La OX27 ....67 C1
Moat The OX7 ....54 C3
Moat's Cres OX9 ....148 A4
Mobbs La OX15 ....30 A4
Moberly Cl OX4 ....141 C4
Moir Ct OX12 ....214 B3
Mold Cres OX16 ....16 A3
Mole Pl 23 OX4 ....142 C1
Mollington La OX17 ....3 A2
Mollington Rd OX17 ....8 B4
Molyneux Dr OX15 ....22 C4
Molyns Ho RG9 ....244 C2
Monarchs Ct OX10 ....203 C2
Monard Terr 10 OX4 ....141 C4
Monique Ct OX16 ....9 A1
Monkley Ct 5 RG4 ....259 B1
Monks Cl
Dorchester OX10 ....182 C1
Oxford OX4 ....142 B1
West Hanney OX12 ....196 C3
Monks Lode OX11 ....200 C2
Monks Mead OX10 ....202 C1
Monks Wlk GL7 ....150 C2
Monmouth Ct 10 RG1 ..259 A1
Monmouth Rd OX1 ....141 B3
Mons Way OX14 ....159 B1
Montabaur Rd NN13 ....24 A4
Montagu Rd OX2 ....140 B4
Montague St RG4 ....259 B1
Montgomery Rd OX27 ..66 A4
Montpelier Dr RG4 ....259 B3
Montrose Way OX9 ....148 A4
Monument Ind Pk OX44 184 C4
Monument Rd OX44 ....184 C3
Monument St OX16 ....16 B3
Moody Rd OX3 ....123 C2
Moor Ave OX28 ....104 A1
Moor La OX15 ....31 C4
Moor Pond Cl OX26 ....65 C1
Moorbank OX4 ....142 C2
Moorbrook OX11 ....200 B2
Moorend La Thame OX9 .129 C1
Thame OX9 ....130 A1
Moorfield Ct OX16 ....16 C3
Moorgate GL7 ....150 A2
Moorhen Wlk OX4 ....142 C1
Moorland Cl OX28 ....103 C1
Moorland Rd OX28 ....117 C4
Moorlands The
Benson OX10 ....204 A2
Kidlington OX5 ....92 C1
Moors Cl OX29 ....118 A3
Moors Drive The OX17 ..17 C4
Moors The Kidlington OX5 .92 B1
Pangbourne RG8 ....256 B3
Morecambe Ave RG4 ..258 C3
Moreton Ave OX10 ....221 A4
Moreton La
Northmoor OX8 ....156 C4
Thame OX9 ....147 C4
Moreton Rd
Aston Tirrold OX11 ....219 C1
Cutteslowe OX2 ....123 A3
Morgan Cl OX16 ....15 C4
Morlais RG4 ....259 A3
Morland Cl OX33 ....144 A4
Morland Rd OX13 ....178 B3
Morlands OX12 ....197 A4
Morrell Ave OX4 ....142 A4
Morrell Cl OX5 ....108 B4
Morrell Cres OX4 ....142 A1
Morrells Cl OX11 ....200 B1
Morris Cres OX4 ....142 A3
Morris Dr OX16 ....15 C4
Morris Ho OX4 ....142 B2
Morse Rd OX11 ....218 B3
Mortimer Dr OX3 ....123 C2
Mortimer Rd OX4 ....141 C2
Morton Ave OX5 ....108 C4
Morton Cl Abingdon OX14 180 B4
Kidlington OX5 ....108 C4
Morton King Cl HP18 ..128 B2
Mosquito La OX10 ....204 B1
Moss Cl RG4 ....259 B2
Motte The OX14 ....179 C4
Moulsford Prep Sch OX10 ....239 A3
Mount Owen Rd OX18 ..135 A2
Mount Pl OX2 ....123 A1
Mount Pleasant
Bishopstone SN6 ....227 B2
Lechlade GL7 ....150 B2
Shipton-u-W OX7 ....85 C4
Wardington OX17 ....5 C1
Mount Pleasant Cotts OX12 ....216 B3
Mount St OX2 ....123 A1
Mount The Reading RG4 .258 C2
Tetsworth OX9 ....166 A4
Mount View RG9 ....244 B1
Mount View Ct RG9 ....244 B1
Mountfield RG8 ....249 B4
Mountfield Rd OX28 ....117 C4
Mousey La 21 OX10 ....221 B4
Mowbray Dr RG30 ....258 A1
Mowbray Rd OX11 ....218 C3
Mowforth Cl RG8 ....240 C1
Mulberries The OX12 ..197 A3
Mulberry Bush Sch The OX29 ....137 B1
Mulberry Ct OX2 ....123 A4
Mulberry Dr
Bicester OX26 ....65 C3
Wheatley OX33 ....144 A4
Mulcaster Ave OX5 ....108 C4
Mullard Way OX14 ....179 C4
Mullein Rd OX26 ....65 C3
Mullens Terr RG4 ....258 B4
Mumbery Hill RG10 ....255 C1
Murcott Rd OX25 ....96 B3
Murdock Cl OX15 ....33 C2
Murdock Rd OX26 ....66 A1
Murray Ct OX2 ....123 B2
Murren The OX10 ....221 B3
Mus Of Modern Art★ OX1 ....123 B1
Mus Of Oxford★ OX1 ..123 B1
Museum Rd OX1 ....123 B1
Musgrave Rd OX39 ....168 B4
Musgrave Wlk HP14 ....188 C3
Musson Cl 10 OX14 ....179 C3
Mustard La RG4 ....260 C1
Myrtle Cl
Long Hanborough OX29 ..90 A1
Reading RG31 ....257 B2

N

Naldertown OX12 ....214 B3
Napier Ct OX14 ....180 A4
Napier Rd OX4 ....142 B3
Nappins Cl HP18 ....129 B3
Narrowby Ct OX16 ....16 B1
Naseby Cl OX9 ....130 A1
Nash Dr OX14 ....179 B3
Nash La OX29 ....106 A4
National Herb Ctr The★ OX17 ....3 A2
Navigation Way OX2 ..123 A3
Neal's La RG9 ....242 A1
Needlemakers HP18 ....129 B4
Neithrop Ave OX16 ....16 A4
Neithrop Cl OX16 ....16 A4
Neithrop Inf Sch OX16 ..16 A3
Neithrop Jun Sch OX16 ..16 A3
Nell Hill SN6 ....227 B2
Nelson Cl OX10 ....221 B4
Nelson Rd RG4 ....259 B1
Nelson St Oxford OX2 ..123 A1
Thame OX9 ....147 C4
Nene Gr OX11 ....201 A1
Nene Rd OX13 ....159 B1
Nether Cl NN13 ....24 A4
Nether Dunford Cl OX3 .142 C4
Netheravon Cl OX18 ..115 C1
Nethercote La OX49 ....167 A1
Nethercote Rd OX5 ....77 B3
Netherton La OX13 ....157 B2
Netherton Rd OX13 ....157 C3
Netherwoods Rd OX3 ..124 C1
Netherworton Rd OX15 ..32 C3
Netley Cl RG4 ....259 C3
Netting St OX15 ....30 A4
Nettlebed Com Prim Sch RG9 ....224 B1
Nettlebed Mead OX4 ..142 C1
Nettleton Dr OX25 ....63 B4
Neunkirchen Way OX26 ..81 A4
Neville Way SN7 ....194 C4
Nevis Rd RG31 ....257 B2
New Alms Hos The RG9 254 C4
New Bldgs SN7 ....211 B4
New Close La OX28 ....117 C3
New Coll OX1 ....123 B1
New Coll Sch OX1 ....123 B1
New College La OX1 ..123 B1
New College Sq OX25 ..48 C1
New Cross Rd OX3 ....124 C2
New High St OX3 ....124 B1
New Hill RG8 ....257 B3
New Hinksey CE Fst Sch OX1 ....141 B3
New Inn Hall St OX1 ..123 B1
New Inn Rd OX3 ....111 A1
New Marston Fst Sch OX3 ....124 A3
New Pl OX17 ....4 C1
New Pond La OX5 ....95 A3
New Rd Adderbury OX17 ..22 C2
Bampton OX18 ....134 C2
Banbury OX16 ....16 B3
Bledington OX7 ....54 B1
Bletchingdon OX5 ....93 A4
Charney Bassett OX12 ..175 C1
Childrey OX12 ....213 A3
East Hagbourne OX11 ..219 A3
Great Tew OX7 ....45 B4
Hailey OX29 ....104 A3
Kingham OX7 ....54 C2
Long Hanborough OX29 ..90 A1
Marcham OX13 ....178 B3
Milcombe OX15 ....21 A1
Oxford OX1 ....123 A1
Radley OX14 ....160 C1
Ratley OX15 ....2 A2
Shiplake RG9 ....255 A2
Shotteswell OX17 ....8 B4
Shrivenham SN6 ....209 C2
Stokenchurch HP14 ....188 C2
Wallingford OX10 ....221 B4
Warborough OX10 ....203 A3
Watlington OX49 ....186 A1
Woodstock OX20 ....91 A3
Wootton OX20 ....75 B4
New Row Ambrosden OX25 81 B2
Bucknell OX27 ....64 C4
New St Abingdon OX14 ..179 C4
Bicester OX26 ....65 C2
Chipping Norton OX7 ....42 C2
Deddington OX15 ....33 C2
Henley-on-T RG9 ....244 C1
New Town Cotts SN6 ..227 B2
New Town La SN6 ....227 B2
New Yatt La OX29 ....104 C4
New Yatt Rd OX28,OX29 .104 B2
Newalls Rise RG10 ....255 C1
Newbery Cl RG31 ....257 B1
Newbold Cl OX16 ....16 C2
Newbury Rd OX12 ....216 C3
Newbury St OX12 ....214 B2
Newcombe Cl OX15 ....21 A1
Newells Cl OX44 ....163 B1
Newfield Rd RG4 ....252 C3
Newgate Rd OX5 ....95 C3
Newington Rd OX44 ....163 B1
Newland OX28 ....104 B1
Newland Cl OX29 ....120 C4
Newland Mill OX28 ....104 B1
Newland Pl OX16 ....16 B3
Newland Rd OX16 ....16 B3
Newland St OX29 ....120 C4
Newlands Ave
Didcot OX11 ....218 C4
Reading RG4 ....259 A2
Newlands Dr OX12 ....196 B1
Newlands La RG9 ....242 A3
Newlin Cl OX4 ....141 C2
Newman Ct Oxford OX4 .123 C1
Witney OX29 ....103 B1
Newman La OX14 ....179 A1
Newman Rd OX4 ....142 A2
Newmans Cl OX11 ....218 B2
Newmill La OX29 ....103 C1
Newnham Gn OX10 ....221 C4
Newnhamhill Bottom RG9 ....242 A3
Newport Cl OX5 ....108 B4
Newport Rd RG1 ....259 A1
Newport Terr 14 OX26 ..65 C1
Newtec Pl OX4 ....141 C4
Newton Ave RG4 ....259 B3
Newton Rd OX1 ....141 B4
Newton Way OX10 ....204 A3
Newtown OX10 ....240 B4
Newtown Gdns RG9 ....254 C4
Newtown Rd RG9 ....254 C4
Niagara Rd RG9 ....254 C4
Nicholas Ave OX3 ....123 C2
Nicholas Rd RG9 ....254 A4
Nicholson Rd OX3 ....123 C2
Nigel Ct NN13 ....24 A3
Nightingale Ave OX4 ..142 C1
Nightingale La SN6 ....208 A3
Nightingale Pl OX26 ....81 A4
Nine Acres Cl OX7 ....73 A2
Nine Acres La OX7 ....73 A2
Nineteenth St OX11 ....217 A1
Ninety Cut Hill OX18 ..102 A2
Ninth Ave OX3 ....142 C4
Ninth St OX11 ....217 A1
Nire Rd RG4 ....259 C1
Nixon Rd OX4 ....141 C3
Nizewell Head OX25 ....62 A4
Noble Rd RG9 ....254 C4
Nobles Cl Grove OX12 ..196 B1
N Hinksey Village OX2 ..140 A4
Nobles La OX2 ....140 A4
Nor Brook Cl OX14 ....160 B1
Norcot Rd RG30 ....258 A1
Norcotts Kiln Cotts HP18 98 A1
Norfolk Cl OX14 ....160 C1
Norfolk St OX1 ....141 B4
Norham End OX2 ....123 B2
Norham Gdns OX2 ....123 B2
Norham Rd OX2 ....123 B2
Norman Ave
Abingdon OX14 ....160 A1
Henley-on-T RG9 ....244 C1
Norman Pl RG1 ....259 A1
Norman Rd RG4 ....259 B2
Norman Smith Rd 20 OX4 ....142 C1
Norman Way OX10 ....221 B4
Normandy Cres OX4 ..142 C3
Norreys Ave OX1 ....141 B3
Norreys Cl OX11 ....218 B4
Norreys Rd Cumnor OX2 .139 C3
Didcot OX11 ....218 B4
Norries Dr OX10 ....203 B1
Norris Cl Abingdon OX14 .160 B1
Adderbury OX17 ....22 C1
Norris Rd OX25 ....96 C4
North Aston Rd OX25 ....47 B3
North Ave OX14 ....160 A1
North Bar Pl OX16 ....16 B3
North Bar St OX16 ....16 B3
North Bush Furlong OX11 ....201 A1
North Cl OX9 ....145 C4
North Croft OX11 ....218 C3
North Dr Grove OX12 ..196 C1
Harwell OX11 ....217 B2
North Gn OX12 ....196 C4
North Hill HP18 ....98 A1
North Hinksey CE Prim Sch OX2 ....140 C4
North Hinksey La OX2 ..140 C4
North Hinksey Village OX2 ....140 C4
North Kidlington Prim Sch OX5 ....92 C1
North La OX25 ....79 A1
North Leigh Bsns Pk OX29 ....105 B4
North Leigh CE Sch OX29 ....105 A3
North Leigh Roman Villa★ OX29 ....89 B2
North Lodge OX2 ....122 B1
North Manor Estate The OX44 ....143 C1
North Mill Rd HP27 ....149 C3
North Oxfordshire Coll OX16 ....16 A3
North Parade Ave OX2 .123 B2
North Pl OX3 ....124 B2
North Quay OX14 ....179 C2
North Rd Didcot OX11 ..200 B1

North Rd *continued*
Moulsford OX10 238 C2
North Side OX25 48 A1
North St Aston OX18 135 C2
Banbury OX16 16 C4
Bicester OX26 65 C1
Fritwell OX27 49 C4
Islip OX5 93 C1
Marcham OX13 178 B3
Middle Barton OX7 60 C4
Oxford OX2 123 A1
Reading RG4 259 A1
Thame OX9 129 C1
Watchfield SN6 191 B1
North Way
Cutteslowe OX2 109 A1
Oxford OX3 124 C2
Steventon OX13 198 C2
Northampton Rd OX1 141 B3
Northbourne CE Prim Sch
OX11 218 C4
Northbourne Ct OX11 218 C4
Northbrook Ho 29 OX4 142 C1
Northbrook Rd RG4 259 B3
Northcot La OX16 16 A4
Northcourt La OX14 160 A1
Northcourt Rd OX14 159 C1
Northcourt Wlk OX14 180 A4
Northern By-pass Rd
Cutteslowe OX2 108 C1
Oxford OX3 124 B3
Northern Ho Sch OX2 123 A4
Northfield Ave RG9 255 A2
Northfield Cl OX4 142 B1
Northfield Ct RG9 244 B2
Northfield End RG9 244 B2
Northfield Rd
Abingdon OX14 160 A2
Oxford OX3 124 C2
Reading RG1 259 A1
Shiplake RG9 255 A2
Northfield Sch OX4 142 B1
Northford Cl SN6 209 B4
Northford Hill SN6 209 B4
Northford Ind Est SN6 209 B4
Northmead La OX12 196 A4
Northmoor Pk OX29 138 B1
Northmoor Rd OX2 123 B3
Northolt Rd OX18 115 C2
Northumberland Ct 4
OX16 16 C3
Northview Cty Prim Sch
SN6 190 A4
Northwood Cres OX18 115 C2
Northwood Rd OX29 103 B1
Norton Cl OX3 124 B1
Norton Pk OX7 42 C2
Norton Terr OX29 102 B4
Norton Way OX18 115 C2
Norwood Ave OX13 156 C1
Nosworthy Way OX10 221 C3
Nottwood La RG9 242 A3
Nourse Cl OX3 110 A3
Nowell Rd OX4 141 C2
Nuffield Cl Bicester OX26 65 C2
Didcot OX11 219 A4
Nuffield Coll Oxford OX1 123 A1
Oxford OX1 123 B1
Nuffield Dr OX16 16 A4
Nuffield Hill RG9 223 B2
Nuffield Ind Est OX4 142 B1
Nuffield La OX10 222 C3
Nuffield Orthopaedic Ctr
OX3 124 B1
Nuffield Rd OX3 124 C1
Nuffield Way OX14 179 B4
Nun's Acre RG8 249 A4
Nuneham Courtenay
Arboretum OX44 161 C1
Nuneham Sq OX14 179 C4
Nunhide La RG8 256 C1
Nunnery Cl OX4 142 B1
Nunney Brook OX11 200 C2
Nurseries Rd OX5 108 B4
Nursery Cl Oxford OX3 124 B1
Shiplake RG9 255 A2
Nursery Dr OX16 16 B4
Nursery Gdns RG8 257 A3
Nursery La OX16 16 B4
Nursery Rd OX29 105 B4
Nursery The OX14 200 A4
Nursery View SN7 173 A2
Nut Hatch Cotts RG8 241 B2
Nuthatch Cl 1 OX4 142 C1
Nyatt Rd OX14 180 B4
Nye Bevan Cl OX4 142 A4

O

O'Connors Rd OX29 102 C1
Oak Ave OX14 160 C3
Oak Cl OX26 65 C2
Oak Dr OX5 92 C1
Oak End Way OX39 168 B3
Oak Farm Cl OX9 166 A4
Oak La Ambrosden OX25 81 B2
Stanford in the V SN7 194 C3
Oak Rd SN6 191 B1
Oak St GL7 150 B2
Oak Tree Copse RG31 257 C2
Oak Tree Rd RG31 257 B1
Oak Tree Wlk RG8 257 B3
Oakdale Ct 5 OX10 221 B4
Oakdene RG8 250 C4
Oakdown Cl RG8 250 C2
Oakes La OX2 121 B1
Oakey Cl OX18 133 B3
Oakfield Ind Est OX29 120 B3
Oakfield Pl OX28 118 A4
Oakfield Rd OX18 115 B1
Oakham Cl RG31 257 B1
Oakham Rd GL56 27 A1
Oakland Cl OX29 105 C4
Oakland Rd OX16 16 B1
Oaklands OX2 121 A2
Oakley Ho OX13 158 B1
Oakley La OX39 168 A3
Oakley Rd Chinnor OX39 168 B3
Horton-cum-S OX33 112 B3
Reading RG4 258 C2
Oaks Rd RG9 255 A2
Oaksmere OX13 158 A3
Oakthorpe Pl OX2 123 A3
Oakthorpe Rd OX2 123 A3
Oasis Pk OX29 120 B3
Oathurst Est OX18 134 C2
Oatland Rd OX11 218 C4
Oatlands Rd OX2 122 C1
Observatory Cl OX10 204 A2
Observatory St OX2 123 A2
Ock Dr OX10 182 B3
Ock Mews 9 OX14 179 C4
Ock Mill Cl OX14 179 B3
Ock St OX14 179 C3
Ockley Brook OX11 201 A1
Octavian Way NN13 24 A4
Oddley La HP27 169 B4
Odiham Ave RG4 259 C3
Odiham Cl OX18 115 C2
Offas Cl OX10 204 A3
Ogbourne Cl OX12 214 A3
Old Arncott Rd OX25 81 B2
Old Bakery The 2 OX1 123 A1
Old Barn Cl Benson OX10 204 A2
Reading RG4 259 A3
Old Barn Gnd OX3 142 C4
Old Bath Rd RG4 260 B1
Old Bix Rd RG9 243 C4
Old Blackalls Dr OX10 221 A2
Old Bldgs 18 OX10 221 B4
Old Bourne OX11 200 C2
Old Bridge Rd OX15 21 C2
Old Burford Rd OX7 54 B1
Old Chapel Cl OX5 92 C1
Old Coachyard The
OX28 104 A1
Old Copse Gdns RG4 252 C3
Old Council Hos The
Horley OX15 8 A2
South Newington OX15 31 C4
Old Croft Cl OX39 167 C2
Old Dashwood Hill
HP14 189 C1
Old Farm Cl
Abingdon OX14 180 B4
Worminghall HP18 127 B3
Old Farm Cres RG31 257 B1
Old Field OX44 164 A4
Old Forge Cl OX7 54 B1
Old Forge Rd OX7 29 A2
Old Foundry The OX14 179 C3
Old George Yd OX18 100 C3
Old Glebe OX15 20 B4
Old Greyfriars St OX1 141 B4
Old Grimsbury Rd OX16 16 C4
Old High St OX3 124 B2
Old Kiln* RG9 224 C1
Old Kiln The RG9 224 C1
Old London Rd
Benson OX10 204 A2
Tiddington OX9 145 C2
Wheatley OX33 144 B4
Chipping Norton OX7 56 B4
Old Luxters Farm Brewery*
HP14 226 C4
Old Maltings The 2 OX9 129 C1
Old Manor Ct OX12 214 A1
Old Marston Rd OX3 123 C2
Old Mill Cl OX12 196 C1
Old Mill The RG8 256 B3
Old Moor OX14 199 B3
Old Moor Cl OX10 221 B4
Old Nursery View OX1 141 B2
Old Orch OX39 149 C1
Old Parr Cl OX16 16 B3
Old Parr Rd OX16 16 B3
Old Place Yd OX26 65 C1
Old Plough Wlk OX15 33 A2
Old Pound The OX13 159 A3
Old Rd
East Hendred OX12 216 C3
Great Tew OX7 45 B4
Oxford OX3 124 C1
Ratley OX15 2 A2
Wheatley OX33 143 C4
Old Reading Rd OX10 221 C3
Old Rectory OX25 48 C1
Old Rectory Ct OX26 80 A2
Old Sawmills Rd SN7 172 C1
Old School Cl
Bicester OX27 65 C4
Stokenchurch HP14 188 C2
Old School End OX15 30 A4
Old School Ho The OX7 70 A1
Old School La OX12 213 C3
Old School Pl OX16 16 C3
Old School The OX4 142 B3
Old Stables The OX3 124 B2
Old Stables Yd OX12 214 A1
Old Station Yd OX14 179 C4
Old Town NN13 24 A4
Old Wallingford Way
OX14 200 A4
Old Warehouse Flats The
OX28 104 B1
Old Well Ct RG4 260 B2
Old Wharf Rd SN7 210 B4
Old Windmill Way HP18 129 B4
Old Witney Rd OX29 120 B4
Oldean Cl RG31 257 B1
Oliver Rd OX4 142 C3
One End La OX10 203 C2
Onley Ct 23 OX1 141 B4
Onslow Dr OX9 130 A1
Onslow Gdns RG4 259 B2
Oracle Parkway RG6 260 A1
Orange Cl SN6 190 A3
Oratory Prep Sch The
RG8 250 B3
Oratory Sch The RG8 251 A4
Orchard Ave RG4 252 C3
Orchard Cl
Abingdon OX14 160 A1
Banbury OX16 16 A3
Buckland SN7 174 C4
Cassington OX29 107 B1
Chalgrove OX44 184 B4
Charney Bassett OX12 175 C1
Combe OX29 90 A2
Didcot OX11 200 C1
East Hanney OX12 197 A3
East Hendred OX12 216 B4
Eynsham OX29 120 C4
Henley-on-T RG9 244 C1
Lechlade GL7 150 B2
Purley on T RG31 257 B2
Salford OX7 41 C2
Shiplake RG9 254 C1
Thame OX9 148 A4
Upton OX11 218 B1
Wallingford OX10 221 B3
Warborough OX10 203 A4
Wheatley OX33 144 A4
Orchard Combe RG8 250 B2
Orchard Cotts OX7 57 A1
Orchard Ct OX4 142 A2
Orchard Field RG4 252 B3
Orchard Field La OX20 91 B2
Orchard Furlong OX12 213 B2
Orchard Gdns OX12 213 B3
Orchard Gr Bloxham OX15 21 B2
Reading RG4 259 C2
Orchard Ground OX7 69 B1
Orchard Haven OX10 202 B4
Orchard Hill SN7 172 C2
Orchard La Cropredy OX17 4 C1
East Hendred OX12 216 B3
Upper Heyford OX25 62 C4
Wootton (Oxford) OX1 140 B1
Orchard Meadow Fst Sch
OX4 142 C1
Orchard Piece OX17 4 A2
Orchard Pl
Upper Heyford OX25 62 C4
Westbury NN13 25 A2
Orchard Rd Ardley OX27 50 A2
Buckland SN7 174 C4
Hook Norton OX15 30 A4
N Hinksey Village OX2 140 A4
Orchard Rise
Burford OX18 100 C2
Chesterton OX26 79 C4
Orchard Row OX18 100 C3
Orchard The
Appleton OX13 158 A4
East Challow OX12 214 A3
Merton OX25 95 B4
Orchard View OX17 4 C1
Orchard Way
Banbury OX16 16 A3
Bicester OX26 65 B2
Chinnor OX39 168 B3
Harwell OX11 217 B4
Kidlington OX5 108 C4
Kingham OX7 54 C2
Marcham OX13 178 B3
Middle Barton OX7 46 C1
Oxford OX4 142 B2
Wantage OX12 214 C2
Witney OX28 118 A4
Orchard Wlk OX49 186 B1
Orchid Cl OX26 65 C3
Orchid Ct OX14 180 B4
Orchids The OX11 235 B4
Ordnance Rd OX11 200 B1
Oregon Ave RG31 257 B2
Oriel Coll OX1 123 B1
Oriel Ct OX11 219 A4
Oriel Sq OX1 123 B1
Oriel St OX1 123 B1
Oriel Way OX26 65 C2
Orkney Pl OX28 117 C4
Ormerod Sch OX3 125 A2
Ormond Rd Thame OX9 130 A1
Wantage OX12 214 C2
Orpine Cl OX26 65 B3
Orpwood Way OX14 179 B3
Orwell Cl RG4 258 C2
Orwell Dr OX11 201 A1
Osberton Rd OX2 123 A4
Osborne Cl Bicester OX26 65 B2
Cutteslowe OX2 122 C4
Kidlington OX5 108 B4
Osiers The OX10 183 A3
Osler Rd OX3 124 B2
Osney Cl OX15 30 A4
Osney La OX1 123 A1
Osney Mead OX2 141 A4
Osney Mead Ind Est
OX2 141 A4
Osney Mews OX2 123 A1
Osprey Cl OX26 81 A4
Osterley Dr RG4 259 C3
Osterley Gr OX16 16 A2
Oswestry Rd OX1 141 B3
Otmoor La Beckley OX3 111 A2
Charlton-on-O OX5 95 A2
Otters Reach OX1 141 C1
Ottery Way OX11 201 A1
Otwell Cl OX14 160 A1
Our Lady's Convent Senior
Sch OX14 180 A4
Our Lady's RC Fst Sch
OX4 142 B3
Ouse Cl OX11 200 C2
Ouseley Cl OX3 123 C2
Outmoor View OX25 95 B4
Outram Rd OX4 142 A3
Oval The Bicester OX26 65 B2
Didcot OX11 200 B1
Oxford OX4 142 A2
Over Norton Rd OX7 42 C2
Overbrooke Gdns OX4 143 A1
Overdale Cl OX3 124 C2
Overdown Rd RG31 257 B1
Overlanders End RG31 257 C2
Overmead OX14 179 C2
Overmead Gn OX4 142 C1
Overstrand Cl OX26 66 A2
Overthorpe Prep Sch
OX17 17 B4
Overthorpe Rd OX16 16 C3
Overton Dr OX9 130 A1
Owlington Cl OX2 122 B1
Ox Cl OX14 180 A4
Oxen Piece OX44 145 B1
Oxeye Ct OX4 161 C4
Oxford Brookes Univ
OX3 124 A1
Oxford Brookes Univ Sch of
Occupational Therapy
OX3 124 B1
Oxford Bsns Ctr The
OX1 141 A4
Oxford Bsns Pk OX2 109 A1
Oxford Bsns Pk N OX4 142 B3
Oxford Bsns Pk S OX4 142 B2
Oxford Cl OX5 77 C2
Oxford Coll of F Ed OX1 141 A4
Oxford Cres OX11 218 B4
Oxford High Sch For Girls
OX2 123 B3
Oxford Hill OX28,OX29 118 B4
Oxford La OX12 196 C1
Oxford Rd
Abingdon OX13, OX14 160 A3
Adderbury OX17 23 A2
Banbury OX15,OX16 16 B2
Benson OX10 203 C2
Bicester OX25,OX26 80 B4
Bletchingdon OX5 93 A4
Burford OX18 100 C2
Clifton Hampden OX14 181 C3
Cumnor OX2 139 C3
Cutteslowe OX2 109 A2
Deddington OX15 33 C1
Dorchester OX10 182 B1
Enstone OX7 58 C3
Eynsham OX29 120 C4
Garsington OX4,OX44 143 B1
Hampton Poyle OX5 93 A2
Kennington OX1 160 A3
Kidlington OX5 108 C4
Kirtlington OX5 77 C2
Marston OX3 123 C3
Middleton Stoney OX25 64 A2
North Aston OX25 47 C3
Oxford OX4 142 C2
Oxford, Littlemore OX4 142 A2
Oxford, Temple Cowley
OX4 142 B3
Reading RG30 258 A1
Stokenchurch HP14 188 B3
Thame OX9 147 C4
Tiddington OX9 145 C3
Woodcote RG8 240 C1
Woodstock OX20 91 B3
Oxford Science Pk OX4 142 A1
Oxford Spires Bsns Pk
OX5 92 A2
Oxford Sq SN6 191 B1
Oxford St Reading RG4 259 A1
Woodstock OX20 91 A3
Oxford Utd FC OX4 142 B1
Oxford Univ Botanic Gdns*
OX1 123 B2
Oxford Univ Inst Of
Experimental Psychology
OX1 123 B1
Oxford Upper Sch OX4 142 A4
Oxhey Hill OX17 4 B2
Oxhey Rise OX15 31 A4
Oxlease OX28 118 B4
Oxlip Cl OX26 65 B2
Oxon Pl SN6 227 B2
Oxpens Rd OX1 141 A4

P

Pack & Prime La RG9 244 B1
Pack La OX7 61 A4
Packhorse La OX13 178 B3
Paddock Cl Benson OX10 204 A2
Chalgrove OX44 184 B4
Sonning RG4 260 C2
Wantage OX12 214 C3
Paddock Farm La OX15 22 B4
Paddock Mews OX13 156 B1
Paddock Rd Ardley OX27 50 A2
Paddock Rd *continued*
Reading RG4 259 B1
Wallingford OX10 221 B4
Paddock The
Chilton OX11 235 B4
Highworth SN6 190 A3
Kennington OX1 160 C4
Longworth OX13 156 B1
Somerton OX25 48 C3
Paddocks The
Bampton OX18 134 C1
Deddington OX15 33 C2
East Hanney OX12 197 A3
Mollington OX17 3 C2
Souldern OX6 35 C2
Yarnton OX5 108 A3
Paddox Cl OX2 123 A4
Paddox The OX2 123 A4
Page Furlong OX10 182 B1
Pages La OX15 7 B3
Pages Orch RG4 252 C3
Paget Rd OX4 142 C3
Pagisters Rd OX14 160 B1
Paines Hill OX25 62 A4
Painswick Cl OX28 103 C1
Painters Cl OX15 21 B2
Palmer Ave OX25 96 C4
Palmer Pl OX14 179 C3
Palmer Rd OX3 124 C1
Palmers OX12 214 C3
Pampas Cl OX18 115 C1
Panbourne Hill RG8 256 B3
Pangbourne Coll RG8 256 A2
Pangbourne Prim Sch
RG8 256 C3
Pangbourne St RG30 258 A1
Panters Rd OX10 221 A1
Paper Mill Cotts OX18 99 B3
Paper Mill La OX11 220 A3
Papist Way OX10 238 C4
Parade The
Kidlington OX5 108 C3
Oxford OX3 124 B2
Paradise La OX15 21 A1
Paradise Mews RG9 244 B1
Paradise Rd RG9 244 B1
Paradise Sq OX1 123 A1
Paradise St OX1 123 A1
Paradise Terr OX7 42 B1
Park Ave Highworth SN6 190 A3
Kidlington OX5 92 B1
Shrivenham SN6 209 B4
Park Cl Avon Dassett CV47 2 C4
Banbury OX16 16 B3
Bladon OX20 91 A2
Cutteslowe OX2 109 A1
Didcot OX11 218 B4
Hanwell OX17 8 C2
Hook Norton OX15 30 A3
Kirtlington OX5 77 C3
Middleton Stoney OX25 64 A2
North Leigh OX29 105 B3
Sonning Common RG4 253 A3
Yarnton OX5 108 A2
Park Cres OX14 179 C4
Park Ct Banbury OX16 16 A3
Thame OX9 148 A4
Park End Bodicote OX15 16 C1
Croughton NN13 36 B4
Park End Cl OX15 16 C1
Park End Ct OX15 16 C1
Park End St OX1 123 A1
Park End Works NN13 36 B4
Park Hill
Hook Norton OX15 30 A4
Wheatley OX33 126 A1
Park Hospl For Children
OX3 124 B1
Park La Appleton OX13 158 A4
Ardington OX12 215 B2
Aston Rowant OX39 167 C2
Bladon OX20 91 A1
Checkendon RG8,RG4 251 C3
Long Hanborough OX29 90 B1
North Newington OX15 15 B2
Stanford in the V SN7 195 A3
Stokenchurch HP14 188 C3
Stonor RG9 225 B3
Swalcliffe OX15 19 C4
Woodstock OX20 91 A3
Park Rd Abingdon OX14 179 C4
Banbury OX16 16 A3
Chipping Norton OX7 42 C2
Combe OX29 90 A3
Didcot OX11 218 B4
Ducklington OX29 118 A2
Faringdon SN7 172 C2
Henley-on-T RG9 244 C1
Hook Norton OX15 30 A4
North Leigh OX29 105 A3
Witney OX28 103 C1
Park Rise OX25 81 B2
Park Side Marcham OX13 178 B3
Woodstock OX20 91 B3
Park St Bladon OX20 91 A1
Charlbury OX7 73 A2
Thame OX9 148 A4
Woodstock OX20 91 A3
Park Terr
East Challow OX12 214 A3
Thame OX9 148 A4
Park The Cumnor OX2 139 C2
Harwell OX11 217 C3
Park Town OX2 123 B2

Rea – St K 279

Reading Rd *continued*
Harwell OX11 217 B3
Kidmore End RG4 252 A2
Pangbourne RG8 256 B3
Streatley RG8 249 A3
Wallingford OX10 221 B2
Woodcote RG8 240 C1
Recreation Rd
Wargrave RG10 255 C1
Woodstock OX20 91 B3
Rectory Cl
Marsh Gibbon OX27 67 C2
Warmington OX17 3 A2
Wendlebury OX26 80 A2
Rectory Cres OX7 60 C4
Rectory Ct OX49 187 A4
Rectory Farm Cl OX12 196 C4
Rectory Gdns OX15 15 B4
Rectory Hill RG9 206 A1
Rectory La
Aston Tirrold OX11 237 C4
Bix RG9 225 B1
Fringford OX27 52 B3
Kingston Bagpuize OX13 176 C4
Letcombe Bassett OX12 231 C4
Lewknor OX9 166 C1
Longworth OX13 156 A2
Middleton Cheney OX17 10 C1
Woodstock OX20 91 A3
Rectory Mdw OX39 168 B4
Rectory Rd
Great Haseley OX44 164 C4
Hook Norton OX15 30 A4
Oxford OX4 141 C4
Reading RG4 259 A1
Streatley RG8 248 B4
Red Bridge Hollow OX1 141 B2
Red Copse Rd OX1 140 C1
Red Cross Rd RG8 249 B3
Red Hill RG9 253 C3
Red House Dr RG4 253 A3
Red House Rd OX15 22 C4
Red La Ewelme RG9,OX49 206 B1
Woodcote RG8 240 B2
Red Lion Dr HP14 188 B3
Red Lion Sq OX1 123 B1
Red Lion St Cropredy OX17 4 C1
Kings Sutton OX17 23 C3
Red Poll Cl OX16 16 A4
Redberry Cl RG4 259 B3
Rede Cl OX3 124 C1
Redland Rd OX3 124 A3
Redlands Cl SN6 190 A2
Redmoor Cl OX4 142 B1
Redmoor Ct OX26 65 B2
Redwing Cl OX26 66 A1
Redwood Cl
Kingston Bagpuize OX13 156 C1
Oxford OX4 143 A1
Redwood Way RG31 257 B2
Reedmace Cl OX4 143 A1
Reedmace Rd OX26 65 C2
Reeds Cl OX12 214 B3
Reema Hos The SN6 190 A1
Regal Ct 13 OX26 65 C1
Regal Way SN7 172 C2
Regency Hts RG4 258 C2
Regent Gdns OX11 219 A4
Regent Mall 5 OX12 214 B2
Regent Mews SN7 172 C2
Regent St OX4 141 C4
Regents Park Coll OX1 123 B1
Regents Riverside 13
RG1 259 A1
Regis Pl OX12 214 A1
Reid Cl OX16 16 A3
Reid Pl OX25 63 A4
Remenham La RG9 244 C2
Remenham Row RG9 244 C1
Remus Gate NN13 24 A3
Remy Pl OX4 141 C3
Renault Ho OX4 141 C3
Rest Harrow 32 OX4 142 C1
Retford Cl RG5 260 C1
Retreat Gdns OX10 221 C4
Retreat La HP14 169 B1
Rewley Abbey Ct OX1 123 A1
Rewley Rd OX1 123 A1
Reynard Ct 3 OX26 65 C1
Reynolds Cl OX7 70 B1
Reynolds Way
Abingdon OX14 179 C3
East Challow OX12 213 C3
Rhigos RG4 258 C3
Rhine Cl RG4 259 B1
Rhodes Ho OX1 123 B1
Richard Gray Ct OX1 123 A1
Richard Nevill Ct 2
RG4 259 B1
Richards La OX2 123 A4
Richards Way OX3 124 C1
Richardson Ct OX4 123 C1
Richens Dr OX18 115 B1
Richfield Ave RG1 258 C1
Richman Gdns OX16 15 C4
Richmere Rd OX11 218 C4
Richmond Rd
Oxford OX1 123 A1
Reading RG4 258 C2
Richmond St OX17 23 C3
Rickyard Cl OX1 123 A1
Rickyard The
Ardington OX12 215 B3
Chalgrove OX44 184 B3
Fulbrook OX18 100 C3
Shutford OX15 14 A3
Riddell Pl OX2 109 A1
Ride The OX13 158 A3
Riders Way OX39 168 B3
Ridge Cl OX16 16 B2
Ridge Hall Cl RG4 258 C2
Ridge The RG8 249 C1
Ridgefield Rd OX4 142 A4
Ridgemont Cl OX2 123 A4
Ridgemount Cl RG31 257 A1
Ridgeway
Wargrave RG10 255 C1
Wootton (Oxford) OX1 140 B1
Ridgeway (YH) The★
OX12 232 B3
Ridgeway CE Prim Sch The
OX12 213 A2
Ridgeway Cl RG9 223 B2
Ridgeway Rd
Didcot OX11 218 C4
Oxford OX3 124 C2
Ridgeway The
Bloxham OX15 21 C2
Nettlebed RG9 224 B1
Reading RG4 259 A2
Wantage OX12 232 B3
Riding La OX29 103 B4
Riding The OX29 86 C1
Ridings Bglws OX29 86 C2
Ridings The Banbury OX16 16 C4
Kidlington OX5 92 B1
Oxford OX3 142 C4
Reading RG4 259 B4
Stonesfield OX29 89 B4
Ridley Rd OX4 142 C3
Riely Cl OX29 90 B1
Riley Cl OX14 179 B3
Riley Dr OX16 15 C4
Riley Ho OX4 142 B2
Rimes Cl OX13 156 C1
Rimmer Cl OX3 123 C3
Ringwood Rd
Oxford OX3 125 A2
Reading RG30 258 A1
Ripley Ave OX29 102 C1
Ripley Rd RG30 258 A1
Ripon Coll OX44 144 A2
Rippington Dr OX3 123 C2
Rise The Adderbury OX17 23 A2
Aston Rowant OX39 167 C2
Islip OX5 93 C1
Reading RG4 259 A2
Rising Hill OX25 48 C1
Rissington Cl RG31 257 C2
Rissington Dr OX28 117 C4
Rivacres RG8 250 C2
River & Rowing Mus★
RG9 244 C1
River Cl OX14 179 C3
River Gdns RG8 257 B3
River Rd RG4 258 B2
River View
Kennington OX1 141 C1
Sandford-on-T OX4 161 A4
Rivermead Rd OX4 141 C2
Rivermead Rehabilitation Ctr
OX1 141 C3
Riverside OX16 16 C3
Riverside Ct Oxford OX1 141 B4
3 Reading RG4 259 A1
Riverside Gdns OX28 104 A1
Riverside Rd OX2 122 C1
Riverview Rd RG8 256 B3
Rivington Glebe GL56 27 A1
Rivy Cl OX14 180 B4
Road Eight OX11 217 A1
Road Eighteen OX11 217 A1
Road Eleven OX11 217 A1
Road Fifteen OX11 217 A1
Road Five OX11 217 A1
Road Four OX11 217 A1
Road Nine OX11 217 A1
Road One OX11 217 A1
Road Six OX11 217 A1
Road Thirteen OX11 217 A1
Road Twelve OX11 217 A1
Road Two OX11 217 A1
Roadside Cotts SN7 171 A3
Robert Palmer Cotts The
RG4 260 B2
Robert Piggott CE Prim Sch
RG10 255 B1
Robert Robinson Ave
OX4 142 B1
Robert Sparrow Gdns
OX10 222 A3
Roberts Cl OX3 125 A2
Robin Hill OX29 90 A2
Robin Pl OX4 142 C1
Robins Cl
Barford St M OX15 32 C3
Great Rollright OX7 29 A2
Robins Field RG8 239 B2
Robins Platt OX39 168 A3
Robins Way OX26 81 A4
Robinson Cl
Blewbury OX11 237 A4
Carterton OX18 115 B2
Robinswood OX16 16 A2
Robsart Pl OX2 139 C2
Rochester Ave RG5 260 C1
Rochester Pl OX7 73 B2
Rochester Way OX17 23 A3
Rochford Gdns OX26 66 A2
Rock Cl OX18 115 B2
Rock Edge OX3 124 B1
Rock Farm La OX4 161 A4
Rock Hill OX7 42 C2
Rock Rd OX18 115 B2
Rock The OX15 32 C3
Rockbourne Gdns RG30 258 A1
Rockhill Farm Ct OX7 42 C2
Rocky La RG9 243 A2
Roding Way OX11 201 A1
Rodney Pl OX13 156 B2
Rodway Rd RG30 257 C1
Roebuck Ct OX11 219 A4
Roebuck Rise RG31 257 B2
Roentgen Ave OX11 217 A1
Rofford La OX44 164 A2
Roger Bacon La 2 OX1 141 B4
Roger Dudman Way
OX1,OX2 123 A1
Rogers St OX2 123 A4
Rokeby Dr RG4 258 B4
Rolfe Pl OX3 124 A2
Rollright Stones★ OX7 28 A1
Rolls Ct OX12 214 B3
Roman Pl OX11 200 B1
Roman Rd OX33 144 B4
Roman Way Beckley OX3 111 A2
Bicester OX26 65 C1
Brackley NN13 24 A4
Lechlade GL7 150 B3
Oxford OX4 142 C3
Wantage OX12 214 B3
Roman Wlk SN6 191 C1
Romany Cl RG30 258 A1
Romany La RG30 258 A1
Romney Rd OX16 8 C1
Romsey Rd RG30 258 A1
Romulus Way NN13 24 A3
Rookery Cl
Abingdon OX13 159 A1
Bodicote OX15 22 C4
Rookery Ho OX44 143 C1
Rookery The OX5 92 B1
Rookery Way OX26 65 B2
Rooks La OX9 147 C4
Roosevelt Dr OX3 124 B1
Roosevelt Rd OX29 106 A4
Rope Way OX15 30 A3
Rope Wlk OX16 16 B3
Roper Rd OX25 63 B4
Rosamund Dr OX20 91 A4
Rosamund Rd OX2 122 C4
Rose Ave OX14 159 C2
Rose Cl Bucknell OX27 64 C4
Carterton OX18 115 B1
Rose Cnr HP14 188 C3
Rose Ct 6 OX4 142 A2
Rose Gdns OX2 140 B4
Rose Hill OX4 142 A2
Rose Hill Fst Sch OX4 142 A2
Rose La OX1 123 B1
Rose Pl OX1 141 B4
Rosebay Cres OX12 214 B4
Rosebery Rd RG4 258 B4
Rosedale Ave OX16 9 A1
Rosehill Ho RG4 259 B4
Rosehill Pk RG4 259 B4
Rosemary Ct OX4 141 C4
Rosemary La OX18 134 C2
Rosemead Ave RG31 257 A2
Roses La OX7 41 C3
Rosina Wlk OX16 9 A1
Ross Rd 11 RG4 259 A1
Rossendale Rd RG4 259 B2
Rotha Field Rd OX2 109 A1
Rother Garth OX11 201 A2
Rother Rd OX16 8 C1
Rotherfield Rd RG9 254 C4
Rotherfield Way RG4 259 A2
Rothwell Gdns RG5 260 C1
Rothwell Wlk RG4 259 B1
Rothwells Cl OX10 221 A1
Rotten Row OX10 182 B1
Round Close Rd
Adderbury OX17 22 C2
Hook Norton OX15 30 A4
Roundham Cl OX5 92 B1
Roundhead Dr OX9 129 C1
Roundhill Rd OX17 4 A2
Roundhills Mead SN6 190 A4
Roundtown OX17 35 B4
Roundway The OX3 124 C2
Rouses La GL7 132 A3
Rousham Pk★ OX25 62 A3
Rousham Rd OX5 77 B4
Routh Rd OX3 124 C2
Roves La SN6 208 A4
Row La RG4 259 C4
Row The Bletchingdon OX5 93 A4
Hinton Waldrist SN7 155 C1
Lechlade GL7 150 C4
Lyneham OX7 70 B3
Mollington OX17 3 C2
Stanton Harcourt OX29 138 A4
Wootton OX20 75 B4
Rowallan Cl RG4 259 B3
Rowan Cl Carterton OX18 115 B2
Kidlington OX5 108 C4
Sonning Common RG4 252 C2
Rowan Gr OX4 143 A1
Rowan Rd OX26 65 C2
Rowans The OX10 220 C1
Rowel Dr OX5 92 A1
Rowell Way OX7 42 C2
Rowland Cl
Cutteslowe OX2 122 C4
Wallingford OX10 203 B1
Rowland Rd OX10 221 A2
Rowlands Ho OX3 125 A2
Rowles Cl OX1 141 C1
Rowles Paddock RG20 235 A1
Rowney Pl OX4 142 A2
Rowstock OX11 217 A4
Roxburgh Dr OX11 200 B2
Royal Berkshire Ct
OX11 218 C4
Royal Mans RG9 244 C1
Royal Military Coll of Science
SN6 209 C4
Ruck Keene Cl OX26 65 B1
Rufus Isaacs Rd RG4 259 A1
Rugge Furlong OX11 201 A1
Rumbolds Cl OX10 203 C3
Rumsey's La OX11 237 A4
Rupert Cl RG9 244 C2
Rupert House Sch RG9 244 C1
Rupert Rd
Chalgrove OX44 184 B3
Oxford OX4 142 C3
Rupert Way OX9 130 A1
Rupert's La RG9 244 C2
Ruscote Arc OX16 16 A4
Ruscote Ave OX16 16 A4
Ruscote Sq OX16 16 A4
Rush Common Cty Prim Sch
OX14 160 A1
Rushall Rd OX9 130 A1
Rushbeds Wood Nature
Reserve★ HP18 98 B2
Rushmead Copse OX14 160 B1
Ruskin Ave OX14 179 C3
Ruskin Cl OX11 219 A4
Ruskin Coll Oxford OX1 123 A1
Oxford,Headington OX3 124 B2
Ruskin Rd OX16 16 B2
Ruskin Wlk OX26 65 C2
Russell Ct OX2 123 A2
Russell Jackson Cl
OX10 182 B3
Russell Rd RG4 258 B4
Russell St OX2 123 A1
Russet Ave GL7 150 C2
Russet Cl RG4 252 C3
Russet Glade RG4 259 B4
Russet Rd OX27 50 B2
Rutherfield Cl OX14 160 A1
Rutherford Ave OX11 217 A2
Rutherway OX2 123 A2
Rutten La OX5 108 A3
Rutters Cl OX5 108 B4
Rycote La OX9 146 B3
Rycotewood Coll OX9 129 C1
Rydal Ave RG30 257 C1
Ryder Cl OX5 108 A3
Rydes Cl OX15 22 C4
Rydes The OX15 22 C4
Rye Cl OX16 8 C1
Rye Grass OX20 91 B3
Rye St Antony Sch OX3 124 A2
Ryecote Chapel★ OX9 146 B3
Ryecroft Cl Sonning RG5 260 C1
Wargrave RG10 255 C1
Rymans Cres OX11 219 A3
Rymers La OX4 142 A3

S

Sackville Cl OX17 8 C2
Sacred Heart RC Prim Sch
RG9 244 B1
Sadler Wlk OX1 141 A4
Sadlers Croft OX44 143 C1
Sadlers Ct OX14 160 A2
Sadlers The RG31 257 A1
Saffron Cl OX26 65 B3
Saffron Ct OX14 180 A4
Sage Rd RG31 257 B2
Sage Wlk 13 OX4 142 C1
St Alban's Ct 13 OX10 221 B4
St Aldates OX1 141 B4
St Aloysius RC Fst Sch
OX2 123 A2
St Amand Dr OX14 179 C3
St Amand's RC Prim Sch
OX12 216 C3
St Andrew's CE Inf Sch
OX39 168 B4
St Andrew's CE Prim Sch
OX39 168 B4
St Andrew's La OX3 124 B2
St Andrew's Rd
Chinnor OX39 168 B3
Didcot OX11 218 C4
Henley-on-T RG9 254 B4
Oxford OX3 124 B2
St Andrews CE Fst Sch
OX3 124 B2
St Andrews Cl OX14 160 B1
St Andrews Ct OX9 147 C4
St Andrews Ho OX39 168 B3
St Andrews Rd RG4 258 C2
St Anne's Cl RG9 244 B1
St Anne's Coll OX2 123 B2
St Anne's Rd
Banbury OX16 16 B2
Oxford OX3 124 B1
St Annes Cl OX26 65 C2
St Annes Ct OX11 219 A4
St Annes RC Prim Sch
RG4 259 A1
St Annes Rd RG4 259 A1
St Anthony's Wlk OX26 66 A2
St Antonys Coll OX2 123 A2
St Augustine of Canterbury
RC/CE Upper Sch OX4 141 C3
St Barnabas CE Fst Sch
OX2 123 A1
St Barnabas Rd RG4 259 A3
St Barnabas St OX2 123 A1
St Bernard's Rd OX2 123 A2
St Birinus Ct GL7 150 B3
St Birinus Sch
Didcot OX11 218 C4
Dorchester OX10 182 B1
St Catherine's Coll OX1 123 C1
St Catherines Ho OX4 123 C1
St Christopher's CE Fst Sch
OX4 142 B3
St Christopher's CE Prim Sch
GL7 132 B1
St Christopher's Pl OX4 142 B3
St Clement's St OX4 123 C1
St Cristopher Cotts SN7 172 C2
St Cross Bldg OX1 123 B1
St Cross Rd OX1 123 B1
St David's Ct NN13 24 A4
St Davids Cl RG4 258 C3
St Denys Cl SN7 194 C4
St Ebbe's CE Fst Sch
OX1 141 B4
St Ebbes St 3 OX1 141 B4
St Edburg's Cl OX26 65 B1
St Edburg's Prim Sch
OX26 65 C1
St Edith's Way OX26 65 B1
St Edmund's La 5
OX14 179 C3
St Edmund's RC Prim Sch
OX14 180 A4
St Edward's Ave OX2 123 A4
St Edwards Ct OX2 123 A3
St Edwards Sch OX2 123 A4
St Francis CE Fst Sch
OX4 142 C3
St Francis Ct OX3 142 C4
St Francis Rd HP14 189 B2
St Frideswides Ct OX11 218 C4
St George's Cl OX10 220 C1
St George's Cres OX16 16 B2
St George's Pl OX1 123 B1
St George's Rd SN7 154 B1
St Georges Gate 6
OX1 123 A1
St Georges Gn OX10 203 B1
St Georges Rd OX10 221 B4
St Giles OX5 93 A4
St Giles Cl OX26 80 A2
St Giles' OX1 123 B1
St Helen's Ave OX10 203 C2
St Helen's Cres OX10 204 A2
St Helen's Ct OX14 179 C3
St Helen's Mews 6
OX14 179 C3
St Helen's Pas OX1 123 B1
St Helen's Way OX10 203 C2
St Helen's Wharf OX14 179 C3
St Hilda's Cl OX26 65 C2
St Hilda's Coll OX4 141 C4
St Hildas Cl OX11 219 A4
St Hugh's Cl
Bicester OX26 65 C2
Stokenchurch HP14 188 C2
St Hugh's Coll OX2 123 A2
St Hugh's Pl HP14 188 C2
St Hugh's Sch SN7 174 A4
St Hughs Cl OX16 16 B2
St Hughs Rise OX11 219 A4
St Ives La OX12 214 C4
St Ives Rd OX12 214 C4
St James OX12 214 B3
St James Cl RG8 256 B3
St James Ct OX29 89 B4
St James Rd OX14 160 C2
St James Terr OX14 160 C1
St James View OX12 197 A3
St James' Tutorial Unit
OX4 142 A2
St John Fisher RC Fst Sch
OX4 142 B2
St John St OX1 123 B1
St John's Cl Didcot OX11 219 A4
Fyfield OX13 157 A1
St John's Coll OX1 123 B1
St John's Ct
12 Banbury OX16 16 B3
Grove OX12 196 C1
St John's Gn OX10 221 B3
St John's Prim Sch
OX10 221 B4
St John's RC Prim Sch
OX16 16 C2
St John's Rd
Abingdon OX14 180 A4
Banbury OX16 16 B3
Grove OX12 196 C1
Reading RG4 259 B1
Wallingford OX10 221 B4
St John's Row OX14 201 B4
St John's St Bicester OX26 65 C1
Lechlade GL7 150 B2
St John's Terr 6 OX10 221 B4
St John's Way OX15 33 A2
St Johns Dr
Carterton OX18 115 C2
Kidlington OX5 92 C1
St Johns Rd OX5 77 B3
St Joseph's RC Fst Sch
OX3 124 A2
St Joseph's RC Prim Sch
OX16 15 C3
St Joseph's RC Prim Sch
OX18 115 B1
St Joseph's RC Prim Sch
OX9 147 C4
St Katherine's Rd RG9 254 B4

St Kenelm's CE Prim Sch OX29 102 C1
St Kenelm's Cl OX29 102 C1
St Laurence's CE Prim Sch OX10 203 A4
St Lawrence Cl OX10 203 A4
St Lawrence Ho OX10 203 A4
St Lawrence Rd
Lechlade GL7 150 B2
South Hinksey OX1 141 A3
St Lawrence's CE Prim Sch GL7 150 B2
St Leonard's CE Prim Sch OX16 16 C3
St Leonard's Cl OX16 16 C3
St Leonard's Ct OX10 221 B3
St Leonard's La OX10 221 B4
St Leonard's Rd OX3 124 B2
St Leonard's Sq 17 OX10 221 B4
St Leonards Cl OX49 186 A1
St Lucian's La OX10 221 B3
St Luke's Rd OX4 142 B3
St Lukes Ct RG4 259 A2
St Lukes Way RG4 259 A3
St Margaret's Rd OX2 123 A2
St Mark's Rd RG9 254 B4
St Martin's Rd OX4 142 A2
St Martin's St OX10 221 B4
St Martins RC Prim Sch RG4 259 C3
St Mary & John CE Fst Sch OX4 142 A4
St Mary's CE Inf Sch OX28 118 A4
St Mary's CE Prim Sch
Banbury OX16 16 B3
Chipping Norton OX7 42 C1
St Mary's Cl
3 Banbury OX16 16 B3
Bicester OX26 65 B1
Chalgrove OX44 184 B3
Henley-on-T RG9 254 A4
Kidlington OX5 92 C1
Oxford OX4 142 A1
St Mary's Ct OX28 118 A4
St Mary's Gn OX14 159 C1
St Mary's Ho OX33 144 A4
St Mary's La OX7 30 C2
St Mary's Mead OX28 118 A4
St Mary's RC Prim Sch OX26 65 C1
St Mary's Rd
Adderbury OX17 22 C1
East Hendred OX12 216 C3
Oxford OX4 141 C4
St Mary's Sch OX12 214 B2
St Mary's St OX10 221 B4
St Mary's Way OX12 214 B3
St Mary's Wlk OX27 50 B2
St Marys Ave RG8 257 B3
St Marys Cl OX33 144 A4
St Michael's Ave
Abingdon OX14 179 C4
Highworth SN6 190 A3
St Michael's CE Prim Sch OX13 198 C2
St Michael's Cl OX27 52 B3
St Michael's La OX5 107 C4
St Michael's St OX1 123 B1
St Michael's Way OX13 198 C2
St Michaels CE Fst Sch OX3 123 C1
St Michaels Cl OX7 85 B4
St Nicholas CE Inf Sch OX10 203 B1
St Nicholas CE Prim Sch SN8 245 C1
St Nicholas Fst Sch OX3 123 C3
St Nicholas Rd
Oxford OX4 142 B1
Tackley OX5 77 B3
Wallingford OX10 221 B4
St Nicholas' Gn OX14 159 C1
St Nicolas CE Sch OX14 179 C4
St Omer Rd OX4 142 B3
St Paul's Cres OX2 140 B4
St Pauls Arts Ctr★ OX2 123 A1
St Peter's CE Inf Sch OX18 133 B3
St Peter's CE Prim Sch OX29 107 B1
St Peter's Cl
Cassington OX29 107 B1
Stoke Lyne OX27 51 A3
Wootton (Oxford) OX13 159 A3
St Peter's Coll OX1 123 B1
St Peter's Cres OX26 65 C2
St Peter's Pl 22 OX10 221 B4
St Peter's Rd
Abingdon OX14 160 B1
Brackley NN13 24 A4
Cutteslowe OX2 122 C4
Didcot OX11 218 C4
St Peter's St OX10 221 B4
St Peters Ave RG4 258 C2
St Peters Cl OX15 31 C4
St Peters Gate NN13 24 A4
St Peters Hill RG4 258 C2
St Philip & St James CE Fst Sch OX2 123 A2
St Ruald's Cl 10 OX10 221 B4
St Rumbold's Rd OX10 221 B4
St Stephens Cl 6 RG4 259 A1
St Swithun's CE Prim Sch OX1 160 C4
St Swithun's Rd OX1 160 C4
St Thomas Moore RC Sch OX5 108 C4
St Thomas St OX15 33 C2
St Thomas' St OX1 123 A1
St Thomas's Cl SN7 155 C1
Salegate La OX4 142 B3
Salesian Gdns OX4 142 B3
Salesian Ho OX4 142 B3
Salford Rd OX3 123 C2
Salisbury Cres OX2 123 A4
Sallow Cl OX26 65 C3
Salmon Cl OX15 21 C3
Salop Cl SN6 209 A3
Salt La OX9 166 C1
Salter Cl OX1 141 B4
Salters La HP18 98 B4
Salvia Cl OX16 9 A1
Samian Way OX10 202 B4
Samor Way OX11 218 B4
Samphire Rd OX4 142 C1
Samuelson Ct 25 OX16 16 B3
Sand Hill SN6 209 A4
Sand View SN7 172 C1
Sandcroft Rd RG4 258 C3
Sandell Cl OX16 16 B3
Sanderling Cl OX26 81 A4
Sanderling Wlk OX16 16 C2
Sandfield Rd OX3 124 A2
Sandfine Rd OX15 15 A1
Sandford Cl
Abingdon OX14 160 A1
Woodcote RG8 250 C4
Sandford Dr RG5 260 C1
Sandford Gn OX16 15 C4
Sandford La OX1 160 C4
Sandford Mount OX7 73 B2
Sandford Pk OX7 73 B2
Sandford Rd OX4 142 A1
Sandford Rise OX7 73 B2
Sandford St Martin Rd OX7 46 B1
Sandgate Ave RG30 257 C1
Sandhill Rd OX5 108 A4
Sandhills Prim Sch OX3 125 A2
Sandleigh Rd OX13 159 A4
Sandpiper Cl OX26 81 A4
Sandpit Hill MK18 39 C3
Sandpit La RG4 259 C4
Sandringham Dr OX11 219 A4
Sandringham Rd OX17 23 C3
Sands Cl Bletchingdon OX5 93 A4
Cumnor OX2 139 C3
Sands La OX15 31 C4
Sands Rd OX11 219 C3
Sands The Benson OX10 204 B3
Milton-u-W OX7 70 A1
Sands Way OX10 203 C3
Sandy La Beckley OX3 111 A1
Cholsey OX10 220 C1
Kingston Bagpuize OX13 156 C1
Long Crendon HP18 129 A3
Oxford OX4 142 C2
Shrivenham SN6 209 A3
Stanford in the V SN7 174 B2
Tiddington OX9 145 C3
Upper Rissington GL54 68 A2
Wootton (Oxford) OX1 140 B1
Yarnton OX5 108 B4
Sandy La W OX4 142 B2
Sandy Lane Ct GL54 68 A2
Sandy Lane Est OX9 145 C4
Sarajac Ave OX12 213 C2
Sarsden Cl OX7 57 A1
Sarum Cl OX18 115 C2
Satin La OX15 33 C2
Satwell Cl RG9 243 A2
Saunders Cl OX49 186 A1
Saunders Ct RG8 257 A3
Saunders Rd OX4 142 A3
Saunders Wood Copse HP14 188 C2
Savile Rd OX1 123 B1
Savile Way OX12 196 B1
Saw Cl OX44 184 B4
Sawpit Rd OX4 142 C2
Sawpits La GL56 40 A1
Saxel Cl OX18 135 C2
Saxifrage Sq 5 OX4 142 C1
Saxon Cl OX10 221 B4
Saxon Ct Benson OX10 203 C2
Bicester OX26 65 C1
Saxon Orch SN6 191 B1
Saxon Pl OX12 214 A3
Saxon Way Oxford OX3 124 A2
Witney OX28 118 A4
Saxons Heath OX14 201 B4
Saxons Way OX11 219 A4
Saxton Rd OX14 179 C3
Sayers Orch OX11 200 B1
Scafell Cl RG31 257 B1
Scampton Cl OX26 66 A2
Schilling St OX25 63 A4
Schofield Ave OX28 104 A2
Schofield Gdns OX28 104 A2
Schofields Way OX15 21 C3
Scholar Cl SN6 191 C1
Scholar Pl OX2 140 B4
Scholars Acre OX18 115 B2
Scholars Cl RG4 258 C2
Schongau Cl OX14 179 B2
School Cl Ickford HP18 128 A2
Long Compton CV36 27 C3
Longworth OX13 156 B2
Steventon OX13 198 C2
School Cotts RG9 243 B1
School End OX17 35 B4
School Hill
Minster Lovell OX29 102 C2
Mollington OX17 3 C2
Wargrave RG10 255 B1
School La
Appleford OX14 200 C4
Aston Rowant OX49 167 C2
Banbury OX16 16 B3
Black Bourton OX18 133 C3
Chilson OX7 71 C2
Coleshill SN6 191 A4
Great Bourton OX17 9 B4
Harwell OX11 217 C4
Kingston Bagpuize OX13 156 C1
Middleton Stoney OX25 64 A2
Milton OX14 199 B3
Milton, Milton Heights OX14 199 B2
Minster Lovell OX29 102 C2
North Newington OX15 15 B2
Reading RG4 259 A1
Reading, Emmer Green RG4 259 A3
Shabbington HP18 128 B2
Stadhampton OX44 163 B1
Stoke Lyne OX27 51 A3
Stoke Row RG9 241 C2
Upper Heyford OX25 62 C4
Wargrave RG10 255 B1
Warmington OX17 3 A2
School of St Helen & St Katherine OX14 179 B4
School Paddock OX27 64 C4
School Pl OX1 141 B3
School Rd
Ardington OX12 215 B3
Finstock OX7 88 B3
Kidlington OX5 92 C1
West Hanney OX12 196 C3
School View OX16 16 C3
School Yd OX44 163 B1
Schooler's La GL56 40 B2
Scotland End OX15 30 A4
Scotsgrove Cotts OX9 130 A2
Scott Cl Bicester OX26 65 B2
Kidlington OX5 108 B4
Reading RG4 259 A3
Scott Rd OX2 123 A4
Scotts Cnr NN13 25 A2
Scotts La OX27 67 C1
Scours La RG30 258 A1
Scrutton Cl OX3 124 C2
Seacourt Rd OX2 122 B1
Sealham Rd OX29 118 A2
Second Ave OX11 200 B1
Second St
Croughton NN13 36 C3
Harwell OX11 217 B2
Sedgefield Cl RG4 252 C3
Sedgemoor Dr OX9 130 A1
Sedgewell Rd RG4 252 C3
Seelscheid Way OX26 81 A4
Seeson Way OX12 214 B2
Sefton Pl OX15 22 C4
Sefton Rd OX3 124 C2
Segsbury Ct OX12 214 A3
Segsbury Rd OX12 214 A3
Selborne Gdns RG30 258 A1
Sellwood Dr OX18 115 C2
Sellwood Rd OX14 159 C1
Selwyn Cres OX14 160 C1
Send Rd RG4 259 B1
Sermon Cl OX3 124 C1
Setler Ho 1 OX16 16 C3
Setts The SN7 172 C1
Seven Acres
Long Crendon HP18 129 A4
Thame OX9 148 A4
Sevenfields SN6 190 A4
Seventeenth St OX11 217 A1
Seventh Ave OX3 142 C4
Severalls Cl OX10 203 B1
Severn Cl OX26 65 A2
Severn Rd
Abingdon OX13 159 B1
Harwell OX11 217 A1
Sewell Cl OX14 160 B1
Sewell's La OX39 167 C4
Seyer Milward Terr 24 OX10 221 B4
Shackleton Cl 4 OX26 66 A2
Shades The OX16 16 B3
Shadwell Rd OX10 182 B3
Shaftesbury Rd OX3 124 C3
Shakenoak OX29 105 B3
Shakespeare Cl RG4 259 B3
Shakespeare Dr OX26 65 B2
Shakespeare Rd OX29 120 B4
Shannon Cl OX12 196 C1
Shannon Rd OX26 65 A1
Sharland Cl OX12 214 C4
Sharman Beer Ct OX9 147 C4
Sharpey Cotts OX26 66 C1
Shaw Cl OX26 65 B2
Shaw's Copse OX14 160 C1
Sheards La SN7 194 C4
Shearings The OX15 30 A4
Shearwater Dr OX26 81 A4
Sheen Cl OX27 65 C3
Sheep St Bicester OX26 65 C1
Burford OX18 100 C3
Charlbury OX7 73 A2
Highworth SN6 190 A3
Sheep Wlk RG4 259 A2
Sheepwash La OX13 199 A3
Sheepway Ct 2 OX4 142 A2
Sheepways La RG4 258 A4
Sheerstock HP17 130 C3
Sheldon Rd HP18 128 A2
Sheldon Way OX4 142 B2
Sheldonian★ OX1 123 B1
Sheldons Piece OX49 186 A1
Shelford Pl OX3 124 B1
Shelley Cl
Abingdon OX14 160 A1
Banbury OX16 16 A2
9 Bicester OX26 65 B2
Oxford OX3 124 C1
Shelley Rd OX4 142 A3
Shellingford CE Prim Sch SN7 193 C4
Shenington CE Prim Sch OX15 6 C1
Shenington Kart Club★ OX15 6 B1
Shepard Way OX7 42 C2
Shepherd Gdns OX14 179 B3
Shepherds Cl
Grove OX12 196 B1
Sibford Gower OX15 19 A4
Weston-on-the-G OX25 79 A1
Shepherds Hill
Sandford-on-T OX4 142 C1
Sonning RG6 260 B1
Shepherds La RG4 258 B3
Sheraton Dr RG31 257 B1
Sherborne St GL7 150 B2
Sherbourne Rd OX28 117 B4
Sheridan Ave RG4 259 A2
Sheriff's Dr OX2 122 C4
Sherwood Ave OX14 180 A4
Sherwood Cl OX26 66 B1
Sherwood Gdns RG9 254 B4
Sherwood Pl RG8 257 A2
Sherwood Rd OX11 218 B4
Sherwood Rise RG8 257 A3
Shifford La OX29 137 B1
Shilbrook Manor OX18 133 C2
Shillbrook Ave OX18 115 B3
Shilldeane Dr OX18 115 B2
Shilson La OX7 73 A2
Shilton Rd Burford OX18 100 C2
Carterton OX18 115 B2
Ship St OX1 123 B1
Shiplake Bottom RG9 252 C3
Shiplake CE Prim Sch RG9 254 C1
Shiplake Coll RG9 254 C1
Shiplake Sta RG9 255 A2
Shipston Rd CV36 27 C4
Shipton Cl RG31 257 B1
Shipton Rd
Ascott-u-W OX7 71 A1
Shipton-u-W OX7 70 A1
Woodstock OX20 91 B3
Shipton Sta OX7 70 C1
Shirburn Rd OX49 186 B1
Shirburn St OX49 186 B1
Shirelake Cl OX1 141 B4
Shires Bsns Pk The NN13 24 A3
Shires Rd NN13 24 A3
Shirley Pl OX2 123 A2
Shirvell's Hill RG8 250 C4
Shoe La
East Hagbourne OX11 218 C3
Oxford OX1 123 B1
Shooters Hill RG8 256 A3
Short Furlong OX11 201 A1
Short St Pangbourne RG8 256 B3
1 Reading RG4 259 A1
Watchfield SN6 191 B1
Short The RG8 257 B3
Shorte Cl OX3 142 C4
Shortlands Hill OX10 238 B2
Shotover SN7 211 B3
Shotover Ctry Pk★ OX3 125 A1
Shotover Kilns OX3 124 C1
Shotover Trad Est OX3 124 C1
Shrewsbury Pl OX18 134 C2
Shrieves Cl OX14 160 A1
Shrivenham CE Prim Sch SN6 209 A4
Shrivenham Hundred SN6 191 B1
Shrivenham Rd
Highworth SN6 190 A2
Longcot SN7 192 B1
Shrubbery The GL7 150 B2
Shute Ave SN6 209 B4
Shutford Rd
North Newington OX15 15 A2
Tadmarton OX15 20 C4
Sibford Gower Prim Sch OX15 19 A4
Sibford Rd
Hook Norton OX15 30 A4
Shutford OX15 13 C2
Sibford Sch OX15 19 A4
Sideleigh Rd OX15 22 C4
Sidings Ind Est The NN13 24 A4
Sidings Rd OX7 55 C3
Sidney St OX4 141 C4
Signet End OX18 100 C2
Silkdale Cl OX4 142 B3
Silver Birches OX33 125 C4
Silver La OX12 213 B3
Silver Rd OX4 142 A4
Silver St Bourton SN6 209 A1
Chacombe OX17 10 C2
Fernham SN7 193 A2
Tetsworth OX9 166 A4
Wroxton OX15 15 A4
Silverdale Rd RG10 255 C1
Silvermead HP18 127 B3
Silverthorne Dr RG4 258 C3
Simmns Cl OX33 125 B4
Simmonds Wlk OX12 214 B3
Simmons Rd RG9 244 B2
Simmons Way OX9 129 C1
Simon Ho OX3 124 B2
Simon's Cl OX33 144 A4
Simons Cl RG31 257 B2
Simons La OX7 85 B4
Simpsons Way OX1 160 C4
Sinclair Ave OX16 16 A4
Sinclair Dr OX16 16 A4
Singers Cl RG9 254 C4
Singers La RG9 244 C1
Singletree OX4 142 A2
Sinnels Field OX7 85 C4
Sinodum Cl OX14 201 B4
Sinodun Rd Didcot OX11 218 C4
Wallingford OX10 203 B1
Sinodun Row OX14 200 C4
Sinodun View OX10 203 A4
Sint Niklaas Cl OX14 179 B2
Sir Georges La OX17 23 A2
Sir Mortimer's Terr OX14 199 B3
Sires Hill OX10 202 B2
Siskin Rd Bicester OX26 66 A1
Upper Rissington GL54 68 A3
Sixpenny La OX44 184 C3
Sixteenth St OX11 217 A2
Sixth St Croughton NN13 36 C4
Harwell OX11 217 A2
Skarries View RG4 258 B4
Skelton Ct OX4 123 C1
Skene Cl OX3 124 B1
Skerrit Way RG8 257 B2
Skilton Rd RG31 257 B2
Skimmingdish La OX27 65 C3
Skimmingdish Rd OX26 66 A2
Skinner Rd OX26 66 B1
Skippett La OX7 88 A2
Skippon Way 6 OX9 129 C1
Skittle Alley OX17 35 B4
Slade Cl OX3 124 B1
Slade End OX10 202 C2
Slade End Rdbt OX10 203 A1
Slade Farm Cotts OX5 63 A1
Slade Rd Cholsey OX10 221 A1
Didcot OX11 200 B1
Stokenchurch HP14 188 C2
Slade The Charlbury OX7 73 B2
Oxford OX3 142 C4
Slaters Ct OX29 90 A1
Slave Hill HP17 130 C3
Slaymaker Cl OX3 124 C1
Sloan Cl RG8 249 B3
Slopes The RG4 259 B1
Small Ho OX15 19 B4
Smith Barry Cir GL54 68 A2
Smith Barry Cres GL54 68 A2
Smith Barry Rd GL54 68 A2
Smith Cl RG4 252 C3
Smith's Cl OX18 135 C1
Smith's Hill OX12 231 C3
Smiths Farm La OX11 200 B1
Smiths Rickyard OX12 216 B4
Snakehill La OX15 33 A2
Snipe Rd GL54 68 A2
Snowdon Mede OX3 124 A2
Snows La OX33 125 B4
Snowshill Dr OX28 103 B1
Snowsill Dr OX28 117 B4
Snowswick La SN7 170 C3
Snuff La OX17 8 B4
Snuggs La OX12 197 A4
Soane End RG4 259 A4
Soden Pl OX13 156 B1
Soden Rd OX25 63 B4
Sollershott OX2 108 C1
Solters Cl HP18 98 B4
Somerton Rd Ardley OX27 50 A2
North Aston OX25 48 A4
Upper Heyford OX25 48 C1
Somerville OX11 219 A4
Somerville Coll OX2 123 B2
Somerville Ct OX17 23 B2
Somerville Dr OX26 65 C2
Songers Cl OX2 140 A4
Sonning CE Prim Sch RG4 260 B2
Sonning Common Prim Sch RG4 252 C3
Sonning La RG4 260 B1
Sonning Mdws RG4 260 B1
Soot La OX17 3 A2
Sopwith Rd GL54 68 A3
Sorrel Mead OX26 65 B2
Sorrel Rd OX4 143 A1
Sotwell St
Brightwell-cum-S OX10 202 C1
Brightwell-cum-S OX10 203 A1
South Ave
Abingdon OX14 159 C1
Henley-on-T RG9 254 C4
Kidlington OX5 108 C3
South Bank RG8 239 B2
South Bar St OX16 16 B3
South Bridge Row OX1 141 B4
South Cl OX5 108 C3
South Dr Harwell OX11 217 B2
Sonning RG4 260 B1
South End
Great Rollright OX7 29 A2
Haddenham HP17 130 C3
South Gate Ct GL54 68 A2
South Hills HP18 98 A1
South Leigh Rd OX29 119 A4

South Lodge The [8]
OX26 65 C1
South Mdw OX25 81 B2
South Mere OX18 116 B2
South Moreton Sch
OX11 219 C3
South Newington Rd
Barford St M OX15 32 B3
Bloxham OX15 21 A1
South Par OX2 123 A4
South Park Ave OX11 218 B4
South Park Ct [6] OX4 141 C4
South Parks Rd OX1 123 B1
South Row OX11 235 B4
South Side OX25 62 A4
South St Banbury OX16 16 C4
Blewbury OX11 237 A4
Letcombe Bassett OX12 214 A1
Lower Heyford OX25 63 A3
Middle Barton OX7 60 C4
Oxford OX2 141 A4
Reading RG4 259 A1
Watchfield SN6 191 B1
South Stoke Cty Prim Sch
RG8 239 A2
South Stoke Rd RG8 240 A1
South View
Great Bourton OX17 9 B4
[4] Wallingford OX10 221 B4
South View Ave RG4 259 B1
South View Pk RG4 259 B1
Southam Rd
Banbury OX16, OX17 9 B2
Mollington OX17 4 A2
Southampton St SN7 172 C2
Southby Cl OX13 158 A4
Southcroft OX3 123 C3
Southdale Rd OX2 123 A4
Southdown Ct SN7 194 C4
Southdown Rd RG4 259 A3
Southend OX44 162 C4
Southend Cotts OX5 78 A2
Southern By-pass Rd
Kennington OX1 141 B2
N Hinksey Village OX2 140 C4
Oxford OX1,OX4 141 C2
South Hinksey OX1 141 A2
Southern Rd OX9 147 C4
Southerndene Cl RG31 257 B1
Southfield Dr OX14 199 C4
Southfield La OX27 49 C4
Southfield Pk OX4 142 A4
Southfield Prim Sch
SN6 190 A3
Southfield Rd OX4 142 A4
Southlands OX18 135 C1
Southlawn OX28 117 C4
Southmead Ind Pk
OX11 200 B2
Southmoor Pl OX2 123 A2
Southmoor Rd OX2 123 A2
Southmoor Way OX14 179 C4
Southrop CE Prim Sch
GL7 131 A2
Southrop Rd OX15 30 A3
Southwold [3] OX26 65 C2
Southwold Cty Prim Sch
OX26 65 C3
Southwood Rd OX29 103 B1
Sovereign Cl OX11 219 A4
Spa Cl SN6 190 A4
Span Hill RG4 260 A4
Spareacre La OX29 120 C4
Sparsey Pl OX2 109 A1
Sparsholt St OX12 212 C2
Spears The OX5 108 A3
Speedwell Croft OX26 65 C3
Speedwell Fst Sch OX4 142 A1
Speedwell St OX1 141 B4
Spencer Ave OX5 108 A3
Spencer Cres OX4 142 A2
Spencer Ct [23] OX16 16 B3
Spencers Cl SN7 194 B4
Spendlove Ctr The OX7 73 A2
Spenlove Cl OX14 159 C1
Spenser Cl OX26 65 B2
Spey Rd OX13 159 B2
Speyside Cl OX18 115 B3
Spier's La OX27 67 C1
Spinage Cl SN7 173 A2
Spindleberry Cl OX4 142 C1
Spindlers OX5 92 C1
Spindleside [1] OX26 65 C2
Spinney Bank OX17 23 C3
Spinney Cl RG4 259 A4
Spinney Dr OX16 16 C2
Spinney Field OX4 142 C1
Spinney The
Abingdon OX14 159 B1
East Hendred OX12 216 B3
Launton OX26 66 B1
Lechlade GL7 150 B2
Spinneys Cl OX14 160 C2
Spinneys The OX7 58 C3
Spitfire Cl Benson OX10 204 A1
[6] Bicester OX26 66 A2
Spleen The OX15 14 A3
Spooner Cl OX3 124 C2
Sprigs Holly La HP14 189 A4
Spring Cl OX28 118 A4
Spring Copse OX1 141 B2
Spring Farm OX25 47 B3
Spring Farm Mews RG8 239 B1
Spring Gdns
Abingdon OX14 179 B4
Lechlade GL7 150 B2
Spring Hill OX13 176 B4
Spring Hill Rd OX5 107 C4
Spring La
Aston Tirrold OX11 237 C4
Great Bourton OX17 9 B3
Horspath OX33 143 B4
Idbury OX7 69 A2
Oxford OX4 142 B1
Oxford,Headington Quarry
OX3 124 C1
Reading RG4 260 A3
Watlington OX49 186 B1
Spring Path OX9 147 C4
Spring Pl OX7 42 C1
Spring Rd OX14 179 B4
Spring St OX7 42 C2
Spring Terr OX14 179 B4
Spring Wlk RG10 255 B1
Springdale OX10 221 B4
Springfield OX17 8 C2
Springfield Ave OX16 16 B2
Springfield Cl
Shrivenham SN6 209 A3
Watlington OX49 186 B1
Springfield Dr OX14 179 C4
Springfield End RG8 249 B4
Springfield Gdns OX39 168 B4
Springfield Mews RG4 259 A2
Springfield Oval OX28 103 C1
Springfield Pk OX28 103 C1
Springfield Rd
Bicester OX27 65 C4
Kidlington OX5 108 C4
N Hinksey Village OX2 140 B4
Stokenchurch HP14 188 C2
Wantage OX12 214 C2
Springfield Sch OX28 103 C1
Springhill Rd RG8 249 B4
Springs The OX28 118 A4
Springwell Hill OX5 78 A1
Springwell Ho [15] OX16 16 B3
Springwood La RG9 253 A4
Spruce Dr OX26 65 C3
Spruce Gdns OX4 161 C4
Spruce Rd OX5 108 C4
Spur The RG10 255 C2
Square Firs OX29 90 A3
Square The
[12] Abingdon OX14 179 C4
Aston OX18 135 C2
Aynho OX17 35 B4
Ducklington OX29 118 A2
Eynsham OX29 120 C4
Great Tew OX7 45 B4
Kings Sutton OX17 23 C3
Long Crendon HP18 129 B3
Longworth OX13 156 A2
N Hinksey Village OX2 122 B1
[2] Oxford OX4 142 B2
Pangbourne RG8 256 B3
Swalcliffe OX15 19 C4
Squire's Wlk OX10 221 B3
Squires Cl OX18 116 B2
Squires Rd SN6 191 B1
Squitchey La OX2 123 A4
Stable Cl Finmere MK18 39 B4
Oxford OX1 123 A1
Stable Cotts GL56 40 B2
Stable Rd OX26 65 C2
Staddlestone Cl RG31 257 B1
Stadhampton Prim Sch
OX44 163 B1
Stadhampton Rd
Drayton St L OX10 183 A3
LIttle Milton OX44 163 C3
Stadium Way RG30 258 A1
Staffordshire Cl RG30 257 C1
Stainer Pl OX3 123 C2
Stainfield Rd OX3 124 A3
Stainswick La SN6 209 B3
Stallpits Rd SN6 209 A4
Stanbridge Cl OX16 16 A3
Standlake CE Prim Sch
OX29 137 B2
Standlake Rd
Ducklington OX29 118 B2
Northmoor OX29 138 A1
Standon Ct OX3 124 B1
Stanford Dr [5] OX14 179 C4
Stanford in the Vale CE Prim
Sch SN7 194 C4
Stanford Rd SN7 173 A2
Stanier Pl OX16 16 C4
Stanley Cl OX2 140 B4
Stanley Rd OX4 141 C4
Stanmore Cres OX18 115 C2
Stansfeld Pl OX3 124 C1
Stansfield Cl OX3 124 C1
Stanton Cl OX28 117 C4
Stanton Cotts OX33 125 B4
Stanton Harcourt CE Prim
Sch OX29 138 A4
Stanton Harcourt Ind Est
OX29 138 A4
Stanton Harcourt Rd
South Leigh OX29 119 B3
Witney OX28 118 B4
Stanton Rd
Forest Hill OX33 125 C2
N Hinksey Village OX2 140 C3
Stanville Rd OX2 140 A4
Stanway Cl OX28 103 B1
Stanway Rd OX3 125 A2
Stanwell Cl OX17 11 A1
Stanwell Dr OX17 11 A1
Stanwell La OX17 9 B4
Stanwell Lea OX17 11 A1
Stapleton Rd OX3 124 B1
Star La SN6 191 B1
Star Rd RG4 259 B1
Starina Croft OX16 9 A1
Starnham Rd OX29 118 A2
Starwort Path [34] OX4 142 C1
Station App Bicester OX26 65 C1
Kidlington OX5 92 B1
Station Field Ind Est OX5 92 B1
Station La OX28 118 A3
Station Rd Ardley OX27 50 B2
Ashbury SN6 228 A4
Aynho OX17 35 A3
Bampton OX18 134 C3
Black Bourton OX18 133 C3
Blackthorn OX25 82 A2
Bletchingdon OX5 93 A4
Brize Norton OX18 116 B2
Chinnor OX39 168 B3
Chipping Norton OX7 42 B1
Cholsey OX10 220 C1
Cropredy OX17 4 C1
Culham OX14 180 C2
Didcot OX11 200 C1
Eynsham OX29 120 C4
Faringdon SN7 172 C2
Goring RG8 249 B3
Grove OX12 214 C4
Haddenham HP17 130 C3
Henley-on-T RG9 244 C1
Highworth SN6 190 A3
Hook Norton OX15 30 B4
Kingham OX7 54 C2
Launton OX26 66 C2
Lechlade GL7 150 B3
Lower Heyford OX25 62 B3
Marsh Gibbon OX27 67 C2
Pangbourne RG8 256 B3
Shiplake RG9 255 A2
Shipton-u-W OX7 70 C1
Shrivenham SN6 209 A3
South Leigh OX29 119 B3
Uffington SN7 211 B4
Upton OX11 218 B1
Wallingford OX10 221 B4
Wargrave RG10 255 B1
Wheatley OX33 144 A4
Station Rd Ind Est OX10 221 B4
Station Yard Ind Est
Adderbury OX17 23 A1
Chipping Norton OX7 42 B1
Station Yd
Steventon OX13 199 A2
Thame OX9 148 A4
Staunton Rd OX3 124 A2
Staverton Rd OX2 123 A3
Steady's La OX29 138 A4
Steep Rise OX3 124 B3
Steeple Cl OX15 21 C2
Steepness Hill OX15 32 C2
Stenton Cl OX14 179 C3
Stephen Ct OX3 124 B2
Stephen Freeman Prim Sch
OX11 200 B1
Stephen Rd OX3 124 B2
Stephenson Ho [14] OX1 141 B4
Steppingstone La SN6 209 A2
Steptoe Cl OX12 196 B1
Sterling Cl
[7] Bicester OX26 66 A2
Kidlington OX5 108 C4
Sterling Rd OX5 108 C4
Sterling Road App OX5 92 C1
Sterling Way RG30 258 A1
Stert Rd OX39 167 C2
Stert St OX14 179 C4
Stevens Cl OX2 123 A2
Stevens La RG9 252 B4
Stevenson Cl OX26 65 B2
Stevenson Dr OX14 179 B4
Steventon Rd
Drayton OX13,OX14 199 A4
East Hanney OX12,OX13 197 C4
Stewart St OX1 141 B3
Stile Rd OX3 124 B2
Stimpsons Cl OX2 122 A1
Stirling Cl
Carterton OX18 115 B2
Reading RG4 259 B3
Wantage OX12 214 C3
Stirling Ct OX16 15 C3
Stirlings Rd [4] OX12 214 B2
Stockey End OX14 160 B1
Stockham Pk OX12 214 B3
Stockham Prim Sch
OX12 214 B3
Stockham Way OX12 214 B3
Stocking La OX15 6 B1
Stockleys Rd OX3 124 A3
Stockmore St OX4 141 C4
Stocks La OX13 198 C2
Stocks The OX7 57 A1
Stocks Tree Cl OX5 108 A3
Stoke Lyne Rd OX27 52 B1
Stoke Pl OX3 124 B2
Stoke Row CE Prim Sch
RG9 241 C3
Stoke Row Rd RG9 252 C4
Stokenchurch Inf Sch
HP14 188 C2
Stokenchurch Jun Sch
HP14 188 C3
Stokes View RG8 256 B3
Stone Cl OX2 122 A1
Stone Ct [20] Banbury OX16 16 B3
Great Rollright OX7 29 A2
Stone Hill OX15 21 B2
Stone House Cl OX13 156 C1
Stone Quarry La OX4 142 A2
Stone St Oxford OX4 142 A4
Reading RG30 258 A1
Stonebridge Rd OX13 198 C3
Stoneburge Cres OX26 65 C2
Stonebury Cl OX12 214 C3
Stonecrop Leyes OX26 65 C3
Stonefield Dr SN6 190 A2
Stonefield Way SN6 209 B3
Stonegables OX28 118 A3
Stonehill La
Abingdon OX14 179 B2
Kingston Bagpuize OX13 176 B4
Stonehill Wlk OX14 179 B2
Stoneleigh Cl OX7 57 A1
Stoneleigh Dr OX18 115 B3
Stonesfield OX11 219 A4
Stonesfield La OX7 73 B1
Stonesfield Prim Sch
OX29 89 B4
Stonesfield Rd OX29 90 A3
Stonesfield Riding OX7 74 B1
Stoney La OX9,OX49 185 C4
Stonhouse Cres OX14 160 C1
Stonor Cl OX11 200 C1
Stonor Gn OX49 186 A1
Stonor Ho* OX49 226 A4
Stonor Pl OX3 124 A1
Stort Cl OX11 200 C2
Stour Cl OX11 201 A1
Stoutsfield Cl OX5 108 A3
Stow Ave OX28 117 B4
Stow Rd Bledington OX7 54 B1
Fifield OX7 69 A1
Stowford Ct OX3 124 C3
Stowford Rd OX3 124 C2
Stowhill OX12 213 B2
Stowood Cl OX3 124 C2
Strachey Cl RG8 256 B1
Strafford Way OX9 148 A4
Strainges Cl OX29 118 A2
Stranks Cl SN6 190 A2
Stratfield Rd
Cutteslowe OX2 123 A3
Kidlington OX5 108 C3
Stratford Dr OX29 120 B4
Stratford La OX20 76 A1
Stratford Rd
Drayton (Banbury) OX15 15 C4
Shenington OX15 6 C4
Wroxton OX15 14 C4
Stratford St OX4 141 C4
Strathmore Cl OX18 115 B3
Stratton Audley Manor
OX27 52 B1
Stratton Audley Rd
Fringford OX27 52 B3
Stoke Lyne OX27 51 A3
Stratton Way OX14 179 C4
Strawberry Hill OX15 21 C3
Strawberry Path OX4 142 C1
Strawberry Terr OX15 21 C3
Stream Rd OX11 218 B1
Streatley & Goring Bridge
RG8 249 A3
Streatley Hill RG8 248 C3
Streatley Lodge [24] OX1 141 B4
Streatley CE Sch RG8 248 C3
Street The
Crowmarsh G OX10 221 C4
Crowmarsh G, N Stoke
OX10 221 B1
Ipsden OX10 240 B4
Moulsford OX10 239 A3
South Stoke RG8 239 A2
Stoke Lyne OX27 51 A3
Tidmarsh RG8 256 B1
Stroud Cl OX16 16 C4
Stuart Cl RG4 259 A3
Stuart Way OX9 130 A1
Stubble Cl OX2 140 A4
Stubbs Ave OX3 142 C4
Stud Farm Cl OX17 5 C1
Studdridge Ct HP14 188 B2
Sturges Cl OX3 124 B3
Sturt Cl OX7 73 B1
Sturt Rd OX7 73 B2
Styles Cl OX27 67 C1
Styles The OX11 217 B4
Sudbury Ct SN7 173 A2
Sudbury La OX13 156 B2
Suffolk Ct OX27 67 C2
Suffolk Ho OX10 204 C2
Suffolk Way OX14 179 B3
Sugarswell La OX15 6 A3
Sugworth Cres OX14 160 C3
Sugworth La OX14 160 B3
Sulham La RG8 256 C2
Summer Fields OX14 160 A2
Summer Ley OX15 32 C3
Summerfield OX1 141 B3
Summerfield Rd OX2 123 A4
Summerfield Rise RG8 249 B4
Summerhill Rd OX2 123 A4
Summers Cl OX17 23 A3
Summerside Rd SN7 174 C4
Summerton Pl OX7 42 C2
Summertown OX12 197 A3
Summertown Ct OX2 123 A4
Summertown Ho OX2 123 A4
Sunderland Ave OX2 109 A1
Sunderland Dr OX26 66 A2
Sundew Cl OX4 143 A1
Sunningwell CE Prim Sch
OX13 159 C3
Sunningwell Rd
Oxford OX1 141 B3
Sunningwell OX13 159 C2
Sunny Rise OX33 143 B3
Sunnymeade Ct [2] OX2 109 A1
Sunnyside Benson OX10 203 C3
Sunnyside *continued*
Oxford OX4 142 B3
Wheatley OX33 144 B4
Surley Row RG4 259 A3
Sussex Dr OX16 15 C4
Sutherland Beck OX11 200 C2
Sutton Cl OX14 179 C4
Sutton Courtenay Rd
OX14 199 C3
Sutton La OX29 120 A1
Sutton Rd Milton OX14 199 C3
Oxford OX3 124 A3
Sutton Wick La OX14 179 B1
Suzan Cres OX12 214 C3
Swain Ct OX28 118 A3
Swalcliffe Lea OX15 14 A1
Swalcliffe Park Sch
OX15 19 C4
Swalcliffe Rd OX15 20 A4
Swale Dr OX11 201 A1
Swallow Cl Bicester OX26 81 A4
[21] Sandford-on-T OX4 142 C1
Swan Cl Grove OX12 196 B1
Lechlade GL7 150 B2
Middleton Cheney OX17 17 C4
Swan Close Rd OX16 16 B3
Swan Ct [7] Oxford OX1 123 A1
Witney OX28 118 A4
Swan Gdns OX9 166 A4
Swan Ind Est OX16 16 B3
Swan La Burford OX18 100 C3
Faringdon SN7 172 C2
Great Bourton OX17 9 B4
Long Hanborough OX29 90 A1
Swan Lane Cl OX18 100 C3
Swan St Eynsham OX29 120 C4
Oxford OX2 123 A1
Swan Wlk OX9 147 C4
Swanhall La OX29 104 A3
Swanlands Ho OX29 120 C4
Swansea Rd RG1 259 A1
Swansea Terr RG31 257 B1
Swansfield Bicester OX26 81 A4
Lechlade GL7 150 B3
Swanston Field RG8 256 B4
Swarbourne Cl OX11 200 C1
Sweeps La OX18 100 C3
Sweet Briar OX13 178 B3
Sweetmans Rd OX2 140 B4
Swerford Rd OX15 30 A3
Swift Cl Bicester OX26 65 B2
[25] Sandford-on-T OX4 142 C1
Swift Way OX10 204 B2
Swin La OX18 101 C3
Swinbourne Rd OX4 142 A1
Swinbrook Cl RG31 257 B2
Swinbrook Ct OX28 118 A4
Swinbrook Rd
Carterton OX18 115 B3
Shipton-u-W OX7 85 C3
Swinburne Rd
Abingdon OX14 180 A4
Oxford OX4 141 C3
Swindon Rd SN6 190 A3
Swindon St SN6 190 A3
Swingburn Pl OX28 118 A4
Swinnerton Ho RG9 244 C2
Swinstead Ct OX44 184 B3
Sworford La OX44 144 C3
Sycamore Cl
Abingdon OX13 159 B1
Long Crendon HP18 129 B3
Sibford Gower OX15 19 A4
Watlington OX49 186 A1
Witney OX28 104 B1
Sycamore Cres OX1,
OX14 160 C4
Sycamore Ct RG8 256 B3
Sycamore Dr
Banbury OX16 16 B1
Carterton OX18 115 B2
Thame OX9 147 B4
Sycamore Gdns OX26 65 C2
Sycamore Pl OX18 114 B4
Sycamore Rd
Ambrosden OX25 81 B2
Launton OX26 66 B1
N Hinksey Village OX2 140 B4
Sycamore Terr OX15 21 B2
Sycamore Wlk OX12 196 B1
Sycamores The OX3 124 C2
Sydenham Gr OX39 167 C4
Sylvester Cl OX18 100 C3
Sympson Cl [12] OX14 179 C3
Syringa Wlk OX16 9 A1

T

Tackley CE Prim Sch
OX5 77 B3
Tackley Pl OX2 123 A2
Tackley Sta OX5 77 C3
Tacks La HP17 130 C3
Tadmarton Pk OX15 21 A3
Tadmarton Rd OX15 21 A3
Taggs Gate OX3 124 C3
Tailsman Bsns Ctr The
OX26 80 C4
Tait Dr OX25 63 A4
Talbot Cl Banbury OX16 15 C4
Reading RG4 259 B1
Talbot Fields OX18 135 A2
Talbot Rd OX2 109 A1
Talbot Way RG31 257 B2

Using the Ordnance Survey National Grid

NG NH NJ NK

NM NN NO NP

NR NS NT NU

NX NY NZ

SC SD SE TA

SH SJ SK TF TG

SM SN SO SP TL TM

SR SS ST SU TQ TR

SW SX SY SZ TV

Any feature in this atlas can be given a unique reference to help you find the same feature on other Ordnance Survey maps of the area, or to help someone else locate you if they do not have a Street Atlas.

The grid squares in this atlas match the Ordnance Survey National Grid and are at 1 kilometre intervals. The small figures at the bottom and sides of every other grid line are the National Grid kilometre values (**00** to **99** km) and are repeated across the country every 100 km (see left).

To give a unique National Grid reference you need to locate where in the country you are. The country is divided into 100 km squares with each square given a unique two-letter reference. Use the administrative map to determine in which 100 km square a particular page of this atlas falls.

The bold letters and numbers between each grid line (**A** to **F**, **1** to **4**) are for use within a specific Street Atlas only, and when used with the page number, are a convenient way of referencing these grid squares.

Example   The railway bridge over DARLEY GREEN RD in grid square A1

Step 1: Identify the two-letter reference, in this example the page is in **SP**

Step 2: Identify the 1 km square in which the railway bridge falls. Use the figures in the southwest corner of this square: Eastings **17**, Northings **74**. This gives a unique reference: **SP 17 74**, accurate to 1 km.

Step 3: To give a more precise reference accurate to 100 m you need to estimate how many tenths along and how many tenths up this 1 km square the feature is. This makes the bridge about **8** tenths along and about **1** tenth up from the southwest corner.

This gives a unique reference: **SP 178 741**, accurate to 100 m.

Eastings (read from left to right along the bottom) come before Northings (read from bottom to top). If you have trouble remembering say to yourself "Along the hall, THEN up the stairs"!

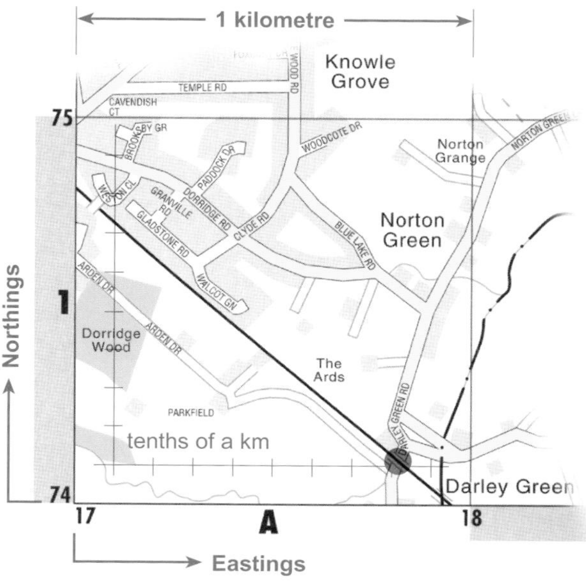